MUSIC
FOR THE PEOPLE

The Sioux Falls, South Dakota,
Municipal Band
1919-1994

By Leland A. Lillehaug
and Laurie L. Anderson

Printed in United States of America

PINE HILL PRESS, INC.
Freeman, S. Dak. 57029

Sioux Falls Municipal Band
75th Anniversary Season
1919-1994

Dedication

Aside from providing music for the people of Sioux Falls and the surrounding area, the Sioux Falls Municipal Band has provided young people with a professional musical group in which to play. As a result, many young Band members learned to appreciate music and continued to play in bands or orchestra as adults.

Unfortunately, early deaths prevented several such players from pursuing their talents. This book is dedicated to them.

Jon Edward Hansen (1944-68)

Jon Edward Hansen was born June 6, 1944, to Lowell and Edith Hansen in Sioux Falls, South Dakota. Jon played the drums in the Sioux Falls Municipal Band in 1960 and 1961 while in high school.

He graduated from Washington High School in 1962 and went on to the University of Colorado in Boulder, where he was a member of Phi Delta Theta fraternity. During his senior year he attended Chapman College's University of the Seven Seas and was elected student council president. He married Helen O'Neill from Midland, Texas, on Septem-

Jon Edward Hansen. *(courtesy Hansen family)*

ber 3, 1966, and graduated January 1967.

Following graduation, Jon returned to Sioux Falls, where he became the vice president of the family-owned Jackrabbit Lines bus company. He was a member of the Lions Club, Jaycees, Elks and Toastmasters.

On July 8, 1968, Jon was on a small plane which disappeared in the Bahamas. Coast Guard, Navy, Air Force and private planes conducted an intensive, unsuccessful search for the missing plane. He was twenty-four years old when he died.

Howard K. Hillman (1920-44)

Howard Hillman, from Lennox, South Dakota, is listed on the Municipal Band roster as a cornet player in 1942 and is the only Municipal Band member known to have been killed during World War II. Lt. Hillman, a P-51 pilot, was reported missing in action over Germany on April 24, 1944. His body was found buried in Germany in 1948 and was returned to Lennox for burial November 7, 1948.

Howard was born in Trent, South Dakota, and lived in Flandreau, Howard and Hawarden, Iowa, before moving to Lennox. He graduated from Lennox High School in 1938 and began college at Augustana in the fall of 1938. He graduated in 1942 and enlisted in the ser-

Howard K. Hillman. *(courtesy Verlyn Hofer)*

vice in January 1943. Howard was stationed in England with the 357th Fighter Squadron and entered combat duty in March, 1944 — only two months before his death. His combat successes during the first weeks earned him two oak leaf clusters.

Myron Floren, in his autobiography, *Accordion Man*, wrote that Howard was his roommate during their freshman year at Augustana College (1938-39). Floren said that "since we were both freshmen and from similar farm backgrounds, we became great friends and helped each other endure those first lonely days away from home." Norman

Sampson, who played clarinet in the Band in 1941 and 1942 and later became the high school band director at Pierre, also had Howard as a roommate at Augustana.

Like his father, Albert, Howard played in the Lennox Municipal Band under Russ Henegar, who also conducted the Sioux Falls Municipal Band.

Denis Kelly (1941-59)

Denis Kelly was introduced to the trumpet and to a community band at an early age, inspiring him to serious study and eventual membership in the Sioux Falls Municipal Band.

Denis, the only child of Marion and Coral Kelly, was born in Buffalo Center, Iowa (near Elmore), on July 22, 1941. He began school in Wanamingo, Minnesota, and moved to Sioux Falls in 1951, during the second half of the fourth grade. Denis started playing trumpet in the third grade, and by the fourth grade he was allowed to sit in with the Wanamingo Community Band.

Denis Kelly. *(courtesy Coral Kelly)*

Denis' musical skills were recognized at Washington High School as well as in city and state musical organizations. He studied privately with Donald McCabe, a local educator and performer, and was first chair in the Washington band during his sophomore, junior and senior years. He was selected for All State Orchestra in 1957 and played for Dr. Leland Lillehaug (Municipal Band conductor 1964-86) in "The Song of Norway" at the Coliseum the same year. At the Washington High School Band spring concert on April 18, 1958, he soloed with "Etude de Concert Number 4" by Ernest Williams. He was principal cornet in the first Augustana Band Festival in 1958.

His academic skills were recognized, too. Denis was talented in creative writing and worked with Ray Shermoe, advisor for the Washington literary magazine, *Chips*. In addition, Denis was a National Honor Society member. At church, he was president of the First Lutheran Luther League.

He became a member of the Sioux Falls Municipal Band and told his parents that he wanted to go to college. He played as an apprentice in the Band in 1957 prior to regular membership in 1958. All the money he earned from the Municipal Band went into savings for college.

However, his plans were not fulfilled, because he died of kidney failure on January 13, 1959, during his senior year of high school. His mother reported that the doctors said her son's good attitude and his love of music, family and friends had extended his life. At his funeral, the Reverend Robert Borgwardt spoke on the theme "Young Man in a Hurry." The Augustana Concert Band dedicated "Built on a Rock" to Kelly at the Concert Band Festival on February 7, 1959. The Denis Kelly Award was established after his death.

Coral Kelly said that when Denis died, the family gave his cornet to Loren Little, their son's good friend and colleague in the Municipal Band. Little said he took the cornet to Vietnam when he served there as a medical doctor.

Denis wrote a piece called "Axiom for Living" for his senior composition class. The piece (see Appendix) was dated December 12, 1958, one month before his death at age seventeen.

Kenneth Lane (1915-47)

Kenneth Lane was a Municipal Band cornetist who became an Army bandsman and later a flier during World War II.

Lane's brother Ronald, three years older than Kenneth, played clarinet in the Municipal Band. Ronald remembered his brother as being "sort of happy-go-lucky" and quite a conversationalist.

In his youth, Kenneth took lessons from the noted Sioux Falls music teacher Vernon Alger, becoming proficient enough to play a solo at the contest in Madison during his final year of high school. He didn't win the contest but did improve his playing, his brother Ronald remembered. Ronald said that his brother could play all the marches the high school band used on parade from memory and never took his instrument out of the case from one concert to the next.

"Well, around 1940," wrote Ronald in a letter in early 1994, "our happy little world came apart." Kenneth was inducted into the Army and had basic training at Camp Claiborne, Louisiana. Henegar had given him a letter of recommendation which got him into the Army band at Framingham, Massachusetts. Kenneth and some of his fellow band members apparently got bored with this routine and resented the low ratings given by their band director. They finally gave him an ultima-

Kenneth Lane, left, with Ruby Porter, Municipal Band member C. R. "Bob" Larson and his bride Doris Porter Larson, September 29, 1940. *(courtesy Doris Larson)*

tum — "Either get us better ratings or we are going to join the Air Force." The director's reply was, "Don't make me laugh; you guys have got the softest jobs in the whole Army, and I can't believe you are about to change that." The director was mistaken. Kenneth transferred to the Air Force, graduated as second lieutenant and was sent to an airfield somewhere in the Southwest to become a test pilot.

When Kenneth arrived home after World War II, his friend Joe Foss talked him into joining the Air Force National Guard. On December 13, 1947, Kenneth was scheduled to fly a small bomber, which needed refurbishing, to the eastern part of the country. He had two crew members — a navigator and an engineer. After a long flight, they lost communication. Late that night while flying over farm country near Scranton, Pennsylvania, hopelessly lost and fuel almost gone, they decided to abandon the plane. Kenneth managed to keep the plane in the air long enough for the two crew members to escape, but was unable to save himself.

Kenneth Lane, then Band president, died just twelve days after presiding at the Band's annual meeting on December 1, 1947. He was thirty-two years old.

Jane Louise Ordal, right. *(courtesy Al and Nona Ordal)*

Jane Louise Ordal (1949-75)

Jane Louise Ordal was a flutist with the Sioux Falls Municipal Band during the 1968 season. She was killed in a car-truck accident in the Rock Springs, Wyoming, area May 20, 1975, at the age of twenty-six years. She was buried in Denison, Iowa, May 25, 1975.

Jane, the daughter of Al and Nona Ordal, was born in Harvey, Illinois, on January 16, 1949. She attended elementary school for two years at Lowell School in Sioux Falls, South Dakota, and for six years in the Denison, Iowa, Community School.

Her musical ability developed early and was evident during each level of her education. She was an outstanding flutist at Denison, Iowa, High School (1964-67) and won a position in the Iowa All State Band all four years of high school. She also attended a six-week session at the famed Interlochen Music Camp the summer of 1967.

While at Augustana College in Sioux Falls from 1967-71, Jane participated in the Concert Band and other musical activities. Following her graduation she taught in the middle school in Amana, Iowa, from 1971-74. Her parents live in Denison, Iowa.

Table of Contents

Foreword

I t's with pride that in 1994 the Sioux Falls Municipal Band completed its seventy-fifth year of providing music to the citizens of Sioux Falls and surrounding communities. Few remaining city-funded bands can boast a history and performance schedule like the Sioux Falls Municipal Band. Still presenting about forty concerts a year, the Band continues to attract high-quality area musicians and enthusiastic audience members.

Although the Band's uniqueness and longevity make it a likely topic for a written history, such a history had never been written. The idea for this book began in 1992, when Dr. Leland Lillehaug, the Band's conductor for twenty-three years (1964-86), was invited by the Minnehaha County Historical Society to speak to the group about the Municipal Band. Dr. Lillehaug spent about a month researching the topic and received a positive response to his lecture. Several of the Historical Society members suggested that a complete history be written for the Band's seventy-fifth anniversary in 1994.

The suggestion was passed on to me. Although such a history may have been better undertaken while original Municipal Band members were living, it was agreed that valuable information from older former and current Band members and audience members could be lost forever if the project were not undertaken soon. After discussion with others, I felt there would be support for such a project.

Because of Dr. Lillehaug's many years with the Band, I — and others — thought that he was the logical person to direct the project. Besides, it was agreed that there would not be resources to engage a full-time researcher/writer to undertake a task of this magnitude. Laurie Anderson, a writer who had previously done a mini-history of the Municipal Band, was engaged to coauthor the book, and a committee was organized to set policies. Fund raising was not easy, but was successful due largely to Lillehaug's determined efforts.

The result is a comprehensive history of the Sioux Falls Municipal Band, personalized by interviews with many of the Band's conductors, players, soloists and guest performers, and sprinkled with interesting facts about Sioux Falls throughout the years. We hope that this book will not only preserve the history of the Sioux Falls Municipal Band but will help ensure its continuation.

> Dr. Bruce T. Ammann, conductor
> Sioux Falls Municipal Band

Our project had two main purposes: First, to gather and record important information about the Sioux Falls Municipal Band before it was lost; and second, to write a book which would be interesting to the players, Band fans and historians.

We recognized the high cost to research and publish a book, even though much of the labor would be donated. We felt that Sioux Falls might have enough businesses, foundations and individuals interested in having the Band's history preserved. We were not disappointed. Our thanks to all those who became a part of this project through their gifts. Their names are found under "Acknowledgments." Any profits from book sales will be used for a Municipal Band endowment fund.

A final purpose in writing this book was to demonstrate the role of music and the arts throughout the history of Sioux Falls. A printed Band program from November 17, 1946, found during our research, aptly describes the value of music:

> Music is a priceless gift, ... not a luxury, but a universal everlasting heritage. Those who enjoy music and use it for self-expression are skilled in the art of gracious living. Their homes reflect an air of comfort, contentment and well-being, ... an environment ideal for instilling in their children an appreciation of the finer things of life.

> Leland A. Lillehaug and
> Laurie L. Anderson, coauthors

Acknowledgments

We realize that we cannot possibly mention and thank all the people by name who have assisted in so many ways, including their encouragement, the assistance and the funding which have stimulated the research and have made this book possible. However, we thank the Rev. Clayton Smith, who started the ball rolling by inviting Dr. Lillehaug to speak to the Minnehaha County Historical Society. The members of the Municipal Band History Project Committee made policy decisions and offered advice. The members, in addition to the authors, are Dr. Bruce Ammann, Earl Bonacker, Sylvia Henkin, Dr. Arthur Huseboe, Dr. Dennis Knutson, Dr. Gary Olson and Trudy Peckham. Our thanks to each of them.

In addition to being on the Project Committee, Dr. Olson served as our research and writing critic. He is a Humanities Scholar, a professor of history at Augustana College and a coauthor of the book *Sioux Falls, South Dakota, a Pictorial History*. His knowledge of regional history, literary style and critical evaluation was invaluable.

We were fortunate to have Dr. Arthur Huseboe as the final evaluator. He is the executive director of the Center for Western Studies at Augustana College and is the author of *An Illustrated History of the Arts in South Dakota*.

We would be remiss if we did not also acknowledge the important help of family members. We thank Ardis Lillehaug for her patient support of this "post-retirement" project and for her helpful suggestions and proofreading. We also thank Jeffrey Anderson for proofreading and encouragement.

We also acknowledge the following for their assistance or support: American Bandmasters Association Library at the University of Maryland; Dr. Bruce Ammann, present conductor, Sioux Falls Municipal Band; Terry Anderson, director, South Dakota Legislative Research Council; the *Argus Leader* for use of photos and reprinting of newspaper articles; Paul Bierley, biographer of John Philip Sousa; Marlin Brown, member of the Municipal Band 1937-43 and 1946; Doris Henegar Dean; Jacquelyn Gunnarson; Loren Koepsell, director of informational services, Augustana College; David Kranz, reporter, *Argus Leader*; Minnehaha County Register of Deeds Office (birth and death records); Minnehaha County Historical Society; Parks and Recreation Department staff; Joseph F. Pekas and the Musicians' Local 733 of Mitchell, South Dakota; Pine Hill Press; Roger Quam; Ron Robinson, professor of English and journalism, Augustana College; Ardyce Samp, writer; Brian Sauer, computer department, Augustana College; Lowen Schuett, director, Sioux Falls Park and Recreation Department; Dr. Donald E. Scott; Sioux Falls City Clerk Office personnel; Sioux Falls Public Library reference librarians; Siouxland Heritage Museums; Thomas Sohre, computer consultant; Dave Sonnichsen, photographer; South Dakota Historical Society; Harry Thompson, Center for Western Studies, Augustana College.

In addition, we thank all who provided information through letters, interviews and photographs. Their names are listed in the bibliography.

Most of all, we acknowledge the continued support of Sioux Falls and area citizens, for whom the Band was formed and for whom the music is played.

• • •

The following foundations, businesses and individuals made the book possible through their financial contributions:

Guarantors ($2,000 and above)

City of Sioux Falls and present Municipal Band members.
Diversified Credit Services of South Dakota.
The First National Bank in Sioux Falls.
Mary Chilton DAR Foundation.
The South Dakota Humanities Council.

Benefactors ($1,000-$1,999)

Argus Leader (contribution in kind).
Midland National Life Insurance Company.
Dr. Howard and Alice Peterson.
Sioux Falls Area Foundation.
Starmark Inc.
Western Surety Co.

Patrons ($500-$999)

Chester and Shirley Anderson.
Home Federal Savings Bank.
Lutheran Brotherhood, East Sioux Falls Branch 8605.
Metropolitan Federal Bank.
Sioux Falls Jaycees.
Western Bank.
Woods Fuller Schultz & Smith PC.

Sponsors ($200 to $499)

Aid Association for Lutherans Branch 5374.
Architecture Incorporated.
Bethany Lutheran Home.
Dempster Christenson.
Disabled American Veterans, Arthur H. Muchow Chapter No. 1.
George Boom Funeral Home.
Good Samaritan Center.
Good Samaritan Luther Manor.
Good Samaritan Village.
Hansen Family Foundation.
Dr. Leland and Ardis Lillehaug.
Dr. Loren Little.
Prince of Peace Retirement Community.
Schmitt Music Centers.
Sioux Falls Music Co.
South Dakota Arts Council.
Southridge Healthcare Center.

Contributors ($50 to $199)

American Legion.
Dr. Bruce Ammann.
David Amundson.
Jeffrey and Laurie Anderson.
Paul and Reeva Bankson.
Best Western Town House Motel (contribution in kind).
Stephen and Catherine Billion.
Marlin Brown.
Earl Colgan.
Cosmopolitan Club of Sioux Falls.
Davenport Evans Hurwitz & Smith.
Dial Bank.
H. C. "Bud" and Norma Doyle.
Elmen Enterprises.
Myron and Berdyne Floren.
Joe and Donna Foss.
Jesse, Mavis, Richard, Sonja Gourley, Pro–Audio.
George Gulson.
Sylvia Henkin.
David and Carole Joyce.
K & M Music.
Dr. Dennis and Mary Ann Knutson.
Koch Hazard Baltzer Ltd. Architects.
Mr. and Mrs. James Kopperud.
Ronald Lane.
David Lillehaug and Winifred Smith.
Dr. Steven Lillehaug and Dr. Tanya Oyos.
Marquette Bank of South Dakota NA.
Marciene Matthius.
Mesirow Financial.
Gary and Geneva Molzen.
Robert E. Nason.
Ray and Lois Nelson.
Nordica Enterprises.
Pat O'Brien.
Dr. James Ode.
R. Alan and Stacey Peterson.
The Printers Inc.
Sioux Falls Chamber of Commerce.
Sioux Falls Chamber of Commerce Cultural Affairs Committee.

Sioux Falls Construction.
Sioux Falls New Car Dealers Association.
Sunshine Food Markets (contribution in kind).
Dr. Kevin and Patti Vaska.
Vern Eide Honda.
Vivian Wegner.
Kathryn Welter.

Friends ($10 to $49)

Jill Bauerle.
Heather Flanery.
Dr. Robert Hanson.
Dale Henegar.
Robert Kindred.
Doris E. Larson.
Thomas L. Little.
Mary Loftesness.
Milt Simons.

We also express our thanks to those donors whose pledges or contributions were received after the book went to press.

Pre-1920

Drumming Up Citizen Support

I nterest in band music was at an all-time high in the late 1800s. Band music was so popular that many Americans believed every town should have its own band. As a result, community bands sprang up throughout the country. In his book *Bands of America,* H. W. Schwartz wrote that hundreds of thousands of bands were formed during 1890 through 1905. The bands were not just for entertainment; Schwartz attributed their popularity to civic pride and a competitive spirit: "Each of these communities had to have a band. It was a rallying point for civic interest. Hardly any event could be properly observed without a band. ... If one town formed a band, all the surrounding towns felt they should have one. ..."

The interest in town bands also may have been influenced by highly successful private bands of the era, such as the bands of Patrick S. Gilmore (founded in 1858) and John Philip Sousa (founded in 1892). Richard Franko Goldman, the son of the founder of the famous Goldman Band (founded in 1918 in New York City), wrote that bands were so popular because of lack of competition from radio and recording and the public's undeveloped taste for symphony music.

While the history of bands such as Sousa's is well documented, Kenneth Berger, in his book *Band Encyclopedia,* said the history of town bands often is difficult to trace since many were short-lived and known only in limited areas. The Municipal Band of Sioux Falls, South Dakota, is an exception. The reasons for the Band's longevity are best explained by looking at the Band's beginnings, when a series of events led citizens — already accustomed to a variety of music and theater — to agree in 1919 to foot the bill to maintain a municipal band. Those events included the passage of a state band tax law, the unsuccessful use of a contracted band for summer park concerts and the performance in Sioux Falls of an outstanding military band.

Music and Theater in Early Sioux Falls

Sioux Falls citizens had been enjoying various types of music and theater for many years before there was any serious discussion of a municipal band. For example, the Great Artist's Course, financially supported by Sioux Falls resident Grace (Mrs. Willis H.) Booth, brought outstanding musical artists to the Coliseum. In 1919, visiting artists included a grand opera quartet consisting of what the *Sioux Falls Press* called "four of the world's greatest artists" (Caroline Lazarri, Francis Ald, Giovanni Martinelli and Giuseppe DeLuca); singer Alma Gluck; Jascha Heifetz, "the marvelous boy violinist"; the Russian Pavley-Oukrainsky ballet with George Barrer's Little Symphony orchestra; and Galli Curci, coloratura soprano. In announcing programs for 1919-20, Mrs. Booth was quoted in the newspaper as saying, "The course represents the best that is obtainable, and I believe that is what the people want."

Theater had been an important part of Sioux Falls entertainment since the 1870s. The *Argus Leader* of October 25, 1919, had the headline, "40 Years of Drama in Sioux Falls, city has long record of stage attractions; famed as show town." The article was based on the memories of the writer, C. H. Craig, and didn't claim to include all aspects of theater in Sioux Falls. Craig said that "Sioux Falls has always borne the reputation among producers of being one of the best theater towns in the entire northwest." The article said traveling shows began visiting Sioux Falls in the 1870s but generally were of poor quality. Better quality shows arrived with the coming of the railroad in 1878. The local playhouse of those days was Clendenning Hall, a theater built on the third floor of a building at the southeast corner of Ninth Street and Phillips Avenue.

The article next discussed Germania Hall, where "numbers of ... prominent stage people of those days, whose names have now passed, appeared. ..." Germania Hall was built in 1880 at the corner of Ninth Street and Dakota Avenue and razed in 1934-35 to make room for the present City Hall. The article said that the "first real up-to-date, honest-to-goodness dramatic company" at the theater was the Edwin Clifford

Germania Hall, located at the corner of Ninth and Dakota, was built in 1880 and razed in 1934-35 to make room for the present City Hall. Germania Hall was used for theater and concerts, but no record was found to indicate that the Municipal Band played there. *(courtesy Siouxland Heritage Museum)*

company, appearing in 1882.

The newspaper article next mentioned the Booth Opera House and Majestic. The Booth was opened in 1885 at West Eighth Street and featured not just opera, but minstrel shows and "many other of the popular attractions of those days." The Majestic was a vaudeville house that burned about 1914.

The New Theater opened in 1898 because "Sioux Falls demanded a more pretentious show house," according to the *Argus Leader*. Located at the southwest corner of Ninth and Main, the New Theater was "the pride of the town," featuring theater companies and singers. The

This early band is identified as the "Sioux Falls Band, Ed Stevens, leader, at Elk's Club, Watertown, May 5, 1909." Those identified are Walter Kleinheinz, bass, far left, first row; Ed Stevens, cornet and leader, fourth from left, first row; and Fred Beecher, trombone, first row far right. Kleinheinz and Beecher later became Municipal Band members. According to the *Sioux Falls Press*, May 6, 1909, this band accompanied 125 Sioux Falls businessmen who traveled by train to Watertown, stopping at fourteen towns along the way. At each town, the men called on merchants and gave out souvenir post cards. *(courtesy Vivian Wegner)*

theater was razed in 1916.

The Orpheum, built in 1913, was designed for vaudeville and motion pictures. Another *Argus Leader* article reported that the Orpheum was on the same vaudeville circuit as Minneapolis, St. Paul, Omaha, Lincoln, Sioux City, Des Moines and Fort Dodge. Fred Beecher, later a Municipal Band member, was manager.

Stout's Band

In addition to live music in some of the theaters, Sioux Falls had professional and volunteer bands. One of the earliest Sioux Falls bands was Stout's Band. The band leader, John H. Stout, was listed as both a cigar maker and a musician in the Sioux Falls city directory 1897-98. Stout's group was described in *Theatre in Spite of Itself*, by L. M. "Barney" Kremer. Kremer wrote that Stout's Band was organized about 1891, managed by Stout and directed by W. G. Wagner. However, Stout's Band didn't appear in the Sioux Falls city directory until 1894-95, listed as "Stout's Band and Opera House Orchestra, J. H. Stout, manager, 404 Syndicate Block." Kremer wrote about the band's skill and fame: "Ten musicians had the ability, after a short rehearsal, to play the score furnished by any traveling drama or music group. Recorded sources maintain they played at all inaugural balls held here, the state inaugural in 1892, and the ball celebrating the opening of the Elks Lodge in 1895. ... It played in all theaters from Germania Hall up to the opening of the State."

An 1894 photo reprinted in 1956 in the *Argus Leader* showed an unidentified nine-piece group which may have been Stout's Band. Although the group contained stringed instruments, it still may have been called a band since several references from the late 1800s and early 1900s used "band" as a generic term for an instrumental group. In fact, the photograph's caption used both terms: "This was one of the earliest professional orchestras in Sioux Falls. ... There was no pianist because 'everyone had a piano at home and didn't care to come downtown to hear someone play a piano.' ... The band played at the old Germania Hall and Booth Opera House and New Theater. ..." The musicians were identified as W. G. Wagner, J. H. Hutchins and Oscar Wagner, violins; Tom Pruner, bass viol; Paul Hanson, flute; A. H. Wagner, clarinet; R. E. Bach, trombone; Connie Holmes, drums; and J. H. Stout, cornet and manager.

Newspaper articles told of Stout's Band giving free concerts. The concerts often were at Seney Island, a wooded island which no longer exists but then was located directly above the Falls of the Sioux River. The following story appeared in the *Argus Leader* of September 10, 1898: "Last Concert of Season, Stout's Band Will Give Their Last Free Outdoor Concert at Seney Island This Evening. The last concert to be given this season by Stout's Band at the pavilion on Seney Island will take place this evening. A delightful program has been arranged and a pleasant time is promised all who wish to spend a couple hours in dancing after the concert." The program was listed as follows:

Overture, Stratmore
Selection, Little Africa
Waltz, Love's Dream
Galop, An Indian Ride
Medley, Around the Metropolis
Two Step, Merry American

Thomas H. Pruner, listed as a bass viol player on the 1894 band photo, was a Sioux Falls pioneer and father of future Municipal Band member Ray Pruner. In a 1923 *Sioux Falls Press* newspaper article, Thomas Pruner told about a band, which he referred to as "the Sioux Falls Band" but which certainly must have been Stout's Band. He said that the ten-piece band was "the pride of the country for miles around in those early days" but that most of the members were no longer living. Pruner also described Seney Island, saying it was where the popular Fourth of July concerts were held: "At that time the island was 'a beautiful place,' ... and the falls were a gorgeous sight in themselves. Now even the trees that we early settlers held so dear, for they were only to be found at the river's edge, are going, and the ... beauty is lost for the people of today."

The Stout Band apparently continued for at least twelve years, but after the leader's death (sometime before June 1907), the band struggled to stay together at all, according to the *Argus Leader*, June 8, 1907. The newspaper article inferred that Stout's Band had been first-rate: "That there is ample material in Sioux Falls for the formation of the best brass band in the state no one will deny. Past experience has shown this. Sioux Falls for years had the reputation of having one of the very best bands in the northwest and with the right sort of backing at home it would again occupy that position."

Sioux Falls Fife and Drum Corps

Another early musical group in Sioux Falls was the Sioux Falls Fife and Drum Corps of Joe Hooker Post, Grand Army of the Republic (the GAR was an association from 1866 to 1949 of Union veterans of the Civil War). A newspaper article from 1904 reported that the "new" drum corps was not new at all, but just the old drum corps reorganized. The article explained that a drum corps had existed in Sioux Falls for many, many years, and had served as a fine advertisement for Sioux Falls, playing at all of the political rallies and old soldiers' encampments, not just in South Dakota but in many other states, including GAR parades

The Sioux Falls Fife and Drum Corps in Boston, Massachusetts, August 22, 1917, during the national parade of the Grand Army of the Republic. From left to right: 8 — J. C. Luce, Groton, S.D.; 7 — Col. C. A. B. Fox, leader, Sioux Falls Drum Corps; 6 — Joseph Fearon, Joe Hooker Post No. 10, Sioux Falls; 9 — J. E. Davis, flag bearer, GAR, Lennox, S.D.; 10 — W. F. McAdam, GAR, Custer, S.D.; 5 — Ed Becker, bass drum; 11 — W. H. Teare, banner carrier, GAR, Onida, S.D.; 4 — Al Seifert, snare drum and fife; 3 — Dan Wagner, snare drum; 12 — Mrs. McAdam; 13 — Lois F. Perry, Joe Hooker WCR; 14 — Lizzie D. Laughlin, Pierre, S.D., WCR; 2 — Fred H. Bishop, drum major, Sioux Falls Drum Corps; 15 — Rebeca Shea, Brookings, S.D., WCR; 1 — John C. Bossidy, M.D.; 16 — T. C. DeJean, Plankinton, S.D.; 17 — Mrs. T. C. DeJean. *(courtesy Sioux Falls Municipal Band)*

The El Riad Shrine Band poses in June 1921 at McKennan Park. Lloyd M. Coppens, holding the baton and standing just to the right of the man in the light-colored uniform, conducted both the Shrine Band and Municipal Band during 1920-21. Many instrumentalists played in both bands. *(courtesy June Beecher)*

at the national encampments in Chicago, Buffalo, Washington, Philadelphia, Cincinnati and San Francisco. According to *Dakota Panorama,* a fife and drum corps from Sioux Falls attended the GAR encampment in 1882 at Huron, South Dakota.

The group captured national attention in 1917, as it marched in the national parade of the GAR in Boston. The *Argus Leader* reported, "In Boston, whenever the (Sioux Falls) Drum Corps appeared in the streets they were surrounded by a large crowd which cheered them, and in the parade the Corps was one of the leading features and was given many words of commendation by the newspapers of Boston." *The Boston Globe* even published a photo of the group.

The El Riad Shrine Band

Another popular band in Sioux Falls was the El Riad Shrine Band, organized December 6, 1910, twenty-three years after the founding of the Sioux Falls El Riad Shrine temple December 27, 1887. An article from the *Argus Leader,* May 9, 1922, recounted the temple's history. It was reported that The El Riad, whose Arabic words mean "The Garden," was the forty-sixth Masonic temple formed in the United States. Fourteen musicians played in the El Riad's first band: F. R. Allen, Fred

Beecher, Walter Kleinheinz, F. W. Daugherty, Jess Zeller, Lou Jacobs, Tony Lee, J. C. Gilbert, E. B. Stevens (who acted as the first director), Dr. R. G. Stevens, H. W. Haugo, Frank Peckham, Henry Jacobs and Phil Beecher. The band first competed nationally with other temples in 1916, traveling to Buffalo, New York.

Even the formation of the Municipal Band in 1920 did not seem to detract from the Shrine Band's popularity. The Shriners continued to be very popular and active during the early 1920s. Newspaper stories described the twenty-five to thirty-five piece volunteer band with such phrases as "one of the best Shrine bands in the Northwest," "well known all over the state" and "the illustrious El Riad Band." With Lloyd M. Coppens as director, the Shrine band made well-publicized trips to imperial Shrine meetings in Portland, Oregon, in 1920 and to Des Moines, Iowa, in 1921. Newspaper stories attested to the band's popularity, with the *Sioux Falls Press* reporting in 1921 that the Shrine Band played at McKennan Park "to a sweltering, perspiring audience that must have numbered into the thousands. ... " and that "half the town went down to the Omaha railroad station Sunday night to wish a happy journey to the Shriners and their famous band who left for Des Moines to attend the annual convention."

Many musicians played in both the Shrine and Municipal Bands. In addition, five out of the nine Municipal Band conductors also directed the Shrine Band. The crossover of musicians may have had a role in the scheduling of the Municipal Band's first summer concert for mid summer, July 11, 1920, since the Shrine Band's sixteen-day trip to Oregon kept Shrine musicians out of town until July 2, 1920.

The El Riad Shrine Band is still in existence today, conducted by former Municipal Band member Marlin Brown.

Other Community Bands in South Dakota

Other bands had been formed in South Dakota before the 1920s. According to Kenneth Berger in *Band Encyclopedia,* Lennox organized a band in 1883; Yankton in 1873, regularly since 1877; and Huron in 1900. Lennox claims to be the oldest continuous band.

Other South Dakota towns organized bands under the provisions of a bill passed in 1915 by the South Dakota Legislature. The South Dakota legislature, at its fourteenth session, passed the bill, "Levying a tax for furnishing musical concerts. An Act Entitled, An Act to Empower Cities and Towns to Levy and Collect a Tax for the Purpose of Furnishing [Free] Musical Concerts to the Public" (see Appendix for complete bill). The act could be put into motion when a petition was signed by at least twenty percent of the electors, filed with the city council and approved in a general election. The bill was introduced by John Wallace Peckham, a Republican who served in the senate from 1915-18. He was from Parkston and represented Hutchinson County.

South Dakota's law preceded the more famous Iowa law by six years. In 1921 Major George W. Landers of Clarinda, Iowa, was a main force in the passage of the Iowa Band Law, which permitted towns and cities under 40,000 to levy a band tax. Although the South Dakota law only uses the term "musical concerts," many South Dakota cities, including Sioux Falls, have interpreted that to mean band concerts.

The Moose Band

Sioux Falls didn't immediately jump on the municipal band "bandwagon" after passage of the bill. Instead, the city contracted a band to provide summer park concerts. In the summers of 1916-18, free public park concerts were provided by a band organized by the Loyal Order of the Moose. Player pay came from profits from the parks' refreshment stands. John L. Johnson was the band's conductor. He later played trumpet and was assistant conductor of the Municipal Band. But the band

— and the citizens — discovered that without consistent funding, a band couldn't provide the desired quality or quantity of music.

Park Board minutes of May 21, 1917, gave details of the contract for that summer: "Moved and seconded that the president and secretary be authorized and instructed to enter into a contract with A. K. Bailey, agent for [the] Moose Band, to play concerts at the city parks at such times and places as the Board of Park supervisors may determine up until the first day of August 1917 at $2 a concert per man and $3 for leader, for not to exceed 18 pieces. Passed unanimously." (Austin K. Bailey later became a charter member of the Municipal Band.)

By some accounts, the band seemed popular enough. In June 1918 — the third season the Moose Band was contracted by the city — the *Argus Leader* of June 19, 1918, reported that the season's opening concert at Sherman Park drew "a large crowd at the park, many autoing in from the country and neighboring towns to spend the day picnicking, swimming and enjoying the music."

But by mid-July 1918 the newspaper reported that the free band concerts might end because of low attendance; low attendance meant no profit from the refreshment stands and no pay for the band. Fred E. Spellerberg, superintendent of city parks, said, "So far there has been an apparent lack of interest and small attendance at the park concerts, due no doubt to the fact that so many of our young men have been called to war, but unless the attendance can be increased, the number of concerts will have to be cut down or discontinued altogether." Spellerberg turned to the daily newspapers for help, pleading with them to "give park band concert announcements a little more prominence."

Newspaper coverage did improve, with the *Argus Leader* printing individual articles about the Moose Band's concert dates and selections. One such article, from August 16, 1918, listed the following musical selections:

March, Old Glory, Barnard
Overture, Northern Star, Grunenfelder
Waltz, Olivette, Meyer
Norwegian Dance No. 2, Grieg
March, They're on Their Way to Mexico, Berlin
Overture, Zampa, Harold
Idyll, Glühwurmchen, Lincke
Medley, Popular Songs, Lampe
Selection, Song of the Nation, Godfrey

But even the improved publicity couldn't keep the concerts going.

Later, in 1919 when a municipal band was being discussed, it was clear that the contract arrangement had satisfied neither the audience nor the Moose Band, and calls for a municipal band became stronger and stronger.

Howard C. Bronson's 51st Field Artillery Band

The municipal band movement seemed to gain the most momentum after Sioux Falls residents heard the 51st Field Artillery Band perform in early February 1919. The band was touted in the *Sioux Falls Press* in November 1918 as one of the best in the Army, and newspapers reported that the two Sioux Falls concerts — a matinee for students and an evening concert — were enthusiastically attended by approximately 2,000 people. Admission to the evening concert was one dollar.

One reason for the audience's enthusiasm was that many of its members were "home town heroes" returning to South Dakota after their World War I service. The *Argus Leader* of February 12, 1919, explained that thirty-five band members mostly were South Dakota "boys" who left in the fall of 1917 with the old South Dakota cavalry for the Mexican border. The band evolved into the 51st Field Artillery Band, as explained in the newspaper: "When the first South Dakota cavalry was disintegrated, the band was attached to the 109th field signal battalion. Later when the 307th cavalry was formed at Del Rio, Texas, the band was assigned to that station. In August last [August 1918] this regiment was reorganized into heavy field artillery and the band then became a part of the 51st field artillery." The printed roster included Sioux Falls musician Floyd Williams, who later became a member of the Municipal Band (1928-29) and for many years operated Williams Piano Store.

Even the director, Lt. Howard Curtis Bronson, was referred to in articles as "a Sioux Falls boy." Many hoped he could be convinced to lead a Sioux Falls municipal band. Bronson was born in Algona, Iowa, in November 1889. However, he had spent time in Sioux Falls attending the School of Business and playing with the Orpheum theater orchestra. *The Heritage Encyclopedia of Band Music, Composers, and Their Music* indicated that Bronson's musical experience included playing clarinet with the Cadet Band in Watertown, South Dakota (1901-04), Peck's 4th Regiment Band (1904-07), the North Dakota National Guard Band (1907-09), and the U.S. Navy Yard Band, Bremerton, Washington (1909-13). It's noteworthy that Bronson later guest-conducted the Sioux Falls Municipal Band July 10, 1949, at Terrace Park.

The band also appealed on a patriotic level in those months following the end of World War I (November 11, 1918). The concert, which was to open with the audience singing "America," was described in the newspaper as "the return of home boys who by their skill in music, have helped to stem, then crush, the German tide that sought to overflow the world." The concert was just one part of an entire week of patriotic singing planned for the city. Patriotic songs were to be sung at public meetings and at churches, and even heard in movie theaters.

But it was the quality of the music that ultimately won the hearts of the audience, according to the *Argus Leader*: It was "not alone the military tinge or the glamor that war throws upon a man that won the plaudits of the crowd at the Coliseum last evening; it was not khaki uniforms or the bronzed faces of Uncle Sam's lusty warriors under the skillful direction of Lt. Harold Bronson, himself a Sioux Falls boy; or yet that they came from the Sunshine State and were being welcomed back. For the music they discoursed stood on its own merits as providing an entertainment one can ill afford to miss."

Days before the concert, Bronson's name was raised as a candidate for leading the proposed municipal band in Sioux Falls. It was said that Bronson "claims this as his home and is said to be anxious to undertake such a project here rather than some other place, if sufficient inducements are offered, but other communities in the state have already made him propositions to locate there." The article said Bronson was "recognized as one of the best directors in the service and his band was highly popular in Oklahoma and Texas where they played for the Army and in public concerts."

Perhaps Bronson indicated he would not be available to start a band in Sioux Falls, because after the concert newspapers reported that the band plan contained no definite arrangements regarding a conductor, "simply assuring the voters that the best possible leader will be employed." Later in the month, when a petition for a municipal band was circulating, band backers were quoted in the newspaper as saying "there need be no questions of a band leader raised as there is ample opportunity to pick the best in the country from among the available list."

As it turns out, when Bronson was discharged from the Army in 1919, he organized the Aberdeen, South Dakota, Municipal Band, a full-time professional organization. His career then included playing clarinet in the Sousa band (1921-29); directing the Kable Brother Company Band and the 129th Infantry Band of Mount Morris, Illinois; serving as music advisor for the War Department during World War II; and serving as chief of army bands 1941-47, according to *The Heritage Encyclo-*

pedia of Band Music, Composers, and Their Music. He also was one of eight ex-Sousa men who founded the Sousa Band Fraternal Society in 1943. Bronson died in 1960. A band room for the 74th Army Band was named Bronson Hall in Bronson's honor February 22, 1987, at Fort Benjamin Harrison, Indiana. The program for the band room dedication said, "Among many notable achievements, Col. Bronson presided over the largest expansion of Army bands in history during World War II."

The Municipal Band Plan

"Various parties interested in the matter" were the driving forces behind the call for a municipal band, according to the *Argus Leader,* March 13, 1919. Those parties included musicians, music lovers and civic organizations, such as the Commercial Club, the Young Men's Booster Association and the Rotarians.

Newspapers reported that the proponents had many convincing arguments for starting a municipal band. One of those reasons was competition with other South Dakota towns. The newspaper cited Watertown and Mitchell municipal bands, saying that those bands "have proven both successful and popular and the cost is not felt by anyone." It was noted that the Watertown Band had won a prize at the Los Angeles Elks national convention and that the Mitchell band was directed by "a member of one of the biggest and best known bands in the country which played at the Corn Palace." The Mitchell band director referred to was Ernest Pechin, who had played with the Sousa Band.

Tied closely to competition was the argument that a municipal band could provide advertising for Sioux Falls. Local attorney T. M. (Theodore) Bailey was quoted in the *Argus Leader* as saying, "I believe that if the question of municipal aid for the maintenance of a band was submitted to the voters of the city it would be found that 90 percent of the people of Sioux Falls favored the project. A first class band is about the best advertising any city can get." Bailey was confident funding could be provided, saying, "I would call the attention of the Commissioners to the old saying that 'where there is a will there is a way,' and cite the laying of the water main to the links of the Minnehaha Country Club. The same situation prevailed, but a way was found to lay the main, and I believe that similar action could and should be taken in connection with the municipal band proposition."

Backers hoped that a city-funded band would be a more dependable source of music. The *Sioux Falls Press* explained, "During past years the city has employed bands at times when needed, but the system has been unsatisfactory to most citizens because it was not always possible to secure an organization to play when desired." Mayor George Burnside expounded upon that idea, quoted in the *Sioux Falls Press* as saying, "There are dozens of times during the year that the services of a band are needed and I am of the opinion that the city should have one of its own which could be depended on to appear when desired."

It was reported that the Commercial Club (which later became the Chamber of Commerce) helped develop a plan for creation of a band. The plan was to pay the director a regular salary, pay band members for rehearsals and concerts, and "provide a crack musical organization available here for all civic purposes at any time."

Promoters of a municipal band began seeking support to get the issue on the ballot. It was reported in the *Argus Leader* of February 19, 1919, that band backers had a meeting and arranged to "send workers through the city with petitions asking that the question of a small levy, sufficient to care for the band, be submitted to the voters at the April city election. Under the law for such elections [which required that a petition be signed by at least twenty percent of the electors as shown by the vote for City Commissioners at the last annual city election], less than 400 signatures will be required and they can easily be obtained in one day."

How much money was needed to fund a band? The original yearly figure cited as necessary for maintenance of the band was one mill — the maximum allowed under the 1915 state law — which equated to about $30,000 a year. In the *Argus Leader,* March 13, 1919, some businessmen and taxpayers argued not against the need for a band, but against a tax-supported band. Thirty thousand dollars, they said, was too much for Sioux Falls taxpayers to bear because the war had caused "increased taxes, increased living expenses and increased prices on all articles." The Associated Retailers argued that "a heavy patriotic duty is now laid on all taxpayers and citizens to contribute to the support of meeting the expenses incurred by reason of the war, and the further fact that on account of the growth of the city of Sioux Falls it is necessary that additional school buildings be built by taxes levied and assessments against property owners of the city." The Associated Retailers suggested that the city save money by continuing to contract out for a band, pointing out that the Park Board had spent $775 for the eleven band concerts in 1918, nowhere near the anticipated $30,000 of a one mill levy. The Association claimed that the Moose Band concerts had been "most popular and well attended with large crowds on each occasion" and that they were "of a high class and greatly appreciated by the citizens."

Various other figures were mentioned for the cost of maintaining a band. One figure was mentioned by C. W. Thompson, identified in the 1916 Sioux Falls city directory as Claude W. Thompson, an automobile salesman. The *Sioux Falls Press* quoted Thompson's speech to the Rotarians, in which he estimated that one season of concerts should cost $4,500: "Figuring on a basis of twenty members in a band with leader at a union scale of wages, allowing one practice a week, concerts at McKennan and Sherman parks and one on the city streets each week, also allowing $500 for new music and running the band for four months, the cost would not exceed $4,500 while the levy calls for $30,000."

Perhaps the clearest explanation of what it would cost to organize and maintain a band came from the voice of experience — the chairman of the Moose Band. That was Walter J. Ellwood, listed in the 1916 Sioux Falls city directory as a lawyer whose office was at 132 South Phillips Avenue. In a lengthy letter to the *Argus Leader*, March 14, 1919 (reprinted in full in the Appendix), Ellwood countered those who said that "the band last year only cost the city $775" by pointing out that "the band cost somebody else a whole lot more than this amount." That somebody else was the Moose Lodge. He estimated that the band had spent $1,200-$1,500 during those three years for the band leader, musical instruments and a rehearsal site. Although band members received union scale "most of the time," he said that many times the musicians donated their services. The only financial assistance they [the Moose] had received, said Ellwood, "was the sum of $200 donated by the Sioux Falls Commercial club, and the further sum of $300 donated by the City Commission. Therefore, the entire amount of outside help, as I have said, was the sum of $500. ..."

He pointed out that the costs weren't just for summer concerts, but for rehearsals. The band practiced from Christmas until the summer season started, with "the players giving their time for these rehearsals, for which they really should have been paid, and the Moose Lodge paying the instructor and standing other expense incident to the operation of the band." He said that people didn't understand how necessary those rehearsals were: "Most people seem to think the organization and maintenance of a band is similar to the organization and maintenance of a bunch of working men, that all you have to do is go out and hire your men and start to work. This is not true, as the only way a band can be a success and credit to the city is in constant rehearsals. ..."

Ellwood said that the Moose Band might continue playing if "some other public spirited organization in the city of Sioux Falls would like to donate a thousand dollars or two for the good of the city and maintain a

band for the coming season." But he said that it was merely a suggestion and didn't anticipate a "great scramble among the various organizations for the first privilege."

Ellwood estimated that it would cost at least $10,000 to properly
maintain and operate a municipal band for one season. He said it would
be a good deal for the city: "It is no doubt true that the city is in great
need of other public enterprises, such as schools and gymnasiums, which
will cost considerable money, but if there is any possible way that $10,000
could be spent to a better advantage, for a thriving, enterprising city
than to place in it a municipal band, properly conducted from a business standpoint, I am unable to ascertain where it could be."

What would one mill really have meant to the individual taxpayer?
The county auditor tried to clarify that for citizens in the *Argus Leader*,
March 13, 1919, saying that one mill levy would increase Sioux Falls
citizens' tax by four per cent, not ten percent as the rumor mill said.
Even so, band backers agreed to change their request from an appropriation of one mill ($30,000) to four-tenths of a mill ($12,000), requiring the signing of new petitions.

A segment of band opponents — and it's not clear who they were
affiliated with — tried a new way to make finances an issue. They lumped
together the issue of forming a municipal band with the issue of building a municipal gymnasium, saying that the two plans together would
raise taxes ninety percent. A defender of the band proposition, Will H.
Round, described that tactic as propaganda of "a questionable nature"
in the *Argus Leader*, March 14, 1919. He said, "Now who is responsible
for the city gymnasium idea I do not know. It has no connection whatever with the municipal band, and I believe that it has been sprung at
this time to handicap the band project. ... In behalf of those who are
behind the municipal band we ask that the proposition be thoroughly
investigated before obstacles are thrown in the way. Just divorce the
band project from any other proposition. We want the band scheme to
stand or fall on its own merits." Nothing further was mentioned about
the municipal gymnasium proposal, and the band issue made it to the
April 15, 1919, ballot as a separate issue.

Sioux Falls in 1919

It's somewhat surprising that some businessmen and taxpayers
were so very concerned with the economic impact of the proposed band
tax levy, because the economic picture in Sioux Falls was favorable in
1919. In their book *Sioux Falls, South Dakota, A Pictorial History,* Gary

Olson and Erik L. Olson wrote that the boom years in Sioux Falls caused by World War I didn't end until 1921: "In 1920 business leaders in Sioux Falls expected that the prosperous boom times of the previous decade would continue. The new auto age was in full bloom in 1920. Sioux Falls car dealers, operating out of large, new buildings, sold cars faster than they could get them from the factory. Implement wholesalers and retailers were doing a brisk business selling new tractor powered farm equipment, and electric home appliances were gaining popularity."

The annual report of the Sioux Falls Commercial Club spoke of a "splendid growth" during 1918. The report said, "This progress needs no explanation. It is simply the result of being located at the center of the most prosperous section of the country and we must build and expand our business to take care of what is actually forced upon us." The Commercial Club said that 1918 had been a banner one in terms of conventions and visitors to Sioux Falls.

An *Argus Leader* headline of January 8, 1920, indicated that construction in Sioux Falls was booming in 1919: "City Shatters All Records in 1919 Building/Two Million Mark Exceeded During Year Ending Tonight/Growth is Remarkable/Plans Completed Already for Buildings in 1920 to Cost $1,500,000."

On all fronts, businessmen and politicians were trying to make Sioux Falls a growing, vital city. City Commission minutes from 1919 and 1920 were full of discussions about modern improvements, such as street paving, sewer lines and electric lighting. Band proponents saw a municipal band as one more way to promote the City.

The Vote

The band proposition was just one of several reasons that the spring election of April 15, 1919, promised to be an exciting one. Another reason was that the election offered city women their first chance to vote on municipal issues and officials. In fact, women all over the state of South Dakota were voting for the first time, since a women's suffrage amendment had been added to the state constitution after the November 1918 vote. In Sioux Falls, women accounted for about one-third of the registered voters, with 4,253 women and 9,179 men. This was about twice as many people as had been registered for previous elections, and a heavy voter turnout was predicted — as high as 8,000 voters.

The big issue was the race between the two mayoral candidates — incumbent George W. Burnside and A. H. Stites. Other major issues on the ballot, besides approving a tax levy for a municipal band, were proposals that the city buy the streetcar system and the gas plant.

Despite predictions to the contrary, there was a low voter turnout, with bad weather cited as a factor. Even so, women accounted for about 2,000 (or two-fifths) of the 5,124 ballots cast. It was a close finish for Mayor Burnside. He defeated Stites by just 172 votes (2,616 to 2,444). The streetcar and gas plant issues were defeated.

It had been said that there was hardly any opposition to the band proposition in Sioux Falls, but it passed by just 170 votes (2,452 to 2,282). The *Argus Leader* editorial said that the newspaper was pleased with the results of the election but added that "there were so many votes against the [band] tax ... that it is manifest a proposal to impose a tax of one mill would have been defeated."

• • •

The band supporters' initial battle had been won when citizens agreed to support a band with tax dollars. But Sioux Falls would have to wait more than a year to finally hear the first strains of Municipal Band music in the parks.

Other bands making appearances in Sioux Falls included the Ferari Bros. Italian band, shown here marching north at the front of a 1903 parade in downtown Sioux Falls. The band's appearance was part of the Midsummer Festival, which ran June 29 through July 4, 1903. The festival created a carnival-like atmosphere in downtown Sioux Falls, with acts and sideshows along the street and items – ranging from "a needle to a threshing machine" – to buy, according to the *Sioux Falls Press*, July 3, 1903. Marching behind the band were Elks members, "dressed in white duck with purple neckties and large purple asters in their caps. They also carried ribboned canes and presented a fine appearance." *(courtesy Vivian Wegner)*.

This photograph of the 1907-08 Lutheran Normal School Band shows that band music was a part of early higher education in Sioux Falls. Parents of two Municipal Band members are pictured. Peter Lillehaug, father of Municipal Band conductor Leland Lille-haug (1964-86), is in the middle row, second from the left, with his cornet. Paul Ode, father of Municipal Band player James Ode (member 1954-57 and 1960-63), is in the second row, second from right. *(courtesy Leland Lillehaug)*

1920-21
Fine Tuning
the Organization

D espite the vote by Sioux Falls citizens in April of 1919 to fund a band, the job of establishing the musical organization was far from over. As the *Argus Leader* said in January 1920, "The mere fact the citizens voted $12,000 as an appropriation this year for the organization and maintenance of a municipal band is just a preliminary step ... and does not in any manner assure the city such a band." Money alone couldn't create music. What was needed was a leader, competent musicians and a plan regarding pay and schedule. It was the determination of a small group of musicians, led by the local musicians union, that caused those issues to be addressed, making the 1920 summer season a reality.

The musicians met for the first time November 2, 1919, at the Labor Temple. Municipal Band minutes show that fourteen people attended that first meeting. Raymond G. Hoyt was elected chairman and manager and was to recruit members and bring the proposition before the City Commission. Others elected to the Band Board were Lloyd M. Coppens, band director; Henry T. Hanson, secretary; Jake Helfert, treasurer; and Sid Drew and Walter Kleinheinz, Board of Directors. Others attending were William G. Wagner, Harry Hobson, Andrew K. Indseth, Charles Hobson, Walter F. Rittman, Roy Meyers, August C. Weich and Oscar G. Dahl. Who were these men and why were they so interested in forming the Band? Of the fifteen who attended the first meeting, only three — Lloyd M. Coppens, Raymond G. Hoyt and William G. Wagner — were listed in the 1921 city directory as musicians. Occupations of the others included secretary of a men's clothing store, letter carrier, cigar maker, grocer, stenographer, student, salesman and post office clerk (see Chapter 12). Whether they just loved music or saw the Band as an opportunity to earn extra money or a combination remains purely speculation. The musicians gathered again November 16, 1919. They voted to give a concert at the Coliseum no later than February 1, 1920. They also voted to ask the musicians union to provide money needed "to cover incidental expenses and procure necessary instruments in order to give [the] concert on date agreed upon." But the concert never took place. There were too many decisions that hadn't been worked out.

The question of leadership was a major issue. The musicians had elected Lloyd M. Coppens as leader, but they didn't have the power to hire him. That was for the city officials to do. In recommending Coppens, who was director of the Sioux Falls El Riad Shrine Band, the musicians argued for local talent, saying that ability should be the only criterion and that there were leaders in Sioux Falls "competent to take hold of and develop a municipal band here that would prove a credit to the city and a source of much enjoyment to the public, the object for which it is intended." However, many other people apparently considered Coppens just a temporary leader until someone could be found who could provide either a music library or name recognition. Reference was made to the Aberdeen, South Dakota, Municipal Band, whose leader was Howard C. Bronson, the man many had wanted to lead the Sioux Falls Municipal Band (see Chapter 1).

Lloyd M. Coppens, first Municipal Band conductor, shown here in his Shrine uniform, 1921. *(courtesy June Beecher)*

Who was Lloyd M. Coppens? Not much was revealed about him during the discussion of a Municipal Band conductor. His name was mentioned more often in connection with his job as conductor of the Shrine Band. That position may have made Coppens a well-known musical figure in the community, because the Shrine Band was a very popular and active volunteer musical group during the early 1920s (see Chapter 1).

A clue to Coppens' personality comes from stories about "Jollies 1920," the 1920 version of the Shriners' annual minstrel show. A newspaper story from September 23, 1920, which gave preliminary information about the show, said that "such funny men as George Talbott and L. M. Coppens will be out for end men 'positions.'" A later story, which named cast members, confirmed that Coppens was chosen to be one of the comedians in the show.

Additional information on Coppens comes from various sources. Records at the Masonic Lodge in Sioux Falls showed that Coppens was born April 19, 1881, in Lowell, Michigan. The federal census of 1920 indicates that Coppens' parents were born in Belgium; that his wife, Yvonne, was born about 1885 in New Hampshire; and that he and his wife rented a room at 821 South Phillips Avenue. Sioux Falls city directories from 1916-18 listed him as leader of the Coppens Orchestra at the Orpheum Theater; the 1919 directory listed him as a salesman at Steens Overland Company, a car dealership that distributed Overland and Willys-Knight cars at 224-226 North Phillips Avenue; and the 1921 directory listed him as a salesman for Home Electric Company, a business that sold Delco light products at 225-227 North Phillips Avenue. He was not listed in city directories after 1921.

In addition to needing a leader, musicians said that they had formed only the nucleus of the Band and needed "first chair" men. Local musicians hoped to induce top-notch players to the city by convincing businessmen to provide jobs for them, saying that the musicians "could not depend on what would be paid them for their concert work."

The Band also needed a plan. Almost a year after the vote, the City Commission certainly hadn't come up with one. The Commission then consisted of George W. Burnside, mayor; Thomas Hardimon, commissioner of streets; and John Mundt, commissioner of water and sewers. The *Argus Leader* reported that the commissioners spent time discussing the "proposed" Municipal Band at their meeting Monday, March 15, 1920, just months before the summer season was to begin. Their apparent lack of action may have been due to political pressure. The newspaper said that the Band's problems were attributed to a "comparatively few" who had been urging the City Commission to withhold the $12,000 appropriation until economic conditions improved. But the newspaper added that those people who objected to the band plan had "apparently failed to take into consideration the keen disappointment this would prove to thousands of residents of the city who do not enjoy automobiles and are largely dependent on the public parks for their summer amusements and outing. The very fact that Sioux Falls, like many another city of its size, does not afford many summer amusements, is additional reason, say the advocates of the Municipal Band, for proceeding this summer to have such an organization."

Local businessmen stepped in to help work out the pay and schedule for the Band. The tentative plan, as of late April 1920, was described in the newspaper as follows:

- Band of 21 pieces to be hired, including several "expert musicians" who would come and help form the Band.
- Salaries totaling about $10,200, leaving the remainder of the $12,000 for "incidentals."
- A schedule of 46 concerts in city parks.

The City Commission's involvement wasn't mentioned again until April 1920 when Mayor George W. Burnside finally named a committee to take charge of the organization of the Band: John Cleaver, Dennis Donahoe and Fred Spellerberg. (Edgar S. Knowles later replaced Donahoe who was unable to serve.) At that late date, Burnside instructed the committee to move rapidly with plans so concerts could begin when the park season opened. The committee met with local musicians in mid-May and amended the earlier plan as follows:

- Twenty-eight players, including about seven "first chair" men from outside of Sioux Falls;
- Thirty concerts in city parks and downtown as needed;
- Paid salaries for the outside talent, with other players being paid for each rehearsal and concert. The timetable was for concerts to begin about June 15.

On May 17 the City Commission finally approved a plan of thirty concerts beginning Thursday, July 1. Four evening concerts were to be played each week, one each at McKennan, Sherman, Covell and Library Parks.

In June, about a month before the first concert, the *Sioux Falls Press* reported that the Band was practicing in the American Legion Hall and would continue to practice every Tuesday night and Sunday morning until concerts began. There were twenty-eight musicians, all local men without the "first chair men" the musicians had hoped to recruit. What then, was the musical quality of the group? On one hand, Coppens was quoted in the *Argus Leader* as saying that the players would be "first class musicians capable of playing popular and worthwhile music that will be a feature of the outdoor life in Sioux Falls this summer." Yet Coppens' comments four days later in the same newspaper made it sound like there was much room for improvement: "This year the Band got a late start and has been unable to obtain the services of some expert outside talent who had previously signed up with other organizations but will give concerts of a character that are expected to give the public a taste of municipal band music and encourage the foundation of a much bigger and better Band next year."

This political cartoon, printed in the *Argus Leader* of May 6, 1920, was titled "Where, Oh! Where Is the Municipal Band." The cartoon shows that while Sioux Falls musicians were practicing in anticipation of Municipal Band concerts, citizens – portrayed as a warrior – were wondering what had happened to the appropriation. *(reprinted by permission)*

1920 Summer Season

The Band had hoped to play the first concert Sunday afternoon, July 11, 1920, at Sherman Park. But three days before the scheduled opener, the newspaper reported that high water had flooded much of lower Sherman Park. So instead, the first concert was played at McKennan Park Sunday, July 11, 1920, between 7 and 9 p.m. Although an afternoon concert was intended, newspaper accounts say that McKennan Park had insufficient shade to comfortably present a concert during that time of day.

Both newspapers gave favorable reviews of that first concert, saying that several thousand people attended. The *Sioux Falls Press* said that the Band "gave an excellent concert, and it was apparent to all that it will be a credit to the city."

However, the *Argus Leader* pointed out some of the problems with the concert. One problem was sound projection: "The question of throwing the sound of the music," stated the newspaper, "is yet to be solved, and sounding boards as used in other public parks may have to be resorted to before the result is satisfactory. Many in the audience but a comparatively few feet away last evening found their enjoyment of the music impaired because there was no way to carry the sound waves in the right direction. Yet the concert could be distinctly heard in scores of homes north of the park because the wind was from the south. It was audible as far north as the post office and many residents of the city sat on their front porches during the two hours and found greater enjoyment than some who went to the park." The *Argus Leader* also reported that noisy children were a problem: "Lack of a reasonable control of the children during the concert also militated against the full enjoyment. Some of the youngsters encountered so little restraint in their playing that they interfered with the members of the Band and numerous little ones kept up an almost incessant shouting that proved annoying to those who were trying to listen to the music." The problem of sound projection was solved in later years as amplification equipment was developed; the problem of noisy children continues today.

The Band's first concert was to include the following selections:

March, Invincible America, Woods
A Garden Dance, Vargas
Waltz, The Spirit of the Dance, Holmes
Overture, The Altar of Genius, King
A Tone Song, Eleanor, Deppen
March, Fraternal Spirit, Scull

Newspaper stories say that the concert actually consisted of some forty selections, although with the above list of repertoire as a guide, it seems unlikely that the Band would have had adequate time to play forty selections in two hours.

It was the first of about twenty concerts that summer, but little is known about the rest of the concerts. The selections were printed in the newspaper only for the first concert, although one newspaper article listed three selections sung by guest vocal soloist Ole Holm on Sunday, August 22, 1920, at McKennan park (see Chapter 10). It's surprising that no photograph of the newly formed Municipal Band was printed in either the *Argus Leader* or the *Sioux Falls Press*.

Sioux Falls Parks

The parks already were very important in the life of Sioux Falls residents in the early 1920s, and the Municipal Band concerts helped bring thousands of people to them. A newspaper article from the *Argus Leader* of March 13, 1920, told about the residents' love of the city parks: "As the city grows and the country becomes more thickly settled, with fences blocking easy access to the spots dear to so many of the old timers, something must be supplied where access may be given to that craving for the great outdoors which all normal men possess. It is with this purpose in view, and also to supply a place where the young folks may safely enjoy themselves, that city parks are maintained." The same article mentioned that the city planned to spend up to $20,000 in 1920 to improve and maintain the parks.

Sherman Park, then described as being in the "western extremity of the city," may have been the first choice for a concert site because in 1920 it was the only park with a permanent band stand. At that time the park consisted of about fifty acres that had been donated by E. A. Sherman in 1910.

McKennan Park (21st through 26th Streets and Second through Fourth Avenues) consisted of almost nineteen acres given to the city in 1906 by Helen G. McKennan for a park and recreation ground for the children of the city. In the early 1920s the park was best known for its beautiful flowers, hedges and trees.

Library Park (now Heritage Park) was a regular concert location. Often used for Wednesday evening concerts, the park was located in the east part of town at the corner of Weber and Sixth Street and consisted of about two and a half acres. The city bought part of the land in 1913 for $1,200 and the remainder in 1917 from Senator R. F. Pettigrew for $25,000. By 1920 the park already had a wading pool, but benches had to be put out and new trees and shrubs planted for the 1920 summer season. There also were plans for a tennis court and playground. Workmen hurried to complete a new combination bath and toilet house before the Band's first concert at Library Park — July 14 — because the Band was to play from the roof of the bath house in the hope that the music would have a better range and be heard by those who did not want to get out of their cars and enter the park.

Covell Park (now Terrace Park) also was used throughout the 1920 season. It then consisted of about twenty acres that had been purchased by the city for $15,000. In 1920 the newspaper reported that the park was "fast becoming one of the most popular of the city's parks. ..." Located in the northwestern part of the city, the park was the site of the Phillips Estate, a large house which was used for private parties and small community meetings. The park also had tennis courts and a small zoo area. Plans were being made in 1920 for a wading pool and refreshment stand.

Other Concert Sites

In addition to outdoor concerts in city parks, the Band played in the 1920 Pageant Parade in downtown Sioux Falls. The *Argus Leader* reported September 6, 1920, that the pageant, "covering the growth and rise of South Dakota from an Indian country to its present status as one of the great agricultural states of the west," consisted of approximately 125 commercial floats, beauty queens, cars by all auto companies and music by "four of the leading bands from this part of the state, led by the Municipal Band of Sioux Falls." The parade was fifteen blocks in length and required thirty minutes to pass a reviewing stand.

For this event the Band was conducted by Henry Busse of the Thurston Management. The *Sioux Falls Press* reported, "Mr. Busse is a musician of note. At one time he directed a division of Sousa's band, and he is a member of the Minneapolis symphony orchestra."

The Municipal Band even traveled during its first season, going to Watertown, South Dakota. The Band went there with the Sioux Falls American Legion delegation to its state convention. The *Sioux Falls Press*, August 22, 1920, reported that although the Band did not have uniforms that first season, some were secured for the trip "through the courtesy of the Army Salvage store recently established in the Chicago hotel building. Commander of the Harold Mason Post Arthur Muchow wore an expansive smile last night. 'Now that the Band is to have uniforms,' he said, 'I'm sure we'll have a snappy looking delegation.'"

Uniforms

Uniforms didn't became a major issue until late 1920. Although the Band had realized their importance, the Band budget hadn't allowed for their purchase. According to Charles A. Smith's *Minnehaha County History,* the appropriation was for maintenance only, and of the

$12,000 appropriated in September 1919 for use during 1920, $10,074 was paid to the Band members, leaving little for other expenses such as uniforms. The *Argus Leader* took up the call for uniforms in an article November 30, 1920, saying that the Sioux Falls Municipal Band had compared unfavorably to three other bands in the September Pageant Parade — the bands of Garretson, Edison township and Lennox — because of lack of uniforms. "Four bands marched up and down the streets of the largest city in South Dakota, three of them with proud air and heads erect, conscious of the fact that they were making something of an impression on their audiences. ... But the Sioux Falls Municipal Band, composed of capable musicians, discoursing good music, alone stepped out without the same confidence. For the three outside bands, all from small communities, were properly uniformed and the Sioux Falls band from the biggest community in the state, marched without."

The newspaper again argued for uniforms in the December 2 edition, saying, "If the police department of Sioux Falls or the firemen, served the city without uniform, citizens would deem it strange. But the Municipal Band of Sioux Falls, gradually being built up into an organization fit to appear on public occasions as representative of the musical development of the city along band lines, must wear ordinary clothing until the funds for uniforms are provided." A few days later, the newspaper added, "Uniforms are about as necessary to a band as a bass drum, for they cannot cut much of a figure when playing out of the city unless clothed in the regulation garments."

Uniform fund raising began in December 1920 with a big dance at the Coliseum, followed by a series of concerts. It was reported that Coppens and several volunteer businessmen of the city even went door to door in an effort to sell the tickets. The dance was called a success, although the *Sioux Falls Press* of December 8, 1920, had few details: "... while the exact amount raised is not known, it is believed that it will go a long way toward the purchase of the desired uniforms. It is estimated that seventy-five or a hundred couples were on the floor at one time." It's not clear if the Band purchased uniforms and began wearing them during the 1921 summer season. Newspaper articles mention that the Band was wearing uniforms by 1922.

1921 Summer Season

One major change and a few small changes occurred in 1921, the Band's second season. One was that the Band quit playing at Sherman Park after one concert. Noise from swimmers – who used the swimming area created with retaining walls and a dam in the Sioux River – detracted the audience too much, the newspaper reported.

Another change was regarding rehearsal pay. The August 13 minutes show that the Board decided to give players one dollar for each weekly rehearsal but no pay for a Sunday morning rehearsal preceding the Sunday concerts. Any member absent without a reasonable excuse from the Sunday morning rehearsal was to be fined one dollar.

It was in 1921 that the Band drafted a constitution and bylaws. Band Board minutes from August 13, 1921, show that the Band Board gave the task to Jake Helfert, Raymond G. Hoyt, Walter Rittman and Henry T. Hanson. Minutes from December 5 show approval of the constitution and bylaws.

But the biggest change was a new director. Although Coppens had been reelected director for the 1921 summer season, the minutes of December 12, 1921, show that fifteen members voted for a new director and seven voted to retain Coppens. The motion was made and carried that Coppens "be allowed 30 days time and to vacate his office as director January 15, 1922." When January 15, 1922 rolled around, the minutes record: "Motion made and seconded that Mr. Coppens be retained as director for two months from January 15th and his service terminate March 15th which resulted in a vote of fourteen yes twelve no." The Municipal Band's first conductor was on his way out.

Indoor Concerts, Starting with Sousa's Band

But before leaving, Coppens conducted a series of free winter concerts in the Coliseum, an idea that may have been spawned by the successful appearance there on November 26, 1921, of John Philip Sousa's band. It was Sousa's first performance in Sioux Falls, and advance newspaper coverage was abundant. One such advance article in the *Argus Leader* of November 4, 1921, put the best light on ticket prices: "Although his [Sousa's] expenses have increased materially in the past few years, Sousa still charges the same prices of $1, $1.50 and $2 for seats. These are the same prices that he has charged for several years." Another article, appearing ten days later on November 14, explained that Sousa's band, "an American institution," was in its twenty-ninth year and that the present tour was its thirteenth. The article said one of the "chief factors in Sousa's unusual success is his ability to give the musical public the class of music it can enjoy. " And according to newspaper reviews, Sousa's organization certainly was enjoyed by the Sioux Falls audience. The *Argus Leader* of November 28, 1921, said the performance

The Coliseum, built in 1917 at Fifth and Main, was used in the Municipal Band's early years for fundraising dances and winter indoor concerts. Sousa's Band appeared there in 1921. In later years, the Coliseum housed the Band's office and library and was used for rehearsals. *(courtesy Siouxland Heritage Museum)*

"might easily be called the most popular musical entertainment ever offered here." Although no attendance count was given, the article said that "all [soloists] were warmly applauded by a good sized audience." Soloists were soprano Mary Baker, xylophone player George Carey, cornetist John Doland and violinist Florence Hardeman. Band selections included Sousa's popular "Stars and Stripes Forever," "El Capitan March," and "The Fancy of the Town," a medley of popular songs from the past ten years. The reviewer concluded the article, "The work of the band might be called part of the triumphal tour of an organization that will live long in the memory of American audiences." Sousa's band returned to Sioux Falls four years later, playing two concerts at the City Auditorium on November 21, 1925.

The Sousa concert must have been a tough act for the Municipal Band to follow. But the Municipal Band did follow with a series of Coliseum concerts beginning Monday, January 2, 1922. The featured soloist was Johanna Downs, a teenage pianist who attended All Saints School in Sioux Falls. She had played with the Band in 1921 and, in the words of the *Argus Leader,* "won much favor." The newspaper of January 3, 1922, reporting on the concert, said: "... to her goes much credit for her interpretation of Weber's 'Invitation to the Dance.' Miss Downs promises to be a pianist of some note. Forced to respond with an encore she played the 'Elegie' of Massenet." The review praised the rest of the concert, too. "Yesterday's concert — they are periodic — was an example of what music means to the community. ... there were several semiclassical and popular selections, too. To please all palates, of course. If we take the audience of yesterday as a fair example of those in the past we will have to admit that the more sedate numbers were better received than the others. 'Semiramide,' that oriental overture of Rossini's was the best thing on the program. It was played with a good deal of appreciation. Schubert's familiar 'Marche Militaire' showed more touches of good handling."

The writer made some observations about the audience, too: "There were probably 1,000 at the Coliseum for yesterday's concert and it was evident if one watched them even a little, that they like music. The applause was never boisterous but nevertheless it was genuine and generous. There were lots of good 'folksy' looking people present that one doesn't see at the concerts where imported talent is used."

The Municipal Band's next indoor concert, on January 15, featured guest vocal soloist John Ross Reed. Reed was musical director of the traveling Biederwolf evangelistic meetings, which had attracted 20,000 people in five nights in Sioux Falls. Reed, formerly a grand opera singer, performed some grand opera pieces, as well as lighter pieces for encores. The program was as follows:

March, The Western World, Price
A Novelette, In Poppyland, Athers
Popular, My Sunny Tennessee, Kalmar
Popular, Fox Trot, One Kiss, Wood
Waltz from Ballet Suite, Sleeping Beauty, Tchaikowsky
Vocal solo, Prologue from Pagliacci, Leoncavallo
John Ross Reed, vocalist
Overture, Barber of Seville, Rossini
Ballet, Egyptian, Luigini
Grand American Fantasie, Herbert

There was a mix-up in scheduling of the Coliseum, which bumped the next scheduled winter concert from January 29 to February 13. The Biederwolf revival party still was using the Coliseum, and, according to the *Sioux Falls Press,* Coppens didn't seem to know anything about it. On January 29, the *Press* reported Coppens as saying, " 'The knowledge that we could not use the Coliseum for the concert came as somewhat of a surprise and also as a disappointment,' Mr. Coppens said last night. 'We had our program complete and had engaged Miss Frances Moore as cello soloist. It was only at the last moment that we found it would have to be called off. The date for the postponed program has not been set as we do not know where we can arrange to hold it but it will possibly be at the auditorium.' "

The soloist, cellist Frances Moore, was able to perform on the new date. She was the daughter of Dr. and Mrs. W. E. Moore, 130 North Prairie Avenue, and recently had completed a tour with a concert company. The *Argus Leader* review of February 14 said that Moore "showed fine technique and power in her solos." She was accompanied by Mrs. Guy Anderson, whose husband was a member of the Band. The review said that the audience was the largest of the year and that the Band was "listened to with a great deal of appreciation by the thousands who came out in the cold to hear it."

The final mention of Coppens in Band minutes was of February 15, 1922: "Meeting held at the court room City Auditorium for the purpose of drawing up a letter or notice to be sent to L. M. Coppens notifying him of his dismissal as Director of the Sioux Falls Municipal Band." Nothing indicated the reasons for Coppens' fall from power.

• • •

Coppens had been an important part of creating the Band, but the organization didn't collapse because he left. The next thirteen years demonstrated even more clearly that the Band's survival depended not only on the leader, but on the combined efforts of the players, the city leaders and the taxpayers.

1922-34
Passing the Baton

S ioux Falls underwent dramatic changes in the 1920s and early 1930s. Not only did the population increase from 25,202 in 1920 to 33,362 in 1930, but transportation changed from horses to cars and from trolleys to buses. The first airport was established. Silent movies gave way to "talkies," a radio station was established and the Coliseum was improved and expanded. Drake Springs swimming pool was opened. Building projects included the sewage plant, Whittier Elementary School (now Middle School), First Lutheran Church and the new Sioux Valley Hospital.

The Sioux Falls Municipal Band was undergoing changes as well. Records indicate that the Band had uniforms by 1922 and that the city's first band shell was built in 1926. But the biggest change was the quick succession of conductors during the thirteen years from 1922-34. They were Charles F. Emmel, 1922; Charles F. McClung, 1923-27; Gerard C. McClung, 1928-29; and Otto H. Andersen, 1930-34. Yet despite the many changes in Sioux Falls and in the Municipal Band leadership, the Band continued to survive, and even thrive.

1922 — Charles F. Emmel, Conductor

Municipal Band minutes dated February 13, 1922, tell of conductor Lloyd M. Coppens' successor, Charles F. Emmel, being chosen unanimously by all eighteen Band members present. There's no indication as to why his name came up for consideration. But it was clear that he was well liked. The *Sioux Falls Press* reported that Emmel, from Vandelia, Illinois, conducted a rehearsal. Afterwards, Raymond G. Hoyt, Band president, was quoted as saying he thought they had obtained the right man for the job: "What we want is a man who can work with the kind of talent which is able to get out and play in a municipal band. ... Mitchell [South Dakota] tried employing a leader highly skilled in directing professionals [Ernest Pechin]. They paid him a large salary but they did not get satisfactory results because he did not know how to work with amateurs. Aberdeen [South Dakota] is trying the use of salaried players. What we are trying to do, however, is to interest the young fellows just starting out and others who may have only moderate ability but willingness to cooperate. In this way we think that we can gradually build up a band of which the city may be proud. ..."

Unlike Coppens and some of the later Municipal Band directors, Emmel did not have the second job of conducting the Shrine Band; instead, Coppens continued conducting the Shriners during 1922, being replaced at the end of the year with the Municipal Band's third conductor, Charles F. McClung.

Emmel's first three concerts were in the Coliseum: March 12, March 26 and April 16, 1922. The *Argus Leader* wrote after the third winter concert that the Band had demonstrated major improvement under Emmel, suggesting that the Band's previous performances hadn't been very good: "Sioux Falls now has a municipal band of which all may be proud. The improvement of the Band has been especially noteworthy during the series of winter concerts just completed and shows what consistent practice, hard work and cooperation can accomplish. ... As the Band gave the excellent program on Easter Sunday, smartly uniformed, alert and competent, it was a complete justification for past and future Municipal Band appropriations. Sioux Falls need no longer be ashamed of her Municipal Band, and the credit is due not alone to the director but to every man within the organization. ... " It's noteworthy that the Band apparently had uniforms by this time.

The article also gave an interesting look at the audience, highly commending it for paying "unusually strict attention during the entire piece," referring to the Band's rendition of "Rigoletto" by Verdi. The newspaper said that although the program lasted a little longer than usual, "every person not only remained seated during the entire final number, but even called and sat through a final encore, which is a very rare occurrence at any musical program. There was no putting on of coats and hats during the final piece and the audience did not leave their seats until the final curtain." The audience's exemplary behavior caused the writer to conclude, "There is no question but that Sioux Falls appreciates good music."

Sectional rehearsals may have been the key to the Band's improvement. Band members were paid one dollar for each regular weekly rehearsal, providing they played the next concert. However, the newspaper reported that players also had begun having nonpaying sectional rehearsals almost every night of the week "just because of [their] interest in the work and in the success of the Band." As a result, Emmel said the Band was in the "pink of condition."

The Band in early 1922 consisted of eighteen members, including "some younger men, two of them high school band players [who] have been worked into the organization as a foundation for the future," according to the *Argus Leader*, April 8, 1922. All the players were "local men who are playing in their spare time," the newspaper reported.

The newspaper also reported that the Band was appropriated "$12,000 for eighteen months last year [1921], but only $5,519.66 was spent for the year's work." The expenses were listed as follows: Leader, $2,400; musicians, $2,000; hall rent, fuel and lights, $865; music, $100; insurance, $28.80; sundries, $125. It was said that the appropriations for 1922 totaled $7,300 and that the leader's salary of $1,800 would come out of that.

The 1922 summer schedule was to include three concerts a week at McKennan, Library and Covell Parks, with Emmel's first summer concert slated for Sunday, May 14, 1922. But that first concert was cancelled because it was too cool and rainy. In fact, it was reported that the entire summer of 1922 was one of the coolest on record, but only the first concert got cancelled due to bad weather. Fortunately, the Band was not scheduled to play on the coolest day (August 10, when the thermometer dropped to 58 at 3 p.m.), nor on the hottest day (June 22, when the temperature reached 96). The Band played at least five concerts in 1922 when the mercury climbed above 90 degrees, including Thursday, August 17, when the temperature reached 94 degrees.

The newspaper predicted that because of the Band's improvement, the summer concerts would "draw double the usual crowds, for Sioux Falls has already demonstrated in the past that good band music well rendered, is enthusiastically appreciated." While crowds may not have doubled, the newspaper did report large crowds. The first 1922 summer concert, Sunday, May 21, at McKennan Park, drew 2,000 people, with the streets around McKennan Park full of cars and all the seats in the park taken. Good attendance continued into the season. In July it was said that "... the Band concert at Covell Park drew the biggest crowd seen there this year, and it was almost difficult to get around in the park, so thick were the spectators."

The crowds were not just large, they were enthusiastic, often calling for encores. After the first concert of the summer season, the *Argus Leader* reported that " 'Morning, Noon and Night' overture and 'The Bohemian Girl' were received with particular enthusiasm by the crowds who demanded encores to every number. Two trombone novelties ... delighted the audience." Later in the summer, it was reported that "cheering crowds almost doubled the program at the concert given by the Sioux Falls Municipal Band at Covell Park yesterday afternoon [Sunday, June 4, 1922], for encores were demanded to every number."

The Band's popularity contributed to the popularity of the parks, where concerts were held. "Never before have the parks in Sioux Falls and vicinity been as popular as they have this year [1922]," said Fred E. Spellerberg, superintendent of city parks, adding that the Band concerts brought many people to the parks for an early supper before the concert. Spellerberg described how people cooked their suppers on fireplaces in the park: "The fireplaces at Covell and Sherman are used more than at McKennan. Especially is this true at Sherman. When folks get out there, they feel more like they are in the country, I guess, and do more cooking. They don't cook just coffee, either; they prepare meat, potatoes, corn and in fact, just about what they would at home." Spellerberg discounted the idea an increase in cars would mean a decrease in park use. "He [Spellerberg] pointed out that while there were many more cars than there used to be, there were many more families in the city, too, and the parks around here do not suffer from neglect."

Park attendance also got a boost in 1922 from the broadcasting of radio concerts by the *Argus Leader* broadcasting station, although at that time the Municipal Band was not yet a part of the broadcasts. A newspaper article of July 14 told of the first public radio concert received in Sioux Falls on Thursday, July 13, 1922. The broadcast was heard at McKennan Park. Local talent was featured, including singer Orville Rennie, violinist Mrs. L. G. Richardson and storyteller Mrs. T. M. Bailey, who ended the program with bed time stories for the children. Radio broadcasts also aired at Library Park.

There still was concern about the Band's ability to adequately project sound at McKennan and Library Park. At McKennan Park, the Band played on a wooden platform near the park house; at Library Park the Band played on the bathhouse roof. By July, a portable covering was used at both parks, and the *Argus Leader* reported that "the success of this portable covering was noticed by all present at Sunday evening's concert [July 16, 1922, at McKennan Park], especially those who were not fortunate enough to get close to the band stand." The newspaper said sound projection was not a problem at Sherman and

Covell Parks because of the natural acoustics. Perhaps Sherman Park's hills created a natural amphitheater effect, but it's not clear why acoustics were good at Covell Park. Before the completion in 1923 of the present amphitheater at Covell (Terrace) Park, the Band played from a wooden platform above the present terraces near the original Phillips house, according to Helen (Mrs. Wilmer) Simmons. Born in 1908, Simmons was the daughter of Joe Maddox, who built the Japanese Gardens at Terrace Park and was a caretaker there for many years. Maddox also supervised the laying of the quartzite steps leading down the terraces to the amphitheater. The steps were replaced by concrete in 1994.

In addition to concerts at McKennan, Library, Sherman and Covell Parks, the Band performed at West Soo Park for the Old Settlers Picnic (the Minnehaha County Early Settlers Association) and in Huron, South Dakota, for the state convention of the American Legion. Band minutes of August 15, 1922, show that the Band Board asked the American Legion to pay ten dollars per Band member per day to travel to Huron but accepted the nine dollars per day offered by the Legion.

One of the surprises of the 1922 season was that the Band didn't play for any Fourth of July celebrations; in fact, Sioux Falls didn't even plan any big patriotic celebration. A June 24 newspaper article said, " 'All quiet on the Sioux' seems to be the order for this Fourth of July with the exception of two ball games between Aberdeen and Sioux Falls and a celebration at West Soo Park. The city will not stage a firework display this year. ..." Although the article added that the Municipal Band would be playing at Library Park, the concert never occurred. A story after the Fourth said, "Not even the expected Band concert materialized to rouse the local populace from a Philadelphian doze."

A special feature of the 1922 programming was inclusion of pieces by Arthur Smith, local musician and composer (see Chapter 13).

The 1922 season was cut short by lack of funds. In early August, Superintendent of Parks Fred Spellerberg said that there would be no more Band concerts. However, the budget eventually allowed the Band to play two more park concerts: one August 17 at Library Park and one September 3 at Covell Park. Financial problems also caused the delay of winter concerts until January 1923. The city changed its fiscal year from October through September to the calendar year, causing the Band's appropriation to run out in September 1922. No more money was given until January 1923, according to the *Argus Leader,* October 25, 1922. The newspaper had earlier reported on April 8, 1922, that the appropriation for 1923 was $7,300, with Emmel's salary set at $1,800.

But Emmel didn't stay to collect that salary. Perhaps it was the

financial problems that caused him to leave or the lack of connections
with the popular Shrine band. Neither minutes nor newspapers gave
an explanation.

1923-27 — Charles F. McClung, Conductor

Band minutes of December 1922 tell of the Band voting for Charles
F. McClung to become the Band's third conductor. The newspaper reported that McClung was "recognized as one of the foremost band leaders in the northwest. ..." Minutes tell of the players' support for McClung:
"Resolution made and carried — that it be the sentiment of the Sioux
Falls Municipal Band that such members pledge themselves to give
their earnest support and cooperation to the newly appointed Band director, Chas. [Charles] McClung, and to assist him in every way possible to build up a successful band organization in Sioux Falls, South
Dakota."

McClung's daughter, Jane (Mrs. Howard) Ice, now living in Beulah,
Wyoming, reported that Charles was born in Kingsbury (near La Porte),
Indiana, in about 1884. He worked in Canada and played in theater
orchestras in Chicago and New York.

The *Sioux Falls Press* reported in January 1923 about McClung's
previous band experience. He had conducted the Tripp, South Dakota,
Municipal Band for three years and the Mitchell, South Dakota, Municipal Band for one year, along with the 147th Field Artillery Band,
also stationed at Mitchell. His salary with the Mitchell Band was listed
at $2,500.

While conducting the Sioux Falls Municipal Band, McClung also
conducted the El Riad Shrine Band, the National Guard band encamped
at Pierre, South Dakota, and a Sioux Falls youth band, which he formed.
The purpose of the youth band, according to the *Argus Leader,* was to
train young musicians for the Municipal Band: "This band will be open
to all youngsters, while older candidates will not be turned away, it is
said, as all interested are felt to be the popular type of material to feed
into the Municipal Band later." Twenty-four young musicians signed
up for the youth band, and rehearsals started at the end of January
1923.

The Municipal Band, meanwhile, was getting ready for the 1923
season. The Band of about thirty-five members was practicing on Monday and Friday nights. The summer outdoor season was to begin Sunday, June 10, continuing to August 30, with concerts rotating among
McKennan, Library and Covell Parks on Sunday and Thursday eve-

nings. Because the first two scheduled concerts were cancelled due to rain, the first summer concert actually took place Sunday, June 17, 1923, at Covell Park.

An article from the *Argus Leader* of August 6, 1923, gave some interesting insights about the Band and the audience. Here's what was said about the large crowd at Library Park and the Band's reaction to the crowd: "... The audience was not confined to residents of the east side as was indicated by the streams of cars and pedestrians who found their way across the river from the west side. Neither can it be said that the listeners were entirely a Sioux Falls crowd, as many cars were noted bearing name plates of surrounding towns, ... the bandsmen are not unappreciative of an appreciative audience. It is a legend of the music profession that a musician or body of musicians can obtain the best results when performing before receptive and responsive audiences."

The story also gave a personal glimpse of tuba player and charter member Austin K. Bailey: "If anyone has the impression that playing one of the big bass horns with one hand is an ideal way to spend a Sunday afternoon, they are advised to interview A. K. Bailey, one of the tuba artists of the Band. Mr. Bailey was unfortunate recently in losing a finger through blood infection, but he has missed almost no concerts and has been manipulating the giant horn with a bandaged hand, which is said to be no pleasant pastime."

Finally, the newspaper article made a plea for building band shells, an argument that continued throughout most of McClung's tenure. Apparently the portable covering used on the bandstands in 1922 was not effective enough. "All metropolitan cities are rapidly adopting the band shell idea for their parks," asserted the writer, "and it is only after hearing a production from one of these shells that full realization can be attained of the wonderful benefits to be derived. Sioux Falls is in dire need of a few band shells and it is the hope of music lovers that the Park Board will be able to realize this need and see their way to erecting one in each park in the near future."

Municipal Band concerts of 1923 were given part of the credit for attracting a large number of people to the city parks, exceeding the 1922 attendance of 100,000.

In late 1923 and early 1924, the Band Board acted on several ideas, including approval of the following items: a trip to Mitchell for Sioux Falls Day at a price of $5 each; dances at the Coliseum to raise money to purchase band equipment; a concert at the South Dakota State Penitentiary; a free concert for dedication of Hawthorne Elementary, 601 North Spring Avenue; and deciding that "not less than sixteen men can play an engagement in uniform and be classified as the Sioux Falls

Municipal Band."

A few changes came in 1924, McClung's second summer season. Concerts were increased from two to four per week; Band membership decreased from thirty-five to thirty; Terrace Park (whose name had changed from Covell Park that year) was added to the weekly rotation of concerts; and Elmwood Park was added as the regular Sunday afternoon concert site.

In 1924, Elmwood Park, located at North Kiwanis Avenue and Russell Street, became five times larger with the city's purchase of 160 acres for $20,000 (the original forty-two acres, known as West Soo Amusement Park, had been purchased in 1923 for $5,500.) It was estimated that close to 5,000 people had heard the Municipal Band at the formal opening of Elmwood Park Sunday, August 3, 1923, causing the Park Board to suggest that the park be used weekly in 1924 for band concerts.

Already in 1924 city officials were envisioning today's Elmwood Park golf course, with D. L. McKinney, a member of the Park Board, quoted in the *Sioux Falls Press* in August 1924 as saying that "perhaps this fall work will be started on an eighteen-hole golf course, which will be finished in two years."

The *Sioux Falls Press* summed up the 1924 summer season by saying on September 6, "The Band has enjoyed an unusually successful park season. ... Thousands of Sioux Falls citizens have heard the performances through the season. Concerts were given four times a week all summer."

Minutes of August 25, 1924, show that the Band Board voted to "request an appropriation of $15,000 for the year 1925 and entire appropriation be applied to Band service." The Board also voted to charge three dollars rather than two for playing at football games.

Apparently nothing startling occurred in 1925, McClung's third summer season. It consisted of fifty summer concerts. Musical highlights included "All King" programs, featuring music written by noted composer Karl L. King of Fort Dodge, Iowa, called a personal friend of McClung. At the end of the 1925 season, McClung was quoted in the newspaper as saying, "The large crowd attending every concert was proof of the fact that the music was enjoyed, and the members of the organization are grateful for this support."

McClung's fourth season, 1926, marked a milestone for the Band with the completion of the McKennan Band Shell. The Cosmopolitan Club of Sioux Falls had taken on the project in 1925, completing fundraising ($4,000) and construction in just one year and two days (the construction took one month). The Club presented the band shell as a gift to the city on Sunday, July 4, 1926.

Local contractor Conrad Knudson designed and built the band shell, located in the southwest part of McKennan Park and facing north. It was described in the *Argus Leader*, July 3, 1926, as follows: "It is of stucco with a metal tile roof. The outside dimensions are fifty-four feet six inches wide; twenty-five feet eight inches deep and thirty-six feet high. The stage is thirty-four feet wide and twenty-one feet six inches deep. The lights in the shell part are concealed in a trough which runs around the shell and reflects the lights into the curved part. The base of the building is painted green and the main part is cream and white."

A plaque, which is still there today, was placed in the center of the front base of the band shell and reads:

Presented by
Cosmopolitan Club
July 4, 1926,
assisted by Municipal Band
Nameplate donated by
[illegible]

The Band tested out the shell before its official dedication on July 4, 1926, and it was reported that McClung gave it high marks. Future conductors were not as impressed with the band shell, finding that it compared unfavorably to the modern "Showmobile" purchased in 1973 (see Chapter 7).

Afternoon ceremonies at McKennan Park to dedicate the band shell drew nearly 4,000 people, while evening ceremonies — also marking the 150th anniversary of the signing of the Declaration of Independence — drew "an enormous audience, estimated by members of the committee in charge at 10,000 persons," according to the newspaper.

Not everyone was pleased with the new band shell, however. Horseshoe enthusiasts, whose courts were located in front of the band shell, didn't like efforts to move the courts to another part of the park. When the Cosmopolitan Club had presented its plan for the band shell, the Park Board had assured the Club that the courts would be moved when a suitable place could be found. Three months later the courts still had not been moved. The Cosmopolitan Club said "if a $4,000 shell could be built in one month, the courts could be moved in much less time." McClung brought the matter to the public attention "when he refused to operate his band in competition with the music made by the clang of 'ringers,' 'leaners,' and the like against the iron stakes. He ... refused to play more concerts until the courts were moved." Band members complained not only of noise but of danger to the public, saying, "Many people have barked their shins against the iron posts which are used, and children have fallen into the courts." Horseshoe players responded that since the courts were in place before the band shell was built, they had "priority rights." They even suggested that the band shell be moved. But the music lovers finally won out, and the horseshoe courts were moved.

With McKennan Park getting the band shell, Library Park inherited the old wooden McKennan bandstand. That meant that Library Park concerts no longer had to be played from the top of the bathhouse: "The bandstand was rebuilt and placed just east of the wading pool. It has been enlarged until it is now twenty-five feet square and will accommodate fifty men. The stand is about three feet from the ground."

The Band continued rotating concerts among McKennan, Library and Terrace Parks in 1926. The plan was for all Sunday afternoon concerts to be played in the new McKennan band shell, but in July the band began playing Sunday afternoon concerts at Sherman Park "to give the large number of out-of-town people who visit the park on Sunday afternoon a chance to hear the concert."

In addition to the building of the McKennan band shell, a major event in 1926 was the dedication of the city sewage plant on August 16. The Municipal Band furnished music, "playing a number of popular numbers and rousing marches, winning considerable applause from the hundreds of persons attending the ceremonies." The $600,000 plant, located "east of the spillway and between the river and the Dell Rapids road [Cliff Avenue]," was called the largest single project undertaken by the city of Sioux Falls. The Izaak Walton League had been instrumental in getting the sewage treatment plant issue on the ballot in November of 1925, and the issue had carried overwhelmingly. It was said that "the river was in such condition, due to the pollution, that no water animal could live in the waters. ..." A. H. Bolton, a Sioux City attorney and a prominent member of the Izaak Walton League, spoke at the dedication and "predicted that in the future all large cities would be required by federal laws to treat their sewage in a manner so that fish and other aquatic life may exist in the streams into which it is diverted."

Another big event of 1926 was a mammoth Labor Day parade, part of a two-day celebration. The Municipal Band, along with the Garretson, South Dakota, band and the Salvation Army Band, provided music. Sponsored by the Trades and Labor Assembly, the event featured contests — including pie eating, doughnut eating and milk drinking — carnival rides, concession and souvenir stands, side shows and dancing.

The final concert of the 1926 summer season was on September 5 and was dedicated to Mayor Thomas McKinnon. The newspaper said that McKinnon was Scottish and, at his request, the concert featured a medley of songs from Scotland, including "Fantasia, Songs from Scotland" by Godfrey.

The 1926 season was summarized in the newspaper as follows: "The Band has played forty-eight open air concerts this season, beginning June 13, and playing four a week when the weather permitted. These concerts were given in the four city parks, McKennan, Sherman, Terrace and Library Parks; ... the Band ... is composed of thirty members."

An important action took place at the end of 1926. Minutes of December 6, 1926, showed that the Board voted "that McClung and McKensie act as a committee to arrange for [a] band concert over radio station KSOO for their first programs."

A newsworthy happening in Sioux Falls in the summer of 1927 was the stopover of Colonel Charles A. Lindbergh in his famous "Spirit of St. Louis." Lindbergh was on a three-month tour to every state in the union, and Sioux Falls was the only stop in South Dakota. In anticipation of the August 27 event, the Band featured "The Spirit of St. Louis" march for the first time at a concert Sunday, July 24, 1927, at McKennan Park. Although the Band didn't actually play for Lindbergh when he landed at Renner Field north of town, the Band did play later that day from the balcony of the Cataract Hotel. But by then Lindbergh was airborne again, on his way to Sioux City, Iowa.

The 1927 summer season, like the 1926 season, included forty-eight concerts, all conducted by McClung. But in 1927, for the first time on record, the Band Board voted to name an assistant director. Raymond G. Hoyt was named to that position August 8, 1927. Perhaps it was a foretelling of McClung's leaving. The September 1927 issue of the Sioux Falls American Federation of Musicians newsletter reported that after the Labor Day concert of 1927, McClung "tied his little red circus wagon on the back of the trusty old Chevrolet, and was off on the big adventure." The adventure was farming a large tract of land near Newell, South Dakota. His daughter Jane McClung Ice recalled that her father stayed on the ranch for a short time. He chose to continue his musical career and moved to Spearfish in 1929 where he became band director in the Spearfish public schools, Black Hills State Normal School and the Belle Fourche Cowboy Band. He died in 1966.

At the December 29 meeting, the Band Board was acting on applications for a new conductor. G. C. McClung, Charles' brother, was chosen for the job. Other applicants included Howard C. Bronson, the man many wanted to lead the Band back in 1919; J. W. Brown; Richard J. Guderyahn, later orchestra and band director at Augustana College and founder of the Town and Gown, forerunner of the present South Dakota Symphony; and Theodore Thorpe.

1928-29 – Gerard Conn McClung, Conductor

In announcing G. C. McClung as the new director for 1928, the *Argus Leader* reported that McClung had been directing bands since 1913. The January 5, 1928, article provided readers a brief biographical sketch: "During the war [World War I] he was in the Navy and was stationed on the *U.S.S. Pittsburgh* for eighteen months as assistant director, having charge of all rehearsals. Until last summer he was located in the South with the C. G. Conn Mobile branch, organizing bands and instructing. He was director of the Capitol City concert band at Tallahassee, Florida, and was with the thirteenth coast artillery band at Pensacola. At one time he directed the boys band at Scotland [South Dakota] and in competition with experienced players, won first prize with his band. Since last summer he has lived at Tripp, [South Dakota], his former home, with his family and has conducted the Tripp band. For the time being he will drive to Sioux Falls for rehearsals each Monday evening and will move his family to Sioux Falls as soon as he can find a house. He has two children." The two children, Virginia and Marjorie, both are living. Virginia (Mrs. James) McClung Maguire reported that her father was born in 1893 in La Porte, Indiana. The McClungs were friends of the Conn family, the famous instrument manufacturers from Elkhart, so they gave their son the middle name of Conn. Gerard chose cornet as his major instrument but also played sousaphone, according to Virginia.

With McClung as conductor, audience-request concerts and guest vocalists gained popularity. The newspaper reported that "hundreds of requests have been sent in to Mr. McClung for special numbers. These requests have varied from popular to classical numbers and for solos. ..." The requests came from "local music lovers, radio fans and people from out of town who drive into the city to attend the concerts. ..."

Band members weren't convinced that they should retain McClung as conductor for 1929. The Band's dissatisfaction with McClung seemed linked with his dismissals of Band members. Minutes of October 15, 1928, read: "Motion made, seconded and carried that G. C. McClung be retained as director of Municipal Band for 1929. Votes cast by ballot thirteen Yes, eight No." Apparently that vote didn't satisfy everyone, because a meeting was to be held November 5, 1928, "for the purpose of electing a director for the coming year." The majority voted against McClung, eleven in favor, fifteen against.

It is clear that the animosity towards McClung was not gone. On January 17, 1929, Mayor McKinnon, appearing before the Board, stated "that it was his desire that the members get together and iron out the trouble so that the members and director could work in harmony and keep up the good record that our band has had in the past." He also stated that he wanted the director "to have charge of the hiring and releasing of the men as it is handled in other departments of the city." The band had one more vote, on January 24, and voted fifteen to seven to retain McClung: "After remarks by several members and the director that all differences and ill-feeling would be forgotten and that all would work together for the best interests of the Band, the meeting adjourned."

After the question of director was finally decided, business went on as usual. Highlights of 1929 minutes included:

- The Board decided to approach the mayor with the suggestion that Band members get paid for all concerts, even if called off because of rain, "for the reason that the musicians are prepared to fill the engagement and many times meet at the place of engagement and find that the engagement is called off" (Minutes, March 28, 1929).
- The Band Board and board of directors of the Musicians Association met to "decide the advisability of accepting a transfer member into the local [union] whose intention it was to become a member of the Band, when there is a local member or members that are in good standing and may be available." The Band Board agreed: "That the Band Board recommend to the board of directors of the Association that no transfers be accepted for jobs when there are any local men available who are capable of playing the job" (Minutes, July 28, 1929).
- A committee working on revision of the constitution and bylaws met and were told that the Mayor wanted the next Band director to have "complete jurisdiction and authority over the Band, especially as to hiring and dismissing men of the Band. It being his intention that the Band should be run the same as any other department of the city" (Minutes August 9, 1929).

Although no record was found, McClung apparently resigned in 1929. His daughter Virginia recalled that he again took a job with the Conn Company, living in Tonkawa, Oklahoma. They moved to Watertown, South Dakota, in about 1930 and later to Deadwood where

McClung became a band director in the public schools. In June 1939, they moved to Spokane, Washington, and he became a salesman for a music store. During World War II he worked at a naval supply depot. A serious head injury while on the job ended his working career. He died in 1978 at the age of eighty-five.

By October 10, 1929, the Band Board was discussing a new director for the next season. The Band president, Raymond G. Hoyt, was to find out if "any arrangements had been made or would soon be made regarding the selection of a director and of work for the next year." The Board also moved to recommend Otto Andersen —a union member, director of the El Riad Shrine Band and possibly a Municipal Band member — for the position, if the city decided to hire someone from the area.

On November 25, 1929, the *Argus Leader* reported that Arthur R. Thompson already had applied for the position of Municipal Band director. Thompson, former high school band director at Madison, South Dakota, and newly hired to conduct the Washington High School Band in Sioux Falls, said he would conduct both the high school band and Municipal Band for a fee of $1,000. He said he hoped that his leadership in both positions would inspire high school musicians to join the Municipal Band.

The musician union's power became obvious in the discussion about a new conductor. The *Argus Leader* reported that Joseph Nelson, water commissioner, told Thompson, a nonunion musician, "that the band in this city was a strictly organized group of musicians and said, 'I would have to insist that you'd have to qualify as a capable leader, and in that way, because of union regulations, I don't believe that you'd be able to work in any high school musicians this year.'" The Commissioners postponed acting on Thompson's application, saying that the city attorney needed to check Thompson's qualifications and discuss the matter with the union men. The Commission also agreed that the musicians must be pleased with the selection in order to perform well. The *Argus Leader* noted on November 25, 1929, that the trades and labor assembly had passed a resolution the week before against the hiring of Thompson. That resolution was not presented to the Commission, but was to have been presented November 25, 1929, to the city auditor.

Four days later the newspaper printed a statement from Thompson, who said he had not only applied for the position but had made a verbal contract with the mayor and City Band Board on August 8, 1929, to be Municipal Band director. City Commission minutes showed no record of such a meeting. It was the beginning of a month of uncertainty about who would become the conductor.

On December 1, 1929, the Band Board called a special meeting to discuss Thompson's statements. The Board stressed that Thompson was not a union musician, and again gave their support to Andersen.

The next day, December 2, 1929, the newspaper reported that despite controversy about his directorship, Thompson was going ahead and naming instrumentation for the Band. The article even told how to get application forms for tryouts.

On that same day, City Commission minutes showed that representatives of the Band appeared before the Commission and urged the appointment of Andersen. Again, "the matter was taken under advisement." Also on that day, Band Board minutes show that the musicians were planning their strategy in fighting Thompson's appointment. They agreed to try to get a union representative and Shrine representative to accompany the Band representative at the next City Commission meeting. For good measure, the Board members themselves unanimously elected Andersen as Band director.

It was just a week later, December 9, 1929, that City Commission minutes indicated that Andersen, not Thompson, was appointed director. In fact, the newspaper reported that "no word was spoken of Arthur Thompson. ..."

On December 15, 1929, Andersen appeared before the Band Board to explain the contract that he expected would be signed the next day. The minutes read: "The contract was read, and he [Andersen] explained it in detail stating that if it is signed by all parties required and he is the director he hopes to have the confidence and cooperation of every member of the Band. Mr. Andersen then retired so that the members could discuss it. After a short discussion it was moved, seconded and carried that Mr. Andersen be called in the meeting and we give him a rising vote of confidence and that our best cooperation will be given him as director. ... This was done and Mr. Andersen thanked the members for the support promised."

But the controversy still wasn't over. On December 16, 1929, City Commission minutes showed that G. J. Danforth, representing the PTA, citizens and taxpayers, along with three PTA members, urged the city to hire Thompson and his high school band to provide part of the summer concerts. The Band appropriation for 1930 was set at $12,500, and the PTA representatives suggested that $5,790 of it be given to the high school band for twenty-two concerts, from January 1 to July 1. From that, they suggested that Thompson receive $1,500. Mayor George W. Burnside's comments about the proposal suggest that perhaps the city had made some sort of verbal agreement with Thompson. Burnside was quoted as saying, "I may say that I feel under obligation to Mr. Thompson, and this city is under obligation to do what is right." Danforth said,

"Mr. Thompson came here under a misapprehension, and since the city hired Otto Andersen last week, has been without hope of aid from the city as director of the Municipal Band." Others spoke of Thompson's training and ability with young musicians.

Although the Commission didn't make a decision at the December 16 meeting regarding the high school band, they did approve Andersen's contract. He was to receive a salary of $2,500 for the first nine months of 1930. " 'That settles that controversy,' Mayor Burnside sighed, as the contract passed," reported the *Argus Leader,* December 16, 1929.

A week later the City Commission agreed to give Thompson's high school band $4,000 of the $12,500 Municipal Band appropriation. In addition to the $12,500 appropriation for 1930, $2,000 was left from the 1929 appropriation of $11,000.

The newspaper said that besides objections from Municipal Band members, one commissioner, Alex Reid, voted against the plan. Reid said, "We're paying the children to go to school if we adopt that resolution. I don't think we should give them anything, and I won't vote for it."

1930-34 — Otto Andersen, Conductor

With all the controversy, little was said about the Municipal Band's new conductor. Apparently Andersen had lived in Redfield, South Dakota, before moving to Sioux Falls. He was listed as church choir director in 1915 of First Congregational Church, Sioux Falls, in the church's centennial history book. In Sioux Falls city directories 1917 through 1936, he was listed as a travel agent, salesman, and director of the Municipal Band. He also was listed on the Shrine Band roster as a horn player in the early 1920s.

Andersen's first summer season probably was the most unusual Municipal Band season on record. Because of the city's contract with Thompson, the high school band played seven concerts before the Municipal Band's playing season of July 2 through September 1. The performance schedule of Thompson's high school band, called the Sioux Falls Symphonic Band, played from June 13 through June 22 at the Wintersteen Building at the corner of Main and Eleventh and at McKennan, Sherman, Terrace and Library Parks.

After that, Andersen's first summer season was rather routine, judging from newspaper accounts. But Band members apparently were pleased with Andersen's work, because in minutes of August 24, 1930, they adopted a resolution recommending Andersen be director for the following season. The resolution said that Andersen "has conducted the band in a very efficient, capable and satisfactory manner to the end that the members of the Band and the director are cooperating to the fullest extent to make the Band as efficient as is possible. ..."

The budget for 1931 was raised to $14,000, and minutes of December 1, 1930, said that "the Municipal Band is assured that the high school band is to receive none of it so that we are benefited financially by $5,500 over last year, which should help materially in providing a better band for the 1931 season."

The subject of uniforms came up at Band Board meetings several times during Andersen's tenure. On February 16, 1931, the Board discussed cleaning and repairing uniforms and possibly getting new caps from Pettibone Brothers of Cincinnati. But the uniform discussion continued because the dress code wasn't being followed. Minutes of June 1, 1931, explain: "The committee further recommends that immediate steps be taken to see that all members are supplied with cap emblems, and that all members be required to obtain the uniform trousers. On recent engagements, several members have appeared in all colors and patterns of trousers, which does not lend anything to the good appearance of the band." The uniform issue was again discussed at the July 13, 1931 meeting: "... a resolution signed by several band members was presented referring to the manner in which some members of the band appear in uniform at concerts and providing a schedule of fines for appearing at a concert in any but the prescribed regulation uniform adopted by the Band and also specifying when a member should be automatically dropped from the band with terms of reinstatement." But the resolution was rejected "for the reason that a previous resolution included a part of this one and further that the director was already empowered by the Mayor with hiring and firing members of the Band." In 1932, the uniform discussion centered on securing white or light trousers for the summer. The idea was voted down.

Again in 1932, new uniforms were discussed. This time Walter Kleinheinz made a motion at the December 5, 1932, meeting "that members of the Band purchase new uniforms before the next Band season starts and that each member pay for his uniform by July 1, 1933, and if it is not paid for by that time, that the secretary hold the amount, to be approximately $20 out of what the member may have coming to him at that time." A committee was appointed to investigate and obtain bids. At the next meeting, December 5, 1932, a lengthy resolution was adopted. The resolution referred to the "designation of uniform, regulations concerning same and penalties for violations of such regulations. ..."

In 1931 minutes suggest that the Band may have been coming

under attack, perhaps because of the tough economic times. The Band had been approached by two groups and asked to play for free. A committee appointed to look into the matter reported on June 1, 1931, saying that in general gratis engagements were to be discouraged. However, the committee added this note: "... with existing conditions in mind and knowing that this organization cannot afford to deliberately make enemies and that we need friends, your committee recommends that the Band agree to play the Peony Show gratis."

Band members began to express dissatisfaction with Andersen after the 1934 season. Vocalist Ed Paul said that Andersen's detractors frequently held meetings after the concert at Terrace Park, meeting behind the building at the top of the hill. Paul said that Anderson had a bad disposition and players felt that he was insulting and embarrassed them. Ultimately there was a mutiny against him. However, Band members realized that appropriation time wasn't the right time to discuss a change in directors. Minutes of August 13, 1934, read: "It was explained to the Board that a petition was being circulated and signed by members of the Band regarding and concerning the Director and after prolonged discussion it was the opinion of the Board that it was not wise to bring this matter any further before the Band members at the present time for the reason that the City Commissioners are now working on the appropriations for next year and as there are some citizens who would be glad to have the Band appropriation eliminated it may give them more arguments to accomplish their ends." Band members voted twenty-two to seven to oust Andersen at the November 18th meeting.

When asked why he thought there were no band records or program books in the Band room from the 1920-34 period, Paul said, "Otto Andersen was very angry when he was fired, and who knows, he may have taken all the records with him when he left." Paul also reported that because of the strife of Andersen leaving, several men quit playing after the 1934 season. Consequently, this created new openings and quite a few new, young people joined the Band in 1935.

• • •

The Municipal Band's leadership had changed five times in fifteen years. The Band needed a new leader who could not only heal the wounds caused by conductor Otto H. Andersen, but also keep the Band alive during years of financial hardship and World War II. That leader was Russell D. Henegar, the Band's first long-term conductor, leading the Band for the next twenty-nine years.

1935-39
The Music ...
and a Lot More

W hile frequent leadership changes had caused few serious problems during the Sioux Falls Municipal Band's first fifteen years, the tough economic conditions of the 1930s threatened the Band's very existence. The Great Depression had a dramatic impact on the Sioux Falls economy. Band Board minutes suggest that the Band's budget, like the rest of the economy, was affected by the Depression. Band members were especially concerned in the summer of 1934 about the following year's appropriation. Band minutes of August 13, 1934, indicate that Band members were careful not to advertise their dissension over conductor Otto H. Andersen until the yearly Band appropriation had been made (see Chapter 3). Despite the careful political maneuvering, the minutes later speak of a reduced appropriation for 1935, causing the Band to "omit a few concerts from the [1935] schedule. ..."

The financial picture for the Band might have continued to worsen had it not been for the leadership of the sixth conductor of the Band, Russell "Russ" D. Henegar. Henegar was hired for the 1935 season and continued to lead the Band through 1963. Henegar's ability to keep the Band going through the mid to late 1930s was a credit to his musical skills and his innovative programming skills and probably to his ability to maintain good relations with city government. No records indicate that the Band received funds under the New Deal programs; the city alone continued to fund the Band because its citizens wanted it.

Henegar's musical credentials were impressive. He was a skilled cornetist, just one of four South Dakotans who had played in the famed band of John Philip Sousa. One former Municipal Band player, Marlin Brown, said he was in awe of Henegar because of his work with Sousa. After all, said Brown, Sousa's name probably was the most widely known in the United States other than Franklin Roosevelt's.

Henegar's showmanship, programming and public relations skills became apparent soon after he took over the Municipal Band. He expanded the traditional Band concert to incorporate guest dancers, twirlers, vocalists and instrumentalists, not just from Sioux Falls but from nearby towns. He also reached out to nearby towns by having the Band make "good will" trips. After Henegar's first year as conductor, Band Board minutes glowingly reported: "New features and specialty numbers were included in the programs the past season by our director, Mr. Henegar, and were partly responsible for bringing out the largest crowds ever appearing at our concerts which were attended not only by local people but by those from miles around. ... I am sure that the members will agree that the first season under the leadership of Russ Henegar has been the most successful and made the Band more popular than any year in the past and that only by such leadership and the cooperation of the members can the coming season be as successful." Such high praises were made throughout the 1930s. Henegar showed that even when finances were a concern, the Band remained a popular way to provide varied entertainment to the community and an effective way to give positive publicity to Sioux Falls.

Henegar's Early Years

Henegar was a South Dakotan, born September 9, 1897, at Chamberlain to Harriet "Hattie" E. Dent Henegar and Leander "Lee" LeRoy Henegar. His father served in various county public offices, including deputy county sheriff, county treasurer and county auditor. Lee Henegar had natural musical talent, often playing piano by ear for the guests at their boarding house. In later years he formed a partnership with his son, Russ, to establish a music store in Mitchell.

Lee and Hattie had two children, Russ and Eileen Pearl Henegar (Mrs. Earl Nason). Both became professional musicians. Eileen became a concert pianist, and was featured with the Municipal Band in 1948, 1952 and 1955 during her brother's tenure (see Chapter 6).

Henegar told reporter David Smith of the *Argus Leader* in an article from the 1950s about the beginning of his musical career: "Dad purchased the first cornet for me when I was thirteen. I had wanted a slide trombone. Didn't slide trombone players have a front seat on the

This photograph of the Lyric Orchestra in Mitchell, South Dakota, dated February 19, 1921, shows a young Russ Henegar (third from left) playing cornet. *(courtesy Doris Dean)*

brightly colored circus wagons of that day? Dad's mind was set on a cornet, however. Soon I was playing first chair and solos in the town band. After about a year, when not in school, I played in my first orchestra with an uncle, W. D. Henegar, who was a harpist and operated his own orchestra."

Henegar graduated from high school in Mitchell, South Dakota, in 1914, and married Gladys Hopkins June 16, 1916. They had two children, Doris Henegar (Mrs. Paul Dean), of Sioux Falls, and Dale Henegar, of Bismarck, North Dakota.

Dean said that for the most part her father was a self-taught musician. She said that although her father couldn't play by ear, he could play anything that was written. Henegar had studied cornet and conducting sometime after high school from outstanding professionals, according to newspaper articles written during his Municipal Band years. An *Argus Leader* article from about 1951 indicated that Earl Flanders was one of Henegar's first cornet teachers. Flanders had directed bands at Rapid City and Mitchell and was a member of a famous Scotch Canadian band that toured the country. Ernest Pechin was another of Henegar's cornet teachers. He was described in the article as "an outstanding cornetist of the day." Frederick N. Innes, who taught Henegar conducting, was "a Chicago concert bandmaster of national repute." Henegar also studied harmony and composition from John Byers at Dakota Wesleyan University in Mitchell, South Dakota.

Henegar's professional musical experience included playing with the Patrick Conway Band of Ithaca, New York, as assistant solo cornet under Pechin, and also playing with the Walter Shaffer Band. According to Albert Powell Graham's book, *Great Bands of America,* the Conway band was a nationally-known band, performing at almost every major music and entertainment center in the country.

Henegar then organized his own dance band in Mitchell, South Dakota. The band toured the Midwest, playing in ballrooms, theaters and hotels and on vaudeville, radio and stage programs. On the back of a postcard showing "Russ Henegar and His Orchestra," Henegar's wife, Gladys, had written about her husband's band: "Seems as if Russell is always busy playing or sleeping. ... This is a picture of the new bunch. ... He says he has the best bunch now he has ever had." No date was given.

Russ Henegar and his Orchestra in the early 1920s. *(courtesy Doris Dean)*

Russ Henegar in
his Sousa Band
uniform, 1924.
*(courtesy Doris
Dean)*

Henegar Joins Sousa's Band

It was in 1923 that Henegar was offered the chance to play cornet
with the Sousa band — an offer that he couldn't refuse. Henegar, in an
undated letter addressed to Eugene "Gene" Slick, editor of the Sousa
Band Fraternal Society newsletter, explained how he "managed to be
with the Sousa band through the recommendations of Ernest Pechin
and Walter Shaffer. ... I had studied and played with both these fine
artists. No doubt Shaffer was the main reason for my getting the chance,
as I played solo cornet with him for several seasons." Shaffer was former
clarinet and assistant director with Sousa. An article in the *Argus Leader*

of August 22, 1954, gave more details about Henegar's offer. The article told how Henegar received a telegram early in 1923 asking him if he would like to become a member of Sousa's band. Henegar recalled that the Sousa band "was considered the greatest band in the world then. ..." Henegar was given ten days to make the decision; it took him just two to accept. "It was quite a jump for me to make. ... It was comparable to the situation of a pitcher playing baseball for the Sioux Falls Canaries one day and for the New York Yankees the next."

Henegar played with the Sousa band 1924-25, making two tours and covering most of the major cities in the nation. Henegar told the *Argus Leader* reporter that Sousa was a musical perfectionist but well-liked and easy to work for. Sousa's sense of humor was admired by the players.

Dean said her father left the Sousa band because "he thought he should be back in South Dakota. He had a dance band playing at the same time in Mitchell." The 1954 newspaper article said the rigorous playing schedule was "too difficult to endure. He left the band after his second season because the work meant being away from his family too long." His wife and son Dale, then just a baby, traveled with him; Henegar's daughter, Doris, stayed in Chamberlain with her grandparents. Henegar was quoted as saying, "I hated to leave the work I enjoyed so much. ... It was a thrill working among such skilled musicians and inspiring working under a man such as Sousa."

Henegar and the Municipal Band

Henegar joined the Sioux Falls Municipal Band, playing cornet 1933-34, about the time that Band members were becoming dissatisfied with their conductor, Otto H. Andersen (see Chapter 3). Dean said the players signed a petition requesting that her father become conductor. Henegar was hired in 1935 as conductor, then a full-time civil service job.

Former players spoke highly of Henegar. They said Henegar had a businesslike, no-nonsense approach to conducting that was easy to follow. They said that he was well liked by the men (like Sousa, Henegar had no women in the Band). Former Band member Marlin Brown said that during rehearsals Henegar seldom spoke other than to announce the next number to be played or when someone dared blow his instrument during intermission or between numbers. If that happened, Henegar would tell the offender, "Practice at home." Yet Brown said that Henegar frequently demonstrated a good sense of humor.

Brown remembered only one time when Henegar was visibly upset. "The only time I can recall the Band messing up was during a concert at Terrace Park. We would be playing Ponchielli's 'Dance of the Hours' from 'La Giaconda.' The Bell Telephone Orchestra had played it the Sunday evening before [on radio] and had started at Letter A instead of at the beginning. Russ decided to do the same thing but the tuba players didn't get the message. It was touch and go for awhile. It was one of the few times that I saw Russ upset."

Henegar "indoctrinated the members with the Sousa philosophy," said former band member Donald McCabe. That philosophy, said McCabe, was "be exact, be precise, be technical, be a musician." McCabe added that Henegar's later membership with an organization consisting of former Sousa band members "allowed him [Henegar] to return from his national meetings with compositions that were not offered for sale by music vendors."

Dean remembered that her father demanded that the players concentrate during rehearsals: "... [one young man], who played in the Band, used to come ... to the Band, and he'd bring a book and sit there and read sometimes in between sets; ... he was a kid, and Dad stopped the Band one time and said, '... if we're bothering you while you're reading, why don't you just go ahead and go in the other room and read?' And he put his book away. ... That's the way he would handle things."

Henegar's granddaughter Kim Dean even recalled her grandfather's businesslike attitude when she tap danced with the Band: "One thing I remember, I was probably five when I danced first with him, and he said, 'Now you go out on stage, you go, you dance, and you get off.' He said, 'You don't talk to me.' And I got up there and I danced and just as we got done I turned around and went, 'Bye, Grandpa.' And he kind of went, 'Uh, oh.'"

Occasionally Henegar would turn over the baton to assistant conductor Vernon Alger so the audience could hear the fine cornet playing that had earned Henegar a spot in Sousa's band. Former player Robert Kindred said that Henegar played a gold Conn Victor cornet. Kindred believed that Henegar was by far the best musician in the Band and was a superb cornet soloist/conductor. Kindred said that Henegar was the only cornet player as far as he knew, with other Band members playing trumpets. Although others have said that Henegar preferred the sound of the cornet, Kindred said that Henegar would never ask anyone to switch from trumpet to cornet. Former player Fletcher Nelson remembered Henegar as a good technician on cornet. McCabe, also a brass player, said Henegar "performed on cornet in the style 'a la-Sousa,' using the music found on the concert programs of the master himself

City Hall, built in 1935-36 at the corner of Ninth and Dakota, housed the Municipal Band office, music library and rehearsal room until the move to the Coliseum in 1963 or early 1964. *(courtesy Siouxland Heritage Museums)*

(opera transcriptions and the like)." Henegar's cornet skill amazed even the very young. A small newspaper clipping found in Henegar's scrapbook told about one of Henegar's nephews, age five, listening to his uncle play a cornet solo at the afternoon concert. "Whew!" he exclaimed as Henegar blew the last long note. "He must have drank a lot of milk when he was a boy!"

New Band Facilities

The new City Hall, completed in 1936 and located at Ninth and Dakota, was where Henegar's office, the music library and rehearsal room were located. The first mention of the Band Board meeting in the new band room was in minutes of February 3, 1936. An interesting reference was made to City Hall almost twenty years later in the May 1956 newsletter of the Sousa Band Fraternal Society, of which Henegar was a member. Editor Eugene Slick had visited Sioux Falls in August

1955 and played a concert with the Band. He commended the Band, saying, "Sioux Falls is one of the live cities of these United States. They support a fine municipal band. As one fellow said, 'They built the new City Hall around Henegar's band stand.'"

It was there that band rehearsals were held, 7 to 10 p.m. Monday evenings. Marlin Brown said they rehearsed fifty weeks a year. The rehearsals continued to be an important part of the members' jobs, so important that on December 6, 1937, a motion was passed that "any member of this Band who misses or stays away from three rehearsals during a year without being first excused by the director automatically tenders his resignation from the Band." A similar policy is still found in the most recent Band handbook.

Players in the 1930s remembered receiving four dollars per concert. Marlin Brown talked about the pay: "Money was hard to come by in those days and the thought of being rained out worried us, at least the younger ones. Once a concert was underway we would have had to get through the third number to be paid. This didn't happen too often as, let's face it, we didn't have much rain." Joe Foss, former South Dakota governor and Municipal Band member 1935 to 1939, said in a recent interview that the money they earned, although not great, was very helpful to them in the 1930s.

It wasn't only dry, it was hot. An *Argus Leader* story of July 11, 1956, of "twenty years ago" recounted, "Russ D. Henegar, director of the Municipal Band, reported today [July 11, 1936] that the extreme heat is causing the valves to stick on many of the horns used by his musicians. To free a sticking valve, they have to douse it with cool water from a pop bottle kept nearby."

But at least the mosquitoes weren't so bad. Brown said that there were *no* mosquitoes in 1937. According to the weather bureau, the rainfall in 1937 was 27.65 inches (close to average). The previous years had usually been below average and may have reduced the mosquito population. There was also a heavy snowfall during the previous winter which may have made the precipitation in 1937 appear normal. The reason that mosquitoes are a topic of discussion for musicians is that it is difficult to use both hands to play an instrument and not be able to swat away the bugs at the same time.

Henegar's Programming

Henegar was a good programmer, a skill he may have learned from Sousa. He was quoted in an *Argus Leader* article, December 15, 1963,

This photo, dated 1938, shows several early members of the Municipal Band. Left to right, front row: Don Foss, oboe; Palmer Kremer, horn; Orville Thompson, flute. Back row: Marlin Brown, clarinet; Ardeen Foss, oboe; Cliff Foss, trombone; and Harry Brown (not a Municipal Band member). *(courtesy Marlin Brown)*

at the time of his retirement that, "A park is not the place for heavy, concert-type music" and that "the Band's programs were designed to entertain rather than to educate." However, an examination of the programs from his first five years as conductor showed that this did not mean that he played trivial or poor music. Although he may have claimed that he was not educating the public, he did it while they were being entertained. His programs reveal that he played many of the great overtures and other compositions which had been transcribed from the orchestral repertoire of the great composers and that he never neglected the Band's mainstay which the public loved — marches. The marches of Sousa, Fillmore, Karl L. King and circus music composers appeared repeatedly on his programs.

Programs show that Henegar often featured Band members in small groups or solos. From 1935-39, instrumental features included solos on cornet, clarinet, bassoon, trombone, saxophone, xylophone and euphonium; duets of flute and cornet, baritone and cornet, two cornets and two clarinets; and a cornet trio, trombone quartet, brass sextet and saxophone octet. One unusual feature was Band member Vernon H. Alger giving the "first demonstration of the new national electrically amplified violin ..." in August 1938. A newspaper article of August 1938 reported that the electric violin had been demonstrated for the first time at Grant Park, Chicago, "only a few weeks ago."

But Henegar's skill in programming went beyond choosing instrumental music. He featured vocalists, community singing, tap dancers, child performers, baton twirlers and even a whistler. Henegar always used vocal soloists at the concerts (see Chapter 10). The oldest living, regular vocal soloist and master of ceremonies is Ed Paul of Sioux Falls who began in 1934, one year before Henegar became conductor. Paul said he had to audition again in order to retain his job. The auditions were held consecutively by having each candidate sing a number with the Band. Paul won the spot over four other candidates and continued to sing with the Band through 1964. Occasionally there were guest vocalists, including bass vocalist Harry Hadley Schyde in 1936. Guest female vocalists during the mid to late 1930s included Patricia Ryan and Frances Loewen in 1939. Even Henegar's daughter, Doris, sang with the Band each year from 1935-39 as part of the "Harmonettes" dance band trio, consisting of Doris, Marion Sather and Lynette Johnson. The El Riad Chanters sang with the Band in 1937, 1938 and 1939.

Community singing with the Band was begun in 1936. An *Argus Leader* article stated, "The innovation in community singing to the accompaniment of the Sioux Falls Municipal Band will be inaugurated at the Band concert Thursday evening at Terrace park, it was announced today. This project is being sponsored by the Sioux Falls Lions Club with the cooperation of other local groups, businessmen, and Russ D. Henegar, Band director, and his musicians. A stereopticon projector and a special screen will be mounted directly behind the Band, and those attending will sing songs chosen especially for the concert, the slides carrying the words and music so that all in the audience may follow them." Another newspaper article about the community singing said that John Morrell and Co. was donating the equipment for the community singing. The Lions Club planned to invite various civic and musical organizations to give suggestions for songs to be put on the slides. A 1937 article reported that because community singing was so popular, six numbers were included in one Sunday evening concert: "Three O'Clock in the Morning," "The Merry-Go-Round Broke Down," "In the Good Old Summertime," "Blue Hawaii," "Let the Rest of the World Go By" and "Auld Lang Syne."

Marlin Brown said that Lawrence Welk may have taken a page

The Clarence DeLong Orchestra, a Sioux Falls dance band popular in the 1930s, included Municipal Band member Robert Kindred, fifth from the left. *(courtesy Robert Kindred)*

from Henegar's book when it came to having children perform at concerts. "I recall ... two brothers, perhaps twelve and ten, who played trumpet duets." The brothers were Donald and Eddie Lias of Humboldt, South Dakota. According to the *Argus Leader* of August 26, 1938, Donald was just eight years old when he first played cornet with the Band. For an encore, he alternately played and sang choruses of "Let Me Call You Sweetheart" (see Chapter 12). There were tap dancers in 1936 from the Florence Bright School of Dancing and from the Tapantoe Studio in 1938. Other children performing with the Band during 1935-39 included twelve-year-old Richard Lanning of Sioux Falls, playing clarinet in 1939; and eleven-year-old Charleen Holdridge, singing and dancing in 1939.

Henegar pulled out all the stops for the final concerts of the summer seasons. For example, the final concert of 1936 included guest vocal soloist Harry Hadley Schyde and tap dancers from the Florence Bright School of Dancing. Fireworks were furnished by Dick Wagner of the Sioux Falls Fireworks Company to accompany the Band's playing of "Nero, the Burning of Rome." The final concert of 1938 had an even bigger lineup: a cornet solo by Donald Lias, tap dance numbers by pupils of Tapantoe Studio, a performance by the VFW Drum and Bugle

Corps of Sioux Falls, fireworks, an electric organ solo by Veda Warner and a demonstration by the firing squad from the 147th Field Artillery.

Concert Sites

Henegar's formula of offering varied entertainment apparently appealed to the audience, because concert attendance increased. Concerts generally rotated between McKennan, Nelson, Sherman, Library and Terrace Parks during 1935-40. About twice as many concerts were played at Sherman Park each season than at any other site. Yet it was Terrace Park that seemed to draw the biggest crowds. Press reports indicate that thousands of people attended each concert at Terrace Park. The number 5,000 occurred frequently, and one news report regarding an August 5, 1937, concert indicated that 15,000 were in attendance. The same figure was given for a concert August 28, 1938. However, Fletcher Nelson, a member of the Band at those concerts and through 1942, thought that the larger figure was much too high, saying 7,000-8,000 would have been more accurate. Even 7,000-8,000 is a large audience compared to those of later years. With no air conditioning, it's likely citizens sought the cooler temperatures of the parks; with little money to spare, they must have appreciated the free concerts; and with Henegar's varied programming, concerts appealed to a wider range of tastes.

In addition to park concerts, the Band played at all the major civic functions in the mid to late 1930s. Events included the laying of the cornerstones at Washington High School and the new City Hall, both in 1935, and the dedication of City Hall on September 24, 1936. Other important events the Band played for during Henegar's first five years included four performances in one day for the Norwegian Royalty which visited Sioux Falls in 1939 and three performances celebrating the fiftieth anniversary of South Dakota statehood. The Band even marched in twenty-seven parades during 1935-39, according to Band minutes.

In 1935 the Band played for a John Morrell and Co. employee picnic at Elmwood Park, just after an announcement by the local union that members would discuss a proposed strike at the plant. Thinking back, former Band member Marlin Brown, who was not yet a Band member at the time, speculated that the picnic was an attempt by the company to foster goodwill to help ward off a possible strike by workers. If so, the plan didn't work. Although the newspaper reported that about 6,000 workers and their families and friends attended the picnic, consuming 1,600 pounds of barbecued beef, workers went on strike two days later. Fifty-four workers were injured in the strike riot July 19, 1935.

The Band, along with the Sioux Falls Musicians' Union, sponsored a dance at the Coliseum in 1936 to provide relief for the city's needy. Admission was one article of food, clothing or fuel. The proceeds were given to the County and City Welfare Association. Henegar directed a fifteen-piece orchestra, which included members of the city's popular dance bands — led by Clarence DeLong, Milt Askew and Nile Running — and augmented by Municipal Band members. In addition, vocalist Ed Paul and the Harmonettes were featured. Henegar was quoted as saying, "That there is an actual need of assistance to the relief agencies of the community cannot be denied. This Good Will Dance affords a splendid opportunity for all to contribute a small amount which will not be missed and yet will do an untold amount of good."

The Band started playing more out-of-town concerts. Initiated by Henegar, these trips often were called "Sunshine Trips," with the Band accompanied by boosters, businessmen and Chamber of Commerce representatives. An article from the Lennox, South Dakota, newspaper, written before the Band appeared there, stated, "The sole purpose [of the concert] is to create a more friendly feeling between the people of the smaller communities and our metropolitan city. ..." In 1935 the Band traveled to Mitchell and Madison for exchange concerts with their municipal bands, as well as to Humboldt, Huron and Luverne (Minnesota). In 1936 the Band traveled to the South Dakota towns of Montrose, Canton, Canistota, Lennox, Garretson and Mitchell; Minnesota towns of Luverne and Pipestone; and the Iowa town of Rock Rapids.

The Band and Radio

Radio was becoming a more powerful medium in the mid-1930s, and the Band wanted to be a part of that. In *Sioux Falls, A Pictorial History,* Gary and Eric Olson wrote that Mort Henkin started KELO radio in 1937 to operate in the evening, supplementing his station KSOO, which broadcast during the daytime. The Band agreed to play for free for the dedication of the KELO station on October 3, 1937, and Band minutes of September 20, 1937, tell why: "... in as much as there is to be an attempt made throughout the country to have less recorded programs and more musicians playing in stations, it was thought well to offer our services free for the dedication and maybe get a few paid winter concerts from the station." The Band's concerts already had been broadcast over KSOO beginning in 1935, perhaps as early as 1926.

Henegar's Other Musical Duties

Henegar's conducting duties extended beyond the Municipal Band. He conducted the El Riad Shrine Band 1934-60, the Lennox Band 1936-48 and the Elks Band 1937-61. According to Verlyn Hofer, former editor of the Lennox newspaper, Henegar also conducted a band of school age students in Lennox for several years. The group's rehearsal was held one day a week, after school, perhaps the same day as Russ rehearsed the town band. In 1937 the Elks Band won first place in its class at a national Elks convention in Denver, Colorado. In 1939 Henegar brought together the Municipal, Shrine and Elks bands — a total of 100 musicians — for a mass concert.

• • •

By the end of 1939, Henegar already had served as long as Otto Andersen, the longest-term Municipal Band conductor to that point. Henegar's musical and programming skills had helped increase the popularity of the Band and kept the Band's appropriation from being cut during the economic problems of the 1930s. His next challenge would be finding enough players in his all-male organization during the turbulent years of World War II, when so many men were sent overseas.

1935. Terrace Park. Standing middle front: Russ Henegar (conductor). Row 1, L to R: William D. Meyer, George Medeck, Ray Benard, Allan Bliss?, Verne Schultz?, O. W. Palmer, Oscar Muller, Ed Paul (vocalist), female vocalist?, Jack Newton, Elmer (Eddie) Edwards. Row 2 (short row): unidentified, empty chair; Right side: Mike G. Hanson, Milt Askew. Row 3: unidentified, Leo Gossman, Raymond G. Hoyt, Guy Anderson, Joe Foss, Joe Thompson (bassoon), Palmer Kremer, L. A. Lewedag? or Walter Rittman?, William G. Wagner, Royal Ellis, Kenneth Lane. Row 4: C. R. Larson, Leonard Paul. (standing): Glen Houdek, Everett J. Reeve, Vernon Alger, Rudy H. Dornaus (string bass). (seated): O. O. Jackson, Austin K. Bailey, Burton S. Rogers, Jake Helfert, Lee Mitchell. (Note: A question mark indicates that the player was in the Band in the given year but could not be positively identified. The personnel of each year's Band may be found in the Appendix.) (courtesy Doris Dean)

1938. By First Lutheran Church in Sioux Falls. L. to R., Row 1: Sidney Jacobs, (vocalist); Glen Houdek, Vernon Alger, Everett Reeve, Russ Henegar, (conductor). Row 2: George Medeck, William D. Meyer, Leo Gossman, Ray Benard, Henry T. Hanson, C. R. "Bob" Larson, Leonard Paul, Ronald Lane, Marlin Brown, Kenneth Lane, Robert Kindred, Royal Ellis, J. M. Newton, Elmer T. "Eddie" Edwards. Row 3: Palmer Kremer, William G. Wagner, L. A. Lewedag, Walter Rittman, Orville Thompson (flute), Oril W. Palmer, Fletcher Nelson, Mike G. Hanson. Row 4: Raymond G. Hoyt, Guy Anderson, Joe Foss, Ardeen Foss, Joe Thompson, Rudy H. Dornaus (string bass), Cliff Foss, Jake Helfert, Burton Rogers, Lee Mitchell. Row 5: Orral O. Jackson and Austin K. Bailey, tubas. *(courtesy Marlin Brown)*

1940-46
Henegar's Fight to Find Players

The economic problems of the 1930s eventually gave way to the prosperity of the war years. Sioux Falls, along with the rest of the country, thrived. The city's population also grew, especially during 1942-45 with the building of the Army Air Corps Technical Training School. According to *Sioux Falls, South Dakota – A Pictorial History,* the school brought fifty thousand servicemen who attended the school for eighteen to twenty-six weeks at a time. Hundreds of family members also came to Sioux Falls during the servicemen's training. But at the same time, Sioux Falls men — including Municipal Band musicians — were being sent overseas to fight. That meant that conductor Russ Henegar had to wage a battle of his own — a battle to find enough players. As he did during the economic problems of the Depression, Henegar once again successfully held the organization together. The *Argus Leader* of August 11, 1946, reported: "Concert schedules were maintained without interruption during the war years despite the fact that twenty of the Band's members were serving in the armed forces."

Band Members in World War II

Throughout 1941-45, Band minutes mentioned members joining the Armed Forces. The first mention was made in 1941, when the Band Board held an election to replace the Band's vice president, Kenneth Lane, who had left for the Army. One year after the attack on Pearl Harbor, minutes of December 7, 1942, reported, "As in 1941, the Band again lost members through removals from the city and to the Armed

Forces." In 1943, the final paragraph of the Band secretary's report poignantly explained the problems that the Band had faced because of the war: "It was probably with a big sigh of relief and a heavy load from the mind of our Director, when after the final descent of the baton, he laid it on the stand at the close of the final concert of the season, as without a doubt this season had more worries for him than any previous year. With still more men being drafted and more difficult than ever to find replacements, the season has probably caused a few more gray hairs to appear on Mr. Henegar's head. We hope next season will be better in that regard. Nevertheless, we think that most obstacles were overcome in good shape and that the season was finished to a satisfactory conclusion." Members who went to war included Alan Bliss, Marlin Brown, Harry Ellis, Don Foss, Joe Foss, Thomas Hanson, John Howard, Bob Kindred, Palmer Kremer, Kenneth Lane, Bob Larson, Donald McCabe, Myron Moore, Fletcher Nelson, Harold Nelson, Robert Niblick, Mark Odland, Ludwig Wangberg and Everett Zellers.

The shortage of players even affected scheduling of band concerts. Minutes of March 27, 1944, reported that Henegar "asked opinions from those present regarding having the Easter concert in the evening instead of afternoon. ... On account of the shortage of personnel in the Band it would also be necessary to get some outside musicians to assist us in the concert in the evening and the director could use his judgment as to who should be asked to help for the concert." In at least one instance the Band did not give a concert because of the shortage of players. In January 1944 the Band Board turned down requests by the Army Airfield to play some concerts for the soldiers because ". . . inasmuch as the personnel and instrumentation of the band is somewhat below the concert standard by losses of members to the armed forces, that for the present and until it can be brought up to a higher standard that the band do [sic] not play at the camp."

Henegar Considers Adding Women

There's evidence that Henegar considered relieving the shortage of players by adding women players. It was not unusual during the World War II years for women to join many segments of the male work force, but Band members weren't ready to break the twenty-five-year tradition of having only male players. Henegar apparently had difficulty finding an oboist. Ardeen Foss moved from Sioux Falls after the 1941 season, and the Band had no oboist in 1942 and 1943. Milt Askew, who had played cornet, saxophone and clarinet with the Band, is listed as the only oboist at a concert on April 9, 1944. The official roster for 1944 is unavailable. Helen Brumbaugh, now Helen Hanson, wife of Wendell Hanson and mother of present Sioux Falls mayor, Gary Hanson, said that Henegar had called her and invited her to rehearse with the Band in early spring of 1945. Just before the summer Band season was to begin, Henegar told her he would have to withdraw the invitation because three veteran Band members said they would quit if a woman were brought into the Band. Hanson said she thought the Band covered the oboe part by having a clarinet play the concert pitch "C" clarinet. Hanson was also a vocalist, and although she was not allowed to play an instrument with the Band in 1945, she sang with the Band on July 15, 1945, and July 31, 1949. Brumbaugh was described in a 1949 *Argus Leader* article as "a former Augustana College student, teacher of vocal and instrumental music at Geddes, South Dakota, now a resident of this city."

Why did Band members have such strong objections to having women play in the Band? Donald McCabe, former Municipal Band member who started playing in 1942, expressed one reason: "At its inception and for many years, the Band was composed of male members only. For many, this was great because it bonded the members, more or less, fraternally. The exception to this being special considerations given to vocalists and dancers. Also, to many, when feminine musicians were allowed membership, there was a weakening of this bond." Tuba player Stan Eitreim, who joined the Band in the early 1960s, suggested another reason: "The old-timers swore they never would tolerate women in the Band. Their vulgar jokes in rehearsal and on breaks would have to cease."

Henegar probably didn't have to consider the issue of women players again, because shortly thereafter, the player shortage was relieved. In 1945 several former Band members were discharged from the service and once more became a part of the Band. It wasn't until 1964, when Dr. Leland Lillehaug took over the Band, that women became regular members of the Band.

Patriotic Concerts

During the war years, the Band provided many patriotic concerts, including the following:

    May 18, 1941: Americanization Day program, Terrace Park.
    May 30, 1941: Decoration Day parade; service, Lyon Park.

October 27, 1941: Parade and a few numbers at Coliseum for
   Navy Day program.
November 11, 1941: Armistice Day parade.
March 16, 1942: Parade to Milwaukee depot for draftees.
April 14, 1942: Parade for defense bond sale.
May 12, 1942: Parade to Omaha depot for draftees.
May 30, 1942: Decoration Day parade; service, Lyon Park.
June 7, 1942: Pearl Harbor Day [six-month anniversary], KSOO.
July 21, 1942: Parade for opening of Navy recruiting station.
July 22, August 6, August 20, and Sept. 3, 1942: Concert, Air
   Corps Training School.
Sept. 18, 1942: Hollywood Star Bond Drive, ball park.
Nov. 11, 1942: Armistice Day Parade; service, Coliseum.
May 4, 1943: Parade for Joe Foss' homecoming.
May 4, 1943: Reception for Joe Foss, ball grounds.
May 4, 1943: 15-minute broadcast on Joe Foss homecoming.
May 31, 1943: Decoration Day parade; service, Lyon Park.
August 1, 1943: Unveiling ceremony of Goddess of Liberty statue,
   McKennan Park.
April 4, 1944: Reception at Coliseum for returned members of
   the 147th regiment from Pacific.
May 7, 1944: Concert at Coliseum during display of German
   War equipment in connection with bond drive.
May 30, 1944: Decoration Day parade; service, Lyon Park.
August 31, 1944: Dedication of Honor Roll of servicemen,
   Lennox.
Nov. 11, 1944: Armistice Day parade.
May 7, 1945: Victory in Europe Day program, Coliseum.
May 30, 1945: Decoration Day parade; program, Lyon Park.
April 6, 1946: Army-Navy parade.
May 30, 1946: Decoration Day parade; service, Lyon Park.

Letters from Henegar's scrapbook show how important those Band
concerts were to people in the war efforts. One such letter was from the
commander of the Sioux Falls American Legion Post, dated March 17,
1942: "May I, in behalf of the members of Harold Mason Post Number
15, extend to yourself and each member of your Band, our sincere appreciation and thanks for assisting us in the send-off for the sons of
many of us and our neighbors who have been called to the line of duty
in the U.S. Army. We have heard nothing but fine compliments over the
occasion and I know that such impressions could only be made through
the splendid cooperation of the Band. The music played was very ap-

The Sioux Falls Municipal Band marched in downtown Sioux Falls, May 30, 1944, as part of a Decoration Day parade. They're shown in front of the Grenada Theater, Eighth and Phillips, marching south on Phillips Avenue. *(courtesy Sioux Falls Municipal Band)*

propriate and I am sure it cheered up those leaving their families and friends. These occasions have been rather sad in the past and we hope to carry on such work and I am sure we shall have to ask your help many times in the future if the state of war exists for any length of time."

A letter dated July 27, 1942, from an officer at the Air Force Technical School read in part: "The men enjoyed the concert immensely, and

look forward to future band concerts. I have heard many of them com-
ment on the excellence of the Band. I am looking forward to your concert on Thursday, July 30th, and to the concerts to be given every other
Thursday thereafter. Needless to say, this will become the most popular
event on the Post." A letter dated July 28, 1945, read: "The patients at
the AAF Regional Station Hospital [in Sioux Falls] are still enthusiastically reminiscing over the Band concert last Thursday evening. We wish
to express the appreciation of both patients and Medical Corps men for
the splendid program. They feel that the selections were exceptionally
well chosen and that the guest artists were excellent. We should like it
very much if you would give a big 'Thank you' to the entire band and to
the vocalists and the tap dancers, too. You all helped to make more
pleasant the hospitalization of many returnees and they are very grateful to you."

Sioux Falls resident George F. Menke, who was born in 1919 and
lived one block north of McKennan Park, remembered seeing many airmen at park Band concerts. He said the airmen went to the park to
hear the Band and meet women.

Guest Features

Despite war concerns, the Band tried to continue business as usual.
Henegar continued his tradition of providing guest features of many
types. Donald Lias, the child cornet soloist, continued to make appearances, as did his younger brother Eddie, who tap danced. Myron Floren
and his accordion students appeared in 1941. Other guest features during 1941-46 were the Elks Quartette, El Riad Shrine Chanters, pianist
Vada Holdridge, dancer Martha Joan Natz, the Kilties organization (from
Decorah, Iowa), Sioux Valley Nurses Chorus; a vocal trio called "The
Three Keys" from Augustana College; and an assortment of dancers
and entertainers from the Alcorn Dancing School.

In 1946, minutes show that Margaret Alcorn, head of the Alcorn
Dancing School, requested payment for furnishing entertainers for the
coming season. " ... the Board decided ... that she was receiving a great
amount of advertising for herself in being able to present her pupils
and also it would set a precedent for other entertainers. On motion by
[Harold] Hoover [Sr.], the request was refused."

In addition to Ed Paul, the regular vocalist, seven women appeared
as vocal soloists. Loretta McLaughlin was the regular female vocalist
during 1941-43 with Anne Bryant taking that spot in 1944 for the next
several years (see more on vocalists in Chapter 10).

Other Happenings

In 1942, the Band purchased new uniforms. A fund-raising dance was held February 9, 1942, and through the sale of tickets, ads in programs, and donations, enough money was raised so that each individual member, had to pay "only $9" for each uniform, according to minutes. It's puzzling that Band members had to pay at all since minutes of January 19, 1942, stated that the new uniforms were to be the property of the Band. The Band had tried unsuccessfully to recruit policemen to sell Band tickets by allowing them a ten percent sales commission. Band members wore the uniforms for the first time in the Decoration Day Parade on May 30, 1942.

Also in 1942 was a unique band dinner: a "pheasant feed." On October 11, several Band members hunted pheasants near Letcher, South Dakota. On October 19, the Band feasted on the pheasants at the Elks Club. Henegar's daughter, Doris Dean, recalled that Band members had to convince her father to go hunting. "They went to Letcher, South Dakota, and they said, 'Come on now, Russ, you've got to try.' So he said, 'OK.' And they told him what he was supposed to do, and so he aimed and he shot and he killed the bird, and he said, 'Is that it?' He didn't like to kill." Dean said her father's disinterest in hunting continued, even though he'd take her brother out hunting. "My mother used to say, 'You've got to do things with Dale,' he liked to hunt and fish; my dad couldn't care less. And so Dad took him out hunting; Dad sat in the car with the heater on and read the paper and Dale went out and walked the cornfields."

Good will trips continued but decreased in frequency. In 1941 to Mitchell, Madison, Lennox and Alcester; no trips in 1942 or 1943; in 1944 to Lennox; none in 1945 or 1946, although minutes of December 2, 1946, indicated that part of an $1,000 appropriation was to be used during 1946 for good will trips.

· · ·

Although the Korean War occurred during the second half of Henegar's reign as Municipal Band conductor, the personnel shortage created during World War II was never again matched. Henegar's next seventeen years would be relatively peaceful.

1943. Terrace Park. Trumpet trio: L to R: Eddie Lias, Russ Henegar, Donald Lias. On podium: Vernon Alger (assistant conductor). Row 1, L to R (straight row in front): Kermit Harrington?, bassoon. Row 2: left side unidentified; second from right J. M. Newton; on outside, Elmer T. Edwards. Row 3 (curved row), left of cornet trio: Ardeen Foss, unidentified, Milt Askew, Everton Little, Guy Anderson (behind and to right of Henegar); Wayne Krumrei (third row to right of conductor); Willard Fejfar? (third row outside right). Row 4: Harry Ellis (third person from left), Glen Houdek (left of chimes on right side); Leon Miller? (outside right). (Note: A question mark indicates that the player was in the Band in the given year but could not be positively identified. The personnel of each year's Band may be found in the Appendix.) *(courtesy Wayne Krumrei)*

1944. Terrace Park. Seated front: Ed Paul (vocalist). Standing center: Russ Henegar (conductor). Row 1: (straight row). Unidentified; O. W. Palmer, flute; Kermit Harrington?, bassoon. Row 2: Ed Gedstad? or William D. Meyer?, Leo Gossman?, others in middle unidentified; On right: Walter F. Rittman?; J. W. Newton, cornet; Elmer "Eddie" Edwards, cornet. Row 3: two clarinets unidentified; Milt Askew, oboe; Everton Little, saxophone; middle of row unidentified; on right: Don Lias?, cornet; Leon Miller?, cornet. Row 4: Two clarinets unidentified; Harry Ellis, tuba; other two tubas probably Austin K. Bailey and O. O. Jackson; euphoniums probably Wayne Krumrei and Bob Aga; unidentified snare drum; Vernon Alger, bass drum; Glen Houdek, tympani; William Tietjen?, cornet; unidentified cornet. Not pictured: Marciene Swenson, vocal soloist. (Note: A question mark indicates that the player was in the Band in the given year but could not be positively identified. The personnel of each year's Band may be found in the Appendix.) (courtesy Sioux Falls Municipal Band)

1947-63
Henegar's March Through the Years

Municipal Band conductor Russ Henegar was used to challenges. The former cornetist with the Sousa Band had led the Sioux Falls Municipal Band through the financial problems of the Depression and the manpower shortages of World War II. But the challenges he faced in the later years of his leadership were less tangible. At a time when air-conditioned homes, replete with radios and televisions, were beginning to tempt people away from concerts in the parks, Henegar's biggest challenge was selling the value of the slightly "old-fashioned" Municipal Band to the taxpaying public. Henegar was well aware of his formidable task, one faced by his colleagues throughout the country. He addressed the topic in an article entitled "Municipal Bands — Their Survival Poses a Problem for the Community," published in the August 1962 issue of the *International Musician*. In the article, Henegar discussed several "musts" in the survival of municipal bands, including tax money and a clear separation between school bands and municipal bands. But his final paragraph indicated that it was the musicians themselves who could make a municipal band survive or die: "The value of the municipal band," he argued, "must be sold to the public, as well as to city officials. It is for each of us professional musicians to do his part in this. Speedy action must be taken to prevent the decline of the municipal band and to do something to supply an outlet for the abilities of the hundreds of musicians finding no place in which to continue their music, following graduation." A look at programs suggests that Henegar's method of trying to "sell" the Band continued to be by programming a wide variety of musical genres and featuring soloists, guest vocal groups, twirlers and danc-ers. The first documented appearance by the American Legion Chorus was in 1947. A juggling act (by Glen Phillips) appeared on a concert program on August 7, 1952. Guest twirlers came from towns nearly one hundred miles away from Sioux Falls — including Delmont and Lake Andes, South Dakota. The first mention of flag twirlers appearing on concert programs was July 26, 1953, when a group from Luverne (Min-nesota) High School performed. Henegar also kept the Band in the pub-lic eye by providing music for important Sioux Falls events. This for-mula helped the Band retain a large and loyal following and continued city support, although crowds might not have been as large as they were in the 1930s and 1940s. It was another challenge — a more per-sonal challenge — that might have been most difficult for Henegar. That was facing a mandated retirement from the Band, after serving as its leader for twenty-nine years.

The ABA Convention in Sioux Falls

One of Henegar's biggest coups was having the Municipal Band host the American Bandmasters' Association annual convention in Sioux Falls from March 18 through March 21, 1948. Henegar had become a member of the prestigious association — consisting of nationally and internationally famous musicians — in 1941 and was elected to the board of directors during the 1948 convention. Newspaper accounts of the event told that welcoming addresses were given by Mayor C. M. Whitfield and Governor George T. Mickelson. The convention consisted of the usual array of addresses, luncheons, dinner meetings and city tours.

But it was the association concert Sunday, March 21, at the Coli-seum that was the feature attraction for Sioux Falls music lovers. The Municipal Band was expanded from its usual forty players to seventy-five for the concert, adding musicians from Northwestern University, Evanston, Illinois; Lincoln, Nebraska; Sioux City, Iowa; and the Sioux Falls area. About 1,800 people attended, paying $1.50 each. Seventeen band directors took the podium: Henegar and Christensen, who "drew prolonged applause"; Karl L. King of Fort Dodge, Iowa, the former cir-cus band leader who conducted his composition "Barnum and Bailey's Favorite"; Henry Fillmore, "colorful band leader from Miami, Florida"; John J. Richards, director of the Long Beach, California, Municipal Band; Col. Howard C. Bronson, chief of the Army music service staff during World War II; Glenn Cliff Bainum, director of music, Northwestern

University; Leo Kucinski, director Monahan Post Band, Sioux City, Iowa; Gerald D. Prescott, director of music, University of Minnesota; Lt. Col. Harold Bachman, Chicago; Capt. R. B. Hayward, Toronto, Canada; Dr. A. A. Harding, University of Illinois, Urbana, Illinois; John J. Heney, DeLand, Florida; J. DeForest Cline, Colorado State College; Col. Earl D. Irons, North Texas State College; Paul Yoder, Glenview, Illinois; and Dr. Edwin Franko Goldman, honorary life president from New York City and one of the charter members of the ABA. The newspaper reported that encores were desired but prohibited: "The concert, racing against a deadline that prohibited encores, was limited to the seventeen numbers on the program. The crowd ... would have applauded King and Henry Fillmore ... into another presentation of their stirring marches but was restrained by the fact that some of the conductors and musicians were due to leave on an afternoon train. As it was, the concert ended a scant fifteen minutes before train time." In addition to the guest conductors' selections, Henegar's sister, Eileen (Mrs. Earl V.) Nason, played Grieg's "Concerto in A Minor" for piano, accompanied by the Band. The newspaper reported that Nason's piece was well received as was "a selection by a ten-man group from Northwestern University combining tympani and a brass section in a novel arrangement. ..."

One of the guest conductors at the ABA concert, Col. Howard Bronson, returned to Sioux Falls on July 10, 1949, to guest conduct the Municipal Band at Terrace Park. Bronson's name had been discussed as a possible leader when the Band was voted on in 1919 (see Chapter 1). His name also came up for consideration in 1927 when the city was choosing a new conductor for the 1928 season. Bronson selected a group of Sousa compositions for his portion of the program, including the following:

March, Glory of the Yankee Navy, Sousa
Looking Upward, from the suite By the Light of the Polar Star, Sousa
March, The Rifle Regiment, Sousa
From Three Quotations, Sousa
March, Liberty Bell, Sousa
Valse, In the Land of the Golden Fleece, Sousa
March, The Stars and Stripes Forever, Sousa

Rehearsal Pay

As early as 1922 Band members were paid for attending rehearsals, but apparently somewhere along the way that practice was discontinued. It was revived in 1951. Minutes of November 27, 1950, indicated that Henegar "had secured a raise in the appropriation which is primarily for the purpose of paying for the rehearsals. ..." In January 1951, rules for receiving rehearsal pay were outlined:

1. The total number of rehearsals is the maximum, and eighty percent of the total is the minimum number at $1 per rehearsal, and those attending fewer than the eighty percent of total rehearsals will receive no bonus payment.

2. That a member of the Band to be eligible to receive the bonus payment must have completed one full concert season with the Band.

3. That the bonus payment is to be made in one payment during the month of December at the time the auditor's office issues the warrants for payrolls, which will probably be about the 15th of the month.

Minutes of December 3, 1951, show that the rehearsal pay was a successful incentive to better attendance: "There were forty rehearsals held during the year. The system inaugurated this year for payment for attending rehearsal helped in the attendance as there was a better average per rehearsal in 1951 over 1950."

Literature

One selection unique to the times was the novelty piece "TV Suite." The piece was first played by the Municipal Band June 21, 1953, shortly after the birth of the city's first television station, KELO, in May 1953. The piece was described as "a novelty arrangement presenting what you might hear and see over your TV," although at that early date probably few Sioux Falls residents had watched a television set. The piece included "Sagebrush Saga," "Whodunit," "Hayloft Hoe Down" and "Big Name Band." A second television station, KSOO (now KSFY), started in Sioux Falls in 1960.

Playing for Annual Events

The Municipal Band was a regular part of several annual events in Sioux Falls. One was the YMCA Friendly Indian Boys' Clubs Pageant, begun in 1944. The Band played for the event through at least 1951. The YMCA's boys' clubs, all named after Native American Indian tribes, met weekly in Sioux Falls. A note on the 1947 printed program explained what the pageant was about: "You are to witness tonight our fourth presentation by white man of this ancient Indian ceremony, dra-

matized especially for the local observance of the 28th anniversary of
the Young Men's Christian Association Boys' Clubs in Sioux Falls, by
the well known Indian interpreter, William J. Bordeaux, of our own
city. He has lived among the Sioux tribes all of his life and we are in-
debted to him for the preparation of the script and the historical accu-
racy of the production." The 1947 concert portion of the program included appropriate musical selections:

Indian March, Edwin Franko Goldman
Transcription, Indian Love Call, Rudolf Friml
Vocal solo, By the Waters of Minnetonka, Thurlow Lieurance
Ella June Whittaker, vocalist
Descriptive, Tartar Dance, William H. Woodin
Vocal Solo, From the Land of the Sky Blue Water, Charles W. Cadman
March, Emblem of Freedom, Karl L. King

Another annual event at which the Band played was the Soap Box
Derby. Begun in 1956, the derby was held on the Fourth of July. The
Band began playing at the derby by at least 1958. In 1963 the *Argus
Leader* wrote about the upcoming derby, "The race will be held, as in
the past, on Derby Hill, one-half mile north of the South Dakota Highway Department building on Interstate 29. The $35 [donated by inter-
ested individuals and businesses] is used by the boy to construct his
racer, and the money is distributed in this way: $15 for official Derby
wheels and axles, $15 for use on the body of the car and $5 for the entry
fee. All work on the car must be done by the boy himself, and it must
pass several inspections before it is entered in the race." Henegar's scrapbook contains a certificate of appreciation for "his organization's cooperation in making the 1958 Soap Box Derby a success." The certificate
reads: "The part played by the recipient of this certificate, did much to
make it possible for those boys who participated to take steps toward
strong citizenship by showing a persevering attitude and displaying
sportsmanlike conduct throughout the building and racing of their cars."
The certificate was signed by representatives of Jay-Shon Chevrolet,
the *Argus Leader* and the Junior Chamber of Commerce.

Playing for Important Sioux Falls Events

One way to sell the public on the value of the Municipal Band was
to be a presence at important events in Sioux Falls. The Band played
for the dedications of the Freedom Train in the airport area on May 12,

1948, and the Royal C. Johnson Veterans' Memorial Hospital on July 24, 1949. An appearance which must have been of special interest to the Band was the dedication of the new bandstand in Library Park on July 10, 1952. Sioux Falls celebrated its Centennial June 15-23, 1956, and the Municipal Band played nine performances during those nine days. There were several other important dedications, especially in the early 1960s. The KSOO TV dedication program was held on July 31, 1960, and the Band was broadcast as part of that program. The Band met at the McKennan band shell at 12:15, evidently to record the music, prior to the three o'clock concert.

On October 29, 1961, the Band played at the dedication of O'Gorman High School, a private Catholic school named after Bishop Thomas O'Gorman, the second bishop of the Sioux Falls diocese from 1896-1921. The one-story structure cost $1.5 million, and according to newspaper articles, had several features not seen before in area schools: "Perhaps the features that will cause the most comment among visitors are the plastic bubble skylights. They eliminate the need for artificial lighting during most of the school day." The school was coed but had separate wings for boys' and girls' classrooms. About 7,500 people toured the school following dedication ceremonies.

The Band also played at the dedication of the Sioux Falls Arena on December 10, 1961. The Arena, a 116,050-square-foot entertainment and sports building, was built on land near West and Russell, part of the wartime Army Radio School grounds that had reverted to the city after the war. The *Argus Leader* of December 9, 1961, called the dedication of the $1,423,328 edifice "one of the most significant events in the city's history. ..." Speakers at the dedication "stressed that the Arena is tied in with and will enhance the progress of Sioux Falls. ... [U.S. Representative Ben] Reifel said it will make Sioux Falls even more of a cultural center. ..." Federal Judge and former South Dakota governor George T. Mickelson, who gave the principal address, was quoted as saying, "I would like to dedicate this Arena to the citizens and taxpayers of Sioux Falls for their foresight, for recognizing that this is a growing community and for doing something to meet expanding needs." The Municipal Band was one of eight musical groups featured in the four-hour program. Other groups included the Augustana College Band, directed by Leland Lillehaug; the Washington High School Band, directed by Ardeen Foss; the Washington High School chorus, directed by Boyd Bohlke; the Sioux Falls College choir, directed by Dr. Lee Bright; the O'Gorman High School Chorus, directed by Sister Mauricia; the Shrine Chanters, directed by Robert Mills; and the Sioux Falls American Legion Men's Chorus, directed by Bright.

The Municipal Band played at dedications of the Minnehaha County Court House, April 19, 1963, and the River Parking Ramp, August 13, 1962.

The dedications and Band performances continued with the unveiling of the new River Parking Ramp on August 13, 1962, and the dedication of the new Minnehaha Courthouse on April 19, 1963. The 60,000 square foot arc-shaped building replaced the old courthouse, constructed in 1889. According to the dedication program, "The past and present buildings, but a few hundred feet apart in distance, are years apart in imagination and efficiency. The old Courthouse is truly a part of our rich Minnehaha County history and heritage." The new three-

GREAT PLAINS ZOO

SIOUX FALLS – SOUTH DAKOTA

GRAND OPENING AND DEDICATION
SUNDAY   2 P.M.   JUNE 30, 1963

The Municipal Band played for dedication ceremonies at the Great Plains Zoo on June 30, 1963.

story courthouse was built at a cost of $1,150,000. According to the *Argus Leader*, "The Minnehaha County Board accumulated funds for eighteen years through a one-half mill levy above budget needs in order to finance construction of a new building. The amount was added to $100,000 in bonds approved by voters in an election." George Barnett, chairman of the Minnehaha County Commission, "tearfully accepted the key to the new Minnehaha County Courthouse presented to him by building architect Howard Parezo at dedication ceremonies. ...."

The Municipal Band also played for dedication ceremonies on June 30, 1963, for the Great Plains Zoo at Seventeenth and Kiwanis, north of the Sherman Park hill. Participants suffered in the 98-degree temperatures. When the zoo opened, there were twenty-seven major exhibits, according to the dedication program. The *Argus Leader* of June 30, 1963, reported that those seeing the zoo would find "a first-rate zoo that has been well worth waiting for. A zoo that, in opinion of experts who have seen it, will rank as one of the finer zoos in the nation in its size category." Admission was twenty-five cents for adults, ten cents for children under sixteen, free for anyone under twelve, accompanied by an adult.

Two months later, on August 30, 1963, Municipal Band members traveled to Lennox, South Dakota, to assist their colleagues in the dedication of the new Lennox band shell. Henegar had been conductor of the Lennox Band 1936-48.

At the Parks

Henegar and the city tried to make the parks more comfortable for the public. The now-questionable practice of using DDT to spray for bugs was first mentioned in 1957. A copy of a press release from that year read as follows: "With the usual fine cooperation and assistance from our Park Superintendent Mr. George A. Pardo and his staff, the Band looks forward to another very successful summer season. Mr. Pardo assures us that the new spraying machine will be used and the very bad mosquito problem of last season will be eliminated." A newspaper clipping from the end of the 1957 Band season, taken from Henegar's scrapbook, showed spraying in progress at Terrace Park. The photograph caption read: "Seating area and lower levels of Terrace Park are being sprayed in preparation for the Sioux Falls Municipal Band's concert Sunday night. The spraying operation is being performed this week to assure band lovers a measure of freedom from mosquito attacks. Insects are a special problem at Terrace Park, due to the nearness of Covell Lake. They have been especially aggressive this summer. T. W. Van Hilten is shown spraying the grounds under the appreciative eyes of George A. Pardoe, city park superintendent, and Russ D. Henegar, Band leader. To combat the mosquitoes nuisance he is using approximately 300 gallons of a mixture of DDT and chloralane [chlordane]."

Uniforms

Henegar knew, as had the earliest band conductors, the importance to the Band of maintaining a professional appearance. To that end, new Band uniforms were purchased twice during Henegar's last seventeen years. The first time was in 1948. According to Band Board minutes of April 5, 1948, total expenditures for forty-four uniforms, including trimmings and cap at $43 each, plus all taxes, charges, etc. made a total of $1,952.88. The uniforms, made by the Mayer Lavity

Some of the features in the 1950s included the Washington High School Majorettes in 1953 (above), Sharon Mullen and Carolyn Denevan of the Margaret Lambert Dance Studio in 1956 (lower left), and baton twirler Joanne Aughenbaugh in 1954 (lower right). *(courtesy Sioux Falls Municipal Band)*

Company, were dark blue, lightweight material. "The manner of paying for them was discussed and Mr. Henegar stated he could give a check for $400 to the Band secretary for services by Band members at the concert for the ABA which would give each member a ten-dollar credit on their uniform and then some manner could be chosen for the payment of the balance to suit the choice of the membership." A newspaper clipping from 1948 told of the new uniforms: "Members of the Sioux Falls Municipal Band will blossom out Sunday in new black tropical worsted uniforms, Director Russ. D. Henegar announced today. The new summer uniforms have double-breasted coats with gold emblem on the left sleeve, just below the shoulder and gold stripes farther down on the sleeve. Gold trouser stripes and gold-braided black summer-style caps complete the ensemble. Each member has purchased his own uniform, Henegar pointed out."

It wasn't easy to unload the old maroon uniforms. Minutes of November 24, 1952, read: "H. T. Hanson suggested that we see about selling the old maroon uniforms" which the Band probably had used for many years. It was stated that inquiries have been made by Mr. Alger with outside organizations but that there was not interest shown by any of them.

The next uniforms were purchased in 1955, and for the first time, the city — not Band members — paid the cost. According to a newspaper article of April 17, 1955, the new uniforms consisted of "a dark blue serge coat, with cap to match, and French gray trousers. ... Director Russ D. Henegar said the new uniforms, recently ordered by the City Commission, will arrive in time for opening of the Band's 1955 park concert season." They were worn for the first time on June 12, 1955.

Henegar's Retirement

Henegar had gradually retired from his conducting positions. He retired from his job as director of the El Riad Shrine Band in 1960. He retired from the Sioux Falls Elks Band in 1961, one year after taking the organization to a competition in Denver, Colorado, where they became the national champions. But it was more difficult to let go of the Municipal Band. In a letter written to Lynn Sams, a friend from ABA, dated December 20, 1962, Henegar wrote, "Have been thinking some about retirement but just can't make up my mind as to what I should decide. Enjoy the work and feel fine so will be here for 1963 at least." But civil service regulations stipulated that Henegar retire at age 65.

**Russ Henegar
retired from his
position as conduc-
tor of the Sioux
Falls Municipal
Band December 31,
1963, after twenty-
nine years.** *(cour-
tesy Doris Dean)*

He was given three extensions during September 6, 1962, to December
31, 1963. His final concert was a Labor Day concert on September 2,
1963, at Terrace Park. Henegar described that concert in a letter to
Sams dated December 22, 1963: "Our final park concert of '63 was an
evening of Labor Day (had been rained out day before in evening) but
still had a packed audience in Terrace Park. The boys surprised me
with a stop in the program, the regular nice speeches, and a fine recorder as a gift, real nice and something I can make good use of at
home. There is something cooking as to an honorary dinner later but so
far I can't seem to get any information out of anyone — only they asked
me just what time we would be taking off for a trip to a warmer cli-
mate??" His final concert featured his grandson, Douglas Dean, as a
cornet soloist (see Chapter 12).

Another letter was written to Sams after Henegar retired: "I am
now Director Emeritus of the Sioux Falls Municipal Band. ... Supposed
to be on vacation for December but have been on the job getting things

in order to move to my home for office and studio. Did move a week ago and certainly a job not knowing I had so darn much filed away after so many years. ... Will remain as secretary-treasurer of the Sioux Falls Musicians Association, A.F.M. and have had many ask me as to whether or not I would again teach brass but really haven't made up my mind as to whether or not I want to get tied up to too strict a schedule. Anyway we will take it easy for awhile and then decide just what is best. It does seem strange to make such a sudden change over to retirement but now I feel real good about the way it is working out." Henegar added that he was pleased with his accomplishments as Municipal Band director: "Have had a real rewarding twenty-eight years [twenty-nine seasons] with the Municipal group and feel I did do a good job for them always having a band that I was happy to work with as well as building it to a point where it was well-known in most parts of the country. It has been one of the few better municipal setups in the nation and still know of none better with the exception of Long Beach and as far as director goes I feel my position was a better one than if I had been in Long Beach. Of course our musicians were part time but the director was full time on a fair salary plus civil service benefits including pension, health and accident, as well as life insurance, and I was allowed to run the department without any kind of problems from any other city dept. or officials."

Band members hosted a retirement dinner for Henegar in 1964. The invitation stated, "You (and any of your guests) are invited to a Testimonial Dinner for Russ Henegar at the Sheraton Cataract [Hotel] on Monday, January 13, at 6:30 p.m. Cost is $1.50 per plate. If you have not already made reservations, call Oscar Loe ... or Leland Lillehaug ... by Friday noon (if possible). Committee." Ninety-four persons attended.

Henegar wrote to Sams about the dinner in a letter dated January 22, 1964: "Want to thank you sincerely and to let you know I certainly did appreciate your nice telegram that was read during the testimonial dinner on the evening of the 13th, held for me at the Cataract Hotel. It was a real nice affair and more of the kind words, letters and telegrams than I had ever expected. [The] president [of the] Chamber of Commerce presented me with a certificate of commendation, [the] president [of the] TV station KSOO gave a fine talk and his program or news director covered it for the station and we did receive nice coverage with TV pictures, radio interviews, etc. The Band president, [the] recorder of El Riad Shrine, Ardeen Foss, and the new director Dr. Lillehaug also gave nice talks as well as others. The many telegrams and letters really made me think they must be talking about someone else. Anyway it was real fine and Mrs. Henegar and the family did enjoy it greatly. All this leaves a fellow with mixed reactions, a little sad but also happy at the same time, wish I could compose a new work for concert band with the title 'Mixed Emotions,' it would cover quite a complete musical panorama, I'm sure."

Typed on the side of the same letter was the following: "Am gradually getting things in order with my office at home and everything working out real fine. Other telegrams included Governor Gubbrud, Senators Karl Mundt and George McGovern, Paul Yoder, Bill Schueller, Herb Johnson, Leonard Smith, Dave Bennett, and Stanley Ballard [secretary of the American Federation of Musicians]. Some letters: Gene Slick, president Sousa Band Fraternal Society, Frank Simon, Bachman, James Berdahl, Merle Evans, Vesey Walker, Carleton Stewart, Karl King, Carl Christensen [ABA]; Al Barto, Allentown, Pennsylvania, Leo Kucinski, Glen Houdek, Florida, signed 'your old sheep skin fiddler' (tymps) – don't know where they heard about it but real fine of them."

According to a letter to Sams dated June 24, 1964, here is what Henegar's life was like after retirement: " ... [retirement] is a complete new way of life for one who has been so darn active over the many years in the field of music – everything is working out fine and it is a relief to not be on a time schedule and to have to worry about the three and four programs each week along with the usual problems of keeping the right men in the right place. Do miss not being with the men and the great fellowship we had over the years but really find it a surprise that I just do not miss the old pressure and schedules. Have the good fortune of better than average health and home and we enjoy our closeness to our son and daughter and their nice families. ... They will all be here for the week of the 4th [of July] and means a great time for all of us — hate to count how many years back that I have never missed doing something in the line of music on that day and for once I'll be able to do as I wish without any 'down beat.' Have my A.F.M. office in my recreation room at home and still secretary-treasurer of our Local 114 (about 380 members which keeps me busy enough without anything else). Have not accepted any private pupils on brass in spite of the possibilities of a full time schedule because I just do not feel ready to go back on such a tight time schedule as yet, may decide later to take a few, possibly a few days per week. ... Mrs. Henegar and I are really getting everything arranged and in good order around the house, making a few changes we had planned for some time and find we are busier than ever, I am finding out I need most of what I thought would be time-off to be "keeper of the yard and hedges" — anyway, everything is fine and certainly nothing will prevent our making the Washington, D.C., ABA. next year."

Henegar served as secretary-treasurer of Local 114 until his death on January 29, 1968. He died in Sioux Falls, at the age of seventy years, four months and twenty days, just twelve days after the death of his wife, Gladys.

• • •

As conductor of the Sioux Falls Municipal Band for twenty-nine years, Henegar provided continuity following the Band's five conductors in fifteen years. By virtue of having played with the enormously popular Sousa band, he brought a sense of prestige to the Municipal Band, yet his entertaining programming assured that the Band appealed to the common citizen. In great part because of his efforts, the Municipal Band became an organization of national repute. It would remain for his successor, Leland Lillehaug, to maintain that tradition.

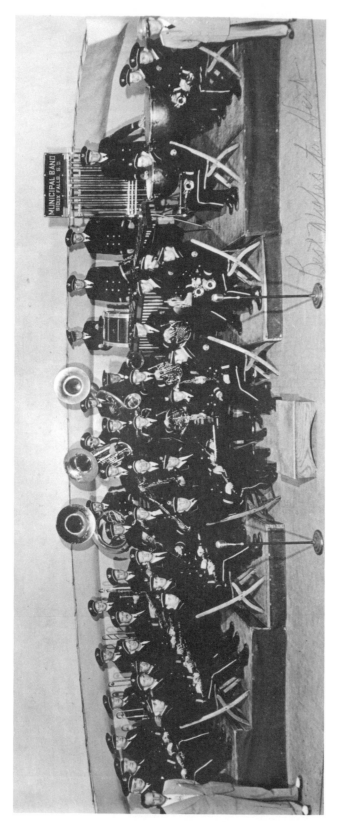

1949. McKennan Park. Standing front left: Ed Paul (vocalist); Standing right front: Russ Henegar, (conductor). Row 1, L to R: O. W. Palmer, Ralph Tyler, Neal Olsen, Ardeen Foss. Row 2: C. R. Larson, Kenneth Pace, Richard Colwell, Henry T. Hanson, R. G. Hoyt, Paul A. Weber, Ron Richardson, William G. Wagner, Glenn Morgan, Robert Griffith, Donald Lias. Row 3: George B. Medeck, Leland Lillehaug, Robert J. Barnett, Ed Gedstad, Milt Askew, Everton Little, Guy G. Anderson, Leonard Lorensen, Stanley Brooks, Wayne Krumrei, Kenneth Ewing. Row 4: Ed Paul, Leo Gossman, C. W. Smith, Harold Hoover, Sr., John Brauch, Jr., Melvin Sunde, James Richardson, Harry Ellis, O. O. Jackson, Everitt Friedhoff, Vernon Alger, Ray Pruner, Robert W. Marker, Robert Niblick, Desmond Kittelson, Leon Miller. *(courtesy Sioux Falls Municipal Band)*

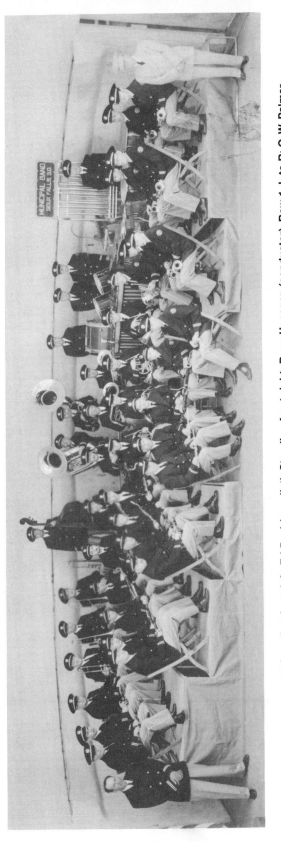

1955. McKennan Park. Standing front left: Ed Paul (vocalist). Standing front right: Russ Henegar, (conductor). Row 1, L to R: O. W. Palmer, Ralph Tyler, Tommy Knutson, Richard Foss, Neal Olsen. Row 2: Ardeen Foss, Ernest Dvoracek, Henry T. Hanson, Gary Harms, A. Ellsworth Winden, William G. Wagner, Paul Anderson, Wayne Burke, Ron Richardson, unidentified cornet, Robert Nason. Row 3: Richard Colwell, James Riemann, Earl Colgan, Jr., Bob Graham, William Warren or William Kramer?, Everton Little, Milt Askew, Harvey Eichmeier, Wayne Krumrei, James Ode, Robert Griffith. Row 4: David Bane?, John Romans? or I. M. Williamson?, Charles Mueller, Harold Hoover, Sr., E. O. Dietrich, Melvin Sunde, Joseph Birkenheuer, Lloyd Kreitzer (string bass), O. O. Jackson, Harry Ellis, J. H. Elgethun, Ray Pruner, Ron Veenker, Glen Houdek, Marvin Mueller, William Byrne. (Note: A question mark indicates that the player was in the Band in the given year but could not be positively identified. The personnel of each year's Band may be found in the Appendix.) *(courtesy Wayne Krumrei and Chris Hill)*

1961. McKennan Park. Standing front left: Russ Henegar (conductor). Right front: Ed Paul (vocalist). Row 1, L to R: O. W. Palmer, Ralph Tyler, Gustav Schuller, Leland Lillehaug, Jurgen Schuller, Chad Boese. Row 2: Ardeen Foss, Oscar Loe, Dennis Olson, Harold Gray, Robert McDowell, Paul Anderson, James Adams, Sam Albert, Donald McCabe, Loren Little, David Wegner. Row 3: Dennis Norlin, Steven Wold, Tom Wegner, Jeff Wold, Everton Little, David L. Johnson, Tom Little, Kenneth Busse, James Berdahl, Wayne Krumrei, James Ode, Ronn Holyer. Row 4: Earl Colgan, Jr., Richard Peik, Harold Hoover, Sr., Harold Hoover, Jr., Melvin Sunde, Keith Knoff, Paul Fialkowski, Robert Collins, J. H. Elgethun, Everitt Friedhoff, Harvey Eichmeier, Harry Ellis, Paul Hoy, Jon Hansen, Ray Pruner, Glen Houdek, Richard Berdahl, Danny Kealey, Robert Griffith. (courtesy Sioux Falls Municipal Band)

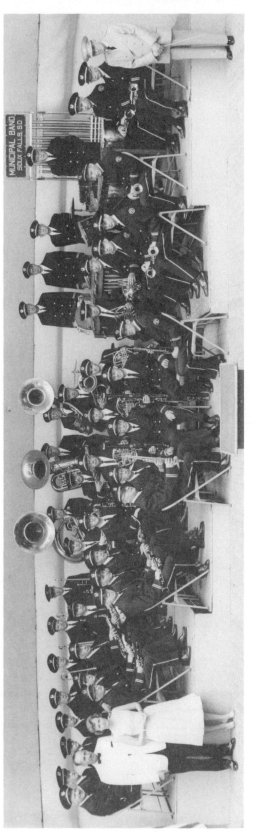

1963. McKennan Park. Standing front left: Ed Paul and Marciene Matthius (vocalists). Front right: Russ Henegar (conductor). Row 1, L to R: O. W. Palmer, Ralph Tyler, Gustav Schuller, Leland Lillehaug, Jurgen Schuller. Row 2: Oscar Loe, Jeff Wold, Dennis Olson, Harold Gray, J. H. Elgethun, Scott Faragher, Robert McDowell, Paul Anderson, Donald McCabe, David Wegner, James Ode. Row 3: Earl Colgan, Jr., Gary Paulson, Everton Little, John Dempster, Tom Little, Kenneth Busse, Wayne Krumrei, Loren Little. Row 4: Milt Askew, Robert Hanson, Robert Mattice, Gerald Kemner, Harold Hoover, Sr., Philip Miller, Ron McGaughey, Harry Ellis, Stanley Eitreim, Harvey Eichmeier, Paul Hoy, Joe Bruun, Ray Pruner, John Solberg, Jack Rembold, Paul Davoux. Not pictured: Chad Boese, Ronn Holyer, Ardeen Foss, David Johnson, Richard Pelk. *(courtesy Marciene Matthius)*

1964-75
A New Director, New Directions

D
r. Leland Lillehaug was director of bands at Augustana College in Sioux Falls in the fall of 1963 when he received a call from then-college president Lawrence Stavig inviting him to a meeting in his office. When Lillehaug arrived, he found that the other person present was Mayor Vinton Crusinberry. Crusinberry told Lillehaug that he was offering him the post of Municipal Band director, now vacant because of Henegar's retirement, but that he had wanted to talk to Stavig first to make sure that the two positions could be handled effectively by one person.

The Municipal Band conductor position was now being designated "part time" but without a change of responsibilities from Henegar's "full time" post. The only difference now was that regular office hours were not required. The position was that of a department head with the same status as the other department managers. All present recognized that it would take a great amount of work, but Lillehaug agreed that he would not let one job interfere with the other. In fact, his acquaintance with many of the top college players turned out to be an advantage to the Municipal Band. It took careful juggling of schedules and a year-round work schedule with very little vacation time, but Lillehaug, then thirty-six, was eager to pursue it.

A letter written by Henegar to his friend Lynn Sams, dated December 22, 1963, shed some light on the selection process for the new Municipal Band director. Although Henegar expressed admiration for Lillehaug, he expressed concern about the new part-time arrangement. About Lillehaug, Henegar wrote: "The new band director is a good fellow and very capable, been with me in our band for quite a few years with the exception of his time away for study. Making a fine record at Augustana College. ..." Henegar said the choice had come down to Lillehaug or Ardeen Foss. Foss, also a Municipal Band member, taught music in the Sioux Falls public schools. Henegar wrote: "Think the mayor had settled on either Foss or Lillehaug, and what tipped the scale seems to be that Foss was already getting a larger salary than the college was paying. He will be called part time (which I was against and tried to get in a full-time man from Washington, D.C., age 46 and retired from Marine and Army field bands) but his [Lillehaug's] salary will be $400 per month, which is not bad for part-time along with his regular salary of I suppose around $7,000. Hope it will work out; he is a good man but I am wondering if he will have the extra time available to handle as he should. Anyway I know he will do his best." Henegar had tried to stay out of the selection process: "As soon as I knew the mayor was planning on a local man I sort of kept out of the picture due to the fact that all the men had worked with and been loyal to me for many years and felt I should not play any favorite or try any pressure in any way."

The official notice of Lillehaug's appointment came at Crusinberry's office in City Hall on November 22, 1963. Lillehaug vividly remembered leaving the Mayor's office, walking into the City Hall corridor and hearing that President John F. Kennedy had been shot.

The new conductor had no way of knowing the changes that would take place in society during the Vietnam War period nor the adjustments that would be needed to keep the Band abreast of new developments. Those changes would include bringing women into the Band, moving the Band facilities to a new building, discovering creative ways to attract listeners, computerizing the Band's music library, purchasing new uniforms and acquiring a new, portable band shell which would allow the Band to play throughout the city. Yet some aspects remained the same. The Band played many concerts each season — forty-six in 1964 and 1969 and forty-seven in 1967. And, like his predecessor, Russ Henegar, Lillehaug had a great concern for quality. With a disciplined approach, he sought to bring the Band's performances back to the high level of previous years.

The remaining weeks of 1963 were spent working with Henegar in making the transition. The two had been friends ever since Lillehaug had joined the Band in 1949 as an Augustana student, and the working relationship was excellent. Lillehaug often gave Henegar credit for his growth as a musician because, he said, "I don't really believe I was good enough to make the Band when I was chosen, but evidently Russ saw some potential for development. I have been forever grateful to him."

Leland Lillehaug became the seventh conductor of the Sioux Falls Municipal Band in 1964. This photo is from about 1968. *(courtesy Leland Lillehaug)*

Women Join the Band

A major decision faced the new conductor early. A few of the older men had chosen to time their retirement with that of Henegar's, under whom they had played for many years. Included in the group were Ardeen Foss, principal clarinet; O. W. "Pic" Palmer, principal flute; J. H. Elgethun, horn; Harold Hoover, Sr., principal trombone; and Ray Pruner, percussion. Their combined number of years was more than 113. In addition, Ralph Tyler, who had played flute alongside Palmer since 1953, decided to return to one of his other performance instruments, the clarinet.

The Municipal Band had consisted of men only, with the exception of vocalists and other soloists. Palmer's retirement and Tyler's switch had left the flute section completely vacant. No male flutists of comparable ability were available in the city. Lillehaug also felt that it was not right that a tax-supported institution kept talented female musicians out of the Band. However, some Band members and citizens suggested to him that the Band should go without flutes until the positions could be filled by men. This was musically unacceptable to Lillehaug.

After considerable thought and investigation, he chose two young women, Kathy Hays and Marilyn Loomis, to fill those spots. Both were top musicians and Augustana College students. Hays was from Yankton and Loomis was a graduate of Washington High School in Sioux Falls. Lillehaug remembered telling them that they were breaking a gender barrier in the Sioux Falls Municipal Band as Jackie Robinson had broken the racial barrier in baseball. (Robinson had become the first black baseball player in the major leagues seventeen years earlier in 1947.) Lillehaug told them, "You have me and you have each other. I don't know what kind of reception you will receive."

Not everyone agreed with his decision. Another woman flutist, older and more experienced than either Hays or Loomis, had considered auditioning but withdrew when told by someone in the Band that she probably wouldn't be comfortable in the group. Some people were upset because of the addition of women. Lillehaug recalled that occasionally he would be stopped on the street and belligerently asked why he was bringing women into the Band. Bob McDowell, who played under both

Marilyn Loomis, left, and Kathy Hays, right, are shown here with Dr. Leland Lillehaug in 1985 receiving plaques honoring them as the first women instrumentalists to join the Sioux Falls Municipal Band. *(courtesy Leland Lillehaug)*

Henegar and Lillehaug said, "There was 'furor' when women were brought into the Band. Some Band members resented not being able to tell dirty jokes anymore."

Fortunately, the strong objectors were in the minority. Most of the younger people thought "it was no big deal"— or were unaware that there was a problem. Some of the band directors in the Band, such as George Gulson of Brandon, thought nothing of it because they worked with young women in their bands every day.

Lillehaug knew that the flutists he chose would have to be impeccable musicians because detractors undoubtedly would cite musical deficiencies to cover the gender bias. Both women played so well that no one publicly criticized their musicianship.

Hays and Loomis continued as the only women members in 1965. However, in 1966 more women auditioned and were accepted into the Band. They included Ann Palmer, Linda Olson, Ann Stauffer, Mary Perrenoud and Barb Johnson Hegg. Soon no one seemed to pay any attention to the percentage of men and women. However, one woman who began in 1966 said she didn't feel any antagonism from any of the men other than her section leader, a Band veteran of many years. She felt uncomfortable until he retired four years later.

Asked if he had checked with his commissioner or others about adding women, Lillehaug said he had not. "I took the action because a good concert band needed flutes, and I knew that including women was the right thing to do. I was willing to face any problems that may have resulted," he said.

Kathy Hays Emmel and Marilyn Loomis Hansen were invited back twenty-one years later and honored for their contributions to the Band. Both said they didn't realize that being the first women in the Band was an important event at the time. They were given a plaque from the Band which read, "You Broke the Barrier! We salute the courage of Kathy Hays Emmel and Marilyn Loomis Hansen — The first women in the Sioux Falls Municipal Band — 1964 Season. Presented August 4, 1985."

Another breakthrough for women took place in 1972 when Merridee Ekstrom was elected as the first woman president of the Band. She served for three consecutive seasons, 1972-74.

Other Changes

Another major change in 1964 concerned facilities. The Band had rehearsed in a large room on the third floor of City Hall for several

**Conductor Leland Lille-
haug directs the Municipal
Band in a rehearsal in 1965
from the Coliseum stage.
The Band started using the
Coliseum for Monday night
rehearsals in 1964.** *(courtesy Sioux Falls Municipal
Band)*

decades. However, City Hall was feeling office space pressures, and it was decided that the Band would be moved to a new home — the Coliseum. The Coliseum stage would be used for the Monday evening rehearsals. Space would be found for the office, the extensive library holdings and instrument storage.

Bob Kunkel was the manager of the Coliseum at that time. In an interview on January 24, 1994, Kunkel said that he wasn't very happy to hear that the Sioux Falls Municipal Band was being moved from the City Hall to the Coliseum because he did not have sufficient storage space at the Coliseum. However, the Band office and library were moved to the northeast corner of the first floor of the Coliseum, and the instruments were stored there. The room was crowded.

Kunkel said that he and Lillehaug enjoyed a good relationship. Lillehaug agreed, saying it was based on mutual respect which has fostered a continuing friendship. The Band sometimes had to find a different rehearsal site for Monday night rehearsals when the Coliseum was rented for other events. Augustana and Axtell Park Junior High were used.

Five members who had served the Band for many years retired during this period, three at the end of the 1963 season and two at the end of 1964. At a May 25, 1964, Board meeting it was voted to give Harold Hoover, Sr., a long-time member who had retired, a radio and plaque similar to those given to O. W. Palmer and Ray Pruner, who also retired after the 1963 season. Ed Paul, who had been the Band's male vocalist and master of ceremonies since 1934, and Marciene Swenson Matthius, regular female vocalist during the 1940s and 1957-64, both retired at the end of 1964. They were succeeded in 1965 by Paul Wegner and Eugenia Orlich Hartig.

One of Lillehaug's first acts was to invite Henegar back to the podium where Henegar conducted grandson Doug Dean in a cornet solo on September 6, 1964, at Terrace Park. Henegar also conducted a concert at the South Dakota State Penitentiary on December 30, 1964, when Lillehaug became ill shortly before the concert. The first record of the Band playing at the Penitentiary was in 1923, and Henegar had conducted the Band there many times. Henegar also guest conducted in 1965. There undoubtedly would have been many invitations for Henegar to guest conduct the Band had it not been for his sudden death on January 29, 1968.

Doug Dean, Russ Henegar's grandson, played a cornet solo when Russ was invited back to conduct in 1964. *(courtesy Sioux Falls Municipal Band)*

The Sioux Falls Municipal Band participated in a major national band project in 1964. During that year, a national committee embarked on a campaign to raise $100,000 toward the establishment of a John Philip Sousa Memorial Fund. The amount would be equally matched by the United States Government for the purpose of building a band stage in the John F. Kennedy Center for the Performing Arts in Washington, D.C. A final date of June 30, 1965, was set for the completion of fund raising. Bands contacted included school, university, armed forces, fraternal, community and professional. Henegar served as area chairman. The Municipal Band Board, on March 8, 1965, passed a motion to contribute. At least forty-three members of the Sioux Falls Municipal Band contributed three dollars each for a total of $129. Any band which raised at least $100 had its name engraved on a plaque which was placed in the band shell area of the Kennedy Center. Lillehaug visited the Center and reported that he had found the Sioux Falls Municipal Band's name on the plaque.

During Lillehaug's second year of leadership, in 1965, a major change was made in the schedule of the Band's weekly midweek concerts — from the traditional Thursday evening to Tuesday evening. The change came about in an interesting way. One day Steven Lillehaug, the conductor's nine-year-old son said to his father, "Dad, why don't we go on out-of-town vacations like some of my friends' families?" Leland explained that there were two concerts on Sunday, rehearsal on Monday, many details to be attended to with personnel and publicity on Wednesday and Thursday, the concert on Thursday evening and preparation for the Sunday concerts on at least part of Friday. That left very little time for a trip of any kind. Thinking that the explanation would satisfy, he was surprised by Steven's question, "Why do you play the midweek concert on Thursday? Why don't you play it on Tuesday? Then wouldn't there be more time?" The answer to that question was, "I don't know; that is the way it always has been done."

However, piqued by the "out-of-the-mouths-of-babes" question, Lillehaug explored the issue. The City Commission and the Chamber of Commerce both said they could see no advantage to the city by playing on Thursday rather than Tuesday. Band members whose jobs required some travel said it would be much easier for them to do their road work Wednesday through Friday rather than having to return to Sioux Falls for the Thursday night concerts. No one could be found who produced any evidence that Thursday night was the preferable evening, so the schedule for the midweek concert was changed to Tuesday where it remained for years.

The Sioux Falls Municipal Band played for the dedication of the Sioux Falls Packers baseball stadium at 6:30 p.m. on June 27, 1965. In addition to the expected "Take Me Out to the Ball Game," the Band entertained with marches and a medley of Glenn Miller tunes. Janine Johnson, who won many regional and national honors as a twirler, including leading the Memorial Day Parade at Indianapolis, performed for an appreciative audience, accompanied by the Band. The first foul ball hit into the stands was caught — and returned — by Lillehaug. The Band could not stay for the entire game because of their 8 p.m. concert at Terrace Park.

The year 1966 included the introduction of a new programming

idea which became an annual event. Paul Hoy, long-time bass drummer, has had a lifelong love for circus music. In 1966 he and Lillehaug
decided that a program of circus music might produce a concert of great
interest and excitement to the listening public. The first circus concert
was scheduled to take place at Terrace Park August 14, 1966. The Band
played only the first seven numbers when they were forced to quit because of rain. A week later rain struck again at Terrace Park, and the
Band moved indoors at the Royal C. Johnson Veterans Memorial Hospital and played circus music. Because of the interest, the concert was
once again scheduled for Terrace and was played on August 28. The
twenty-ninth consecutive annual circus concert took place in 1994.

Hoy, who joined the Sioux Falls Municipal Band in 1957, and Lillehaug enjoyed a wonderful relationship throughout their years together.
Lillehaug once told the Band members that if the Sioux Falls Municipal Band were the National Football League, the one no-trade, pro-
tected player would be Hoy, the bass drummer. In a letter to Paul Hoy
(then sixty-three years of age), on September 14, 1970, conductor Lillehaug wished him "... at least another two decades of playing." By 1994
Hoy had exceeded that wish by nearly half a decade. The veteran circus
drummer still plays bass drum and picks the programs for each year's
circus concert.

Also in 1966, Lillehaug was looking for ways to attract an audience of young people and their families, and implemented the idea of a
"Children's and Youth Concert," which was first held July 17, 1966, at
Terrace Park. The Band began with "Children's March" by Edwin Franko
Goldman. It was followed by Ray Loftesness narrating "The Man Who
Invented Music." Loftesness, well-known radio personality, served as
master of ceremonies and demonstrated his ability to hold the attention of young people. Dr. Harold Krueger played the solo, "The Toy Trumpet," which seemed to fascinate the children as did the duet arrangement of "Wizard of Oz" by Eugenia Hartig and Loftesness. Four Band
members put their instruments on their chairs and came forward to do
a dance quartet, with the Sioux Falls Municipal Band playing "Parade
of the Wooden Soldiers." The four Band members were Ann Palmer,
Mary Ellefson, Keith Peterson and Earl Sherburne. The children's interest didn't flag as the Band closed with "Who's Afraid of the Big Bad
Wolf," "Dry Bones" and "The Stars and Stripes Forever." The concert,
later simply called "Children's Concert," became an annual event, being played at a midweek concert and Sunday evening at Terrace Park.
The seventy-fifth anniversary year in 1994 featured the twenty-ninth
consecutive Children's Concert.

The Band members decided to join the fun at Children's Concerts

Having Band members wear costumes became a traditional part of the annual Children's Concert, begun in 1966. Shown here in the mid 1970s are Laurel Paulson, front; Mindy Braithwaite, center; and Jeff Kull, back. *(courtesy Sioux Falls Municipal Band)*

by changing their appearance. The Band members dressed up in all types of outlandish costumes, a tradition that has been a hit with the children and has continued through the years. Merridee Ekstrom related one incident at a Children's Concert which was humorous to Band members but perhaps not to all members of the audience. "It occurred on a Sunday night at Terrace Park just prior to the Children's Concert. Al Berdahl [who had been born with one partial arm but who never seemed to be self conscious about it] and Scott Faragher came as cowboys and staged a duel in front of the stage. Al uncovered his partial arm, which was covered with ketchup or something red, and claimed

Right: Children
and Band mem-
bers enjoy dress-
ing up for the
Children's Con-
cert. This photo,
from 1970, shows
vocalist Paul
Wegner (far left)
and conductor
Leland Lillehaug
(far right). *(cour-
tesy Sioux Falls
Municipal Band)*

Flutist Pat Masek and her son,
below, dressed up as hobos for
1970 Children's Concert at Terra
Park. *(courtesy Sioux Falls Mun-
pal Band)*

Above: Steve Rinder (left), guest
master of ceremonies, joined con-
ductor Leland Lillehaug and vocalist
Paul Wegner at this 1974 Children's
Concert. *(courtesy Sioux Falls
Municipal Band)*

that Scott had shot off his arm. Several kids were sitting on the grass fairly close to the stage and began to scream. To those of us who knew that Al never had all of that arm and hand, it was funny."

Patricia "Pat" Masek recalled that the various sections of the Band often coordinated their clothing to illustrate a theme. The flute section often wore mouse costumes. At one of the concerts, Oscar Loe tied Masek's costume tail to the chair, causing an unexpected problem when she attempted to stand to take a bow with her fellow Band members. In later Children's Concerts, children were encouraged to wear costumes. Paul and Amy Hoy furnished balloons for all children and commercially printed programs for the audience.

Because of the wide acceptance, the Children's Concert format changed very little. Below is the program from the tenth annual Children's Concert in 1975, which was performed July 22 at Crippled Children's Hospital and School (now Children's Care School and Hospital) and July 27 at Terrace Park. The theme of the concert is based on animals, birds and fish:

Grand Opener and Star Spangled Banner
Talk to the Animals, Bricusse/Ken Whitcomb
The Pink Panther, Henry Mancini
The Adventures of Pinocchio, Paul Yoder
Parade of the Wooden Soldiers, Leon Jessel/Carl F. Williams
Vocal solo, Jonah and the Whale, Robert MacGimsey/Gene White
Paul Wegner, baritone
Three Little Fishies, Saxie Dowell/George Briegel
Toy Tiger, Henry Mancini/Howard Cable
The Elephants Tango, Bernie Landes/Alfred Reed
Golden Eagle, Harold L. Walters
Vocal solo, Oliver, Lionel Bart/Norman Leyden
Eugenia Hartig, soprano
Donkey Serenade, Rudolf Friml/Moffitt
A Horse A-Piece, Paul Yoder
Children's March, E. F. Goldman
Bear Dance, Bela Bartok/Erik Leidzen
Tiger Rag, La Rocca/Paul Yoder
Encore: Talk to the Animals, Bricusse/Ken Whitcomb

The only exchange concerts during this period were with the Sioux City Municipal Band on July 30, 1967. On the same Sunday, the Sioux City Band conducted by Leo Kucinski played two concerts in Sioux Falls, and the Sioux Falls Municipal Band played concerts in Sioux City at

Riverside Park in the afternoon and at Grandview Band Shell at 8:15 p.m. Kucinski is well known in the Sioux Falls area because for many years he was conductor of the Sioux Falls (now South Dakota) Symphony. The Sioux City band's appearance at Terrace Park was marred when some young pranksters threw eggs over the back of the bandstand. The eggs broke on some of the players.

Sealed bids on new Band uniforms were due on May 9, 1966. On May 30, 1966, the J. C. Penney Co. (representing The Fechheimer Bros. Co.) was notified that it was the successful bidder over five other companies. The new lightweight uniforms were delivered in 1967. The material was a light ten-and-a-half ounce fabric. This was a dramatic departure from the heavy sixteen-ounce whipcord which had been used for at least two decades. The color was blue-black so that the old uniforms could be used as fill-ins when necessary. The coats were double breasted with two buttons and a roll lapel. Sixty uniforms were purchased at $56.85 each for a total of $3,411 plus one conductor's uniform at $60.75. George Gulson remembered that Mayor Crusinberry was a former fireman and didn't like the big, round hats Band members had worn before. Crusinberry insisted that the caps be oval.

The Monday night rehearsals at the Coliseum were always intense, especially during the summer when the group was preparing for three, and sometimes four, concerts during the week. However, on Monday evening June 24, 1968, Band members were allowed to leave before the customary 10 p.m. closing time. During the evening, some of the Band members smelled smoke somewhere in the stage area, but the source could not be located. The fire department was notified, and the fire truck was there so quickly that Band members were amazed. The next day the *Argus Leader* reported that a fire truck was returning from the incident in which a North Central plane toppled a television tower east of Sioux Falls and was within two blocks of the Coliseum when it was called there. Some of the Band members joked that as long as no flames were evident, Lillehaug would keep rehearsing. However, the Band was dismissed when the fire department said they were going to have to work there to determine the cause of the smoke. No damage was visible in the stage area.

The Band's 50th Year and Beyond

The Band's 50th year anniversary was celebrated in 1969, and two players shared the conducting duties. Lillehaug was on leave from February 1 to September 1 doing a music research project for the U.S. Office of Education. Donald McCabe and Dr. Harold Krueger were appointed co-conductors by the City Commission on the recommendation of the Band Board and Lillehaug. Because there were several players who were also conductors, the choice was not an easy one. Oscar Loe, who had been serving as assistant conductor, felt that he should have been chosen. Consequently, he dropped out during the 1969 season but returned in 1970 upon Lillehaug's return. Long-time member Harvey Eichmeier retired as of the annual meeting on December 1, 1969.

McCabe wrote a march "The Golden Year" in honor of the anniversary, and the piece was used to open every concert during the summer season. McCabe and Krueger each conducted half the concerts during the season and played in the Band when not conducting.

In 1971 Mary Harum Hart, presently a star of "Entertainment Tonight," sang with the Band at Terrace Park on July 25 (See Chapter 11).

The Sioux Falls Municipal Band has provided concerts for towns in the surrounding area since early in its history (a full list of concert sites is in the Appendix). This practice continued in 1964-75 and included performances at the Salem Harvest Festival, Valley Springs, Canistota, Lennox, Canton, Hudson and Hills, Minnesota. Attendance was excellent at each concert. That was also true at the Sioux Falls appearances, which were reported to be the best attended in at least ten years.

Theme concerts, other than patriotic titles, probably had their origin in the 1966 Circus and Children's Concerts mentioned earlier. They increased in numbers slightly during the next few years, but it was not until 1977 that the year's schedule listed them in abundance — approximately forty percent of the season's offerings. In 1977, themes included Flag Day, Government Employees' Appreciation Night, All March Concert, Humor in Music, Circus Concert, Salute to News Media, Children's Concert, Golden Age of Radio, International Night, All American Music, Music of the '40s — The Big Bands, and Grand Finale. Since that time, the creativity of the conductors has produced more than 220 theme titles. Contributing to many of the theme concerts were the sparkling musical arrangements of Gene White (see Chapter 13) which gave new life to old and new tunes alike.

Administrative actions in 1972 included an August 29, 1972, Band Board decision not to begin rehearsals until February 5. Previously the Band had started its winter rehearsals in mid to late January. A short document "Responsibilities of a Principal (first-chair player) in the Sioux Falls Municipal Band" was distributed, dated July 14, 1972. At the 1972 annual meeting concerns were voiced about getting air-conditioning for the Coliseum stage because of the intense heat in the Coliseum during summer rehearsals. That goal was never achieved.

A new "Opener" and "Closer" for the concerts were used in 1972. They were written by former Sioux Falls resident and now professional musician Lloyd Norlin.

The year 1973 began with the excitement of a fire in the Coliseum annex on January 5 and included a number of important events for the Band — the acquisition of a portable shell (Showmobile), a serious difference of opinion between members of the Park and Band Boards and playing for the dedication of the new facilities at EROS.

Lillehaug remembered waking up early and turning on the radio on Friday morning January 5, 1973. What he heard was a major shock. The Coliseum annex was on fire! His first thought was of the wonderful Municipal Band library and the equipment which was housed in the Coliseum portion of the building. He dressed quickly and headed for the Coliseum on a morning when the temperature had dropped to a minus fourteen degrees. When he arrived on north Minnesota Avenue and Seventh Street, Lillehaug was told by the police that no one was allowed in the area. However, after learning that he was the Municipal Band conductor they let him through and he was able to talk to the fire chief. Lillehaug was told that it was possible that the Coliseum might burn as well. Lillehaug and volunteers began carrying out uniforms that would be damaged by smoke and planned to remove the music if the fire spread. Fortunately, the fire wall at the back of the stage held, and the Coliseum and the Band facilities were saved.

With the loss of the annex, the Coliseum management needed all the first floor space for storage. The decision was made to move the Municipal Band to the second floor of the Coliseum. Two storage rooms which were next to the steps in the second floor balcony area on the north side were renovated for the Band office, instrument storage and library. A space next to the stage was enclosed, and the instruments used weekly were stored there, saving much movement of instruments before and after rehearsals. The move gave the Band office and library more space.

Although the Sioux Falls Municipal Band played regularly in four of the established parks (Terrace, McKennan, Sherman and Heritage), Lillehaug wanted to reach people who could not or did not choose to attend those concerts. How could one bring the music to people in their own neighborhoods and to nursing homes and also have acceptable acoustics?

The acquisition of the "Showmobile" in 1973 allowed the Sioux Falls Municipal Band to embark on a program of "taking music to the people" by playing in residential neighborhoods, at retirement and nursing homes and in many other places that previously were not possible for outdoor concerts. The forty-foot vehicle could be used to create a stage with a sixteen-foot or twenty-four-foot depth that seated the entire Band comfortably. It was purchased from the Wenger Corporation in Owatonna, Minnesota, in a cooperative venture between the Band and the Sioux Falls Parks and Recreation department. Each was to share the use and each put in $10,252.50 for a total cost of $20,505. The purchase was not a sudden decision. The manufacturer had allowed the the Band to use such a vehicle on July 20, 1965, when it was used for a concert at Heritage Park. The audience and Band member responses were positive, but efforts to get funding took another eight years.

Stan Eitreim has been Band equipment manager and mover for many years. He wrote of some of his experiences: "One of Dr. Lillehaug's pet ideas was to bring music to the people, so we began moving to other

The Showmobile, a moveable stage acquired in 1973, allowed the Municipal Band to give concerts at locations throughout the city. The Showmobile is shown here at Sherman Park, where there is no band shell. *(courtesy Sioux Falls Municipal Band)*

The Showmobile is shown here all packed up and ready to move on to its next concert site. *(courtesy Sioux Falls Municipal Band)*

locations with the Showmobile on Tuesday nights [and eventually on other nights of the week]. We would go into a neighborhood where a contact person had been established, set up on the street or in a cul-de-sac, run an extension cord to somebody's house to run the sound system and play for whoever showed up. Flyers were taken around the neighborhood in advance to try to get an audience."

Until the Band got the Showmobile, Eitreim hauled four-by-eight-foot platforms, which were borrowed from the Sioux Falls Community Playhouse, to a grassy location in lower Sherman Park. He wrote, "The Band had started alternating between McKennan and Sherman parks on Sunday afternoons, and at first set up on the asphalt parking lot at Sherman. The midsummer hot sun beating down on the asphalt caused problems, so we moved onto the grass, but since there was no hard surface to reflect the sound, the audience couldn't hear us. So we solved that problem temporarily with the platforms, which were old plywood and three-by-four concrete frames that someone had donated to the Playhouse. Sundays were not my favorite days during those years — I had to start in early morning to load the platforms onto a Munce Brothers flat bed truck and take them to Sherman Park, drop them off, take the truck back and get a moving van, load the Band equipment out of the Coliseum and get it to the park around noon. After the afternoon concert, we loaded the truck and went to Terrace Park with a short break for dinner, set up on the Band shell and played the concert, then loaded the equipment back to the Coliseum and changed trucks again to get the platforms back to the Playhouse. It was usually close to midnight when I got done. I usually hired a high school or college student to help with the loading, especially when dealing with the platforms."

George Gulson, a former Band president, said that the Showmobile was a very important addition because it enabled the Band to move around the city. Notices of the concert were passed out to the area residents a few days prior to the concerts.

Scott Faragher, a veteran Band member, wasn't as positive regarding playing at many different locations. He said, "It [the Showmobile] allowed the Band to move around the city, but I often wonder whether it might be more beneficial to have a few fixed concert sites where the Band would play on the same days and times each week. However, in spite of this possible advantage it would be a shame to eliminate playing for the residents of the nursing homes."

Associated with the purchase of the Showmobile was a disagreement in 1973 between the Band Board and the Park Board about playing at McKennan Park. The conflict was finally resolved at an evening meeting at City Hall. Lillehaug recalled that there were two aspects to the problems at McKennan. First, although the shell may have been a noteworthy landmark, its physical condition had been allowed to deteriorate. Steps were broken, and vandals had spray painted the interior walls repeatedly. The backstage area was dirty. There were no gates on the shell, so there was no way of keeping vandals out. Ken Munro, Parks and Recreation director, had not been receptive to the conductor's requests to get the shell in shape for the upcoming season. Secondly, and more important, the McKennan shell did not have good acoustics. It is reported that if one listened to a concert sitting in the audience area on the left side, moved to the center and finally to the right side, one would hear "three different bands." Members of the audience were hearing different sounds depending on where they sat, none of them representing the true sound of the Sioux Falls Municipal Band. When the Showmobile was purchased in 1973, the Band Board felt that the situation would be improved in both areas and wanted to quit playing in the McKennan shell.

Lillehaug had been on a trip to Europe and returned on June 18 to find a number of startling developments. In spite of the previous resistance of the Director of Parks to improve the condition of the McKennan shell, there evidently had been some change of heart shortly before the 1973 season started, and the Park Department had made some improvements in the physical condition of the shell. The Park Board had ordered the Band to use the old band shell at McKennan Park even though the new, better, recently acquired acoustical Showmobile was available. A threat was made that the Band would not be permitted to play in McKennan Park unless they played from the shell.

After a meeting of the Band Board on June 28, 1973, a letter was sent to the Park Board, dated July 2, 1973, citing the Band's position. Band Board members began by thanking the Park Board for their cooperation in buying the Showmobile and went on to say that the Band Board had taken no stand as to whether or not the McKennan shell should have been repaired or remodeled and that this decision was within the province of the Park Board. "However, the Municipal Band Board feels strongly that the decision of the Park Board prohibiting the Band from playing in McKennan Park unless it plays from the 'old shell' is an arbitrary and unfair one. Since we are an independent department of the city we feel that we should have been consulted previous to a decision which concerned us so directly."

The letter went on to state the acoustical superiority of the Showmobile as outlined above and stated, "Mrs. Smith [of the Park Board] asked why we did not complain before [about the McKennan acoustics previous to the Showmobile]. There seemed to be no reason to complain when there seemed to be no way to better the situation. The Sioux Falls Municipal Band has always attempted to do its best under the situations which prevailed."

The Band Board concluded by saying that in order to demonstrate the Sioux Falls Municipal Band's cooperation and to avoid a public confrontation, the Sioux Falls Municipal Band had played two concerts from the McKennan shell and hoped that the Park Board would review the situation and reach the conclusion that the previous prohibition should be withdrawn. There was no question that the McKennan shell was typical of the old style often used by bands throughout the country and had a certain appeal to some people. David Krueger, a former Band president, liked to play in the shell for that reason, but he recognized the acoustical shortcomings. After the meeting between the two boards, the Park Board relented, and the Band played its McKennan concerts from the Showmobile, positioned at Twenty-Third Street and Fourth Avenue.

The 1973 season included an unusual three concerts in one day, July Fourth. The Band played at the Battleship South Dakota reunion

in the forenoon, at the Sioux Falls Airport for the Blue Angels air exhibition
in the afternoon and at the W. H. Lyon
Fairgrounds in the evening.

The Band also played for the EROS
(Earth Resources Observation Systems)
dedication on Tuesday, August 7, 1973,
at 9:10 a.m. The appearance allowed the
Band to be heard by the many nationally prominent guests who were in South
Dakota for the dedication. The facility
proved to be an important asset for this
area. An *Argus Leader* news story of
June 1, 1994, told of additional new construction starting at the EROS facilities,
which when completed, would require
an additional 150 employees.

Long-time members Harry Ellis
and Gustav Schuller retired at the end
of the 1973 season. The Band presented
them with plaques and thanks for their
service.

**Bassoonist Gustav
Schuller, a long-time
Municipal Band member,
retired at the end of the
1973 season. *(courtesy
Sioux Falls Municipal
Band)***

Reviving Ideas from the Past

In order to play earlier in the year and to be able to play classical
music, the Band once again began to give winter indoor concerts in the
Coliseum. The Band had begun the tradition in 1921, but the last such
concert, according to programs found, had been in 1952. On March 25,
1974, the Band played a concert with the theme "Music from Many
Lands" with music of Mozart, Delibes, Richard Wagner, Vaughan Williams and Grieg in addition to marches by E. F. Goldman and Sousa.
The concert was well received and was followed by another performance
at the Coliseum on March 17, 1975, as a part of the area "Fine Arts
Month." The concert was divided into four theme sections. Because of
the March 17 date, the first was "Salute to the Irish — St. Patrick's Day
1975" and included a number of Irish compositions. It was followed by
"A Salute to the Arts and Fine Arts Month." At this concert Mayor Rick
Knobe guest conducted a march "The City of Champions" in a tribute to
democracy and local government. Knobe also guest conducted on March
22, 1976, at the Coliseum. Mayor Knobe, in a 1994 interview, reported

that he had performed on stage many times, given speeches and presided over meetings, but the times he remembered having the most
butterflies were the narration appearance with the South Dakota Symphony and his first guest conducting of the Municipal Band.

Although the Band had always tried to answer requests from the
public for specific musical numbers, Lillehaug became pro-active and
began publicly soliciting requests. Many concerts contained compositions which had been requested by listeners. Soliciting requests was a
procedure used by conductors during the early years of the Municipal
Band. Printed programs have been found from 1934 and earlier, which
indicated that the Band was attempting to please the public by playing
its specific requests.

In 1974, the Sioux Falls Municipal Band received an invitation to
perform at the Spokane World's Fair. Lillehaug and several members of
the Board felt that this would be an excellent way to publicize Sioux
Falls at a major national event. However, after much consideration, the
Band decided not to go because too many of the members would not be
able to make the trip because of work commitments and other conflicts.

Computerization of the Band Library

Lillehaug began a reorganization of the music library shortly after
becoming conductor in 1964. The card files which were used were standard for the time, but Lillehaug felt that computers, then in their relatively early stages, might provide some assistance.

Although it hardly seems innovative in 1994, the computerization
of the Band's large music library is thought to be one of the first, if not
the first, in the nation, other than the Library of Congress music section. Lillehaug, although not originally trained in the area of computers, had been an Army band librarian and was looking for a way to look
at the library in different ways as he pursued the large task of programming forty concerts each season. A system which could quickly
sort and print out the holdings by composer, arranger, title, musical
type and accession number seemed to be a possible solution. He took
his ideas to Ed Castle, head of the computer area at City Hall, and to
Glenn Wika, who occupied a comparable position at Augustana College.
Both agreed it was possible and subsequently had programs written to
do it at both institutions. This resulted in the computerization of the
Municipal Band and Augustana Band music libraries over the next few
years. The city's system cross-indexes over 4,000 musical compositions
in multiple ways, enabling one to locate a piece of music in a matter of

seconds. An article written by Lillehaug and published in a national music magazine, *The School Musician* in November 1982, brought inquiries about the system but no statements from anyone indicating that a comparable idea had been implemented. The early computerization of the library saved thousands of work hours through the years.

Playing at Heritage Park

Mayor Crusinberry, a strong supporter of the Band, had felt that it was important that the Band continue to play in Heritage Park on the East Side, long the blue collar section of town. He felt that although the size of the audience had shrunk for those concerts, the people deserved to be able to hear the Band in their own area. Consequently, weekly concerts were held in Heritage Park during the early part of the 1964-75 period but dwindled to one per season near the end. Smaller audiences and inability to control noisy and mischievous youth led to a switch to other concert sites. At one concert, young boys climbed the walnut trees in the park during a late summer concert and threw green walnuts at the Band members during the concert. Mary Jacobson and representatives of the citizens' group ACORN provided some help in policing the area and kept the concerts at Heritage Park longer than would have been the case without their assistance.

The Vietnam War and Its Influences

Anyone who lived through the Vietnam War years knows that it was difficult in many ways, especially for the youth. The establishment was being challenged, and loyalty to traditional social structures was breaking down. The emphasis was on individualism and "doing their own thing." When the Municipal Band began in 1920, much of the classical music it played was popular among the listeners. During the '30s and '40s Big Band music was popular and was easily performable by a concert band. In the 1960s the attitudes and music were different. Many of the youth felt that the music of concert bands was not "their" music. The music of the day did not fit organizations like the Municipal Band nor could it be easily adapted to the large group. During those years there also was greater than normal turnover in personnel in the Municipal Band. Some of it was normal — some came to Sioux Falls to attend one of the colleges and left the city when their college days ended. Other Sioux Falls students left the city to work or attend college elsewhere.

George Gulson remembered when some older members wanted to force long-haired younger male members to get haircuts. Lillehaug remembered a high school band director telling him that it was his (Lillehaug's) responsibility to see that no long hair be allowed. Lillehaug replied, "It is not my or the Band's responsibility to mandate personal hair style as long as it is clean and properly taken care of." The matter was ultimately dropped. Lillehaug – and the Band Board – weren't as lenient about bare feet. A few young people would have liked to come to rehearsals barefoot, but the conductor told them that shoes were expected. At the Board meeting on May 29, 1972, a motion was passed that Band members had to wear shoes during rehearsals.

The Challenges of Playing Outside

South Dakota can become extremely hot in the summer, especially noticeable when one has to expend the energy required to play an instrument in the sun. However, the Band never canceled a concert due to the heat because the "show must go on." Whenever fifty members are part of an organization more than seventy times each season, and often for many years, many stories about the weather are remembered and retold.

For instance, there is the story of the extremely hot concert in 1969 and the "disappearing" stage. Several Band members remember the incident related by Merridee Ekstrom: "On a hot Sunday afternoon at Sherman Park before we had the Showmobile, we sat on folding chairs on the blacktop parking lot. I sat next to a trumpet player who was quite a large person. During the concert, he seemed to be getting shorter, and we realized that his chair was sinking into the hot blacktop. All four legs of his chair had sunk far enough so that all the rubber tips were totally submerged." David Krueger reported the depression as being nearly two inches and recalled that on another hot day at the Battleship Memorial, his wife Donna was sitting in a position unprotected from the sun. Her skin was burned through her trousers.

Pat Masek verified the above story about the Sherman concert but stated that there was another equally hot day at Tuthill Park in later years when Alan Taylor was the conductor. "It was so hot that Oscar Loe and I had to leave the bandstand. Jane Quail [piccolo] didn't leave but didn't feel well the next day." On another hot day at a concert at the Nordland Fest on the Augustana Campus, water had to be passed to the Band members throughout the concert. It was probably at the Tuthill concert that Taylor allowed the Band to break another tradition. Because of the heat they were allowed to remove their ties.

Lillehaug recalled that on the Showmobile the conductor frequently had no shade because the Showmobile top did not extend far enough. The only day the heat made him ill was a 103 degree day at McKennan. However, the players didn't let the temperatures, hot or cold, deter them from their appointed musical tasks. Terry Walter remembered that Tom Ellwein, a trombonist who had spent his career as a member of the United States Marine Band in Washington, D. C. (see Chapter 11), told her that the heat was a factor in his retirement from the Sioux Falls Municipal Band.

One would think that heat would be the only temperature problem during the summer months. However, during the Taylor years (1987-91) there was a concert at the Prince of Peace Retirement Community when the temperature was in the 40s, cold enough that the players could see their breaths.

The temperature was not the only problem for players on a stage. At some sites, such as Heritage Park, where there was no back on the risers or the bandstand, there was the ever-present danger of Band members in the back row falling over backwards. This happened to trombonist Paul Bankson at Sherman Park during one concert. Luckily the riser was less than a foot in height, and he was not injured nor was his instrument damaged.

One member recalled that there were problems getting to and from the Terrace Park band shell. "Parking was often a problem at Terrace, and our normal parking spot was accessible via a short cut by walking along a dirt path. When it got dark later in the season, there was always the danger of falling into a ravine along the path," said David Krueger.

Band Members' Recollections

Scott Faragher remembered one concert when the Band was playing a woodwind ensemble feature in which each solo instrument followed the previous one with the same melody in the cadenza (a passage without band accompaniment). Milt Askew played several wrong notes on his cadenza on the clarinet. Ev Little then followed with the same cadenza on the alto sax and purposely tried to put in the same wrong notes that Milt had done.

Faragher also remembered the perseverance of member Harry Ellis, whose health problems caused him to be very short of breath. The Band once played the Soap Box Derby in northwest Sioux Falls and met at the state highway department building near the present Ramkota Inn. They then marched to the top of the hill, played for a short time and marched to the bottom of the hill for additional numbers. Ellis was physically unable to march up to the top of the hill with the Band so he drove his car up so he could play with the Band when it reached the top. When the Band finished he ran to his car, put his horn away, drove to the bottom of the hill and hurriedly put his horn together in time to play there even though he was still short of breath. Lillehaug said that Ellis was determined to carry his part of the load in spite of his health problem.

Tuba player Harry Ellis was remembered by other members for his perserverance. *(courtesy Sioux Falls Municipal Band)*

Band Governance

Although the conductor, as department head, had the final responsibility for all areas of the Band, the members of the Band Board played a major role in Band governance and in assisting the conductor with the internal administration of the Band. The minutes of the Band Board, beginning with the first Band in 1920, show this to be true. There was a great concern on the part of the conductor and Board members that Band members should always "look sharp" when in public. It appears that in the early years the members may have been responsible for their own uniforms. Later, the city provided uniforms to assist in the Band's appearance, and members had a responsibility to wear all parts of the uniform properly and to appear with uniforms properly pressed and shoes shined. Because all members did not always adhere to the established codes, the Board imposed fines for infractions. Minutes from 1972 and other years indicated that some members were fined for being out of uniform at concerts.

Band and audience members enjoyed the occasion when conductor Lillehaug was fined on a "trumped up being out of uniform" charge. He had donned a cowboy hat presented to him on stage by a farm group to whom Lillehaug had dedicated the concert. Band president Robert McDowell came out of his section in the Band and told Lillehaug that it would cost him a two-dollar fine. McDowell collected on the spot. Repeated new motions were passed that stipulated a fine for being out of uniform. Evidently Board members or players had forgotten that rules already existed

The minutes also indicate the Board's concerns for maintaining the Band's quality. On August 27, 1973, a motion was passed that "any apprentice or regular member returning from leave of absence be required to audition in order to become a regular member." In 1974 the Board agreed that a contract should be drawn up for players to sign each season committing to play the entire season.

Lillehaug Philosophy and Player Reactions

There is little or no disagreement that when Lillehaug became conductor in 1964, the musical discipline became tougher. Henegar had been a good conductor, and for much of his tenure the Band was blessed with a rather high percentage of veteran players with considerable playing ability. However, some of the veterans played beyond their good playing years, and some of the members said that the quality of the Band had gone down during Henegar's later years. Consequently, Lillehaug was forced to make several replacements after 1964. In addition, he believed that the highest quality Band could be produced only with a complete combination of the following items:
- The best conductor available.
- The best players available, both in terms of talent and willingness to prepare for rehearsals and concerts.
- Sufficient rehearsal time.
- Disciplined rehearsals in which players work hard and as a result receive great satisfaction from the high quality result of their efforts. This creates pride in the organization and leads to even higher attainments.
- A conductor has no right to waste the player's time. This stems from a feeling of respect for the players and also for the tax monies.
- Strong support from the administration, not only the Commissioner in charge but the entire Commission.
- An audience which comes out to hear the Band and appreciates the product when it is done well.
- Although requests for excuses are considered and honored on an

individual basis, each person who wants to be a "full time" player with the attendant privileges also has the responsibility of being at all rehearsals and concerts, unless excused in advance.

Lillehaug believed that unless all the above were at a proper level, it would not be possible for the group to reach its full potential. Not all were willing to discipline themselves in the way which the conductor expected. Some would leave and would be replaced. Fortunately, it was usually the best players who liked the challenge and the results and remained with the group.

Responses from Band members on the topic of discipline included: "Some people couldn't take it and quit. But we always found good people to take their places" (Paul Bankson). Bob McDowell, who played under both Henegar and Lillehaug, said that when Lillehaug became conductor the discipline was tougher. Another change he saw, but which he felt was more related to social conditions than conductors, was that it appeared that the better musical players tended to be less social: "Competition, rather than camaraderie, later become the vogue." Doug Lehrer commented, "Lillehaug might have been hard on the clarinets, expecting that they should produce more quickly than might normally have been the case. This may have been because he was a clarinet player and had a thorough knowledge of the instrument. I enjoyed his giving background on the music and/or the composer. He may have come down hard on sections sometimes, but I don't remember that he focused publicly on any one individual." And from Linda McLaren Roach came this remark: "He knew the music. He had high expectations and occasionally may have 'come down too hard' on the Band members and became upset when they were not playing up to his expectations."

Paul Bankson remembered what he considered an amusing quip from the conductor: "Someone came in on rests during a rehearsal. The passage was repeated several times without much improvement. Finally, in desperation, Lillehaug said, "See those little curlicues? They are rests. Don't play them!"

Other comments about Lillehaug include this from Stan Eitreim: "Under Lillehaug's direction, the Band literature went more toward modern original Band works rather than so many orchestral transcriptions. Patriotic medleys and marches, of course, continue to be a mainstay of the Band's literature." George Gulson said, "[Conductor Alan] Taylor was a definite change from Lillehaug. He fostered a more relaxed atmosphere. Lillehaug 'leaned' on people, but he had a great ability to properly program." Jeanette Paulson, who played oboe in the Band beginning in 1977, said that "discipline makes for a fine ensemble. Lillehaug knew exactly what he wanted out of a rehearsal and how to put on

Baton twirlers Nancy Mehlum, left, and Janine Johnson, above, were two of the many guest performers who appeared with the Municipal Band. *(courtesy Sioux Falls Municipal Band and Augustana College Edda)*

a 'good show' for the concerts, even down to instruction of proper deportment while in uniform. A disciplined approach to music is invaluable." Ralph Tyler, who played under both Henegar and Lillehaug said, "I didn't feel that the transition from Henegar to Lillehaug was difficult because music is still music."

Instrumentation

During the Band's first decade, there were about thirty players. When Henegar became conductor in 1935, the roster showed thirty-seven players plus the conductor. There also may have been a sound person who was not listed, and female vocalists soon appeared on the programs. During Henegar's early years, the instrumentation was similar to that of 1935, often using two flutes and piccolo, only one oboe and one bassoon, eight clarinets, three saxophones, five cornets, four horns, three trombones, one baritone (euphonium), two tubas, one string bass, three percussion and one or two vocalists. The number of players in several sections increased over the years until the instrumentation stabilized at about forty-six members. Because players were paid, the instrumentation was dependent on the personnel budget. Lillehaug tried to increase the clarinet section to ten and have a four-person double reed section. The membership was supplemented by many guests, including dancers, vocalists, twirlers, whistlers and instrumentalists. A typical instrumentation of fifty during Lillehaug's years was:

3 flutes (one player doubling piccolo)
2 oboes
2 bassoons
10 B flat soprano clarinets (or nine sopranos and one E flat alto clarinet)
1 bass clarinet
4 saxophones (2 altos, tenor and baritone)
6 cornets, with two playing the trumpet parts
4 horns
4 trombones
2 euphoniums
3 tubas
4 percussion
2 vocal soloists (one male, one female)
1 MC (sometimes the same person as the male vocalist)
1 sound technician
1 conductor

In 1972 the instrumentation was forty-seven players, two vocalists, one sound person and conductor, for a total of fifty-one. In 1973 the player number was raised to forty-nine but, because of finances, it dropped to forty-six in 1974.

• • •

In spite of the many changes, the Band's performance quality grew during 1964-75, and the audiences were generally large. Women members contributed to that growth. Band facilities were firmly established at the Coliseum. The Showmobile permitted the Band to give concerts where concerts had never been given. The Vietnam War was approaching an end, and some of the wounds of that period began to heal. The nation looked forward to celebrating its Bicentennial in 1976.

1964. McKennan Park. Standing front left: Ed Paul and Marciene Matthius (vocalists). Standing front right: Dr. Leland A. Lillehaug (conductor). Row 1, L to R: Kathy Hays (Emmel), Marilyn Loomis, Gustav Schuller, Jurgen Schuller. Row 2: Oscar Loe, Jeff Wold, Harold Gray, Russell Tiede, Scott Faragher, Robert McDowell, Donald McCabe, Loren Little, David Wegner. Row 3: Richard Peik, Ralph Tyler, Kenneth Busse, Everton Little, Keith Peterson, Tom Dempster, Wayne Krumrei, Robert Ortman, Robert Frick, George Gulson, Robert Holyer, Jack Rembold. Row 4: Robert L. Hanson, John Mattice, Gary Hoiseth, Philip Miller, Harold Hoover, Jr., Ronald McGaughey, Keith Knoff, Paul Bankson, Harry Ellis, George Runyan, Harvey Eichmeier, Paul Hoy, Robert Doescher, Stanley Eitreim, Kenneth McClain, Paul Davoux. Not pictured: Dennis Olson, Milt Askew, Paul Skattum. *(courtesy Marciene Matthius)*

1965. McKennan Park. Standing front left: Paul Wegner and Eugenia Orlich Hartig (vocalists). Standing front right: Dr. Leland A. Lillehaug (conductor). Row 1, L to R: Kathy Hays Emmel, Marilyn Loomis Hansen, Steven Olson, Gustav Schuller, Jurgen Schuller. Row 2: Oscar Loe, John Mattice, Robert L. Hanson, Ralph Olsen, Jr., Richard Peik, John Dempster, Ralph Tyler, Gary Hoiseth, Loren Little, Jack Rembold. Row 3: Harold Gray, Kenneth Busse, Everton Little, Robert J. Barnett, Keith Peterson, Stephen Heetland, Scott Faragher, Robert McDowell, Donald McCabe, Robert Holyer, George Gulson. Row 4: Tom Ellwein, Paul Bankson, Keith Knoff, Robert Hansen, Robert Ortman, Harry Ellis, George Runyan, Harvey Eichmeier, Paul Hoy, Robert Doescher, Alfred Boysen, Stan Eitreim, Paul Skattum. (courtesy Sioux Falls Municipal Band)

1967. Sioux Falls Coliseum. Standing front left: Paul Wegner and Eugenia Orlich Hartig (vocalists). Standing front right: Dr. Leland A. Lillehaug (conductor). Row 1, L to R: Ann Palmer, Kathy Hays Emmel, Linda Olson, Don Olson, Jurgen Schuller. Row 2: Ralph Olsen, Jr., Richard Peik, Gary Hoiseth, Gary Schaefer, Dan Runyan, John Mattice, Mary Perrenoud, Ann Stauffer, Harold Gray, Gustav Schuller, Doug Dean, Terry McCabe. Row 3: Kenneth Busse, Lon Wright, Robert Barnett, Everton Little, Greg Helland, Barb Johnson Hegg, Scott Faragher, Robert McDowell, Donald McCabe, Dr. Harold Krueger, Ken McClain, George Gulson, Paul Davoux. Row 4: Stan Eitreim, Gary Nelson, Robert Doescher, Paul Hoy, Wayne Krumrei, George Runyan, Harvey Eichmeier, Harry Ellis (sound), Earl Sherburne, Robert Schoppert, Dennis Hegg, Tom Ellwein, Paul Reeg, Paul Bankson, Hans Arlton. (courtesy Sioux Falls Municipal Band)

1968. Sioux Falls Coliseum. Standing front left : Paul Wegner and Eugenia Orlich Hartig (vocalists). Standing right front: Dr. Leland A. Lillehaug (conductor). Row 1, L to R: Pat Masek, Linda Mitchell, Jane Ordal, Oscar Loe, Gustav Schuller, Steven Olson. Row 2: Gary Schaefer, James Johnston, Dan Runyan, Ann Stauffer Flisrand, Mary Perrenoud, Earl Colgan, Jr., Richard Flisrand, Lon Wright, Doug Dean, Terry McCabe. Row 3: Jolayne Owen Hanson, Everton Little, Kenneth Busse, Linda Johnson, Greg Helland, Barb Johnson Hegg, Robert McDowell, Donald McCabe, Dr. Harold Krueger, George Gulson, Paul Hanson, Del Bickel. Row 4: Gary Nelson, Randy Hink, Robert Doescher, Paul Hoy, Wayne Krumrei, Harry Ellis, Dennis Hegg, Harvey Eichmeier, Mark Aspaas, Robert Schoppert, Paul Reeg, David Mitchell, Paul Bankson, Hans Arlton. (courtesy Sioux Falls Municipal Band)

Sioux Falls Municipal Band
Director Leland Lillehaug
Photo by 'Harolds'

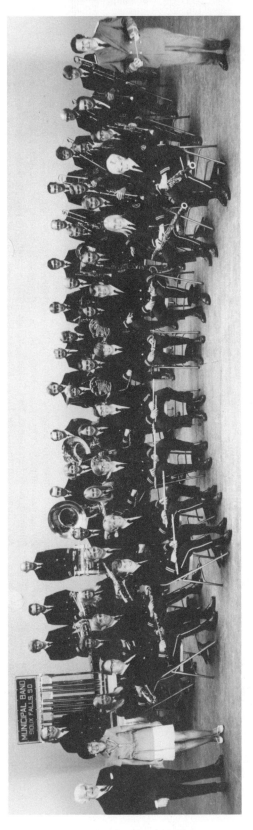

1970. Sioux Falls Coliseum. Standing front left : Paul Wegner and Eugenia Orlich Hartig (vocalists). Standing right front: Dr. Leland A. Lillehaug (conductor). Row 1, L to R: Pat Masek, Donna Van Bockern Krueger, David Lillehaug, Ralph Olawsky, Jeff Kull, Ove Hanson, Connie Wombacker Blanchard, Mindy Braithwaite. Row 2: Oscar Loe, Gary Schaefer, Dan Runyan, Sheila Haraldson, Anne Juul, Curtis Braa, Natalie Olson, Colin Olsen, David Krueger, David Gudmastad. Row 3: Kristi Elgethun, Don Newcomb, Mary Warren, Kenneth Busse, Deb Johnson Helland, Maureen Warren, Greg Helland, Dr. Harold Krueger, Loren Little, George Gulson, Merridee Ekstrom, Del Bickel. Row 4: Stan Eitreim, Greg Daniels, Robert Doescher, Paul Hoy. (seated): Wayne Krumrei, Donald M. Nelson, Jeff Bowar, Harry Ellis (sound), Michael Olson, Robert Ortman, Tom Ellwein, Scott Shelsta, Scott Stroman, Paul Bankson, Lon Alness. (courtesy Sioux Falls Municipal Band)

1972. Terrace Park. Standing in back on right: Paul Wegner and Eugenia Orlich Hartig (vocalists), Dr. Leland A. Lillehaug (conductor). Row 1, L to R: Pat Masek, David Lillehaug, Doug Olawsky, Jeff Kull, Ove Hanson. Row 2: Oscar Loe, Peg Larson, Debra Moe, Natalie Olson, Suzanne Prieb Olawsky, Anne Juul, Laura Frakes, Cindy Nelson, Steven Lillehaug, Tom Hartig, Gustav Schuller, Mindy Braithwaite. Row 3: James Albright, Janet Person, Mary Temanson, Don Newcomb, Garneth Oldenkamp Peterson, Tom Braithwaite, Randy Bingner, Connie Tornberg, Scott Faragher, Jack Reynolds, Jack Rembold, Merridee Ekstrom, Carol Ackerman, James Kirkeby, David Krueger. Row 4: Stan Eitreim, Greg Daniels, Jean Hoiseth, Paul Hoy, Harry Ellis (sound), Paul Runyan, Robert Runyan, Alan Berdahl, Michael Olson, Vinson Weber, Tom Ellwein, Paul Reeg, David Evenson, Paul Bankson, Lon Alness. *(courtesy Leland Lillehaug)*

1973 Sioux Falls Municipal Band
Director Leland Lillehaug
Photo by Harolds'

1973. Terrace Park. Standing in back on right: Paul Wegner and Eugenia Orlich Hartig (vocalists), Dr. Leland A. Lillehaug (conductor). Row 1, L to R: Pat Masek, Ann Faragher, David Lillehaug, Doug Olawsky, Kathy Moe, Jeff Kull, Connie Wombacker Blanchard, Mindy Braithwaite. Row 2: Oscar Loe, Richard Rath, Natalie Olson, Mary Rauk, Tom Hartig, James Albright, Martha Vegge, John Roth, Patsy Larson, Mark Lotz, David Krueger. Row 3: Anne Juul, Yvonne Johnson, Linda McLaren, Gus Schuller, Garneth Oldenkamp, Tom Braithwaite, Connie Roth, Tom Keleher, Susan Anderson, Connie Tornberg, Scott Faragher, Dr. Harold Krueger, Jack Rembold, George Gulson, Merridee Ekstrom. Row 4: Rick Paulsen, Jean Hoiseth, Lynn Peterson, Paul Hoy, Harry Ellis (sound), Greg Smith, Paul Runyan, Al Berdahl, Mike Olson, Anna Hamre, Paul Reeg, Paul Bankson, Scott Shelsta, David Evenson. Not pictured: Jack Reynolds (trumpet). *(courtesy Sioux Falls Municipal Band)*

1974. Terrace Park. Standing in back on right: Paul Wegner and Eugenia Orlich Hartig (vocalists), Dr. Leland A. Lillehaug (conductor). Row 1, L to R: Pat Masek, Ann Palmer Faragher, Donna Van Bockern Krueger, Kathy Moe, Jeff Kull, Mindy Braithwaite. Row 2: Oscar Loe, Natalie Olson, Mary Rauk, Steven Lillehaug, Tom Hartig, Janice Trumm, Terry Walter, Martha Vegge Nelson, John Roth, Sandra Person McAllister, Mark Lotz. Row 3: Linda McLaren, Anne Juul, Arlene Kleinsasser, Barb Griffith, Michael Engh, Connie Roth, Susan Anderson, Scott Faragher, Robert McDowell, Dr. Harold Krueger, David Krueger, Merridee Ekstrom, Tom Bierer. Row 4: Rick Paulsen, Jean Pinard, Greg Daniels, Jean Hoiseth, Paul Hoy; (seated) Stan Eitreim, David Joyce, James Taylor , Alan Berdahl, Loren Fodness, Robert Ortman, Paul Reeg, Paul Bankson, Paula Jorgensen, Kathy Schmidt. *(courtesy Leland Lillehaug)*

1975. On Showmobile. Front left : Dr. Leland A. Lillehaug (conductor). Front right: Eugenia Hartig and Paul Wegner (vocalists). Row 1, L to R: Pat Masek, Ann Palmer Faragher, Donna Van Bockern Krueger, Kathy Moe, Jeff Kull, Mindy Braithwaite, Laurel Paulson. Row 2: Oscar Loe, Steven Lillehaug, Thomas Hartig, David Amundson, Barb Griffith, Linda McLaren, Martha Vegge Nelson, James McWayne, John Roth, Sandra Person McAllister, Janet Bruns Hallstrom, Jeff Bowen. Row 3: Floyd McClain, Rosalie Jorgensen, Kevin Vaska, Barb Hanson Johnson, Kathy Bangasser, Tom Braithwaite, Michael Engh, Connie Roth, Susan Anderson, Scott Faragher, Robert McDowell, Dr. Harold Krueger, David Krueger, George Gulson, Merridee Ekstrom, Terry Anderson. Row 4: Jean Pinard, Julie Kahl, Tom Keleher, Paul Hoy; (seated) Stan Eitreim, Michael Seto, Paul Runyan, Robert Ortman, Loren Fodness, Kathy Schmidt, Paula Jorgensen, Paul Bankson, Paul Reeg. (courtesy Leland Lillehaug)

1976-86
Lillehaug Leads Through 1986

A n editorial in the July 16, 1977, *Argus Leader* reported that the nostalgic part of yesteryear's America was still alive and well in Sioux Falls. The headline read, "Sunday picnics and band concerts in the park." The editorial continued, "Sioux Falls is fortunate in having a combination of both parks and concerts that please families, old and young, during this very enjoyable summer of 1977. ... Sunday's afternoon concert at Sherman Park is an example. The program was a salute to the media and included compositions and verses typifying the press, television and radio. While the Band played, youngsters romped nearby, families lingered at picnic tables and others in the audience sprawled in the grass and enjoyed music." The review caught the essence of what has made band music popular throughout the history of this nation.

1976 — The Bicentennial

The patriotic nature of the nation's 200th year was a natural for community bands, a part of the country's national heritage since the beginning. The 1976 Sioux Falls Municipal Band season opened with a concert at the Coliseum on March 22, 1976. From the opening "Colonial Legend" (Grundman) to "Overture and March 1976" (Charles Ives), through the "Overture to a Celebration" (Hastings), and "We Hold These Truths" (Washburn), the patriotic nature of the occasion was emphasized. American music was in evidence — from the "Tournament Galop" of Louis Gottschalk, the celebrated pianist and composer, to "Suite from 'Unicorns and Butterflies' " by native South Dakotan Floyd McClain of Yankton. Other American composers represented on the program included Robert Russell Bennett, Jared Spears, Natalie Sleeth and Richard and Robert Sherman. With a probable unintentional nod to English composers Malcolm Arnold and Ralph Vaughn Williams, also represented on the program, the signal was given that all was forgiven from the events of 1776.

Mayor Rick Knobe showed that he could handle the baton as well as a radio microphone and the mayor's gavel by guest-conducting Sousa's famous "Washington Post March." Sponsorship for the concert came from the Recording Trust Funds obtained through Local 114 of the Musicians' Union, The National Bank of South Dakota, Schmitt Music Company, Sunbank of South Dakota and Williams Piano Company. Sharing the evening was the Bicentennial Chorus of Sioux Falls, conducted by Rolf Anderson.

The Municipal Band continued the patriotic theme by playing for the dedication of the Bicentennial Sundial at Fawick Park on July 4, the Independence Day evening celebration at the W. H. Lyon Fairgrounds and at the Royal C. Johnson Veterans Memorial Hospital on July 28. Fittingly, the final three numbers at the 1976 final summer park concert at Terrace Park were "Red's White and Blue," Sousa's "Semper Fidelis" and "Battle Hymn of the Republic."

During the 1976 summer concert season the Band played at Terrace Park every Sunday evening and alternated between McKennan and Sherman Parks on Sunday afternoons. Midweek concerts were played at various locations throughout the city. One out-of-town concert was played at the Harvest Festival in Salem on August 11. In addition to patriotic marches and vocal solos, many of which had similar themes, the Band played twenty-one different patriotic compositions during those concerts. Historical themes relating to the nation included "Salute to Rural America," "Our Ethnic Heritage," "Big Band Night," and an "All American Music Program."

One of the favorite concerts during the 1976 season was "The Golden Age of Radio" which featured local radio personality Ray Loftesness. Loftesness wrote the script which told the story of many major radio shows and personalities through the years. Lillehaug located or wrote the arrangements which musically identified and introduced the programs. The concert was so popular that it was repeated in 1977. Some of the pieces included in the program were "William Tell Overture" from "The Lone Ranger"; "Seems Like Old Times" from the Arthur Godfrey show; "The Perfect Song" from the Amos 'n Andy show; "Thanks for the

Memory" from the Bob Hope show; and "Love in Bloom" from the Jack Benny show.

1977

One of the Band's main goals in the statement of objectives for 1977 was increasing audience size. During the summer season 10,000 fliers and 500 posters were distributed. Lillehaug appeared on several television talk shows, and individual Band members spread the word about the concerts. The commissioner in charge of the Band, Vernon Winegarden, gave the Band strong support.

The previous enthusiastic support of indoor concerts led to a March 21, 1977, concert at the Coliseum entitled "Hands Across the Sea — Europe and America Meet With Music." Perhaps this was a wise choice — looking at the entire world after turning attention to the United States in 1976. The concert was a part of several Fine Arts Month performances in Sioux Falls. The Coliseum gave the Band an opportunity to feature compositions which lent themselves better to an indoor setting. Dr. Harold Krueger performed with vocalist Paul Wegner in "The Trumpet Shall Sound," and four outstanding performers were featured in Val Hamm's "Dialogue for Four." They were Patricia Masek, flute; Jeffrey Kull, oboe; Oscar Loe, clarinet; and Scott Faragher, horn. Selected high school musicians from the bands of Washington, Lincoln and O'Gorman performed with the Band on part of the program.

Special theme concerts and events during the season included "Government Employees Appreciation Night," the International BB Gun Shoot Championships held at Augustana College, "Salute to the News Media" and an "Audience Request Concert." Concerts were also played for Sioux Falls' neighbors in Centerville and Salem, South Dakota, and Hills, Minnesota.

Major overtures still held the important number two location on many of the Band's programs. "War horses" such as "Poet and Peasant" by von Suppe, "Il Guarany" by Gomez and "Ruy Blas" by Mendelssohn appeared along with "Walt Disney Overture" by Christensen and "Festive Overture" by Alfred Reed.

1978

Once again the Band opened its season with a winter concert at the Coliseum, this time on March 13, 1978. The varied program was built around the theme "Strike Up the Band." Featured soloists included

Dr. Harold Krueger, trumpet; Oscar Loe, clarinet; and Paul Wegner, vocalist. The final concert of the season was played on Veterans Day, November 11, at Lincoln High School.

During each season, instrumentalists who had solo capabilities frequently were given the opportunity to perform either as a soloist or in a small group. Soloists during 1978 were Oscar Loe, clarinet; Dr. Harold Krueger, trumpet; Carl Hallstrom, euphonium; and Terry Walter, alto saxophone. Instrumental feature groups included a trumpet quintet, trombone duet, Dixieland combo, flute trio, trumpet quartet, three different trumpet trios and a tuba trio.

Regular vocal soloists were Eugenia Hartig and Paul Wegner. Three female vocalists were featured during the season: Ruth Tobin, Joyce Nauen and Cammy Iseminger. Diana Borgum appeared as a narrator, and Linda Gednalske was a featured twirler.

Research on new band uniforms, begun in 1976, led to their purchase in 1978. The new uniforms, first worn at the opening of the park season on June 18, 1978, cost $9,252.30. A city ordinance No. 6-77, adopted January 24, 1977, listed supplemental appropriations for Federal Revenue Sharing Projects, including band uniforms in the amount of $7,700. The uniforms were purchased from Sol Frank Uniforms, Inc., of San Antonio, Texas, with Roy Olson Music of Fergus Falls, Minnesota, as the manufacturer's local representative. The items included were:

> 70 caps at $11.65 each
> 70 coats at $68.31 each
> 70 trousers at $36.74 each
> 80 extra coat patches at $2.35 each
> 250 shirt patches at $1.75 each
> 108 ties at 85 cents each
> 1 complete director's uniform at $150

The bid specifications indicated that the material should be Hamburger number 333, fifty-five percent dacron, forty-five percent virgin wool, and weight not less than ten to ten-and-one-half ounces (the manufacturer later recommended fourteen ounce material). The basic colors were red, white and blue. The coats were lipstick red, single-breasted with two gold buttons. The coats had blue stripes on the forearms with white piping, and blue epaulets with white piping and gold buttons; the trousers were royal blue and had three-quarter-inch red stripes with white piping; the caps were Air Force style with white bills and crowns with red bands with blue piping and eagle emblems.

One of the memorable moments of the season occurred on August 13, 1978, at Mom and Dad's Nursing Home. Before the concert began, a nurse brought a blind and deaf woman from the home. The elderly woman was seated next to the Showmobile stage, close enough so that she could put her hands on the stage surface. During the entire concert the conductor and adjacent players could see a smile on her face. Evidently, she was getting vibrations through the stage floor which pleased her. It was heart warming to all who watched. One person remarked that if one of the national news networks would have filmed the episode it certainly would have made the national evening news.

"Municipal Band Week" was inaugurated in 1978, during which time the Band played eight concerts in eight days at various sites in Sioux Falls. The summer park season ended on Sunday, August 20, with musical and celestial fireworks. Out-of-town trust fund concerts were played at Canistota, Centerville and Salem.

1979

A new idea, open rehearsals, was implemented in 1979 and continued fairly regularly for several years. Rather than playing a late winter or spring concert in 1979, the Municipal Band invited the public to an open rehearsal on Monday evening, March 19, to show how music was readied for performance. The event was not well attended, but the coffee and doughnut reception gave players and fans an opportunity to get acquainted with one another. Open rehearsals also were held in March 1982, March 1983 and April 1984 in the Augustana College band rehearsal room. That location provided better seating facilities for the public than the Coliseum did for that type of event. In 1984, a new twist was added. During the break, the Band members served refreshments and talked with the visitors, and during the second half the guests who brought their instruments played with the Band.

A program distributed to the audience called attention to the community band movement in the nation. It read: "No other type of musical organization has been so much a part of the grass roots fiber of our nation as the concert band. From Revolutionary times to the present, it has occupied an important place in community life. Although many participatory activities suffered during the early years of television, we now see a resurgence and a growth, especially in community musical organizations. The development of our school music programs has trained hundreds of thousands of performers who need community organizations in which they can continue to practice their art." It was

Open rehearsals, begun in 1979, allowed the public to see and hear how the Municipal Band prepared for concerts. The Band is shown here on the Coliseum stage in 1982. *(courtesy Sioux Falls Municipal Band)*

also noted that just as band music had raised citizens' spirits during the Depression of the 1930s and World War II, it could serve a similar function "as the nation faces economic problems." The statement may have been even more apropos following the large stock market drop eight years later in October 1987, when the Dow Jones Industrial Average fell 508 points or nearly 22 percent. It almost equalled the two-day loss of the historic crash of 1929.

The sixtieth anniversary banquet was celebrated Saturday, July 28, 1979, at the Airport Holiday Inn with 105 persons attending. A social hour, buffet dinner, program and a short rehearsal were held that evening, and the "Reunion Band" performed three numbers on the Terrace Park program the following evening. The Reunion Committee was co-chaired by George Gulson and Merridee Ekstrom. Gordon Olson, Chamber of Commerce manager, served as master of ceremonies. Several speakers shared past experiences as members of the Band, including Bob Niblick (1940s), Earl Colgan (1950s), Oscar Loe (1960s) and

executive proclamation

OFFICE OF THE
GOVERNOR

THE STATEHOUSE   PIERRE, SOUTH DAKOTA

WHEREAS, The Sioux Falls Municipal Band has contributed greatly to the cultural and recreational life of our state since 1919; and,

WHEREAS, The band has provided professional music utilizing the talents of a cross-section of South Dakota occupations such as realtors, medical technicians, secretaries, beauticians, homemakers, bank employees, students and educators; and,

WHEREAS, The band has been dedicated to bringing music to the people through free summer concerts; and

WHEREAS, The band has served as an example of the pride and talent of the citizens of South Dakota; and,

WHEREAS, The band will celebrate the Sixtieth Anniversary of its founding during this session, including a reunion of former band members, during the week of July 22-29:

NOW, THEREFORE, I, WILLIAM J. JANKLOW, Governor of the State of South Dakota, do hereby proclaim July 22-29, 1979, as

SIOUX FALLS MUNICIPAL BAND WEEK

in South Dakota.

IN WITNESS WHEREOF, I have hereunto set my hand and caused to be affixed the Great Seal of the State of South Dakota, in Pierre, the Capital City, this Twenty-Ninth Day of June, in the Year of Our Lord, Nineteen Hundred and Seventy-Nine

WILLIAM J. JANKLOW, GOVERNOR

ATTEST:

ALICE KUNDERT, SECRETARY OF STATE

This executive proclamation, signed by Governor William J. Janklow in 1979, proclaimed July 22-29 as "Municipal Band Week" and congratulated the Band on its sixtieth anniversary.

Doug Olawsky (1970s). Former Governor Joe Foss sent a tape telling of some of his experiences as a member from 1935 to 1939. Remarks were also given by Dr. Leland Lillehaug and by family members of the late Russ Henegar. Vera Moss, pianist, favored the group with dinner music. A printed program commemorating the event was distributed at the McKennan and Terrace Park concerts on July 29, 1979.

Governor William J. Janklow proclaimed July 22-29 as "Municipal Band Week" and congratulated the Band on its sixtieth anniversary, stating that, "The Sioux Falls Municipal Band has contributed greatly to the cultural and recreational life of our state since 1919, [and that] ... the Band has served as an example of the pride and talent of the citizens of South Dakota."

Two female vocalists from the Henegar years were invited back and performed at the July 29 Terrace reunion concert. Marciene Matthius joined regular vocalist Eugenia Hartig to sing the duet "I Waited for the Lord," and Anne Bryant Fisher sang "Italian Street Song," a number which she often had sung as regular vocalist.

The Band's annual schedule had not changed greatly during the past two decades with the exception of the rehearsal season, which included January during the Henegar years. Rehearsals were held on Monday evenings from 7:30 to 10 p.m. beginning the middle of October and continuing through the end of November with an appearance on Veterans Day. Monday evening has been the normal rehearsal night throughout the Band's history. The Band took December and January off and began rehearsals the first Monday in February. During some years there was a winter concert and two concerts prior to June 15, with the park season beginning the middle of June. The Band rehearsed once a week during the summer and played three or four concerts each week until near the end of August. By this time most members were tired and welcomed being off until the middle of October. The annual meeting normally was held following rehearsal on the final Monday of November. There was a large turnover of personnel at the end of the 1979 season, but the reasons seemed to be individual rather than being caused by any common problem.

Three national magazines recognized the work of the Sioux Falls Municipal Band during 1979. A picture and a story about the Band appeared in the spring issue of the national publication of the National Federation of Music Clubs, the *Music Clubs Magazine*. A 1979 article in the *International Musician*, a national publication of the American Federation of Musicians, cited conductor Lillehaug's statement that many of the group's accomplishments were due to the support of the City Commission, the dedication of the individual members and the work of the

Board of Directors. Another leading national music publication, *Wood-wind World, Brass and Percussion*, devoted the entire cover of its July/ August 1979 issue to a picture of the Band against the backdrop of the Terrace Park band shell and included a story about the Municipal Band written by oboist Jeanette Paulson. A booklet, published by the Convention-Visitors Bureau of the Sioux Falls Chamber of Commerce, included a color photo and paragraph of the Municipal Band as a part of "The Arts" section. The 1979 publication also included other facts about Sioux Falls at that time: Population 87,000, annual average temperature 45.5 Fahrenheit, annual precipitation 24.72 inches and average wind speed 11.1 miles per hour.

A new feature in 1979 was the concert of music by women composers and arrangers. Women represented were Marian Morrey Richter, Cecile Chaminade, Julia Smith, Cecile Vashaw, Carole King, Ruth Roberts, May H. Brahe and Rosemary Lang. The composition "Deadline" by Band member and former Band president Merridee Ekstrom also was programmed. Gene White's arrangement "Women's Lib Medley" added humor to the occasion.

Four out-of-town concerts were played during the summer of 1979: Lake Benton, Minnesota; Salem, Canistota and Freeman, the latter through a South Dakota Arts Council grant.

Other items of note during 1979 included an All-Sousa concert which was greeted with enthusiasm by the audience; the Band's becoming a new member of the Association of Concert Bands, the national organization for community bands; and the retirement of regular vocalists Eugenia Hartig and Paul Wegner.

1980

During 1980, publicity was extended through many outlets. Jeanette Paulson developed one of the best promotional efforts in many years for TV and radio spots and newspaper and periodical publications. Consequently, the crowds were consistently good at all concerts throughout the season. A "Municipal Band Week," during which the Band played additional concerts, was proclaimed by the mayor.

Ray Loftesness served as the new master of ceremonies in 1980, replacing Paul Wegner who had retired in 1979. In addition to Loftesness, five different guest masters of ceremonies were used during the 1981 season: Denny Oviatt, Paul Wegner, Ray Peterson, Dr. Olaf Malmin and Lillehaug. In 1980, Lillehaug decided to have auditions for guest vocalists and postpone choosing permanent replacements for Hartig and

Wegner. Thirteen different guest vocalists appeared during 1980 and six in 1981 (see Chapter 10). This gave added opportunities for talented people from the community to appear on stage with the Band. The vocal numbers were part of a total of 206 different compositions performed by the Band during the 1980 season.

During 1980, the city of Sioux Falls published a brochure called "Your Property Tax Dollars" indicating that the typical homeowner in Sioux Falls paid $255.09 to the city in annual property taxes. Some representative departments and the amounts were:

Police	$ 32.25
Fire	$ 26.10
Storm sewers	$ 4.84
City Commission	$ 1.91
Attorney	$ .77
Municipal concerts (Band)	$ .63

Since the Band played approximately forty concerts per season, it cost each citizen approximately one and one-half cents per concert.

More attention was being given to the "Dakota Proposition," a proposed law before the state legislature which, had it passed, could have cut budgets of many arts organizations, including the Band.

1981

The Band began its outdoor concert season earlier in 1981 by making its first appearance at Armed Forces Day on May 16. The event, held on the grounds of the Royal C. Johnson Veterans Memorial Hospital, was sponsored by the Military and Veterans Affairs Committee of the Sioux Falls Chamber of Commerce and paid tribute to the men and women of the armed forces. Three out-of-town concerts helped celebrate centennials — at South Dakota State University in Brookings, at Hartford and at Baltic. The Band also played for the Jaycees International BB Gun Shoot. The Band closed the season by helping veterans observe Veterans Day on November 11. A total of thirty-nine concerts (thirty-three city, six Trust Funds) were played during the 1981 season. One concert was rescheduled because of rain.

New publicity ventures included the new Arena computerized sign through the courtesy of Arena manager Bob Kunkel and an enclosed Band display on the Downtown Mall all summer. Lillehaug continued doing radio interviews and speaking to local service clubs about the

Band. A display also was set up on July 26 for the Civic Dance Association's "Sunday on the Grass," an event which allowed citizens to become acquainted with arts organizations and artists in the area.

1982

The 1982 season featured two new vocal soloists, a number of special concerts, the creation of a new fund to assist the Band with special projects and good audience attendance. Dr. Monty Barnard became the regular male vocalist and Roma Prindle the regular soprano soloist, with Paul Wegner making guest appearances. Ray Loftesness was master of ceremonies. A concert took place on July 28, to celebrate the centennial of Sioux Falls College, and out-of-town concerts were played in Hartford, Dell Rapids and Hudson. During "Municipal Band Week" seven concerts were played in eight days. The attendance at the final concert at Terrace Park was the largest in several decades, according to the

Roma Prindle, who became the regular female vocalist in 1982, is shown here in rehearsal with conductor Leland Lillehaug. *(courtesy Sioux Falls Municipal Band)*

conductor and several veteran members.

Lillehaug, in negotiations with Mayor Rick Knobe and city commissioners, was able to establish a "Sioux Falls Municipal Band Trust Fund" which could accept donations. The income from this fund was to be used for mileage expenses for out-of-town players. Initial gifts to the fund were a Hammond organ from Doug Lehrer's father and $400 from Dr. James Marvel, a horn player in the Band. Later in 1985, this special projects fund received contributions from local corporations, especially Northwestern Bell, which increased its annual donation to the Band Trust Fund from $500 to $750. No monies from tax revenues were used for this fund.

Because the Band's 1982 budget had been cut due to a 1981 Commission action, the season had been reduced by four city-sponsored concerts – from thirty-four to thirty – in addition to the five recording trust fund concerts. Conductor Leland Lillehaug's request to the Commission in its 1983 budget hearings was for a 12.8 percent increase in order to regain the lost concerts and increase the Band members' pay. An *Argus Leader* article of September 1, 1982, carried the headline, "Band's budget request hits sour note with city." According to the article, Commissioner Peterson asked Lillehaug to come back to the Commission with a plan for how the Band could operate on a $73,500 budget, which would be a 6.5 percent increase. The article further stated that the city library was asked to reduce its request from a 12.5 percent increase to 10 percent. That budget request had been "about a million." The final number of concerts was thirty-one city and five trust fund, for a total of thirty-six.

Paul Bankson, trombone, observed his twentieth anniversary with the Sioux Falls Municipal Band and announced his retirement. A banquet honoring him was held Sunday, August 8, 1982, at Nordic Hall. Lillehaug spoke of the tremendous service that Bankson had given during those years as a player, a Board member, a Band manager, a public relations worker and as an individual. The Band members presented Bankson with a gift as an expression of their appreciation.

Band member Terry Walter was commissioned by the South Dakota Department of Tourism to write a two-and-one-half minute composition based on the department's promotional theme, "Feel Free Again." It was premiered on Sunday, August 15, at McKennan and Terrace Parks. The major ceremonies were held at the evening concert in Terrace Park. Walter was introduced, Lt. Governor Lowell Hanson spoke briefly and Lillehaug presented the score on behalf of the composer to Susan Edwards, tourism director. The piece was distributed by the South Dakota Tourism Department to bands throughout the state.

1983

The Band helped the Lennox Municipal Band, reputedly "the oldest continuous musical organization in South Dakota," celebrate its centennial on June 10. The Lennox Band began in 1883, only four years after the town was founded in 1879. John Buus, conductor of the Lennox Band since 1955, guest conducted the "Washington Post March." Ties between the two bands included having Russ Henegar as the Lennox Band director from 1936 to 1948, Lennox buying band uniforms from the Sioux Falls Band in 1942 at a cost of five dollars each, and at least ten appearances by the Sioux Falls Band in Lennox from 1939 to 1983, including the dedication of the new Lennox band shell on August 30, 1963. The latter was one of the last concerts Russ Henegar conducted before retiring from the Sioux Falls group. Several members of the Sioux Falls Band played with the Lennox Band through the years.

The first written mention of the emerging need for a history of the Sioux Falls Municipal Band is found in the minutes of the January 31, 1983, Board meeting. Mary Jensen, chairperson of the publicity and concert attendance committee, brought a list of suggestions, one of which was "printing a book about the Municipal Band." Like suggestions from many committee reports, it was not something that anyone could undertake at that time.

On August 4-7, 1983, the Band played host to the national convention of Windjammers, a circus music organization. Seven Band members played in the Windjammers band at the Terrace Park concert on Saturday, August 6. Lillehaug was one of the conductors and also played in the band. Members of the Windjammers were guests at the Sunday,

---

Ardis and Leland Lillehaug enjoy the July 26, 1983, Municipal Band banquet honoring Lillehaug for twenty years as conductor.
(courtesy Leland Lillehaug)

**Senator Larry Pressler is shown here with conductor Leland Lille-
haug at the 1983 Memorial Day Concert at the Royal C. Johnson
Veterans Memorial Hospital.** *(courtesy Sioux Falls Municipal Band)*

August 7, concerts. The concerts featured Windjammer president Ron
Grundberg as euphonium soloist and Bob Hills as guest conductor at
McKennan and at the Terrace circus concert dedicated to Karl L. King.

On September 19, 1983, the Band Board considered an invitation
from Hungary to participate in a 1984 summer music festival. Cost and
scheduling problems made it impossible to accept the invitation.

Through the years the conductor's programming procedures seemed
to have met with wide acceptance. However, in 1983 Board members
suggested that more contemporary "pop" music be programmed. Although there was not a great increase in new "pop" compositions, one
notes "Summer of '42," "New York, New York," and "Star Wars Medley,"
along with "pop" tunes from the Big Band era. Rock tunes were played
infrequently.

Concert attendance was lower during the 1983 season, in contrast
to a steadily growing attendance in previous recent years. Most of the
problems were blamed on the weather — unusually cold and rainy early
in the season and very hot later in the summer. The budget proposal for
the 1984 season was cut by one concert by the Commission, with a warn-
ing that if John Morrell and Co. should close other cuts could be forth-
coming.

1984

The 1984 season was standard in terms of the number of concerts, but it did include one new concert site and a number of guest conductors. A total of thirty-nine concerts were scheduled and all were performed. There were no rain outs. Out-of-town concerts were played at Dell Rapids, Brookings and Canistota. A concert was played at a new concert site on June 28 — on the grounds of the historic Berdahl-Rolvaag House at Menlo Avenue and Thirty-Third Street. Guest conductors during the season included Gunnar Malmin, who conducted the Band and Minnehaha Mannskor on June 19 and 24; Lt. Col. Charles Erwin (assistant conductor of the United States Marine Band in Washington, D.C.); Butler Eitel of Brookings; and Dr. Darwin Walker (director of bands at South Dakota State University). Eitel and Walker both conducted at the Band's concert in Brookings on July 7, 1984.

During the year, the Band Board discussed the founding of a citizens' support group for the Band, an idea which had been proposed by conductor Lillehaug earlier and which had been discussed and tabled in January 1983. Lillehaug believed that although the Band members were certainly competent to handle the Band's day-to-day affairs, it would be helpful to have a board of citizens to bring in wider perspectives. There was insufficient support, and the proposal was dropped. The idea reappeared at Board meetings on January 7, April 15 and June 10, 1985, but again nothing was implemented.

The Band continued trying to reach a greater audience, this time by purchasing a thirty-second spot on KELO which ran numerous times. Television advertising had been used as early as 1975.

Three items of a different nature were discussed by the Band Board in 1984. First, in an effort to get more of the members involved in Band projects, five committees were formed: social, recruiting and retention, publicity, financial, and music selection. Secondly, some members, concerned with insufficient rehearsal time during the summer, suggested that a few Sunday afternoon concerts be cut and replaced with extra rehearsals. Although the Board recognized that it was difficult to play three or four concerts a week with a two-and-one-half hour rehearsal, the Sunday afternoon concerts were well established, and the Board decided it would not be wise to cut any of them. Thirdly, another tradition of not changing a player's seating rank if the person were playing satisfactorily was sustained by the Board. During the year a bassoonist challenged for the principal's chair, but the Board denied the request.

One of the most successful projects ever sponsored by the Band took place October 8, 1984, when the Municipal Band sponsored the

THE SIOUX FALLS MUNICIPAL BAND
IN COOPERATION WITH
ARGUS LEADER • CITIBANK • KELO-LAND RADIO & TV
MIDLAND NATIONAL LIFE INSURANCE COMPANY
proudly presents

THE UNITED STATES

MARINE BAND

The President's Own

Sioux Falls
Coliseum

Monday
October 8, 1984
8:00 P.M.

This is the program from the October 8, 1984, concert of the United States Marine Band. The event was sponsored by the Municipal Band, in cooperation with the Argus Leader, Citibank, KELO-Land Radio and TV and Midland National Life Insurance Company.

U.S. Marine Band from Washington, D.C., in two concerts at the Sioux Falls Coliseum. The matinee for students and senior citizens sold out, and the evening concert was well attended. The two concerts attracted a larger audience at the Sioux Falls Coliseum than most performances of any type in many years. The fifty-two-page program featured articles on Sioux Falls, the arts in South Dakota, information about the U.S. Marine Band and the Sioux Falls Municipal Band (then in its sixty-fifth year), the conductors, commissioners, Band personnel, committees and soloists. Colonel John Bourgeois, the Marine Band conductor, led the elite group through an exciting program beginning with "Black Horse Troop" and ending with "The Stars and Stripes Forever," both by John Philip Sousa. Numbered among the other compositions on the program were the difficult overture "Masquerade," by Carl Nielsen, Mussorgsky's "Pictures at an Exhibition," Ravel's "Bolero" and features for the group's vocal and instrumental soloists. Lillehaug had guest conducted the Marine Band in Tempe, Arizona, in March 1984.

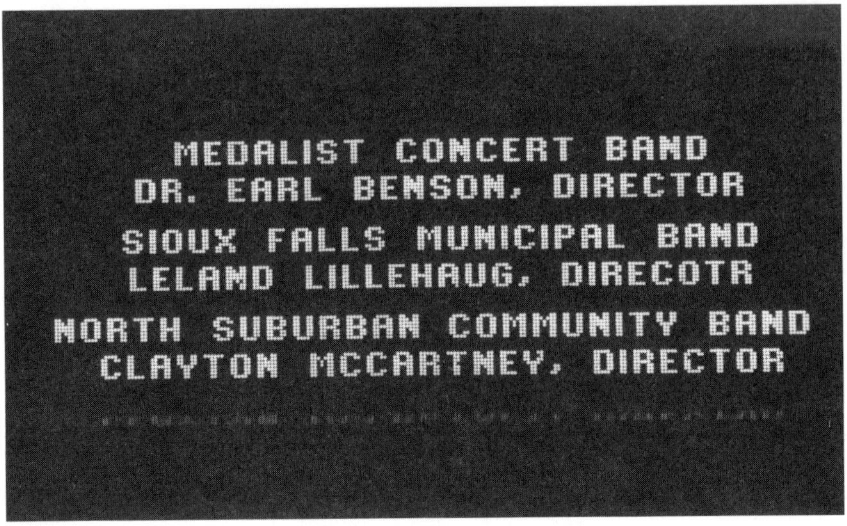

MEDALIST CONCERT BAND
DR. EARL BENSON, DIRECTOR
SIOUX FALLS MUNICIPAL BAND
LELAND LILLEHAUG, DIRECOTR
NORTH SUBURBAN COMMUNITY BAND
CLAYTON MCCARTNEY, DIRECTOR

The Sioux Falls Municipal Band was one of three bands chosen to play at the 1985 baseball All Star Game in Minneapolis July 16, 1985. The scoreboard, shown above, listed the three bands and their directors. *(courtesy Sioux Falls Municipal Band)*

1985

Although there were no major scheduling changes each year, there was normally something new in the venues, the occasion or in the guests. The Band played at the Delbridge Museum of Natural History for the dedication of a panda exhibit. A concert was also played in the Empire Mall, but no concerts were played at Heritage Park in 1985. Groups performing with the Band included the American Legion "Singing Legionnaires" and the South Dakota Dance Theatre. A "Big Jazz Band" was formed from the membership, and it appeared as a part of the concert on the Downtown Mall on July 18.

An unusual situation occurred in 1985 — no competent oboists were found, and the entire season was played without that instrument. During the 1985 season, the playing instrumentation varied between forty-three and forty-six, plus two vocalists (Roma Prindle and Dr. Monty Barnard), one sound person and one master of ceremonies. Terry Walter was librarian.

A highlight of 1985 was the invitation extended to the Municipal Band to join selected bands, one each from Wisconsin, Minnesota and

North Dakota, to participate in the ceremonies at the national baseball All Star Game in Minneapolis on Tuesday evening, July 16. The Band left Sioux Falls Monday noon July 15, played a concert at Peavey Plaza in downtown Minneapolis Tuesday noon and returned to Sioux Falls at 1:30 a.m. on Wednesday following the game. The only out-of-town concert, besides the Minneapolis trip, was at Dell Rapids.

Another event which is remembered fondly by many Band members is the guest appearance of Merle Evans, ninety-two-year-old former conductor of Ringling Brothers and Barnum & Bailey Circus, for two circus concerts on June 23. Ray Loftesness served as ringmaster. The circus bandmaster's appearance in Sioux Falls was sponsored by the Midland National Life Insurance Company. Evans, called the "Toscanini of the Big Top," had toured with the circus for fifty years, beginning the same year the Sioux Falls Municipal Band was authorized (1919) and continuing until 1969. According to *The Heritage Encyclopedia of Band Music*, Evans conducted more than 18,250 performances without ever missing.

Lillehaug and bass drummer Paul Hoy were personal friends of Evans. Lillehaug said that he had questioned the story of Evans never missing a performance in fifty years. When asked about it, Evans told Lillehaug that the story was true and said, "I was blessed with good health, but of course there were times when I went to work even if I wasn't feeling well." Evans told Lillehaug that he had promised the rights to his biography to writer Gene Plowden but that if he didn't get it written Lillehaug would have the next rights. However, Plowden completed the book, which was published in 1971 by the E. A. Seemann Publishing Co. Evans suffered a stroke on December 15, 1987, and died December 31.

Hoy spoke of his association with Evans and the first time Hoy played with a circus: "The year I graduated from high school, Ringling Brothers were in Sioux City. I knew Merle Evans already because I knew him in Sheldon when Ringling came there so I said to him, 'Can I play a march in your concert before the show starts?' And he said, 'Sure.' He said, 'I'll tell the bass drummer.' So he motioned for me to come and play, and instead of a march, there was 'Night in June,' ... it had about six beats in it for the bass drum and I was flabbergasted. Then Leland [Lillehaug] had Merle Evans come to Sioux Falls in 1985 to direct our circus concert, and Merle was sitting here and I said, 'Merle, do you remember back in about 1925, I asked you if I could play a march?' And Evans said, 'Yes,' and ... 'Now I'll tell you what you played — 'A Night in June.' That was over fifty years after that. Now, that is what I call a memory."

1986

The Band began its 1986 season by playing for Armed Forces Day on May 17 with assistant conductor Oscar Loe serving as conductor. The season closed with the November 11 Veterans Day observance. A total of thirty-eight concerts were played during the year.

Special guests during the season included composer/conductor Al Davis on June 15, the Sioux Emperians Barbershop Chorus, and the Masterworks Mixed Chorus and Salem Zion Mens' Chorus from Freeman, conducted by Band member Dennis Graber. James Christensen, music director at Walt Disney World, appeared with the Band on July 8, in the roles of guest conductor and trombonist in a concert called "Happy Sounds of Disney" on the Downtown Mall. The final guest of the season was M/Sgt. Scott Shelsta, former Band member, who is trombone soloist with The United States Army Band in Washington, D.C. His solo artistry was enthusiastically received at the McKennan and Terrace concerts on August 10, 1986.

A study of the programs through the Lillehaug years indicated that he did not make any major changes from the procedures with which he started in 1964. Every concert contained standard marches, most notably by Sousa, Karl L. King and Fillmore but with a good representation of circus march composers as well. European march writers such as Fucik and Kenneth J. Alford (pseudonym of Frederick J. Ricketts) were represented along with the Germans Blankenburg and von Blon.

One change may have been fewer performances of the orchestral transcriptions of overtures such as "Il Guarany" (Gomez), "Sicilian Vespers" (Verdi), and "Zampa" (Herold). Lillehaug commented that he personally loved these and other overtures but there were fewer veterans in the Band who knew that literature. Many of the classic overtures are very difficult, especially in the high woodwinds, and require sufficient rehearsal to do them well. With rehearsal time always in short supply, Lillehaug made some concessions and played more recently arranged medleys by Porter, Kern, Gershwin and Youmans in the number-two spot on the program. However in the 1985 and 1986 programs one finds Wagner's "Die Meistersinger ...," "Chester Overture" (William Schuman), "American Overture for Band" (Jenkins), "Eighteen-Twelve Overture" (Tschaikowsky) and others of the heavier type.

It is interesting to compare Henegar's final program of September 2, 1963, at Terrace and Lillehaug's final program at the same park on Sunday, August 17, 1986, twenty-three years later. These concerts were the last summer concerts before retirement for both. Programs read as follows:

Monday, September 2, 1963, Terrace Park, 8 p.m.
Russ Henegar, Director

1. March, Bombasto, O. R. Farrar.
2. Overture, The Marriage of Figaro, W. A. Mozart.
3. Trumpet solo, Carnival of Venice, Herbert L. Clarke.
        Soloist: David Wegner
4. Excerpts from the Ballet, The Sleeping Beauty, Peter I.
    Tschaikowsky.
5. Vocal solo, Danny Boy (Londonderry Air), old Irish melody.
        Soloist: Marciene Matthius
6. Ebony Rhapsody, Edgar L. Barrow.
        Features the entire clarinet section of the Band.
7. Cornet solo, The Charmer, Louis F. Boos.
    Soloist: Douglas Dean. Douglas is the son of Mr. and Mrs. Paul Dean
        of Rock Valley, Iowa The guest soloist is making his first appear-
                ance with the Band in Terrace Park.
8. A Salute to Grofe, Ferde Grofe.
9. Vocal solo (request), A Perfect Day, Carrie Jacobs-Bond.
        Soloist: Ed Paul
10. Presenting the sisters Marilyn and Rita Aughenbaugh of Iroquois,
    South Dakota, daughters of Mr. and Mrs. Burdette Aughenbaugh.
    They are senior state baton twirling champions of 1962 and 1963
    and will present both regular and fire baton routines including
    their duet that was featured on the Ted Mack Original Amateur
    Hour from New York City. This fall they will be head majorettes
    and featured twirlers with the South Dakota State College Band.
11. Presenting a song and dance revue of talented youngsters from
    the Tanglefoot Studio under the direction of Lila Lee Christy
    accompanied by the Municipal Band.
12. Finale: Grand display of fireworks produced by the Rich Bros.
    Fireworks Company of Sioux Falls under the supervision and in
    charge of Mr. Dale Dodge. Background music by the Band.
The National Anthem.

It is noteworthy that David Wegner was the featured trumpet soloist in 1963, and his son, Nathan, was a member of the trumpet trio in
the 1986 program.

Sunday, August 17, 1986, Terrace Park, 8 p.m.
"Grand Finale and Fireworks" concert
Dr. Leland A. Lillehaug, Conductor

Opener and Star Spangled Banner
1.   Marche Militaire   C. Saint-Saens / M. L. Lake.
2.   Chester Overture   William Schuman.
3.   Feature, Bugler's Holiday   Leroy Anderson.
         Trio: Eric Knutson, Nathan Wegner, Steve Sommers.
4.   Vocal solos, The King and I   Richard Rodgers / R. R. Bennett.
     Memories of You   Eubie Blake.
             Soloist: Roma Prindle, soprano.
5.   March, Trouping Days   Karl L. King.
6.   John Denver   John Denver / Andrew Balent.
7.   Vocal solos, Oklahoma   Richard Rodgers / Paul Yoder.
     America Our Heritage   Helen Steele/Hawley Ades.
             Soloist: Dr. Monty Barnard, baritone.
8.   March, On the Mall   Edwin Franko Goldman / Lake.
9.   America the Beautiful   Samuel A. Ward / Dragon.
10. The Stars and Stripes Forever   John Philip Sousa.

Fireworks music:
     March, Black Horse Troop   John Philip Sousa
     March, Monte Carlo   Karl L. King
     March, Washington Post   John Philip Sousa
     March, Semper Fidelis   John Philip Sousa
     March, University of Idaho   Karl L. King
     Eighteen-Twelve Overture   Tschaikowsky

Lillehaug said that he normally programmed the final concert with slightly "lighter" music because: 1) The crowds were large and there was more audience noise; 2) More solos and feature numbers were desirable; and 3) Many of the people present may have attended few or no concerts during the season and were less acquainted with the standard band literature.

An organization must always stay up-to-date, requiring the constant testing of new compositions and necessitating additional rehearsal time. Because variety was a trademark of Lillehaug programming, he also used many vocal and instrumental soloists — regulars and guests. These required more rehearsal time, minute for minute, than did the straight band compositions.

Lillehaug had intended to retire on December 31 but was asked by Mayor White to stay on through the Band's appearance at the national convention of the Association of Concert Bands on April 25, 1987, in Chatfield, Minnesota, and until a new conductor was hired.

This and That

There has been threatening weather at concerts through the years. One night there was a tornado threat and the concert was terminated early. Sirens went off as the Band members were on their way home. Severe storms happened at least twice — at Terrace and at Luther Manor. After the Luther Manor concert several Band members went to Lillehaug's home (close to the concert site) to ride out the storm.

One night at a Heritage Park concert, Lillehaug shortened the concert slightly because many of the players wanted to get to a television set to see the final episode of "The Fugitive" series, a very important event to some of them.

The Dispute with Commissioner Dick Peterson

A different kind of storm brewed during Lillehaug's last five years as the conductor of the Municipal Band. Although good will between Sioux Falls city officials and Municipal Band leaders has been a key ingredient in the longevity and success of the Band, a conflict began in 1983 that nearly jeopardized one summer's concert schedule and caused the Band's leader to sue the city and its officials. The conflict centered around three issues. The first was a raise and subsequent rollback of conductor Lillehaug's salary. A secondary conflict, which entered the picture at the same time, was the suggestion by then Commissioner Richard "Dick" Peterson — who oversaw the Band — that the Band cease to be an independent department and be put under control of the Park Department. Peterson did not succeed in his attempts to move the Band to Park Department supervision while Lillehaug was conductor, and complete resolution of the salary conflict didn't occur until Lillehaug's retirement in 1987. Thirdly, Peterson wanted to make the position contractual rather than that of a city employee as it had been since at least 1935. In a recent interview, Sioux Falls finance director Manfred Szameit said the purpose of the change evidently was to cut the benefits associated with the position and save money. The Commission removed the conductor's job from the employee salary matrix and established it as a contractual position in 1984. Peterson declined to discuss these or any other issues relating to his tenure as commissioner for this book. Information comes from newspaper articles, documents and other interviews.

The issue of Lillehaug's salary began when he wrote to Commissioner Peterson on August 11, 1982, asking for an evaluation of his po-

sition as Band director. Lillehaug wrote: "... I would like you and the
other commissioners to examine my salary in relationship to the job I
am doing and in relationship to comparable positions in city government and in the community. As I mentioned, I have never raised the
salary issue once during my nineteen years and consequently no one
else has examined it." He pointed out possible areas of comparison, including part-time city attorneys and the conductor of the South Dakota
Symphony. Lillehaug concluded the letter by saying, "This is not a request for a raise as such in the usual sense, but a look at the job classi-
fication, such has been done with other department heads in the past. I
have a Ph.D. with thirty years of conducting and management experience. Thank you for your consideration. I would be happy to discuss it
with you further in person, if you desire." Lillehaug indicated that he
was doing the same work as his predecessor, Russ Henegar, who had
been classified as full time, and that the job had grown in complexity
through the years. Lillehaug said Peterson referred him to Doug Meyers,
then the city's personnel director, who said the city was planning a comprehensive study of all positions and salaries and asked if Lillehaug
could wait a few months. Lillehaug said he agreed.

It was in January of 1983 that the city initiated the comprehensive wage and benefit study mentioned by Meyers. The study was conducted by Touche Ross & Co., an independent consulting firm from Minneapolis. According to a copy of the project summary written by Touche
Ross & Co., the objective of the project was "to develop and implement
an equitable pay plan for all employees of the city. In order to accomplish this objective, specific activities were undertaken to: (1) Conduct
fair evaluations of each job in the city; (2) Design a pay plan to attract
and retain competent employees; and (3) Provide for an expeditious
adoption and implementation of the plan to best serve the needs of the
city." The project activities included:

- A review of all job descriptions by appropriate department directors;
- Job site interviews, revisions and new job descriptions as needed;
- Review of job descriptions and evaluation of components of the
  jobs by employee committees. An interoffice memo indicated that
  the employees on the committees "represented a cross-section
  of departments and positions. These committees evaluated individual positions and ultimately ranked them relative to one
  another. These evaluations and rankings led to the assignment
  of classifications to pay scales within the new plan."
- Wage and salary surveys were reviewed and analyzed. The same
  memo explained that Touche Ross "collected wage and salary

information from local and regional organizations in both the private and public sectors. They also utilized other salary surveys that were available to help them review and analyze salary levels." According to a quote in the newspaper from then-personnel director Kaye Paul (Byrnes), the consultants also judged officials "on what operations they are responsible for, the knowledge required to do the job, and the availability of people to fill the position." The combination of the findings yielded two new pay plans, one for general and middle-management employees and one for department heads. Lillehaug recalled furnishing job specifications for the study.

The results of the study were revealed to city leaders later that year, beginning with the Commission in late May 1983. Department heads, including Lillehaug, were briefed on the recommendations on June 13, 1983. Readings of the new pay ordinance occurred June 20 and June 27, 1983. The Commission put their final stamp of approval on the Touche Ross study, including any changes, and the recommendations went into effect July 18, 1983.

What were the results of the study? The briefing memo given to department heads June 13, 1983, indicated that "under the new plans, ninety-seven percent of the employees would receive a salary increase." The study recommended raises of ten to fifty percent for "most of the city's top-level managers," according to newspaper articles. Band conductor Lillehaug was at the high end of the pay increases. The study recommended that his salary of $15,927 be raised to $24,413, an increase of $8,486 or fifty-three percent. The salary of city attorney Roger Schiager, another part-time department head, was raised $8,361 (from $24,326 to $32,687) or 34.8 percent (*Argus Leader* article, December 9, 1983). Raises of two assistant city attorneys were each about $6,000. A letter was given to Lillehaug by city officials, informing him "of the impact of the study on you individually." No objections were made by commissioners as they studied the results of the report. In fact, on July 25, 1983, the Commission transferred $2,918 to the Municipal Band budget for the Band salary increase. On the same resolution, funds of $16,137 were transferred to the city attorney department, also part-time employees, ostensibly for the same reason.

But two months later — September 28, 1983 — Lillehaug said Commissioner Peterson told him that he was planning to roll back the salary to the previous level. Peterson was later quoted in newspaper articles as saying the reason for the rollback was that the study treated Lillehaug's job as a full-time position when the raise was given. In an article from the weekly *Tribune* of April 20, 1984, Peterson said, " 'Back last year, when the city was having the Touche Ross study conducted to study city employee salaries, they told us that it was designed to study salaries for full-time employees. We told them that we had a couple of part-time people we also wanted salaries evaluated for. ... They were evaluated as full-time employees, and we were going to take the fact that they were part-time employees into account when we determined their salaries.' Somewhere along the line, Lillehaug slipped through the cracks, Peterson said. 'In our haste to implement the new salaries established from the survey, Dr. Lillehaug's salary slipped on by. One day last fall, the finance office called me up and asked where the money was going to come from to pay Lillehaug's new salary. I asked them, what new salary?' " In the same article, Peterson denied he was singling out Lillehaug: " 'The bottom line is money,' Peterson said . 'I have no complaints with how Lillehaug has been doing his job. If I had any complaints, you would have heard about them by now.' " An *Argus Leader* article, dated December 9, 1983, also had Mayor Rick Knobe saying that the study looked at employees as full time: "Mayor Rick Knobe said the salary study had looked at the three lawyers and the Band director as full-time employees. There's some question about whether those positions should be considered full-time, and the Commission will review the increases next year. ..."

Lillehaug objected to the salary rollback because he thought it was unfair that only he was getting his salary rolled back when there were others, including the city attorneys, in the same category. He also felt he deserved the pay based on his responsibilities, his education and experience and the product he produced, whether that was considered full-time or part-time work. He said he asked Peterson if he was planning to do that to any other employees. "He told me I was the only one. I told him I couldn't accept that if I were being singled out from all employees." In the *Tribune* article of April 20, 1984, Lillehaug said, "This job used to be full-time with the previous director, Russ Henegar. This position is not so lowly that it deserves the salary they want to pay. Look at the other department heads, their education and qualification — I should rank up there, too." Lillehaug said the job is not one that requires a time card, and that his professionalism should rank higher in this salary discussion.

Additional meetings between Peterson and Lillehaug occurred in 1983 and on into 1984. Lillehaug said he met with Peterson on September 30, 1983, with Peterson referring to the rolled back salary and telling him to "take it or leave it." That same day the City Commission approved the 1984 budget with Lillehaug's salary at the rolled back figure. The next meeting between Lillehaug and Peterson was Monday,

January 30, 1984. Lillehaug said Peterson had no new proposals.

A second source of conflict — the suggestion of restructuring the supervision of the Municipal Band — occurred February 13, 1984. Lillehaug said that Peterson then told him that he was doing an excellent job as conductor but added that he was thinking of putting the Band under the Park Department. "I stated that I thought this would be an unwise move because it would reduce the effectiveness of the adminis- tration of the Band which had been functioning directly under a mayor or commissioner without any problems for decades," Lillehaug said. At another meeting with Lillehaug on February 23, Lillehaug recalled Peterson saying that he definitely had decided to propose having the Band under the Park Department.

According to Lillehaug's time line of events, on March 23, 1984, he was given a contract to sign. The contract — patterned after the city's golf pro's contract — would have placed the Band under the Park De- partment. Lillehaug objected to having a change in structure when the Band members were being given no opportunity to express their opin- ions. He said that there were several items that "did not properly relate to a musical organization at all." The contract also would have elimi- nated an important benefit to the conductor — the city pension pro- gram. Lillehaug called the contract "ludicrous" and consulted a lawyer, John Gridley. Gridley was later quoted in the *Argus Leader* as saying, "The contract is an incomprehensible document. I don't think there's a lawyer in Sioux Falls who would write such a ridiculous contract." Peterson asked for a meeting April 5, 1984. Lillehaug wanted his law- yer to attend the meeting, but said Peterson refused to see him with Gridley present. At the meeting, Peterson asked Lillehaug to sign the contract, but Lillehaug refused. Peterson asked for a decision by 2 p.m. the following day. Lillehaug again refused to sign.

The issue drew public attention after the City Commission meet- ing of April 10, 1984, when the Commission introduced a proposal to delete the Band director position from the city employee matrix. Lille- haug said he had not been notified that such action was going to be taken. The *Argus Leader* reported, "The City Commission wants the city's band director to take an $8,000 pay cut, and if he refuses, it could jeopardize thirty-five Municipal Band concerts scheduled for summer." The article quoted Peterson as saying, " 'I will simply not concede to a fifty-percent pay increase.' " In addition to arguing against the con- tract, Gridley, Lillehaug's lawyer, accused Peterson of "unreasonable demands." He was quoted as saying, "Commissioner Peterson's conduct has been an outrageous abuse of his position." Although the article in- dicated that Peterson was "ready to drop Lillehaug from the city payroll at Tuesday's Commission meeting," it was added that Mayor Rick Knobe and Commissioner Loila Hunking wouldn't agree to that. A tape of the meeting indicated that Mayor Knobe said, "You are not treating him as you are the others." Peterson agreed to try to negotiate further with Lillehaug. Peterson did not have a replacement in mind for Lillehaug, but said, "I'm sure there's all kinds of talent .... that would be delighted at the opportunity of conducting the band." Lillehaug stated that Peterson never tried to negotiate the salary increase but always tried to get him to agree to the complete rollback.

The Commission chamber was packed for the next meeting of Monday, April 16, 1984. The *Argus Leader* indicated that about seventy citizens attended, more than half of them Band supporters and musicians. They "filled every seat and lined the walls of the Commission chambers Monday to voice their opposition to an ordinance proposed last week." Lillehaug had cancelled that evening's Band rehearsal so Band members could attend. On the agenda was a vote on an ordinance that proposed eliminating four city-appointed positions: sanitary landfill supervisor, director of the Great Plains Zoo and Museum, superintendent of public works and bandmaster. The Band director and museum director would become contractual positions, meaning they would be hired by the Park Board instead of by the Commission and no longer head their own department. The newspaper reported that "After forty minutes of discussion, Mayor Rick Knobe suggested that the bandmaster position, held for the past twenty years by Lillehaug, be eliminated from the ordinance. "Until you have a replacement or a signed contract, you should leave that position as an appointed position by the city," Knobe told Peterson. "I know I'm not going out and conduct the Band. The question becomes, who is going to do it? It's not appropriate to discuss this until we have someone else in mind." The amended ordinance was approved unanimously, with Peterson voting against his own proposal. The meeting did not address the issue of the salary rollback.

The Commission met the following day (April 17, 1984), and Peterson proposed the first reading of the rollback of the conductor's salary. Resolution of that issue occurred April 23, 1984, when the second reading on rollback and removal of the position from the matrix occurred. The Commissioners left the council chambers and went into executive session taking the city attorney with them. According to Knobe this was the first action of this type during his tenure. When they returned, they voted unanimously for the rollback and removal of the position from the matrix. That meant there were no possibilities of normal career ladder advancements for the conductor. Knobe said in a November 3, 1994, interview that Peterson's wish to roll back the conductor's salary may not have been fair or equitable, but that it was the normal practice not to interfere with a commissioner's action within the departments he supervised unless there was evidence of illegal activity. Knobe also said there was probably no consideration of rolling back the attorneys' raises.

Reaction to the Commission's action varied. Lillehaug objected, saying, "The city attorney — who has a direct conflict of interest in this matter — advised the City Commission in a closed meeting." The *Argus Leader* editorial of April 20, 1984, urged passage of the ordinance. "There's no question that Commissioner Dick Peterson and his colleagues on the City Commission made several mistakes on Band director Leland Lillehaug's salary last summer. Now, to their credit, they're trying to rectify the problem by cutting Lillehaug's salary by $8,000. ... That salary represents two-thirds of what Sioux Falls is paying its mayor. It is a gross distortion of city pay scales and values for part-time work, no matter how well Lillehaug has performed. Peterson should have caught the mistakes much sooner than he did, but he deserves credit for taking action last December to make amends. He has attempted to negotiate a settlement with Lillehaug, to no avail. We think Lillehaug has done a fine job as Band director for the city of Sioux Falls. He has given a great deal of effort to this role and has contributed much to the public's enjoyment of band music. Even so, this does not warrant continuing the imbalance in what the city pays for a part-time position."

Comments from citizens were recorded in the "Sound Off" column of the *Tribune*. One opinion was: "To the City commissioners: Why are you jeopardizing the Municipal Band? Professor Lillehaug is worth his weight in gold." While another opinion was: "Who says the Band is free? With Dr. Lillehaug getting a raise like that, who goes to the Band and doesn't pay?"

Lillehaug next filed a lawsuit seeking $100,000 in damages, saying the city officials "arbitrarily and capriciously denied him his constitutional rights when they decided to cut his salary $8,000." Those named in the lawsuit included Peterson, who was sued for $50,000 in punitive damages, with Lillehaug accusing him of acting in "a malicious and oppressive manner"; Commissioner Loila Hunking, who approved the salary reduction; and Mayor Joe Cooper, who took office later; and the city of Sioux Falls. The lawsuit, filed in U.S. District Court in Sioux Falls, asked for a court order directing the defendants to restore Lillehaug's salary and position as recommended by the consultant, and monetary damages.

Lillehaug's suit was dismissed by Judge John B. Jones in June 1985, so Lillehaug appealed the decision. A three-judge panel of the

Eighth U.S. Circuit Court of Appeals upheld the earlier court's decision. The *Argus Leader* of April 22, 1986, reported that "the judges said Lillehaug had no constitutional protection for his salary level." The federal court held that the claim did not rise to the level of a civil rights violation but could be pursued in a contract action in state court. Lillehaug chose a negotiated settlement.

But the conclusion of the matter really came with Lillehaug's retirement in 1987. As reported by the *Argus Leader*: "Municipal Band director Leland Lillehaug will retire and accept a one-year job as City Band consultant. In return, he agreed to waive any rights to legal claims against the city over a 1983 pay raise controversy. Lillehaug, sixty, is retiring after twenty-three years as director of the Sioux Falls Municipal Band. The retirement will become effective April 1, but Lillehaug will remain on the city payroll for one year as a $6,000 consultant to the Band. The City Commission voted four to one Monday to hire Lillehaug as a consultant. Commissioner Dick Peterson opposed the measure. The city will hire a new Band leader." The paper also quoted city officials as saying that the decision to hire Lillehaug as a consultant "was not an attempt to buy out the Band leader." Mayor Jack White negotiated the agreement with Lillehaug when discussions broke down between Lillehaug and Peterson. According to the newspaper, "Peterson said he refused to agree to demands made by Lillehaug. 'When I informed them I wasn't going to do anything, that's when the mayor stepped in,' he said. 'I think if he (Lillehaug) wanted to retire, he should have gone ahead and retired.' [Commissioner Susan] Randall said Peterson opposed Lillehaug's new appointment because he refused to negotiate the retirement agreement. 'Commissioner Peterson may choose to call it buying off because he was a little ruffled as the rest of us went over his head,' Randall said."

• • •

The years 1976-78 featured spring concerts at the Coliseum. New uniforms were purchased in 1978, and the Band celebrated its 60th anniversary in 1979. Vocalists Hartig and Wegner retired in 1979. Ray Loftesness became emcee in 1980, and Prindle and Barnard began as regular vocalists in 1982. Special events included the sponsorship of the U. S. Marine Band in 1984, an appearance at the national All-Star baseball game in 1985 and guests Merle Evans, James Christensen and Scott Shelsta. Budget cuts and problems between the Band and Commissioner Peterson clouded the late 1980s. Lillehaug retired in April 1987, and Dr. Alan Taylor was hired.

1976. On Showmobile. Front left: Paul Wegner and Eugenia Orlich Hartig (vocalists); Front right: Dr. Leland A. Lillehaug (conductor.) Row 1, L to R: Pat Masek, Pam Hansen, David Lillehaug, Jeff Kull, Linda McLaren, Mindy Braithwaite, Laurel Paulson. Row 2: Oscar Loe, David Amundson, Janice Trumm, Kevin Vaska, Barb Hanson, Barbara Boschee, Martha Vegge Nelson, John Roth, Sandra Person McAllister, Janet Bruns Hallstrom, Clayton Lehmann, Row 3 (standing): Barb Griffith, Charlotte Hedeen, Kathy Bangasser, Terry Walter, Mary Avery, Lori Blauwet, Steven Lillehaug, Tom Braithwaite, Connie Roth, Susan Anderson, Scott Faragher, Robert McDowell, Harold Krueger, David Krueger, Jeff Bowen, Merridee Ekstrom, Terry Anderson. Row 4: Jean Pinard, Julie Kahl, Tom Keleher, Paul Hoy, David Joyce, Stanley Eitreim, Michael Seto, Dennis Hegg, Jeff McAllister, Laurel Cluts, Paula Jorgensen, Paul Bankson, Paul Reeg. *(courtesy Sioux Falls Municipal Band)*

1977. On Showmobile. Front left: Paul Wegner and Eugenia Orlich Hartig (vocalists). Right front: Dr. Leland A. Lillehaug (conductor) and Tom Block (sound). Row 1, L to R: Pat Masek, Mary Jensen, Donna Krueger, Mary Auen, Jeff Kull, Linda McLaren Faragher, Laurel Paulson. Row 2: Oscar Loe, David Amundson, Kathy Bangasser, Kevin Vaska, Barb Hanson, Barb Boschee, Martha Vegge, Terry Walter, Steven Lillehaug, James McWayne, Janet Bruns, Tom Bierer. Row 3: Charlotte Hedeen, Gayle Becker, Mary Avery, Lori Blauwet, Vonnie Endahl, Michael Engh, Scott Faragher, Dr. Harold Krueger, David Krueger, George Gulson, Merridee Ekstrom, Kellie Brinkman. Row 4, (standing) Luanne Warner, Julie Kahl, Robert Patterson, Paul Hoy; (seated) David Joyce, Stanley Eitreim, Al Berdahl; far right: Carl Hallstrom, Laurel Cluts, Paula Jorgensen, Paul Bankson, Paul Reeg. Not pictured: Rahn Anderson (bassoon), Sandy McAllister and Gary Tanouye (saxophones), Susan Anderson (horn), Jeff McAllister (euphonium). (courtesy Sioux Falls Municipal Band)

1978. Terrace Park. Standing front left: Paul Wegner and Eugenia Orlich Hartig (vocalists): Standing center: Dr. Leland A. Lillehaug (conductor). Row 1, L to R: Pat Masek, Pam Hansen Barnard, Donna Van Bockern Krueger, Linda McLaren, Cindy Jurisson, Jeanette Paulson, Carol Buckwalter Pederson, Laurel Paulson. Row 2: Kathy Bangasser, Steven Lillehaug, Charlotte Hedeen, Kevin Vaska, Barbara Hanson Johnson, Barbara Boschee, Martha Vegge Nelson, James McWayne, Gary Tanouye, Everton Little, Janet Bruns Hallstrom, David W. Erickson, Row 3: Terry Walter, Marlene Graber, Susan Ackerman, Donna Schettler Hoogendoorn, Mary Avery, Lorie Simon, Kathy Johnson, Vonnie Endahl, Robert McDowell, Scott Faragher, Dr. Harold Krueger, David Krueger, George Gulson, Merridee Ekstrom, Kellie Brinkman. Row 4: Luanne Warner, Julie Kahl, Robert Patterson, Paul Hoy; (seated) David Joyce, Stan Eitreim, Alan Berdahl, Carl Hallstrom, Rick Skatula, Laurel Cluts, Steven Pfeiffer, Paul Bankson, Paul Reeg. (courtesy Sioux Falls Municipal Band)

1979. On Showmobile at Robert Frost School. Front left : Paul Wegner and Eugenia Orlich Hartig (vocalists); Right front: Dr. Leland A. Lillehaug, (conductor); Row 1, L to R: Pat Masek, Renee Fillingsness, Donna Van Bockern Krueger, Jeanette Paulson, Jeff Kull, Linda McLaren, Carol Buckwalter Pederson, Laurel Paulson. Row 2: Kathy Bangasser, Barbara Hanson Johnson, Donna Schettler Hoogendoorn, Cathy Green, Mary Avery, Kevin Vaska, Terry Walter, Mary Michael, Martha Vegge Nelson, Jim McWayne, Janet Bruns Hallstrom, Robin Steinke; Row 3: Marlene Graber, Kathy Clausen, Kristi Reierson, Barb Gilchrist, Mary McDonald (front and left of tuba on left), Kathy Johnson, Robert McDowell, Scott Faragher, Dr. Harold Krueger, David Krueger, Doug Lehrer, Merridee Ekstrom, Kellie Brinkman. Row 4: (standing) Dan Bailey and Dave Hall (percussion); Deb Aning and Teresa Wells (clarinets); Robert Patterson (percussion); Lori Blauwet (clarinet); Paul Hoy (percussion); David Joyce, Stan Eitreim, Carl Hallstrom, Lois Hendrix, Brad Widness, Faye Fossum, Paul Bankson, Steve Pfeiffer. Not pictured: Mary Jensen (flute), Susan Anderson (horn), Kerchal Armstrong (trombone). *(courtesy Sioux Falls Municipal Band)*

1980. Terrace Park. Standing left front: Ray Loftesness (emcee); Standing center, Dr. Leland A. Lillehaug (conductor). Row 1, L to R: Pat Masek, Mary Jensen, Martha Barnett, Claudia Hasegawa, Jeanette Paulson, Carol Buckwalter, Lori Quanbeck. Row 2: Barbara Hanson, Marlene Graber, Kristi Reierson, Kathy Bangasser, Cathy Green, Barb Gilchrist, Teresa Wells, Terry Walter, Jim McWayne, Martha Vegge, Everton Little, James Perkins, Robin Steinke. Row 3: Deb Aning, Mary Avery, Judy Soukup, Charlotte Hedeen, Curt Hammond, Barb Hegg, Joan Haugen, Gina Waltner, Scott Faragher, Tom Bierer, Doug Lehrer, Kellie Brinkman, Merridee Ekstrom, Janet Bruns Hallstrom. Row 4: (standing) Dan Bailey, Loni Winter, Dan Hatfield, Paul Hoy; (sitting) Tad Smith, Stan Eitreim, David Joyce, Lois Hendrix, Dennis Hegg, Brad Widness, Faye Fossum, Paul Bankson, Laurel Cluts, Steve Pfeiffer. Not pictured: Faith Stahl (bari sax), George Gulson (trumpet), Linda McLaren (bass clarinet). *(courtesy Sioux Falls Municipal Band)*

1981. Terrace Park. Standing center: Dr. Leland A. Lillehaug (conductor). Row 1, L to R: Pat Masek, Mary Jensen Ryrholm, Martha Barnett Lyons, Betty Swanson, Jeanette Paulson, Linda McLaren, Carol Buckwalter Pederson, Lori Quanbeck. Row 2: Kristi Reierson, Charlotte Hedeen, Marlene Graber, Teresa Wells, Donna Schettler Hoogendoorn, Cathy Green, Barb Gilchrist, Deb Aning, Terry Walter, Kathy Kuyper, John Roth, Eddie Johnson, Mark Levsen, James Perkins. Row 3: Karen McLinn, Jackie Larsen, Mary Avery, Delight Jensen Elsinger, Sandra Weikel, Dr. James Marvel, Scott Faragher, Phil Bajema, Doug Lehrer, Janet Bruns Hallstrom, Gary Holman, Steve Sommers. Row 4: Eric LeVan, Kathy Huether Moklebust, Dan Hatfield, Paul Hoy, Toby Schmuck, Stan Eitreim, David Joyce, Paul Weikel, Michael Dailey, Brad Widness, Faye Fossum, Paul Bankson, Laurel Cluts, Steven Pfeiffer. *(courtesy Sioux Falls Municipal Band)*

1982. On Showmobile. Standing front left: Ray Loftesness (emcee); Monty Barnard and Roma Prindle, (vocalists); Dr. Leland A. Lillehaug, (conductor). Row 1, L to R: Pat Masek, Pam Hansen Barnard, Martha Barnett Lyons, Melissa May, Jill Gibson, Carol Buckwalter Pederson, Lori Quanbeck. Row 2: Mark Isackson, Charlotte Hedeen, Teresa Wells, Steven Lillehaug, Donna Schettler Hoogendoorn, Carole Ahlers, Delight Jensen, Terry Walter, Ed Johnson, Martha Vegge Nelson, R. Gail Bachand, Mark Levsen, Rolf Olson. Row 3: Jackie Larsen, Mary Avery, Nancy Negstad, Deb Aning, Curt Hammond, Michelle Youngquist, Sandra Weikel, Jeanette Duerksen, Scott Faragher, Doug Lehrer, James Perkins, Janet Bruns Hallstrom, Gary Holman. Row 4: (standing) Eric LeVan, Cathy Huether Moklebust, Dan Hatfield, Paul Hoy, Toby Schmuck, Stan Eitreim, David King, David Joyce, Vince Aughenbaugh, Rich Woolworth, Bill Glenski, Faye Fossum, Paul Bankson, Paul Weikel, Brad Widness. *(courtesy Sioux Falls Municipal Band)*

1983. Terrace Park. Standing front left: Ray Loftesness (emcee) and Roma Prindle (vocal soloist). Standing middle: Dr. Leland A. Lillehaug (conductor). Row 1, L to R: Pat Masek, Pam Hansen Barnard, Mary Jensen Ryrholm, Karen Nogami, Claudia Hasegawa, Linda McLaren, Carol Buckwalter Pederson, Katherine Peterson. Row 2: Mark Isackson, Oscar Loe, Kathy Bangasser, Charlotte Hedeen, Kathy Boullion, Delight Jensen, Donna Hoogendoorn, Carole Ahlers, Terry Walter, Janelle Schweim Johnson, Martha Vegge Nelson, R. Gail Bachand, Gary Horsley, Steven Sommers. Row 3: Laurie Stephens, Jackie Larsen, Judy Engh, Mary Avery, Curt Hammond, Sandra Weikel, Michelle Youngquist, Scott Faragher, Doug Lehrer, James Perkins, Mark Levsen, Janet Bruns Hallstrom. Row 4: Cathy Huether Moklebust, Dan Hatfield, Eric LeVan, Paul Hoy, Toby Schmuck, Stan Eitreim, David King, Rolyn Beaird, Vince Aughenbaugh, Dan Engh, Paul Reeg, Faye Fossum, Laurel Cluts, Brad Widness. Not pictured: Dr. Monty Barnard (vocalist), Gary Holman (cornet), Paul Weikel (euphonium). *(courtesy Sioux Falls Municipal Band)*

1984. The Empire mall. Standing left: Ray Loftesness (emcee). Standing middle: Dr. Leland A. Lillehaug (conductor). Standing right: Roma Prindle and Dr. Monty Barnard (vocalists). Row 1, L to R: Pat Masek, Pam Hansen Barnard, Mary Jensen Ryrholm, Karen Nogami, Tami Huse-Kerr, Linda McLaren, Lori Quanbeck, Katherine Peterson. Row 2: Oscar Loe, Kathy Bangasser, Delight Jensen, Kathy Boullion, Donna Hoogendorn, Laurie Stephens, Judy Engh, Eddie Johnson, Janelle Schweim Johnson, Martha Vegge Nelson, James Parker, Steven Sommers. Row 3: Jackie Larsen, Mary Avery, John Titus. Row 3, right side: Lissa Robertson, Curt Hammond, Doug Lehrer, James Perkins, Janet Bruns Hallstrom, Gary Holman, Eric Knutson. Row 4, standing: Cathy Huether Moklebust, Sara Levsen, Dan Hatfield, Paul Hoy. Row 4, seated: Stan Eitreim, David King, Rolyn Beaird, Vince Aughenbaugh, Dan Engh, Susan Howard, Faye Fossum, Robert Streemke, Laurel Cluts. Not pictured: Charlotte Hedeen (clarinet), Terry Walter (alto saxophone), Gail Bachand (baritone saxophone), David Miller (string bass). *(courtesy Sioux Falls Municipal Band)*

1985. Terrace Park. Standing front left: Ray Loftesness (emcee), Roma Prindle, (vocalist). Standing center: Merle Evans (Ringling Brothers Circus Bandmaster), Dr. Leland A. Lillehaug, (conductor); Row 1, L to R: Pat Masek, Mary Jensen Ryrholm, Linda McLaren, Lorie Quanbeck, Katherine Peterson. Row 2: Oscar Loe, Charlotte Hedeen, Kathy Boullion, Susan Rogotzke, Kari Reyner, Jennifer Stansbery, Eddie Johnson, Terry Walter, Chris Olkiewicz, Beth Ahlers, Kevin Groskurth, Nathan Wegner, James Parker. Row 3: Jackie Larsen, Dennis Graber, Brenda Zacharias, Kara Jorve. Right side: Dennis Kaufman, Rolf Olson, Scott Faragher, Doug Lehrer, William Freitag, Marc Mueller, Janet Bruns Hallstrom, George Gulson, Eric Knutson. Row 4: (standing): Cathy Huether Moklebust, Ann Cameron, James P. Carlson, Paul Hoy; right side: Wayne Krumrei, Stan Eitreim, David King, Carl Hallstrom, Rolyn Beaird, Dawn Hanson, Paul Reeg, Faye Fossum, Robert Streemke, Laurel Cluts. *(courtesy Sioux Falls Municipal Band)*

1986. Phillips Avenue. Standing front left: Dr. Monty Barnard and Eileen Bauermeister (vocalists). Standing front right: Ray Loftesness (emcee), Dr. Leland A. Lillehaug, (conductor). Row 1, L to R: Pat Masek, Pam Hansen Barnard, Mary Ryrholm, Linda McLaren, Lori Quanbeck, Katherine Peterson. Row 2: Oscar Loe, Charlotte Hedeen, John Titus, Jennifer Stansbery, Brenda Bahnson, Ed Johnson, Yvonne Lange, Judy Soukup, Janelle Johnson, Diana Christiansen, Beth Ahlers, Chris Olkiewicz, Steve Sommers, Vicki Savage. Row 3: Dennis Graber, Brenda Zacharias, Mary Fritz, Tom Merrill, Michelle Youngquist, Lois Nelson, Mary Devaney, Jane Preheim, Beth Duerksen, Lawrence Price, Eric Knutson, Nathan Wegner, Steve Stombaugh, Janet Bruns, Gary Holman. Row 4: Kathy Welter, Ann Cameron, Ken Yoshida, Paul Hoy, Wayne Krumrei, Stan Eitreim, David King, David Larson, Rolyn Beaird, Carl Hallstrom, Dawn Hanson, David Jans, Faye Fossum, Laurel Cluts, Not pictured: James Perkins (trumpet). *(courtesy Sioux Falls Municipal Band)*

1987-94
New Faces
on the Podium

I mportant changes occurred during the eight years of 1987-94. There were two new conductors, Dr. Alan Taylor and Dr. Bruce T. Ammann; the City Commission recently had changed from three to five persons; and the Band lost its independent department status, being placed under the Park Department rather than reporting directly to the mayor or one of the commissioners. Two new conductors in eight years represented a break in continuity because the previous two conductors, Henegar (1935-63) and Lillehaug (1964-86), had led the Band for fifty-two years. The drop in the number of players who were members of the musicians' union made it impossible for the Band to secure Recording Trust Funds, which had funded an average of six concerts per year for several decades. Taylor had to struggle with this problem in addition to a belief by some of the players that the Band was not playing up to its potential. Other events during this period included the repair of the Terrace Park band shell and budget cuts which Dr. Ammann faced when he became conductor.

It appears that the Municipal Band conductor had reported to the mayor or a commissioner as early as 1928. Both Henegar and Lillehaug had department head status. In 1987, there were two issues involved — which commissioner was to supervise the Band and/or whether the Band was to be placed under the Park Department rather than functioning as an independent department. Just before 1987, it appeared to Lillehaug and many of the Band members that their commissioner, Richard Peterson, was not a strong supporter of the Band. Band members did not like Peterson's asking the Park Board to take over the control of the

Band without consulting them first, nor his treatment of the Lillehaug salary issue (see Chapter 8). As a result, they did not want Commissioner Peterson to control the Band, preferring that the mayor assume jurisdiction. They also wanted to remain as an independent department.

Peterson decided that he wanted the Band placed under the Park Department and made the proposal to the Park Board on January 20, 1987. He said, " ... this arrangement is common in many cities. In Sioux Falls the Municipal Band certainly uses several parks for their performances, and the portable stage is the property of the parks." This was partially incorrect. The Band and the Park Department shared equal ownership in the portable stage, called the Showmobile. Its purchase had been initiated by the Band. On February 3, 1987, the issue was discussed again, but the Park Board postponed further action. Subsequent Park Board minutes do not indicate that the question of placing the Band under the Park Department was discussed any further or that any action was taken.

An *Argus Leader* article from March 5, 1987, with the headline, "City Band wants Peterson replaced," indicated that the Band members, through the Band Board, had asked Mayor Jack White to take over supervision of the Band from Peterson. On February 23, 1987, Band president Gary Holman sent a letter to Mayor White stating that the Sioux Falls Municipal Band Board of Directors felt that past associations with Commissioner Peterson "have been difficult at best." Holman proposed that the Band Board of Directors immediately be involved in assisting in the selection of a new conductor to replace Lillehaug, who was retiring, and that the Band be placed under the supervision of the mayor. Mayor White replied on March 10, 1987, indicating that no decision had been made regarding the placement of the Band under the supervision of the mayor but seemed sympathetic to the Band's desire to assist in choosing the new conductor. The mayor also stated that the first advertisement of the bandmaster position had taken place on March 8, 1987, with deadlines for application set for March 20, 1987.

Commissioner Peterson was quoted as saying, "They [the Band Board?] have been very unkind. I think it's politics. Certainly the Board of Directors has never spoken to me and don't know what my feelings are." Holman said in the article that the Band members also did not want to operate under the director of the Park Department, believing that such a move would simply place another layer of bureaucracy upon the Band. "I think it should be maintained as a separate department of the city, as it is now," Holman, the Band president, said. "If you're under one commissioner or mayor, there's just one person you have to go talk to."

On May 4, 1987, the commissioners made their annual assignment of departments. Both the Band and the Park Department were transferred from Peterson's jurisdiction to the mayor. There were no dissenting votes to the reassignment. In addition to Mayor White and Dick Peterson, other commissioners present were Loila Hunking, Susan Randall and Joe Vanderloo. At the same meeting department heads were appointed or reappointed. Although "Municipal Concerts" (Municipal Band concerts) is listed separately, there is no mention of a department head for the Band. Lowen Schuett was reappointed as department head of Park and Recreation. It seems clear that the commission had made the decision to place the Band under the Park Department at this time. This was first mentioned in a letter from Mayor White to Gary Holman on May 14, 1987, in which the mayor thanked Holman and Stan Eitreim for their participation in the interview and selection process of the new bandmaster. White told Holman, "As the result of reassignment of departments, I am in charge of the Park and Recreation Department which is now also responsible for the Municipal Band. ... Mr. Schuett and the Park and Recreation Board assure me they will cooperate in every possible way to effectively handle the day to day procedures so the Municipal Band is a continued success in the community." From that point – May 1987 – the Band was supervised by Lowen Schuett who had begun his job as director of Parks and Recreation in July of 1986. Dick Justman, controller of the Finance Department, said that the Band is still an independent department with its own budget but that the bandmaster reports to the director of Parks and Recreation rather than to a commissioner.

Since the Band had been an independent department for decades, some observers expected that the Band members would strongly resist what was considered a "demotion" in their status. It is not clear how strong an effort was made, but the Band members did not succeed in preventing the Band being placed under the Park Department.

Selecting a New Director

Although Lillehaug had asked to retire January 1, 1987, the city had not succeeded in finding a new conductor. Mayor White asked Lillehaug, and he agreed, to stay on until at least through the next major appearance of the Band — a concert at the national convention of the Association of Concert Bands in Chatfield, Minnesota, on April 25, 1987.

The mayor appointed a search committee to bring a recommendation for a new Band director to the City Commission. Appointees included Sylvia Henkin, community representative; Julie Simko, Park Board member; Lowen Schuett, director of Park and Recreation; and Stan Eitreim and Gary Holman, Band representatives. Jennifer Iveland, director of the Personnel Office, assisted but was not a voting member. Some Band members said that they thought they should have had a majority on the committee since they would be working with the conductor.

Lillehaug had hoped that the city would conduct a nationwide search to find the best conductor available. He had prepared a computerized mailing list of top college music departments and noted band directors in the country and notified the Personnel Office of its availability. The list was never used. Schuett said that the job description was sent to high schools and colleges in the area. Dr. Alan Taylor, eventually chosen as the new director, was band director at Southwest State University in Marshall, Minnesota, and received the announcement and job specifications through his chairman. The specifications, which he received in 1987, listed a date of March 1983. They apparently had not been redesigned for the recent changes in structure because they stated that the conductor was to be responsible to the "Parks and Utilities Commissioner" and made no mention that the new conductor would report to the director of Parks and Recreation.

A search of Park and Personnel Department records yielded no minutes or records of the work of the committee, and Jennifer Iveland was not able to furnish additional details. Schuett said that it is not typical to keep the records of this type of committee. The committee — not the Personnel or Park Department offices — controlled the job description content, he said. But Sylvia Henkin, a committee member who later served as park commissioner (and the Band) from December 1990 to July 1991, said she never saw a job description for the post that was being considered, even though Schuett said the committee was responsible for the job description.

The Interviews

Nine people were considered, and the choice was narrowed to four: Oscar Loe, principal clarinet and the Band's assistant conductor; David Mitchell, former band director at Vermillion High School who had served for one year as band director as a one-year sabbatical replacement at Augustana College; Dr. Alan Taylor, director of Bands at Southwest State University at Marshall, Minnesota; and George Whaley of Yankton.

Taylor recalled that he was invited for an interview which took place in City Hall. He said Henkin, Iveland, Eitreim, Holman and Schuett attended. Simko remembered Taylor's interview and said, "He didn't push, he was a polite person and didn't offend."

There had been no mention of conducting auditions so Taylor suggested it would be wise to have them before selecting the conductor. He didn't think it had been considered before he mentioned it. Committee member Henkin remembered differently. She recalled that at a final committee meeting she had said, "We should be able to see them conduct." She said even the Band representatives hadn't demanded this. Although it is not clear who suggested it first, both Henkin and Taylor recognized the need to see a conductor in action before hiring him.

The Conducting Audition

Mitchell, Taylor and Whaley, all from out of the city, were invited back for the conducting audition with the Band at its regular Monday evening rehearsal, probably April 27, 1987. The audition committee had selected one piece for the candidates to conduct; the candidates could choose the second. One of the candidates wanted to sit in on the auditions by others, but the committee decided not to allow it since Taylor was to conduct first and intended to leave immediately after he had finished. After his audition, Taylor said that he and Schuett went upstairs to the Band room to visit for a few minutes, after which Taylor returned to Marshall.

The choice of the new conductor was made shortly after the conclusion of the conducting auditions, but it was not unanimous. Following the conducting auditions, the Band members held their own vote and instructed their representatives that David Mitchell was their first choice. It reportedly was based primarily on his conducting and rehearsal procedures and the feeling of the Band members that he had done the best of the three in the conducting audition. However, Dr. Alan Taylor was chosen by a majority vote of the committee. Sylvia Henkin, voting with the majority, said she felt that Taylor had performed the best at the audition. She said that he seemed willing to be a good promoter and would be able to market the Band. Julie Simko, a member of the selection committee, said committee members who were not Band members may not have been extremely knowledgeable about band music. However, she said they believed that the Sioux Falls Municipal Band was an asset to the community and wanted to keep the tradition going. They believed Taylor would best fulfill that goal. Band member Linda McLaren Roach recalled that many of the Band members said they felt "frustrated" and "violated" when the committee chose someone else since they would have to work with the conductor.

Why did the committee choose Taylor over the other candidates and over the recommendation of the Band members? There is general agreement on the part of the committee members that the following items played a part:

- Taylor's doctorate.
- Taylor's more professional demeanor.
- Taylor's employment, especially at a university level. The committee believed the salary was too small to attract anyone who was not already employed. They were looking for continuity and longevity and thought that if someone were hired who was not otherwise employed, the person might quit in a short time because of the salary. They wanted to make sure that the successful candidate also had another relatively permanent position. Some committee members reported that the interview with Mitchell did not go well and that Whaley did not receive strong consideration.

Taylor's travel distance (about 180 miles round trip) was perceived as a negative but not enough to counteract the positive. There were others outside the committee who recognized the difficulty of the drive, especially for the winter rehearsals. Taylor later acknowledged that handling the job and living that far from Sioux Falls was not easy. Since it would be too difficult to commute to Marshall during the busy summer concert season, Sylvia Henkin found a home for Taylor to rent for the summer.

Oscar Loe didn't think he got a "fair shake" when it came to the choice of Lillehaug's successor. Loe applied and was given an interview. However, Loe was not one of the three chosen for conducting auditions. Loe believed that since he had been assistant conductor under Lillehaug, he should have been shown the courtesy to be in the final conducting auditions.

It appears that it was on Friday evening May 1, 1987, that Taylor received a call saying that he had been selected by a majority vote of the committee.

An article in the *Argus Leader* on May 16, 1987, began with the headline "Alan Taylor Named Bandmaster." However, Taylor couldn't be given a contract until the Park Board agreed and the City Commission affirmed the choice. Park Board minutes show that on June 2, 1987, the Park Board reviewed Taylor's contract for $14,500. Mayor White was at that meeting. Taylor was hired for the period May 8, 1987, through December 31, 1987. The contract included a thirty-day notice before the end of the contract, evidently giving the Park Board an option as to whether they wished to renew the contract.

Dr. Alan W. Taylor

Taylor, who became the eighth permanent conductor of the Sioux Falls Municipal Band, is a native of Melbourne, Australia, and received his bachelor's degree in music education and a doctor of music degree from the Indiana University School of Music. After teaching for seven years at Scotch College, a Presbyterian Church School for boys in Melbourne, Taylor taught for one year at a high school for music in Adelaide, Australia. In the United States, Taylor was an associate instructor of trumpet at Indiana University and acting director of bands and instructor of trumpet and music education at Wright State University in Dayton, Ohio. Prior to going to Southwest State University in the fall of 1985, he was director of instrumental ensembles at Arkansas College. He was active as a clinician, conductor and trumpet soloist. While conductor of the Sioux Falls Municipal Band, Taylor retained his position as director of bands at Southwest State University in Marshall, Minnesota.

Although Lillehaug had no part in recommendations, selection or the hiring process, he was anxious to see the new conductor succeed. Both he and Taylor agreed that they had a very professional and friendly relationship during Taylor's five years with the Band. Lillehaug offered assistance when asked and Taylor never appeared defensive about inviting his predecessor back to the podium. Taylor and the Band sponsored a retirement concert for Lillehaug on July 26, 1987, during which Taylor conducted the opening number and turned over the baton to Lillehaug for the remainder of the concert. Both have said that they felt comfortable in each other's company.

A look at the programs from the five years indicated that Taylor continued the basic programming procedures of Henegar and Lillehaug. The programming suggested that the Band would play the highest quality of literature possible that was suited to the outdoors without losing sight of the fact that it was entertainment. The pleasure of the audience had to be a high priority. Taylor's programming stressed variety plus instrumental and vocal features. Taylor said he never made a commitment to a local soloist that the soloist would play a solo in public until the person had a successful rehearsal with the solo. Band members sometimes complained about the amount of time used to rehearse vocal soloists. Taylor said that the Sioux Falls Municipal Band has a

Dr. Alan Taylor became conductor of the Sioux Falls Municipal Band in 1987. *(courtesy Alan Taylor)*

wonderful music library and he enjoyed selecting programs from it. "It was tough generating that many programs (nearly forty) each season, " he said.

In an effort to create additional variety, Taylor used a jazz band one year to play after a regular Band concert. He said that he didn't do it again because the players didn't want to stay after the regular rehearsal to rehearse further or have extra rehearsals.

Unlike his predecessors, Taylor never designated an assistant conductor. If he had to miss a rehearsal, he usually appointed four members, who were also conductors, to take the rehearsal. Each would prepare approximately twenty-five percent of the music which was to be rehearsed that evening.

There were two highlights from 1991 that were singled out by Taylor and many of the members. One was the appearance of the great tuba player Harvey Phillips as the guest soloist at a Sunday evening concert on August 14, 1988. The Band's only rehearsal with him was after the Sunday afternoon concert. The other memorable performance was the Band's being chosen as one of the guest bands for the national convention of the Association of Concert Bands in Omaha, Nebraska, on April 5, 1991. It was the second time the Sioux Falls group had been chosen during the thirteen-year history of the association. Dr. Leland Lillehaug, who was national president of the association at the time, guest conducted a number at the concert.

One sour note tempered the excitement of the Band's appearance at the convention. The city would not pay the Band members for the concert they played at the Association of Concert Bands Omaha convention or for the mileage expenses of the trip. Some band members said that it seemed unfair that the city would not fund the Band when they were being a public relations vehicle for Sioux Falls and South Dakota at a national convention of their own association.

The Trust Fund Problems

During the years prior to Taylor, members of the Band had been union members. However, during Taylor's first year, 1987, some members chose not to join the union, causing problems in securing funding from the national Recording Trust Funds, which then came through the local union office. Those funds financed five or six free concerts a year by the Band in Sioux Falls and surrounding towns in addition to free music in hospitals and for other benevolent purposes. Those who were not union members played the five or six trust fund jobs as volunteers. In 1990, some union Band members complained about the difference between their regular city per-concert pay and what they received from trust fund jobs, the trust fund jobs being less. Band members wanted the city to pay the difference. Rather than do this, Taylor applied for only one trust fund job in 1990 and paid all the other concerts from city funds, thinking he had solved the wage differentiation problem. Then the union members said, "Why did we join the union and pay union dues when we don't get more Trust Funds?"

During 1991, Taylor applied for more Trust Fund concerts but did not pay the Band members any differential pay. Taylor negotiated the Trust Fund contracts directly with the New York office rather than going through the union local in Sioux Falls. However, by that time, the union musicians' Local 114 in Sioux Falls was almost ready to close down, and there were fewer union members in the Band. The demise of the once-powerful Sioux Falls Musicians' Union Local didn't just cause frustrations, it resulted in the loss of six free Municipal Band concerts each year.

Other Recollections from the Taylor Years

When Ray "Lofty" Loftesness was unable to continue as master of ceremonies in 1991 because of health problems, it left a great void and a challenge to Taylor to find a capable replacement. Loftesness had been a popular master of ceremonies for eleven years (see Chapter 13). Taylor looked for a replacement but couldn't find the right person, so he did the announcing during the rest of the season. At first he put a microphone clip on his uniform and made announcements from the podium area. This went too quickly and did not allow Band members sufficient time to get ready for the next piece. He then used a standing mike which took slightly more time between numbers. It was difficult being conductor and master of ceremonies, he said.

Free media coverage of the Band had declined in the 1980s. Consequently, Taylor sought other ways to publicize Band concerts. He bought advertising in the *Argus Leader* to announce the concerts and used commercially printed fliers for the weekly neighborhood concerts. Printed programs were used for the Circus Concert, grand finale and concerts that had a noted guest.

The Parks and Concert Scheduling Procedures

Taylor generally continued the pattern of concert scheduling which he had inherited. There were Sunday afternoon concerts at McKennan and Sherman, Sunday evenings at Terrace, week nights at retirement homes and veterans and patriotic-type events and concerts at residential neighborhoods and smaller parks. A new special concert was the Mayor's Picnic, beginning in 1987 and continuing each year through 1993. During the first seven years of this event, three of the concerts were at Sherman, three at Terrace and one at Laurel Oak. The concert at Laurel Oak in 1993 was in connection with the dedication of the new swimming pool. The 1991 concert at Sherman helped celebrate the Park Department's seventy-fifth anniversary and a Great Plains Zoo anniversary. The June 14, 1992, concert and picnic were built around the rededication of the band shell at Terrace.

Repair of the Terrace Park Band Shell

The favorite site of most band fans through the years has been Terrace Park and its Sunday night summer concerts. In the early 1920s the Band played from a temporary bandstand in the park. On June 12, 1923, a "Terrace Garden Theater" opened, although the area was not completely finished. The first program was by the McBride Studio of Dancing and Expression, according to the *Argus Leader* of June 12, 1923. The news article indicated that the program probably would be "the only program there until late summer on account of the new condition of the terraces." There is no mention of the Band's using it at that time. The original flooring of the stage was wood, which was replaced with concrete in 1933. Mayor George Burnside was quoted in the *Argus Leader* of July 25, 1933, as saying, "Myself, I wouldn't walk across the old stage for fear it would cave in with me." As with any outdoor facility, the weather through the years took its toll on the physical condition of the bandstand at Terrace Park. It is not unusual that the Park Department would be concerned about its deteriorating condition in the late 1980s.

In early 1989, a master plan was submitted by the Park Department for creating new facilities in the Terrace Park area, including a new bandstand or band shell across Covell Lake to the west. Schuett, the Park Department head, thought that the plan was a good one. A planning committee of Terrace Park area residents approved the master plan on September 20, 1989, but implementation of the plan was not completed as proposed because of strong opposition from residents of the Terrace Park area. Park Board minutes show that on June 4, 1991, nearly two years later, the Park Board met with members of the "Community Committee" that had been established to consider the Terrace Park band shell. Members present were Dick Dempster of Architecture Incorporated, Jamie Halworth-Smith and Hugh Grogan. Also present were two members of the Municipal Band, Steve Stombaugh and Craig Alberty. Dempster reported that he had met and discussed acoustics with a consultant from Chicago regarding the science of sound projection for stages and outdoor amphitheaters. He mentioned five options with costs ranging from $10,000 to $200,000. Band representative Steve Stombaugh indicated a concern about the acoustical consequences of any decisions. Halworth-Smith said that she "thought people coming to the Band concerts were not that concerned about the sound, and that the setting for the band was much more important." Grogan said that he "thought the music was not as important as the setting, and it is more of a social aspect of a band concert that people enjoy; ... it does become cost prohibitive to build a new structure that would provide the quality of sound the Band may be asking for with acoustical properties." Jack Marshman, Park Board member, asked how much it would cost to get information on acoustic treatment for the bandstand,

and Dempster promised to research it. Halworth-Smith and Grogan planned to check on Terrace neighborhood people regarding their wishes.

On June 18, 1991, Larry Weires of the Park Department said that Dempster of Architecture Incorporated had submitted a letter recommending that the existing band shell be repaired but not totally renovated. Grogan and Halworth-Smith said residents of the Terrace Park neighborhood wanted the Park Department to restore the existing band shell and not build a new one. After further discussion, it was the consensus of the Park Board to accept the suggestion that the existing band shell be renovated to correct structural problems but not to replace completely or change the appearance of the band shell. The matter was discussed again on July 2, 1991, with Schuett saying that this would only be a major repair project and not a total reconstruction or renovation. The Park Board discussed the various alternatives, and after discussion decided to delay any action pending further information and the on-site inspection of the bandstand by the Park Board.

No further record of discussion or action was found until the minutes of October 1, 1991, when Dick Dempster of Architecture Incorporated spoke to the Board. He listed things which needed to be done with the Terrace Park band shell and estimated the cost to be about $40,000. On March 3, 1992, the Park Board reviewed a construction change order from the Henry Carlson contract relating to the Terrace band shell. It was for $6,040 to "provide structural stability for the walls of the bandstand." The motion was passed unanimously. On May 19, 1992, the Park Board reviewed and approved the color scheme for the renovation of the shell. It was also announced that the ribbon cutting marking the completion of the renovation would occur on June 14, 1992, the day of the Mayor's Picnic.

As a result of the major repair project, the following improvements were made to the present Terrace Park band shell:
- Reinforced walls.
- A new concrete floor.
- Floor electrical outlets.
- All new lighting.
- Repair of stone work on the front of the stage.
- Loading dock for stage.
- A ramp to make the stage accessible for the handicapped.
- Improved storage room.

According to Larry Weires of the Park Department, the final cost of entire renovation was $77,885.

Other work was in progress to accommodate citizens who go to the Terrace Park concerts and use the park in other ways. In the minutes of

October 12, 1993, it was noted that the main stairway that leads from the top of the Terrace Park hill down to the band shell was in bad condition and would be remodeled as part of the project: "The fifteen-foot-wide staircase would be replaced with a concrete and cobblestone stairway that would meet safety requirements but still provide an aesthetically pleasing staircase." The Terrace Park staircase work was in progress during the 1994 Band season and completed in the autumn.

Taylor's Resignation

While Taylor claimed that he had approached the Band Board in 1987 regarding setting up a process to evaluate the conductor, nothing was done until 1990, when the Band Board began looking at it seriously. Park Director Schuett reported that a request for an evaluation of Taylor came from the Band near the end of Taylor's five years (1991). The Band Board created the evaluation instrument based, at least partially, on symphony evaluations documents which they had seen. The August 20, 1991, Park Board minutes show that Lowen Schuett briefed the Park Board on an evaluation form that had been developed. Later in 1991, the conductor evaluation took place.

Taylor and the Band members remembered the evaluation outcome differently. Taylor said that the evaluations were mixed while Band members thought a high percentage of the returns were negative. Since Taylor had already considered resigning, he concluded that this was the right time. His stated reasons for resigning were the stress of commuting, additional responsibilities assumed at Southwest State University and family. Taylor said that he was glad he conducted the Band for those five years and considered it a real privilege. His resignation was effective on or about October 1, 1991.

Taylor's Accomplishments

The items which Taylor felt were noteworthy during his five-year tenure were the Band's fine performance at the Association of Concert Bands Convention in Omaha, keeping the Band on track after following a conductor who had conducted the Band for many years, and recruiting. Craig Alberty, the Band's president from 1991-93, added three accomplishments by the Board: the constitution and by-laws were revised (approved November 1992), a handbook of procedures was created for the members and a conductor evaluation was established.

Alberty said future goals include more actively seeking the Band's audience and inviting other groups to perform with the Band. No consideration had been given to the creation of a citizens' board for the Band, a suggestion which has surfaced from time to time in past years.

Taylor was undecided as to whether the change of structure from serving directly under a commissioner to his working under the Park Department was positive or negative. Because of his commute, he said it was helpful having the Park office take care of phone calls and details.

Taylor, still a member of the music faculty at Southwest State University in Marshall, Minnesota, now lives in Pipestone, Minnesota. His wife, Georgia, teaches instrumental music in the Pipestone schools. They have two daughters: Patricia, age fourteen, and Melinda, age twelve.

Another New Conductor – Dr. Bruce Ammann

When Taylor resigned in September of 1991, he recommended Bruce Ammann as his successor. Ammann had been playing alto saxophone in the Band and was the director of bands at Augustana College. Band president Craig Alberty, on behalf of the Band members, agreed with Taylor. Dr. Ammann was appointed a temporary conductor through the November 11, 1991, concert. At least two Band members said that they would have applied for the conductor's post had it been open to other candidates.

At the November 19, 1991, Park Board meeting, Board members reviewed the search process to find a band conductor for 1992. Schuett said the process would be similar to the one used when Taylor was hired in 1987. It was decided that Ann Louise Kuehn would represent the Park Board on the selection committee. Other members would be a Band member and someone from the public schools music department. Board member Jack Marshman recommended that the arts reporter from the *Argus Leader*, Ann Grauvogl, be asked to join the committee, but there was no indication of any action on his suggestion. By the December 3, 1991, Park Board meeting, the Band Board had recommended to Schuett that Ammann be appointed as the interim conductor for 1992, beginning January 1992. Because the position was then considered a "contracted professional service position," there was no legal requirement that the job opening be published. The Park Board agreed, and the search for a permanent conductor was postponed until later in 1992. On December 17, 1991, the Park Board approved Ammann's 1992 contract for

$16,000.

The Park Board planned to begin a search process for a permanent conductor for the Band during the last half of 1992 and agreed that the position should be open to anyone. On June 2, 1992, Schuett reminded the Board of the need to select a permanent conductor for the Band beginning in 1993. He suggested that the Board start the screening process and invite prospective candidates to direct the band during the summer of 1992. It is not clear whether the intent was for the candidates to conduct at rehearsals or concerts, but it was probably the former, even though rehearsal time is at a premium during the summer. Had the candidates been asked to conduct concerts, they would have needed even more rehearsal time. Park Board minutes of June 1, 1992, stated, "The Board directed Mr. Schuett to proceed with the process of starting the interview sessions."

Following the Board's instructions, Schuett brought a plan to the Park Board on June 16, 1992, which listed these procedures:

- The job announcement would be made approximately June 24, 1992.
- The Park Department would receive applications and a committee would shorten the list of applicants to three or four, followed by personal interviews.
- In October, the committee would watch candidates conduct the Band during rehearsals for the Veterans Day program. Schuett suggested that the committee would consist of two Park Board members, two Band Board members and someone from the public school music department. Gerald Lotten of the Park Board requested that someone from the South Dakota Symphony be involved, and Schuett agreed. Marshman suggested that there be just one Park Board member, and the others agreed.

However, on August 4, 1992, Schuett told the Park Board members that he had been contacted by Craig Alberty, president of the Municipal Band, and that the Band Board was asking that the current director, Bruce Ammann, be offered the conductor's contract for 1993. With this news, the search procedures outlined above were dropped, and the Park Board unanimously agreed that Ammann would be offered a one-year contract for 1993. Schuett reported that Ammann had been evaluated by the Band members and that the results were positive. At the Park Board meeting on November 24, 1992, Ammann's contract for 1993 for $17,000, a raise of $1,000 from the previous year, was approved unanimously. Ammann said that he was notified in the fall of 1992 that he would be permanent conductor of the Municipal Band in 1993.

Dr. Bruce Ammann become conductor of the Municipal Band in 1992. *(courtesy Bruce Ammann)*

Ammann's Background and Training

Previous to his appointment at Augustana in 1989, Ammann was on the faculty of Arizona State University, where he spent two years completing the doctor of musical arts degree in instrumental conducting. From 1984 to 1987, Ammann was assistant director of bands and professor of saxophone at the University of Florida. He has a bachelor of music degree in music education and the master of music degree in saxophone performance from the University of Arizona. Prior to his appointment at the University of Florida, Ammann taught all levels of public school instrumental music. His last five years of public school teaching were as director of bands at Sahuaro High School in Tucson, Arizona. While he was at Sahuaro High School, his bands consistently earned superior ratings in concert, marching and jazz festivals throughout the Southwest.

Ammann has won many honors and held important professional offices. He was the recipient of the American School Band Directors Association Stanbury Award for the Outstanding Young Band Director in the State of Arizona, 1983-84. He is active as an adjudicator and clinician throughout the country and holds membership in many of the top professional organizations. Ammann was elected to serve on the governing board for the South Dakota Music Educators Association 1992 through 1996. He also is the South Dakota state chairman both for the College Band Directors National Association and the Association of Concert Bands. In the spring of 1994, Ammann completed his fifth year as director of bands and associate professor of music at Augustana College in Sioux Falls. He assumed the chairmanship of the music department in the fall of 1993.

The Band Budget

The Band suffered cuts in its proposed budgets for both 1993 and 1994. At the September 30, 1992, Park Board meeting, Schuett said cuts had been requested by the Commission and made from several areas of the Park Department budget for 1993, including $2,000 from the Band. A year later, September 28, 1993, Schuett announced that the proposed Band budget for 1994 had been cut $4,060. This represented a cut of two rehearsals and two concerts. As a result, the first and last proposed concerts of the 1994 season were dropped. These cuts hit veterans' groups especially hard because the first outdoor appearance normally was Armed Forces Day in May and the final was Veterans Day in November. Veterans' groups and the Military Affairs Committee of the Chamber of Commerce expressed special concerns about the action. No budget changes were made; consequently the Band did not play at the Veterans Day program.

Goals for the Future

Ammann's primary goal is to create a band which will be recognized as a truly professional organization and will command the respect he feels the group deserves. That means attracting the best players and training them well. It means adequate rehearsal time, proper facilities and sufficient funding. If he can receive good support from the news media in informing the public, he is convinced that audience support will follow. He believes that the sound of a band is directly related to its instrumentation. There were fifty players represented in the instrumentation chart for the 1994 Band: Woodwinds: three flutes, two oboes, two bassoons, ten clarinets, one bass clarinet, four saxophones. Brasses: eight cornets and trumpets, six horns, five trombones, two euphoniums, two tubas. There were five percussion. In addition there was a sound person, two vocal soloists and the conductor for a total of fifty-four. Ammann said he believes the Band would be strengthened by the addition of another bass clarinet, two soprano clarinets and a tuba if budget were available. The Band has been enlarged slightly in the past few years in order to accommodate the demands of the music being written today.

Ammann believes proper programming procedure is important. His programs include instrumental solos and ensembles and male and female vocals. He schedules one instrumental feature on each program. The soloists or featured players are given the pieces they are to perform early in the rehearsal season. By the end of May he has rehearsed two-thirds to three-fourths of the literature. He plans one-hour concerts which require forty-five minutes of music. The other fifteen minutes include the "Star Spangled Banner," "Opener," "Closer" and announcements. His programming concept includes theme concerts, general variety, features, variety in lengths of the pieces, three or four marches and vocals. Special arrangements normally are done by Band member Craig Alberty who utilizes new technology, employing a computer program, "Finale," which creates the parts from the score, thus eliminating the need of a copyist. The cost for score and parts of a typical arrangement is $125.

Ammann sees efficient and proper administrative procedures as necessary for the job. To him, the nonmusical areas such as publicity, promotion and administration are among the most difficult tasks of the position. "There are so many time constraints," he said. Finding and buying new music and proper maintenance of the present library requires much time. Although Lillehaug had supervised the organization and computerization of the library, it never is a static facility and needs constant care. Other aspects include maintenance of equipment, rehearsal and concert site management and complete responsibility for personnel. The conductor also is in charge of auditions, with designated band members assisting as necessary.

One of Ammann's major immediate concerns is acquiring new uniforms. Although additional uniforms of the same color and style have been purchased in the past few years, a new set of uniforms has not been purchased since 1978. The Band first wore the present uniforms on June 18, 1978, to open the 1978 park season. The uniforms have been worn for seventeen years. Wearing them an average of thirty-eight times a season for seventeen years means that each of the originals has been worn about 646 times, most performances being in very warm weather. Ammann said that is a long time for any garment.

Another goal of the present conductor is to have the Band record tapes and compact disks. He is considering the possibility of radio broadcasts, following up a proposal made by officials from the WSN radio station, who approached Alan Taylor about broadcasting a couple of concerts per season. Schuett said he would have the city attorney check regarding recording rights, but Taylor reports nothing further materialized.

Ammann is a firm believer in having guest soloists. However, he said guests are a supplement to, rather than a substitute for, solos and ensembles by Municipal Band members. He said the fact that major guest soloists are willing to play with the Band gives credibility to the organization. In addition, he said the guest artists are professional role models for the players and allow the audience to hear a variety of outstanding soloists on the various instruments. Ammann has featured Dr. Robert Spring, clarinet; Paul Hankins, trumpet; and M/Sgt. Scott Shelsta, trombone. The budget provides for one soloist per year.

Although he has not been able to bring in any guest conductors to date, he plans to do so. "It is important," he said, "for a Band to play under different conductors because both the players and the regular conductor gain by seeing how someone else handles the group."

The Band Board recently established the policy of performance evaluations. Beginning in the fall of 1994, they will have performance evaluations for all the Band members every other year. The conductor and section principal will evaluate each player's attendance record, music preparation during the season and past performance. When section principals are evaluated, another section principal will assist the conductor. The evaluations also will be used for placement within the section.

Ammann changed the schedule for fall and winter rehearsals. The Band now rehearses 7:30 p.m. to 9 p.m. without a break, instead of until 10 p.m. with a break.

Other Challenges

That weather is always a problem with outdoor concerts is illustrated by the 1993 year, which was the wettest year in Sioux Falls history. Nevertheless, the Band was fortunate. Only one concert was canceled, and the Band moved another concert indoors when bad weather threatened. There is always stress with the decision of whether to cancel a concert. "When you awake to sunshine it relieves the stresses," Ammann said. The Band uses a telephone calling chain to notify members of a cancellation. The Park and Recreation Department also has a fax service which allows announcements to be sent out quickly to all media. The fax also is used for news releases. The weather problem involves heat in addition to rain. Ammann said, "It was a hot, humid day (August 9, 1992) when Dr. Robert Spring was our guest clarinet soloist. My glasses fogged up so bad I couldn't see the notes I was conducting. That, plus trying to relate to the guest soloist, made it tough going for several minutes." Wind is often a problem — trying to hold the music down and turn pages with one hand while still conducting with the other. Players use clothes pins to try to prevent the music from blowing away, and when there are two players per stand they can assist each other. "I much prefer heat to wind," Ammann said. Perhaps that doesn't sound too unusual for a man who spent much of his life in Arizona.

And what does he find most satisfying? Ammann says he enjoys the people the most. A musical group like the Band merges many age groups — high school students, college students and professional people from the community. The Monday night rehearsal is the reward for the planning and preparation because he then has the opportunity to work with the talented musicians. The other reward is seeing the response of the audiences at the concerts. Ammann has enjoyed the aesthetic improvement resulting from the recent renovation of the Terrace Park Band shell. It didn't result in any acoustic improvement but it looks much better, he said.

The Reunion and 75th Anniversary Concerts

Because 1994 was the 75th anniversary year, Ammann and the Band planned special concerts and events to commemorate the year. Special theme concerts related to the past were held on June 15, 1994, when the Band played "Concert from the 1940s," and on June 28 with "Selections from the Past." On July 12 the theme was "Concert from the 1970s," and on July 31, "Concert from the 1960s." The reunion event was held on June 25 and 26. A reunion banquet was held for present and returning past members at the Morrison Commons at Augustana College. Members came from as far as Texas and California plus from neighboring states.

Robb Hart, the Band's master of ceremonies, served in that capac-

The three living Municipal Band conductors, from left to right, are Dr. Leland Lillehaug, Dr. Bruce Ammann and Dr. Alan Taylor. All took turns conducting the Municipal Band at a concert Sunday afternoon, June 26, 1994, at McKennan Park for the Band's 75th reunion. *(courtesy Leland Lillehaug)*

ity at the banquet. Speaking on the program were conductor Dr. Bruce Ammann, conductor emeritus Dr. Leland Lillehaug, former members Marlin Brown (1937-43), George Gulson (1964-85), David Joyce (1975-83) and Eugenia Orlich Hartig, regular soprano soloist (1965-79). (Years in parentheses indicate their year with the Band.) Musical entertainment was furnished by Sheila Wulf, piano, and Joan Van Holland, soprano. Band members had the opportunity to view Band photos and memorabilia that were displayed in the banquet room. Each member who attended the banquet was given a Municipal Band 75th anniversary coffee mug.

The three living Municipal Band conductors, Ammann, Taylor and Lillehaug, led the Municipal Band at the McKennan Concert on Sunday afternoon, June 26. The Sunday evening concert at Terrace featured the present Municipal Band playing the first half of the program and the Reunion Band playing the second half. The Reunion Band consisted of past members together with present members. The Reunion

Band rehearsed on Saturday afternoon, prior to the banquet. Each of
the three conductors mentioned above conducted two pieces with the
Reunion Band.

 The following are those involved with the reunion:

Band alumni joined the 1994 Band for the concert. Alumni Band members
included the following: Flute: Linda Olson, Pat Penn, Ralph Tyler; bassoon: Carol
Buckwalter Pederson; clarinet: David Amundson, Catherine Green Billion, Marlin
Brown, Barb Gilchrist Christwitz, Earl Colgan, Donna Schettler Hoogendoorn, James
Johnston, Oscar Loe, Charlotte Hedeen Miller, Dick Peik, Norman Sampson; saxo-
phone: Sandy Person McAllister, Terry Walter; trumpet: Terry Anderson, George
Gulson, James Ode, James Perkins, Brian Smith, David Wegner; horn: Robert

**A large crowd attended the Municipal Band's 75th Reunion Concert
Sunday evening, June 26, 1994, at Terrace Park.** *(photo by Dave
Sonnichsen, courtesy Sioux Falls Municipal Band)*

Euphonium player
Michael Cwach, left,
and cornet player
Jeremy Hegg talk
before a Band
concert in 1994.
*(photo by Dave
Sonnichsen, cour-
tesy Sioux Falls
Municipal Band)*

McDowell; trombone: Dick Flisrand, Faye Fossum; euphonium: Rolyn Beaird, Jeff
McAllister, Robert Ortman; vocal soloists: Lisa Wiehl Grevlos, Eugenia Hartig,
Marciene Matthius, Joan Van Holland. Conductors: Dr. Leland A. Lillehaug, Dr. Alan
W. Taylor.

Other alumni who attended the reunion events but are not listed above in-
clude: Paul Bankson, Chad Boese, Marty Braithwaite, Mindy Braithwaite, Brenda
Zacharias Clark, David Joyce, David Krueger, Donna Van Bockern Krueger, Kristi
Reierson McWayne, James McWayne, Leon "Curly" Miller, Martha Vegge Nelson,
Paul Runyan, and Kathryn Welter. Current members attending the reunion banquet
were: Alan Berdahl, Dr. Bruce T. Ammann, Kathy Bangasser, Pam Hansen Barnard,
Michael Cwach, Dennis Graber, Mark Gross, Jeral Gross, Robb Hart, Paul Hoy,
Amy Millikan, Lois Nelson, Julie Pachoud, Lori Quanbeck, Mary Jensen Ryrholm
and Sheila Wulf.

The committee members for the reunion were the following: Craig Alberty, Dr.
Bruce T. Ammann, Pam Hansen Barnard, Laura Britton, Delight Jensen Elsinger,
Dennis Graber, Paul Hoy, Eric Knutson, Lois Nelson, and Mary Jensen Ryrholm.

Plans for the future include a newsletter mailing to alumni band
members and additional reunions. A positive result of the reunion was
the updating and computerization of the band mailing list to be used in
future communication with alumni members.

The Municipal Band Moves to a New Temporary Home

An unusual incident led to the Municipal Band leaving the Sioux Falls Coliseum for a new, hopefully temporary, home. A portion of the Coliseum ceiling – hundreds of pounds of plaster, wire netting and nailed laths – crashed onto the auditorium seats on February 18, 1994; more ceiling fell in early May 1994. No one was hurt in either incident. Although the auditorium was closed to the public in February, the Band continued to rehearse on the stage and use its office, library and storage facilities elsewhere in the Coliseum. During the late summer and early fall of 1994, there were speculations that the city might sell or give the Coliseum to Minnehaha County and that the auditorium portion of the building might be torn down. On December 20, 1994, the Sioux Falls City Commission agreed to sell the Coliseum and Rec Center to Minnehaha County for one dollar. The county will keep the Coliseum closed but will lease back the Rec Center. The *Argus Leader* re-

The former Church of the Bible building, located at Thirty-Fifth and Summit, is the new, temporary home of the Municipal Band office. *(courtesy Bob Elmen)*

ported on December 21, 1994, "Though the agreements call for the Coliseum to remain closed, commissioners agreed that they would consider the possibility of allowing private groups to pay for renovation of the structure if they so desire. At this point, no such groups have come forward."

Bob Elmen, a local businessman, had negotiated an assignable purchase of the Church of the Bible – a wooden structure located at Thirty-fifth Street and Summit Avenue – in 1992 on behalf of a potential purchase by Our Savior's Lutheran Church for use as a parking lot. Our Savior's then voted to purchase the church building and grounds. Following the ceiling problems at the Coliseum in 1994, Elmen learned that the Municipal Band and the South Dakota Symphony would need rehearsal space until the Washington Pavilion is completed. He contacted W. Mack Richardson, executive director of the Soth Dakota Symphony, about the potential for the former Church of the Bible building as a rehearsal site. Richardson was interested and contacted Ammann and the Park Department. All parties concerned agreed that the building would be a good temporary location for the groups, and a contract was signed between Our Savior's and the city of Sioux Falls for use of the building.

Ammann and a group of assistants moved most of the Band's holdings from the Coliseum to the church on the weekend of October 1, 1994. The contract with Our Savior's allows the Band and the Symphony to use the building for rehearsals until the new Pavilion Arts Center is available.

The building has two small rooms on each side of the entrance corridor for storage of music, uniforms and equipment and for work space and desks. The former church sanctuary is large enough to seat large music groups comfortably during rehearsals. Ammann is attempting to make the room acoustically acceptable. The stage curtain from the Coliseum is draped from the balcony to the floor, and sound panels are being attached to the walls in an attempt to absorb excessive "ring." Adequate parking for the players is available.

Player Comments about Ammann

After three years, comments from the players have been very positive. One player said, "I really like him. He is well prepared and knows what he wants. He is able to communicate his wishes. I also like his selection of music" (Linda McLaren Roach). Another stated, "The Band has improved under Ammann. He is outstanding as a person and as a musician" (Pat Masek). A third remarked, "Bruce Ammann is very organized and is a personable leader" (Greg Handel). Thus, it appeared that both Ammann and the players were enjoying their relationship as they made music together during the Band's seventy-fifth anniversary.

• • •

The adjustments for Sioux Falls Municipal Band were many during 1987-94. In 1987, the Band was placed under the Park Department rather than reporting directly to the mayor or one of the commissioners. During the period, the players had to become accustomed to working with two new conductors, Taylor and Ammann, and the Band went from union to nonunion, resulting in the financial loss of about six Recording Trust Fund concerts each season. The Terrace Park band shell, continuing to draw large crowds for the Sunday evening concerts, was repaired and repainted and was rededicated on June 14, 1992. Special events were held during the 75th anniversary season in 1994 including a reunion of past players, conductors and guest performers. In spite of budget cuts in its financial proposals in 1993 and 1994, it appears that the Sioux Falls Municipal Band will continue to move forward.

1988. Sioux Falls Coliseum Stage. Standing on left (white coat) Ray Loftesness (emcee). Standing on right: Dr. Alan Taylor. Row 1, L to R: Pat Masek, Jane Quail, Linda McLaren Roach, Lori Quanbeck, Katherine Peterson. Row 2: Oscar Loe, Dan Irvin, Kathy Bangasser, Brenda Bahnson, Brenda Zacharias, Jackie Larsen, Dennis Graber, Terry Walter, Todd Novak, Martha Vegge Nelson, Lori Neprud, Craig Alberty, Eric Knutson, Mary Fritz, Ann Barrett, Linsey Langford Duffy, Ann Natvig, Denise Noble, Lois Nelson, Lawrence Price, Doug Lehrer, Janet Bruns Hallstrom, Nathan Wegner, Steve Stombaugh. Row 4: (standing) Eric LeVan, Stan Eitreim, Scott Fenton, Paul Hoy; (seated): David Larson, Craig Rostad, Wallace Waltner, Rolyn Beaird, Lyn Alberty, Robert McDowell, Jr., Faye Fossum, Eric Christensen, Carl Hallstrom.

1992. Terrace Park. Standing front left: Dr. Monty Barnard and Lisa Wiehl (vocalists) and Robb Hart (emcee); Standing front right: Dr. Bruce Ammann, (conductor). Row 1, L to R: Pat Masek, Pam Hansen Barnard, Jane Quail, Sheila Wulf, Kristen Sonnichsen. Row 2: Dan Irvin, Kathy Bangasser, Delight Jensen Elsinger, Jackie Larsen, Dennis Graber, Nancy Barnes, Lois Nelson, Steve Spieker, Jason McFarland, Barbara Johnson Hegg, Dawn Dalseide, Lori Quanbeck, Katherine Peterson, Row 3: Kristi Tharp McDowell, Mary Fritz, Nikki Maher, Barb Hanson Johnson, Lynda Rasmussen, Deann Golz, Brian Smith, Pam Sonnichsen, Janet Bruns Hallstrom, Greg Handel, Craig Alberty, Jeremy Hegg, Rolyn Beaird, Lyn Alberty, Jason Schwans, Martha Vegge Nelson, Brenda Bahnson, Laura Busdicker Britton. Row 4: (standing) Michael Smith, Robert Kramer, Mike Hart, Paul Hoy; (seated) Stan Eitreim, Craig Rostad, Gary Pederson, Robert McDowell, Jr., Mark Gross, Carl Hallstrom, Faye Fossum, Deb McConahie. *(courtesy Bruce Ammann)*

1993. Terrace Park. Standing front left: Dr. Monty Barnard and Joan Van Holland (vocalists). Standing front right: Robb Hart (emcee) and Dr. Bruce Ammann (conductor). Row 1, L to R: Pam Hansen Barnard, Jane Quail, Mary Jensen Ryrholm, Sheila Wulf, Kristen Sonnichsen. Row 2: Dan Irvin, Kathy Bangasser, Delight Jensen Elsinger, Jackie Larsen, Dennis Graber, Lois Nelson, Steve Spieker, Carrie Baird, Jason McFarland, Marian Ost, Dawn Dalseide, Linda McLaren Roach, Lori Quanbeck, Katherine Peterson. Row 3: Kristi Tharp McDowell, Mary Fritz, Nikki Maher, Angela Larson, Lynda Rasmussen, Deann Golz, Brian Smith, Pam Sonnichsen, Janet Bruns Hallstrom, Eric Knutson, Steven Stombaugh, Greg Handel, Jeremy Hegg, Kris Whitely, Carl Hallstrom, Lyn Alberty, Jason Schwans, Amy Millikan, Brenda Bahnson, Laura Busdicker Britton. Row 4: (standing) Michael Smith, Derek Hengeveld, Robert Kramer, Mike Hart, Paul Hoy; (seated) Stan Eitreim, Gary Pederson, Michael Andersen, Robert McDowell, Jr., Mark Gross, Bill Gibson, Faye Fossum. *(courtesy Bruce Ammann)*

1994. Terrace Park. Standing at left: Robb Hart (emcee), Monty Barnard and Lisa Wiehl Grevlos, (vocalists). Standing at right: M/Sgt. Scott Shelsta (guest trombone soloist), Dr. Bruce Ammann, (conductor). Row 1, L to R: Pat Masek, Pam Hansen Barnard, Mary Jensen Ryrholm, Kristen Sonnichsen, Cara Soper, Row 2: Kathy Bangasser, Nikki Maher, Delight Jensen Elsinger, John Titus, Angela Larson, Lois Nelson, Shad Fagerland, Steve Spieker, Jason McFarland, Teri Naber, Marian Ost, Linda McLaren Roach, Deann Golz, Katherine Peterson. Row 3: Kristi Tharp McDowell, Mary Fritz, Dennis Graber, Anne Weiland, Amber Sittig, Jeremy Nygard, Craig Alberty, Janet Bruns Hallstrom, Eric Knutson, Steve Stombaugh, Greg Handel, Jeremy Hegg, Jeral Gross, Heidi Olson, Michael Cwach, Lyn Alberty, Jason Schwans, Amy Millikan, Sheila Zweifel, Brenda Bahnson. Row 4: Standing at back: Kevin Meyer, Derek Hengeveld, Michael Smith, Kelly Bradbury, Paul Hoy. (seated) Stan Eitreim, Alan Berdahl, Michael Andersen, Mark Gross, Scott Loftesness, Carl Hallstrom, Tony Dresbach, Cindy Ellison. (courtesy Bruce Ammann)

 **10** **Regular and Guest Vocalists**

T he first conductors of the Sioux Falls Municipal Band discovered that having vocal soloists on the program drew additional listeners to their concerts, just as John Philip Sousa
earlier had found that noted female vocal soloists helped attract audiences. Sousa's biographer, Paul Bierley, said that Sousa had three requirements for female vocalists: talent, beauty and stage presence.
Marjorie Moody sang with Sousa longer than any other vocalist (more
than 2,500 concerts), starting in 1917. The most renowned Sousa vocalist was the coloratura soprano Estelle Liebling, who like the others,
performed without the assistance of a microphone. Because of Sousa's
national and international fame, millions of listeners were accustomed
to hearing vocal soloists at band concerts. It was not unusual for conductors of town bands to use that very successful formula. Gerard C.
McClung, the fourth conductor of the Sioux Falls Municipal Band, said
in 1928 that other singers would be appearing on the programs because
previous singers had been so popular with the audience.

Vocal music was emphasized at area colleges as early as the late
1800s, which not only indicated the importance of vocal music to the
community but also provided a source of vocalists for the Municipal
Band. Vocal music at Lutheran Normal School in Sioux Falls was "classed
with the regular subjects and obligatory upon all who are not by nature
disqualified for singing," according to the school's 1893-94 catalog. Both
Augustana College, which moved to Sioux Falls from Canton in 1918
and merged with Lutheran Normal School, and Sioux Falls College offered vocal music in their early years. Because of these factors, it does

206

not seem unusual that there are references to vocal soloists — and to their popularity — with the Sioux Falls Municipal Band from the first season in 1920 and continuing to the present. Several, including the first male vocalist and the present male vocalist, have had roots with Augustana College. Some sang just once with the Band, while others, like Ed Paul, sang for many years. Their selections have included the entire musical spectrum from classical to popular. Because audience members often refer to vocalists by their first names, the same is done in this chapter.

Ole Holm

Ole Holm is the first vocal solo-ist with the Band on record, singing during both the 1920 and 1921 seasons while Lloyd M. Coppens was conductor. Newspaper accounts show Ole's selections as "Somewhere a Voice is Calling," "The Sunshine of Your Smile," and "Dear Old Pal O' Mine" at the concert Sunday, August 22, 1920, at McKennan Park.

Ole was known locally as head of the Augustana College music department and director of the Augustana band. The 1921 Augustana yearbook indicated that Holm "studied at 'Sivertsen's Middelskole,' Trondhjem, Norway, 1895-96, and in the Army Music School, Christiania, Norway, 1896-1900. He specialized in music under Rolf Hammer and Morten Swendsen, 1902-07. In 1908-09 he was a student in Concordia College, Moorhead, Minnesota, since which

Ole Holm, shown here in the 1921 Augustana yearbook, was the Municipal Band's first vocal soloist. *(courtesy Augustana College)*

time much of his time has been devoted to concert and church choir work until he came to Augustana in 1919 as director of music in the school."

Holm also had a national reputation, having been the leading tenor in grand and light operas and having been employed in what the *Argus Leader* called "the choirs of some of the larger churches of the Northwest." During his two years in Sioux Falls, Ole also was in charge of the First Lutheran Church choir and the Minnehaha Mandskor, a men's choir. It was reported that he moved to Minnesota in 1921, where he was an administrator at the Saint Paul Musical Academy.

Royal S. Barnes, Gerhard H. Dahl, Rolla Dickenson, James Ballard, John Ross Reed and Lyda Pallansch

The experiment with vocalists in 1920 evidently was successful because the practice was continued — and expanded — during the remainder of Coppen's tenure, to include five male vocalists and one female vocalist.

The male vocalists included Royal S. Barnes, called a tenor in one news article and "a baritone known to all Sioux Falls music lovers" in another. Royal, who sang with the Band in 1921, was involved in some way with First Methodist Church, but it's not clear if as a member or as a choir director. Another male vocalist, baritone Gerhard H. Dahl, sang Handel's "Honor and Arms" and "Thank God for a Garden" by Riego in 1921. Roland "Rolla" E. Dickenson, also a guest in 1921, sang "I Gathered a Rose" by Lee and "Give Me All of You" by Schwarzwald. Rolla was also the drum major with the Shrine Band, according to later Municipal Band vocalist Ed Paul. James Ballard also was mentioned in 1921 as a baritone soloist, presumably a baritone vocalist and not a baritone (euphonium) player. His selection was "The Perfect Song" by Brell. John Ross Reed's selection with the Band was "Prologue from Pagliacci" by Leoncavallo. John was in Sioux Falls in 1922 as the choir leader of the Biederwolf evangelistic services which took place in the Coliseum. The revival meetings drew an average of 1,900 people each night for about two weeks in January of 1922.

It appears that Lyda Pallansch was the first female vocalist with the Band, singing in 1921. Lyda received a good review from the *Argus Leader* on February 21, 1921, for her renditions of "Slave Song" by Teresa del Riego (a female composer) and "Your Eyes Have Told Me So" by Blaufuss.

Alice Barr

No vocal soloists were found during conductor Charles Emmel's tenure (1922). Just one was found during conductor Charles F. McClung's tenure (1923-27): Alice Barr in 1923.

The only information given about Alice is that she sang "Love Sends a Little Gift of Roses," by Openshaw.

Eugene Cashman, Norman Mathers, and Mrs. R. L. Van Ellis

Vocal soloists again appeared on the programs during the 1928 and 1929 seasons during G. C. McClung's tenure. Eugene "Gene" Cashman, "The Singing Policeman," performed in both 1928 and 1929. The *Argus Leader* called Gene the first vocal soloist with the Band, but other accounts disprove this as indicated by the above listings of soloists. His selections included "My Ohio Home," "Ramona," "Back in Your Own Backyard" by Berlin, "Girl of My Dreams" by Jack Mills, "That's How I Feel About You," and "Mean to Me." Another male vocalist, Norman Mathers also sang in 1929, with his selection "Mighty Lak' a Rose" by Nevin. Also in 1929 one woman is known to have sung. Mrs. R. L. Van Ellis sang "From Sunrise to Sunset" and "Weary River," both by Berlin.

Ed Paul

It wasn't until 1934 that a regular soloist was chosen. Conductor Otto H. Andersen selected Ed Paul as a regular baritone soloist and master of ceremonies. Ed served in that capacity for thirty-one years (1934-64), excluding a one-year leave in 1938, giving him more years of service than any other vocalist or emcee.

Ed, like Ole Holm, came to the Municipal Band via Augustana College. He was born in 1909 and came to Sioux Falls from Bryant, South Dakota, in 1928 to attend Augustana College. During college, he became well known for his vocal and drama

Ed Paul, shown here in about 1945. *(courtesy Ed Paul)*

activities. Ed also played guitar and violin, playing the latter in the Augustana College Orchestra. Graduating in 1932, he went to Luther College, Decorah, Iowa, where he taught drama for a year.

When he returned to Sioux Falls, he was billed as the "Midwest's Finest Baritone," singing, playing bass viol and fronting the Herbie Lowe Dance Band and later the Jimmy Barnett Band. He also started his career with the Municipal Band. Ed's first audition for the Municipal Band was at the McKennan Park band shell in 1934. At that time, some Monday rehearsals took place in the band shell rather than indoors. It's not clear if it was too hot to rehearse indoors or if a good rehearsal facility was not available. It was in 1934 that the bond issue was passed for the new City Hall which was completed in 1936. It's possible that the old City Auditorium, which was replaced by City Hall, was being torn down at that time. At Ed's audition there were problems with the sound system and he didn't think it was a good audition. He sang "Wagon Wheels" and "There's an Old Spinning Wheel." Despite the problems, Ed was hired.

Also during that time, he taught at Luverne, Minnesota (1934-37), married Evelyn Kemper of Sioux Falls (1937) and taught at Father Flanagan Boys Home in Boys Town, Nebraska (1938), where his choir was in the movie "Boys Town." He said that he never missed a Municipal Band concert for thirty-one years except for his leave of absence when he taught at Boys Town.

At the first Municipal Band concert Ed ever sang (at McKennan), the audience demanded six encores after his first number. After he sang a scheduled number later in the program, an encore was demanded again. The audience demanded so many encores that next time a note was put on the printed program saying there would be no vocal encores until the end of the program. Loretta McLaughlin Hartrich, regular female vocal soloist 1941-43 and a colleague of Ed, understood the audience's reaction. She recalled Ed singing "in his resonant, appealing tenor voice."

In the early years, Ed wore dress clothing at the concerts. But he was forced to wear a uniform, because several Band members felt he looked out of place with everyone else in uniform. After a year Band members agreed it probably was better for him to return to his previous attire, which he did.

Ed sang with three conductors: Otto H. Andersen in 1934, Russ Henegar during his entire tenure (1935-63) and with Leland Lillehaug for one year. Ed retired after the 1964 season.

Some of the compositions Ed sang with the Band during the mid-1940s included: "Sweet Dreams, Sweetheart," "My Dreams Are Getting

Better All the Time," "Memories," "Don't Fence Me In," "Mighty Lak' a Rose," "That's an Irish Lullaby," "I'll See You in My Dreams," "Always" and "The Rose of Tralee."

Mid-1950s choices included "Just a Cottage Small," "A Perfect Day," "The Lonesome Road," "Vaya Con Dios," "My Buddy," and a first performance with the Band of "I Believe," which had just sold one million records. Many of the tunes were Irish and many others were sung in answer to requests. Band members during his final years with the Band recalled the popularity of "Cruising Down the River."

Ed was involved with several musical activities in addition to singing with the Municipal Band. He was president of the American Federation of Musicians for seventeen years and sang with the Elks and Shrine Bands. He also sang with the Lennox Municipal Band.

As this book was written, Ed was living in northeast Sioux Falls with his wife, Evelyn. He has an excellent memory of events during his years with the Band.

Loretta McLaughlin (Hartrich)

Loretta McLaughlin was the regular female vocalist from 1941-43. Writing from her current home in Orland Park, Illinois, she recalled, "The Sioux Falls Municipal Band — Lee Bright introducing me to Russ Henegar, the members of the Band, all so dedicated, all so attuned to the harmony of music, the conductor and each other. What a privilege to sing with them!"

Loretta was a native of Sioux Falls. She was the oldest in a family of eight girls and two boys — all were redheads. Three sisters, Mary (Mrs. William Novetzke), Elizabeth and Irene McLaughlin live in Sioux Falls as does her uncle Earl McLaughlin, a supporter of the arts and retired architect.

Loretta wrote in a letter dated February 18, 1994, that although she sang all through grade and high school at churches, weddings, social groups, and for her family, she had realized that she needed a voice teacher. The name of Lee Bright — music professor at Sioux Falls College — frequently was mentioned in the *Argus Leader*. Although she had never met him, she made up her mind that she would. Money was scarce, but she persisted and made an appointment to audition. "He was a gracious man and supportive of my efforts." After agreeing to teach her, he mentioned his fee. She was startled, and recalled that she didn't have the money, even for bus fare that day. So she proposed to pay by baby-sitting for the Bright children, Rosemary and Bill. Bright

Loretta McLaughlin (Hartrich), shown here in 1994 with former Band member Marlin Brown, was the Municipal Band's regular vocal soloist from 1941 through 1943. *(courtesy William Novetzke)*

agreed with a chuckle, and the deal was made.

She attended Sioux Falls College for two years. While there, Loretta sang with the choir and loved the bus tours to many small towns in South Dakota, Iowa and Minnesota. There, the church families were her hosts — kind and sincerely religious. She recalled an evening in Parker, South Dakota, where her hosts, a family of seven, with bowed heads and holding hands, thanked the Lord for His blessings and welcomed her into their circle. She was deeply moved by that family's faith.

People still remember Loretta from Sioux Falls College. Glenna Rundell, later supervisor of music in the Sioux Falls public schools, was her accompanist at lessons and recitals. Glenna said Loretta McLaughlin was an excellent soloist with the Sioux Falls College Choir: "She was also an attractive redhead and a fun person." Anne Bryant Fisher, who followed her as the Band's soloist, remembered, "Loretta McLaughlin had a beautiful voice."

After her two years at Sioux Falls College, Loretta taught music in the Montrose schools. She later completed her four years of college by attending the University of South Dakota with the financial help of the Sioux Falls Women's Club. Then came one-and-a-half years teaching Morse code to newly recruited soldiers at the Air Base, located near the present Joe Foss Field.

It was during those years that Loretta starting singing with the Band, 1941-43. She had vivid memories of those concerts: "Standing near Russ, looking out and up at the terrace sitting places, at our Sioux Falls neighbors, friends and folks — relaxing and enjoying the music of the togetherness — I was both happy and a little nervous." Loretta remembered what she called the simple life: "The parks were havens of relaxation — picnics, friends and families, children all enjoying swings, the seesaw, tennis — a chance to see the softball players and finally to relax and listen to the Band. How lucky I was — we all were. A memory in time."

It was the time of Jeanette MacDonald, a popular operetta singer, and she was Loretta's idol. In fact, Jeanette MacDonald was the idol of both Loretta and Anne Bryant Fisher, Loretta's successor as vocalist with the Sioux Falls Municipal Band. Loretta sang many of the popular songs from the pens of respected composers of the day. Some were popular earlier in the century but had already become standards, such as Rudolf Friml's "Indian Love Call" from the operetta *Rose Marie* in 1915. "Ah, Sweet Mystery of Life" from *Naughty Marietta* had been written in 1910 by Victor Herbert and was revived in 1922. Another Herbert tune, "A Kiss in the Dark," was written in 1922. Loretta sang tunes by Sigmund Romberg, which, although written in the 1920s. were extremely popular during Loretta's years with the Band. Romberg, like Loretta, had served as an entertainer for the troops, but in World War I rather than World War II. Other compositions included works by classical composers and great European operetta composers such as Oscar Straus and Lehar:

> Will You Remember, Romberg
> Il Bacio, Arditi
> Ave Maria, Schubert
> Serenade, Schubert
> Ouvre Ton Coeur, Georges Bizet

Loretta was not the only member of her family who appeared with the Sioux Falls Municipal Band. Her brother, Joe, danced with the Band in 1936. He studied with Florence Bright, wife of Sioux Falls College music professor Lee Bright. "At the concert, Joe was one of ten dancers. The men wore dark suits and white shirts. The girls wore long dresses, full skirts in pastel colors and the audience loved them," said Loretta.

Loretta's job with the Municipal Band ended in 1943. Loretta applied to the Marines and to the American Red Cross and received telegrams from both — accepting her on the same day. Her sister Lavonne suggested that she toss a coin — heads for the Marines and tails for the Red Cross. The Red Cross won, and her life was directed from Sioux Falls to Europe, sailing to England in 1943 on a Liberty ship. She met several members of a USO entertainment group who were to entertain American troops with "Oklahoma." However, half of the cast members were on another ship in the same convoy so they had to wait until they landed to get together. She sang with a professional group (the USO entertainers) for the first time. "What a joy!" she wrote. While in England, France and Germany with Patton's Third Army, she continued to sing from a special vehicle. It was a one and one-half-ton truck built with one side that could be lowered to form a stage. It also was equipped with a mini-piano and a public address system. She and her partner, Pat, also enjoyed singing for the troops in an open field with the GIs sitting on their helmets. Then Loretta would invite the GIs to sing, tap dance and entertain. And she said they did — with gusto.

It was after she met her husband, Edwin Hartrich, in Germany in 1946 after the war that her singing career ended, she said. He had just been demobilized from the Army there and was a foreign correspondent for the *New York Herald Tribune*. Yet music has remained an element in her life: "Music of all kinds is a very important pleasure in my life. And the Sioux Falls Municipal Band was a springboard to a lifelong appreciation of music."

Maud Runyan

English mezzo soprano Maud Runyan appeared with the Band during the 1941, 1942 and 1943 seasons. The *Argus Leader* of August 3, 1941, said that Maud was born in Colchester, England, and studied at the Royal College of Music in London. She sang for a year in Europe before going to the United States. A printed Band program from a concert of August 3, 1941, described her as possessing "a magnificent voice that has been royally acclaimed on both sides of the Atlantic. Winner of the much-coveted scholarship of the Royal College of Music in London, toured Europe and the United States, scoring as soloist with prominent symphony orchestras as well as with the Philadelphia Opera Company and the National and Columbia Broadcasting Systems."

Maud sang with the Municipal Band on August 17, 1941, for the unveiling and dedication of "The Pillars of the Nation" at McKennan Park. The Pillars — whose name was suggested by Paul Meyers, secretary of the Sioux Falls Chamber of Commerce — are columns in McKennan Park along Second Avenue between Twenty-Second and

Twenty-Sixth Streets. They consist of stones from all the states.

Programs show Maud's other appearances. She sang in the summer of 1942 at least once each month: June 28, 1942, and July 19, 1942, at McKennan Park; August 16, 1942, at Terrace Park. The last time her name appeared on a program was August 8, 1943, at Terrace. No records have been found indicating what she did when she left the city.

Ed Paul remembered Maud — especially one incident. She told him that she was scared to death about singing with the Band even though she had sung opera. Maud said that singing opera, with orchestral accompaniment, was much different from singing with a band. Ed said she was literally shaking after performing with the Band that day.

Anne Bryant (Fisher)

Anne Bryant was the regular female vocalist for twelve years (1945-56), following Loretta McLaughlin and preceding Marciene Swenson Matthius. She also sang guest appearances in 1943, 1944, 1957, 1979 and 1980.

Fifty years later, Anne's love of music and her joy from those days still were apparent: "In 1943, there were no air conditioners and no television. On hot Sunday afternoons, a huge army of perspiring Sioux Falls citizens flocked to McKennan Park with their lawn chairs to sit under the cool shade of the ancient elm trees — or lie on a blanket on the grass to hear our Band. Even more beautiful was the Sunday evening concert at Terrace Park, where an even bigger crowd packed the area. It seemed all of Sioux Falls was there in that lovely place that always reminded me of a scene from 'A Midsummer Night's Dream.' We had two old fellows who were quite deaf and played off key. However, this just made the audience love us more. One August evening toward the end of the 1943 season, Mr. Henegar let me sing, and thus began a fourteen-year [twelve-year] career. In those days, there were two teen-age sopranos, Deanna Durbin and Jane Powell, who were the rage of the movies, and classical music was in style. I fit right into that era."

Anne's musical career really began at Washington High School in Sioux Falls where she had been singing in the chorus for three years without the director, Boyd Bohlke, ever knowing she was there. Anne said that she wasn't noticed because she was a tall, shy, skinny girl who needed eye glasses to remedy astigmatism. "No way could I have won a part in the spring operettas," she said. Without her glasses she could not see her way around the stage, and she would have towered over any leading man with her five-foot, eight-inch height. It seemed that she would never get the recognition she desperately wanted.

Some of the desired recognition came in April of her junior year. The Washington High Orchestra, under Harold Hoover, was planning the spring concert. One of the selections was "Il Bacio" by Luigi Arditi. Her friend, Maxine Prescott who played violin, told Hoover that Anne could sing that song. Hoover needed some soloists to liven up the show, so he put her on the program. The performance went well and the wild applause of the parents was the recognition she had been seeking. She recalled that she appeared on the stage without her glasses and wearing a three dollar formal from the "White Elephant" shop (an early secondhand store). She learned she could stride out on the stage, blind without her glasses, and find the spot where she was to stand. Performances during that time were done without a microphone, and the soloist had to be able to project above the orchestra.

Anne Bryant (Fisher) was the regular female vocalist 1945-56. *(courtesy Anne Fisher)*

It was Hoover, a trombone player in the Sioux Falls Municipal Band, who brought Anne to the attention of Russ Henegar. Her voice had a wide range from A below middle C to the high C and E notes coloratura sopranos love, so she could handle any arrangement the Band had. However, what really endeared her to Henegar was the fact that she seldom needed to practice with the Band. Once she did a song, she never forgot it. "Mr. Henegar could put out my songs for the week and everything went off great every week." She said that this was not as difficult as it sounds, because the Band arrangement was almost always the same as her piano copy. In all that music, she remembered only three songs that were slightly different arrangements. Evidently Henegar trusted her abilities, because she did not rehearse with the Band during the winter. With this ability to stay out of his way and not bother him, her job with the Band was secure. She sang three concerts a week all those years and never once had to miss a concert. Even after she married and moved to Centerville forty miles away, she managed to continue the concerts from 1953 through the 1956 season.

Then, one day in 1957 she had to sit in Henegar's office and tell him the fun was gone and the driving all summer was becoming a grind. However, she could not leave without helping to find someone to take her place. She said that she called a classmate, Marciene Swenson, who had been the star of the high school operettas all four years at Washington High School, and talked her into taking her job. Anne recalled that Marciene didn't think she wanted to take on the work but finally decided it might be fun and a little extra money would be nice. Anne sang at least one guest appearance in 1957.

How did Anne's love of music begin? It began one day in 1934 when she was ten years old and her mother left her at the old State Theater while she went shopping. The show was Victor Herbert's "Naughty Marietta" with Jeanette MacDonald and Nelson Eddy. Anne got lost in the romantic story, and when Jeanette began to sing "The Italian Street Song," she felt the theater spin in space for a few seconds! When the theater stopped whirling, she knew she was in love with Jeanette's voice. From that moment she wanted just one thing in life — to sing like Jeanette. Those were the days of the Great Depression, and her father was barely keeping the family afloat with his little barber shop in the Stock Exchange Building. Anne begged for lessons until he finally started her with Mrs. Hilda Thatcher in 1937, when she was thirteen. The lessons cost $1.50 per week, plus sheet music. She said that today when she hears television people insisting that what children see on TV doesn't influence them, she thinks of that day when the old State Theater spun in space and sent her on a lifelong love of vocal music.

Her parents could not afford to send her to college, so the day after graduation from high school she began a six-month course at Stewart's Beauty School which was located in the attic over Kopel's Dress Shop. In those days it cost sixty dollars to attend school for six months. The idea was to get a job and be able to afford college. She found that she had very little talent for beauty work. It took her six months to learn to set the old-fashioned finger waves so popular in those days. She finally got through the course, and by some miracle, passed the state board exams. The Egyptian Beauty Shop hired her but fired her a few months later when she wanted a few hours off to go to Sioux Falls College. She realized her scheme was not going to work. She also learned that the salary for beauticians was next to nothing unless she owned her own shop. So Anne decided to work and save in order to buy a shop. A good job became available at Williams Piano Co., where two good buddies from the Band worked. Milt Askew and Ernie Dvoracek recommended her, and she got the job. She saved every penny and skipped lunch every day for two years to save the money to open a shop in her parents' home on their big sun porch. Her business was an instant success, and the money began rolling in. She was doing better than her friends who were teachers and nurses, and she could afford a year at Sioux Falls College and even take a taxi to get there!

Although she had dreamed of being a famous singer at the Met, it was beginning to dawn on her that she was never going to get to New York. She began to feel satisfied with her life. She had a fine business in her shop, she had the Band and she was the soloist at St. Joseph Cathedral. Something told her that life in New York, even if she got to the Met, would not be any better than this life in Sioux Falls — maybe not as good. So, she quit dreaming of New York.

Her memories of the Sioux Falls Municipal Band include the beautiful cornet solos Henegar played once in a great while, with so much soul, and "the artistry of Milt Askew who got the most beautiful sound out of his clarinet that anyone has ever heard." She recalled the huge crowds in the parks, and the children who loved to play with the loud speakers out in front of the band shells until someone chased them away. She also remembered the dog at East Side Park who insisted on singing a mournful duet with her. When the song was finished, she thanked the dog for his impromptu performance, got a great laugh from the audience and Ed Paul.

One Sunday at the McKennan concert, Myron Floren was on the program and heard her sing. He hired her to sing on several shows he put on in the few months before he and his wife left Sioux Falls. One of these shows was in Winner, South Dakota, for the Metz Baking convention. It was a hot day, and Myron's old Dodge car kept overheating and stalling. It took all day to get there — they arrived just in time for the show.

Bryant remembered the trips the Sioux Falls Municipal Band took to Hills, Minnesota, every summer, and sometimes to Salem and Mitchell. Henegar always put her in a car with the "old fellows." Anne and Raymond Hoyt were riding in the back seat of Ardeen Foss' car one evening and he said, "Why doesn't Russ let you ride with the young guys?" She said she had never thought of that, but it was a good question. Other female vocalists attested that Henegar took good care of them.

She remembered her dad going with her on the rare occasions down to the City Hall band room when she had to try out a new song. She mused, "This is probably why none of the young fellows ever tried to date me. It's hard to approach a girl who has her dad along."

Anne believed that a magic thing happened every time Henegar put the song "Brazil" on the program for her to sing. Every time she had this song on the program someone came backstage to see her. Sometimes it was a classmate home from the war, or a friend she hadn't seen in years. This magic didn't work when *she* asked to have "Brazil" on the program. It only worked when Henegar used it. She said that Ed Paul always got to do the popular songs of the day, while Henegar kept her on classics. She finally did wrangle a few "almost popular" solos like "Embraceable You," "Brazil" and Gershwin's "Summertime." But, she said, "Ed got the good ones!" She remembered sitting quietly behind the Band getting ready to go on. She would watch Harry Ellis on tuba, Harold Hoover on trombone and Vernon Alger on the drums. They enjoyed the Band so much! Bryant said that she never had stage fright, that she loved being in front of the Band and loved the lights and the audience, even though she could not see the audience without her glasses. She added that she probably would have been scared to death if she had ever seen the audience.

Anne had two regrets about her years with the Municipal Band. One was missing a Band picture — the only one she that she remembered being taken during her years as soloist. Another was that the microphone in use during her years with the Band was a crude, temperamental ogre which was hard to control. It would overload at the slightest change in volume. They joked that it had been rained on so often it was rusty inside. At the Band's 1979 celebration, Anne was amazed at the marvelous mike being used. She said it was like velvet. She thought that this was probably the first time anyone had heard her voice perfectly amplified.

She concluded, "My years with the Band were pure enjoyment, and I wish everyone could have . . . such fond memories."

James Cabbell

James B. Cabbell was a black man who sang at least twelve times in 1953 and also in 1954 and 1955. Most of his selections were spirituals, such as "Deep River," "Sometimes I Feel Like a Motherless Child" and "Go Down Moses."

James' obituary indicated that he was born December 4, 1919, in Sioux City, Iowa. More information came from a copy of a 1953 press release found in the Band office. The release indicated that James had moved to Sioux Falls in 1952, having been "a G.I. student at the Sioux City School of Music for four years, a member of the Sioux City Choral association and vocal soloist for many church and civic organizations.

While in [the] service he sang under Jess Hairston, MGM choral director of Negro music."

Anne Bryant, who was singing during that period recalled in a
letter in 1994, "One summer we had a handsome, tall, young man named
Jim Cabbell singing with the Band. He was an African American with a
rich baritone voice. We were sitting behind the bandstand one evening
when he said he and his wife wanted to buy a house. I said, 'Yes, it's
hard to get that down payment.' He said, 'No, that's not the problem.' I
realized that even Sioux Falls had prejudice. How sad that these two
well-educated, beautiful people were denied a house."

James and his wife, Geraldine, stayed in Sioux Falls for many years.
City directories list him from 1953 through 1961 as an employee of Modern Cleaners and from 1962 through 1972 as a nursing assistant at the
Royal C. Johnson Veteran's Memorial Hospital. He was listed as retired
in 1973 through 1974. Geraldine apparently preceded him in death.
James died November 27, 1974, at his home in Sioux Falls. Graveside
services were held in Sioux City, Iowa.

Elizabeth Swanson (Kuhn)

Soprano Elizabeth Swan-
son of Larchwood, Iowa, made
her first guest appearance with
the Sioux Falls Municipal Band
on July 17, 1955, at Terrace
Park. She was the regular female vocalist in 1956 and made
guest appearances during 1957-
59.

She grew up on a farm near
Larchwood, Iowa, and at an
early age sang for band concerts,
weddings and funerals. Her
mother, a concert pianist and
organist, accompanied her at
contests, county fairs and school
programs in Iowa, Minnesota
and South Dakota. At the age of
six, Elizabeth already felt im-
bued with music, seeing that
music not only stirred emotions

**Elizabeth Swanson was a regular
vocal soloist with the Band in
1956.*(courtesy Elizabeth Swanson
Kuhn)*

of other people but also her own.

The 1955 Band printed program indicated that she attended Minnehaha Academy in Minneapolis and was then a student at North Park College in Chicago, Illinois. The program stated, "She is an honor student in the department of music and is a voice major. During the past year she also appeared as soloist in Orchestra Hall in Chicago."

She went on to sing professionally in Europe – Germany, Switzerland and Austria. She sang operas, operettas, Lieder recitals and made a film of "Die Fledermaus," which still is shown. The marvel of singing grew stronger, but an illness abruptly ended her promising career.

Elizabeth founded and owned the Lafayette Restaurant in Sioux Falls with John Anderson in the late 1970s. She currently lives in Palm Desert, California.

In a conversation with Dr. Monty Barnard, now vocalist with the Sioux Falls Municipal Band, it was discovered that he had known Elizabeth when he was an undergraduate and she was a graduate student at the American Conservatory in Chicago. They performed together in chamber operas in the Chicago area and studied with the same voice teacher. Monty remembered that she had a beautiful coloratura voice.

Marciene Swenson Matthius

Marciene Swenson Matthius was the Band's regular, soprano soloist in 1944 and 1957-64. She made guest appearances in 1942, 1943, 1947, 1948, 1965, 1967 and 1979. She also sang with other former Band vocalists in 1994.

Marciene Swenson, born in 1924, in Inwood, Iowa, was one of four children. Her father, Swen Swenson, came from Norway at age four. Her mother, who died when Marciene was twelve years old, was also of Norwegian heritage. Her parents had musical talent, but Marciene said they didn't really use it, although Swen played the fiddle and her mother tried to teach Marciene piano. Marciene moved to Sioux Falls when she was seven.

It was at Washington High School that Marciene's interest in music developed. She sang leads in operettas and was a member of the chorus conducted by Boyd Bohlke, the school's vocal teacher. She never had private lessons – just a natural voice. She said she couldn't afford lessons but sang with records by opera singers. One of her uncles was a music director, and he'd give her pointers when he visited. He suggested that she take French to help get rid of her slight Norwegian accent. "I didn't have a strong Norwegian accent, but I think I hung on my s's ...

So I took French, and I think that helped me."

After high school, she took some classes at Augustana, but the funds ran out. She was a guest vocalist with the Municipal Band in 1942 and 1943 and a regular vocalist in 1944. During those years she also worked for area engineers who were building the Air Base. The starting salary was $125 a month, which she said was a lot of money then. She moved up to become secretary for the quartermaster, quitting in 1944 when she married a captain at the Air Base. They lived in Virginia but moved back to Sioux Falls in 1945.

She made guest appearances again with the Municipal Band in 1947 and became the regular soprano in 1957 following Anne Bryant's retirement. Marciene quit after the 1964 season "for personal reasons." She returned to sing a duet with Eugenia Orlich Hartig during the Band's sixtieth anniversary reunion concert in 1979 and to sing with other former Municipal Band vocalists for the Band's seventy-fifth anniversary concert in 1994.

Marciene and Ed Paul sang many duets together for Band concerts. She remembered Ed as being friendly and helpful.

Marciene Swenson Matthius, shown here in the early 1960s, was a regular vocal soloist in 1944 and 1957-64. *(courtesy Marciene Matthius)*

Marciene said that she didn't get to know the players very well. Part of that was due to having four young children at home. "Having a family like that, I'd necessarily come in just before my number, sing my number, and I'd leave." It was also because she was the only woman in the Band. She said that Henegar was a little protective of her and didn't introduce her to many players. "He arranged for me to ride with some of the more mature men when the Band went out of town!"

She said Henegar didn't like to spend a lot of time rehearsing. She would go to Monday night rehearsals, and if she got to go through her number a couple of times, that was about it. But she added that Henegar was easy to work with. "Russ was kind of laid back. He was pleasant and treated everyone with respect. I think of Russ a lot with the greatest amount of affection. He was so great about my being a soloist, always watching me and breathing with me and pausing with me, even if I sang it differently every time."

Although the pay of three dollars a concert was nice, the music was the main reason Marciene sang with the Band. Previous solo work had been with piano accompaniment, and she enjoyed having the entire band accompany her.

Marciene said that she preferred to sing light opera and said that she never was able to do modern songs (ballads, folk songs). A study of her first season indicated that she sang many light opera selections. They included: "Kashmiri Song," "Summertime," as well as Romberg's "One Kiss," "Deep in My Heart" and "Will You Remember." However, lighter selections also appear with equal frequency: "I've Never Been in Love Before," "People Will Say We're in Love," "It's a Grand Night for Singing," "Danny Boy," "When Day is Done" and "You are Free."

There were special challenges associated with singing outdoors. Marciene said the mosquitoes were terrible, especially at Terrace Park. And summer temperatures soared. She didn't think that acoustics were a problem and later learned to work with the old-style freestanding microphone, moving closer and further away as necessary to help control her volume.

McKennan Park was her favorite place to perform. It was there that her father had worked with the Park Department, patrolling during Band concerts. And it was there that she had heard the Band perform when she was twelve and thirteen years old.

Marciene added a touch of glamour to the concerts. She always wore formals or, on very hot days, pretty sun dresses. Originally it was her decision: "Since the men were all dressed in uniform and the audience had come here to listen to us sing and play, I thought, 'We're going to give you a show.' And I thought it was part of my obligation to present them with something a little bit out of the norm, so I wore a lot of formals." She said Henegar didn't stipulate her dress, but he later said that since she had set a precedent, she would have to continue dressing up. Marciene even had a private source in New York for designer gowns that were supposed to have sold for $2,000-$3,000. She said that she was able to buy them for "an acceptable price."

Marciene sang for weddings, funerals and anniversaries for many years in addition to owning The Galleria store in downtown Sioux Falls for thirteen years. She is now retired and living in Sioux Falls. She said people still remember her from her years of singing with the Band.

Marty Braithwaite

Although Marty Braithwaite never sang as a regular vocal soloist with the Municipal Band, she was well known as a vocalist in the Sioux Falls area and sang guest appearances in 1957-59, 1969 and 1973.

She was born in Ida Grove, Iowa, and was a 1943 graduate of East High School in Sioux City. Even as a young child, she enjoyed entertaining. She sang as a guest with the Sioux City Municipal Band at age fourteen and again in 1973.

Like other members of the Municipal Band, she remembered the heat, including the many blistering Sunday afternoons at McKennan Park. As the mother of two former Municipal Band members, Mindy (bassoon) and Tom (horn), she remembered that players were happy when the new lightweight uniforms were purchased to replace the heavy 100 percent wool uniforms. One of the hot days that she remembered was the performance of the "Blue Angels" on a July 4th, probably in 1973. Although the program doesn't mention the "Blue Angels," the concert was at Joe Foss Field where the air show would have occurred. She tried to help the Band members beat the heat by providing homemade ice cream at McKennan after one concert.

How did Marty prepare for performances? She said that it was easy for her to learn the words to the songs so she didn't have to spend much time on that but could concentrate on the vocal production. She would do some vocalizing before concerts and not eat heavily. Marty also did a lot of walking to build up stamina.

Marty sang in many musicals and operettas on stage and also sang with dance bands from her youth. Her favorite tunes are: "It Might as Well Be Spring," "Just in Time" and "Bill Bailey." As a contralto, Marty had difficulty finding vocal arrangements with band in the right key because most arrangements fit sopranos better. She said that singing with a dance band is different and that microphone facilities allow vocalists to be more subtle.

Marty lives in Sioux Falls.

Paul M. Wegner

Paul Martin Walter Wegner served as master of ceremonies and regular baritone vocalist from 1965-79. He made guest appearances in 1964, 1980, 1981 and 1982.

Paul did not have an easy life during his childhood years. He was

Paul M. Wegner was the Municipal Band's regular baritone vocal soloist 1965-79. This photo is from 1963. *(courtesy Vivian Wegner)*

born September 8, 1915, in Milwaukee, Wisconsin, to Gotthold and Meta Wegner. Paul's mother died of cancer when Paul was ten years old. His alcoholic father lost his job and the family home and was unable to care for him. Paul lived with relatives and continued his education (at several schools) through the eighth grade, graduating as salutatorian in 1929. At the age of fourteen, he got a job as a Western Union messenger, moved into a boarding house and enrolled at a vocational school where he studied commercial art one day a week for the next four years. He sang with the school glee club and the St. Stephens Arcadian double quartet and played organ every Sunday for the Evangelical Lutheran Mission. In 1934, at the age of nineteen, Paul moved to Towner, North Dakota, where he lived with and worked for an uncle who owned a grocery store. In 1936, he moved to Minot, North Dakota, where he joined the Lutheran Church choir and met his future wife, Vivian Beaudry. They married October 3, 1937, in Minot, North Dakota. On June 6, 1939, he sang for Crown Prince Olav of Norway and Crown Princess Martha during their visit to Minot.

After moving to Sioux Falls in 1941 he took voice lessons intermittently in the 1940s from Professor Clifford Olson of Augustana College.

Paul opened his own business, the Wegner Display Service (creating window displays for businesses). His son, Paul, Jr., traveled with his father in the 1940s and early 1950s. Paul, Jr. remembered his father practicing his voice warm-up routines as they drove between towns. Paul, Jr. also recalled his father at home listening to recordings of some of the songs he was trying to learn, as they were sung by the finest baritones of the day. He also remembered hearing him practice songs, sometimes accompanying himself at the piano with what Paul, Sr. referred to as his "hammer touch." He prided himself on never referring to note cards when he sang.

After a series of mild heart attacks, Paul opened an electric model train sales and repair shop at the back of his home.

Paul's musical involvement was extensive. In addition to being regular vocal soloist with the Municipal Band, he landed leads in various local musicals, including "The Sound of Music," "South Pacific," "Damn Yankees," "Showboat," "Little Mary Sunshine" and "Fantasticks." He also sang with the Sioux Falls Symphony Chorus, the First Lutheran Church choir and soloed for twenty years for the First Church of Christ Scientist. In 1968 he recorded twenty Lutheran hymns for the national television show "Lutheran Vespers," which was broadcast every Sunday evening. In addition, he sang for numerous weddings, funerals and other occasions.

Paul knew how many songs he had performed from memory over the years, but Paul, Jr. has forgotten what that number was — it must have been at least in the several hundreds. A list typed by Paul, Sr., found by Vivian Wegner, listed 125 different compositions programmed with the Municipal Band, 1965-77. Paul, Sr.'s notes indicated that he had sung four of them in both English and German, one in Hebrew, two in English and Latin. He had served as narrator with the band on six other compositions and listed nine new songs that he was hoping to do in 1978. He undoubtedly sang additional songs during his final two years with the Band and with his many other singing jobs.

Paul and soprano Eugenia Orlich Hartig, who both began and retired from the Municipal Band the same years, were honored at the final concert of the summer season at Terrace Park on August 19, 1979. For his final selections on that day, Paul chose "Letter from Camp" by Ponchielli at the McKennan Concert and "A Perfect Day" by Carrie Jacobs-Bond for his Terrace Park presentation.

In addition to his master of ceremonies and vocal responsibilities with the Band, he served as stage decorator for special events such as the Circus Concert, Children's Concert and the final gala season-ending performances at Terrace Park. This came easily for him because of his experience in creating advertising displays. He also designed the familiar Municipal Band logo of the bass drummer in 1965. This logo is still used on Municipal Band publicity and throughout this book.

Paul must have gotten some personal satisfaction from his sing-ing, but Paul, Jr. doesn't recall feeling that his father really enjoyed it — he always seemed to be trying so hard to do better. He also appeared to be so frustrated by his minimal formal training and other demands on his time that prevented him from achieving the skill level that he wanted. Nevertheless, Paul, Jr. believed that "Pop" reveled in the ap-plause.

Paul, Jr. remembered the last visit he had with his father at their family home, about a month before Paul, Sr. died of cancer August 25, 1986, at the age of seventy. He had been undergoing chemotherapy and radiation and, as a result, looked thin and wan and was nearly bald. His model train shop was open for business, so the Band's former vocal soloist was dressed in his bright red shop jacket and an engineer's cap to cover his now nearly-bald head. They were sitting in the dining room, which was adjacent to the shop, when "Pop" heard a customer come in. He immediately stood up and hesitated a moment while he squared his shoulders, adjusted his jacket and cleared his throat — as he would before any performance — then entered the shop to greet his customer. Band members can undoubtedly remember him doing that very thing as he rose to walk to the microphone.

Paul's friends and Band associates remembered him as dignified, courteous and a perfectionist. He was always prompt, had a wonderful sense of humor and took pride in his appearance. Municipal Band mem-ber Terry Walter remembered Paul's good sense of humor. One evening at a concert when, as the master of ceremonies, he was bothered by the children riding bikes back and forth in front of the stage, he said to them, "Tie it to a tree, feed it some oats, but don't ride it." Leland Lille-haug, who conducted during Paul's entire tenure with the Band, re-membered him as one who always came to every rehearsal and perfor-mance completely prepared. "He was a professional in every sense of the word — the consummate professional," said Lillehaug.

Paul and his wife, Vivian, had three sons who played with the Mu-nicipal Band: Tom, clarinet; David, trumpet; and Paul, Jr., bassoon and clarinet; and a grandson, Nathan, trumpet. It appears there never has been another instance of a father and three children (plus a grandson) in the Municipal Band.

Eugenia Orlich Hartig

Eugenia Orlich Hartig was the regular soprano soloist with the

Eugenia Orlich Hartig was the regular soprano soloist with the Municipal Band 1965-79. *(courtesy Eugenia Hartig)*

Municipal Band for fifteen years from 1965 through 1979, when she retired. She made guest appearances in 1980.

She was born April 23, 1923, a first generation American. Both her parents were born in Yugoslavia but met in the United States after her father escaped from Yugoslavia. Eugenia and a twin sister are the oldest, with three younger brothers. Chisholm, Minnesota, is her home town. Eugenia moved to Sioux Falls in 1957 after having lived in California and Nebraska.

Eugenia completed graduate work, taught at various locations and had numerous professional music and theater experiences before coming to Sioux Falls. Her advanced degree is from the University of Minnesota, with majors in English and theatre. She appeared as a vocalist with the West Coast Navy Band and Chorus, the St. Paul Civic Opera, the Minneapolis Opera and Shiek's Singing Sextette (at a German restaurant in Minneapolis). She was with the University of Minnesota touring theater and Minnesota Summer Stock. Eugenia taught English, creative dramatics and speech in Minnesota, California and Nebraska.

She moved to Sioux Falls in 1957, where she was a broadcaster with KELO-TV for twenty-five years, as well as an adjunct faculty member in the speech and music departments at Augustana College since

1964. She has served as a vocalist in many community groups: soloist with First Lutheran Church, as well as First Congregational Church and Mount Zion Temple. Many people in the area remember her best for her starring roles in numerous community musicals and theater productions, including, "The Merry Widow," "The King and I," "The Sound of Music," "Mikado" and "Show Boat." She also starred in many plays, including "Applause" and "Death of a Salesman."

Eugenia said that highlights of her musical career included appearing as vocal soloist with the Sioux Falls Symphony Orchestra (now South Dakota Symphony) under the direction of Leo Kucinski. She was the only local soloist chosen for the "Music of Lerner and Loewe" concert in 1969. Another memorable performance was as a soloist at the University of Minnesota International Yugoslav Conference (poets and philosophers invited to do readings), where she sang material from American musicals and Yugoslav songs that her mother and father sang to her.

Other awards and achievements include listings in *Who's Who in American Women* and *Who's Who in the Midwest*. She also received the 1974 Woman of the Year in Communication Award and other acting awards.

Eugenia said she had to convince then-conductor Leland Lillehaug to let her audition for the position of vocal soloist in 1965. "The first thing I'll tell you is that I got mad at him, I really did. ... He never asked me to audition for the Band. And I remember once he came to KELO. I said, 'Leland, why don't you ask me to audition for your Band. You know I'm good.' 'Oh, oh, do you want to?' And I said, '... Of course I want to.' 'Well come on, go ahead, you can.' And then I was asked to be their vocal soloist."

She said she had to learn to follow his conducting and not just sing the way she wanted to: "... He said, 'All right, come to my office, we don't have time for rehearsals.' ... I was singing, and he was doing like this [was looking at his watch], and I said, 'What are you doing?' And he said, 'I'm seeing how many beats to the minute you're going.' I said, 'I don't sing like that.' And he said, 'Well, you're going to sing like that for me.' I said, 'Leland, you know what? I put passion into my singing, and I'm not going to sing by a watch.' ... And then at the first rehearsal he said, 'That's not what you did in the office.' And I said, 'Do you suppose you could just follow me?' ... I learned ... I knew it but, I really didn't put it into practice. I knew as a vocalist without much rehearsal I'd darn well better follow the Band. And if there was any fooling around, I had to do it within the measure."

Lillehaug and Eugenia became colleagues and friends, she said. In addition to their association in the Municipal Band, the two worked together in community musicals and at Augustana College.

Like many performers Eugenia was nervous before concerts. "There were a lot of nerves. I get very nervous. Unglued." To overcome it, she said she got "over prepared." She would sit backstage, looking at her music, then a couple of seconds before she would go on she would go to the equipment van and warm up and vocalize, and then walk on stage and think, "Oh, God, what's my name, let alone what's the first word. And you'd just do it."

She, like other vocal soloists, spoke of special challenges with singing outdoors. She immediately mentioned the heat and said that she needed to have water readily available backstage. She was always afraid a bug would go down her throat, but one never did.

Eugenia, like her predecessor Marciene Swenson Matthius, wore formals and fancy dresses. Eugenia said her "uniform" was a long red/white/blue dress since the Band also wore red, white, and blue.

Her favorite musical medleys were "I Do, I Do," "Oliver," "Camelot" and "Fiddler on the Roof." Lillehaug said she sang them with flair and great feeling. But special arrangements were a necessity, and she said Lillehaug had a lot of tunes arranged for her. "Once we had a many nations [concert], and he arranged a couple of Yugoslav songs. ... He was very good about that."

Where did she most like to sing? The Fairgrounds concert on July Fourth was a favorite because it attracted such a big audience. But she still thought that the Terrace Park concerts were the most fun. She liked looking out and seeing many of the same people each Sunday night, waving at them and having them return the wave.

Eugenia pointed out reasons for the continued success of the Band: "... on a Sunday afternoon or Sunday night, families can come and just relax and hear beautiful music and they're not even aware that they're listening to classical music. And that's it: Hey, isn't this neat — we can bring our lunch, we can sit on a blanket, and if you told them it was classical music, they wouldn't come, a lot of them. And it's just like these people: 'I don't like violins, I don't like orchestra,' when on all these trashy dramas they watch on television, the background music is classical, with violins and instruments. ... It's listenable, and it's fun, and you smile. And look at all the people's children who are getting a musical education at the concerts."

Eugenia was admired by her colleagues. Dr. Monty Barnard, present baritone soloist and a colleague at Augustana College, commented, "Eugenia Orlich Hartig had a big following and was very professional." Perhaps Paul Hoy, secretary-treasurer of the Band, put it best in a letter dated September 3, 1975: "You put a touch of beauty, color, and 'the works' into every song you perform with the Band."

She has many fond memories of the Band. What she remembered most was the support of the members, especially Paul Hoy, Paul Bankson and Harold Krueger. "When I want to smile, I think about the days of performing, because it was fun. It was a period in my life that I will treasure always."

Dr. Monty Barnard

Any successor to vocalist Paul Wegner would realize that he had large shoes to fill. Conductor Lillehaug also understood Wegner's popularity and the importance of finding a competent replacement. Dr. Monty Barnard made guest appearances in 1980, and in 1982, he was hired as regular baritone soloist.

Monty's undergraduate work was done at the American Conservatory of Music in Chicago, where he also earned his master's degree. He received his doctorate from Northwestern University. He taught voice at the American Conservatory of Music from 1967 to 1969, then joined the faculty at Augustana College as an assistant professor of music. After coming to Augustana, Monty took leaves to study with Margaret Hoswell at the Manhattan School of Music and with Frank Corsaro of the New York City Opera. In May of 1981, Monty had the distinction of making his debut appearance at Carnegie Recital Hall in New York City. He is a member of Phi Alpha Sinfonia, the National Association of Teachers of Singing and the Music Teachers National Association. He presently is a professor of vocal pedagogy, music theory and voice at Augustana.

Monty said that he has enjoyed his tenure with the Band immensely and that he welcomed a chance for additional performing opportunities. The opportunity came when he was extending his performing capabilities in 1980-81 with studies in New York during a sabbatical leave from Augustana College. "As a regular soloist, one has to be ready to produce immediately, correctly and effectively," he said. Monty emphasized that no matter how casual the atmosphere, one still must sing his best. The relaxed atmosphere of the outdoor concerts helps him when he returns to the indoor concert hall.

He smiled broadly as he remembered one humorous incident which occurred at a rehearsal with the Band. He was singing a Mozart aria from the opera *Marriage of Figaro.* He sings of one of the characters, Susannah. During rehearsal the Band members followed that with "Oh,

**Dr. Monty Barnard became
the Municipal Band's regular
baritone vocal soloist in 1982.**
(courtesy Monty Barnard)

Susanna, don't you cry for me" — the Stephen Foster tune. At the performance, in jest, he changed the words in the aria and sang, "Susanna, don't you cry for me." Roma Prindle, the soprano soloist at the time, remembered the incident: "One time, the Band thought they had played a trick on Monty, but he had the last laugh."

Roma Prindle

Lillehaug had originally thought that a one-season search in 1980 might produce a female soloist to replace the popular Eugenia Orlich Hartig who had retired in 1979. Such was not the case. However, in 1981 a petite soprano named Roma Prindle sang guest appearances with the Municipal Band and subsequently was chosen as the full-time soloist beginning with the 1982 summer season. She sang through the 1985 season after which career opportunities took her elsewhere. She returned for guest appearances in 1986.

A native of Kentucky, Roma came to Sioux Falls to teach vocal music at Augustana College, occupying that position from 1980-86. She received a bachelor of arts degree from Transylvania College in Kentucky and a master's degree and course work for a doctor of musical arts from Hartt School of Music in Connecticut. She had studied voice and operatic coaching with noted teachers and had sung professionally with performances in thirty states. In addition, she taught at Westfield State College (Massachusetts), Clarion State College (Pennsylvania), James Madison University (Virginia), Hartt School of Music (Connecticut), and currently is an assistant professor at Morehead State University in Morehead, Kentucky, where she is acting chair of the voice department.

Prindle said the preparation for solo performances and one's personal life experiences are closely related. "The wonderful thing about being a singer is that part of preparation for performance involves living! Every day experiences are celebrated in every song we sing. The challenge lies in learning how to transform love and heartbreak, joy and sadness, beauty and anger, and spin them into a phrase that communicates the song's message to the listener. So a lot of my preparation for Sioux Falls Municipal Band concerts involved living — as fully as possible!" She said that a singer's personal life is reflected one way or another in performance and that, "It's a great catharsis, or therapy, to release these emotions into the air. It's a bit frightening, too, since you always run the risk of rejection or of being

Roma Prindle was the regular soprano soloist with the Municipal Band 1982-85. *(courtesy Sioux Falls Municipal Band)*

misunderstood. After all, you are up there virtually oozing 'your-selfness' all over the audience! But it is exhilarating to live on the edge. Some people drive race cars or jump out of airplanes. I sing!"

She has many memories from her years with the Municipal Band. The former Band soprano was nervous only twice during her appearances. Once was when the theme of a concert honored John Philip Sousa. Lillehaug had found a little-known song Sousa had written called, "Smick, Smack, Smuck," and asked her to sing it. "I hated that song! It was silly and the words were even slightly dirty. But I agreed to sing it."

She says that experience taught her a valuable lesson. Her dislike of it betrayed her and she forgot half of the words in the performance. Ray Loftesness, the master of ceremonies, laughed heartily as she left the stage! The second time that Roma was nervous was at Terrace Park when she was not feeling well and realized there were no bathrooms near. Fortunately, she made it through the concert.

She said that she and fellow vocalist, Monty Barnard, had a great relationship. Roma said that they had so much fun sitting next to each other during concerts and making wisecracks along with Lofty. "We had so much fun, in fact, that once we were scolded and told to behave on stage when we weren't singing!" Monty said that she was fun to be with and to sing with and that she had a fine voice.

Other memories include Sunday evening concerts at Terrace Park. Her statement is a synthesis of what many others have mentioned: "... meeting other band members walking down the hill, the sounds of laughter and instruments warming up, the smell of bug spray, seeing the terrace steps slowly fill up with people, joking with people before the concert, the transformation that took place as we took the stage, the sound of Lofty's voice over the microphone, the slow descent of darkness, and the final strains of "I'm from Sioux Falls, South Dakota" played by the Band. How I miss it all."

Eileen Bauermeister

Eileen Bauermeister was the regular soprano soloist during the greater part of the 1986 season. She graduated from Augustana College where she studied with Roma Prindle and, later, with Dr. Monty Barnard. Barnard remembered her as having a beautiful, warm, soprano voice. She married Jan Tjeerdsma. In 1993 she was teaching vocal music in the South O'Brien School District in Cherokee, Iowa.

Lisa Wiehl Grevlos

As a child Lisa Wiehl lived near McKennan Park and attended concerts there while in junior and senior high school. She envisioned herself singing on that stage. Her home was directly across the street from the park and they often listened from the front steps.

Lisa, a soprano, is a graduate of Augustana College. In 1987 she was appointed assistant choral director at Washington Senior High

School. After guest appearances in 1987, she began singing with the Municipal Band as a full-time soprano soloist the next year. Lisa has been the regular soprano soloist through 1994 with the exception of 1993 when she was on leave. During the school year of 1989-90 she studied at Northwestern University in Evanston, Illinois, receiving two master's degrees in 1991. She was appointed to the music faculty at Augustana College in 1993 with the rank of instructor.

Her most memorable experience with the Band was seeing the courage of Ray Loftesness, his serious illness unknown to most of the public, announcing his final concert at Terrace Park. Lofty often said "You're in good voice" after she had sung. Lisa appreciated that.

Lisa Wiehl Grevlos is the regular soprano soloist with the Municpal Band. *(courtesy Lisa Grevlos)*

She remembered the Children's Concert when she sang "Anything You Can Do I Can Do Better" from "Annie Get Your Gun." She sang a duet with Monty Barnard, who wore a Hawaiian costume and had coconut shells on his chest as if emphasizing the words of the song. Lisa and Monty sang duets on numerous occasions. "Barnard is very easy to work with," she said. He in turn said, "Lisa Wiehl Grevlos has matured into a wonderful singer."

Joan Van Holland

Joan Van Holland was the regular soprano soloist with the Municipal Band in 1993, substituting for Lisa Wiehl Grevlos, who was on leave. Van Holland, from Rock Valley, Iowa, received her master of music degree from the University of South Dakota, and her bachelor of arts degree from Dordt College in Sioux Center, Iowa. In 1993 she was working on an education degree at the University of South Dakota. Conduc-

**Joan Van Holland was the
regular soprano soloist with
the Municipal Band in 1993.**
(courtesy Joan Van Holland)

tor Ammann described her as having a strong voice, being well prepared, reliable and a pleasure to work with. He said the Band was fortunate to get Joan.

• • •

Vocal soloists have been part of the Sioux Falls Municipal Band
since its first season in 1920. Some have appeared just once with the
Band; others, like Ed Paul, have spent decades with the Band. With
their wide range of selections and personalities, vocalists have added a
unique dimension to Municipal Band concerts.

The following list includes vocal soloists with the Sioux Falls Municipal Band from 1920 through 1994. Names and years printed in bold face indicate regular vocalists. All other entries indicate guest appearances. Names are listed as they appeared in programs or newspaper articles. When a woman's last name is in parentheses, it is known to be a married name added after her appearance(s) with the Band.

Kathleen Arend	1965
Leslie Arneson	1951-1952
Janet Austin	1980
James Ballard	1921
Dr. Monty Barnard	1980, **1982-94**
Royal S. Barnes	1921
Robert Barnett	1981
Alice Barr	1923
Eileen Bauermeister	**1986**
Joyce Becker	1970
Roger Blunk	1965
Diana Borgum	1974?, 1975-1978, 1981
Marty Braithwaite	1957-59, 1969, 1973
Lyndall Brogdon	1957
Donna Brown (Robinson)	1943
Helen Brumbaugh (Hanson)	1945, 1949
Anne Bryant (Fisher)	1943, **1944-56,** 1957, 1979-81
Ricki Bryant (Anderberg)	1981
James Cabbell	1953-55
Donna Carlson	1950-52
Eugene "Gene" Cashman	1928-29
Margaret Barnard Cavitt	1954
Carla Connors	1980
Gerhard H. Dahl	1921
Roland "Rolla" E. Dickenson	1921,1932
William Dickenson	1938
Mrs. James Donahue	1949
Betsy Doyle	1975
Kristine Ann Farkas	1963, 1965
Marilyn Fialkowski	1959
Joan Forrette	1946
Nancy Gardner	1944
Lisa Grevlos	See Wiehl
Florence Gunderson-Soutar	1932
Mike Haley	1956
Helen Hanson	See Brumbaugh
Joyce Harris	1980
Eugenia Orlich Hartig	**1965-79**, 1980, 1994
Mary Harum (Hart)	1971
Dee Hemphill	1979
Betty Hoeger	1968
Pat Hoffman	1972
Mary Ann Hohman	1965

Ole Holm 1920-21
Faye Hurley 1987
Cammy Iseminger 1978
Sidney Jacobs 1937, **1938**
Arlene Julson 1943
Myrtle Stolt Kaponin 1941-42
Linda Lang 1979
Marion Larson 1943
Loren Loe 1942
Frances Loewen 1939
Dr. Olaf Malmin 1975-76, 1980-81
Norman Mathers 1929
Marciene Swenson Matthius ... 1942-43,**1944**,1947-48,**1957-64**,1965,
                                                                                          1967,1979
Loretta McLaughlin (Hartrich) **1941-43**
Robert Morris 1931
Hope Mosher 1965
Janet Whitfield Muxfelt 1944
Joyce Nauen 1977-78
David Nield 1980
Allen Opland 1945
Ertis Osterberg 1980
Julie Overseth 1972
Lyda Pallansch 1921
Ed Paul **1934-37, 1939-64**
A. Richard Petersen 1966
Ray Peterson 1980,1981
Shirlene Peterson 1976
Roma Prindle 1981, **1982-85**,1986
John Ross Reed 1922
Ruth Stene Reistroffer 1947, 1956
Gertrude (Mrs. E. M.) ReQua 1932
Connie Roth 1945
Maud Runyan 1941-43
Patricia Ryan 1939
Dean Schultz 1975
Harry Hadley Schyde 1936
Pat Sisson 1980
Gary Sona 1965, 1966
Tom Steever 1979
Elizabeth Swanson (Kuhn) 1955, **1956**, 1957-59
Marciene Swenson .... See Matthius
Ruth Tobin 1975-78
Nellyebelle Reardon Tolpo 1943
Mrs. R. L. Van Ellis 1929
Joan Van Holland **1993**
Joyce Van Steenwyk 1945
John Voss 1980
Kay Webster 1986
Paul Wegner, Sr. 1964, **1965-1979**, 1980-82
Donald Westerlund 1954
Mitzi Westra 1987

Julie Overseth, left, sang a Hawaiian song and played the ukulele with the Municipal Band in 1972. *(courtesy Sioux Falls Municipal Band)*

Hope Mosher, right, sang with the Municipal Band in 1965. She is shown in this photograph striking a pose from her role as Carmen in the Sioux Valley Hospital musical, which played at the Coliseum in 1964. *(courtesy Sioux Falls Municipal Band)*

11 Prominent People and Playing Pros

Most of the people discussed in this chapter would not consider themselves "celebrities." Yet these people are representative of many involved with the Sioux Falls Municipal Band, past and present, who went on to important and successful careers. Some made professional music their vocation, while others became well-known in other areas, including the military, major pageants and the media. Most viewed their association with the Sioux Falls Municipal Band as a formative experience in their progress toward success in their professional careers.

Jimmy Barnett

Jimmy Barnett, a trumpet player, was the leader of the "Jimmy Barnett Orchestra," one of the best known dance bands in the Midwest, playing an area from Chicago to Denver during the late 1930s and early 1940s. He is on the Sioux Falls Municipal Band player rosters of 1933-35.

In his early years Barnett showed ambition and ability, but his life probably was not that much different from the lives of many of his contemporaries. Born in 1906, he came from a family of five girls and five boys. According to his sister Margaret, their mother sang and played piano by ear, and all the girls played piano. Barnett graduated from Cathedral High School in Sioux Falls, went to Columbus College in Sioux Falls — formerly located on the grounds of the Royal C. Johnson Veterans Memorial Hospital — for about a year and later transferred to Marquette University in Milwaukee. Playing with dance bands helped Barnett pay his way through college.

He operated his own dance band in the Sioux Falls area until 1943. He employed Charles and Paul Reagan, who were members of the Sioux Falls Municipal Band in 1935 and perhaps even earlier. In 1943 Jimmy Thomas, another well-known dance band leader, fronted Barnett's band under the Jimmy Barnett name. When Thomas established his own band in 1946, Johnny Soyer became the playing leader of the Barnett band. Soyer is a Sioux Falls musician who had been the drummer in the band in 1943. Soyer bought the band and ran it until 1952 and still owns the library. Soyer said, "Jimmy Barnett was a duplicate of Lawrence Welk. He treated the members of his band very well. He was honest."

An *Argus Leader* story of May 19, 1947, called Sioux Falls the "approximate center of the world's biggest one-night stand territory for dance bands." It was reported that there were nearly forty territory bands playing within a 300-mile radius of Sioux Falls, including three bands from the city — Jimmy Barnett, Pat Boffman and Fats Carlson. Barnett is quoted as crediting Lawrence Welk with introducing the sleeper bus to this territory in 1934 and talking him into getting one in 1935. The sleeper bus enabled musicians to sleep as they traveled to the next town for the following night's gig.

After Barnett retired from the music business, he operated Sioux Falls Roof and Siding Company and ran a band booking agency. He joined the Civil Air Patrol and was killed in an airplane crash in Evansville, Indiana, on a routine mission on September 24, 1950, at age forty-four. He was a pilot, but his sister Margaret didn't think he was piloting that day. He is buried in the Barnett lot at St. Michael's Cemetery in Sioux Falls.

Robert Barnett

Robert Barnett sings professionally with the United States Field Band at Fort George G. Meade, Maryland, and has made numerous tours with them, sometimes singing in the Sioux Falls area. He made a guest appearance with the Sioux Falls Municipal Band in 1981.

Born in 1952, he is the son of Dr. and Mrs. G. L. Barnett of Sioux Falls. He was a music major graduate in voice at the University of South Dakota in 1974. Following graduation he performed at Disney World for one year. He then joined the Navy and was chosen to tour with the

Bicentennial Band and chorus for two years as a vocalist. He joined the Army Field Band and Chorus in 1977. He sang in France in 1994 for the D-Day observances.

Justin Berger

Justin Berger, who rose to the rank of brigadier general in the South Dakota Air National Guard, appeared as a tap dancer with the Sioux Falls Municipal Band with the Florence Bright School of Dancing group in 1936.

Berger remembered that it was "scary" to perform with the Sioux Falls Municipal Band. He recalled one occasion when he came on stage and was embarrassed when he tipped over a player's music stand.

Berger, born in 1922, was an outstanding athlete (football, basketball and track under coach Howard Wood) at Washington High School and said the balance he learned in dance helped him as an athlete. He graduated from the University of Nebraska and later joined the Air National Guard. He was a part of a four-plane acrobatic team that gave air shows from the East Coast to Wyoming. The leader of his group was Joe Foss, also a former Municipal Band member. Berger flew second in the formation as Foss' wing man.

Berger is now retired and lives in Sioux Falls.

James Burge

James Burge is a former part-time player in the Sioux Falls Municipal Band who found a career in a professional band. He was born in 1945 in Marion, South Dakota, and graduated from Marion High School in 1963. He received a bachelor of arts degree in music education from Augustana College in 1967. Although never a full-time member in the Sioux Falls Municipal Band, Burge served as a substitute player in 1964, 1965 and 1967. He served as band director in the Ida Grove, Iowa, school system from 1967-72. He joined the United States Army Field Band in 1972 and has continued to play with that group. He has served as principal alto saxophonist and now is the noncommissioned officer in charge of the concert band.

The United States Army Field Band is the official touring representative of the United States Army and is stationed at Fort Meade, Maryland. The band performs concerts throughout the nation and oc- · casionally overseas. Approximately 110 days are spent each year on tour. While on a national tour in 1993, the band played at Freeman, South Dakota, and in northwest Iowa. In July 1994, the Band returned from a thirty-day tour of England, Belgium, Luxembourg and Germany as the Army's representative for D-day celebrations.

William Byrne

William Byrne, a trumpet player with the Municipal Band from 1954-57, played with major jazz bands during his career. Born in 1936, he graduated from Flandreau (South Dakota) High School in 1954. After graduation, his friend and colleague in the Municipal Band, Bob Niblick, suggested that Byrne contact nationally known trumpet player Frank Simon about future training. Simon got him a scholarship to the Cincinnati Conservatory of Music, which Byrne attended from 1954-59. While at the conservatory he played as a substitute with the Cincinnati Symphony Orchestra. He was a member of the Naval Academy Band in Annapolis, Maryland, from 1959-64 and then played in New York from 1964-65. He was hired to play trumpet with the Woody Herman Band after a friend recommended him for an opening. He played trumpet with Herman beginning in August 1965 and served as the road manager from 1967-90. Byrne made about thirty albums with the Herman Band and played about ten times in Carnegie Hall. The Herman Band traveled forty-eight weeks per year, including tours to forty different nations. In addition to his membership in the Herman Band, Byrne played with Ralph Marterie in 1958, Larry Elgart from 1964-65 and did a national tour of "Hello Dolly" with Mary Martin.

Byrne, who now lives in Pierre, said that as a youth he wanted to study privately with Russ Henegar, but Henegar had quit teaching and sent him to Ardeen Foss. Byrne admired Foss, Henegar and Milt Askew and felt that playing in the Band was wonderful training.

Betsy Doyle

Vocalist Betsy Doyle made a guest appearance with the Sioux Falls Municipal Band in 1975 when she was "Miss Sioux Falls." Doyle has performed in the Chicago area for eleven years, appearing at such places as the Palmer House, the Swissotel, the Whitehall, Convito Italiano and the Fairmont Hotel. She currently is performing as a singer and keyboard player in Chicago's famed Pump Room.

Doyle graduated from Augustana College in 1978, with majors in

Betsy Doyle, a former "Miss Sioux Falls" and now a professional singer in Chicago, made a guest appearance with the Municipal Band in 1975. *(courtesy Betsy Doyle)*

music and French. She studied in France and performed two extended playing engagements in Düsseldorf and Wiesbaden, Germany.

Doyle recalled her performance with the Sioux Falls Municipal Band: "I can remember thinking what a nice benefit it was being asked to sing with a group I had heard on family park outings. I was terribly nervous, this being my first time singing a solo with a band. ... I had known Dr. Lillehaug through Augustana College, so I knew I was under excellent leadership. As expected, his cues and tempi gave me the security I needed to sail through my numbers. It was incredibly sunny the day of my performance, and I recall a feeling of joy while singing outdoors with such a great ensemble. To this day, I like nothing better than to stand up and sing with a band."

Tom Ellwein

Tom Ellwein was a trombonist with the world famous United States Marine Band in Washington, D.C., through most of his career. He returned to Sioux Falls after he retired from that group and played with the Municipal Band 1965-72 and 1975.

Mrs. Marge Overby, Ellwein's sister, recalled that music was very important in their home. Her brother, born in 1923, appeared to be musically talented as a young child and won all the contests in which he participated. Ellwein graduated from Bridgewater High School in 1940. His band director through his junior year was Ron Best followed by Municipal Band member Ardeen Foss during his senior year. It is interesting to note that Bridgewater, a relatively small town (population 633 in 1988), managed to attract some of South Dakota's best band directors. In addition to Best and Foss, directors included Marlin Brown, a Municipal Band member from 1937-43, and Elden Samp, who was secretary-treasurer of the South Dakota Bandmasters Association for many years. After high school, Ellwein attended the University of South Dakota for two years.

When Ron Best became a Coast Guard band director at Curtis Bay, Maryland, he called Ellwein, informing him about musical opportunities in the Coast Guard. Ellwein enlisted in the Coast Guard to play in Best's band in about 1943. After World War II, Ellwein returned to the University of South Dakota. When an opening developed in the Marine Band, Tom was selected and began playing immediately, serving from 1945 to 1963.

Ellwein liked dance band music as well. He played with Kai Winding, an internationally known trombonist and writer, when both were members of the Coast Guard Band. He also played with the Wally Jerome dance band in Sioux Falls.

Edna Ellwein said that her husband had difficulty making the adjustment to amateur groups after playing with the elite Marine Band. However, Leland Lillehaug, who conducted the Municipal Band when Ellwein was a member, said that Ellwein gave no indication of that and was a valued leader and was highly respected. Ellwein died in 1987.

Myron Floren

Myron Floren has been a household name in the area for decades. He is best known as the accordion soloist and frequent band leader on the "Lawrence Welk Show." He appeared as a soloist and with featured groups with the Sioux Falls Municipal Band during 1940-43.

"It was a big thrill for me to be with the Sioux Falls Municipal Band," Floren recalled. "It was fun to be accepted by the musicians. Henegar was a big supporter of me and gave me a lot of encouragement. Appearing with the Sioux Falls Municipal Band gave me added expo-

Nationally-known for his accordion playing on "The Lawrence Welk Show," Myron Floren appeared with the Municipal Band during 1940-43. *(courtesy Myron Floren)*

sure, and that helps one's career in the entertainment field." He said he enjoyed watching Henegar conduct, and when he observed him, he was reminded of what Sousa may have been like. Floren remembered seeing all the people who ate picnic lunches in the Sioux Falls parks and then came to the concerts.

Former Municipal Band members remembered Floren. Vocalist Anne Bryant told about a difficult car trip to Winner on the way to a playing job with Floren's combo (see Chapter 10). Floren said that he remembered the incident well: "It was the only time I have ever experienced vapor lock with a car." Former Band member Ronald Lane said about Floren, "The memory of one concert which seems to have stuck in my mind was a Thursday evening concert at McKennan Park. We had as soloist Myron Floren, who at that time was in Sioux Falls attending Augustana College. His playing was well received, as he was already quite a virtuoso on the accordion. He played two selections, and I still remember the title of one, 'The Dancing Tambourine.' Who would ever have thought he would one day be appearing on national TV?"

Floren, born in 1919, was a graduate of Webster High School in 1938, having moved to Webster from Roslyn after his father became a county officer. He came to Sioux Falls in 1939 to attend Augustana College, where he was a student about two and one-half years. From 1940 to 1944, Floren taught up to one hundred students per week and gave them one-hour private lessons. He organized an accordion quartet — which included his future wife, Berdyne Koerner — and an accordion band. Berdyne, who was thirteen or fourteen years old when she started playing accordion, studied with Floren for about five years. Floren also played with the dance band of Milt Askew, a Sioux Falls Municipal Band member.

Floren, who is living in Southern California, was elected to the South Dakota Hall of Fame in 1994. Although he's still on the road playing solo concerts, usually with backup bands, he is cutting back so that he can spend more time with his family.

Joe Foss

General Joe Foss, World War II flying ace, played baritone saxophone with the Sioux Falls Municipal Band from 1935-39. He was governor of South Dakota from 1954-58 and commissioner of the American Football League from 1959-66.

Foss was born in 1915 on a farm near Sioux Falls. He tried playing violin but didn't like it. He started saxophone in the seventh grade and said he loved it. His first saxophone instructor was Vernon Alger, Municipal Band assistant conductor. Alger was a disciplinarian. "You'd get chewed up and spit over your shoulder if you didn't do what he wanted," Foss recalled. Foss took lessons at Alger's studio between Ninth and Tenth Streets on Phillips Avenue on the east side of the street. At Washington High School his band director was Arthur Thompson (see Chapter 3). "Thompson ran a tight ship but we got along fine," said Foss. Foss graduated from high school in 1934.

Joe's father, Frank, had played the E flat alto horn, saxophone and violin. Frank played in the Orpheum Theater Orchestra with William G. Wagner, Sioux Falls Municipal Band horn player and 1920 charter member. Frank was accidently electrocuted in an accident in 1933.

Foss started playing with the Municipal Band in 1935. From his home in Scottsdale, Arizona, he recalled those days: "I was playing in the Municipal Band during the drought and Depression. It was so dry that a cow had to go on a gallop to get a mouthful of grass. Henegar was a good friend. He was a good director who didn't put up with foolishness. I earned four dollars a concert, so with three concerts per week that was twelve dollars. That was good money at that time. In 1936-37, I worked at Tolly's Service Station with Duke Corning and we earned twenty-five cents an hour." Foss enjoyed having his relatives Cliff and Donald in the Band, but was especially close to his cousin Ardeen. Although Foss' conductor in the Municipal Band was Russ Henegar, Foss said that he also remembered Charles "Charlie" McClung, who conducted the Municipal Band 1923-27. He said the Band taught him discipline, how to wear the uniform and how to work with lots of people. "In music you are part of a team," he said.

Foss' love of good music has continued. He still owns a straight soprano sax (some were curved) and an E flat alto sax but said that he always played baritone sax in the Sioux Falls Municipal Band. He recalled hearing Sousa's Band perform in Sioux Falls.

Former Municipal Band member Kenneth Lane had an association with Foss. Lane became a test pilot and when he arrived home following World War II, his friend Joe Foss talked him into joining the Air Force National Guard.

Foss has been honored in many ways, including by musical compositions. Former Municipal Band member Palmer Kremer wrote and scored "Major Joe Foss March" for concert band. Other composers honoring Foss included Washington High School senior Donna Moran ("American Ace," first performance August 13, 1944), F. E. White ("Major Joe Foss" played June 17, 1943) and Austyn R. Edwards ("Pride of the Marines", programmed August 7, 1955). During "Joe Foss Day" in Sioux Falls May 4, 1943, the Municipal Band played for a 11:30 a.m. radio broadcast, a 12:15 p.m. parade and a 2:30 p.m. program at Howard Wood field. More recently, Foss was elected to the Marine Hall of Fame and the South Dakota Hall of Fame in 1994.

Mary Hart

Mary Harum Hart, a soloist with the Sioux Falls Municipal Band when she was "Miss South Dakota" in 1970, has become a national figure in the entertainment industry and now co-hosts the national television program "Entertainment Tonight." She made two guest vocal appearances with the Municipal Band: July 20, 1971, at Heritage Park and on July 25, 1971, at Terrace Park. She sang "Love Story" and "What the World Needs Now is Love."

Mary Harum Hart, former "Miss South Dakota" and now star of the television show "Entertainment Tonight," sang with the Municipal Band in 1971. *(courtesy Mary Hart/Paramount Pictures Corporation)*

Born in South Dakota, Hart lived in Sioux Falls until the age of six, when her father's career took the family to Europe. After spending four years each in Denmark and Sweden, she returned to South Dakota to attend boarding school (Augustana Academy at Canton) and later earned a degree in English from Augustana College.

It was during her college years that Hart was bitten by the television bug. She recalled, "The first time I was on camera, I knew that's where I belonged. I felt that very, very strongly, right away." Following graduation from Augustana, Hart taught high school English in South Dakota for three years and began hosting a local talk show. Moving to Oklahoma City in 1976, she began producing and hosting the successful midday talk show "Dannysday," as well as numerous specials.

In 1979, Hart moved to Los Angeles to co-host the local edition of "PM Magazine." Less than two years later, she was selected by Regis Philbin to join him as co-host of his daytime series on NBC. In June 1992, Hart celebrated her tenth anniversary with "Entertainment Tonight." During that time she had met many of her favorite stars, including Julie Andrews, Dolly Parton, Mary Tyler Moore and Sammy Davis, Jr.

A talented singer, dancer and entertainer, she has performed in Las Vegas and Atlantic City. Hart frequently is tapped to sing the national anthem at major sporting events. She has sung at the White House and the Kennedy Center.

Along with her nightly appearances on "Entertainment Tonight," Hart has been a guest on the television shows "Late Night with David Letterman," "The Arsenio Hall Show," "The Today Show," "The Tonight Show" and "Circus of the Stars." Of special interest to South Dakotans is her July 1991 appearance with fellow South Dakotan Tom Brokaw when they hosted the nationally televised dedication of Mount Rushmore. In the summer of 1994 she was the narrator for "Peter and the Wolf" in the Flathead Valley Music Festival in Montana.

Most recently Hart revived her singing career with the release of the compact disc "Mary Hart Sings from the Heart." The disc features lullabies for children, including one written for her young son, AJ. Most of the profits will go to the March of Dimes.

Hart said her performances with the Municipal Band have not been forgotten, and that she has wonderful memories of the concerts. "I knew at that time that I wanted to be in show business, but then it was only a dream," she recalled. She added, "I hope I never lose that little extra adrenaline I get driving through the Paramount gates, the 'Gee Whiz' factor that says, 'I've come all the way from South Dakota and I'm doing this!' "

Sandra Kay Hart Golding

Sandra Kay Hart, "Miss South Dakota" in 1952, performed a solo twirling exhibition with the Sioux Falls Municipal Band on July 12, 1953, at Terrace Park. Sandra, who now lives in San Rafael, California, remembered the appearance and her nervousness. She had some burns, not yet healed, from a fire baton performance about a month earlier. The injury hindered her skills. However, she reported that the performance "went extremely well and I recall, as well, a sense of the feeling of support and encouragement that this professional music organization provided me." She remembered that being asked to appear with the Band was important to her because the Band had such a good reputation. She added, "The Band's summer concerts set a standard for South Dakota, and its guest performers were considered to be excellent. My parents, my brother Monte and I had attended numerous concerts because we all liked band music."

Sandra Kay Hart Golding has adult twin children — Natasha and Jesse. Both play musical instruments and although they make their homes in California, they have spent much time in South Dakota.

Sandra Kay Hart (Golding) was "Miss South Dakota" in 1952 and performed a solo twirling exhibition with the Municipal Band in 1953. *(courtesy Sandra Kay Hart Golding)*

Sally Jo Iverson

Sally Jo Iverson represented Augustana College when she won the "Miss Sioux Falls" pageant competition in 1967. In June of the same year, she was elected "Miss South Dakota."

She did a solo baton twirling exhibition with the Sioux Falls Municipal Band on July 21,1963, at McKennan and Terrace Parks. At the time of her Municipal Band performance, Iverson had just finished her sophomore year at Brandon High School. She had performed many times as a twirler and a percussionist but remembered holding the members of the Municipal Band in awe because of their great expertise on their instruments. Because of this she was very nervous as she approached her performance.

Iverson, now Mrs. Doug Wells, lives in Sioux Falls.

Jean Kopperud, who played clarinet with the Municipal Band in 1971, is a professional musician in New York City. She's shown jumping out of an airplane with her clarinet in this publicity photo. *(courtesy Jean Kopperud)*

Jean Kopperud

Jean Kopperud, who played clarinet with the Sioux Falls Municipal Band in 1971, is now a professional clarinetist in New York City. In early 1994 she appeared on the nationally televised program "Sixty Minutes" in a story about minority students at the Juilliard School of Music.

In addition to playing, she is teaching at Juilliard. She has three private students, a class of nine clarinet players and an experimental class called "On the Edge," a course to practice performing. It is a class modeled after an acting class and is aimed at dealing with playing music in public. "The class provides a safe place for people to open up and explore what is going on so that they can perform with their whole being and not shut down under pressure," Kopperud added.

At the time of her letter to the author in 1993, Kopperud was preparing for numerous public appearances. She played a recital which included music of Finzi, Brahms, Vaughan-Williams, Bernstein, Gershwin's "Rhapsody in Blue" and a new virtuoso bass clarinet work. This was followed by new music concerts in New York, San Francisco and Los Angeles followed by a trip to Chicago to do performance art. "I am playing the title role in *Peer Gynt* and Satan in a new work about creation. Then off to Rhode Island to play a nightingale. Works are in progress for a possible three-week tour of China of a mix between my old show 'Cloud Walking' and some 'straight' playing. Hope that works out!"

Kopperud, born in 1953, moved during her youth with her family from Lake Preston to Sioux Falls and graduated from Lincoln High School. She said that her first paying job was with the Sioux Falls Municipal Band through Leland Lillehaug, her clarinet teacher. She recalled that summer with the Band as being fun, and she felt proud that she was earning money playing an instrument. At that time she still was planning to be a veterinarian, so playing was her hobby. "Who could guess that twenty-two years later I would be a professional musician?" she asked. "Just look what trouble it has gotten me into! I jump out of airplanes with the thing [the clarinet], dance, swing from ropes, ride unicycles, eat fire — all in the context of being a clarinetist. I even play regular music!" She does indeed jump out of airplanes with her clarinet as a publicity photo attests.

She concluded, "The Sioux Falls Municipal Band was the beginning of a lifelong quest for perfection, risk-taking and continual pleasure as a New York City professional musician."

Dr. Loren Little

Dr. Loren Little is an ophthalmologist in Las Vegas, Nevada, but he plays trumpet about twice a week with top bands in that city. He has been trumpet soloist for numerous entertainers including Tony Bennett, Burt Bacharach, Jack Jones and Sammy Davis, Jr. Little told what membership in the Municipal Band had meant to him: "The classical training from the Sioux Falls Municipal Band was of vital importance in my being able to attain any status [as a musician] in Las Vegas. It helped me to do almost anything." That included total earnings of nearly a quarter of a million dollars during his part-time career in music plus residuals each year.

Dr. Loren Little, born October 28, 1941, remembered going to concerts as a child and smelling the wonderful aroma of popcorn at Terrace Park. On many occasions he and his younger brother, Tom, accompanied their father, Everton, a saxophonist with the Band, to the concerts. In his memory, Little can still see the people on the terraces showing their appreciation for the Band and can still hear the beautiful sounds produced by Wayne Krumrei and Harvey Eichmeier, then members of the euphonium section.

Little said that he played one concert with the Municipal Band in 1956 — he thinks he substituted for Curly Miller at a trust fund concert. In 1957, at the age of fifteen, he auditioned for conductor Russ Henegar, was accepted and started playing regularly. He had great respect for Henegar because of his accomplishments. He still has an earnings statement from a 1957 Music Performance Trust Fund concert. He said the $5.25 he earned went a long way in 1957, when the allowance for most children his age was about twenty-five cents a week. He recalled prices from those days included fourteen cents for a hamburger, twenty-one cents for a malt from Dairy Queen, fifty cents for a movie, ten cents for a bus ride and transfer, one cent for peanuts or gum at the gas station and fourteen cents for a gallon of gasoline. One year Little played principal trumpet for nearly

Dr. Loren Little plays trumpet about twice a week with top bands in Las Vegas. *(courtesy Sioux Falls Municipal Band)*

the whole season but on the annual photo he was asked to sit in the second chair spot for some reason. He said he can still see the anger on his face in the picture. He remembered the cornet soloists at that time: Robert Nason, David Wegner, Bill Byrne and Denis Kelly. Denis Kelly (see Dedication) was his best friend. As a high school student, Little studied with soloist Bill Byrne during the summers, taking three lessons per week. He admired Byrne's musical playing and accurate high register playing. Little thought that he was in an elite unit when he played with the Sioux Falls Municipal Band. After Little graduated from high school he couldn't get to Macalester College in time for the start of football practices because Henegar said he had to finish the Band season. He received bachelor's degrees from Macalester in 1963 and the University of South Dakota in 1965. Little later became a medical doctor (1967) and interned in Sioux Falls in 1968. He was the doctor in charge in the hospital when Henegar became seriously ill and died.

Little, a Lieutenant Colonel, served as a medical doctor in the Vietnam War and was seriously wounded shortly before he was to return home. He was awarded the silver star, purple heart, bronze stars and other medals during the course of his service. At his first concert with the Sioux Falls Municipal Band after returning from Vietnam, the concert ended with fireworks. When the first blast went off Little hit the deck, a reaction to his time in the war.

Pat O'Brien

Pat O'Brien, formerly of Sioux Falls, has been seen by hundreds of millions of viewers as a commentator for CBS sports. He danced at Municipal Band concerts in the late 1950s and early 1960s.

His mother, Vera Moss of Sioux Falls, recalled that Pat, born in 1948, seemed to want to dance as a young child. The late Lila Lee Christy, director of Tanglefoot Studio in Sioux Falls, started him at age four. Christy's students danced at many Sioux Falls Municipal Band concerts both for Russ Henegar and Leland Lillehaug. O'Brien said about Christy, "She was the greatest. We all loved her. Her son, Ted, was like my brother, and I spent a great deal of time at their home." O'Brien's mother played piano for all of Christy's student recitals in return for lessons for O'Brien. "It seemed very natural having my mother at the piano. She was my partner," he recalled.

O'Brien danced in contests in Iowa and Minnesota and received monetary awards for winning. He also danced in recitals while in high school. One of his major early appearances was at the Farm Show at the Coliseum Theater in the variety show where Ray Loftesness (see Chapter 13) was the master of ceremonies. O'Brien mentioned that Loftesness was a strong positive influence in his life.

Printed programs record that O'Brien danced at Municipal Band concerts between the ages of eight and thirteen. He danced on August 30, 1956 (at East Side Library Park with Joyce Becker); August 29, 1957 (at East Side Library Park with the Tanglefoot Studio Dancers and partner Joyce Becker) and September 3, 1961 (duet with Patty Strong and in a quartet with Patty Strong, Sandra Point and Nila Nester

CBS television's sports commentator Pat O'Brien tap danced with
the Municipal Band three times in the late 1950s and early 1960s.
He is shown here in about 1955 with dance partner Joyce Becker.
(courtesy Vera Moss)

at Terrace Park). O'Brien said appearing with the Band was different
from appearing in the many recitals: "It caused me to feel a special
sense of responsibility. And interestingly, the stage seemed bigger outside even though we had danced on the same size stages indoors." Because the "Star Spangled Banner" was always played at band concerts,
he said he still recalls some of those moments as he listens to the national anthem at the games he broadcasts.

Dance partner Joyce Becker, currently a real estate agent in New
Jersey, started dancing at age five and danced with him through grade
eight. Becker said that she got along well with O'Brien and that he was
an excellent dancer. She recalled that they practiced their routines with
taped music. She, too, enjoyed dancing with the Sioux Falls Municipal
Band and found it fun, rather than scary.

What did dancing do for O'Brien? "It gave me confidence, poise,
coordination and helped me conquer my innate shyness." O'Brien recently appeared on the David Letterman show. He said it wasn't an
easy task. However, he said, "If I am asked back, I'm going to tap dance

on his show." Can he still do it? "Once a hoofer, always a hoofer," was his quick reply.

Dancing isn't the only thing that people remember from O'Brien's boyhood. While in high school in 1964 he played guitar and sang in a rock band, "Bill Gregory and the Shouters." After high school O'Brien got a degree at the University of South Dakota and danced in the Strollers Show, which he also later directed. He was a political science major, and after college he went to Washington, D.C., to work for George McGovern. He then worked on the NBC nightly news and researched for David Brinkley and John Chancellor. He went to Chicago as an anchor and reporter and then to Los Angeles. His boss went into the sports area of broadcasting and took him along.

O'Brien currently lives in Los Angeles. He said that sometimes he reflects about the past during those minutes before a major game that he is working, such as at the World Series in 1993. He knows that when the camera rolls he soon will be seen by 130 million people over the medium of television, but he said, "I know that during my youth in Sioux Falls I was a part of the 'real America.' A night under the stars at a band concert is a part of the grass roots of our nation." Like Johnny Carson (from Norfolk, Nebraska), O'Brien is not hesitant to talk about his pride in his home town and native state. His voice had a special passion when he said, "So much of my life is in South Dakota. I've worked with kings, presidents, and The Beatles, but my heart is always in Sioux Falls and South Dakota. When I return home to visit, I stop at various places and talk to people." He recently made commercials for selected Sioux Falls business firms. The commercials are currently being aired on television. Undoubtedly the reason for his not being identified by name in the commercials is that the sponsors feel confident that viewers will readily recognize him.

Because CBS lost the contract for NFL football in 1994, O'Brien will be looking toward other projects and challenges. He plans to save time to play golf with some of his "name" sports personality friends — like Michael Jordan. And there is another former baseball great with a reputation for heavy partying from whom O'Brien once got this famous quotation when he interviewed him: "If I had known I was going to live this long, I would have taken better care of myself." Baseball buffs will remember that statement coming from Mickey Mantle, with whom O'Brien was going to play golf the day after the interview for this book.

O'Brien travels a lot with his job and often works on weekends. He did the Super Bowl and the Winter Olympics in Lillehammer in 1994. His wife, the former Linda Anderson, is from Sioux Falls. They have a seven-year-old son, Sean.

Ralph Olsen, Jr.

Clarinetist Ralph Olsen, who now plays professionally on Broadway, was outstanding as a clarinetist during his school days and credits the Sioux Falls Municipal Band with motivating him toward a musical career. Olsen, who played in the Municipal Band 1964-68, has a contract to play "Phantom of the Opera" in New York City until the play closes.

Olsen, born in 1946, spent his early years in Sioux Falls, then moved with his family to Pipestone, Minnesota, in 1960 and graduated from high school there. He attended Augustana College, graduating in 1968. His first season with the Sioux Falls Municipal Band was in 1964, Lillehaug's first season as conductor. Olsen played from 1964 through most of the 1968 season, playing assistant principal clarinet to Oscar Loe as well as playing solos. He said that playing in the Sioux Falls Municipal Band was his first exposure to a real professional atmosphere. He got paid for doing something he really loved and it gave him the feeling that this might be something he would want to do in his life, at least part time.

The Band required discipline and learning and this was very important to Olsen. "It wasn't 'Let's get together and play a few tunes,' but was serious musical endeavor. And it was fun, too. It opened my eyes," he said. In the Band, his major friends were Ev and Loren Little. He especially liked the setting of the Terrace Park concerts.

Scott Shelsta

Scott Shelsta is solo trombonist and trombone section leader of The United States Army Band, Washington, D.C. which he joined in 1974. He was a member of the Sioux Falls Municipal Band 1968-70 and in 1973.

Born in 1948, Shelsta is a native of Hayti, South Dakota. While at Augustana College, he studied with Tom Ellwein (see this chapter). Shelsta graduated from Augustana in 1971 and later received his master's degree from the University of Northern Colorado where he studied with Edwin "Buddy" Baker.

Shelsta's professional playing experiences include Bob Hope Specials, Wayne Newton Orchestra, tour with Glenn Miller Orchestra, Bobby Vinton Orchestra, Dean Martin Orchestra and appearances with Arthur Fiedler, Maxine Andrews, Ubie Blake, Nashville Now and Reba's Christmas Card (NBC). He has played for all United States presidents since

President Richard Nixon, and their guests, including foreign heads of state. He recently was a part of tours to Japan, Australia, Sweden, Norway and the Netherlands.

Shelsta recalled that being accepted as a member of the Sioux Falls Municipal Band was a new and purposeful venture for him as a 1967 Augustana student: "As a college musician, I was constantly competing with my peers for special placements, positions, ratings and grades. But the Sioux Falls Municipal Band was my first step into the real

world of music. I joined the local musicians' union and then auditioned for our conductor, Dr. Leland Lillehaug. Once in the Band, my outlook and attitude were immediately different. It was at this point in my life that I began to feel comfortable as a musician." Shelsta felt that members of the Sioux Falls Municipal Band turned his thinking and life into a more positive direction. He liked the idea that music has no respect for the age of a performer, and that he could be playing for a long time. He felt that beat the prospects of being used up by the time he was twenty-five years old in a sports program. This was from a man who played on a high school basketball team that was in the state tournament!

Now a trombonist with The U.S. Army Band, Scott Shelsta was a Municipal Band member 1968-70 and 1973. *(courtesy Scott Shelsta)*

"But it was the people in the Sioux Falls Municipal Band who made me feel welcome," Shelsta recalled. "What a comfortable feeling. Music was created so differently, so comfortably, more socially, more relaxed; and the job still got done." He liked being able to perform five to six solos in a summer or try them out during the off-season rehearsals. He said it would have been inconceivable to consider soloing like this in any college or university music program; the time is simply not there for any one student. Shelsta said that the Sioux Falls Municipal Band filled this void in his life and left him with skills that could be "tried and experienced" only in this type of professional hands-on setting. The idea of playing trombone, making adult friends, being accepted as a contributing union member, and getting paid were much needed steps in his confidence as an adult artist. Shelsta recalled that all of them touched him with their gracious, humble and sincere musical guidance. Even today, he continually relies on this rich and beautiful past as an enhancement to his way of life as an adult, not just as an artist. He still has many friends in the Sioux Falls Municipal Band who, he said, he will not forget.

Everyone in the Sioux Falls Municipal Band knew how difficult a life as a professional musician would be and is, but never once did Shelsta's family tell him, "You can't do it!" or "This profession is not for you!" He recalled that everyone was positive and supportive. "Where else could one get this type of education for future work?" he asked. "The caring and love I experienced were not for sale but were freely and willingly given by fellow union band musicians. When I now audition great musical talents, the spirit, resilience and resourcefulness of a successful musician's life are usually missing in their young lives. If I could only let them step into my ... past with the Sioux Falls Municipal Band, their lives also would be rich and constantly full of goals, interest, and a love of my 'mistress,' which is music."

Shelsta returned to Sioux Falls during the Municipal Band's 75th year celebration as the featured trombone soloist at McKennan and Terrace Parks on Sunday, August 7, 1994. He performed "Air Varie" and "Blue Bells of Scotland," both by Arthur Pryor, and the encore "76 Trombones." He was enthusiastically received by the large audiences.

• • •

Although these people have had a variety of life experiences, there is a common thread present — their love of music. Some have made professional music performance their career and still are involved in it. Others were involved with the Sioux Falls Municipal Band for a short time and went on to success in other vocations. All have indicated or demonstrated that the association with the Band and with music has been very important to them.

12 Notes About the Players

R egardless of the conductor's competence, the audience size, sponsor support and guest performer quality, it is the players who determine how good a musical organization will be. This chapter spotlights players who have made significant contributions to the Sioux Falls Municipal Band. Undoubtedly, there may have been others who contributed as much or more. The players highlighted below were charter members, members who played in the 1920s and early 1930s before conductor Russ Henegar, later players whose musicianship was admired, soloists and others who served as officers for several terms. Others were respected section leaders, played for a long time or contributed information which illuminated some aspect of the Band. Information regarding other members who rightfully might have found a place in this chapter are included in Chapter 10 (Regular and guest vocalists), Chapter 11 (Prominent people and playing pros) or Chapter 13 (Noteworthy people, tasks).

Each season, the players in the Municipal Band represent a cross-section of the community in terms of their work outside of musical performance. During 1983 the following vocations were represented: musician and music teacher, personnel supervisor, college student, bank employee, nursing home medication aide, band director, arts management person, restaurant employee, homemaker, marketing employee, nurse, secretary, teacher (non music), newspaper circulation manager, telephone equipment engineer, recording studio owner, child care employee, high school student, factory employee, office assistant and retired newspaper circulation employee. Two years later, the list included additional job descriptions: management information specialist, professional musician, bee keeper, credit manager, music store employee, law office manager, clerical worker, bookkeeper, college music professor and radio show host. During the years the members have represented most of the major vocations in the city. Few doctors or lawyers have been members of the Municipal Band, probably because of the time demanded of the musicians. However, the recently established Augustana/Community Band, operating with a different schedule, has enabled several very competent people in those professions to begin playing again. As in most organizations, there has been a core of veteran players who have played for many years, supplemented by those who play for only a short time.

Players leave the Sioux Falls Municipal Band for a variety of reasons. Most leave because they move due to job transfers or because they are seeking employment elsewhere. Others have played for a long time and are either burned out or choose to retire. Others have changes in family responsibilities that no longer allow them to attend the seventy to eighty concerts and rehearsals each year. Occasionally someone quits because he or she is dissatisfied with the conductor, a fellow player or a policy. Some have been terminated by the conductor and Board because of problems with their performance or conduct. Most appear to leave regretfully. A sampling of resignation letters in the files include statements such as, "I have enjoyed and cherish my six-year association with the Sioux Falls Municipal Band. Each year I look forward to the time when rehearsal and concert activity begin. I likewise cherish the friendships that I have developed during my association with the Band" (Janet Bruns Hallstrom, who later rejoined the Band). A 1980 letter complimented Sioux Falls for the support of the Band with, "It is really great that Sioux Falls provides an opportunity for musicians to keep playing after the high school band days are over. I only hope that the fine tradition the Band has established for sixty-one years [in 1971] can continue for at least another sixty-one years" (Robin Steinke). Another, who became a professional artist, wrote, "As excited as I am about moving towards new experiences in art and music, ... I also feel bittersweet about leaving this fine organization. The last five years in the Band have taught me many fine things about musicianship, character and band camaraderie that I'll never forget. Thanks again for the opportunity to play, the friendships and the inspiration to always play good music" (Brad Widness). A young person who later became a prominent school band director in the state wrote, "My primary objective as a teacher is that of learning and growing as a practicing professional musician and to pass on that current knowledge to my students. The

Band provided that for me in my rather short stay. The artistic quality and professional atmosphere was greater than any group I have ever been a member of, and I will miss that aspect most" (Fred Ellwein).

• • •

Players included in this chapter are grouped where they played the most years or, in some cases, in the period during which they entered the Band. They are listed alphabetically within the following time periods:

- Charter Members (1920)
- Players from the Early Years Through 1934.
- 1935-63: The Henegar Years.
- 1964-86: The Lillehaug Years.
- 1987-1994: The Taylor and Ammann Years.

Charter Members (1920)

No rosters remain from the early years, but the names of twenty-two probable charter members were gleaned from Band Board minutes, newspaper articles and interviews. In addition to the sketches below, information on charter members Guy Anderson and Henry T. Hanson is found in Chapter 13. No further information was found on charter member Sidney Drew (a 1920 Board member). Much of the information on early members came from *Argus Leader* obituaries.

Austin K. Bailey

Austin Kerr "Bill" Bailey, tuba, played with the Municipal Band 1920-52. He was born September 29, 1871, in South Salem, Ohio, and moved to Sioux Falls in 1908 from Anderson, Indiana. He married Josephine Dougherty on January 18, 1915.

A 1948 newspaper article told about his musical experience: Bailey "helped pep up the sixth and seventeenth regiments of the Ohio National Guard in 1890, performing at the Chicago world's fair in 1893. He was in the Indiana Union Traction Co. band, under Director George Payson, from 1900 to 1904 and for a time was with the Robinson circus. He has played in various Sioux Falls bands since 1908."

Bailey worked for the Detlie Horseshoe Company in Sioux Falls

1908-11, and as a machine operator at Jordan Brothers for the next forty years, retiring in 1951.

He was president of the Sioux Falls Musicians Association Local 114 1923-53. He had been a member of the local Elks and El Riad Shrine Bands for many years until illness forced his retirement in 1952. He was a member of First Presbyterian Church.

Bailey died August 15, 1953, in Sioux Falls.

Austin Bailey was a charter member of the Municipal Band, playing through 1952. *(courtesy Doris Dean)*

Frederick John Ludwig Beecher

According to Fred Beecher's daughter, June Beecher, who died shortly before publication of this book, her father was a charter trombone player in the Municipal Band, and her brother Curtis later played percussion in the Band.

A 1957 centennial edition of the *Argus Leader*, called Fred Beecher "probably the best-known man in the entertainment business." Beecher managed the New Theatre, the Majestic and Orpheum Theaters and the Coliseum during his career in Sioux Falls.

More about Beecher's early years comes from *Theatre in Spite of Itself – A Century of Action on Sioux Falls Stages Cues Its Schools' Evolvements in the Fine Arts*, by the late L. R. "Barney" Kremer. Kremer wrote that Beecher was "born in Illinois in 1879, came to Sioux Falls with his parents, Mr. and Mrs. Jacob Beecher, at the age of two." Robert Beecher, Fred's great-nephew, said the family went by "Becher" until approximately World War I.

Kremer wrote more about Fred Beecher: "Fred saw his first plays at Germania Hall. An early job was water boy for the concrete gang on a construction crew. At night he found his way to the Booth [Theater], where he performed any necessary task."

In addition to playing in the Municipal Band, Beecher was one of the fourteen original members of the El Riad Shrine Band, formed December 6, 1910.

Beecher died September 27, 1947, at the age of 68.

Oscar G. Dahl

Oscar Dahl, trombone player, was documented as a member of the Municipal Band 1920-22 but since the rosters are not available from that period, he may have played longer.

Dahl was born August 25, 1886, in Sioux Falls. He was married June 3, 1911, to Laura Johnson. He worked at Fenn Brothers before working for thirty-six years at the post office (1919-55).

Dahl died October 2, 1965, in Sioux Falls.

Dr. E. O. Dietrich

E. O. (Ernest) Dietrich, born October 26, 1887, in Sibley, Iowa, was probably a charter member trombonist who evidently played for several years, dropped out for many years and played again 1951-56. Marlin Brown, a Band member from the 1930s now living in Sioux Falls, said that Dietrich was a dentist and that the last patient he worked on before he retired was Marlin's mother. Dietrich was married to Marie McGilvray. According to Brown, Dietrich had one adopted son, Robert, and one adopted daughter.

He died March 17, 1959, in Sioux Falls. He was buried at Hills of Rest Cemetery.

Jacob "Jake" Helfert

Jake Helfert, trombone, played with the Band 1920 through early 1946 when he died.

Helfert was born January 13, 1883, at Sabula, Iowa. He came to Sioux Falls with his parents when he was four years old. He married Edith Wright September 11, 1906. One of Helfert's sisters was married to another Municipal Band member, Ray Pruner.

More about Helfert comes from an article from the *Argus Leader*, July 3, 1920, about the El Riad Shrine Band, of which he was a member. The article told about him during their 1920 trip to Portland, Oregon: "Jake Helfert was the clown of the return trip. He kept everyone around him in a good humor by his witty sallies, and through British Columbia when we went through so many tunnels, he was a busy man. He declared that he was the protector of the women on the train during these emergencies, and apparently he played no favorites for they all agreed that Jake was strictly on the job and he even made the young bloods of the party who had been diligently rushing numerous girls, look to their laurels."

In addition to membership in the Municipal Band and Shrine Band, Helfert played with earlier city bands and Elks bands and was a member of the Sioux Falls Musicians' Union.

Helfert started working for the post office January 10, 1905, working there for forty-one years. His obituary called him "Sioux Falls' genial mailman," saying that "for twenty years [he] extended his friendly greetings on the Phillips and Main Avenue route of business places, as he made letter deliveries." He was featured in the philosophical sayings of a section called "Jake the Mailman Says" in an *Argus Leader* Sunday newspaper column, "The Party Line."

He died July 28, 1946, in Sioux Falls.

Charles Hobson and Harry Hobson

Charles and Harry Hobson were father and son, according to William Hobson, a Sioux Falls real estate agent and relative. He also said the family moved to California, and Charles died in 1939.

Raymond G. Hoyt

Raymond G. Hoyt played saxophone and bass clarinet with the Band 1920-54.

Hoyt was born February 20, 1876, at Orfordville, Wisconsin. He lived in Mitchell, South Dakota, 1882-90 and studied violin in Chicago before moving to Sioux Falls in 1901. He was married July 18, 1904, in Sioux Falls. More about his early years comes from a 1948 *Argus Leader* article: Hoyt "was a violin pupil of Emil Richter in Chicago for four years, coming to Sioux Falls in the fall of 1901. He traveled with a dance orchestra until Thanksgiving of 1902 when he started his own orchestra [Hoyt's Orchestra] here. He conducted the orchestra at the New Theatre for eight years, played a concert every Sunday at the Cataract Hotel for eleven years and played at the Orpheum Theatre for about four years."

Hoyt was instrumental in founding the Sioux Falls Musicians' Union, was concertmaster of the Sioux Falls Symphony Orchestra and worked as a piano tuner.

In addition, he was one of the oldest members of the Sioux Falls Elks Club, having joined in 1903. He was a member of St. Joseph Cathedral. Hoyt died April 1, 1959.

Andrew K. Indseth

Charter member Andrew K. Indseth, a trombone and baritone horn player, played in the Band 1920-33. Records indicate that he soloed 1924-26, 1929, 1931 and 1933.

Indseth served as a band director for area bands. An *Argus Leader* article of December 21, 1929, told of the brass quintet consisting of Indseth and his four sons entertaining Christmas shoppers on Phillips Avenue and elsewhere in the business district as part of the newspaper's Christmas music program. The article described Indseth as "director of the East Side Community Band and ... bands at Bridgewater and several other neighboring towns." He conducted the Humboldt-Montrose combined school band at a shared concert with the Municipal Band at Terrace Park on August 25, 1935.

Walter L. Kleinheinz

Walter Kleinheinz, a tuba player, was a Municipal Band Board member during the Band's first year in 1920. He became president in 1926 and played in the Band through 1933.

William D. Meyer

William Daniel Meyer, clarinet, was a charter member of the Sioux Falls Municipal Band.

He was born in 1879, married in 1902 and had five children: Roy, Marie, Marguerite, Hazel and Florence. The family moved to Sioux Falls about 1910, living at 126 North Spring Avenue. They later moved to 1025 West Fifteenth.

Meyer was a stone monument carver who worked for Ballard Monument for many years. A photo dated February 1939 showed that he also owned his own monument works.

According to his daughter Florence Meyer Brown, 88, who lives in Sioux Falls, Meyer was kind, generous and good to his family. Her dad was a friend of conductor Russ Henegar and of charter member Henry T. Hanson. Brown said that Hanson, a neighbor living on Grange Avenue, gave her father a ride to the concerts because they did not own a car. Brown said that her father was a musician at the State Theater, the Orpheum and the Strand.

Former Band members recalled Meyer's musical skills. Former clarinetist Ronald Lane (see this chapter) said that he took lessons from Meyer for at least two years. Lane admired Meyer's technical ability and was continually amazed at Meyer's ability to play anything put in front of him. Lane said that Meyer seemed old when he knew him, didn't speak very clearly and was hard of hearing. Lane's lessons undoubtedly occurred before Lane joined the Band in 1937, so Meyer would have been in his 50s.

Charter member Willliam D. Meyer played clarinet with the Band 1920-40. He is shown here in 1902 when he was married. *(courtesy Florence Brown)*

Former Band member Donald Lias described Meyer as a "machine" in terms of his great playing technique and said that Meyer played with a "German" type clarinet sound.

Lias remembered Meyer's stories about other musicians. Meyer spoke often of a Rudolph Ringwald, whom he apparently knew and considered an absolute virtuoso on the clarinet. He told the story of Ringwald trying out for some musical organization. It seems Ringwald took the music from the stand and promptly turned the music upside down and played the entire composition — and what beautiful tone! "Ringwald had tone that would knock your ears off," Meyer had said.

Meyer also liked to tell of his experience playing alongside the composer and clarinetist Rosenkranz. It wasn't clear what band that was, but it may have been that Rosenkranz was a guest of the Sioux Falls Municipal Band or was a professional musician who played in one of the theaters.

Meyer bought mail order instruments and sold them locally. He once ordered a clarinet for someone and told the supplier that it had better be well in tune or he would send it back "right now." He would order reeds by the box for anyone who wanted to buy them that way.

Apparently Meyer had difficulty marching with the Municipal Band in later years, because Band minutes of June 26, 1939, indicated that he and H. T. Hanson were asked not to appear in parade. Minutes from 1940 indicated that William was entirely incapacitated and could no longer play with the Band. He was called "a faithful member of the Band for many years. ..." Meyer died June 20, 1946, after a long illness.

In addition to Florence, two of Meyer's other daughters, Marguerite Meyer Block and Marie, also live in Sioux Falls.

Roy W. Meyer

Roy William Meyer, clarinetist and son of charter member William Daniel Meyer, also was a charter member, according to his sister Florence Brown.

Roy was born January 26, 1903, at Stillwater, Minnesota. He moved with his family to Sioux Falls in 1910. His obituary said that in addition to playing with the Municipal Band, he worked as a card dealer at various clubs. Florence said Roy went to high school for two years but didn't graduate. Former band member Ronald Lane remembered that William Meyer had told him that Roy had attended a music school in Minneapolis run by Clarence Warmelin, principal clarinetist with the Minneapolis Symphony.

Roy died May 13, 1976, in Sioux Falls at the age of 73.

Roy Meyer, son of charter member William D. Meyer, also was a charter member. *(courtesy Marguerite Block)*

Lee Mitchell

It is thought that Lee Mitchell, trombone, played from his charter year through 1941 but there are some years in the middle period that cannot be verified. He was president of the Band in 1921 and 1924, vice president in 1923 and a member of the Board 1931-34. He soloed in 1930 and 1933.

John "Jack" M. Newton

Cornet player John "Jack" M. Newton played with the Municipal Band 1920-45. He was working for National Tire and Repair Company when he first played with the Band.

Cornet player Jack Newton was a charter member of the Municipal Band. *(courtesy Doris Dean)*

In 1981, Newton — believed to have been the only living charter member at that time — gave a short telephone interview about the Municipal Band. Newton said that although he was not a professional musician, he played both trumpet and cornet with the Municipal Band for twenty-six years: "I played, sort of moonlighted, ... and I had played down here in the East before and ... then when I went out West I was in the automobile business for a good many years." Newton said there were twenty-five to thirty men in the band, mostly middle-aged, older professional players and businessmen. He said that the first concerts were very successful: "Big crowds and it was very, very nice. The music was not rock 'n' roll in any way whatever. All the popular tunes that came out were played and marches and also old show tunes of all types." He said the band spent three hours a week in rehearsals: "We first started in the old City Hall which was just east from the City Hall that's there now. There was an old building, a big old building [City Auditorium], and then a hotel, and that was torn down, when the new one [City Hall] was built. Then we had a nice band room up there."

Oril "Pic" W. Palmer

The earliest record found of Oril W. "Pic" Palmer's being in the Municipal Band was a 1922 newspaper article. But Ralph Tyler, who played flute in the section with Palmer beginning in 1953, said that Palmer had said he was a 1920 charter member on flute and piccolo. Palmer's obituary of 1974 suggested that Palmer had been a charter member. The obituary stated that he had played in the Municipal Band for forty-five years; however, since he retired from the Band in 1963, the maximum number would have been forty-four years even if he had been a charter member. Band programs show him as a frequent soloist, especially during his early years.

Palmer was born April 26, 1898, in Minneapolis. He married Mina Jensen September 19, 1921, in Luverne, Minnesota.

Former Band members remembered Palmer for his playing and his personality. According to Curly Miller, Palmer had a fine ear and was adept at playing harmonies without the music. Ralph Tyler remembered Palmer getting tired of vocalist Ed Paul singing "Mother Macree" a lot and saying he'd do something desperate if Ed sang that number again. Don Lias said that Palmer "had the manners of a wart hog but he could really play!"

Palmer's musical experiences included playing with bands and working in an instrument repair shop. He played clarinet and sax with the Pete Erickson Band, with the Augustana Symphony and in local theaters. He owned the Midland Sax Shop, an instrument repair shop at 302 South West Avenue in Sioux Falls, and invented a new type of flute which had bigger tone holes. He thought the tone was larger than that produced by the traditional flute and hoped that his invention would be bought by a major flute company. His hopes were never realized.

Palmer retired in 1973. He died in Sioux Falls, October 3, 1974, at the age of seventy-six.

Walter F. Rittman

Walter F. Rittman was a horn player and charter member of the Municipal Band.

Rittman was born July 14, 1889, in Brookings County. He attended

Brookings schools and South Dakota State University in Brookings, after which he farmed for several years. He moved to Sioux Falls in 1916 to attend business college and work in the federal meat inspection division. A newspaper article of 1948 reported that Rittman "began playing the cornet in the Brookings junior band when twelve years old." In addition to playing with the Brookings city band for nineteen years, he played with the South Dakota State University band and symphony orchestra. He also was a member of the Sioux Falls Symphony Orchestra in 1916 and 1917.

Rittman served in World War I, and when he returned from the war in 1918, he was employed by John Morrell & Co. in the plant operations division and later in the job and rate analysis department. He married Martha Knodt April 20, 1932, in Sioux Falls. He was a member of the local Musicians' Union and Our Savior's Lutheran Church.

Rittman died May 5, 1949, in Sioux Falls.

Arthur N. Sears

Band minutes indicated that Arthur N. Sears, clarinet, was a charter member of the Band, playing through 1934.

Sears was born in Illinois. He married December 20, 1889, in Sioux Falls. In 1921 his occupation was listed in the city directory as director of the Sears Orchestra. His obituary indicated he was a compounder with the Brownell Oil Corporation until shortly before his death. Sears died September 11, 1934, at the age of 54. Municipal Band Board minutes of December 3, 1934, told of his death: "Members of the Band were shocked to learn of the sudden death of Arthur N. Sears on September 11. Art was a member of the Municipal Band since its organization and had played in local bands for many years prior to that. He was a faithful member and although he was quiet and had little to say when with the Band, he was always a friend to all."

William G. Wagner

William G. Wagner was a horn player with the Municipal Band from its inception through 1957.

He was born February 5, 1871, in Dubuque, Iowa and attended school in Dubuque.

Wagner was active in music for fifty years. He studied music in

New York before moving to Sioux Falls in 1889, playing in what was described in a 1948 *Argus Leader* as "the community's first band, directed by J. B. Reynolds." Research has indicated that there were several early bands that, at one time or another, were called "the first band." Wagner studied violin at the Chicago Conservatory of Music in 1894. In 1900 he joined the C. A. Elmendorf orchestra in Sioux Falls and studied violin with Frank S. Henes. He played in the Booth Theater and taught guitar, banjo and mandolin at the Sioux Falls Conservatory of Music. As an orchestra leader, Wagner had the honor of opening all the vaudeville houses in Sioux Falls such as the New Theater in 1898, Orpheum in 1911, Majestic in 1918 and State in 1926. He traveled one season with the "Birth of a Nation" show and was first violin with Stout's Band. According to the February 1905 Lutheran Normal School *Mirror,* a monthly publication, Wagner conducted the "reorganized" Lutheran Normal School Band consisting of sixteen pieces. Although it is not

Horn player William G. Wagner played with the Municipal Band from 1920-57. *(courtesy Sioux Falls Municipal Band)*

clear if Wagner was just beginning as the conductor at that time, the *Mirror* stated that as of that month the instructor was Peter Myhre. Lutheran Normal was located on what is now the campus of Augustana College and merged with that institution when it moved to Sioux Falls from Canton in 1918. At one time Wagner sold flowers and vegetables raised in his greenhouse next to his home at 643 South Main Avenue. Wagner, also a member of the Sioux Falls Musicians' Union and the Shrine Band, died on April 3, 1960, in Sioux Falls.

August C. Weich

Very little is known about charter member August C. "Gus" Weich. He was born in Scotland, South Dakota, and was accepted into the Sioux

Falls Musicians' Union on August 22, 1915. His instruments were cornet and horn. His wife's name was Lydia.

Players From the Early Years Through 1934

Information was found about four persons who were players during the Band's early years but who could not be positively identified as charter members. John L. Johnson played under conductors Charles F. Emmel and Charles F. McClung; Everett Zellers under Otto H. Andersen and Russ Henegar; and Orral O. Jackson, Sr. under Charles F. McClung, G. C. McClung, Andersen and Henegar. Marson Metzger played under Andersen and Henegar but not for any of the previous conductors.

Orral O. Jackson, Sr.

During his career with the Sioux Falls Municipal Band, O. O. Jackson, Sr. served as Band president six years (1928 and 1944-48), one of the longest number of years in that position of any member. He also served on the Board in other capacities through the years. He played tuba in the Band for thirty-three years (1925-57), until he retired and moved away from Sioux Falls.

His son, Orral O. Jackson, Jr., of Louisiana, Missouri, wrote that he remembered going with his dad to many concerts and rehearsals. His father had lost a leg in World War I, and the younger Jackson wanted to help him whenever he could. He remembered Sunday afternoons at Sherman Park and Sunday evenings at either McKennan, Terrace or East Side Park, and Thursday rotating between the last three. He said that his father received one dollar for rehearsals and three dollars for concerts.

The elder Jackson had a variety of educational, music, Army and other work experiences during his life. Born July 25, 1895, he started his music career in 1913 or 1914 traveling with a circus, playing with the Mighty Haag shows and the Gollmar Bros. shows. He told his son that one of the directors of a circus band he played with was a Mr. James, who was father of Harry James, the famous dance band leader of the 1930s and 1940s, and husband of movie star, Betty Grable. In 1915, he was called to serve in the Army and lost his leg in France just days before the Armistice. The younger Jackson said that at war's end, his father probably thought making a living as a musician wasn't going to take care of his new wife and son (Orral, Jr.), so he went to college at the University of Missouri and Washington University in St. Louis. He moved to Sioux Falls in 1923 or 1924 and started a grocery store (Little Soo Grocery Store) on Phillips Avenue, a couple buildings up from the old Palace of Sweets restaurant. In 1926, he went to work for the Northern States Power Company and retired in 1957. Jackson also played from 1931 to 1957 in the El Riad Shrine Band.

After Jackson retired, he moved to Oklahoma where he stayed until his wife died in 1960. He then moved back to the old home in Louisiana, Missouri, and married a cousin of his late wife. Jackson died in 1962.

John L. Johnson

John L. Johnson, the conductor of the Moose Band in Sioux Falls in 1918, is documented as having played cornet in the Municipal Band in 1922, 1923 and 1926. He conducted the Band for conductor Charles McClung on June 21, 1923, and served as assistant conductor. He is listed as a "musician" in the city directory of 1919. Minnehaha County records do not indicate that he was born in the county but he is recorded as having died February 28, 1935.

Marson Metzger

Marson Metzger, born 1914, is one of two living persons located who played in the Sioux Falls Municipal Band as early as 1933. He played cornet 1933-34 for O. H. Andersen, whom he described as a "good conductor."

Metzger moved with his family to Sioux Falls in 1927 from Hartford. His father was a painter in Hartford and later worked for Wilson Storage in Sioux Falls. Metzger said that he started at Washington High School in 1929, the same year that Arthur Thompson arrived as band director. Metzger played in the high school band and graduated in 1933. He said he played with the Municipal Band for two seasons (1934-35), then joined the Civilian Conservation Corps in the Black Hills for one year, returning in the winter of 1935. Although Henegar's printed roster does not show him as a regular member in 1935, Henegar sometimes did not record the name of a person who may not have played the full season. Metzger worked at John Morrell and Co. for forty-two years, interrupted by serving two years in the Navy, 1940-42. Because of union problems at the Morrell plant he hesitated to join any union; thus he didn't return to the Municipal Band.

Metzger retired in 1977 and lives in Sioux Falls.

Everett Zellers

Everett Zellers, born in 1918, is one of two living persons located who played in the Sioux Falls Municipal Band as early as 1933.

He said that he liked band music and began playing the clarinet at an early age. He, like many other young musicians of his time, took lessons from Vernon Alger, a Sioux Falls studio teacher and member of the Municipal Band.

Zellers stated that he thought he played in the Municipal Band under G. C. McClung in 1928-29. However, he would have been only ten years old at the time — probably too young to be accepted into a professional organization regardless of the talent. G. C. McClung also conducted a youth band at that time and that may have been the organization in which Zellers played. However, Zellers said that he definitely remembered playing in the Municipal Band under McClung's successor, Otto H. Andersen, and believed he played full time under Henegar until the beginning of World War II. Zellers graduated from high school in 1936. He also said that he played the latter part of 1945-49 when he commuted from Sacred Heart, Minnesota, where he taught. Henegar's personnel records show Zellers as a full-time member of the normal eight-man clarinet section 1940-42, but the rosters from 1946-48 are not available so the latter dates could not be verified. However, Henegar's records did not always show substitutes or part-time players and it is possible that Zellers may have occupied that position prior to 1940. In addition to clarinet, Zellers played the oboe and English horn and still has his instruments.

He remembered that his years with the Band were very enjoyable and that he especially liked becoming acquainted with a lot of music. He reported that he received three dollars per concert when he began. Zellers played in the Elks and Shrine Bands but never did dance work. He remembered that as conductors "both Andersen and Henegar were good men." The players that he admired most were principal clarinetist William Meyer, who "despite his deafness was an excellent clarinetist," and O. W. Palmer, flute, both charter members of the Band.

During his career, Zellers was a band director, science/math teacher, school administrator and college professor.

He is now living with his wife in Flandreau, South Dakota.

1935-63: The Henegar Years

Information about members who played during the Henegar era was easier to locate because written records were available in the Band office and because players – even from the 1930s and 1940s – are living today. The 1940s were the years of World War II, and many of the members went to war (see Chapter 5). Many did not play after the war.

Washington High School in Sioux Falls supplied several "home grown" players for this period. The 1928 Washington High School yearbook listing of the school's band included eight players who became Municipal Band members in the 1930s: Paul and Charles Reagan, Ronald and Kenneth Lane, Royal and Harry Ellis, Jr., Everton Little and Paul Bankson. Little was a saxophone player in the Municipal Band but was listed as a baritone (horn) player in the Washington Band. That may have been an error and may have been confused with baritone saxophone or he later switched to saxophone. The 1936 Washington High School band had six students who were members of the Municipal Band at the time or who later became members of the Municipal Band. They were Orville Thompson, Marlin Brown, Rodney Bray, Donald Foss, Everett Zellers and Clifford Foss.

Milt Askew

When players from 1930-66 were interviewed, Milt Askew's name surfaced again and again because of his musicianship and performance ability. He also played for many years with the Band. No personnel records are available previous to 1935, but Askew's name appeared on the roster steadily from 1935 through 1966.

Askew was described by several of his fellow band members as "a natural musician" and a "personable man," and was well liked by most people. Don Lias remembered Askew "as a truly great musician." Askew had his own dance band, playing clarinet and saxophone. He may have played the oboe part on clarinet in 1945 when Henegar was having problems finding oboists that year, according to Helen Brumbaugh Hanson. However, players also told of Askew's ability on brass instruments. He once worked at Williams Piano Company and later had his own music store.

However, colleagues also mentioned Askew's weakness for liquor. "He once emptied a half-pint of whisky in one swallow while getting ready for a job at the Arkota," said drummer Johnny Soyer, a friend and one-time leader of the Jimmy Barnett orchestra. Askew told Soyer that he (Askew) was going to donate his body to the University of South Dakota School of Medicine and wanted Soyer to do the same for comparison purposes between one who had abused his body and one who had not.

Curtis Beecher

Curtis Beecher, born March 1, 1918, learned stage management from his father, Fred (see this chapter), and used his experience to serve as a stage manager in New York after he moved from Sioux Falls. The Washington High School yearbook of 1936 listed him as a senior, and his name appeared as a percussionist on the 1952 and 1962 Municipal Band rosters. Marlin Brown (Municipal Band member 1937-43), remembered that Beecher played as a substitute in the Municipal Band as early as 1935 and also played in the Sioux Falls College Band. He was not a student at Sioux Falls College but the college permitted community adults to participate.

His sister, the late June Beecher, said that Curtis had lived in Sioux Falls much of his life, but she didn't remember if he did anything else for a living other than play drums for dances. It is reported that in addition to working at the Sioux Falls Coliseum, he worked as a sales representative for a liquor company in Sioux Falls.

Beecher married Beverly Best, sister of the late Robert Best, a Sioux Falls business man. Beecher's adopted son, Robert, said that the family moved from Sioux Falls to New York, where Curtis became a stage manager in a television studio. The studio housed the Dinah Shore Show and the Ed Sullivan Show. Betty Best said that Beecher loved his work at the studio. She also said Beecher and his wife divorced, and he moved to California where he died in about 1963 in Los Angeles, following a long struggle with alcoholism.

Marlin Brown

Marlin Brown, born in 1918, was one of several Washington High School players whose abilities and love of band music gained them entrance into the Municipal Band. Brown joined the Band in 1937, immediately following his graduation from Washington High School, and played through 1943. He played a clarinet solo with the Municipal Band ("Carnival of Venice"), but he was not a regular soloist.

Clarinet player Marlin Brown played in the Municipal Band beginning in 1937. He is shown here playing at his senior recital in 1941 at Sioux Falls College. *(courtesy Marlin Brown)*

Brown had experienced early musical success, including taking an E flat clarinet solo to the national contest in Ohio, where he received a division I rating. Participation in the national, which was one of the highlights of his life, followed wins at district and state. Brown tried out for the Stokowski Youth Orchestra in 1939 and 1940; the orchestra was open to anyone through age twenty-five.

Numerous career opportunities followed after Brown's graduation from Sioux Falls College in 1941. He taught and was band director at Bridgewater and Madison, later becoming an ensign in the Navy in 1944. Following World War II he worked as a telephone company executive in Chicago, Virginia and California.

Brown stayed involved with municipal bands. While in Virginia, he conducted the Municipal Band of Charlottesville, Inc. When he moved to California, he helped found the Indio Municipal Band. He was the clarinet teacher of Elsa Ludewig Verdehr, an internationally known clarinet performer, when Elsa was in grade school.

Brown is retired and living in Sioux Falls. He is the president and conductor of the El Riad Shrine Band.

Ernest Dvoracek

Ernest Dvoracek, born in 1908, came to Sioux Falls in 1942 from Tyndall, South Dakota, but soon found a place in the musical life of Sioux Falls, playing in the Municipal Band during the 1940s and 1950s.

His wife, Libbie Dvoracek of Sioux Falls, has vivid memories of her late husband and the music he loved so much, including their dog's howling whenever her husband practiced his clarinet.

Dvoracek was young when his father bought him a fifteen-dollar wooden clarinet. That clarinet was accidently burned years later when a fellow dance band player tossed a cigarette into the equipment vehicle and it caught fire.

Dvoracek's work experiences were primarily in the field of education following his graduation from Tyndall High School in 1926 and Southern State College in Springfield, South Dakota. Teaching jobs included band director and principal in the Tabor city schools and county superintendent of schools in Bon Homme County (Tyndall). He later became a code instructor at the Air Base in Sioux Falls. Dvoracek took piano tuning instruction from Municipal Band charter member Raymond G. Hoyt.

Dvoracek died in 1959.

Donald Foss

Donald Foss, part of the musical Foss family, went on to significant careers in the military and business fields. Born in 1920, he played oboe in the Municipal Band 1937-41, beginning at age sixteen. Foss went into the Marine Corps in 1942 as a carrier-based pilot and served on several aircraft carriers. He remained in the service for thirty years and was discharged as a colonel in 1972. As a civilian, he built tennis and racket clubs in Spokane, Washington, where he now lives. He also has been a banker and a mortgage business chairman and is now in banking and development. His father, Henry, was a farmer in the Sioux Falls area, a builder, a real estate agent and a policeman on the Sioux Falls force.

Foss played in the Sioux Falls Municipal Band with his brother, Ardeen; his two cousins, Joe and Cliff, who were brothers; and another cousin, Edgar. He said his close friends in the Band were Marlin Brown, Orville Thompson, Cliff Foss, Fletcher Nelson, Joe Foss, Ardeen Foss and "last but not least, money."

Donald Foss played in the Washington High School Band, Elks

Band, Shrine Band and Sioux Falls College band and orchestra. He and Ardeen went to Sioux City and played in the Monahan Post Band under Leo Kucinski. Donald also did a little dance work – for free – at high school dances. Foss' instruments were clarinet, oboe, sax, English horn and flute.

He felt that the top musicians of his period included Vern Alger, Glen Houdek, Milt Askew, Palmer Kremer, Marlin Brown, Jake Helfert, Ardeen Foss, Henegar and Fletcher Nelson. Other memories include outstanding flutist "Pic" Palmer, who Foss said was always late and continually dropped his music. Foss had the opportunity to meet the Crown Prince and Princess of Norway who were in attendance at a concert at Terrace Park on June 14, 1939.

He recalled a concert by the Municipal Band in Mitchell during Corn Palace week. The Band played on a stand on the midway during the afternoon. It was a very cold day but many of the younger men went hunting for ducks and pheasants after the afternoon concert. Luckily, each of them previously had won a blanket at a bingo game, and they used the blankets to keep themselves warm. The Band members went to the Corn Palace show in the evening. Foss remembered that Paul Whiteman was featured at the Corn Palace that year, but Whiteman got so drunk before the show that he couldn't appear that night.

Foss said band experiences helped him in later life. "I learned to work closely with others and to rely on others to do their respective jobs. Comradeship was very important and necessary to make things 'click.' "

Foss thought he started at two dollars per afternoon concert and three dollars for evening and out-of-town concerts. This was later raised to three dollars for afternoon and four dollars for evening which gave the players seven dollars for a Sunday. "That was good money at that time," he recalled. He did not believe they were paid for rehearsals.

Edgar J. Foss

Most of Edgar J. Foss' career was spent in the newspaper business, including being publisher of the Siskiyou *Daily News* in northern California. He began as a publisher in 1947. He is presently living in California.

Foss was a cousin to four other members of the Foss clan who played in the Municipal Band: Ardeen, Donald, Joe and Clifford. Edgar said he was in the Band for two years in the 1930s (probably as a sub), graduated from Washington High School in 1939, and went into the armed forces in 1942. He studied under Ardeen Foss and played in the Sioux Falls College band and orchestra, which Ardeen Foss conducted. He was a dance musician, playing tenor sax, and said that he joined the union although he said he didn't really want to.

Foss is currently living in Yreka, California.

Richard Foss

Richard, the son of Ardeen, played oboe with the Band 1955-57. He graduated from West Point in 1962 and rose to the rank of lieutenant colonel. He is retired and living in Colorado Springs, Colorado.

Robert Griffith

Robert Griffith was recommended for the Municipal Band by his teacher, Harold Hoover, the Washington High orchestra director from whom Griffith took cornet lessons on Saturday mornings. He said he did not play in the school band because he had heard that conductor Arthur Thompson was too regimented. He graduated from Washington High School at midterm in January 1947 and immediately enrolled at Augustana College. Griffith later became principal cornet in the Augustana band and orchestra.

Griffith played with the Municipal Band 1947-62. One high moment occurred at a Library Park concert. He was playing assistant to principal cornet Donald Lias. The concert was to start at 8 p.m. and Lias had not showed up — and Lias had the music. The first march was "High School Cadets," and Griffith played it from memory. Band members and Henegar were impressed. Lias, who had a flat tire on the way to Sioux Falls from the Humboldt area, arrived in time for the second number.

Richard Guderyahn

Richard Guderyahn, born 1904, appears to have been the only cellist with the Sioux Falls Municipal Band. During World War II many of the players were being called into the armed forces, and it was not easy for Henegar to maintain proper instrumentation. It seems likely that he was short of low brass players and in 1945 invited Guderyahn to play cello.

Guderyahn, a member of the Augustana College music faculty and conductor of the college orchestra, also taught at Cathedral School. Steven Barnett, now a priest, had Guderyahn as his band director at Cathedral. He recalled that Guderyahn had great rapport with the children. Catholic students who were in band or orchestra were allowed to leave school to attend Guderyahn's funeral in 1959 at First Lutheran Church, the first time that Barnett and others had been to a non-Catholic church.

Greg C. Hall

Greg Hall is a retired South Dakota state trooper now living in Pierre, South Dakota, who was a percussionist with the Band in 1957-61 and 1963 as a part-time (substitute) Municipal Band member. He said that he played partly for the pay but more for the enjoyment of playing. Hall especially liked Sousa marches. His close Band friends were Chad Boese, Ardeen Foss and Paul Reagan.

Hall started playing percussion in the Sioux Falls grade schools. He continued playing at Washington High School and the University of South Dakota. Besides playing with the Municipal Band, he played with dance bands such as Myron Lee and the Caddies.

Wayne Krumrei

Wayne Krumrei, now retired and living in Sioux Falls, reputedly had a very beautiful and classic euphonium sound. Don Lias, solo trumpet of the Municipal Band beginning in 1944, called Krumrei one of the finest euphonium players he has heard. Former Band member Curly Miller agreed.

Krumrei, born in 1922, began playing cornet in the sixth grade and had Esther Gunderson as his director throughout his school years. He became bored with cornet, and after falling off a tractor and breaking some teeth, he switched to tuba as a high school junior. He bought an upright tuba at Odland Music without realizing it was an E flat instrument instead of the more common BB flat. He graduated from Harrisburg High School in 1940. Shortly after high school he took lessons in the Sioux Falls City Hall band room from Henegar. He also played E flat tuba in the Harrisburg town band conducted by Neil Bellach.

Wayne Krumrei played euphonium with the Municipal Band beginning in 1943. *(courtesy Wayne Krumrei)*

There was an opportunity to join the Band in 1943. That year there were no tuba openings, but there was an opening on euphonium because Fletcher Nelson was going to the service. Krumrei, who had played euphonium in the Canton Community Band, was chosen for the spot. He considered playing in the Sioux Falls Municipal Band "a big step upward."

Krumrei was baritone (euphonium) soloist during many of his years in the Band. Two of his favorite solos were "Ballad for Evening" by John J. Morrissey and "American Fantasia" by E. F. Goldman. He also played several professional engagements, including Shrine circuses and the Ringling Brothers circus.

His closest friend in the Band was Harvey Eichmeier — an area farmer, self taught and likeable. Other memories about Band members included: Guy Anderson was a great guy; O. O. Jackson had an artificial leg; Vernon H. Alger conducted when Henegar soloed; and Henry T. Hanson was always trying to sell insurance to the Band members. Krumrei enjoyed going out of town to small town celebrations, especially to Hills, Minnesota. His high point musically was when he played in the 1948 American Bandmasters Association Convention band in Sioux Falls.

Ronald Lane

Ronald Henry Lane, born May 25, 1912, is one of the few living former Municipal Band members who can say that he was recommended for membership by a charter member of the Band. His sponsor was clarinetist William Meyer. Lane joined the Band at age twenty-five, playing 1937-40. "I wanted to play in the Sioux Falls Municipal Band because it was the preeminent musical organization in Sioux Falls at that time. Also, one had contact with the Band almost all year long, either through rehearsals or concerts. Now if you ask why did I want to play in a band, any band, this is a question I have pondered for many years. I had always gotten more enjoyment from blowing my horn with a musical group than any other activity. It didn't matter whether the ensemble was large or small, good or bad, it was a lot of fun. Why this was so completely eludes me."

Lane recalled how he got started playing clarinet. He said that in the early years of the Municipal Band the conductor had to organize and conduct a junior band. However, Lane said director Charles McClung had neglected this until close to the end of his career with the Municipal Band. When McClung finally organized the youth band, Lane's younger brother, Kenneth, got interested, acquired a cornet and joined the group. This got Lane interested, too, so he abandoned his piano lessons and chose a clarinet to take to the junior band rehearsals and added mightily to the cacophony. "Poor Charlie [McClung]!" he said.

About the time Lane entered Washington High School, Vernon Alger was director of the high school band, and Lane started taking lessons from the Alger School of Music where one could learn to play any instrument, all taught by Alger. Lane also played in the Sioux Falls College band and orchestra, which Alger directed. The college band emerged as a full-blown concert band. The years and experiences in the Washington High School band and in another student-led group proved to be motivating factors for Lane. "Progress in learning to play the instrument seemed to be very slow at this time, but I attributed this to the fact that I had been grossly shortchanged when the natural music ability was passed out," Lane said. He said things got better when Arthur Thompson took over the high school band during Lane's last year in school. The citation under Lane's picture in his senior yearbook at Washington High School was "One is never so happy or unhappy as he imagines." Lane said that at this time a group of like-minded students organized a little band of their own which they called the Paramount Band. He stated that it miraculously existed for several years, mostly because of the effort and persistence of one member, Bruce McLeod. McLeod played trombone but never made the Sioux Falls Municipal Band. Others who played in the Paramount Band and who later were accepted into the Municipal Band were Marlin Brown, Joe Foss, Fletcher Nelson, Rodney Bray, Ronald Lane and Kenneth Lane. Curtis Raines and Robert Shenkle, not Municipal Band members, also played in the Paramount Band.

Lane said involvement in the Sioux Falls College Band and the Paramount Band kept him from laying away the "old horn" and made him a better member of the Sioux Falls Municipal Band. Like many other Municipal Band members, he also played in the Elks Band.

The Municipal Band normally made several out-of-town trips each year, and Lane remembered one that was especially eventful to him. "An event that must have been humorous to some people occurred on an out-of-town trip. I can't remember where to [probably Huron, South Dakota], but it was a considerable distance from Sioux Falls, so the Band and entourage employed a whole railroad train, complete with steam locomotive that is. Entertaining the local crowd was finished at about noon, and the train was not scheduled to head back to Sioux Falls until late in the afternoon. After traversing both sides of the main drag, I was a little tired and bored, so I decided to relax in a movie theatre. Little did I dream that I would soon be dreaming the happy hours away while my transportation was preparing to desert me. Remarkably, I suddenly awoke just before the scheduled departure time and rushed into the street, wondering whether to make a run for it. That question was answered by a long lonesome sound, [which] wafted toward me on the evening breeze — the sound that could only come from the whistle of a locomotive. Later, I headed to a traffic signal on a street that led to Sioux Falls, to hitch a ride. It was hard to believe, but no one was going as far as Sioux Falls. I could only go back to the middle of town and to the hotel to see if there hopefully would be a room available. Of course, there was not. I was lucky though to get a pillow, blanket and a carpeted floor to lay them on. Not bad at all, really. After a leisurely ride to Sioux Falls the next day, I finally walked out of the depot to the guffaws of a couple of friends who had come to pick me up."

Although he loved music, he chose a different vocation — a machinist. "Not a very prestigious position," he said," but to me it was a source of great satisfaction that I pursued past retirement into the hobby stage, just like the postman's vacation."

Lane is retired and living in Hemet, California. He never played his clarinet after leaving the Municipal Band and just recently parted with the instrument.

C. R. "Bob" Larson

C. R. "Bob" Larson was described by musicians who knew him as a "really nice guy" and an "excellent musician and clarinetist." Don Lias, trumpet, remembered him as "one of the nicest persons that ever lived, and he played very well."

Larson was born November 22, 1917, in Sioux Falls. He was a graduate of Washington High School in 1936 and later of court reporting at the Gregg College of Business in Chicago, Illinois. His musical training began on violin. He later played clarinet under Arthur Thompson at Washington High School in Sioux Falls. Larson found that Thompson was "a strict director," said Larson's wife, Doris, whom he married September 29, 1940.

Larson played in the Municipal Band from 1935 through the early 1950s. In 1940, he worked as a court reporter for Judge Knight in Brookings and drove back and forth to Sioux Falls for the 1940 Band season. Larson was always conscientious about attending rehearsals and concerts, and he and his wife drove to Sioux Falls for the Armistice Day concert November 11, 1940. It was canceled because of a blizzard, and they were forced to follow the snow plow in order to get back to Brookings. He moved to Sioux Falls in approximately 1942 to work for judges.

In addition to playing in the Municipal Band, Larson was a member of the Elks Band, having joined while still in high school. He also played pit band jobs but did no dance work. The fact that he didn't play saxophone may have been an important factor in his not playing dance jobs.

Larson had a low draft number (eight), and went into the Army July 21, 1943. He was discharged September 10, 1945. During World War II, he served in the 70th Infantry Division.

Larson was honored at a retirement reception June 15, 1989, at which Governor George Mickelson proclaimed July 1st as "Bob Larson Day." Larson died of Lou Gehrig's disease August 27, 1989, at age 71. He is buried at Hills of Rest in Sioux Falls.

Donald Lias

It appears that Donald Lias holds a record for the shortest span of time between starting on an instrument and playing a solo with the Sioux Falls Municipal Band. Lias was born August 21, 1929, near Humboldt, South Dakota. He was so interested in playing trumpet (cornet) at age eight that his father, Bill, took him to Mr. Gulson, band director in Hartford, to see about lessons. Gulson was gone, so Lias' father checked with Russ Henegar in Sioux Falls about lessons. Henegar agreed to take him as a student beginning in the fall, and Lias soloed with the Municipal Band the next summer. A newspaper photograph from 1938 showed him at about age eight, dressed in a band uniform which his mother had made for him. Lias confirmed an August 26, 1938, *Argus Leader* article which indicated that at age eight a playmate shot

Lias in the mouth with a slingshot, dislodging a tooth. This required a temporary crown and forced Lias to play off to one side of his mouth. He was able to change to the more traditional center position after about a year and was never bothered by the injury.

As a boy of about twelve he played duets with his younger brother, Eddie (born 1932), at the Municipal Band concerts. Donald played in the Municipal Band in 1944-50 and substituted in 1958. He was the regular trumpet soloist during most of the period. Solo repertoire most often included "Josephine," by Kryl, "Atlantic Zephyrs," by Simon, "The Premier," by Llewellyn, "The Southern Cross" and "Showers of Gold," both by Clarke.

As he grew older, his musical experiences continued on new levels. Lias won the regional music contest playing a cornet solo in about 1947. He graduated from high school in 1947 and attended Augustana 1947-48. He recalled that his experiences in the symphony there were not especially satisfying. Brass players tend to count many more rests in symphony playing than in band performance. This frustrated Lias when, as a member of the Augustana Symphony, the orchestra rehearsed a Sibelius work for nine weeks and never got to the spot where the trumpets came in.

Colleagues included clarinetist Dick Colwell, with whom he played many road shows that came to Sioux Falls; Glen Houdek, "a good percussionist who earlier had played in vaudeville"; and trumpet colleague David Wegner, who had "institutional memory" — once he learned something he never forgot it. Lias didn't believe that the Municipal Band was as good immediately after World War II as it was prior to the War.

Lias said that Henegar picked on him a lot, but that Henegar wouldn't say anything to some of his "cronies" if they fouled up. It may have been that Henegar demanded more from Lias than from others because Lias had been his prize student.

Everton "Ev" Little

Everton Little is remembered as a true veteran of the Municipal Band, a part-time professional musician in the area and a man with a wonderful sense of humor.

He was born in Worthington, Minnesota, on June 29, 1909. He graduated from Washington High School in Sioux Falls in 1928 and later from Sioux Falls College. The 1928 Washington High School annual described him as "audacious, clever and gracious."

Dr. Loren Little remembered that his father started playing saxophone in the Sioux Falls Municipal Band in the early 1940s (rosters indicate 1943) and played through 1980, the last few years as a substitute. Everton and his two sons, Loren and Tom, played a total of more than fifty years in the Municipal Band.

Little was involved with other musical groups. He played in the El Riad Shrine Band. Little also played dance jobs, but according to Loren, his father tried to keep it a secret because his employer, John Morrell and Co., took a dim view of any of their employees playing dance jobs. Little worked for Morrell for forty years before retiring in 1974. He worked in sales prior to becoming manager of the purchasing department.

His sense of humor was evident in his many stories. Little said there are two things you don't do on a playing job: First, don't shake hands with the other musicians while you're getting ready or the audience will know you may be meeting for the first time (many times dance or show bands are put together and have never played together previous to the public performance); and secondly, don't yawn — the audience will think you are bored.

Ev Little played saxophone with the Municipal Band from the 1940s through the 1980s. He is remembered for his sense of humor. *(courtesy Sioux Falls Municipal Band)*

Little died in Las Vegas on September 16, 1989. The stories of his wonderful sense of humor were related at his funeral on September 19 at First Presbyterian Church in Sioux Falls. It was reported that Wendell Hanson told this story as part of the eulogy: Little said that he was mowing his lawn at his home one day when a woman pulled up in a car. Thinking that he was a commercial lawn mower, the lady said, "You do a good job; what do they pay you?" Little answered, "The lady doesn't pay me anything, but she lets me sleep with her." The visitor left quickly not knowing that the woman Little was speaking of was his wife. His love of good humor had followed him to the end.

George Medeck

The exact year that clarinetist George Medeck began playing in the Municipal Band has not been definitively determined, but he was an early member and was a member of the Board in 1929. His wife, Helen, believed he started by 1927 and played until about 1950.

Medeck, born January 21, 1904, followed a variety of interests as he matured, including music, accounting and photography. Medeck, the oldest boy in the family, grew up on a farm near Ravinia and Lesterville, South Dakota, and was a graduate of Lesterville High School. Lawrence Welk played at the White Star Pavilion which Medeck's father, William, had built on the home farm. The band which Welk led was called the "Little Red Robin Band." Medeck came to Sioux Falls and attended Sioux Falls Business College and later became a certified public accountant and held the fourth license in South Dakota. He took organ lessons as an adult and also played with the Shrine and Elks bands. According to his daughter Bonnie, Medeck gave private clarinet lessons. Photography was also a hobby, as was being a member of the Audubon Society.

Playing in the Sioux Falls Municipal Band was very important to him, Bonnie recalled. She remembered hearing her father play "Clarinet Polka" in his practice sessions and remembered going to Municipal Band concerts as a child. As an adult, she went to concerts when her husband, Bob Griffith, played trumpet in the Band.

Medeck died of a heart attack in 1963.

Leon "Curly" Miller

Leon Miller, affectionately called "Curly," developed into an extremely capable trumpet player with the Sioux Falls Municipal Band even though he had never had a lesson. The records show him beginning in 1947 and playing at least twenty-seven years, part of the time as a substitute.

Miller, born October 7, 1917, borrowed his first cornet from Verdi, Minnesota, school system, where he later graduated from the high school in 1935. After starting to learn the instrument, Miller figured out how to play some German tunes. His father called a friend on the telephone and told Miller to play "Acht du Lieber" over the phone. Miller's performance pleased his father, and he agreed to purchase a cornet for his son as a result — a rebuilt instrument that cost twenty dollars.

Miller started playing in dance bands as a sophomore in high school and did dance work until recently. One of his memorable events was a rehearsal night during the Henegar years. Miller drove a motorcycle to rehearsal and had to go over the railroad tracks on the way. On one of the trips his case jumped out of his bike saddle bags. The car behind him drove right over the cornet and ruined it. Miller then bought a new Selmer trumpet.

Miller also played in a combo with pianist Bob Shaw, a brother of area big-band leader, Don Shaw. When Shaw moved away, Miller became leader of the combo.

Robert Nason

Robert Nason is a former member and cornet soloist with the Municipal Band, 1950-57, who became a certified public accountant and is presently the chief executive officer of Grant Thornton in Chicago, the seventh largest accounting and consulting firm in the world.

Nason had a special interest in the Municipal Band because Russ Henegar was his uncle, and his mother, Eileen Henegar Nason, was a piano teacher in Sioux Falls who soloed at least twice with the Band.

"I cannot recall exactly when I began playing with the Band," Nason said, "but I think it was before I entered high school. That means my first summer could have been in 1950. Russ, of course, had been giving me cornet lessons from the time I was old enough to blow air through a horn. I did play cornet solos from time to time as well as duets and trios." He has not played since 1957 but still has his cornet. He played in the Washington High School and University of South Dakota bands, the Shrine Band, stage bands, circus bands, Milt Askew's dixieland band and while in college, he led his own dance band.

Fletcher Nelson

Fletcher Nelson was euphonium soloist with the Municipal Band 1936-41. He was born in 1918 in Viborg and graduated from Sioux Falls Washington High School in 1936, where he played euphonium under Arthur Thompson. He had personality problems with Thompson so he quit the Washington High School band. Nelson bought his euphonium new at Williams Piano Co. for $37.50. Nelson played with the Sioux Falls College band which was then conducted by Municipal Band member Ardeen Foss.

In 1937, Nelson joined the Elks Band and went with the band to the 1937 National Elks Convention in Denver. He and other eighteen- and nineteen-year-olds were taken along to strengthen the group. They were sworn into the Elks even though they were not twenty-one years of age, the normal minimum joining age.

Playing with the Sioux Falls Municipal Band was his biggest challenge musically up to that point in his life, he said. He learned a lot from Mike Hanson, euphonium section principal. Once Nelson smashed a finger the day before he was to play a solo, but, in the spirit of show business, he played the solo and the concert anyway. Donald Foss, a Band oboist at that time, said that Nelson had "great articulation and technique and a fine sound."

Francis Peckham

Cornetist Francis Peckham, born 1914, played the 1945 season with the Municipal Band.

He had South Dakota relatives who played important roles in the band arena in the early decades of this century. His father, Frank D., was bank president in Alexandria, South Dakota, and conducted a community band there. Frank also served as a state senator. John Wallace Peckham, a state senator who sponsored the South Dakota band law (see Chapter 1), was Francis' uncle. Deecort Hammitt, Alcester Community Band director and composer of "Round Up," chosen as a South Dakota state song, was married to Francis' sister. Deecort moved to California from Alcester.

Francis lives in Sioux Falls and still plays dance jobs.

Norman Sampson

Norman Sampson played in the Municipal Band during 1941 while a student at Augustana College. Although Henegar's personnel rosters do not show it, Sampson thought he also played in 1940 or 1942.

Sampson became interested in playing with the Band partly because of playing in a dance band with Band members Bob Niblick, Milt Askew, Ev Little and Russ Henegar. Playing in the Augustana band and orchestra also influenced him to play in the Municipal Band. He was a student director and music major at Augustana, playing clarinet and saxophone.

He said that the Municipal Band was his first chance to play with a professional band. The musicians he admired most were the players mentioned above and Ardeen Foss. Because he played clarinet, he especially admired the way Mark Odland, another Band member, played the glissando opening of "Rhapsody in Blue," something none of the other clarinetists could do. He especially remembered the Band's Easter concerts. He remembered conductor Russ Henegar as being "very competent." Band members received about five dollars per concert and had to be members of the musicians' union. Like many Municipal Band members, Sampson also played in the Elks and Shrine bands.

The Municipal Band helped him develop musically and eventually led him to choose music as a career. During World War II, he played four years in an Army band in Washington, D.C., playing concerts for patients at Walter Reed Hospital, for funerals at Arlington and for bond drives. After military service, he was high school band director at Lemmon and Pierre, South Dakota, until retirement.

Sampson presently lives in Pierre and spends the winters in Texas.

Mel Sunde

The records list 1943 as the first year that Mel Sunde, a trombonist, played in the Municipal Band, but his wife Tillie, said he may have played some concerts in 1942. She recalled that Sunde had a good sense of humor and loved to play. He'd say, "The reason I play is I love it." Sunde was born in 1901. Both he and Tillie grew up in Madison. Sunde was a graduate of Madison High School and studied law for one and one-half years at the University of South Dakota. At that time one could study law without being a college graduate, Tillie said. He decided against law and worked at the post office in Sioux Falls for thirty-eight years, part of the time as a supervisor.

Their close Band friends included Russ and Gladys Henegar, Dr. E. O. Dietrich, Cliff Foss, Ev Little, Milt Askew and Paul and Vivian Wegner. Sunde also played in Henegar's dance band.

Mel and Tillie, married in 1926, celebrated sixty-five years of marriage prior to his death in 1991.

Ralph Tyler

Ralph Tyler has been performing music in Sioux Falls for nearly sixty years, beginning with a concert with the Luther College Band on tour on November 7, 1935, through a performance with the Augustana/ Community Band on November 12, 1993, and with the Sioux Falls College/Community Orchestra in 1994. During that period he played second flute, piccolo and clarinet in the Municipal Band (1953-65), other professional music jobs and had a family orchestra consisting of himself, his wife and children. When O. W. Palmer, his best friend and the principal flutist of the Municipal Band retired before the 1964 season, Tyler switched to his original instrument, the clarinet. He recalled that there was very little amplification of the Municipal Band sound at concerts in the earlier days and that the pay scale in 1953 was five dollars to six dollars per concert.

Although performance was important to him, most of Tyler's days were spent in the field of music education. Born in 1912, he graduated from Luther College in 1937 and taught in Montana in 1937, Lyons, South Dakota, in 1938, at several Sioux Falls grade schools in 1954, followed by Axtell Park Junior High in 1956. Tyler recalled that Martin Luther said that music is second only to theology in importance.

There was another outstanding musician in Tyler's immediate family. His uncle, George Tyler, was cofounder of the noted Long Beach, California, band in 1909 and was the assistant conductor and cornet soloist for thirty-two years, including most of the years when famed trumpet soloist and conductor Herbert L. Clarke was the director (1923-43). The Long Beach band played twelve concerts per week. George Tyler was elected to the elite American Bandmasters Association in 1932 and resigned in 1948. Ralph recalled that his dad bought George a cornet for two dollars. *The Heritage Encyclopedia of Band Music* lists George Tyler with one known work, "Pacific Echoes," cornet solo (Rubank, 1939), but Ralph says George also wrote "Freedom of the Air March." George Tyler's march "The Sentinel" was performed from manuscript on July 31, 1960. Ralph heard his uncle solo with the Long Beach band in 1939.

The Three Wegner Brothers – Paul, Jr., David, and Tom

Three Wegner brothers played in the Sioux Falls Municipal Band as a part of a family that included Paul, Sr. (master of ceremonies and vocalist), and David's son, Nathan. David recalled, "As Band members, the Wegner brothers wore dark wool uniforms, and in combinations of one or two brothers per summer, they contributed great amounts of perspiration to Band concerts over a period spanning twelve years. Do they think it was worth it? You bet!"

Band membership by the second generation members of the Wegner family preceded that of their father, Paul, Sr. (See Chapter 10). Their acceptance into the Sioux Falls Municipal Band as ninth graders in the 1950s was facilitated by their teacher, Ardeen Foss, clarinetist and oboist with the Municipal Band. Foss had started each boy on his instrument at "ground zero": Paul, Jr. in 1948, David in 1949 and Tom in 1952. Before recommending an instrument, Foss always examined the prospective students' jaw and teeth structures. He recommended clarinet to all three boys. Paul and Tom accepted Ardeen's recommendation, with Paul switching to bassoon in later years. David chose the cornet. Foss told his students to practice one hour per day, no exceptions. Mother Vivian took this requirement to heart, enforcing it constantly and consistently, with Paul, Sr., occasionally joining a practice session with appropriate chords on the piano.

The Wegners recounted many benefits from the Municipal Band: sight-reading large amounts of challenging music, opportunities to play in dance bands that resulted from Municipal Band associations, consequent development of lips and lungs through frequent and lengthy playing, satisfaction from performing in surrounding communities where appreciation flowed freely afterwards, and association with other musicians that continued through the years. Participation in the Sioux Falls Municipal Band, they said, contributed to higher levels of success in other endeavors throughout their school years and beyond.

Personal circumstances of the second-generation Wegners in 1994 are as follows: Paul, Jr., born 1938, lives in south-central New York where he is semiretired after many years with the IBM Corporation; David, born 1939, lives in Sioux Falls and is semiretired after serving in various educational and business capacities; and Tom, born 1943, lives in Eden Prairie, Minnesota, where he is employed as an IBM executive with global responsibilities. David still plays trumpet in the Shrine and Lennox bands. Neither Paul, Jr. nor Tom have played their instruments since leaving the Band. David's son, Nathan, played trumpet in the Band (see sketch later in this chapter).

Milo Winter

The records do not show Milo Winter as having played any concerts with the Municipal Band, but he rehearsed with the Band, and his stories are worth recording. Winter is band director at Rapid City Stevens High School.

Winter recalled, "I was a college student at Augustana College when

I was invited (or accepted) for winter rehearsals of the Sioux Falls Municipal Band directed by Russ Henegar. It was with a sense of awe and apprehension that I joined the musicians in the City Hall for rehearsals, taking my place in the lower end of the six-man cornet-trumpet section to the director's right. My fears were soon confirmed as Leroy Anderson's 'Irish Washerwoman' was called up, with its fast trumpet solo featuring some wicked cross fingerings. I knew I would never pull this solo off quickly enough as written and I also knew that Mr. Henegar was very familiar with each and every cornet/trumpet part. As panic began to set in, I suddenly had a flash of inspiration. I pulled out my main tuning slide to throw my trumpet into the key of A (sort of) and used conventional fingerings to get through the incidental solo as best I could, not pretty, but at least without disaster. Upon completion of the tune, Mr. Henegar turned to the trumpet section and said, 'I'll be #$#@$. What's your name, son?' This was a compliment from a demanding taskmaster which I'll never forget!"

Winter said that rehearsing with the Sioux Falls Municipal Band had a great impact on his musical development. "I will always be grateful for the experience and the many friends and advisors I met through this organization."

1964-86: The Lillehaug Years

When conductor Russ Henegar retired at the end of the 1963 season, there were fourteen players who left the Band. Several members of the Band chose to retire because of their age, others graduated from college and left the area and still others quit for various reasons. Forty-five members from the previous season (regulars and substitutes) were the nucleus of the 1964 Band under Leland Lillehaug, the new conductor. Seventeen others (including substitutes) replaced those who had left. Although the turnover was slightly more than occurs in a normal year, the transition was relatively smooth.

All the following are living and all but three live in the Sioux Falls area.

Scott Faragher

Scott Faragher played his first season in the Municipal Band during Henegar's final season in 1963. He played full time from 1963-83, with the exception of three seasons when he was in the Air Force. He was a section principal for several years. Faragher resigned from the Band because of the summer time commitment. He has played as a substitute since then as well as playing in the Sioux City and South Dakota symphonies.

Faragher began on cornet but later switched to horn. Russ Tiede, Faragher's horn teacher, encouraged his love of music. Faragher was also highly motivated by the fine horn players he heard in the Strategic Air Command Band in Omaha, Nebraska, in which he played.

George Gulson

George Gulson, born 1939, played trumpet in the Municipal Band as a regular member 1964-80 and as a substitute for several years after that. He was Band president for four consecutive years 1968-71 and was on the Board during other seasons.

Gulson, formerly the band director at Brandon High School and now superintendent of schools in Brandon, said that the most important thing to him during his participation was having an opportunity to play through vast amounts of musical material. It helped him professionally and with his own music groups. He recalled that the Band schedule was very demanding, adding that when he quit playing with the Band it was as if someone had let him out of jail! Gulson also remembered the twentieth anniversary dinner for Lillehaug in which he was a speaker and the good time he had "roasting" the conductor.

Curt Hammond

Curt Hammond's years in the Municipal Band were one step toward a doctorate in music and a teaching position in a college music department. Hammond played horn in the Band 1980-85 and was assistant librarian 1983-85.

After graduating from Lincoln High School in 1982, he attended Concordia College in Nebraska for three years before earning his degree from the University of Nebraska at Lincoln. He received a master's degree at Cleveland Institute and in 1994 was almost finished with a doctor of musical arts degree at Florida State where he played principal horn in the band.

He said that one of the important musical skills he acquired with the Sioux Falls Municipal Band was learning to read E flat horn parts which required transposing everything down one step. He also learned how to listen and how to learn the music quickly. He was able to transfer what he had learned from other compositions to music he had not seen before because the material in both compositions had similarities.

Although the horn parts are not especially interesting to play in circus literature, Hammond enjoyed the Circus Concerts because of their overall effect: "They made an impression on me figuratively and literally." The "literally" referred to the deep ring around his lips from the sustained playing. Hammond also enjoyed playing music not ordinarily played in college bands. Two of his favorite pieces were "First Swedish Rhapsody" by Leidzen and Sousa's march "U. S. Field Artillery." He said he hated "Kentucky Babe."

Gary Holman

Gary Holman, trumpet player and Band president, played full time 1981-88 and two concerts in 1989 before being transferred to Omaha, Nebraska. He served as Band president in 1983 and 1985-87. He auditioned for the Municipal Band because he liked the kind of music they played.

Holman's memories of the Municipal Band include Paul Hoy because of his helpfulness and finesse as a bass drummer and Stan Eitreim for his ability to identify a wrong note and give the correct one. He enjoyed the trips to smaller communities to play concerts. Holman especially enjoyed the guest conductors — he said it always seemed that the Band worked harder and paid more attention to the details of the music with a guest

Gary Holman played trumpet in the Municipal Band 1981-88 and served four years as band president. *(courtesy Sioux Falls Municipal Band)*

conductor. Special memories are the pregame show at the 1985 All Star game in Minneapolis and the Association of Concert Bands convention concert in Chatfield, Minnesota. One thing that was reinforced in the Band that he carried into his work was that all commitments must be honored.

He currently is playing in three groups in the Omaha area: The Nebraska Wind Symphony, a community symphonic concert band; N. W. S. Swingtones, a twenty-piece Glenn Miller style dance orchestra; and the Papillion Area Community Band, which plays in the park in the summer and also plays some indoor concerts.

While in Sioux Falls he also played in other bands: El Riad Shrine Band, Lennox Municipal Band, Midnighters Dance Band and the American Legion Band. While a Sioux Falls Municipal Band member, he was employed with Northwestern Bell Telephone Company (now US West) as an engineer — working with microwave radio and fiber optic communications systems.

David Krueger

David Krueger, trumpet, was a member of the Band Board 1973-76 and 1979, and was Band president for two seasons, 1977-78. He also appeared frequently in featured trumpet trios.

Krueger joined the Band because he really liked to play. The money helped but was not the main reason. Occasionally, the Municipal Band has been called "Muni Band" and "Money Band." He didn't like the latter term because it seemed like a negative term to him. He resigned after the 1979 season because both he and his wife Donna played, and once their second child arrived the schedule was too difficult. He had founded K & M Music in Sioux Falls with Robert McDowell in 1976, and business responsibilities were demanding more time.

The Municipal Band helped him in many ways, he said. It helped him keep in touch with band directors, increased his sight reading skills, made fall auditions for the Augustana College band much easier, kept him in shape all year and taught him interpersonal relationships.

Many elm trees were cut down during the height of the Dutch elm disease problem during the 1970s. The removal of the large elms at Terrace Park was a shock to everyone. Krueger was not aware of their removal one evening when he came to a concert because he had come in a back way. Before the concert, he was on stage putting his music in order. He looked up toward the audience area and couldn't believe what he saw. It was as if the "forest" which they were used to seeing was suddenly gone. It took several years for trees to grow back.

Other memories of the Band include:

- Fourth of July at W. H. Lyon Fairgrounds.
- He enjoyed seeing Paul Hoy's excitement at the circus concerts.
- He liked ending the season at Terrace with the "1812 Overture" and the fireworks, a tradition which had existed for many years.
- He didn't like dressing up for the special Children's Concerts.
- The trumpet features he played challenged him and helped him to improve.
- He enjoyed playing under his father during the 1969 season when Dr. Krueger was co-conductor.

Harold Krueger

Dr. Harold Krueger played cornet with the Municipal Band 1965-79 and co-directed with Donald McCabe in 1969. He also served as vice president in 1970 and trustee in 1971.

Krueger said he became acquainted with the Sioux Falls Municipal Band long before he moved to Sioux Falls, because his wife, Phyllis, was from Hurley, South Dakota, and they would hear the Band during visits to Sioux Falls in the 1950s. He remembered meeting Henegar and being impressed with the Band. When he moved to Sioux Falls in 1965 to join the Augustana College music faculty, he said joining the Band seemed like the natural thing to do, since he had been involved with municipal bands almost everywhere else he had lived.

Krueger was born to Walter and Anna Krueger on June 15, 1928, in Wabasso, Minnesota, the

Dr. Harold Krueger played cornet with the Municipal Band 1965-79 and co-directed with Donald McCabe in 1969. *(courtesy Sioux Falls Municipal Band)*

oldest of eleven children. A tricycle accident at age five injured his left arm — he can't completely straighten it — and his mother thought playing an instrument might be a good activity for him. His parents bought him a trumpet, paying one dollar a week for forty weeks. His only music teacher from fifth grade through high school was the Redwood Falls, Minnesota, high school band director, Stanley Limburg.

Krueger's training prepared him for a career in music education on both the public school and college levels. He graduated from high school in 1946, going on to earn a bachelor's degree from Luther College in Decorah, Iowa, in 1950. He earned a master's in 1955 and doctorate in 1964 from the University of Northern Colorado. Krueger taught high school music in Calmar and Britt, Iowa, and Glencoe, Minnesota. He went on to teach at the college level, first at St. Cloud State University in Minnesota and then at Augustana College, 1965-93.

Krueger was a frequent trumpet soloist with the Band. Representative of his solo repertoire are the following pieces: "The Magic Trumpet," by Burke; "Trumpeter's Lullaby," by Anderson; "American Caprice," by E. F. Goldman; "Fairy Tale," by Smith; "Willow Echoes," by Clarke; "Napoli," by Bellstedt; and "Quixote," by Klein. One solo particularly popular with children in the audience was "Toy Trumpet" by Scott. For this piece, Krueger wore an animal puppet on one hand as he played. The tricky performance was the brainchild of his predecessor in the section, Loren Little.

Krueger's memories of the Municipal Band include joys and difficulties. His favorite outdoor concert site was Terrace Park, but it was the rare indoor concerts at the Coliseum that he really enjoyed, because the music was more challenging. He said having his son David sit next to him in the section during 1969-79 was "very special." Less enjoyable were the Circus Concerts because of the many marches. "Marches kill a brass player," he said.

Krueger said a major benefit of the Municipal Band is that it provides an outlet for adults to play their instruments. Former students who weren't music majors often tell Krueger they lack opportunities to play in groups and miss it. "We as educators owe that to them."

Retired and living in Sioux Falls, Krueger practices regularly and plays for church, weddings and occasionally "The Star Spangled Banner" for local sports events.

Doug Lehrer

Doug Lehrer, an East Coast man who joined a Navy band, ended up in Sioux Falls through a series of circumstances and later became a member of the Municipal Band. He was a member of the cornet section 1979-92, served as principal trumpet and played frequently in trumpet feature groups. He was a member of the Board in 1980 and 1983 and was president in 1981 (filled unexpired term) and 1982.

Lehrer graduated from high school in New Jersey, went to the Navy School of Music at Little Creek, Virginia (near Portsmouth), serving in the Navy a total of four years as an enlisted man. Lehrer's only instrument was cornet. Lehrer moved to Sioux Falls in February 1976, at the invitation of Gene McGowan, a Sioux Falls financial broker who had been his bandmaster in the Atlantic Fleet Band. Lehrer left the Navy in September 1975, and McGowan, who was from Minnesota, was later discharged. McGowan invited Lehrer to South Dakota to join him in a publishing venture which was discontinued after about six months. Lehrer then found employment at the *Shopping News*.

How did Lehrer get into the Sioux Falls Municipal Band? Lillehaug was impressed with his playing in a First Lutheran Church brass group one Sunday, saw him outside after the church services and invited him to audition. Lehrer's first partner on the second cornet stand was Janet Bruns Hallstrom.

Lehrer said he always felt that Lillehaug conducted circus marches too fast until Merle Evans, former conductor of the Ringling Brothers Circus, guest-conducted the Municipal Band and took the marches much, much faster. Lehrer said he grew as a musician while in the Sioux Falls Municipal Band, even more than when he was in the Atlantic Fleet Band in the Navy. Lehrer said he never had enough time to practice so he had to be able to play the music at sight at the rehearsals.

His years with the Band were filled with enjoyable trips to area towns and to a national convention, an appreciation of the importance of good acoustics to musical performance, development of a fondness for particular compositions and occasional interesting incidents. He agreed with several other members that the Band had played very well at the Association of Concert Bands National Convention in Omaha, especially the Shostakovich "Festive Overture." His favorite pieces are "Stars and Stripes Forever," the Vaughan Williams "English Folk Song Suite," and the Holst "Suites." Acoustically, he thought that the Terrace Park shell was a hard place to play because it was difficult to hear the other sections of the Band. "On the Showmobile one can hear the other sections better," he said. An unusual incident he remembered was a Veterans Day Concert on November 11, 1981, when Phil Bajema, a fellow trumpet player, and he played taps early in the program. Bajema accidently played some wrong notes, and Lehrer was supposed to play the echo. Lehrer purposely imitated the wrong notes so that the echo would be identical. Someone from the military group came to them and asked them to repeat it correctly at the end of the program, which they did.

Robert McDowell, Sr.

Robert McDowell, Sr. joined the Sioux Falls Municipal Band in 1961 and told of numerous learning experiences during those first years. He played full time 1961-69 and 1973-76, spending the intervening years in the Air Force. He was Band president in 1975 and 1976.

McDowell was only fourteen when he began rehearsing and fifteen — fresh out of ninth grade — when he played his first concert. "It was scary at first," McDowell said. At one rehearsal he was the only horn and the Band played "American in Paris," which contained major horn parts. Another night he forgot both of his mouthpieces, went home to get them but was too embarrassed to return that evening. That taught him to check his equipment. Another learning experience resulted one time when the Band was playing on a ball field. McDowell said he inverted his horn to dump out the condensation. The mouthpiece fell into the dirt and he couldn't get it cleaned enough to play the rest of the concert. Other young colleagues in the horn section were Sam Albert, who had just graduated from Washington High School, and Jim Adams, who was still at Washington. Other players who were about the same age were Richard Peik and Harold Gray.

Robert McDowell, Sr. started playing with the Municipal Band when he was fourteen years old. *(courtesy Sioux Falls Municipal Band)*

Jeanette Paulson

Jeanette Paulson, former principal oboist, Band president and staff member of the Sioux Falls Municipal Band 1977-81, is now living in Duluth, Minnesota. She was vice president in 1979 and 1980 (partial term), and served partial terms as president in 1980 and 1981, before moving from Sioux Falls. She has played in several other adult bands since her days in Sioux Falls: Rochester Summer Parks Band, Bethany

College/Community Band (Mankato), Mankato State Symphonic Band, Mankato Municipal Band, Duluth Band and the Twin Ports Wind Ensemble. She finds much to admire in the Sioux Falls program by comparison.

Paulson said that discipline in the Sioux Falls Municipal Band made for a fine ensemble. "A disciplined approach to music is invaluable." She said she was not sure how many people knew or appreciated Lillehaug's efforts to keep a full schedule of concerts and keep the player's pay from dwindling. She recalled Lillehaug telling players to appreciate their pay because there are places where musicians pay for the privilege of playing in a band. "I know this to be true now. I am playing in a community band here in Duluth which is run as a part of community education. I just wrote a check for twenty-four dollars so my daughter and I can play with the group for one quarter [of the year]."

She recalled that concerts could be entertaining from the vantage of the stage. There were frequent budding conductors, three and four-year-old children, who stood behind the conductor, mirroring his moves — something the conductor never got to see. However, that vantage was frightening once. Paulson reported that one July 4th, a dark cloud bank grew to tremendous proportions. "The Band faced west and could see it coming. We shortened the concert, saw the most condensed fireworks display in history, and were just making it to our car in the pouring rain when the tornado sirens sounded."

In her letter of February 1, 1994, she added this note about a Band member: "One last thought. I can't write of memories of the Sioux Falls Municipal Band without mentioning Paul Hoy. His faithfulness to the Band and love of circus music were a real inspiration."

Linda McLaren Roach

Linda McLaren Roach said that playing in the Sioux Falls Municipal Band has made her feel like a professional. She appreciates the support of the community and the City Commission through the twenty years she has played in the Band. She also served as librarian, as a member of the Board, as vice president in 1985 and 1987 and as president 1988, 1989 and 1990.

The Band taught her valuable lessons: "A group becomes a team when members are confident enough of their own skills that they can praise others." She has tried to carry that over into her daily work. She thought the Band governance structure had been democratic and had worked well.

There are always memories of things that did not go smoothly for players and conductors. McLaren Roach remembered being in the middle of a home move and rushing before a concert. She quickly put on her uniform and drove to McKennan. Once there she realized that she had forgotten her instrument, and Lillehaug told her to go home and get it. He delayed the concert slightly, and she returned in time to play the concert. She also recalled when Lillehaug started wearing bifocals and needed a different pair of glasses for conducting. He would sometimes start the rehearsal and realize he couldn't see the music clearly. As librarian, she would dash up to the office on the second floor of the Coliseum to retrieve his conducting glasses. Lillehaug added, "Linda was a great librarian. She was organized and was able to anticipate what might be needed in different situations. Her experience as the Augustana band librarian prepared her for her duties as Municipal Band librarian."

Linda McLaren Roach was active as a player and Board member. *(courtesy Sioux Falls Municipal Band)*

Most of the Band members related how they enjoyed the out-of-town concerts; that was not true for McLaren Roach, but she's not quite sure why. Perhaps the bugs always seemed to be worse. She remembered problems concentrating at the Salem concerts because the concert site was close to the carnival midway, and the players could see the Ferris wheel in the distance as they watched the conductor.

Memorable moments for McLaren Roach were the patriotic concerts. When she was younger she grumbled about having to take a half-day of vacation time because of playing those weekday concerts. However, at one Veterans Day concert she looked into the faces of veterans in the audience, many of them elderly or bearing the injuries of earlier battles, and realized what they had done for the country. She never grumbled again.

Roach also remembered that Band members Al Berdahl and Jeff Bowar had a bet as to who could go the longest without washing their

Band shirts. It ended in a tie — each got through the season without washing his shirt. But they endangered many friendships in the process, especially of those who sat nearest them. The conductor didn't learn about it until twenty years later.

1987-94: The Taylor and Ammann Years

It often happens that when there is a conductor change, there is a greater change in personnel. During Taylor's first year in 1987, nineteen players (regulars and substitutes) from the 1986 roster did not appear in the 1987 listing. In the transition from Taylor to Ammann, an identical number of players (nineteen regulars and substitutes) did not continue from 1991 to 1992. During both transitions replacements were found, and the instrumentation remained nearly the same.

Pam Hansen Barnard

Pam Hansen Barnard, flute and piccolo, graduated from Lennox High School in 1972 and from Augustana College in 1976 with a degree in music education. She is presently employed by Turning Point and is married to the Band's vocal soloist, Monty Barnard.

Hansen Barnard played in 1976, 1978 and 1982-94, under Lillehaug, Taylor and Ammann. She served as the Band's president during 1994 and had an important part in organizing and implementing the special activities associated with the Band's 75th anniversary year and the reunion.

Pam Hansen Barnard. *(courtesy Monty and Pam Barnard)*

Carl Hallstrom and Janet Bruns Hallstrom

The evening trip home on the bus from a Band performance at a national convention in Chatfield, Minnesota, led to the first date between Janet Bruns and Carl Hallstrom. They were married in September 1988, and both have continued to play in the Municipal Band.

Carl Hallstrom began playing in the Sioux Falls Municipal Band in 1977 and graduated from Augustana College in 1979. He said that his reasons for playing in the Municipal Band are a combination of enjoyment and the pay. His first instruments were the trumpet and euphonium but he also played trombone in college. Later he played in the 686th Air Force Band in Europe (Ramstein Air Base), the group that was a descendent of the Glenn Miller Band. He also was stationed in California with the 15th Air Force Band. Hallstrom has been a featured soloist with the Band on both euphonium and trombone.

Carl Hallstrom began playing euphonium in the Municipal Band in 1977. *(courtesy Sioux Falls Municipal Band)*

Janet Bruns Hallstrom, a native of Lennox with experience in that band, started in the Sioux Falls Municipal Band after college years. She told of an embarrassing moment at her first concert of her first season. She arrived at the McKennan band shell, thinking it was the concert location. No one was there. She then drove to an alternate site (Sherman Park) and found no Band members there. In near panic, she called Ardis Lillehaug and learned that the McKennan Park concert location was not the band shell but the Showmobile near the tennis courts. She barely made it in time for the concert.

Highlights of her years in the Band include performances at the Association of Concert Bands national conventions in Chatfield, Minnesota, (1987) and Omaha, Nebraska (1991). She was sorry to see the fireworks, another highlight, discontinued at the final concert of the season at Terrace Park.

Other Band members helped make her experience memorable. She said Scott Faragher and Al Berdahl were two of the people who furnished the most humor in the Band. Hallstrom credits her improved social skills to her participation in the Band. Her loyalties to the group have grown as have her sight reading skills. When asked about her colleagues, she mentioned the positive attitude that bass drummer, Paul Hoy, demonstrated on a very hot day in 1988. Everyone was complaining about the heat except Hoy, who said, "It's just right."

Greg Handel

Greg Handel joined the Band in 1991 after graduating from Augustana College. A native of Freeman, South Dakota, he is band director at Patrick Henry Middle School and assists at Washington High School in Sioux Falls.

Handel said that the Municipal Band helps him because it keeps him playing. Busy band directors sometimes lose their playing abilities, and he doesn't want that to happen. It also provides him with exposure to literature one may not get in a college band. "It makes you feel as a professional — getting paid for your services and the time and money you have spent to reach a certain level of playing."

Favorites for Handel include guest soloists and the grand finale concert in August at Terrace Park.

He said he's had few disappointments playing in the Municipal Band. However, because of turnover, some sections may not be as strong as they should be some years, the time commitment is great and there is never enough rehearsal time. "One can't postpone — one must be ready because there is no tomorrow. One cannot cancel the concerts because of lack of preparation," he added.

Humorous events include trying to swat mosquitoes during the rests and hearing Stan Eitreim say "hats off" after the first number. Eitreim brings the members on stage about three minutes before concert time with the familiar "Let's go," reminiscent of Harry Ellis who performed the same task decades ago.

Nikki Maher

Nikki Maher, born in 1972, graduated from Lincoln High School in 1990 and will receive her degree in instrumental music education from Augustana College in 1995. She played in the Band 1990-94 and soloed on clarinet 1992-94. Her solos included "Concertino" and 'Polacca' from "Second Concerto" by von Weber and "Fantasie Caprice" by Lefebvre.

Maher liked the variety of music which she played and believed that the guest soloists and vocalists added greatly to each concert season. She hopes to teach music in public or private schools on the elementary and middle school levels but also is interested in teaching woodwinds at the college level. Maher plays alto saxophone as a secondary instrument.

Stephen "Steve" Stombaugh

Steve Stombaugh played cornet solos with the Band 1987-94, having joined the group as a part-time player in 1986. He was the Band's librarian in 1988. Favorite works performed include Haydn's 'Rondo' from the "Trumpet Concerto," "Carnival of Venice" and "Trumpeters Lullaby."

Born in 1960, Stombaugh graduated from O'Gorman High School in 1979, received a bachelor of music degree from the University of South Dakota in 1984 and a master of music from the University of Nebraska, Omaha, in 1986. He is a member of the 147th Army National Guard Band. He plays in several other musical organizations, including the South Dakota Symphony. Stombaugh credits participation in the Municipal Band with increased sight reading ability and added performing confidence. He currently works in Sioux Falls as a computer programmer.

Nathan Wegner

David Wegner's son, Nathan, is the fifth member of the Wegner clan to have been a member of the Band. He joined the Sioux Falls Municipal Band as a tenth-grade trumpet player in 1985. He continued as a member for five consecutive summers. Wegner was particularly grateful for opportunities to earn money in activities that were so enjoyable to him. He earned extra money as a band setup/take-down helper during most of those years.

Wegner was introduced to music at an early age. As a student of the Margeson music studio in Sioux Falls from age four through seventeen, he received an appreciation for good music and a solid foundation in rhythm and harmony. Weekly fifth grade school lessons got him started on the trumpet. He and his father began playing frequent trumpet duets a year later, and his improvement and natural talent became very noticeable. Summer lessons from Dr. Harold Krueger of Augustana College, followed by several years of weekly lessons from South Dakota Symphony trumpeter Conte Bennett, led Wegner to explore trumpet performance as a possible career. Wegner's undergraduate degree from the University of Kansas is in trumpet performance. While living in Lawrence (1987-92), he was a member of many musical organizations, including the Lawrence Symphony, the Lawrence Chamber Players, the Topeka Symphony and the University of Kansas's symphonic band and orchestra.

Wegner completed his second year of medical school in Kansas City in the spring of 1994. Although his time is limited, he continues to play for weddings and other church functions in the Kansas City area.

• • •

The key people of a musical organization are the players. During seventy-five years society has changed in many ways; however, the players have not changed that much from 1920 to 1994. Today, they may be somewhat better educated than their colleagues of yesteryear and they play a somewhat different repertoire. As in earlier decades, most of them have families and jobs outside of music. Their methods of playing their instruments are largely the same, and when the downbeat is given they strive to produce their best music. They take pride in the moments of exhilaration that come from the aesthetic experience — produced when everything jells. They want to please their audiences and hope to be appreciated. They are human and fret about the heat or the cold that make them uncomfortable and make it more difficult to produce music at the top level of excellence. The players in the 1990s look forward to their paychecks as did the Band members of the 1920s and all the decades in between, just as do business people, construction workers, secretaries and circus acrobats. The players and their conductors have been striving to sustain and raise the level of musical performance in Sioux Falls and the Sioux Empire. The players will continue to provide this type of service if their community will support them. Most play because there is something within them that demands realization and utilization of their God-given abilities.

13 Noteworthy People, Tasks

I n the history of any organization, there are always people who are of extraordinary value or who bring something unique to the group. Some of them operate behind the scenes and may not be well known to the public. For the Sioux Falls Municipal Band these special people have included composers and arrangers, assistant conductors, masters of ceremonies, fans and a number of special individuals. Composers and arrangers furnish the music that is performed. Masters of ceremonies make the music more meaningful to many listeners through their descriptions and anecdotes. Still others leave their imprint just because of the type of people they are and what they do. Although it is difficult to determine exactly who should be included in this category, it is hoped that the persons selected might be representative of many others known and loved by the musicians and audience.

Composers and Arrangers (1920-94)

The Sioux Falls Municipal Band is fortunate to have a fine music library consisting of thousands of pieces — transcriptions of the classics, a major collection of marches and the latest popular tunes of each decade. The composers and arrangers represent, for the most part, the elite writers for band. However, creativity never ceases, and the library is being augmented each year. Local arrangers fill the need for pieces for special occasions and for soloists, such as those with voice ranges which may require a key different from the published version.

311

Arthur Smith

Arthur Revington Smith was best known as an arranger in the early years of the Sioux Falls Municipal Band but was a composer as well. He came from Wisconsin in 1901 and joined the established Hoyt's Orchestra as a piano player. He was considered a genius by some, including longtime vocalist Ed Paul, who knew him personally. David H. Smith, a staff writer for the *Argus Leader*, described Smith in about 1965 as an "impoverished Bohemian who, more than twenty years ago, left to the city of Sioux Falls a musical legacy which has yet to be fully and fairly evaluated." He also wrote that Arthur had studied French, German and Spanish and was "an engaging conversationalist." Arthur was described as being soft spoken and without any unusual physical characteristics. Apparently Arthur lived in dim quarters in the basement of the Strand building on the southeast corner of Eighth and Phillips and performed tasks such as washing dishes in a restaurant to gain a livelihood. Later in life, Smith lived at the County Farm for indigent persons (located northeast of Sioux Falls). In his later years, the local Musicians' Union made gifts of clothing and food to Smith at the County Farm.

Although *Argus Leader* writer David Smith believed Smith may have turned down some attractive offers from music publishers, a letter found in one of Arthur Smith's scores appears to refute this. Arthur wrote to Davis Schmegler Company (obviously a publisher), in Los Angeles, California, on May 19, 1941 — near the end of his life — as follows:

Dear Mr. Manager:
    Have sent you several songs in the past but none found favor in your sight. However, I hereby submit "This Little Old Man," hoping. Have had one song taken by Joe McDaniel but have not sent this to him. Thot [thought] perhaps it would be a case of 'too much Smith.' Awaiting your decision I am
Very Truly,
Arthur R. Smith
Sioux Falls, South Dakota c/o Band Room, City Hall

Only one page of manuscript (thirteen measure segment) of "This Little Old Man" has been found in the Municipal Band library. The letter demonstrates that Smith had been attempting, with little success, to get a publisher to take his pieces but was continuing to try to persuade someone to believe in their musical worth. According to the Band program of

July 13, 1941, "Joe McDaniel Music Co. was a publisher from New York City" which recently had published a Smith piece. It was probably a firm that the Schmegler Company recognized since Smith "dropped" the name. Smith also was aware of the sensitivities of publishers when he wrote that the piece he was sending to them had not been sent to anyone else. Giving first right of refusal is a common practice today. The "too much Smith" probably indicated that Smith had sent many things to Joe McDaniel and didn't want to burden him further.

Ed Paul remembered that one season he needed a vocal arrangement of "Prayer Perfect," so he and Henegar drove out to the County Farm to see if Smith could do the arranging. A week later Smith had the arrangement ready and all parts copied. Former Band member Marlin Brown said that Smith arranged a clarinet solo, "The Carnival of Venice," for him for five dollars.

Many of Smith's arrangements are in the Sioux Falls Municipal Band library. His music notation is very small but legible. One reason that his arrangements have not been played as much as they may deserve may be because most musicians prefer to play from printed, rather than manuscript, parts. Other pieces may not currently be in vogue. Among his arrangements are "The Lord's Prayer," "Good-bye Sweet Day," "Fairy Tale," "In the Gloaming" and "Passing Thought."

The Sioux Falls Municipal Band library contains at least fifty-seven pieces (or parts of pieces) which appear to be Smith's original compositions, rather than arrangements. The dates on the pieces range from 1907 to 1943, the year of his death. In 1922 the newspaper reported that the Municipal Band had played Smith's "Spring Dance No. 1" and "Red Arrow." The latter was dedicated to the men of the Thirty-Second Division, which the article said consisted mainly of Wisconsin men, "for the composer was originally a Badger and knew many of the officers and men." Another of his compositions, "The President's Own," was dedicated to the United States Marine Band. It was given its first public performance on August 20, 1931, at McKennan Park. In addition, it was reported in 1922 that Smith also had written "Waltz Rhapsody" but that it required a larger band than the Municipal Band to play it.

The newspaper described Smith's methods of composing. It was reported that Smith "never goes near a piano while he is improvising [probably composing] because he says the fingers instinctively stray where they have been before and make creation difficult. When he has what he calls an idea, he gets no peace of mind until he writes it down. 'It is not the music musicians write that makes them go crazy,' Mr. Smith said, 'but the music they don't write. The only way to be happy when you have the feeling is to let it have full sway.'" Smith added that com-

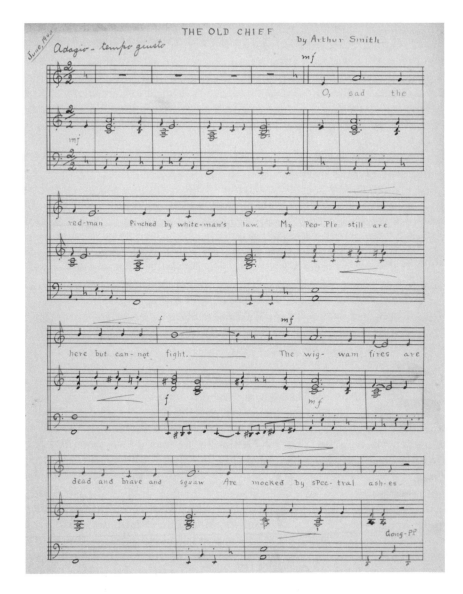

This is the first page from Sioux Falls composer Arthur Smith's manuscript "The Old Chief," dated June 1940. The Municipal Band music library contains at least fifty-seven pieces (or parts of pieces) which appear to be Smith's original compositions, rather than arrangements.

posing was not a money-making proposition "but is an essential occupation to the musician with the feeling for it." Smith was a pianist at the Liberty theater during or previous to 1922, according to an August 4, 1922, article in the *Argus Leader.*

Four of Smith's compositions have Native American themes. The lyrics of his "Old Chief" show compassion for the plight of Native Americans. The score bears the date of June, 1940. The lyrics read:

O, sad the red man
Pinched by white man's law.
My people still are here but cannot fight.
The wigwam fires are dead, and brave and squaw
Are mocked by spectral ashes gleaming white.
Now but in dreams I see the buffalo,
Nor elsewhere do I see the antelope.
The forest no more knows the buck and doe
Relaxed at noon on some sequestered slope.
O, pain is mine to see the white man gloat
O'er spoils awarded him by War's decree
The rising war whoop dies within the throat;
The ghost of Glory grins derisively.
The oak, bereft of half its quondam self,
Still proudly stands, repressing grief and fears.
While I the fated take my empty shelf
To mutely mourn thru out the closing years.

A second composition, "A Sioux Serenade," contains love lyrics. A third, "Winnewissa," recounting the love thoughts of an "Indian Maid," is scored for orchestra and is dated November 30, 1942. A fourth is entitled "An Indian Love Lyric."

Some of his scores have a handwritten inscription showing they were written at the City Band Room, City Hall. Others come from "c/o County Farm, R. F. D. #2, Sioux Falls, South Dakota" and another shows an address, "Room 300 Minnehaha Block. ..." (southwest corner of Ninth and Phillips). One score, "Lovelit Eyes," bears the inscription, "Band Room, City Hall, Sioux Falls, So. Dak. Oct. 1919." This indicates that some provision had been made for Band facilities after the passing of the tax levy to fund the Municipal Band on April 15, 1919, and before the first season in 1920.

Love is an ever-present theme — often love lost. One apparently original composition is "I Want a Girl, Want a Girl, Want a Girl." The lyrics may have represented a wish in his life:

I'm lonesome, dejected, And this is why
I can't get a girl friend tho I try and try.
Refrain:
I want a girl, want a girl, want a girl,
That's why I'm sad.
If one would be all my own, I would be a diff'rent lad
But it becomes worse and worse all the time
It's got so bad if I have a date, she is always late,
Never shows up at all sometimes. I wish I knew
What it is keeping them away from me.
And anytime anyone puts me wise, I'll grateful be
I want a girl, one to call "Baby,"
If I keep a-looking I will find her, maybe.
I want a girl, want a girl, want a girl,
That's why I'm sad.

Others treating the subject of love were, "Life Was Just Apple-Sauce" ("until you came and made it peaches and cream"). Several of the scores indicate that Smith wrote both the lyrics and the music.

The cover of one score called "Reminiscent" has a tribute: "This song was written to Ethyl Davis, now deceased, the most nearly perfect being I ever have known. Originally written in April, 1907, this revision was made December 11, 1942. The poem may be found in the April 25, 1907, issue of the *Bohemian Magazine.*

Some of the titles, such as "Life" and "Strange Road" (April 23, 1940) are contemplative. The lyrics of "Strange Road" state: "Sometimes I get to wond'ring just what Life means. Life with its countless actors, numberless scenes. Sometimes the skies are blue, then clouds come again. Constantly changing puzzle, baffling mere men. We reach its culmination, where do we go? (Creed is but speculation). We do not know. One thing I hope won't be." At this point the music suddenly cuts off and there is a pause, as if Smith didn't know the answer to the thing he hoped wouldn't be. Finally he added, "Ambitions keen goad." He concluded with, "Meanwhile we wander, hoping, down this STRANGE ROAD." Apparently Smith still was searching near the end of his life.

The earliest dates found on scores are the 1907 date (above), and a date of November 29, 1908, on a second score. His activity continued through the decades with two scores dated February 1, 1943, and April 6, 1943, only a few months previous to his death on September 16, 1943.

Smith died at the age of sixty-six. His obituary in the *Argus Leader* (September 17, 1943) was extremely short. It said that his address was 136 North Phillips Avenue and that he was formerly a musician who had not been active during recent years. His body was sent to relatives in Plattville, Nebraska, for funeral services and interment. Present maps do not show the post office or hamlet of Plattville. It was located in Saunders County on the Platte River, three miles south of Fremont.

Argus Leader writer David Smith gave a fitting summing up of Arthur Smith's life. Smith died "after a long career of striving for recognition, fraught with poverty and adversity but brightened by the hopeful pride of unfaltering endeavor." He was a talented recluse, "whose greatest failing seemed to be his inability to commercialize his work."

Robert Kindred

Robert Kindred was a player and arranger with the Sioux Falls Municipal Band who went on to play and write for several "Big Bands" and became a member of the Glenn Miller Army Band during World War II.

Kindred, born in 1913, was a Washington High School graduate in 1931. The citation by his picture in the 1931 yearbook predicted, "A place in rank awaits him." He joined the Sioux Falls Municipal Band in about 1935 when he was twenty-three years old. He also played in both the Shrine and Elks bands. He had played in a dance band with Russ Henegar since 1932 and thus no recommendation was needed to get into the Municipal Band. Kindred had ten years of formal study on violin, trumpet and cornet. He studied with two Sioux Falls teachers — theory and composition with Leon Jelinek and piano with Alexander Wurzburger. Wurzburger had studied in Vienna, Austria. Kindred remembered that the first chair players in the Municipal Band were "the best."

One Municipal Band concert stood out in Kindred's memory. He had arranged a suite for band from some piano pieces by Rimsky-Korsakov (they still are in the Municipal Band library). Ed Paul was vocalist and announcer and gave him such a nice introduction that he was a little embarrassed when he had to take a bow. He called that evening a highlight in his career.

Kindred said that his vocations have all been in music. He played with several name bands until 1965 and was also a full-time arranger, writing many "charts" (music) for the bands. He played several different brands of trumpets: Bach, King, Besson, Conn and Benge, in addition to cornets. While playing in New York, he used cornet a lot when playing jazz at the "Nut Club" in the Village. Kindred did dance work with leaders Woody Herman (as a sub), Dick LaSalle (a society band) in

Municipal Band member Robert Kindred, second from left, is pictured with the brass section of the Clarence DeLong Orchestra in 1935. *(courtesy Robert Kindred)*

Las Vegas after World War II, Clarence DeLong, Chuck Church, Milt Askew, Pee Wee Victor, Herbie Lowe and Jimmy Barnett. He also had his own Bob Kindred band. He continued arranging even after discontinuing trumpet.

When interviewed, Kindred seemed very happy to be "rediscovered." He celebrated his eight-first birthday on July 21, 1994.

Palmer Kremer

Palmer Kremer's musical credits include being a french horn player, a director and a composer. Kremer received his training at Yankton High School and at Augustana College. He played french horn in the Sioux Falls Municipal Band 1936-41, part time in 1943 and 1946, and was a member of the Elks and Shrine Bands. He was band director at

Colome, South Dakota, during World War II (1941-43), and at Canton, South Dakota, and Fort Dodge, Iowa, after the war. He wrote and scored "Major Joe Foss March" for concert band in honor of World War II hero and former governor Joe Foss. Although not published, it has been programmed several times by the Sioux Falls Municipal Band, by the Palomar College Band and the Army Transportation Band, of which he was a member in 1943-46. He also composed the Palomar College fight song.

Kremer later taught forensics, debate, history, political science and speech, most recently at the Community College in San Marcos, California. He also served as a councilman and mayor in that city. He died May 9, 1993.

Donald McCabe

Donald McCabe played trombone and french horn with the Sioux Falls Municipal Band in 1942 and from 1952 through 1969, playing for both Henegar and Lillehaug. During much of that time he was horn section principal and also served as Band president.

McCabe is a graduate of Washington High School and Sioux Falls College. He received his master of arts degree from Western Reserve University and did doctoral studies at Western Reserve, University of Minnesota and the University of South Dakota.

McCabe held various educational and professional positions during his musical career in Sioux Falls. He started teaching in the Sioux Falls public schools in 1950, organized the grade school music contest in Sioux Falls and was founder of the All-

Donald McCabe arranged and wrote several pieces that were programmed by the Band. *(courtesy Sioux Falls Municipal Band)*

City Junior High School Marching Band. He was band director at Edison Junior High School and assumed a similar position at Washington High School in 1965 when Ardeen Foss moved to Lincoln High School. At Washington, McCabe emphasized concert and jazz performances. Other professional positions included serving as principal horn with the Sioux Falls Symphony (now the South Dakota Symphony), and sharing the Municipal Band conducting duties with Dr. Harold Krueger in 1969, when Lillehaug was on leave.

McCabe held several national, state and local offices during his career in music. He is a member of the American School Band Directors Association and served as national secretary, vice-president and president. He chaired the national convention and guest conducted The United States Army Band in 1965 and compiled and edited a "Curriculum Guide" for school bands in 1969. McCabe was president of the South Dakota Bandmasters Association and was awarded the South Dakota High School Activities Association Distinguished Service Award in 1986.

Several of McCabe's arrangements and compositions were programmed by the Band. They included "The Search," a published composition, and "The Golden Year," which was written for the Band's fiftieth anniversary year in 1969 and was played to open each concert. McCabe wrote chamber music and choral compositions in addition to the following for band:

Greater Sioux Falls March — 1960
Weismarchen (March)
Stadium March
The Marching Warrior
Burgundian Overture
Soliloquy and Night Dance
Fantasia a due
Justification — tone poem
Beguinium
Rhapsody of Impressions
Band arrangements:
Fanfare and Tuba Tune — Stanley Saxton
To the West (Trumpet solo) — J. Gustat

Jeffrey Kull

Jeffrey Kull, an oboist from 1970 to 1979 with the Municipal Band, wrote "Sioux Empire March." It was programmed as recently as July 1994. Another composition, "Jeff's March," was given its first performance by the Sioux Falls Municipal Band on August 19, 1975. Kull now is a court reporter in Richmond, Virginia.

Leland Lillehaug

Dr. Leland Lillehaug, Municipal Band conductor 1964-86, did several hymn tunes and vocal arrangements during his tenure as conductor. Vocal accompaniments included "Rising Early in the Morning," "Serbian Medley," "Seems Like Old Times" and "Twelfth of Never."

Gene White

Gene White, trombonist and arranger, was thirty years old when he came to Sioux Falls. He already had been writing music while in high school and had run a band for eight years. White was in the NORAD (Air Force) Band in 1962. He then went to Dallas and to school at North Texas State in Denton, following which he went into the business world for eight years.

White was a friend of Mark Miller, son of "Curly" Miller, a former member of the Sioux Falls Municipal Band. White and Miller had been students at North Texas State in Denton, Texas. White was planning to go to Chicago to find work but decided to accompany Miller when he visited his parents in Sioux Falls in January 1971. While in Sioux Falls White met Loren Little, and they organized a six-piece band which included the Olsen brothers, Ralph and Greg.

In Sioux Falls, White soon met Charlotte Carver of the South Dakota Arts Council. That led to a grant from the Council to take jazz programs to the schools of the state during the 1971-72 school year.

Lillehaug, then conductor of the Sioux Falls Municipal Band, invited White to arrange for the Band, and White accepted. White said that arranging kept him in "rent money" and gave him a chance to hear immediately what he wrote. He also wrote for Augustana instrumental music groups. He made guest solo trombone appearances with the Sioux Falls Municipal Band in the late 1970s. Lillehaug said he was highly impressed with White's talents and that White contributed wonderful, much needed arrangements to the Band's library. Many of them have been played often throughout the years, especially White's arrangement of the "Armed Forces Medley," a collection of the songs of the various branches of the military.

White was described as a fun person, compassionate, concerned about people's feelings, but thoroughly disorganized in many respects except when he sat down to write. Then the music flowed from his pencil in a steady stream. He seldom had to erase or redo. He was a very creative person, open in his relationships and easily forgivable. He was a night person and often worked late into the night, even all through the night.

White currently has a twenty-one piece orchestra in Las Vegas, with four trumpets, two trombones plus himself, four saxes, guitar, bass, drums, four violins and two cellos. He works with the "Rockabillies," a Country Western band during the week. White plays with his own group on Sunday night and on special dates including New Year's Eve at the Sands.

Merridee Ekstrom

Merridee Ekstrom, trumpet, arranged several compositions for the Band, most of them for vocalists, from 1969 to 1980. The Band also programmed her composition "Deadline."

Ekstrom played in the Sioux Falls Municipal Band during the same period and was elected as the first woman president, serving during the 1972, 1973 and 1974 seasons. She completed her music major degree at Augustana College in 1973.

Ekstrom wrote at least twenty-one arrangements, some of which are listed below:

Merridee Ekstrom arranged pieces for the Band and was the Band's first female president. *(courtesy Sioux Falls Municipal Band)*

American Hymn
And This is My Beloved
At the River
Daddy Wouldn't Buy Me a Bow-Wow
Green-Eyed Dragon
Jerusalem, Jerusalem
Kukavica

Love in Bloom
Love Nest
Much More
My Ship
My White Knight
One Day at a Time
Sam You Made the Pants Too Long

Ekstrom presently lives in Plymouth, Minnesota, with her husband, Arne.

Gary Michaels

Gary Michaels of the Sioux Falls area did a limited amount of arranging for the Band in 1975.

Stan Eitreim

Stan Eitreim, possessing the attribute of absolute (perfect) pitch, has been an asset to the Band in many ways. He has played tuba and percussion in the Sioux Falls Municipal Band continuously since 1962 with the exception of two years with the Air Force Academy Band (1968-69) and one year with the Black Hills Playhouse (1973). Eitreim has been the equipment hauler for many years and he arranged several pieces for the Band including the following titles:

Big Band Medley
Bubbles in the Wine
I Wish You Love
In the Garden of My Heart
Those Were the Days
Let's Dance
Way Down Yonder in New Orleans
Whiffenpoof Song
The Waltz You Saved for Me

Eitreim was a music major graduate of Augustana College in 1967 and now works at Augustana.

Stan Eitreim, dressed for a Children's Concert.

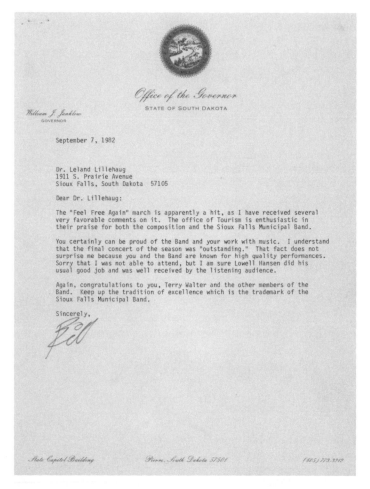

Municipal Band member Terry Walter was commissioned by the South Dakota Department of Tourism to arrange "Feel Free Again" for concert band. Governor Bill Janklow wrote this letter to congratulate Walter on her work and the Municipal Band on its performance of the piece.

Terry Walter

Terry Walter (Mrs. Don Cooper) is a 1972 graduate of Freeman High School and 1976 graduate of Augustana College. She did graduate study at the University of Iowa in saxophone performance. Walter is currently doing studio teaching in Sioux Falls. She plays professionally on piano and saxophone and has soloed on saxophone with the Sioux Falls Municipal Band. Many of her arrangements were written for vocal soloists Paul Wegner, Dr. Monty Barnard and Roma Prindle. They include:

Bedtime at the Zoo
Come to the Fair
Concerto for Two Horns
Give Me Your Tired, Your Poor
If I Were a Rich Man
I'll Walk With God
Johnny One Note
My Heart Belongs to Daddy
There is Nothing Like a Dame

Walter was commissioned by the South Dakota Department of Tourism to arrange "Feel Free Again in South Dakota" for concert band. The tune was used in promotion, and the band arrangements were distributed to all the school bands in South Dakota. The premiere performance took place at McKennan Park on Sunday August 15, 1982, and was repeated at Terrace Park in the evening. South Dakota Tourism Director Susan Edwards and Lieutenant Governor Lowell Hansen attended. Governor William Janklow wrote to Lillehaug, "The 'Feel Free Again' march is apparently a hit, as I have received several very favorable comments on it. The Office of Tourism is enthusiastic in their praise for

Terry Walter has been a player, librarian and arranger for the Sioux Falls Municipal Band. *(courtesy Terry Walter)*

The Sioux Falls
Municipal Band has
played many pieces
by area composers.
Shown here are "Hail,
South Dakota!" by
Deecort Hammitt,
above, and "Sunshine
& Smiles" by D. O.
Jones, right.

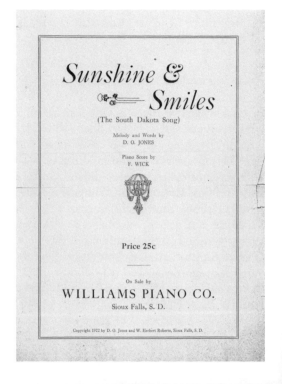

both the composition and the Sioux Falls Municipal Band. Again, congratulations to you, Terry Walter and the other members of the Band. "

Craig Alberty

Craig Alberty, a more recent addition to the arranging staff, is a 1970 graduate of Washington High School and a 1974 graduate of the University of South Dakota. He received his master of music education degree from Arkansas State University in 1976. Alberty was band director at Washington High School 1986-88. He currently teaches electronic music at the University of South Dakota and operates a production studio specializing in educational materials.

Alberty has done about twenty-five arrangements for the Sioux Falls Municipal Band, many of them for the vocalists. Two of his favorite creations are "Someone to Watch Over Me" and "A Whole New World," from *Alladin*. He creates his musical arrangements on a Macintosh computer using the "Finale" program.

Vernon Alger

Vernon Alger wrote numerous compositions for band. His work in this area is discussed below under "assistant conductors."

Other Area Composers

Other area composers whose works have appeared on Municipal Band programs include W. S. Peck (1935), S. A. Wise of Mitchell (1936), Dag Hagen (1937), D. O. Jones (1938), Ira Vail of Canton (1941), Deecort Hammitt, Alcester (1942), Frederic E. White (1942), Howard Bronson (1944), E. L. Van Walker, Milbank (1945), Gust Henle, Irene (1955), Felix Vinatieri, Yankton, (1955), Dennis Hegg, Dell Rapids (1966), Wally Ost (1966), Mrs. Donald Wohlenberg (1966), John Cacavas (1966), Rich Ricke (1966), and Lloyd Norlin (1966). The 1966 performances were at a "Music of Area Composers and Arrangers" concert which Lillehaug programmed on September 4, 1966, at McKennan Park. Donna Moran, a Washington High School senior, wrote a piece called "American Ace" in 1944 and dedicated it to Joe Foss. C. H. Moen of Inwood, Iowa, was not a member of the Band but had a composition performed by the Band under Russ Henegar.

Assistant Conductors

In addition to the composers and arrangers, another group who performed valuable musical and administrative services were the assistant conductors. Similar to a person elected as a vice president, each assistant conductor had to have musical and administrative capabilities which would allow him/her to assist the conductor and to perform his duties when needed.

Although Russ Henegar and Leland Lillehaug seldom missed rehearsals or concerts, they occasionally found it necessary to be gone because of professional responsibilities and needed someone to conduct in their absence. Each year they usually appointed one person to be assistant conductor and to assume conducting responsibilities as needed. That person was usually a playing member who was also a professional and/or school conductor. Alan Taylor did not designate assistant conductors, and Ammann has not.

John L. Johnson

John L. Johnson was one of the Band's earliest assistant conductors, but the exact dates of his tenure are uncertain.

Vernon Alger

Vernon Alger was assistant conductor to Russ Henegar during some of the years he was with the Band and was also a composer. He substituted for Henegar on June 8, 1947, when Henegar was in Detroit for a convention.

Born April 15, 1889, in Wessington, South Dakota, Alger was a violinist, percussionist and teacher. An *Argus Leader* article of July 21, 1929, described his father as "a musician of no mean ability." Alger began his musical studies in Huron after moving there as a small boy. The 1923 Washington High School yearbook faculty section listed his educational background as "Huron College." Huron is only thirty miles from Wessington, his birth place. He reputedly started studying violin before age five and had fairly advanced techniques by age six — an unusual achievement. He taught at Northern State College beginning in 1908 at age nineteen, continuing for six years. During that time he was director of the violin and orchestral departments. He had planned to go to Europe to study in 1914, but the beginning of World War I changed his plans.

Alger came to Sioux Falls in 1917, directly from a position as director of one of the "Birth of a Nation" orchestras which he had joined in 1914. His group was called "the largest orchestra with a road show that ever toured the United States at that time." He was musical director of the Strand Theater orchestra for four years, resigning in 1921, according to an *Argus Leader* article of September 5, 1921, "to devote his entire time to teaching." The article added that he was "head of the violin and orchestral departments at Sioux Falls College, the head of the violin, orchestral and band departments of Columbus College, director of the high school orchestra and band and conductor of the Sioux Falls Orchestral Art Society."

One source indicated that Alger directed the Washington High School band and orchestra for ten years (1919-29). However the 1920-21 Washington High School yearbook stated, "In 1921, Mr. V. H. Alger took Miss Toohey's place [as orchestra director] and has produced results that have surprised even himself." Alger was praised for his "pleasing personality," "good judgment," and "tact and ability in dealing with players." The 1925 Washington High School year book stated that the orchestra had grown from twelve to sixty-two players during Alger's first five years as conductor.

Alger was involved with several other musical organizations. He was in charge of violin, band and orchestra at Columbus College in Sioux Falls 1921-24. A story in the *Argus Leader* of July 25, 1927, announced Alger's appointment as professor of violin and director of the band and orchestral departments at Sioux Falls College. At that time, according to the article, he had his private studio in the Smith Block. Alger also was hired by Fred Beecher, manager of the popular Orpheum Theater, to direct the playhouse's six-piece orchestra during the season which began in August 1926, according to the *Argus Leader* of August 18, 1926. The orchestra furnished the overture and the music between the various acts that played at the Orpheum. Because of the small size of the group, the director would also be a playing member — in this case playing the violin. In 1931 Alger set up the Alger School of Music in Sioux Falls.

Also a composer and an arranger, Alger wrote violin solos under the name of Jan Ricardo. He wrote thirty-four military band marches and published most with Carl Fischer under assumed names. His compositions include: "El Riad Temple March" and "The Orange and Black," the latter dedicated to Washington High School. The following Alger march compositions, arranged by Arthur Smith, are in the Sioux Falls Municipal Band library. Most of them are in manuscript.

City Progress
El Riad Temple (his 25th march)
El Riad Golden Jubilee
Flying Colors (Alger's first march, 1926)
Jupiter March
King of the Campus
Little Mischief (trumpet solo)
Passing in Review
Pride of West Point
South Dakota State College
Those Trombones Ahead
Under the Big Top

An *Argus Leader* article of July 21, 1929, credited him with more than 200 compositions, encompassing the areas of band, orchestra and solo instruments. He gave his concert orchestral library to the Sioux Falls Public Schools.

Alger retired at the age of sixty-three and died at age sixty-four in 1953. He was buried in "Our Mother of Mercy Cemetery" in Centerville, South Dakota, his wife's original home.

Ardeen Foss

Ardeen Foss (1916-77) wore many hats as a musician in Sioux Falls — principal oboist and clarinetist and assistant conductor to Russ Henegar in the Sioux Falls Municipal Band, a performer of professional caliber, a teacher, and a leader in band music in South Dakota.

Foss, a 1934 graduate of Washington High School, received a bachelor of arts degree from Sioux Falls College in 1938. He attended the Eastman School of Music in 1938-39 and did graduate work at the University of South Dakota 1941-43 and 1950-52. Foss was band director in the schools of Bridgewater, 1939-41, and Vermillion, 1941-44. He was com-

Ardeen Foss. *(courtesy Sioux Falls Municipal Band)*

missioned in the U. S. Navy in 1944 and was discharged in 1946. Beginning in 1946, he served as professor of music education at Sioux Falls College before assuming the position of supervisor of instrumental music in 1948 in the Sioux Falls public schools. Foss became band director at Washington High School in 1950, continuing until 1965, when he became the first band director at the new Lincoln High School. He was the *Argus Leader* "Citizen of the Week" in September 1962.

Foss' stature in his profession is reflected in his election as president of the American School Band Directors Association (1971) and the American Bandmasters Association (1977). He also held important posts in the South Dakota Bandmasters Association.

Foss began playing in the Sioux Falls Municipal Band in 1931 at age fifteen, during the tenure of conductor O. H. Andersen. A program shows that Foss played a clarinet solo, "Long, Long Ago," at McKennan Park on August 5, 1934. He had great facility on both clarinet and oboe and played in the Sioux Falls Municipal Band and in the Sioux Falls Symphony Orchestra. Foss also was director of the Shrine Band and played in the Elks Band and in the Sioux City (Iowa) Symphony.

His home for many years was at 1504 South Spring Avenue. He later moved to Woodwind Lane in southeast Sioux Falls. He and his wife, Rachael, had three sons. Foss died on May 28, 1977 at the age of sixty-one. He was buried at Woodlawn Cemetery on June 1, 1977.

Oscar Loe

Oscar Loe was assistant conductor of the Sioux Falls Municipal Band during part of Lillehaug's tenure and conducted in Lillehaug's absence several times. He also served on the Band Board and as president in 1963.

Loe, born in 1932, had extensive opportunities for performance studies and for practical experience in conducting. His first music lessons on piano began at age three, followed by clarinet in seventh grade at age twelve. He spent grades one through twelve in Hudson, South Dakota, and graduated in 1950. While in the seventh grade he was given the opportunity to direct the high-school band. Loe was also student director throughout high school. Joe Thompson, who played in the Sioux Falls Municipal Band from 1935-41, was his director for a time and started him on clarinet. Ron Best was also one of Loe's conductors. Loe received a bachelor of fine arts, *cum laude*, degree in 1954 and master of music in 1957 from the University of South Dakota. During his four years at the University he played solo clarinet in the band. He was assistant director from 1953-55 and was director of the ROTC Detachment Band. Loe has had additional graduate study at the University of South Dakota, Augustana and South Dakota State University and earned over two hundred total hours of academic credit. He was elected to ASBDA (American School Band Directors Association) in 1969.

Loe's playing experience includes many area jazz groups, lead saxophone with the Ringling Brothers Circus and other traveling shows and more than two dozen musicals, including directing performances of the Sioux Valley Hospital Auxiliary musical, "A Funny Thing Happened on the Way to the Forum." He played oboe and principal clarinet with the South Dakota Symphony for twenty-four years.

Oscar Loe served as assistant conductor during part of Leland Lillehaug's tenure. *(courtesy Oscar Loe)*

Loe's first experience with the Sioux Falls Municipal Band was as a substitute during the summers of 1953 and 1954. He began playing in the clarinet section as a full-time member in 1960, playing principal clarinet during most of his twenty-seven year tenure. He also filled in on oboe, saxophone and percussion when needed. Loe was the drum major of the El Riad Temple Brass Band for ten years during the time when they marched and was president for two years.

Loe said one of the highlights of his career with the Municipal Band was the Chatfield, Minnesota, concert at the national convention of the Association of Concert Bands. He described the Sioux Falls concert with circus conductor Merle Evans as "a joy." Loe enjoyed serving as host chauffeur for Evans when he was in the city.

Loe also played solos with the Band. He said that his solo preparation included late night and early morning practicing. He frequently practiced between midnight and two a.m., averaging two hours of practice per day in preparing for performances and looked forward to each public performance with anticipation. "Immer Kleiner" was one of the "fun" solos. He said the job of section leader was sometimes satisfying but sometimes trying when young players did not want to accept suggestions for improvement.

Loe has taught all levels of students during his career as a band director/teacher. He was band director at Scotland, South Dakota, from 1957-59. In 1959, he moved to Sioux Falls as band director at Axtell Park Junior High and for nine years also assisted with the Washington High School Marching Band. He is currently in his thirty-sixth year as band director at Axtell Park Middle School and three elementary schools. College teaching experience includes winds and percussion at Sioux Falls College and oboe/saxophone at Augustana College.

Patricia Masek

Patricia "Pat" Masek first joined the Sioux Falls Municipal Band as principal flutist in 1968 and has held that post for the past twenty-seven years. She served as assistant conductor to Lillehaug in the late 1970s and early 1980s. The players on the second flute and piccolo stands have normally been Masek's former students.

A native of Illinois, Masek completed her formal music training before working in Sioux Falls as a music teacher in the public schools 1962-67. She received a bachelor's degree in music education from the University of Illinois in 1960 and a master's degree in flute performance from the University of Kentucky in 1962.

In Sioux Falls, Masek has pursued numerous professional opportunities in music. She has played flute with the South Dakota Symphony from 1962 to the present (principal 1962-84) and was a charter member of the Dakota Wind Quintet (1982-

Pat Masek has played flute in the Municipal Band since 1968 and has served as assistant conductor. *(courtesy Sioux Falls Municipal Band)*

84). Masek has been the librarian with the Symphony since 1973 and an instrument repair person at K & M Music since 1978. She has done other professional playing in the area and has been an adjunct member of the Augustana College faculty since 1966, teaching applied flute, flute pedagogy, theory, music education and ensemble literature. She has occupied a similar position at Sioux Falls College since 1978.

Masek has made solo flute appearances with several South Dakota musical groups and is well-known in the area as a flute clinician.

Guest Conductors

In addition to members of the Band who occasionally were given a chance to conduct, a number of out-of-town guest conductors also appeared. Henegar's guests included Joseph P. Tschetter, conductor of the Mitchell Municipal Band, during 1941, 1942, 1950 and perhaps other years; Col. Howard Bronson on July 10, 1949; Paul Christensen, conductor of the Huron Municipal Band, September 3, 1950; and Carl Christensen, director of bands at South Dakota State College, on September 5, 1954. Bronson, Carl Christensen and other prominent conductors also guest conducted the Sioux Falls Municipal Band at the American Bandmasters Convention on March 21, 1948.

Lillehaug's guests included Dr. Leo Kucinski of Sioux City, August 20, 1967; John Buus of Lennox, August 17, 1967, and June 10, 1983; and Robert Hills of Ohio, August 7, 1983. Others who wielded the baton in front of the Band were Butler Eitel, a member of the American Bandmasters Association from Brookings, South Dakota, July 7, 1984; Charles Erwin, assistant conductor of the United States Marine Band, 1984; and Dr. Darwin Walker, director of bands at South Dakota State University, July 7, 1984. Walker also conducted a rehearsal in Lillehaug's absence. During Lillehaug's final two seasons Band members had the opportunity of working with Merle Evans, Ringling Brothers Circus conductor, June 23, 1985; Al Davis, composer , June 15, 1986; and James Christensen, Disney Corporation, July 8, 1986.

Dr. Alan Taylor invited Lillehaug to guest conduct at Lillehaug's retirement concert on July 26, 1987, and for the Band's appearance at the Association of Concert Bands annual convention in Omaha, Nebraska on April 5, 1991.

Dr. Bruce Ammann used Taylor and Lillehaug as guest conductors during the reunion concerts on June 26, 1994.

Merle Evans, left, former conductor of the Ringling Brothers and Barnum & Bailey Circus band, guest-conducted the Municipal Band in 1985. *(courtesy Sioux Falls Municipal Band)*

Guest conductors in 1986 included James Christensen (left), music director at Disney World, and Al Davis (above), composer and conductor. *(courtesy Sioux Falls Municipal Band)*

Masters of Ceremonies

Masters of ceremonies have always played an important role at Municipal Band concerts. They have set the tone and created a personal type of relationship between the audience and the Band. Depending on their personalities, they have provided humor, anecdotes, stories about the music, the composers and the Band members. They usually have been the first voices heard at "downbeat time" as the conductor and the Band are introduced and the last voices that thanked the audience for coming, often with the admonition, "Drive safely; we want you back here next week!" They have motivated the featured performers with their introductions and have related to members of the audience who came to the bandstand with requests and dedications. They have been the voice of the Sioux Falls Municipal Band.

Ed Paul and Paul Wegner

Ed Paul served as master of ceremonies from 1934-64 (with the exception of 1938) and Paul Wegner served in that capacity 1965-79 (see Chapter 10, Regular and Guest Vocalists).

Ray Loftesness

Ray "Lofty" Loftesness, born June 15, 1922, brought a special talent to his role as master of ceremonies. His mellow voice, easygoing personality, understanding of the makeup of the audience and great knowledge of music made him a natural as the voice of the Band. Loftesness was the Sioux Falls Municipal Band master of ceremonies in 1980 and from 1982 until his death in 1991. He had made guest appearances as master of ceremonies and vocalist beginning in 1965.

Loftesness worked for KSOO and KELO radio and later KSOO TV and KELO FM radio. KELO and KSOO were both owned by Mort Henkin and were in the same building at Ninth and Phillips. In the early days, Loftesness would keep a show on each station going at the same time by running up and down the stairs to keep the recordings playing. There also was a short period in the 1980s when he had a morning show on another radio station. He worked approximately forty years with KSOO, beginning as a music librarian at age fourteen. His radio show "Holiday Inn," which ran daily from Thanksgiving to Christmas for fifty-four years, was a favorite with listeners in the Sioux Empire. He also worked for the Fred Waring organization beginning in 1968.

Scott Loftesness said that people depended on his father to answer all kinds of musical questions. Lofty would get telephone calls, some after midnight, from people at parties, asking the names of tunes.

Lofty's interests were not restricted to radio and music. He was a voracious speed reader. His children eventually quit buying him books as gifts because they were disappointed that he read a new book in one sitting. He read many books, mainly histories and biographies, and major magazines such as the *New Yorker.* Because Lofty loved music, his son Scott said that the children grew up in a home where music was a very important part of the environment. From this, Scott (now the band director at Roosevelt High School in Sioux Falls) developed a deep respect for music and musicians.

After leaving KSOO in 1975, Loftesness had several jobs including Director of the Minnehaha County Bicentennial Commission, convention promoter for Holiday Inn Downtown, executive director of the Community Blood Bank and announcer for KELO FM's "Big Band Show" on Saturday nights. He worked long hours. He began his career with KSOO and ended it with KELO FM, working until Christmas, 1990, when he became ill.

Loftesness prepared and studied well for his Sioux Falls Municipal Band appearances as master of ceremonies. His casual

Ray "Lofty" Loftesness brought humor and musical knowledge to his job as master of ceremonies with the Municipal Band. *(courtesy Loftesness family)*

stage appearance made some people believe he knew so much about music and probably needed little or no preparation. However, he kept the "cue cards" (listing the composition title along with some information about the music) on a shelf by his front door so he wouldn't forget them on the way to the concert.

One of the things that made him so good as a master of ceremonies was that he was able to relate the music or the composer to this geo-

graphic area and to his audience. He could personalize the music because he knew many major composers personally. Like a good story
teller, he often exaggerated. Sousa's "Washington Post March" was an
audience favorite and appeared fairly often on Band programs. Often
Lofty would say something like, "I have checked the records and this is
the 1,832nd time that the Sioux Falls Municipal Band has played this
piece in its history." Because he changed the number each time (sometimes increasing or decreasing the previous number by several hundred on subsequent announcements), Band members listened eagerly
to see where he was heading on that particular concert. He often gently
scolded the large audience at the final concert of the season at Terrace
Park — knowing that many had come primarily to see the traditional
fireworks. After thanking them for attending the concert he would ask,
"Where have you been all season? Don't forget to come back next year
— the Band begins playing in June."

It was traditional that at the Band's annual Circus Concert the
master of ceremonies would become the ringmaster and don the red
and black ringmaster's uniform with the high black hat. Loftesness hated
to wear that uniform. For one thing it didn't fit very well, especially
after he had gained quite a few pounds in his belt area. Besides, it was
hot many Sunday evenings at Terrace Park. The hat was constructed
somewhat like an accordion and could be pressed together until it re-
sembled a plate. This he would do periodically and then suddenly in-
flate it to full size by tapping the underside with his fist. He loved to
surprise an unsuspecting onlooker with this gesture. Scott Loftesness
said that his father often would do a Groucho Marx imitation at home
after putting on the uniform.

Monty Barnard, a vocal soloist with the Band, remembered
Loftesness saying that performing "alfresco" was an asset for a soloist.
The word means "in the open; outdoors." Lofty's point was that a vocalist singing outdoors had to project the tone in order to reach the listeners. Barnard added, "Ray had a wonderful manner that helped one to
perform better than one otherwise would."

Roma Prindle, a former soprano soloist with the Band, also remembered the support Loftesness gave to the soloists. She told of the
evening when she was on her way to a concert at Heritage Park. A
motorcycle ran into her car, and the driver and his girlfriend were thrown
off the cycle and flew over the hood of her car. Fortunately, no one was
injured. She thought she had handled the situation pretty well emo-
tionally until she got to the concert site. When she saw familiar faces,
she said she "kind of fell apart" and didn't feel much like singing.
Loftesness did his best to console and distract her with his inimitable

brand of humor. His last words to her before the concert began were, "I know you'll do fine. Just relax. And if the police show up to arrest you, Lillehaug and I will pay your bail!"

Prindle also recalled a very hot Sunday afternoon in Sherman Park when she wore a "backless" sun dress. Loftesness really liked that dress and asked the audience if *they* liked it. "I made it," he said. "It isn't finished yet." Another time Prindle said she and Loftesness sat listening to a piece the band was rehearsing. It was a new piece and it was a pretty messy rehearsal for a few minutes. Prindle asked him what he thought of the piece. "I like it," he replied, "and there must be a melody in there somewhere!"

In 1990, when he began to talk about not feeling well, his family persuaded him to go to the doctor. He was in the Sioux Valley Hospital in June 1990, for two weeks. His son, Scott, said his father thought about other people rather than dwelling on his own problems. On June 11, Scott's birthday, Scott visited his father in the hospital. Scott said he wasn't leaving until Lofty told him about the illness. Loftesness finally said he had pancreatic cancer, and Scott became the first one in the family to learn the details. Loftesness knew that Scott was going out that evening with his friend Rolf Olson, a trumpet player who played in the Municipal Band. As Scott departed, he and his father hugged; Loftesness slipped him a twenty-dollar bill and told him to have a good time and to buy Rolf a drink.

In the summer of 1991, Loftesness was very ill and had not been able to continue as master of ceremonies. The Band members decided to honor him at a concert at Terrace Park, on Sunday evening, July 14, 1991, presenting him with a certificate for his nine years as full-time master of ceremonies. The concert theme was "A Night in Vienna." Even though he was very ill, he decided to attend, and moreover, he would be on stage as master of ceremonies. Very few people in the audience knew of the seriousness of his illness. As band member Janet Hallstrom said, "One couldn't tell from his actions that he was terminally ill."

On that same afternoon, Lillehaug had spent much of the afternoon with Loftesness. They discussed the years of their friendship, Lofty's accomplishments, the Band, life and death. Taylor had told Lillehaug about the Band's plans to honor Loftesness that evening, but Lillehaug thought there was no way that Loftesness could go to the concert and decided not to discuss the subject. Lillehaug could not believe it when, arriving at Terrace Park about 7:30 p.m., he saw Loftesness by the bandstand preparing to be master of ceremonies. It was his final appearance with the Band. He died approximately one month later, on August 16, 1991.

Loftesness was loved by the band members and many commented on their sadness at his sudden passing. "Lofty's illness and death left a great impression on me and the other players," said bass clarinetist, Linda McLaren Roach.

Robb Hart

Robb Hart, master of ceremonies since 1992, was awarded the master of ceremonies position on the basis of an audition.

He received a bachelor of arts degree in speech communication from Northeast Louisiana University. At one time he worked with Ray Loftesness at KELO Radio but now is the news producer at KSFY Television.

Guest Masters of Ceremonies

Others who served as guest masters of ceremonies include Dr. Monty Barnard, Dave Dedrick, Eugenia Hartig, Dr. Olaf Malmin, Denny Oviatt, the Reverend A. Richard Petersen, Tom Steever and Gene White.

Other Noteworthy People

There are three other people who have been especially memorable to Band members during the past thirty years. One did not play in the Band but was a dedicated Band fan; a second is a former player who has been a major promoter of the Band in the community; the third is the oldest player in the Municipal Band and has the longest tenure in the group.

Owen Foster

Owen Foster may have been the most devoted fan of the Sioux Falls Municipal Band. Beginning in about 1975, he attended every Monday night rehearsal and every concert of the Band, unless illness prevented it.

Foster, who had an identical twin brother Ivan, was born in Conde, South Dakota, in 1919, but grew up in Sioux Falls and graduated from

Owen Foster was one of the Band's most loyal listeners, attending concerts and rehearsals. He is shown here in 1982 at a rehearsal at the Coliseum. *(courtesy Sioux Falls Municipal Band)*

Washington High School where he played in the band. He spent a twenty-year career in the Air Force, beginning in 1937. Following his discharge, he lived in California through 1975, working as a security guard.

Foster loved band music. On Monday evenings he would choose a seat in one of the front rows of the Coliseum and listen to the Band rehearse. Before the rehearsal, he would sit just inside the south stage entrance, usually with a cigarette in his mouth, and greet the players as they entered. At intermission he was back in the corridors visiting with anyone who would stop to chat. He said that he had played the euphonium in the Sioux Falls Municipal Band, but his name does not appear on any of the membership records. When Foster couldn't get to the concerts on his own, Bob Roach, husband of bass clarinetist Linda McLaren Roach, picked him up at the Royal C. Johnson Veterans Memorial Hospital.

Foster died April 25, 1991, leaving a family of two sons, two daughters, one brother and one sister, Drusilla Sisson of Sioux Falls. The Band members sent flowers to his funeral in memory of him and of his devotion to them.

Paul Bankson

There are many who feel that the success of the adult community band movement in the future, as in the past, depends directly on the tremendous love of band music on the part of many of the players. An

embodiment of that deep love for band music in the Sioux Falls Municipal Band has been Paul Bankson. He does not relate to band music
because of prestige, perceived business connection advantages, or of
seeing or being seen. He just loves the music.

Lillehaug said that he has not known a person for whom band
music was so important and recalls that Bankson said that recording
the titles of music he has heard almost got him in trouble. Bankson has
been known to make notes on napkins while sitting in a cafe, docu-
menting a tune which he has just heard on the radio or juke box so that
he can make a suggestion to the
conductor regarding future performance. The titles of popular
tunes which he had written on
a restaurant napkin were
rather amorous, such as "I'll See
You In My Dreams," "I Can't Do
Without You," or "Love Me Tonight." When he retired on a
particular night he placed the
napkin on the dresser along
with the other contents from his
pockets. His wife noticed the
titles the next day and asked for
an explanation. Evidently she
understood and the explanation
was accepted.

How did he get in the Mu-
nicipal Band? Bankson recalled
that after the Sioux Falls Municipal Band played at the
Arena dedication, December 10,
1961, he talked to saxophonist

**Paul Bankson has been a major
supporter of the Municipal Band
through the years. *(courtesy Sioux
Falls Municipal Band)***

Ev Little, who suggested that he
join the Band. So Bankson contacted Henegar. There were no openings,
so Bankson waited until 1963, Henegar's last season, when he was allowed to play as a fill-in. He remembered that at his first rehearsal he
was assigned to the first trombone part. They played the "Peer Gynt
Suite," which contained "In the Hall of the Mountain King." It was difficult and Bankson said, "I was in trouble." He became a full member
under Lillehaug in 1964 and played through 1982.

Bankson, a native of Canton, South Dakota was born May 29, 1910.
He participated in music from an early age and developed a love for

music that led him to play in community groups as an adult. He took piano lessons but thought the piano was "a girl's instrument." He didn't want to be considered a sissy so he started playing trombone in the ninth grade in Canton. Later he was one of the community players who performed in the Town and Gown Orchestra at Augustana College. He had to quit that group in 1938 because it conflicted with his doorman job at the State Theater. Although he played in orchestra, he preferred playing in bands.

Bankson held several jobs in the 1930s before entering the armed forces in World War II. He was head usher at the State Theater from about 1930-33 after which he became a car salesman at Hartman Motor. Later he was doorman at the Arkota 1934-38 when Ben Abel was manager. Bankson went into the Air Force March 19, 1942, and served until November 5, 1945, much of the time in the South Pacific. Following the war, he spent most of his working life in real estate and insurance claim work.

Although he did not play his trombone while in the armed forces, he soon found opportunities to play after he got out of the service. He played in the State Legion Band, in the Lennox band for about thirty-six years and in the Sioux Falls Municipal Band. Bankson said that it was a big opportunity being able to play in a band like the Sioux Falls Municipal Band for nearly twenty years (1963-82), serving as Band president, member of the Board and Band manager.

Bankson also was impressed with many of the young people in the Band and said he was proud to sit in the same section as Scott Shelsta, now solo trombonist with The United States Army Band (see Chapter 11). He remembered Shelsta saying, "You gotta have fun." Bankson, at age eighty-four, has recently been playing with the Augustana/Community Band.

Paul Hoy

Paul Hoy, born December 12, 1906, in Sheldon, Iowa, is the oldest playing member of the Band at age eighty-eight. Although there were no other musicians in his own family, he possesses musical talent to the degree that he is considered by his colleagues as a "musician's musician." Hoy and his wife, Amy, were married in 1949 and had one son, Robert, now deceased. They have four grandchildren.

A graduate of Sheldon, Iowa, High School in 1925, Hoy spent most of his life in the newspaper business — first in Sheldon and then at the Sioux Falls *Argus Leader,* where he worked in the circulation department from 1956-72. Hoy had an ice cream shop in Sheldon for six years, following six years on a Wonder Bread route and twenty-five years as a printer for the *Sheldon Sun*. He also spent several years as office manager for the American Federation of Musicians, Local 114.

Hoy's musical training/experience includes participation in the first Sheldon band, organized when he was a freshman in high school (1922). He never had any private instruction. "George Wilcox was our band director. I don't think George gave private lessons to anybody. We learned by playing, I guess; ... we only had one rehearsal a week. That was bad, because everybody in the band loved it. And we never had a rehearsal until after four o'clock when school was out. I guess in those days they didn't consider the band much."

The Sheldon band had limited funds and music during its first year. Paul recalled, "I'll tell you something funny about the band. When it started, the school didn't have any money for music, and we each brought a dime, and in those days, times were tough. A dime meant a lot of money. So the school gave us fifteen cents, and we bought a [Karl] King book with sixteen numbers in it. That was all the music that we had for a year. And after that there was tax money for music so we did have different music after that year."

Although Hoy was a snare drummer in the Boy Scouts, he always admired bass drummers and took up that instrument when a position became available. He began playing with the Sheldon Municipal Band about 1930 and played with that band until it disbanded in 1944. Snare drum and bass drum are the only instruments that Hoy has played.

Hoy has always been fascinated with the circus and with circus music. "Half of my blood is still circus blood," he said. "People in the circus never get out of it." At the age of ten, he was working at the *Sheldon Sun* and received comp tickets for the circuses that came to town. In the afternoon show he would sit on one side of the band, and at the evening show he would sit on the other side of the band to get the full effect of the musical group.

He got his first job playing with a circus band in approximately 1924 when he was still in high school. The circus was the now defunct Atterburg Circus, which performed in Sheldon. He had an offer to travel with a circus band in 1925 but turned it down because his mother was a widow, and he didn't want to leave her alone. After his first job, he traveled with circuses on and off for months at a time from 1926-55. He also played with circus bands during vacation times. "Every time I got a vacation I went with the circus. ... It was fun. I wouldn't take a million dollars for the fun I've had playing with shows." The circuses included Mills Brothers, Dailey Brothers, Gil Gray, the Cole Circus, and

Bass drummer Paul Hoy is the oldest playing member of the Sioux Falls Municipal Band. He has been secretary-treasurer of the Band since 1964. *(courtesy Paul Hoy and the Argus Leader)*

Kelly-Miller. Hoy had to learn a few tricks of the trade to continue playing: the bass drummer often had to play without any music; there were no rehearsals; tempo was determined by watching one finger of the trumpet-playing conductor; and the piece was identified by hearing only one note. The last time he played with a circus was in 1961. Hoy said he quit because he was too old and because so many circuses started using tape instead of live music.

One outlet for Hoy's fascination with circuses is provided by planning a circus concert every summer for the Municipal Band. He presented the idea of a circus concert to Lillehaug, and the first annual circus band concert at Terrace Park took place August 14, 1966. "Typical" circus music actually is "a mixture of everything," said Hoy, who named marches, galops, waltzes, Spanish numbers and pop tunes as examples. He said that the Municipal Band gives an accurate representation of music from actual circus bands.

Hoy played one concert in 1957. During the 1958 season he played snare drum and bass drum. "The first year I was in the [Sioux Falls] City Band I played ... bass drum until nine o'clock and then ... the bass drummer that they had came and played for the last hour. ... And that went on for one year, and it seems like every concert night Russ Henegar would call and say, 'He isn't going to play tonight; you're going to play bass drum!' And that went on for a year, and Russ said, 'After this, if he [the other player] wants in the Band, he can play baritone.' ... I've never played anything but bass drum in the Band. The fact is the bass drum we have now he [Leland Lillehaug] and I went to a music store and ordered the drum from a store owned by Milt Askew. Nobody's ever played it but me." The drum cost $126.40.

Hoy has played with the Band for thirty-eight years and has been secretary/treasurer of the Band since the 1964 season, a total of thirty-one years. How long he will play depends on his health, he said.

Hoy said the Municipal Band has kept him young: "There's one thing about the Municipal Band as far as it concerns me — it has kept me young. There are so many young folks in the band, and, I shouldn't say it, but I've gotten along with all of them. They make you feel young. None of them ever said, 'Well I think you're too old to play in the band' or anything. All the years that I've been in the band, all the kids that I've played with have been just wonderful. You don't play in the Band for the money because you're not going to get rich. You play because you like it, and you like the people that are in the Band, the ones you work with. I know it's done me a lot of good in trying to stay young."

Band Secretaries

During its seventy-five years, the Municipal Band has had only four people serve as secretary/treasurer. Paul Hoy has served for the longest time (thirty-one years), followed by Guy Anderson (twenty-four), Ray Pruner (eleven) and Henry T. Hanson (nine).

Henry T. Hanson

Henry T. Hanson, born October 30, 1885, near Dell Rapids, was a 1920 charter member and was elected as the first secretary on November 2, 1919. Jake Helfert was elected treasurer at the same time, but nearly a year later, on October 15, 1920, the office of secretary and treasurer were combined into one position and Henry T. Hanson was elected to occupy that post. Hanson served until December 3, 1928, a total of nine years. A 1948 newspaper article said he "began his musical career by playing with the Dell Rapids [South Dakota] band from 1905 to 1917. He was director in 1916 and 1917, also directing a theatre orchestra there for seven years before coming to Sioux Falls."

Hanson, a soprano and alto clarinetist, played with the Sioux Falls Municipal Band from its first season in 1920 through 1958, one of the longest tenures of any player.

When the Band was formed he was a secretary at F. H. Weatherwax Company in Sioux Falls. Later, he was a clothing salesman at the Shriver Johnson Department Store. His obituary said he worked in various clothing stores 1905-44 and worked as a bookkeeper and accountant for the Masonic Grand Lodge 1944-58 when he was retired.

He was married September 15, 1920, in Sioux Falls to Myrtle C. Hanson. Musicians' Union records show that he applied for membership in the Local on May 24, 1918, and that he died at the age of seventy-eight on July 23, 1964.

Guy G. Anderson

Guy G. Anderson, born November 23, 1888, in Adrian, Minnesota, was a saxophonist with the Band from its first season in 1920 through 1954, a total of thirty-five years.

According to a 1948 newspaper article, he also played the trombone, although that seems like an unlikely combination. The article reported that Anderson had played the trombone "in the Sioux Falls high school orchestra under the direction of Prof. C. A. Wilkinson in 1908. He continued on that instrument when playing in a city band here under the direction of John L. Johnson in 1912."

Anderson was listed in the 1921 Sioux Falls city directory as an assistant cashier at Mutual Life Insurance Company of New York. He worked in the treasurer's office at City Hall, served as Band secretary-treasurer 1929-52, a total of twenty-four years. In a letter dated August 1978 to then-conductor Leland Lillehaug, Anderson commented on the quality of the Band musicians: "It was a fine thing when they started teaching band instruments in the schools as it has brought out many fine musicians, much better as a group than our old group of players."

He died at the Good Samaritan Village in Sioux Falls November 4, 1978, shortly before his ninetieth birthday.

Ray Pruner

Ray Pruner, who had been the Band president since 1947, became the secretary/treasurer in 1952 and held the post for eleven years until 1963, when he retired. Pruner, who had worked for the Panama Railroad for twenty-seven years, had returned to Sioux Falls and joined the Band in 1945, playing percussion.

Pruner was born January 4, 1883, in Sioux Falls. He died May 4,1966, according to Sioux Falls Musicians' Union records.

Pruner's nephew Thomas E. Pruner, Sr., a Sioux Falls resident, remembered going to the back of the Terrace Park band shell on Sunday evenings during the late 1940s to say hello to his uncle Ray. "He would give me a quarter almost every time," Thomas said. He said that Ray always

Ray Pruner served as the Band's secretary/treasurer for eleven years. *(courtesy Sioux Falls Municipal Band)*

had a big cigar in the side of his mouth, most of the time unlit. He also told of Ray's love for his 1940 Buick.

Ray Pruner was the son of Thomas H. Pruner, who played with Stout's Band (see Chapter 1) and was a part of professional music life of Sioux Falls, including being one of the founding signers of the Federation of Musicians charter for Sioux Falls Local 114, on April 2, 1906.

Paul Hoy

As mentioned earlier in this chapter, Paul Hoy was elected secretary-treasurer of the Band at the annual meeting on January 13, 1964, and is still serving in that post in 1994, a total of thirty-one years.

• • •

Although the conductor and all the players are critical to the smooth performance of a band, there are other contributors whose work is often overlooked. These include the composers/arrangers, assistant conductors and masters of ceremonies. In addition, although they have not been mentioned above, there are other important groups of people: those who arrange the stage, drive and set up the Showmobile, work in the music library, write publicity pieces, handle the sound system and office business, serve as officers and care for the uniforms. The conductor often must be a part of many of the tasks, but assistance is always needed.

Finally, one must not forget the support of spouses and family during the players' seventy to eighty events each season or the audience whose attendance makes all the efforts worthwhile.

14 Leadership from City Hall

Producing a top musical organization takes a combination of several factors: the best players available, an outstanding conductor, audience support and administrative and financial support. The administrative and financial support is crucial because it is not possible to have the other three factors without it. Those who supported the establishment of a municipal band in Sioux Falls and the legislators who passed the 1919 law (see Chapter 1) understood that, and the positive results of their action are evident in the success of the Band through seventy-five successive years.

Decisions on financial support in Sioux Falls are made by the City commissioners who supervise the various departments and vote on budgets. Support has been quite stable throughout the seventy-five-year history of the Sioux Falls Municipal Band, ebbing and flowing slightly because of local social and economic conditions and the interest, or lack of interest, on the part of individual commissioners.

Elections for Sioux Falls commissioners normally are held in April or June, and the winners take office in May or July. Although it appears that the Band director reported to the Park Department during its early years, the Sioux Falls Municipal Band functioned as an independent department during much of its history. The Band director was a department head and made budget requests directly to the mayor or one of the commissioners. In 1975 the Band was placed under the jurisdiction of Earl McCart, city commissioner. Previously it had been under the mayor. In 1987, the Band was placed under the jurisdiction of the Park Department. Since that time, the Band budget request goes to the Director of the Park Department, who makes judgments on it and incorporates the request into the Park Department budget request to the City Commission. The original Band budget request will fare well or poorly depending on the attitude toward it of the director of the Park Department, followed by the response of the commissioners.

Several of the present and past mayors and commissioners were interviewed, hopefully representing a cross-section of the officials through the years. All of them indicated that they were supporters of the Band and its service to the community. Some said that there are some years in which financial considerations do not allow for any increase in budget and sometimes require cuts.

Questions most often asked regarding the change in Band structure is why the commission changed the position of band conductor from a department head to an independent contractor and moved the supervision of the Band from a mayor or commissioner to that of the Director of Parks and Recreation (in 1987) when it had seemingly functioned so well for many decades. Although it is difficult to ascertain the answer with precision, the following have been suggested:

Hiring the Band conductor as an independent contractor rather than as a city employee eliminated the need to pay benefits; the Band plays a large number of its concerts in the parks so having it report to the Park Department makes coordination easier; the Park Department has a staffed office to which calls from the public can be directed; Commissioner Peterson, who had first suggested the change, didn't want to be bothered with direct supervision of the Band.

Gary Holman, representing the Band as president of the Band Board during the mid 1980s, and Leland Lillehaug (conductor at that time) were very much against the change and stressed that the Band had functioned without administrative problems for many years when it worked directly under mayors or commissioners. They said that it was unwise to make a change with a structure that was working well. They felt that because the Band represented the entire city, it was simpler and more efficient to have the conductor report directly to the mayor or one of the commissioners. Past commissioners and Band supervisors Mike Schirmer, Earl McCart and Jack White agreed as did past commission members Rick Knobe, Harold Wingler and Joe Cooper. Commissioner Matt Staab said he felt that the Band was not a big enough department to report directly to a commissioner and that it should remain under the Park Department. Past commissioner Richard Peterson declined to be interviewed.

It probably will take a few years in the present relationship to ascertain if the Band will function better or worse under the director of

Parks as compared to having the director report directly to the mayor or a commissioner.

In 1994, the citizens of Sioux Falls voted in a new form of government, effective January 1, 1995. It will consist of a mayor and eight part-time council members, one elected from each of five districts and three at large.

Terms of the mayor and council members will be four years. After the first election, four of the council members will serve for two years and four will serve for four years. Every two years four council members will be up for election. The council will set policy and vote on ordinances and the mayor will be the chief executive officer. It is not clear at this time as to whether the Band will remain under the Park Department under this new system.

Mayors and Commissioners in Charge

Mayor Thomas McKinnon

Band minutes of 1928 indicate that the Band was responsible to Mayor McKinnon, at least during part of his term. Minutes of August 20, 1928, speak of drawing up a contract with the mayor for certain playing jobs. This probably means that the mayor, who served from 1924-29, was supervising the Band at that time. In October 1928 there is evidence of problems between the first-year conductor G. C. McClung and members of the Band, seemingly because he had begun action to terminate employment of some of the players. The mayor found it necessary to step in. On November 5, 1928, at a meeting of the entire Band at the City Auditorium, the Band president read a letter from Mayor McKinnon relative to employing a director for the coming year. A motion to retain G. C. McClung was defeated fifteen to eleven by the Band members. As a result, a Band committee was appointed to meet with Mayor McKinnon and E. J. Wintersteen, who was a member of the "City Band committee." The minutes of that meeting indicate that a brief discussion took place but do not record any decisions

The dissension in the ranks caused Mayor McKinnon to attend a special meeting of the Band on January 17, 1929. He stated that it was his desire that the members get together and iron out the trouble so that the members and director could work in harmony and keep up the good record that the Band had in the past. He also stated that he wanted the director to have charge of hiring and releasing of the men as it was handled that way in other departments of the city. McKinnon evidently proved to be a good negotiator because at a meeting of the Band on January 24, 1929, the members voted to retain McClung. The minutes stated that "After remarks by several members and the director that all differences and ill-feelings would be forgotten and that all would work together for the best interests of the Band, the meeting adjourned."

Mayor George W. Burnside

Mayor Burnside assumed jurisdiction of the Band when he was elected in 1929 and was in office through 1934. E. J. Wintersteen continued to serve as a representative of the city in its business with the Band. The Band offered to play at a reception in the Coliseum on Wednesday, May 1, in honor of Burnside, the newly elected mayor but for some reason it was not held.

Negotiations regarding a new director to replace G. C. McClung were held with Alex Reid of the City commission and Mr. M. G. Luddy (a Band representative?). A problem existed because Arthur Thompson and O. H. Andersen (the Band's choice) both claimed they had been hired by the city. The minutes do not describe the outcome further, but O. H. Anderson was selected as the conductor. However, probably to pacify Thompson, the city hired him to play seven concerts with high school musicians early in the 1930 season (see Chapter 3).

Mayor A. N. Graff

It seems that the new mayor became involved with Band personnel because he requested that the Band use a Mr. Moen on baritone horn if possible. The May 27, 1935, Band minutes stated that president Edwards was to "interview" the mayor and "explain that it would mean adding another member to the Band and also that Mr. Moen was not a member of Sioux Falls Musicians Local." In an evident effort to placate the mayor, Edwards said Moen would be given permission to sit in and play gratis if he would obtain a uniform. It is not clear if players were required to own their own uniforms at this time or if the statement meant that Moen would simply need to check out a uniform from the Band.

During the 1935 season, Graff approved an exchange concert with the Madison band in response to a request by the mayor of Madison. It is clear from the minutes that Graff was paying attention to the activities of the Band, including giving his advice on such items as transferring a concert from one of the regularly scheduled sites to the Sioux Falls College campus and purchasing a loud speaker system rather than renting it. Graff's term ran 1934-39.

Mayor John T. McKee

Band minutes 1940-42 show that there were periodic discussions with the mayor regarding the operation of the Band during his 1939-42 term. Among items discussed were personnel and the purchase of new instruments. McKee died in 1942, and at the final concert of the summer season on September 6, 1942 (played at the Coliseum because of rain), Ed Paul sang "The Prayer Perfect" as a memoriam to the late mayor.

Mayor C. M. Whitfield

Mayor Whitfield continued the supervision of the Band 1942-49 and was consulted regarding special requests for concerts (Band minutes August 23, 1943). On August 5, 1946, president Jackson and conductor Henegar were instructed by the Band Board to meet with the mayor to see if there could be an extra appropriation for the next season which would allow the Band to play "Trade Relations Trips" to neighboring small towns that had requested concerts. However, at about this time the Recording Trust Funds through the Local Musicians Union became available (in 1947), and the Band played eight concerts with those funds, six of them in small towns in the Sioux Falls area. In 1949, the Moose Lodge sponsored a benefit for the March of Dimes and requested the Band to play. Henegar informed them that he would have to check with the mayor. This indicates that the conductor felt it necessary to check with his supervisor, the mayor, when matters of policy were involved. He was afraid that if the Band honored this request they would feel obliged to do the same for other groups — ultimately taking concerts away from the parks.

A paucity of minutes during the terms of Mayor H. B. Saure (1949-54) and Mayor Fay Wheeldon (1954-61) makes it impossible to determine definitely that Henegar reported to the City commission during those years, but it seems very likely because Crusinberry supervised the Band during his term.

Mayor Vinton L. Crusinberry

Earl McCart, who became acting mayor following Crusinberry's death in December 1967, said, "Crusinberry was an honorable man. He may be one of the better mayors we have ever had." McCart said that Crusinberry, a former fire chief, considered himself a public servant. Crusinberry hired Lillehaug in late 1963 and was an active supporter of the Band until his death while still in office. Crusinberry's term was 1961-67.

Mayor M. E. (Mike) Schirmer

Mayor M. E. Schirmer supervised the Band 1968-74. He recalls that at one time the commissioners were looking for ways to lower the city budget. Schirmer thought that perhaps the Band would be one department whose budget could be cut. However, after he accompanied the Band to a concert at the Harvest Festival in Salem he changed his mind. When he heard the fine quality of the Band's performance and saw the response of the crowd, he realized what a good public relations vehicle the Band was for Sioux Falls and opposed any budget cuts for the Band that year.

Mayor M.E. "Mike" Schirmer was the commissioner who supervised the Municipal Band 1968-74. *(courtesy Argus Leader)*

Schirmer had been a bareback rider in a circus in his younger days and he observed that the gait of the horse changed according to the tempo of the music. "If that can affect a horse that way, think what it can do to the emotions of a human being," he stated. He was born in Baraboo, Wisconsin, a famous circus town, and began touring at the age of fifteen. He played Chicago in 1925.

Schirmer has lived in Sioux Falls for fifty-six years. He feels that the Band brings cultural values to the community and likes the idea of music in the open air. He emphasizes that it also introduces young children to good music, consequently providing them educational benefits. The live performances also introduce youth to the various instruments. The personnel in the Band demonstrate that music can be a lifelong endeavor and shows that citizens from various vocations can join together to practice their musical skills. In terms of audience, the concerts bring the family unit together because people of all ages can enjoy a band concert. "The Band is an organization that can play all types of music," Schirmer said. "The money that is put in by the city produces something important. The results may be less tangible than buildings, but they are there."

During his administration, Schirmer said it was his experience that many more people said, "Don't cut the budget for the Band," than those who said "cut the budget." The former mayor hopes that the public will always maintain their support of the Band and realize the benefit it has been to the city of Sioux Falls. "The Band is one of the things that is as needed as much as anything we have. ... It has an important influence on young people," he added.

Earl J. McCart

McCart supervised the Band from December 27, 1967, to May 1968, while he was acting mayor, and 1974-76 as a commissioner. He said that he considered himself a strong advocate for the Band. Former mayor Rick Knobe agreed, saying that he believed that Commissioner Earl McCart was the strongest advocate of the Band during his years on the commission. McCart was a "people program person," Knobe stated. McCart remembered that during the period he served, the Band was highly regarded by the commission. He reported one situation that might not be accepted today. Henegar, as secretary-treasurer of the Musicians Union, ran the musicians' union business from his Band office in City Hall. Some commissioners were con-

Earl McCart. *(courtesy city of Sioux Falls)*

cerned about it, but since there was no criticism from the public and since it didn't seem to cause problems, the commissioners decided to "let sleeping dogs lie."

McCart remembered that there was some argument regarding the purchase of the portable stage (Showmobile). As indicated in Chapter 7, the decision to purchase the Showmobile took nearly eight years. It is not clear whether it was Parks Director Ken Munro, the Park Board, the commissioners, or some combination of the three, that caused the delay. McCart said that after the purchase of the Showmobile, Ken Munro wanted to tear down the McKennan band shell. He presented his proposal to the Park Board but it was defeated. McCart credited Park Board member Peder K. Ecker as being one of the strongest advocates of historic preservation in regard to the band shell. Ecker, in a recent interview, said that he indeed had opposed the destruction of the McKennan shell.

Prior to his position on the commission, McCart worked for the United States Public Health Service, the Conservative Bond and Mortgage Company and was Minnehaha County's first democratic county auditor (1957-61). During World War II he served with the 147th Field Artillery in the Pacific Theater 1940-45. The unit left Pearl Harbor three days prior to the bombing on December 7, 1941.

He said that the Sioux Falls Municipal Band "is a part of the history and tradition of Sioux Falls and should be sustained in perpetuity."

Vernon G. Winegarden

Vernon Winegarden, originally from Wessington Springs, supervised the Band 1976-81. Lillehaug remembers him as being easy to work with and as a strong Band supporter.

Prior to being commissioner, Winegarden had served for fourteen years as Sioux Falls city treasurer, had worked at Midwest Oil Co. and had served in the Army.

Winegarden was defeated by Richard Peterson in 1981. He and his wife moved to Rapid City in 1983, where he died April 28, 1988, at the age of 61.

Vernon Winegarden. *(courtesy Argus Leader)*

Richard E. Peterson

Richard E. Peterson supervised the Municipal Band 1981-87. Leland Lille-haug, conductor during those years, said Peterson seemed supportive of the Band early in his term but later seemed antago-nistic toward it. Peterson lost the support of many members of the Municipal Band during the controversy with Lillehaug (see Chapter 8).

Peterson began as commissioner in 1981, was reelected for a four-year term in 1986 and resigned in 1988.

He declined to be interviewed for this book.

Richard Peterson. *(courtesy Argus Leader)*

Mayor Jackson "Jack" White

Mayor Jack White served a five-year term beginning in 1986 and was reelected in 1991 for another five-year term. He took over the Band and Park Department from Richard Peterson in early 1987. The Band was placed under the supervision of the Park Department in early May of 1987, and White supervised parks until May 1989.

White heard the Municipal Band when he was a child because he lived near McKennan Park and sold pop-corn there.

When asked how he thought he would feel if 1994 were 1919 and he had to make a decision as to whether to found a municipal band, White said he would support such action. "The Band is a great asset to the commu-nity and I have enjoyed the Band."

Mayor Jack White took over supervision of the Band from Commissioner Peterson in 1987. *(courtesy Jack White)*

Kenny Anderson

Kenny Anderson was elected to fill Peterson's unexpired term in 1988 and was reelected for a five-year term in 1990 but died in November 1990. He assumed jurisdiction over the Park Department, and thus the Band, on May 1, 1989.

Sylvia Henkin

Sylvia Henkin was appointed as commissioner from December 1990, to July 1991, and supervised the Park Department (and the Band). She remembered no problem with the Band budget or the Band.

When asked what she would like to see that might involve the Band, she replied that a Fourth of July parade and celebration in addition to the evening fireworks would be a good addition.

Matt Staab

Matt Staab assumed responsibility for the Park Department, and through it, the Band in 1991. He feels that the Band is important to the community as a quality of life factor. He would vote to institute such a band today if it were not in existence, and feels that such a proposal would pass in a citizen vote.

Normally, commissioners are sworn in at City Hall. However, Staab requested that he be sworn in as commissioner before a Sioux Falls Municipal Band concert at Terrace Park on June 23, 1991. It is thought that he is the first Sioux Falls commissioner to be sworn in at a band concert during the past several decades — perhaps ever. Staab wanted something that symbolized many of the good things in Sioux Falls — parks, recreation and the Band.

Other Mayors and Commissioners

Mayor Rick Knobe

Rick Knobe was mayor from 1974-84. He remembers that people

came in at budget time to support the Band. He felt that it was a good procedure for the Band to play in many locations, strengthening the concept of "arts for everyone." "The Band, like the city library, is accessible to the regular people," he said. Knobe felt the concerts had an air of sophistication but were not highbrow. He sensed that the conductor was trying to elevate the music appreciation of the listeners.

Knobe felt the Band budget was small compared to most city expenditures and that many times the commissioners unnecessarily haggled over small items in the Band's budgets. Knobe considered himself to be an advocate of the arts and recreation programs as well.

How did people respond regarding the Band at annual budget hearings? "There were responses from both sides," Knobe said. There were some concerns that the ordinary player could not get into the Band because the demands were too great.

Knobe says he attended quite a few concerts. His interest in instrumental music stems from having been a saxophone player and having an aunt who was organist in the church George Washington attended. Positive influences on Knobe regarding the Band were Ray Loftesness, Eugenia Hartig, Paul Bankson and Paul Wegner.

He felt that the acquisition of the Showmobile (portable stage) was very important to the Sioux Falls Municipal Band.

Harold Wingler

Harold Wingler served as commissioner from 1978-83 for one five-year term, following David Witte and preceding Loila Hunking.

Even though Wingler was not the Band's commissioner, he said he supported the Band with his votes. He felt the concerts had special value, particularly for the older citizens. Wingler served with Knobe the entire term, with Winegarden, who was the commissioner in charge of the Band at that time, and with Peterson, who followed Winegarden.

Mayor Joe Cooper

Joe Cooper was mayor from 1984-86, following Rick Knobe. He did not complete his five-year term because of the change of government. He chose not to run again for mayor in the election, which enlarged the governing body from a three- to a five-person commission. He has a very positive attitude about the Sioux Falls Municipal Band and often attended concerts at McKennan and Terrace.

Cooper knew band music, being a baritone and trumpet player and having played with the Karl King Band in Ft. Dodge, Iowa, about 1946-49. King was once the conductor of the Barnum and Bailey Circus Band and was a noted composer. Cooper started on the clarinet but liked brass better. He also played bass viol in the orchestra in high school and attended junior college in Ft. Dodge.

It is Cooper's belief that the Sioux Falls Municipal Band should work to reach the young people, and feels that the Band should try to play in the schools if possible. He realizes that it may be difficult to implement because of problems with players' work schedules, but he feels it is worth investigating. When Cooper hears a good march done well, the hair on the nape of his neck often stands up — demonstrating that good music does have an emotional impact!

He doesn't remember any big hassles about the Band budget. When he attended Band concerts he came away thinking that the time was well spent. Cooper is now the executive director of the South Dakota Broadcasters Association and works out of his home in Sioux Falls.

A Message from Mayor Gary Hanson

"Congratulations on your successful endeavor to provide a history of the Sioux Falls Municipal Band. I have fond memories of listening to the Band as a young boy at the McKennan Park and Terrace Park band shells. My mother, Helen Brumbaugh Hanson, sang guest appearances with the Band in 1945 and 1949. I am especially pleased for her that this project has been successful.

"I hope that our citizens enjoy your sounds of music for many more generations."

• • •

The evidence is strong that nearly all of the mayors and commissioners in the seventy-five year history of the Band have recognized the value of the Band to the city and its citizens and have given it strong moral and financial support. Even some who may not have been personally interested in music were aware of what the organization meant to a broad spectrum of the public.

15 Fans Reminisce, Look to the Future

W
hy has the Sioux Falls Municipal Band survived for seventy-five years, and what is the value of the Sioux Falls Municipal Band to the Sioux Falls area? In other chapters, several of the players mentioned how important the Band was to them in preparing for professional careers in music, in providing a musical outlet and in helping music teachers get acquainted with vast amounts of band literature. City commissioners stressed the Band's role in improving quality of life in the community. In the Band's early years, the Chamber of Commerce used the Band as a public relations tool in trips to surrounding towns. Pat Masek, the veteran principal flutist, said the Band's success has hinged on the variety of music, including the popular music of the 1940s. Others affirm that the Band's success has been due to the high quality of the performances, produced by skilled conductors and proficient players. Still others complimented the city's steady financial support — producing concerts that are free, clean, enjoyable family entertainment, something increasingly difficult to find. Perhaps the answer to the Band's longevity is a combination of all of the above.

But one of the main ingredients in the musical formula is the listeners who, for seventy-five years, have attended the concerts. Listeners come as singles, couples and families. They are the elderly, children and, recently, an increasing number of people in their late teens and twenties. Concerts are readily accessible because the Band plays about four times a week in many parts of the city during the summer and occasionally in the winter. The Municipal Band is taken for granted by many, but to others it remains a valued entertainment and arts organization. Eight senior citizens explained what the Band meant to them:

Margaret Barnett, a resident of Prince of Peace retirement community, said that her family never missed a Sunday night Band concert. They always looked forward to concerts because of the variety. Barnett said she "really loved" band music.

Anna Schartz, now living at Bethany Home, was born in 1908 and came to the Sioux Falls area before World War II. When she was a child, her father sometimes took all four children to the concerts in their Model T Ford. She married a farmer near Hartford and later lived in Hartford. She would try to get to the concerts if the "Mister," her name for her husband, didn't have to work. Sometimes they went to Sioux Falls on Sundays during the summer, swimming at Sherman Park and attending the Band concerts. Although they attended concerts in other parks, Sherman was the handiest. Access seemed to make a difference even when Sioux Falls was smaller. Park Board minutes indicate that residents of Northwest Iowa tended to favor McKennan Park because it was on "their side" of the city.

Hallie McBride, also a resident at Bethany Home, had no friends or relatives in the Sioux Falls Municipal Band, but she lived near McKennan Park so she attended concerts there as well as at Terrace Park. She especially enjoyed marches and selections from Broadway musicals. McBride moved to Sioux Falls with her husband, Fred, from Kansas City during World War II. She is the mother of state legislator Barbara Everist, who remembered that they often had picnics in conjunction with the concerts.

Another reason for attending concerts was given by **Esther Schroeder**, now nearly ninety years old. She said concerts were relaxing and gave her a chance to "get out of the house." Born in 1905 in Chancellor, South Dakota, she has lived in Sioux Falls since World War II. Schroeder is a single woman who did house work for the Milton Pay family. She lived close to McKennan Park and was able to walk to those concerts. Because she didn't have a car, her father, who once played in the Emery Community Band, would take her to Terrace Park concerts. She loved marches and enjoyed hearing Ed Paul sing.

Bands have always been associated with patriotic events. **Gladys Bairey**, a resident at Good Samaritan Village, moved to Sioux Falls

This is the scenic view — from the upper terraces at Terrace Park —
Municipal Band fans have enjoyed since the Terrace Park band-
stand was built in 1923. This photo is from about 1992. *(courtesy
Sioux Falls Municipal Band)*

from Brookings in 1930. She said there is something thrilling about
"The Stars and Stripes Forever": "It just makes you feel patriotic." She
commented on how much children seem to love the concerts. She remembered when her daughter was about two-and-one-half years old
and slipped away from her parents, ran up in front of the Terrace Park
stage and danced around.

   Helen De Velde, who moved to Sioux Falls from Parkston in about
1942, agreed with Bairey about the march "Stars and Stripes Forever."
She liked the piece because of the melody and the rhythm. She heard a
lot of band music because her husband, Harry, was once band director
in Oldham, South Dakota, and taught music at Whittier School in Sioux

Falls. De Velde is living at Good Samaritan Village.

Helen (Mrs. Wilmer) Simmons, born in 1908, didn't have to go far to hear Municipal Band concerts because the family lived in the former Phillips House at Terrace Park. Simmons says that her father, Joe Maddox, was a caretaker at Terrace Park for many years and built the Japanese Gardens. She said that the Band played from a wooden platform near the Phillips House, which was above the present terraces. She also recalled that the early bands played on a wooden platform near the Park House at Terrace Park, before the band shell was built in 1923. Simmons lives with her daughter, Joan Gerry, in Sioux Falls.

Bob Heege, a retired judge, now plays in the Augustana-Community Band. Heege and his wife took their family to band concerts, usually to McKennan Park because they lived in that area. Hegge was impressed with the quality of the Band and said the whole family loved the concerts.

Band Fans Look to the Future

Arts advocates in Sioux Falls were heartened by the decision to create a new Arts Pavilion in the former Washington High School building in downtown Sioux Falls. Many Band supporters thought that the facility would house rehearsal facilities, office space, library space and instrument storage for the Band. But the news about the Band's future in the facility is uncertain as of November 1994. Band fans find it difficult to understand why an organization which is funded by the city of Sioux Falls should not automatically be housed in the new facility, which is partially funded with tax monies.

Pam Hansen Barnard, the current Band president, stated, "The Band members are hoping to be a part of the new facilities and eagerly look forward to the completion of the Pavilion." She said that being in a facility with good acoustics would provide more opportunities for winter concerts and would enable the Band to move indoors in the summer when bad weather prevents outdoor performances.

Conductor Bruce Ammann said that the Sioux Falls Municipal Band is a vital part of the arts community in Sioux Falls. "If the Washington Pavilion is to be the center of arts in our community, I feel that the Sioux Falls Municipal Band should be a part of that," Ammann added.

Commissioner Bob Jamison is the chairman of the Washington Pavilion of Arts and Science implementation committee. He is the only elected official from the city of Sioux Falls on the committee and reports back to the City Commission. Jamison is optimistic that the Washington Pavilion will be able to provide suitable accommodations for the Municipal Band. This optimism is shared by Lowen Schuett, director of Parks and Recreation, who supervises the Band. Schuett said, "I hope that the physical arrangements will accommodate the rehearsal needs for the Band in the Pavilion."

Bob Winkels, project manager for the construction phase of the Washington Pavilion, was hired by the city of Sioux Falls in January 1994 to represent the City's interest in the project. He is aware of the space needs of the Municipal Band and the South Dakota Symphony and said the committee hopes to find a satisfactory solution. In addition to rehearsal and performance facilities, the two groups need space for library and equipment storage.

• • •

This book has attempted to give an overview of seventy-five years in the life of the Sioux Falls Municipal Band, tracing the Band's history from its establishment by a vote of Sioux Falls citizens. The Band struggled for identity from 1920 to 1934, then grew and developed into one of the leading organizations of its kind in the United States. The trials of making music during the Depression and World War II tested the mettle of the conductor and players. The Band adjusted to changes in the social conditions and weathered the problems of the Vietnam era. Women became a part of the previously all-male Band in 1964.

The innovation of a computerized library and a portable band shell changed the way the Band prepared for its concerts and performed. New programming ideas with theme concerts, circus tunes and music for children brought new band fans to the parks and increased audience attendance. Reviving indoor concerts at the Coliseum allowed the Band to play an even greater variety of music. After the continuity of two conductors during fifty-two years, the Band has adjusted to two new conductors during the past eight years.

The Band has survived because of people — the conductors, the players, vocalists, leaders from City Hall and audience members. All are bound together by one common factor — their love of music. This common bond makes it possible to play and to listen regardless of differences of age, economic level, vocation, gender or race. This red, white and blue community band, celebrating seventy-five years of life in 1994, is truly a part of the grass roots tradition of the United States of America. The Sioux Falls Municipal Band is alive and well and eager to serve its citizens as it points toward the year 2019 and its centennial.

In addition to its regular park concert sites, the Municipal Band has performed at various locations throughout Sioux Falls and surrounding communities. When park benches are not available, audience members take along their own lawn chairs or blankets. This photo was taken in 1986, when the Band played in downtown Sioux Falls in front of the First National Bank Building at Ninth and Phillips. *(courtesy Sioux Falls Municipal Band)*

Appendix

1915 South Dakota Band Tax Law

1915 South Dakota Legislature
(Fourteenth Session)
Senate Bill 21

"§ 1. Tax to be levied and duty of city council, board of commissioners and board of trustees. That the city council, board of commissioners or board of trustees in all cities and towns organized under the general laws of the state, or under special laws, unless otherwise provided for in their charters, may levy a tax of not exceeding one (1) mill each year on all taxable property within the city, or town, for the purpose of creating a fund for the furnishing of free musical concerts to the public, provided, that before any levy of said taxes shall be made, there shall be filed with the city council, or commissioners of such city, or board of trustees of such incorporated town, a petition signed by at least twenty (20) per cent of the electors thereof, as shown by the vote for members of the city council or commissioners or board of trustees at the last preceding annual election held in such city or town, and requesting that the levying of said tax be submitted to the electors thereof at the next general election preceding the meeting of the city council, board of commissioners or board of trustees held for the purpose of making the annual appropriation, such petition to be filed with the city auditor or town clerk at least ten days preceding the date set for any general city or town election. Upon the filing of said petition as aforesaid it shall be the duty of the city auditor or town clerk to submit such proposition to the voters of such election, said question to be submitted upon a separate ballot. If a majority of the electors of such city or town voting at such election shall vote in favor of such proposition, then the levy of said tax shall be deemed authorized, otherwise no such levy shall be made herein.

"Said tax shall be used for no other purpose than herein before provided. Said tax levy shall be made by said city council, or said board of commissioners, at their first regular meeting in September, and by the board of trustees before the third Tuesday in May. Said tax levy shall thereupon be immediately certified by the city auditor, city clerk or town clerk, to the county auditor of the county in which said city or town is situated.

"§ 2. Duty of City or Town Treasurer: It shall be the duty of the city or town treasurer to keep all moneys collected or received from the county treasurer under the provisions of this act, in a special fund separate and apart from any other moneys that may come into his hands as such city or town treasurer.

"§ 3. Duty of County Auditor: The county auditor shall calculate and fix the rate per centum of the tax in the same manner as all other city and town taxes are levied, and shall enter the same on the tax lists for collection as other city or town taxes are collected.

"§ 4. Repeal. All acts or parts of acts in conflict with this act are hereby repealed.
Approved March 11th, 1915."

South Dakota Constitution and The Laws Passed at the Fourteenth Session of the Legislature of the State of South Dakota, official edition, Pierre, SD: Hipple Printing Co., pp. 695-696.

W. J. Elwood Letter to the Editor, 1919

Letter to the editor from W. J. Elwood, chairman of the band committee for the Loyal Order of the Moose, 1916-18.

"That there will be no band in Sioux Falls this year unless municipally supported and that the Moose lodge in the past have generously provided the funds for maintaining the band, is the statement of W. J. Ellwood. Mr. Ellwood says: 'I have read with a great deal of interest the extensive articles appearing in the *Argus Leader* in regard to the municipal band proposition, and the lengthy discussions of some of the gentlemen on this subject are almost amusing.

"For the past three years the only band organized in Sioux Falls has been that of the Loyal Order of Moose, and at the time the local Moose lodge decided to organize and assist in the operation of a band for the city, not fully realizing the difficulties to be encountered, I consented to be chairman of the band committee, and served as such for the period of time mentioned. During that period of three years, the only outside help that I can recall that the band received, other than the union scale paid to the various members for their services, most of the time, but not all of the time, as on many occasions their services were donated by the musicians, was the sum of $200 donated by the Sioux Falls Commercial Club, and the further sum of $300 donated by the City Commission. Therefore, the entire amount of outside help, as I have said, was the sum of $500; the remainder of the expense incident to the operation of this band for three years was borne directly by the Sioux Falls Order of Moose and some of its patriotic members, and as near as I can estimate at this time, the expense of the lodge and the individual members who donated for the expense of the band for three years past was between $1,200 and $1,500, this money being spent in various ways, for band leader, for musical instruments, and for the maintenance of a place for the band to practice.

"Most people seem to think the organization and maintenance of a band is similar to the organization and maintenance of a bunch of working men, that all you have to do is go out and hire your men and start to work. This is not true, as the only way a band can be a success and credit to the city is in constant rehearsals, and in the years past the Moose band practiced practically the entire winter. At least each year from Christmas on until the band concerts opened in the parks, the players giving their time for these rehearsals, for which they really should have been paid, and the Moose lodge paying the instructor and standing other expense incident to the operation of the band.

"I notice from the articles I have referred to, that some of our generous citizens say that they are satisfied with the band for the past few seasons, and that they are opposed to the municipal levy, and point out the fact that the band last year only cost the city $775, but they are not aware of the fact that the band cost somebody else a whole lot more than this amount.

"It is to be remembered that when a lodge or such organization maintain and operate a band that members of the various committees donate their time for the good of the cause, and this time amounts to a great deal. If anyone disputes this statement, I only invite them to try it. In maintaining a municipal band much of the service that is rendered for nothing, as in the case just referred to, would have to be paid for, which it should be, and while I am not in a position to state definitely how much it would cost to maintain and operate a municipal band for the coming season, I would not put the figures under $10,000. Of course, the amount necessary would be governed by the extent of the services rendered, the number of concerts played and whether or not the band would receive pay from other sources save from the levy, for rendering services not strictly considered to be for the city, such as public speakers, conventions, and the like.

"It is no doubt true that the city is in great need of other public enterprises, such as schools and gymnasiums, which will cost considerable money, but if there is any possible way that $10,000 could be spent to a better advantage, for a thriving, enterprising city than to place it in a municipal band, properly conducted from a business standpoint, I am unable to ascertain where it could be.

"I hope and trust that the good citizens of Sioux Falls will support the band proposition, as I feel sure that without the municipal support to the amount of at least $10,000, Sioux Falls for the coming season will have no band."

– The Daily Argus-Leader, **March 14, 1919, pp. 14-15.**

• • •

Sioux Falls Musicians' Union Charter

Articles of Incorporation of the Sioux Falls Musicians Union of Sioux Falls, South Dakota, Local No. 114. American Federation of Musicians.

KNOW ALL MEN BY THESE PRESENTS:

That we, the undersigned, Russell A. Dotson, Fred Becher and R. E. Bach for ourselves, our associates and successors, have associated ourselves together for the purpose of forming a corporation under and by virtue of the statutes and laws of the State of South Dakota, and we do hereby certify and declare as follows, viz:

FIRST.

The name of this Corporation shall be The Sioux Falls Musicians Union of Sioux Falls, South Dakota, Local No. 114, American Federation of Musicians.

SECOND.

This corporation is formed and organized for scientific, charitable and benevolent purposes, and for the mutual assistance and betterment of those who become members thereof; to promote and encourage their social and physical improvement and culture; to provide for them the convenience of club house, club rooms and pleasure grounds; to buy or receive voluntary grants of real and personal property and to sell, encumber or otherwise dispose of the same; to lease real and personal property as lessor or lessee; to loan and borrow money; to receive and hold bequests, legacies or devises; to organize and unite the instrumental portion of the musical profession for the better protection of its interests in general and the establishment of a minimum rate or prices to be charged by its members for their professional services; to provide for the assistance and support of sick, indigent or unemployed members and their families and for the assistance and support of the families of deceased members; to promote, encourage and enforce good faith and fair dealing among its members; and to do and perform any and all acts and things necessary or incidental to the carrying on of the business of such corporation.

THIRD.

This corporation shall be located, and its principal place of business, shall be at the city of Sioux Falls, South Dakota.

FOURTH.

The term for which this corporation shall exist shall be perpetual.

FIFTH.

The number of directors of this corporation shall be five, and the names and residence of such who are to serve until the election of their successors are as follows:

Names	Residences
L. M. Coppens	Sioux Falls, S.D.
Carl Bodley	Sioux Falls, S.D.
H. H. Howe	Sioux Falls, S.D.
R. G. Hoyt	Sioux Falls, S.D.
William Meyer	Sioux Falls, S.D.

SIXTH.

There shall be no capital stock of this corporation, but each individual member, in good standing, shall be entitled to one vote at all meetings of said corporation.

SEVENTH.

This corporation shall be subject to the jurisdiction of the American Federation of Musicians of the United States of America.

EIGHTH.

The amount of property which this corporation may hold shall not exceed Fifty Thousand ($50,000) Dollars, and, in case of dissolution, the same shall be divided among its members in good standing as provided in the bylaws of the corporation.

NINTH.

Private property of the members of this corporation shall not be liable for its corporate debts.

IN WITNESS WHEREOF, said incorporators have hereunto set their hands and affixed their seals, together with their respective places of residence, this ___ day of August, A.D., 1915.

Russell A. Dotson
Fred Becher
R. E. Bach

• • •

An Axiom for Living, by Denis Kelly

Much emphasis these days is placed on the number of activities engaged in by certain individuals; and this tabulation forms the basis for deciding how well-received he is by those around him. If he is participating in a large total of activities, he is ascertained by the critical public as being well-rounded and developed in the arts of living with society. By the same token, and in the opposite extreme, he who takes part in a small number of activities is labeled as warped and underdeveloped, and not quite up to par with the rest of his fellow beings. However this view of the worth of humans is very unjust and unfair. If we answer a few pointed questions for ourselves, we should be able to see readily that this is true. First have you considered the fact that maybe those persons engaged in few activities have not the abilities to allow them to carry more? Maybe also those few things that they can do, they do well. Certainly much credit should be given them for this. Secondly, are those with "something-going-all-the time" doing all those things with topmost efficiency? Are they accomplishing the best job in each and every activity, or is mediocrity the standard? Thirdly, do people that are busy-busy-busy all the time———do they really have time to sit back, collect their thoughts, and relax? In their hurry-scurry of running from one thing to another, people have forgotten how to relax. . . . . .So if someone seems to look somewhat "down" on you or one of your friends because you aren't doing quite as many things as they, just make this very short but meaningful explanation to him: "I'm satisfied doing what I'm doing, because I'm doing it well. I hope you're doing the best sort of job you can, and that you still have time to enjoy the best things in life."

Sioux Falls Municipal Band Family Relationships

It has not been uncommon to have persons in the Band who were related. They included playing members, conductors, guest soloists and office staff. Relationships are confirmed unless otherwise indicated.

Last Name   **First Names**

Aasheim .... Rod and Ann Barrett Aasheim (husband and wife).
Ackerman .... Carol and Susan (sisters).
Ahlers .... Beth and Carole Ahlers Joyce (sisters).
Alberty .... Craig and Lyn (husband and wife).
Andersen .... Otto H. and Mrs. O. H. Andersen (husband/conductor and wife/guest violin soloist).
Bailey .... A. K. and Roy W.
Barnard .... Monty and Pam Hansen Barnard (husband and wife).
Barnett .... Robert P., Martha Barnett Lyons (siblings).
Barnett .... Jimmy, Robert J. (cousins).
Barnett .... Robert J. uncle of Robert P. and Martha.
Beecher .... Fred and Curtis (father and son).
Berdahl .... Arthur and James (brothers), Alan and James (brothers), nephews of Arthur and James.
Braithwaite .... Marty; daughter Mindy and son Tom.
Brooks .... Douglas and Stanley.
Christensen .... Eric and Heather Christensen Flanery (siblings).
Dean .... Doug (grandson of conductor Russ Henegar).
Dick .... Charlene and Rachel (sisters).
Doescher .... Robert and Robin (father and daughter).
Duerksen .... Beth, Greg, Jeanette (siblings).
Edwards .... Elmer T. (Eddie) and Harold (Professor). Relationship not confirmed.
Elgethun .... J. H. and Kristi (father and daughter)
Ellis .... Harry and Royal (brothers).
Ellwein .... Tom and his cousin's son Fred. Both are related to Brian and Michael Smith (see below).
Engh .... Dan, Judy, and Michael (siblings).
Flisrand .... Richard and Ann Stauffer Flisrand (husband and wife).
Fodness .... Loren and Kathy Schmidt Fodness (husband and wife).
Foss .... Ardeen and sons Robert and Richard.
Foss .... Cliff and Joe (brothers). Cousins of Ardeen, Donald and Edgar.
Foss .... Ardeen and Donald (brothers). Cousins of Cliff, Joe and Edgar.
Foss .... Edgar (cousin of Cliff, Joe, Ardeen, Donald).
Gedstad .... Ed and Warren (father and son).
Gibson .... Bill and Beverly (husband and wife).
Griffith .... Robert and father-in-law George B. Medeck.
Gross .... Mark and Jeral (brothers).
Hallstrom .... Carl and Janet Bruns Hallstrom (husband and wife).
Hansen .... Robert and Marilyn Loomis Hansen (husband and wife).
Hanson .... Paul and Jolayne Owen Hanson (husband and wife).
Hanson .... Paul and Barb Hanson Johnson (siblings).
Hartig .... Eugenia and Tom (mother and son).
Hartwig .... Stephen and Tiffin (siblings).
Hasegawa .... Sam and John (siblings).
Hatfield .... Warren and Dan (father and son).Warren guest soloist, Dan regular member.
Hays .... Rex and Stan (father and son). Guest players. Daughter, Kathy Hays Emmel.
Hegg .... Dennis and Barb Johnson Hegg; sons Jason and Jeremy.
Helfert .... Jake's sister married Ray Pruner.
Helland .... Greg and Deb Johnson Helland (husband and wife).
Helland .... Connie and Greg (siblings).
Henegar .... Russ and grandson Doug Dean.
Hillman .... Albert and Howard (father and son).
Hobson .... Charles and Harry (father and son). William a cousin.
Hoiseth .... Gary and Jean Hoiseth Peterson (siblings).
Holyer .... Robert and Ronn (brothers).
Hoover .... Harold, Sr. and Harold, Jr. (father and son).
Howard .... Susan and John. Relationship not confirmed.
Johnson .... Eddie and Janelle Schweim Johnson (husband and wife).
Joyce .... David and Robert (brothers). David married Carole Ahlers.

Last Name   First Names

Knutson .... Charles and Tommy (brothers).
Knutson .... Eric and Brian (brothers).
Kramer........................... Kerry, Robert, William. Relationship not confirmed.
Krueger .... Harold and David (father and son).
Krueger .... David and Donna Van Bockern Krueger (husband and wife).
Lane .... Kenneth and Ronald (brothers).
Larson .... Patsy Larson Holzwarth and Peg Larson Cummings (sisters).
Levsen .... Mark and Sara (siblings).
Lias .... Donald and Eddie (brothers). David is distant cousin?
Lillehaug .... Leland, father of sons David and Steven and daughter, Laurie.
Little .... Everton and sons Loren and Tom.
Loftesness .... Ray and Scott (father and son).
Masek .... Patricia and Brian (mother and son).
McAllister .... Jeff and Sandy Person McAllister (husband and wife).
McCabe .... Donald and Terry (father and son).
McClung .... Charles F. and G. C. (brothers).
McDowell .... Robert, Sr. and Robert, Jr. (father and son).
McDowell .... Robert, Jr. and Kristi Tharp McDowell (husband and wife).
McWayne .... James and Kristi Reierson McWayne (husband and wife).
Medeck .... George B. and son-in-law Robert Griffith.
Meyer .... William D. and Roy (father and son).
Meyers .... Mark and Nancy (husband and wife).
Miller .... Leon and David (father and son).
Mitchell .... David and Linda (husband and wife).
Morris .... Robert and S. O. Relationship not confirmed.
Mueller .... Charles and Marvin (brothers).
Nason .... Mrs. Earl and Robert (mother and son). Mother was guest soloist.
Olawsky .... Doug and Ralph (brothers).
Olawsky .... Doug and Suzanne Prieb Olawsky (husband and wife).
Olkiewicz .... Chris and Beth Duerksen Olkiewicz (husband and wife).
Olsen .... Greg and Ralph, Jr. (brothers).
Olson .... Linda and Heidi (mother and daughter).
Omanson .... Darrrell. Son-in-law of Paul Reagan.
Opland .... Allen. Daughter Pam Opland Sonnichsen and her daughters Kristen and Kari.
Perkins .... James and John (brothers).
Person .... Janet and Sandra Person McAllister (sisters).
Peterson .... Lynn and Jean Hoiseth Peterson (husband and wife).
Pfeiffer .... Steven and Gina Waltner Pfeiffer (husband and wife).
Polzin .... Geraldine, Linda and Brenda (sisters?).
Pruner .... Brother-in-law of Jake Helfert. Ray's wife was Helfert's sister.
Reagan .... Paul and Charles (brothers). Paul was father-in-law of Darrell Omanson.
Richardson .... James and Ron (brothers).
Roth .... Connie and John (husband and wife).
Runyan .... George, Dan, Paul, Robert (four brothers).
Runyan .... Paul and Robyn Lenker Runyan (husband and wife).
Schuller .... Gustav and Jurgen (father and son).
Shelsta .... Scott and Kay Amerson Shelsta (husband and wife).
Siverson .... Glennis, Sayra, Jay (siblings).
Smith .... Brian and Michael (brothers). Their father, James, is Fred Ellwein's first cousin.
Taylor .... Alan and Georgia (husband and wife).
Thompson .... Joe, Orville, Lawrence (brothers).
Warren .... Mary and Maureen (sisters).
Wegner .... Paul, Sr., three sons David, Tom, Paul, Jr. and David's son, Nathan.
Weikel .... Paul and Sandra (husband and wife).
Williamson .... I. M. and Mark. Relationship not confirmed.
Wold .... Steve and Jeff (brothers).
Woolworth .... Rich and Cathy Huether Moklebust (siblings).

• • •

Performance Sites and Special Appearances

The following represents the Sioux Falls Municipal Band documented sites, special appearances and years played. All sites are in Sioux Falls unless otherwise indicated. Towns and cities are in South Dakota unless otherwise indicated. Events in the "Special Events" section are not necessarily repeated at the sites listed below unless it was the only event ever played at that site. "Gratis" indicates that the Band members donated their services.

Geographic Sites   Years

Aberdeen .... See Elks convention, special events.
Airport .... See special events, inauguration of night flying.
Alcester .... 1941, Legion Community Band Shell dedication; 47, 58.
Army Air Base (Technical School) .... 1942, 45.
Army Air Base Hospital .... 1945.
Army Reserve .... 1986.
Augustana Campus .... 1977 and 81, International BB Gun Championships.
Augustana Campus, primarily Nordland Fest .... 1968, 72, 74-76, 79-83, 85-86, 88.
Augustana College Kresge Hall .... 1988.
Augustana stadium .... See special events.
Baltic .... 1952, 81.
Bancroft School .... 1973.
Baseball Parks (various locations) .... 1931. Canaries?, American Legion benefit?; 32-37, 39-42, 50.
Battleship South Dakota Memorial .... 1970, 73, 75-77, 79, 81, 83, 85 ,87, 89, 91, 93.
Beaver Creek Lutheran Church (33rd & Prairie) .... 1994.
Beresford .... See special events, Highway 77 formal opening.
Bethany Home .... Sponsor with Children's Care Hospital & School. Usual site.
Bridgewater .... 1935, 47.
Brookings .... 1959, 80-81, 84.
Canistota .... 1930, 36, 59, 72, 78-79, 84.
Canton .... 1935-36, 67.
Cataract Hotel .... See special events, VFW convention, druggist convention, Lindbergh.
Centerville .... 1977-78.
Chamberlain .... See special events, Nation's Highway.
Chatfield, Minnesota .... 1987, National convention Association of Concert Bands.
Children's Care Hospital and School .... 1969, 70, 73-94.
Children's Home .... 1930s. Band played on Easter Sunday mornings.
Children's Home Society (801 North Sycamore) ...... 1992-94.
Christian Reformed Church Grounds .... 1980.
City Hall .... 1936 (gratis); 67, Veterans Day
Cleveland School .... 1968, 70-73, 75, 84.
Colton .... 1957.
Covington Heights Health Care Center .... 1986, 88, 90, 92-94.
Dell Rapids .... 1933, 38, 49, 57, 80, 82, 84-85, 87-88, 91 and see special events, National Corn Husking.
Dow Rummel Village .... 1974-86, 88-93. Rained out in 1994.
Downtown high-rise apartments .... 1973-74, 76.
Downtown Mall .... 1974, 1976, 78, 79-82, 83 (Nordland Fest), 85-89.
Drake Springs .... 1934-35, 40.
East Side Ball Park .... 1930; 1931, Band played for pageant.
East Side Community Club .... 1930.
East Side Park .... See Library Park.
Elmwood Park (concerts) .... 1924-26, 28-32.
Empire Mall .... 1975, 78, 84-89.
EROS (northeast of Sioux Falls) .... See special events.
Fawick Park .... 1976, Bicentennial Sundial.
Frank Olson Park .... 1976-78, 90-94.

Geographic Sites   Years

Geographic Sites	Years
Freeman	1979.
Garretson	1936, 47, 49, 53, 61.
Good Samaritan Center	1968-69, 81-94.
Good Samaritan Luther Manor (was L.M.)	1968-69, 73-82, 84, 86-94.
Good Samaritan Village	1970-79, 81, 83, 85, 87, 89, 91 ,93-94.
Great Northern Railroad Depot	1939, met Good Will delegation from MN. Parade followed.
Great Plains Zoo	85-86, 89, 91.
Hartford	1947, 81-82.
Hawthorne School	See special events.
Hayward School	1974-75.
Heritage Park	See Library Park.
Hills, Minnesota	1940, 47-50 (rain), 51-58, 60, 1964, 77.
Horace Mann School	1972-73.
Hospitals	1930s. Band played on Easter Sunday mornings.
Howard Wood Field	1965-66, July 4th.
Hudson	1938, 40, 48, 52, 60, 67, 82.
Humboldt	1935, 37, 39-40, 42, 45, 47-48.
Hurley	1953.
Huron (State Fair)	1934-35, 37, 39. See special events, American Legion (Huron).
Jane Addams School	1974.
Joe Foss Field	See special events, Centennial Air Show.
Lake Benton, Minnesota	1979.
Larchwood, Iowa	1938.
Laura Wilder School	1973.
Laurel Oak Park (49th and Laurel Oak Drive)	1993.
Lennox	1936, 39, 41, 44 (gratis), 61, 63, 65, 67, 69, 75, 83.
Lester, Iowa	1948.
Library Park (also East Side and Heritage)	A usual performing site.
Lincoln Senior High School	See special events, Veterans Day.
Luverne, Minnesota	1934-35, 37, 39, 48, 58.
Lyon Park	1940-49, 90-94.
Madison, Garden Theatre	1935, 37 (location uncertain).
Madison, Library Park	1941.
Marion	1954, 59.
McKennan Park	A usual performing site.
Meldrum Park	1968-69, 82-83.
Minneapolis, MN, Peavey Plaza, downtown	1985.
Minnehaha County Courthouse	See special events, Minnehaha County Courthouse.
Mitchell Corn Palace	1934, 38-39, 46.
Mitchell, Courthouse Lawn	1940-41, 55.
Mitchell, Hitchcock Park	1935-36.
Mom and Dad's Nursing Home	1977-92, 94.
Montrose	1936, 1954 (Golden Jubilee Celebration).
Nelson Park — Drake Springs	1935-36, 40.
Neptune Park	See special events, Labor Day Celebration.
O'Gorman High School	See special events.
Omaha Depot (Sioux Falls)	1942 (parade for draftees, gratis).
Omaha, Nebraska	1991, National convention, ACB, April 5, 1991.
Packer Stadium (baseball)	1964 opening; June 27, 1965 dedication; 67.
Parker	1937, 40, 59.
Pinney Addition Residential Area	1968.
Pioneer Park	1987.
Pipestone, Minnesota	1935, 36.
Prince of Peace Retirement Community	1987-94.
Postmaster Farley, met train, Railroad Depot	1934.
Ramkota Inn	See special events, Air Guard, SD Centennial, SD Homecoming.
Renner	See special events, Minnehaha County Fair.
River Tower Apartments	1975, 77.
Robert Frost School	1970-73, 78-80.
Rock Rapids, Iowa	1936-37, 39.
Rock Valley, Iowa	1954, 56-57, 63.
Rolvaag House, 33rd Street and Menlo	1984, A Scandinavian Salute.
Ronning Addition	1971, 74.
Rushmore Bridge	See special events.
Salem	1948-49, 52, 55-80.
Senior Citizens' Center	1974.
Sherman Park	A usual performing site.

Geographic Sites   Years

Sioux City, Iowa, Grandview Park .... 1967 exchange concert.
Sioux City, Iowa, Riverside Park .... 1967 exchange concert.
Sioux Empire Fairgrounds .... 1939-40, 43, 51-56, 59, 61-77.
Sioux Empire Fairgrounds (July 4) .... 1967, first year July 4 concert & fireworks this site; 69-94.
Sioux Falls Air Field National Guard Hangar .... See special events, Air Force Day.
Sioux Falls Arena .... 1961(dedication),See special events, Veterans' Appreciation Day
Sioux Falls Care Center .... 1970, 82, 84.
Sioux Falls Coliseum .... 1922 and many other years, Easter concerts.
Sioux Falls Coliseum Annex .... See special events, Sioux Falls Coliseum opening; war exhibit.
Sioux Falls College (concerts) .... 1971, 82-94.
Sioux Falls downtown .... See special events, several items.
Siouxland Heritage Museum, 131 North Duluth .... 1992-94.
Softball park .... See special events.
South Dakota School for the Deaf .... 1990-91.
South Dakota State Penitentiary .... 1937-38, 41, 42 (gratis), 54, 56-57, 62, 64-69, 71?, 72-73, 85.
Speedway Race Track .... 1929.
Spencer Park .... 1990-91, 93.
Sunnycrest Retirement Village .... 1990-94.
Terrace Park .... A usual performing site.
Tuthill Park .... 1956 (first appearance?), 71-72, 75, 87-89.
Valley Springs .... 1970.
Veterans Administration, Sioux Falls .... 1949-54, 56-57, 60-94.
VFW Building .... 1969.
W. H. Lyon Fairgrounds .... See Sioux Empire Fairgrounds.
Washington High School .... See special events.
Watertown .... See special events, American Legion.
West Soo Park .... See special events, Early Settlers Picnic.
West Soo Race Track .... See special events, Minnehaha County Fair.
Western Heights .... 1971.
Wintersteen Building, Main and 11th .... 1930.
Worthington, Minnesota, Chautauqua Park .... 1937.
Yankton Diamond Jubilee .... 1936.
Yankton Trails Park .... See special events, Great Plains Hot Air Balloon Race.

• • •

Special Events   Years

Air Fair concerts and/or parades, Sioux Falls .... 1930-31.
Air Force Day, Sioux Falls Air Field National Guard hangar .... 1947.
Air Guard anniversary, Ramkota Inn .... 1986.
Alcester band shell dedication .... 1963.
All Star baseball Game, Minneapolis, Metradome .... 1985.
American Legion Chorus back from Philadelphia, Milwaukee Depot .... 1949.
American Legion Chorus welcome, no site listed. .... 1950.
American Legion convention electric parade .... 1930.
American Legion convention industrial parade .... 1930.
American Legion convention, Sioux City .... 1939.
American Legion parade. Location not indicated. Probably downtown .. 1937.
American Legion state convention, Arkota Ballroom .... 1930-31.
American Legion state convention, Huron .... 1922.
American Legion state convention, Mitchell .... 1929.
American Legion state convention, Sioux Falls Coliseum .... 1952, 1954.
American Legion state convention, Watertown .... 1920.
Anniversary (134th) of U.S. Constitution, Sioux Falls Coliseum .... 1921.
Arena dedication .... 1961.
Armed Forces Day parades .... 1950, 1959, 1961.
Armed Forces Day concerts .... Many appearances.
Armistice Day concerts .... 1932, 1948 at City Hall; elsewhere other years
Armistice Day parades .... 1930, 35-39, 41-42, 44.
Army Day .... 1960.
Army-Navy Day parade .... 1946.

Special Events   Years

Barn dances .... ?
Bond drive, display of German war equipment .... 1944.
Bond election parade and rally .... 1933.
Boy Scout circus and parade .... 1936, 37 (circus); 40 (concert) gratis.
Boy Scout Jamboree, Fairgrounds .... 1941.
Broadcasting program, Community Chest drive. .... 1932-33.
Centennial Air Show, Joe Foss Field .... 1973, 85, 89.
City employees party, Coliseum .... 1941 (gratis).
Clean Up Week parade .... 1932.
Community Chest drive .... 1931.
Cosmopolitan Club "Made in SD Exposition," Sioux Falls Coliseum ...... 1927-31, 34.
Dance to raise money for uniforms, Sioux Falls Coliseum .... 1920, December 7.
Decoration Day (Memorial Day) parades .... Normal during 1930s and 1940s.
Dedication and corner stone laying at new City Hall, August 15 .... 1935.
Defense bond sale parade .... 1942 (gratis).
Democratic rally .... 1930, 36 (rally & parade paid by Demos).
Downtown Mall .... Sept. 27, 1986, ribbon cutting. May 17, 1993,
                                                                                                              opening.
Drake Springs swimming pool opening .... 1934.
Druggist state convention, Cataract Hotel .... 1921.
Early Settlers picnic, West Soo Park .... 1921-1922.
Easter concerts at Coliseum and other sites .... Frequent during Henegar years.
Elks convention, Aberdeen .... 1921.
Elks convention, concert and parade .... 1930.
Elks Flag Day .... Most years.
Elmwood Park formal opening. .... 1924.
EROS dedication .... 1973.
Farm Show, Sioux Falls Coliseum .... 1954.
Fine Arts Month .... 1974-78.
Flower Show, Coliseum all or most years. .... 1927-32, 37-39.
Football game for charity .... 1931.
Four H Club concert at Fairgrounds .... 1943.
Freedom Train, Airport .... 1948.
Freedom Train, Sioux Empire Fairgrounds .... 1975 (September 7).
Friendship program, Coliseum .... 1948.
Girl Scout House dedication, Elmwood Park .... 1936.
Goddess of Liberty Statue unveiling, McKennan .... 1943.
Goodrich Silvertown Fleet parade .... 1929.
Goodwill concert, Coliseum .... 1940, for Spencer, Iowa group; 1941.
Great Plains Hot Air Balloon Race, Yankton Trails Park,
     S. Minn. Ave. & I-229 .... 1994.
Great Plains Zoo dedication. .... 1963.
Greater Sioux Falls celebration, (sponsored by Junior Chamber) .... 1935-1936 (gratis).
Greek Order of Ahepans parade .... 1935.
Hawthorne School dedication .... 1923? (or early 1924?).
High School Band returned from Eastern trip .... 1939, met by Municipal Band (gratis).
Highway 77 formal opening, Beresford .... 1940.
Hollywood Star bond drive .... 1942.
Inauguration of night flying, Airport .... 1940.
International BB Gun Championships .... 1977, 81.
IOOF Grand Lodge parade .... 1936.
Joe Foss Day, Howard Wood Field .... 1943.
Joe Foss homecoming parade and reception .... 1943.
Junior Chamber of Commerce Industrial parade .... 1937.
Knight Templar parade, Sioux Falls College .... 1933.
Knight Templar state convention, Augustana Campus .... 1954.
KSOO radio broadcast, Arkota Ballroom .... 1940.
KSOO radio broadcast of Coliseum concert, March 24 .... 1940.
Labor Day celebration, Neptune Park .... Year unavailable.
Labor Day parade, Sioux Falls downtown .... 1926-27, 1935-36, 38-42.
Laurel Oak swimming pool dedication .... 1993.
Library Park bandstand dedication .... 1952.
Lindbergh, Charles, welcome, Cataract Hotel .... 1927.
Lions Club district convention, Coliseum .... 1946.
Midwest Conference (Midwest meeting of Musicians' Locals) .... 1940.
Minnehaha County Courthouse dedication. .... 1963.
Minnehaha County Fair, Location? .... 1932.

Special Events   Years

Minnehaha County Fair, Fifth and Main .... 1921.
Minnehaha County Fair, Renner .... 1929, 33-34.
Minnehaha County Fair, West Soo Race Track .... 1934, horse races.
Morrell Picnic, Elmwood Park .... 1935, 1936. Paid by Morrell.
Motor Transportation Progress parade, Sioux Falls downtown .... 1946.
Municipal Airport dedication .... 1939.
Municipal Employees concert, Coliseum .... 1940 (February 3).
NAIA track meet, Howard Wood Field .... 1965.
National Corn Husking field dedication, Dell Rapids .... 1938.
National Security Seminar .... 1963.
Nation's Highway Celebration parade and concert, Chamberlain .... 1938.
     (Completion of Highway 16 across South Dakota)
Navy Day program, Coliseum .... 1941 (gratis).
Navy Recruiting Station opening, parade .... 1942 (gratis).
New Coliseum Exposition Annex opening, Sioux Falls Coliseum .... 1932.
Nordland Fest .... See sites, Augustana Campus.
Norwegian Royalty events, Sioux Falls downtown and Terrace Park .... 1939.
O'Gorman High School dedication, O'Gorman High School .... 1961.
Old Home Bakery basketball game, Coliseum .... 1942 (gratis. Old Home gave $50 to uniform
                                                                            fund).
147th National Guard welcome, Joe Foss Field, Nat'l Guard Armory .... 1962.
     (Visit of General Moses, Fifth Army Deputy Commander)
Pageant parade, Sioux Falls downtown .... 1920, 42.
Parade for draftees (gratis), Milwaukee Depot .... 1942.
Pearl Harbor Day, KSOO .... 1942 (gratis).
Policemen's Ball, Arkota Ballroom .... 1931.
Public School May Day Festival .... 1929.
President's Ball, Sioux Falls Coliseum .... 1936.
Reception, 147th Regt. from Pacific, Coliseum .... 1944.
Republican parade .... 1936 (paid by Republicans).
River Parking Ramp dedication .... 1962.
Retail Merchants concert at Coliseum .... 1940.
Rushmore Bridge dedication., East 10th Street .... 1934.
Sandstorm Division reunion parade .... 1940.
Sangerfest convention parade, Sioux Falls downtown .... 1938.
Sioux Falls Arena dedication .... 1961.
Sioux Falls Canaries game, baseball field .... 1941. See sites, Baseball Parks.
Sioux Falls Centennial, Augustana stadium .... 1956.
Sioux Falls College centennial .... 1982.
Sioux Falls Day in Mitchell .... 1923.
Sioux Falls Diamond Jubilee Celebration, concerts and parade. .... 1931.
Sioux Falls Packer Stadium opening .... 1964.
Sioux Falls Park Department 75th anniversary, Sherman Park .... 1991.
Sioux Falls River Parking Ramp dedication .... 1962.
Sioux Falls Sewage Plant dedication .... 1927.
Soap Box Derby (Sioux Falls Jaycees), Northwest Sioux Falls .... 1959-72.
Softball Recognition evening, softball park .... 1964.
South Dakota Centennial Homecoming, Ramkota Inn .... 1989.
South Dakota Crop Show .... 1931.
South Dakota fiftieth anniversary pageant, Augustana stadium .... 1939.
South Dakota Homecoming Gala, Ramkota Inn .... 1983.
South Dakota Municipal League convention, Sioux Falls Coliseum .... 1974.
State Federation of Labor convention, Coliseum .... 1940 (gratis).
State Retail Association convention, Coliseum .... 1942.
Sunshine Special Boosters trip .... 1924.
Terrace Park Band Shell rededication .... 1992.
Union Railway Employees parade, Sioux Falls .... 1935.
VE (Victory in Europe) Day Memorial Service, Coliseum .... 1945 (May 7).
Veterans Appreciation Day, Sioux Falls Arena .... 1991.
Veterans Day, Lincoln High School .... 1978-93.
VFW dance, Neptune Park .... 1933.
VFW convention, Cataract Hotel .... 1932.
War Exhibit program, Sioux Falls Coliseum Annex .... 1944.
Washington High School, cornerstone laying, center section of school. .. 1935.
Washington High School football game vs. Mitchell
     (field on E. 10th St.?). .... 1920.

Concert Themes

The following 222 concert themes represent most of them since their use began in the early 1970s.

Theme Title   **Years**

Across the USA .... 1988-89, 92-93.
Air Guard Anniversary .... 1986.
All American Music .... 1977-78.
All City Picnic .... 1987.
All March Concert .... 1974, 76-78.
All Nations Concert .... 1975.
America the Beautiful .... 1993.
American Music .... 1982, 84.
American Popular Theater .... 1983.
Armed Forces Day .... 1981-93.
Around the World .... 1991-93.
Arts Festival Happy Sounds .... 1984.
At the Movies .... 1992-93.
Audience Request Program .... 1927, 30, 76-81, 84, 86.
Bach and Baroque—300 Years .... 1985.
Band's Best, The .... 1984.
Battleship SD Reunion .... 1973, 75-77, 79, 81, 83, 85, 87, 89, 91, 93.
Belles, Ballads & Barkers .... 1986.
Best of Broadway .... 1974.
Bicentennial Preview .... 1975.
Big Band Era .... 1975.
Big Band Jazz .... 1974, 84.
Big Band Jazz, Sounds Of .... 1985, 87.
Big Band Night (40s and 50s) .... 1976.
Big Band Revisited .... 1992.
Big Band Showcase .... 1993-94.
Big Bands .... 1977-79.
Big Jazz Bands Revisited .... 1986, 88-91.
Broadway Show Time .... 1986, 89, 94.
By Land, Sea and Air .... 1991.
Celebration Days .... 1988.
Centennial Celebration (SF College) .... 1982.
Centennial Celebration (Canistota) .... 1984.
Centennial Concert (Dell Rapids) .... 1980.
Centennial Concert (Hartford) .... 1981.
Centennial Concert (Lennox Band) .... 1983.
Centennial Homecoming .... 1989.
Children's Concert .... Every year from 1966.
Circus Concert .... Every year from 1966.
Classics for All Ages .... 1994.
Classics Remembered, The .... 1981.
Coast to Coast .... 1994.
Concert for Children and Animals, A .... 1986.
Concert from the 40s .... 1994.
Concert from the 60s .... 1994.
Concert from the 70s .... 1994.
Conductors' Concert .... 1994.
Dad's Day Delights .... 1983, 93.
Dad's Delights Delivered .... 1988.
Dad's Night .... 1986-87, 89.
Disney Favorites .... 1993.
Down Memory Lane .... 1980.
Elderhostel Welcome, An .... 1985, 87.
Election Preview, An .... 1972.
Ethnic Evening, An .... 1986.
Evening in Space, An .... 1989.
Evening of Pops, An .... 1991-93.

Theme Title	Years
Evening with Porter, Kern & Gershwin	1984.
Fanfares and Fireworks	1985.
Fathers' Day Tribute	1984, 90-92, 94.
Fathers' Day Special	1981.
Favorites Old and New	1983-84, 86-94.
Featuring SD Dance Theater	1985.
Fine Arts Month Concert	1977.
First Chair Players Featured	1986.
Flag Day	Normal concert beginning in 1920s.
Freedom Train	1975.
Gay '90s and Good Old Summertime	1985.
Gershwin Salute	1992.
Golden Age of American Operetta	1984.
Golden Age of Radio	1976-77, 83.
Good Neighbor Salute	1984.
Government Employee Appreciation Night	1977.
Grand Finale	1976-94.
Hands Across the Sea	1979.
Happy Birthday America	1985, 91-94.
Happy Birthday USA	1983, 87, 89, 90.
Happy Sounds of Disney	1986, James Christensen, guest conductor.
Heritage from Broadway, A	1990-92.
History of Broadway	1975.
Humor in Music	1977.
Independence Day (July 4)	Most years beginning in 1920s.
In the Good Old Summertime	1984, 93.
International Festival, An	1983.
International Night	1976-78.
International Theme	1986, 90.
Jerome Kern & Friends—100th Birthday	1985.
June is Busting Out All Over	1985-87, 90, 93.
Let's Talk to the Animals	1988-89.
Light Listening	1986-94.
Lilt of the Latin	1983.
Little Night (Band) Music, A	1984.
Lost at Sea	1989.
Mainly Broadway Musicals	1975.
Marches for a Sunday Afternoon	1985-86.
Marching Around the World	1986-87.
Marching Down Broadway	1984.
Mayor's Family Picnic	1988-93.
Memorial Day	Played almost every year.
Midsummer's Eve, A	1980.
Mixing Pleasure With Business	1988.
Mostly Marches	1980, 83-84, 94.
Music and Dance	1985.
Music Around the World	1982.
Music for a Midsummer Night	1993.
Music for a Summer Afternoon	1980.
Music for Midsummer	1987-92.
Music for Midsummer Eve	1986.
Music for the Birds	1983.
Music from Broadway	1987.
Music in Three-Quarter Time	1984.
Music of Many Lands	1975.
Music of the Dance	1976.
Music of Women Composers	1979.
Music That Tells a Story	1976.
Music With a Latin Beat	1984.
Musical Carousel, A	1988-94.
Musical Celebration, A	1988, 93.
Musical Fun on a Monday Night	1985.
Musical Heritage, A	1987-93.
Musical Hits—Dirty 30's Revisited	1985.
Musical Kaleidoscope	1986.
Musical Potpourri	1980, 84.
Musical Pyrotechnics	1984.

Theme Title   Years

Theme Title	Years
Musical Sunset, A	1990-94.
Musical Travelogue, A	1994.
Night at the Ballet, A	1980, 84.
Night at the Opera, A	1984.
Night in Vienna, A	1984, 85, 90-92.
Night of Classics, A	1992-93
Night on Phillips Avenue, A	1990-93.
Night on the Town, A	1988-89, 94.
Night with the Stars, A	1988.
Nordland Fest	1975, 79-83, 85-86, 88.
Old Fashioned Band Concert, An	1984, 88-93.
Olympic Spirit	1992.
On Broadway	1993.
On the Mall	1987.
Our Ethnic Heritage	1988 (see also Nordland Fest).
Our Ethnic Heritage in Music	1976.
Our Musical Heritage	1994.
Pandas and Pachyderms	1985.
Parade of the States	1983.
Past, Present and Future	1985.
Picnic Pops	1983-92, 94.
Pleasure for Business	1983.
Pops Emphasis Concert	1973.
Porter, Kern, Gershwin, Youmans	1987.
Porter, Kern,& Gershwin	1986, 88-90.
Quarry Days Celebration (Dell Rapids)	1991.
Red, White and Blue	1986.
Reunion Year	1987, 89.
Riverside Picnic	1987.
Romantic Evening, A	1987, 89-93.
Sacred Meets Secular	1986-90.
Sacred Songs and Sounds	1985.
Salute to Agriculture	1976.
Salute to Broadway	1980.
Salute to Dads	1977-80.
Salute to Karl King	1925, 27, 73.
Salute to Maturity (Senior Citizens Center)	1974 (November 18).
Salute to Richard Rodgers	1979.
Salute to Rural America	1976, 85.
Salute to the News Media	1977.
Salute to the Pioneers	1973.
Salute to Youth	1984.
Scandinavian Salute	1984.
Selections from the Past	1994.
Senior Games Blast-off	1991.
Seventy-Fifth Anniversary Band Reunion	1994.
Shop, Look and Listen	1985.
Sing, Stomp and Whistle	1985, 87-88, 90.
Sioux Falls Area Veterans Appreciation	1991 (Picnic).
Sit in the Sunshine Musical Day	1985.
Sixtieth Year Band Reunion	1979.
Sixty-Sixth Kickoff	1985.
Something for Everyone	1984.
Songs of the Seasons	1980.
Sounds of the Season	1975.
Sounds on the Mall	1986.
Sousa and Friends, John Philip	1986.
Sousa Concert, All	1979.
Sousa, Fillmore, Goldman & Friends	1988, 90-91.
Sousa, King and Fillmore	1983.
Sousa Spectacular	1992.
Sousa-Style Concert, A	1994.
Sousa Tribute	1993.
Sousa, USA's March King	1985.
South Dakota Centennial Folk Festival	1989.
South Dakota Homecoming Gala	1983.
Spanish-American War Veterans Salute	1922.

Theme Title   Years

Spirit of Patriotism, The .... 1979-80.
Sports Day Salute (Canistota) .... 1979.
Spotlight on King and Sousa .... 1982.
Strike Up the Band .... 1984, 87-92, 94.
Summer Bouquet, A .... 1986-87, 89-91.
Summer Celebration, A .... 1994.
Summer Delights .... 1987.
Summer Kaleidoscope .... 1985.
Summer Season Farewell .... 1984.
Summer Serenade, A .... 1984, 86-94.
Summer Sounds .... 1994.
Summer Sounds and Sunshine .... 1987-93.
Sun Dial Dedication .... 1976.
Sunday Matinee .... 1987-94.
Sunset With Music .... 1984.
Swings the Thing .... 1982.
There's No Business Like Show Business .... 1989.
Tops in Pops, Old and New .... 1986.
Tribute to Duke Ellington and Big Bands .... 1974.
Tribute to Irving Berlin, A .... 1990.
Tribute to John Philip Sousa, A .... 1987.
Uncle Sam #210 .... 1986.
Uncle Sam's Birthday Party .... 1984, 88.
Up, Up, and Away .... 1993-94.
Veterans Day .... Many years.
Women's Rights .... 1973.
Wonderful World of Disney .... 1988-91.
You, the Night and the Music .... 1985.
Zippity Zoo concert .... 1986.
Zippity Zoo Day .... 1989.

• • •

Sioux Falls Municipal Band Officers 1920-94

The first three names listed are president, vice president and secretary/treasurer. The Band minutes sometimes gave only last names and often members used the initials of their first and middle names. A question mark after the first name indicates that the name was not given but evidence indicates that it probably is the person who would have filled the office. First names are listed the first time they appear if they are known and the initials subsequently. All terms are for one year unless otherwise indicated.

1920. Raymond G. Hoyt, No Vice President listed, Secretary, Henry T. Hanson, Treasurer, Jake Helfert; Secretary and treasurer positions combined on October 15,1920, in the person of Henry T. Hanson. Board members: Sid Drew, Walter Kleinheinz; Conductor, Lloyd M. Coppens.

1921. Lee Mitchell, Austin K. Bailey, Henry T. Hanson; Board members: Jake Helfert, Guy Anderson, Walter F. Rittman; Librarian and band custodian, J. F. Rhoda; Conductor, L. M. Coppens.

1922. R. G. Hoyt, A. K. Bailey, Henry T. Hanson; Board members: Jake Helfert, Walter F. Rittman, J. L. Johnson; Conductor, Charles F. Emmel.

1923. John "Jack" M. Newton, Lee Mitchell, Henry T. Hanson; Board members: Burton S. Rogers, Jake Helfert, Guy Anderson: Conductor, Charles F. McClung.

1924. Lee Mitchell, J. M. Newton, Henry T. Hanson; Board members: Burton S. Rogers, Jake Helfert, Guy Anderson; Conductor, Charles F. McClung.

1925. Burton S. Rogers, Orral O. Jackson, Henry T. Hanson; Board members: J. W. Helfert, Arthur N. Sears, Guy Anderson; Conductor, Charles F. McClung.

1926. W. L. Kleinheinz, O. O. Jackson, Henry T. Hanson; Board members: Walter F. Rittman, Guy Anderson, Arthur N. Sears; Conductor, Charles F. McClung.

1927. J. M. Newton, O. O. Jackson, Henry T. Hanson; Board members: Everett J. Reeve, W. F. Rittman, J. W. Helfert; Publicity man, Roger Brown; Conductor, Charles F. McClung. Assistant Conductor, R. G. Hoyt appointed August 8, 1927.

1928. O. O. Jackson, Elmer T. Edwards, Henry T. Hanson; Board members: Austin K. Bailey, Guy Anderson, W. F. Rittman; Conductor, G. C. McClung. Assistant Conductor, R. G. Hoyt?

1929. A. H. Hanson (R. G Hoyt replaced A. H. Hanson as president on October 10, 1929. Hanson moved out of the City), W. F. Rittman, Guy Anderson; Board members: A. K. Bailey, Floyd Williams, Burton S. Rogers; Publicity man, Tom? or James? Sessions; Conductor, G. C. McClung.

1930. E. T. Edwards, Henry T. Hanson, Guy Anderson; Board members: Lee Mitchell, R. G. Hoyt, Glen G. Houdek; Conductor, Otto H. Andersen.

1931. E. T. Edwards, Henry T. Hanson, Guy Anderson; Board members: Lee Mitchell, R. G. Hoyt, Glen G. Houdek; Conductor, Otto H. Andersen.

1932. E. T. Edwards, J. M. Newton, Guy Anderson; Board members: Lee Mitchell, A. R.? Rock, Glen G. Houdek; Conductor, Otto H. Andersen.

1933. E. T. Edwards, J. M. Newton, Guy Anderson; Board members: Rudy H. Dornaus, Lee Mitchell, Glen G. Houdek; Conductor, Otto H. Andersen.

1934. E. T. Edwards, Burton S. Rogers, Guy Anderson; Board members: A. K. Bailey, Lee Mitchell, Glen G. Houdek; Conductor, Otto H. Andersen.

1935. E. T. Edwards, Burton Rogers, Guy Anderson; Board members: A. K. Bailey, Jimmy? Barnett, George Medeck; Conductor, Russ D. Henegar.

1936. E. T. Edwards, Burton S. Rogers, Guy Anderson; Board members: A. K. Bailey, J. M. Newton, George Medeck; Conductor, Russ D. Henegar.

1937. E. T. Edwards, Burton S. Rogers, Guy Anderson; Board members: A. K. Bailey, J. M. Newton, George Medeck; Conductor, Russ D. Henegar.

1938. E. T. Edwards, Ardeen Foss, Guy Anderson; Board members: A. K. Bailey, J. M. Newton, George Medeck; Conductor, Russ D. Henegar.

1939. E. T. Edwards, A. K. Bailey, Guy Anderson; Board members: J. M. Newton, Glen G. Houdek, Burton S. Rogers; Conductor, Russ D. Henegar.

1940. Kenneth Lane, A. K. Bailey, Guy Anderson; Board members: J. M. Newton, Glen G. Houdek, Burton S. Rogers; Ed Paul elected as the Band's (first?) business manager (minutes of December 4, 1939). Conductor, Russ D. Henegar.

1941. Lee Mitchell, Kenneth Lane, Guy Anderson; Board members: J. M. Newton, Glen G. Houdek, Marlin Brown; Business Manger, Ed Paul; Conductor, Russ D. Henegar.

1942. Milt Askew, Burton S. Rogers, Guy Anderson; Board members: E. T. Edwards, Norman Sampson, Glen G. Houdek; Business Manager, O. O. Jackson; Conductor, Russ D. Henegar; Assistant conductor, Vernon Alger. First mention of assistant conductor for Henegar.

1943. Milt Askew, George Medeck (replaced by A. K. Bailey), Guy Anderson; Board members: R. G. Hoyt, E. T. Edwards, J. M. Newton; Business manager, O. O. Jackson; Conductor, Russ D. Henegar; Assistant conductor, Vernon Alger.

1944. O. O. Jackson, A. K. Bailey, Guy Anderson; Board members: Robert Niblick, Harold Hoover, Sr., Glen G. Houdek; Business manager, Ed Paul; Conductor, Russ D. Henegar; Assistant conductor, Vernon Alger.

1945. O. O. Jackson, Harold Hoover, Sr., Guy Anderson; Board members: E. T. Edwards, Ray Pruner, Milt Askew; Business manager, Ed Paul; Conductor, Russ D. Henegar; Assistant conductor, Vernon Alger.

1946. Kenneth Lane, Melvin Sunde, Guy Anderson; Board members: Robert Niblick, Ray Pruner, Milt Askew; Business manager, Ed Paul; Conductor, Russ D. Henegar; Assistant conductor, Vernon Alger.

1947. Kenneth Lane, Melvin Sunde, Guy Anderson; Board members: Robert Niblick, Ray Pruner, Milt Askew; Business manager, Ed Paul; Conductor, Russ D. Henegar; Assistant conductor, Vernon Alger.

1948. Ray Pruner, Melvin Sunde, Guy Anderson; Board members: Robert Niblick, Don Lias, Milt Askew; Business manager, Ed Paul; Conductor, Russ D. Henegar; Assistant conductor, Vernon Alger.

1949. Ray Pruner, Melvin Sunde, Guy Anderson; Board members: Robert Niblick, Harold Hoover, Sr.; W. H. Tietjen; Business manager, Ed Paul; Conductor, Russ D. Henegar; Assistant conductor, Vernon Alger.

1950. Ray Pruner, John Brauch, Jr., Guy Anderson; Board members: Ardeen Foss, Harold Hoover, Sr.; C. R. "Bob" Larson; Business manager, Ed Paul; Conductor, Russ D. Henegar; Assistant conductor, Vernon Alger.

1951. Ray Pruner, Melvin Sunde, Guy Anderson; Board members: Ardeen Foss, Harold Hoover, Sr., C. R. "Bob" Larson; Business manager, Ed Paul; Conductor, Russ D. Henegar; Assistant conductor, Vernon Alger.

1952. Ray Pruner, Melvin Sunde, Guy Anderson; Board members: Ardeen Foss, Harold Hoover, Sr.; O. O. Jackson; Business manager, Ed Paul; Conductor, Russ D. Henegar; Assistant conductor, Vernon Alger.

1953. Melvin Sunde, Vernon Alger, Ray Pruner; Board members: Ardeen Foss, Harold Hoover, Sr.; O. O. Jackson; Business manager, Ed Paul; Conductor, Russ D. Henegar; Assistant conductor, Vernon Alger.

1954. no record. Business manager, Ed Paul; Conductor, Russ D. Henegar; Assistant conductor, Ardeen Foss?

1955. no record. Business manager, Ed Paul; Conductor, Russ D. Henegar; Assistant conductor, Ardeen Foss?

1956. no record. Business manager, Ed Paul; Conductor, Russ D. Henegar; Assistant conductor, Ardeen Foss?

1957. Donald McCabe, Ernest Dvoracek, Ray Pruner; Board members: Glen G. Houdek, Ardeen Foss, Ralph Tyler; Business manager, Ed Paul; Conductor, Russ D. Henegar; Assistant conductor, Ardeen Foss.

1958. Ardeen Foss, Leland Lillehaug, Ray Pruner; Board members: Mel Sunde, Donald McCabe, Ralph Tyler; Business manager, Ed Paul; Conductor, Russ D. Henegar; Assistant conductor, Ardeen Foss.

1959. Ardeen Foss, Ralph Tyler?, Ray Pruner; Board members: Earl Colgan, Robert Griffith, Harvey Eichmeier; Business manager, Ed Paul; Conductor, Russ D. Henegar; Assistant conductor, Ardeen Foss.

1960. Ardeen Foss, Wayne Krumrei, Ray Pruner; Board members: Earl Colgan, Paul Hoy, David Wegner; Business manager, Ed Paul; Conductor, Russ D. Henegar; Assistant conductor, Ardeen Foss.

1961. Ardeen Foss, Wayne Krumrei, Ray Pruner; Board members: Oscar Loe, Paul Hoy, David Wegner; Business manager, Ed Paul; Conductor, Russ D. Henegar; Assistant conductor, Ardeen Foss.

1962. Ardeen Foss, Oscar Loe, Ray Pruner; Board members: Earl Colgan, Ralph Tyler, David Wegner; Business manager, Ed Paul; Conductor, Russ D. Henegar; Assistant conductor, Ardeen Foss.

1963. Oscar Loe, Leland Lillehaug, Ray Pruner; Board members: Earl Colgan, Ralph Tyler, Ardeen Foss. Business manager, Ed Paul; Conductor, Russ D. Henegar; Assistant conductor, Ardeen Foss ?.

1964. Oscar Loe, Harvey Eichmeier, Paul Hoy; Board members: Wayne Krumrei, Kenneth Busse, Ralph Tyler; Band Manager, Earl Colgan; Conductor, Dr. Leland A. Lillehaug.

1965. Oscar Loe, Harvey Eichmeier, Paul Hoy; Board members: Donald McCabe, Everton Little, Gus Schuller; Band Manager, Paul Bankson; Conductor, Dr. Leland A. Lillehaug. Elected at annual meeting on November 30, 1964.

1966. Paul Bankson, Robert McDowell, Paul Hoy; Board members: Gus Schuller, Harvey Eichmeier, Ralph Tyler (Tyler later decided to take a year's leave and was replaced by Stan Eitreim on February 21, 1966); Band Manager, Jurgen Schuller; Conductor, Dr. Leland A. Lillehaug. Elected at annual meeting on Monday, November 29, 1965.

1967. Paul Bankson, Dr. Harold Krueger, Paul Hoy; Board members: Delbert Bickel, George Gulson, Gus Schuller; Band manager, Stan Eitreim; Conductor Dr. Leland A. Lillehaug. Elected at the annual meeting on November 28, 1966.

1968. George Gulson, Tom Ellwein, Paul Hoy; Trustees: Paul Bankson, Donald McCabe, Dr. Harold Krueger; Band Manager, Robert Doescher; Conductor, Dr. Leland A. Lillehaug. Assistant conductor, Oscar Loe.

1969. George Gulson, Tom Ellwein, Paul Hoy; Trustees: Delbert Bickel, Robert Doescher, Robert McDowell (McDowell went to Air Force mid-season 1969 and was replaced by Wayne Krumrei); Band Manager, Paul Bankson; Conductor, Dr. Leland A. Lillehaug. (Dr. Harold Krueger and Donald McCabe conducted during summer season). No assistant conductor.

1970. George Gulson, Dr. Harold Krueger, Paul Hoy; Trustees: Delbert Bickel, Donald McCabe (replaced by Stan Eitreim March 30, 1970 when McCabe went on leave), Wayne Krumrei; Band Manager, Paul Bankson; Conductor, Dr. Leland A. Lillehaug. Assistant conductor, Oscar Loe.

1971. George Gulson, Merridee Ekstrom, Paul Hoy; Trustees: Pat Masek, Dr. Harold Krueger, Tom Ellwein; Band Manager, Paul Bankson; Conductor, Dr. Leland A. Lillehaug. Assistant conductor, Oscar Loe.

1972. Merridee Ekstrom, Patricia Masek, Paul Hoy; Trustees: Scott Faragher, George Gulson, Deb Johnson, James Kirkeby; Band Manager, Paul Bankson. Conductor, Dr. Leland A. Lillehaug. Assistant conductor, Oscar Loe.

1973. Merridee Ekstrom, George Gulson, Paul Hoy; Trustees: David Krueger, Oscar Loe, Jack Rembold; Band Manager, Paul Bankson; Conductor, Dr. Leland A. Lillehaug. Assistant conductor, Oscar Loe.

1974. Merridee Ekstrom, George Gulson, Paul Hoy; Trustees: David Krueger and Jack Rembold (one year terms), Oscar Loe (two year term); When Rembold later resigned, Robert McDowell was appointed to take his place. Band Manager, Paul Bankson; Conductor Dr. Leland A. Lillehaug. Assistant conductor, Oscar Loe.

1975. Robert McDowell, George Gulson, Paul Hoy; Board members: Merridee Ekstrom (one year), David Krueger (second year of two year term), Oscar Loe, Paul Reeg; Band manager, Paul Bankson; Conductor, Dr. Leland A. Lillehaug. Assistant conductor, Oscar Loe.

1976. Robert McDowell, Sue Anderson, Paul Hoy; Board members: Merridee Ekstrom, Donna Van Bockern Krueger (on leave), David Krueger, George Gulson (appointed February 9, 1976 to fill vacancy caused by Donna Krueger's leave). Donna returned in the fall. Uniform Manager, Paul Bankson; Conductor, Dr. Leland A. Lillehaug. Assistant conductor, Oscar Loe.

1977. David Krueger, Jeff Kull, Paul Hoy; Board members: Donna Krueger, Tom Keleher (replaced by Kathy Bangasser), Martha Vegge; Uniform Manager, Paul Bankson; Conductor, Dr. Leland A. Lillehaug. Assistant conductor, Oscar Loe.

1978. David Krueger, Donna Krueger, Paul Hoy; Board members: Charlotte Hedeen, Martha Vegge, Mary Jensen. Uniform Manager, Paul Bankson; Conductor, Dr. Leland A. Lillehaug. Assistant conductor, Oscar Loe.

1979. James McWayne, Jeanette Paulson, Paul Hoy; Board members: David Joyce, Kathy Bangasser, Mary Jensen, David Krueger; Later in the season Kathy Bangasser and David Joyce left the Band (and the Board) and Martha Vegge and Patricia Masek were appointed as Board members; Uniform Manager, Paul Bankson; Conductor, Dr. Leland A. Lillehaug. Assistant conductor, Pat Masek.

1980. James McWayne, Jeanette Paulson, Paul Hoy. Board members: Mary Avery, Marlene Graber, George Gulson; James McWayne resigned on October 22 (going to school) and vice-president Jeanette Paulson became president. Charlotte Hedeen was appointed to fill the vacant post of vice-president. Doug Lehrer was appointed to the vacant Board spot resulting from the resignation of Marlene Graber, and Pat Masek replaced George Gulson on November 5. Band manager, Paul Bankson; Conductor, Dr. Leland A. Lillehaug. Assistant conductor, Pat Masek.

1981. Jeanette Paulson, Doug Lehrer, Paul Hoy; Board members: Mary Avery, Charlotte Hedeen, Terry Walter; President Jeanette Paulson moved out of the city. Doug Lehrer assumed the presidency and Pat Masek was appointed to fill the vacant vice-president spot. Band Manager, Paul Bankson; Conductor, Dr. Leland A. Lillehaug. Assistant conductor, Pat Masek.

1982. Doug Lehrer, Pat Masek, Paul Hoy; Board members: Terry Walter, Charlotte Hedeen, Dan Hatfield; Band manager, Paul Bankson; Conductor, Dr. Leland A. Lillehaug. Assistant conductor, Pat Masek.

1983. Gary Holman, Mark Isackson, Paul Hoy; Board members: David Joyce, Mary Jensen, Dan Hatfield, Doug Lehrer. Vince Aughenbaugh replaced David Joyce who moved out of the city after playing his final concert on July 4; Band manager, Faye Fossum; (Paul Bankson had served in the manager position for many years). Mary Jensen replaced Hoy in the position of recording minutes of meetings. Conductor, Dr. Leland A. Lillehaug. Assistant conductor, ?

1984. Vince Aughenbaugh, Laurel Cluts, Paul Hoy; Board members: Janet Bruns, Donna Hoogendoorn, Mary Jensen and past president, Gary Holman; Aughenbaugh resigned the presidency on August 20 and Gary Holman was appointed to finish the unexpired term. Band manager, Pam Hansen. Conductor, Dr. Leland A. Lillehaug. Assistant conductor, Oscar Loe.

1982 Municipal Band Board members were, from left to right standing: Leland Lille-haug, conductor; Doug Lehrer, president; Dan Hatfield, two-year member. From left to right sitting: Paul Hoy, secretary-treasurer; Paul Bankson, manager; Terry Walter, one-year member; Charlotte Hedeen, two-year member. *(courtesy Sioux Falls Municipal Band)*

1985. Gary Holman, Linda McLaren, Paul Hoy; Board members: Faye Fossum, Mary Jensen, Stan Eitreim (two year term); Uniform Manager, Terry Walter. Conductor, Dr. Leland A. Lillehaug. Assistant conductor, Oscar Loe.

1986. Gary Holman, Lorie Quanbeck, Paul Hoy; Board members: Faye Fossum, Charlotte Hedeen, Linda McLaren, Dennis Graber, Stan Eitreim (second year of term). Linda McLaren replaced Mary Jensen Ryrholm as recording secretary. Band manager? Conductor, Dr. Leland Lillehaug. Assistant conductor, Oscar Loe.

1987. Gary Holman, Linda McLaren, Paul Hoy; Board members: Wayne Krumrei, Lois Nelson, Eric Knutson, John Titus, Lori Quanbeck (two year term); Conductor, Dr. Leland Lillehaug (through May 1 and assisted through July 31) and Dr. Alan W. Taylor. No assistant conductor.

1988. Linda McLaren Roach, Rolyn Beaird, Paul Hoy; Board members: Gary Holman, (Past president), Faye Fossum, Brenda Bahnson , Lori Quanbeck (second year of term), Lois Nelson?, Lawrence Price?; Conductor, Dr. Alan W. Taylor. No assistant conductor.

1989. Linda McLaren Roach, Rolyn Beaird, Paul Hoy; Board members: Faye Fossum, Brenda Bahnson, Lori Quanbeck (two year term); Conductor, Dr. Alan W. Taylor. No assistant conductor.

1990. Linda McLaren Roach, Rolyn Beaird, Paul Hoy; Board members: Brenda Bahnson, Kathy Bangasser, Steve Stombaugh (two year term); Conductor, Dr. Alan W. Taylor. No assistant conductor.

1991. Craig Alberty, Rolyn Beaird, Paul Hoy; Board members: Dr. Bruce T. Ammann, Craig Rostad , Faye Fossum (two year term), Steve Stombaugh (second year of term). Conductor, Dr. Alan W. Taylor. No assistant conductor.

1992. Craig Alberty, Jackie Larson, Paul Hoy; Board members: Gary Pederson, Lyn Alberty, Kathy Bangasser (two year term), Faye Fossum (second year of term); Conductor, Dr. Bruce T. Ammann. No assistant conductor.

1993. Craig Alberty, Brenda Bahnson, Paul Hoy; Board members: Pam Hansen Barnard, Lyn Alberty, Barb Johnson (two year term) resigned June 1, 1993, Kathy Bangasser (second year of term); Conductor, Dr. Bruce T. Ammann. No assistant conductor.

1994. Pam Hansen Barnard, Mary Ryrholm, Paul Hoy; Board members: Craig Alberty, (Past President), Dennis Graber, Eric Knutson, Laura Britton (two year term), Lois Nelson (one year term to fill unexpired term of Barb Johnson); Conductor, Dr. Bruce T. Ammann. No assistant conductor.

Sioux Falls Municipal Band Personnel, 1920-94

Personnel records from the following years are unavailable, and rosters may be incomplete: 1920-34, 1946-48 and 1950-51.

Codes: Sub = substitute; part = partial season; fall = played concert(s) in autumn only. Question mark (?) indicates not verified.

Name	Instrument	Years
Aasheim, Rod	trombone	1988 sub
Ackerman, Carol	cornet	1972
Ackerman, Susan	clarinet	1978
Adams, James	horn	1957-61
Afdahl, Peter	cornet	1993 sub
Aga, Robert	euphonium	1944
Ahlers, Beth	sax, tenor	1985-86
Ahlers, Carole	clarinet	1981 sub; 82-83
Ahlness, Robert	clarinet	1945
Albert, Samuel	horn	1958-62
Alberty, Craig	cornet	1972 sub; 88-94
Alberty, Craig	euphonium	1987 sub
Alberty, Lyn	euphonium	1987 sub; 88-94
Albright, James	sax	1971-73; 74 sub
Alcorn Dance Studio	dance	1942; 44-47, 53-54, 56 guest
Alger, Vernon Herman	conductor, asst.	during many of Henegar's years
Alger, Vernon Herman	percussion	1933-53
Alger, Vernon Herman	violin soloist	1930-33 guest
Allen, Betty	twirler	1950, 52-53 guest
Alness, Lon	trombone	1970-72
Ament, Jean and Tommy	dance and song	1950 guest
American Legion Aux. 6	vocal group	1964 guest
American Legion Chorus	vocal group	1947-50; 57, 70; 75-76 guest
American Legion Quartet	vocal group	1949 guest
Ammann, Bruce	conductor	1992-94
Ammann, Bruce	sax, alto	1989-90; 91 sub
Amundson, David	clarinet	1975-77
Andersen, Michael	tuba	1992 sub; 93-94
Andersen, Mrs. O. H.	violin soloist	1933, guest
Andersen, Otto H.	conductor	1930-34
Anderson, Curt	showmobile driver	1978
Anderson, Guy G.	sax	1920-54
Anderson, Jeanice	twirler	1953 guest
Anderson, Mark	sound	1982
Anderson, Pat	clarinet	1968 sub fall
Anderson, Paul	horn	1954-57; 60-63
Anderson, Rahn	bassoon	1977
Anderson, Ron	percussion	1970 sub
Anderson, Susan	horn	1973-79
Anderson, Terry	cornet	1975-76
Aning, Deb	clarinet	1979-82
Arend, Kathleen	vocal soloist	1965 guest
Arlton, Hans	trombone	1967-68
Armstrong, Kerchal	trombone	1978 sub; 79
Arneson, Leslie	vocal soloist	1951-52 guest
Arneson, Marianne	twirler	1951-53 guest
Askew, Milt	clarinet	1964-66 sub
Askew, Milt	cornet	1935
Askew, Milt	sax	1936 sub; 40-60; 62-63 & 68-69 sub
Aspaas, Mark	euphonium	1968
Auen, Mary	oboe	1977
Aughenbaugh, F. W.	conductor, guest	1954 guest
Aughenbaugh, Joanne	twirler	1955 guest
Aughenbaugh, Marilyn and Rita	twirlers	1954, 60, 62, 63 guest
Aughenbaugh, Vince	euphonium	1982-84

Name	Instrument	Years
Augustana Vikingette Duo	twirler	1954 guest
Austad, Brett	horn	1989-91
Austin, Janet	vocal soloist	1980 guest
Avery, Mary	clarinet	1976-84
Avery, Mary	library asst.	1980
Axelson, James	cornet	1962
Bachand, Gail	sax, baritone & tenor?	1981 sub; 82-84
Bachman, Harold (Lt. Col)	conductor, guest	1948 guest
Bagpipe Band, Winnipeg, Canada	instr. group	1942 guest
Bahnson, Brenda	clarinet and saxophone	1986-94
Bahnson, Bruce	euphonium	1969 part
Bailey, Austin K. "Bill"	tuba	1920-52
Bailey, Daniel	percussion	1979-80
Bailey, Daniel	showmobile asst.	1980
Bailey, Roy W.	tuba	1939-40
Bainum, Glen C.	conductor, guest	1948 guest
Baird, Carrie	horn	1992-93
Bajema, Phil	cornet	1979-80 sub; 81
Baker, Charles	clarinet	1945
Bale, Gloria	twirler	1951 guest
Ballard, James	vocal soloist	1921 guest
Bane, David	clarinet	1956-59
Bangasser, Kathy	clarinet	1975-80; 82-84; 87-94
Bankson, Paul	trombone	1963 sub; 64-82
Barlow, Nicole	percussion	1990 sub
Barnard, Monty	vocal soloist	1980 guest; 82-94
Barnes, Nancy	clarinet	1992
Barnes, Royal S.(Royl?)	vocal soloist	1921 guest
Barnett, Jimmy	cornet	1931; 33-35
Barnett, Robert J.	clarinet	1947-49; 50?, 51, 53, 61, 64-69
Barnett, Robert	vocal soloist	1981 guest
Barnett Lyons, Martha	flute	1979 sub; 80-85; 86 sub
Barr, Alice	vocal soloist	1923 guest
Barrett, Ann	clarinet	1986 sub; 87-89
Bauermeister, Eileen	vocal soloist	1986
Beaird, Rolyn	euphonium	1983-88; 89 sub; 90-92; 93 sub
Beck, Buddy	accordion	1953 guest
Beck, Buddy	percussion	1953
Becker, Gayle	clarinet	1977, 79
Becker, Joyce	dance	1956 guest
Becker, Joyce	vocal soloist	1970 guest
Bedient, Larry	showmobile driver	1987-94
Beecher, Curtis	percussion	1935 sub; 52 sub, 62 sub
Beecher, Fred	trombone	1920 and ?
Benard, Ray	clarinet	1935-37
Bennett, Conte	cornet	1986 sub; 87-88
Berdahl, Alan	tuba	1971-74; 77-78; 90-91; 94
Berdahl, Arthur	euphonium	1923
Berdahl, James N.	euphonium	1961-63
Berdahl, James	string bass	1941
Berdahl, Richard	cornet	1961-62
Berg, Jon	percussion	1967 sub; 68
Berg, Tiffany	horn	1991 sub; 93 sub
Berge, Gloria	twirler	1953-55 guest
Berger, Justin	dance	1936 guest
Bicentential Choir	vocal group	1976 guest
Bickel, Del	cornet	1965 sub; 66-70
Bierer, Tom	cornet	1974; 77-80
Bierer, Tom	showmobile asst.	1978 sub
Bierer, Tom	sound	1978 sub
Bild, C. E.	horn	1931-32
Bingner, Randy	horn	1971-72
Birkenheuer, Joseph	trombone	1954-57
Bjorklund, Barb	cornet	1990
Blauwet, Lori	clarinet	1976; 79 sub
Bliss, Allan	clarinet	1929; 30-31?; 32-33; 34?; 35
Block, Tom	sound	1974-77; 78-80 sub; 82-86 sub; 88, 89 & 91 sub

Name	Instrument	Years
Blunk, Roger	vocal soloist	1965 guest
Boese, Chad	oboe	1957-63
Boffman, Mark	percussion	1978 sub
Boffman, Pat (Baughman)	trombone	1957 sub
Boise, James	trombone	1954
Bonfoey, Mark	percussion	1978 sub
Borgum, Diana	vocal soloist	1975-78 & 81 guest
Borneman, Roy	sax	1940-45
Boschee, Barbara	clarinet	1976-78
Boullion, Kathy	clarinet	1982-85
Bowar, Jeff	tuba	1970-71
Bowen, Jeff	cornet	1975-76
Bowen, Jeff	showmobile asst.	1975-76
Boysen, Alfred	percussion	1964 sub; 65
Boysen, Allan	horn	1958
Braa, Curtis	clarinet	1970-71
Bradley, Linda	twirler	1953-54 guest
Braithwaite, Marty	vocal soloist	1957-59; 69, 73 guest appearances
Braithwaite, Mindy	bassoon	1968 sub; 69-76; 78
Braithwaite, Tom	horn	1972 sub; 73; 74-76 sub
Brandland, Curt	clarinet	1957 sub
Brandon HS Twirlers	twirler	1959 guest
Brauch, John, Jr.	trombone	1949-50
Bray, Rodney O.	sound	1938-39
Brendtro, Kristi	twirler	1960 guest
Brick, Norma	publicity	1975
Brinkman, Kellie	cornet	1975 &77 sub; 78-79; 81 sub
Britton, Roger	cornet	1993-94 sub
Brogdon, Lyndall	vocal soloist	1957 guest
Bronson, Howard C.(Col.)	conductor, guest	1948-49 guest
Brooks, Douglas	clarinet	1942
Brooks, Stanley	euphonium	1949
Brosz, Brian	trombone	1982 sub
Brown (Robinson), Donna	vocal soloist	1943 & 48 guest
Brown, Marlin	clarinet	1937-43; 46 sub
Brown, Nancy	horn	1982 & 85 sub
Brown, Roger	publicity	1926-28
Brumbaugh (Hanson), Helen	vocal soloist	1945 & 49 guest
Bruns Hallstrom, Janet	cornet	1975-94
Bruun, Joe	percussion	1962-63
Bryant (Anderberg), Ricki	vocal soloist	1981 guest
Bryant (Fisher), Anne	vocal soloist	1943 & 44 guest; 45-56; 57, 79 & 80 guest
Buckwalter Pederson, Carol	bassoon	1978-83
Burge, James	sax, alto	1964, 65 & 67 sub
Burk, Wayne	horn	1951-56
Busdicker Britton, Laura	sax, baritone	1990 & 91 sub; 92-94
Busse, Henry	conductor, guest	1920 guest
Busse, Kenneth	sax, baritone	1957 sub; 58-70
Buus, John D.	clarinet	1929-31?
Buus, John D.	conductor, guest	1967, 83 guest
Byrne, William	cornet	1955-57
Cabbell, James	vocal soloist	1953-55 guest
Cameron, Ann	percussion	1985-86; 90 sub
Carlson, Cherie	sax, baritone	1987 & 88 sub; 89
Carlson, Donna	vocal soloist	1950-52 guest
Carlson, James Paul	percussion	1985
Carlson, Shannon	clarinet	1994
Carpenter, Kenneth	clarinet	1975-76 sub
Cashman, Eugene "Gene"	vocal soloist	1928-29 guest
Cavitt, Margaret Barnard	vocal soloist	1954 guest
Chambers, Roland	trombone	1956-57
Christensen, Carl	conductor, guest	1954 guest
Christensen, Eric	trombone	1986 sub; 87; 88 sub; 89-90
Christensen, James	conductor, guest	1986 guest
Christensen, Lisa	clarinet	1993 sub
Christensen, Paul	conductor, guest	1950 guest
Christiansen, Diana	sax, alto	1986; 87 sub

Name	Instrument	Years
Clarke, Dean	inst. soloist, saxophone	1945 guest
Clausen, Kathy	clarinet	1978 sub; 79
Clinch, Timothy	oboe	1987 sub
Cline, J. De Forest	conductor, guest	1948 guest
Cloud, James or Rex?	trombone	1928-30
Cluts, Laurel	library asst.	1980-81
Cluts, Laurel	trombone	1976-78; 80-86
Colgan, Earl, Jr.	clarinet	1952-64; 68
Collins, Robert	string bass	1961
Colwell, Richard	bassoon	1949
Colwell, Richard	clarinet	1944-48; 50-51?; 52, 55; 56 & 59 sub
Colwell, Richard	inst. soloist, clarinet	1941 guest
Colwell, Richard	librarian	1946-51?
Community Chorus	vocal group	1921 guest
Connors, Carla	vocal soloist	1980 guest
Cook, Duane	horn	1969
Cooper, Marvin	percussion	1943 sub?; 45
Coppens, Lloyd M.	conductor	1920-21
Crowley	cornet	1931
Cwach, Michael	euphonium	1989; 94
Cyrus, Sara	horn	1989 & 92 sub
Dahl, Gerhard H.	vocal soloist	1921 guest
Dahl, Oscar G.	trombone	1920-22
Dailey, Michael Patrick	euphonium	1980 sub; 81
Dalseide, Dawn	bass clarinet	1992-94
Dance Quartet	dance group	1966 guest
Daniels, Greg	percussion	1970-74; 76 sub
DAV Junior Drum & Bugle Corps	inst. group	1942 guest
Davoux, Paul	cornet	1963-67
Dean, Doug	cornet	1963 & 64 guest; 66 sub; 67-69; 70 sub
Dean, Doug	librarian	1968
Dedrick, Dave	MC	1965 & 83 guest
Dempster, John Tom	sax, alto	1963-65
Devaney, Mary	horn	1986
Devaney, Patsy	twirler	1951-54 guest
DeVilbiss, Ray	cornet	1967, 74, 75, & 86 sub
Dewald, Brian	trombone	1987
Dick, Charlene	cornet	1990
Dick, Rachel	horn	1991
Dickenson, Roland "Rolla" E.	vocal soloist	1921 & 1932 guest
Dickenson, William	vocal soloist	1938 guest
Dietrich, E. O	trombone	1920?; 21-29; 51-56
Dody Thill Dancers	dance group	1966 guest
Doescher, Robert	percussion	1964-70
Doescher, Robin	bassoon	1980 sub
Donahue, Mrs. James	vocal soloist	1949 guest
Dornaus, Rudy H.	string bass	1933-39
Downs, Joanna	piano soloist	1921-22 guest
Doyle, Betsy	vocal soloist	1975 guest
Drawbaugh, Robert	clarinet	1960
Dresbach, Tony	trombone	1993-94
Drew, Sid		1920
Duerksen, Beth	horn	1986; 87 part time
Duerksen, Greg	tuba	1976 sub
Duerksen, Jeanette	horn	1982
Duffy, Linsey	clarinet	1991
Duncan, Isa	violin soloist	1922 guest
Dunn, Jack		1922
Dvoracek, Ernest	clarinet	1943 sub?; 44-45; 46-48?, 50?, 51?; 52-57
Dyvig, Clifford	cornet	1965 sub
East, Judy	twirler	1950 guest
Eberle	trombone	1952
Edward, Elmer T. (Eddie)	cornet	1923-47
Edwards, Harold (Prof.)	violin soloist	1934 guest
Eichmeier, Harvey	euphonium	1951-60
Eichmeier, Harvey	tuba	1961-69
Eitel, Butler	euphonium	1982 sub

Name	Instrument	Years
Eitel, Butler	guest conductor	1980; 83; 84, SDSU campus (Brookings) guest
Eitel, Butler	inst. soloist, euphonium	1980 guest
Eitreim, Stan	percussion	1964-67; 69 sub; 70-72; 87-88 perc. & tuba; 89-91
Eitreim, Stan	stage manager	1988-94
Eitreim, Stan	tuba	1962-63; 74-86; 87-88 tuba & perc.; 92-94
Ekholm, Jimmy	inst. soloist, euphonium	1956, 58 guest
Ekstrom, Merridee	cornet	1968-80; 85 sub
Ekstrom, Merridee	library asst.	1975-76
El Riad Chanters	vocal group	1937-45; 48, 49-52; 53 guest
Elgethun, J. H	horn	1962-63
Elgethun, J. H.	percussion	1954-59
Elgethun, J. H.	tuba	1961 sub?
Elgethun, Kristi	sax, alto	1970-71
Elks Quartet	vocal group	1942 guest
Ellefson, Mary	flute	1966 sub; 69
Ellis, Harry	sound	1967-73
Ellis, Harry	tuba	1942-44; 46-66
Ellis, Royal	cornet	1935-41
Ellison, Cindi	trombone	1994
Ellwein, Fred	euphonium	1983
Ellwein, Tom	inst. soloist, trombone	1940 guest
Ellwein, Tom	trombone	1965 sub; 66-72; 75 sub
Elrod, Kathie	twirler	1954, 60, 62, 63 guest
Emmel, Charles F.	conductor	1922
Endahl, Vonnie	horn	1977-78; 79 sub
Engh, Dan	trombone	1983-84
Engh, Judy	clarinet	1982 sub; 83-84
Engh, Michael	horn	1974 sub; 75-77; 78 sub
Engh, Michael	showmobile asst.	1977
Erickson, David Walter	cornet	1978
Erickson, Jon Richard	showmobile asst.	1973 sub
Erickson, Rosemary	twirler	1951 guest
Erwin, Charles (Lt. Col)	conductor, guest	1984 guest
Evans, Merle	conductor, guest	1985 guest
Evensen, Stuart	euphonium	1972
Evenson, David	trombone	1972-73
Ewing, Kenneth	cornet	1948-49
Fagerland, Shad	horn	1994
Faragher, Scott	horn	1963-67; 71-83; 84 sub; 85; 89-91 sub
Farkas, Kristine Ann	vocal soloist/dance	1963 & 65 guest
Feiock, Arlo	trombone	1958
Fejfar, Willard	cornet	1943 sub?; 44
Fenner, John	horn	1964 sub
Fenton, Scott	percussion	1987-90
Ferrell, Rob	percussion	1974 sub
Fialkowski, Marilyn	vocal soloist	1959 guest
Fialkowski, Paul	string bass	1960-62
Fillingsness, Renee	flute	1979 sub
Fillmore, Henry	conductor, guest	1948 guest
Finck, Stanley	twirler	1953-55 guest
Flanery, Heather	flute	1990-91 sub
Fleming, Mark	sound	1981; 82 & 83 sub
Flisrand, Richard	euphonium	1964 sub; 66; 67 sub; 68
Flisrand, Richard	trombone	1960, 62
Floren, Myron	accordion	1940-43 guest; 48 guest
Floren Accordion Quartet	accordion	1941, 43 guest
Florence Bright School of Dance	dance	1936 guest
Fodness, Loren	euphonium	1974-75
Fodness, Loren	showmobile asst.	1974-75
Foland, Lori	clarinet	1990-91
Forrette, Joan	vocal soloist	1946 guest
Foss, Ardeen	clarinet	1934; 1952-63
Foss, Ardeen	oboe	1931-33; 35-41; 46-51
Foss, Cliff	trombone	1936-45
Foss, Donald	oboe	1937 sub; 38-41
Foss, Edgar	sax, tenor	1937-38?
Foss, Joe	sax, baritone	1935-39

Name	Instrument	Years
Foss, Richard	oboe	1955-57
Foss, Robert	flute	1957 sub
Fossum, Faye	trombone	1979-93; 94 sub
Four Blue Notes, Pipestone	vocal group	1954 guest
Frakes, Laura	clarinet	1971 sub; 72
Frank, Stephanie	sax, baritone	1987 sub fall
Freitag, William	cornet	1985
Freitag, William	library asst.	1985-86
Frick, Robert	euphonium	1963 sub; 64
Friedhoff, Everitt	tuba	1948-49; 59-61
Fritz, Mary	clarinet	1985 sub; 86-88; 90-94
Fuller, Anne	twirler	1954 guest
Gaalswyck, Joel	sound	1965; 67 sub
Gardner, Nancy	vocal soloist	1944 guest
Gednalske, Linda	twirler	1980 guest
Gedstad, Ed	clarinet	1943-51
Gedstad, Warren	clarinet	1952-59
Gerry, Kathy	clarinet	1969 sub
Gibson, Beverly	clarinet	1992 sub; 93
Gibson, Bill	trombone	1993
Gibson, Jill	bass clarinet	1981 sub; 82
Gilbertson, W. J.		1921
Glenski, Bill	trombone	1981 sub; 82; 84 sub
Goheen, Bob	percussion	1983
Goldman, Edwin Franko	conductor, guest	1948 guest
Golz, Deann	clarinet	1992-94
Golz, Deann	library asst.	1994
Gossman, Leo	clarinet	1935-53
Graber, Dennis	clarinet	1985-94
Graber, Marlene	clarinet	1978-80
Graham, Robert	sax	1955-56
Gran, Ellen	twirler	1952 guest
Gray, Harold	bass clarinet	1961-67; 69
Green, Cathy	clarinet	1979-81
Greive, Tyrone	violin soloist	1971 guest
Grevlos, Lisa	See Wiehl, Lisa	
Griffith, Robert	cornet	1948-52; 54-62
Groskurth, Kevin	sax, baritone	1985
Gross, Gene	horn	1962
Gross, Jeral	cornet	1994
Gross, Mark	trombone	1992-94
Guderyahn, Richard J.	cello	1945
Guderyahn, Richard J.	inst. soloist, violin	1945 guest
Gudmastad, David	cornet	1970-71
Guenevere Gustad Ballet Studio	dance	1953, 55-57, 59 guest
Gulson, George	cornet	1964-78; 79 sub; 80, 81, 85 & 86 sub
Gunderson, James	cornet	1993-94 sub
Gunderson-Soutar, Florence (Mrs. F.J.)	vocal soloist	1932 guest
Gustafson, Ramona	sax, baritone	1978
Gym-O-Rama Gymnastics School	gymnastics	1958 guest
Haaland Paddock, Joan	inst. soloist, cornet	1989 guest
Haanstad, Morris	cornet	1958-59
Haley, Mike	vocal soloist	1956 guest
Hall, David Charles	percussion	1979
Hall, Greg	percussion	1957 sub; 58; 59 sub; 61, 63
Hallstrom, Carl	euphonium	1977-79; 85-87; 93
Hallstrom, Carl	showmobile asst.	1978
Hallstrom, Carl	trombone	1988-92; 94
Hamilton, Claude, Jr.	dance	1944 guest
Halvorson, Donald	horn	1943 sub?; 44
Hammond, Curt	horn	1980-85
Hammond, Curt	library asst.	1983
Hammond, Curt	publicity	1984
Hammond, Paul	horn/cornet	1943-44?
Hamre, Anna	euphonium	1973
Handel, Greg	cornet	1991-94
Hankins, Paul	inst. soloist, cornet	1993 guest

Name	Instrument	Years
Hansen, Jon	percussion	1960-61
Hansen, Robert	euphonium	1965-66
Hansen, Robert	trombone	1964 sub
Hansen Barnard, Pam	flute	1976, 78, 82-94
Hansen Barnard, Pam	librarian	1975
Hanson, A. H.		1929
Hanson, D. M.	euphonium?	1922
Hanson, Dawn	librarian	1986
Hanson, Dawn	showmobile asst.	1985
Hanson, Dawn	trombone	1985-86
Hanson, Henry T.	alto clarinet/clarinet	1920-28; 29-30?; 30-33; 34?; 35-58
Hanson, M. T. (G?)	euphonium	1922-28?; 29
Hanson, Merlin (same as above?)	euphonium	1927
Hanson, Mike G.	euphonium	1930-33; 34?; 35-43
Hanson, Ove	oboe	1968 sub; 69-72
Hanson, Paul	cornet	1967 sub; 69-72
Hanson, Paul Nathan	sound	1985 sub
Hanson, Robert L.	clarinet	1962-66; 67 sub
Hanson, Tom	flute	1942
Hanson Johnson, Barbara	clarinet	1975-80; 89 sub; 92; 93-94 sub
Haraldson, Sheila	clarinet	1969-70
Harding, Dr. A. A.	conductor, guest	1948 guest
Harmonettes	vocal group	1935, 38 & 40 guest
Harms, Gary	bass clarinet	1955-61
Harms, Gary	clarinet	1954
Harrington, Kermit	bassoon	1942-44
Harris, Donald	horn	1969; 70 sub; 71
Harris, Joyce	vocal soloist	1980 guest
Hart, Mike	percussion	1992-93; 94 sub
Hart, Robb	MC	1992-94
Hart, Sandra Kay	twirler	1950, 53 guest
Hartig, Eugenia Orlich	vocal soloist	1965-79; 80 & 94 guest
Hartig, Thomas Daniel	clarinet	1972-75
Hartshorn, Larry	oboe	1953-54
Hartwig, Stephen	cornet	1991 sub
Hartwig, Tiffin	flute	1989-91 sub
Harum (Hart), Mary	vocal soloist	1971 guest
Hasegawa, Claudia	oboe	1980; 82 sub; 83
Hasegawa, Sam	clarinet	1966; 67 sub
Hatfield, Dan	percussion	1979 sub; 1980-84
Hatfield, Warren	inst. soloist, alto saxophone	1980 guest
Hattervig, Charlene	twirler	1951 guest
Haugen, Joan	horn	1979 sub; 80
Hays, Rex	clarinet	1964, 65 & 68 sub
Hays, Stan	clarinet	1964-65 sub
Hays Emmel, Kathy	flute	1964-65; 67; 85 guest
Hays Emmel, Kathy	librarian	1964-65
Hayward, R. B. (Capt.)	conductor, guest	1948 guest
Headley, Jack	twirler	1940 guest
Hedeen, Charlotte	clarinet	1976-78; 81-86; 87 & 94 sub
Heetland, Stephen	horn	1965-66 sub
Hegg, Dennis	euphonium	1966 sub; 67; 76; 79 sub, 80
Hegg, Dennis	MC	1994 sub
Hegg, Dennis	tuba	1968
Hegg, Jason	sound	1994
Hegg, Jeremy	cornet	1990-91; 93-94
Heiden, Tami	horn	1984 sub
Heinemann, Wayne	horn	1984
Heinemeyer, Dick	trombone	1965 sub
Heisel, David	sound	1991
Helfert, Jake	trombone	1920-25; 26?; 27-46
Helland, Connie	percussion	1969
Helland, Greg	horn	1967-71
Helwick, Cindy	clarinet	1989-90
Hemphill, Dee	vocal soloist	1979 guest
Hendrix, Lois	euphonium	1979-80
Henegar, Russell D.	conductor	1935-63; 64, 65 guest

Name	Instrument	Years
Henegar, Russell D.	cornet	1933-34
Heney, John J.	conductor, guest	1948 guest
Hengeveld, Derek	percussion	1992-94
Henning, Linda	dance	1959 guest
Hering, George	sound	1949-64; 65 sub
Herman, Amy	horn	1994 sub
Herr, Jackson	cornet	1958-59
Herting, S. J.	string bass	1956-59
Hill, Gregory	trombone	1991 sub
Hillman, Albert R.	horn	1943 sub?; 44-48
Hillman, Howard	cornet	1942
Hiniker, Thomas	oboe	1992 sub
Hink, Randy	percussion	1968-69
Hobson, Charles		1920; also later?
Hobson, Harry		1920; also later?
Hobson, William	euphonium	1948
Hoeger, Betty (Mrs. August)	vocal soloist	1968 guest
Hoffman, Pat	vocal soloist	1972 guest
Hohman, Mary Ann	vocal soloist	1965 guest
Hoiseth, Gary	clarinet	1963 sub?; 64-69; 71
Hoiseth, Jean	percussion	1972-73
Holdridge, Charleen	dance/vocal	1939 guest
Holdridge, Pat and Barbara	dance	1936 guest
Holdridge, Vada	piano soloist	1939 & 42-43 guest
Holm, Ole	vocal soloist	1920 & 21 guest
Holman, Gary	cornet	1980 sub; 81-88
Holyer, Robert	cornet	1964 sub; 65
Holyer, Ronn	cornet	1960-64
Hood, Gary	showmobile driver	1979-86
Hoover, Harold, Jr.	trombone	1959-65
Hoover, Harold, Sr.	trombone	1943-63
Horsley, Gary	cornet	1983
Horsted, Don	bassoon	1959; 60?
Houdek, Glen G.	percussion	1930-48; 50-51; 53-61
Howard, John	cornet	1943
Howard, Susan	trombone	1984
Hoy, Paul	percussion	1957-94
Hoyt, R. G.	bass clarinet	1920-54
Huether Moklebust, Cathy	percussion	1982-85
Huisman, Mark	sound	1985 sub
Hurley, Faye	vocal soloist	1987 guest
Huse-Kerr, Tami	oboe	1984
Indseth, Andrew K.	trombone	1920-33
Ireland, William	euphonium	1950-51?
Irons, Earl D. (Col.)	conductor, guest	1948 guest
Irvin, Dan	clarinet	1988-93
Isackson, Mark	clarinet	1981 sub (alto sax?); 82-83; 81, 85, 89 & 90 sub
Iseminger, Cammy	vocal soloist	1978 guest
Iverson, Sally Jo	twirler	1963 guest
Jackson, Orral O.	tuba	1924-31; 34-57
Jacobs, Deb	twirler	1973 guest
Jacobs, Sidney	vocal soloist	1937 guest; 38
Jankowski, Phil	sound	1985 sub; 86-87
Jans, David	trombone	1986-87; 88 sub; 89-91
Javurek, Anton "Tony"	whistler	1965, 73, 75?, 82 all guest appearances
Jensen Elsinger, Delight	clarinet	1981-84; 90-94
Jensen Elsinger, Delight	librarian	1990-94
Jensen Ryrholm, Mary	flute	1977-81; 82 sub; 83-86; 89-90 sub; 93-94
Jensen Ryrholm, Mary	librarian	1977-79
Jensen Ryrholm, Mary	library asst.	1984
Jetvig, Laurie	horn	1988 sub
Jodie's Dance Studio	dance group	1964 guest
Johnson, David L.	inst. soloist, alto saxophone	1958-59 guest
Johnson, David L.	sax, alto	1960-63; 66; 67 sub
Johnson, Eddie	sax, baritone	1981-82; 83 sub; 84-86
Johnson, Eddie	showmobile asst.	1981-82
Johnson, J. L.	conductor, asst.	1926

Name	Instrument	Years
Johnson, J. L.	cornet	1922-26
Johnson, Janine	twirler	1963-64, 66-67 guest
Johnson, Kathy	horn	1978-79
Johnson, Linda	horn	1968-69
Johnson, Mark	tuba	1972, 74 & 86 sub
Johnson, Yvonne	clarinet	1973
Johnson Hegg, Barbara J.	horn	1966-68; 79 sub; 80, 92; 93 sub
Johnson Hegg, Barbara J.	librarian	1966-67
Johnson Helland, Deb	horn	1970-71
Johnston, James	clarinet	1968-70
Jones, Evan	sound	1979-80
Joneson, O. A.	cornet	1953
Jonsson, Jon	percussion	1967 sub; 68
Jorgensen, Paula	trombone	1974-77
Jorgensen, Rosalie	clarinet	1975
Jorve, Kara	clarinet	1985
Joyce, David	euphonium	1983
Joyce, David	showmobile asst.	1980-81
Joyce, David	tuba	1974-82
Joyce, Robert	percussion	1984-85 sub
Julson, Arlene	vocal soloist	1943 guest
Jurgensen, Mary	twirler	1952 guest
Jurisson, Cindy	oboe	1978
Juul, Anne	clarinet	1969-74
Kahl, Julie	percussion	1975-78
Kaiser-Frazer Quartet	vocal group	1950 guest
Kamolz, Fred	euphonium	1945
Kaponin, Myrtle Stolt	vocal soloist	1941-42 guest
Kaufman, Dennis	horn	1985, 90
Kealey, Danny	cornet	1959-62; 63 sub; 64, 65, 67, 68 & 74 sub
Keleher, Tom	horn	1973-76; 77 part time
Kelly, Bradbury	percussion	1994
Kelly, Denis	cornet	1957 sub; 58
Kemner, Gerald	clarinet	1963
Kindred, Robert	cornet	1936-42
King, David	tuba	1982-86
King, Karl L.	conductor, guest	1948 guest
Kirkeby, James	cornet	1971-72
Kittelson, Desmond H.	cornet	1949-51
Kleinheinz, Walter L.	tuba	1920-33
Kleinsasser, Arlene	clarinet	1974
Knoff, Keith	trombone	1961-66; 67 sub
Knutson, Brian	sax, alto	1987 sub
Knutson, Charles	bassoon	1951-54
Knutson, Eric	cornet	1984-88; 91-92 sub; 93-94
Knutson, Eric	showmobile asst.	1985-86
Knutson, Tommy	bassoon	1953-58
Koolbeck, Dean	clarinet	1951?; 52
Kopperud, Jean	clarinet	1971
Koupal, Carrie	clarinet	1993 sub
Kramer, Kerry	sax, baritone	1987-89 & 91 sub
Kramer, Robert	percussion	1992-94
Kramer, William	sax	1954-55
Kreitzer, Lloyd	string bass	1953-57
Kremer, Palmer	horn	1936-41; 43 & 46 sub
Krueger, David	cornet	1969-79
Krueger, Harold	co-conductor	1969
Krueger, Harold	cornet	1965 sub; 66-71; 72 sub; 73-79
Krumrei, Wayne	euphonium	1943-64
Krumrei, Wayne	tuba	1967-70; 85-87
Kucinski, Leo	conductor, guest	1948 & 67 guest
Kull, Jeff	oboe	1970-77; 78 sub; 79
Kuyper, Kathy	library asst.	1981
Kuyper, Kathy	sax, alto	1980 sub; 81
Lafleur, Joe	oboe	1988 & 89 sub
Lambert Dance Studio	dance	1955-58 guest
Landech	trombone	1922 sub?

Name	Instrument	Years
Lane, Kenneth	cornet	1935-40; 46-47
Lane, Ronald	clarinet	1937-40
Lang, Linda	vocal soloist	1979 guest
Lange, Yvonne	clarinet	1986
Langford Duffy, Linsey	clarinet	1987-91; 94 sub
Lanning, Richard	inst. soloist, clarinet	1939 guest
Larsen, Jackie	clarinet	1974 sub; 80 sub; 81-85; 86 sub; 87-93
Larson, Angela	clarinet	1993 sub; 94
Larson, Britt	bass clarinet	1992
Larson, C. R. (Bob)	clarinet	1935-43; 46-51
Larson, Carol	gymnastics	1959 guest
Larson, David A.	stage asst.	1990-91
Larson, David A.	tuba	1986-91
Larson, Elaine	inst. soloist, trombone	1935 guest
Larson, Gayle	inst. soloist, piccolo	1957 guest
Larson, Larry	trombone	1958-59
Larson, Marion	vocal soloist	1943 guest
Larson, Mary	euphonium	1973 & 77 sub
Larson, Patsy	sax, baritone	1973-74
Larson, Peg	clarinet	1971-72
Lee, Doug	tuba	1977 sub
Lehmann, Clayton	cornet	1976 sub
Lehrer, Doug	cornet	1978-85; 86 sub; 87-92
Lenker Runyan, Robyn	flute	1975 fall, sub
LeVan, Eric	percussion	1980 sub; 81-83; 85-86 sub; 88-91 sub
Levsen, Mark	cornet	1981-82; 83 sub
Levsen, Sara	percussion	1984
Lewedag, L. A.	horn	1932; 33-34?; 35-38
Lias, David	horn	1957-58
Lias, Donald	cornet	1944-50; 58 sub
Lias, Eddie	inst. soloist or duets, guest	1939 & 41-46 guest
Lien, Lyle	sax, tenor	1952
Lillehaug, David	flute	1970-76
Lillehaug, David	library asst.	1976
Lillehaug, Laurie	library asst.	1976, 78, 80
Lillehaug, Laurie	publicity	1982
Lillehaug, Leland	bassoon	1957-58; 61-63
Lillehaug, Leland	clarinet	1949, 50? 56 sub; 59
Lillehaug, Leland	conductor	1964-86; 87 & 94 sub
Lillehaug, Steven	clarinet	1972-75; 76, 77 & 78 sub; 82
Lillehaug, Steven	library asst.	1975-76
Lillehaug, Steven	sax	1979 sub
Lillehaug, Steven	showmobile asst.	1977
Lillehaug, Steven	sound	1978
Limburg, James	trombone	1966 sub; 69
Lippert, Michelle	clarinet	1991 sub
Little, Everton	sax	1943 sub?; 44-69;70 sub; 71,72 &75 sub; 77-79 sub
Little, Loren	cornet	1957-65; 67 & 68 sub; 70; 71 sub
Little, Tom	sax, tenor	1961-63; 65 sub
Loe, Loren	vocal soloist	1942 guest
Loe, Oscar	clarinet	1953, 54 & 59 sub; 60-67; 71-78; 82-88
Loe, Oscar	conductor, asst.	1972-78; 83-87 (through April in 1987)
Loe, Oscar	oboe	1968; 70, part time.
Loewen, Frances	vocal soloist	1939 guest
Loftesness, Ray	MC	1965 & 68, 73 & 75 guest; 80-90; 91 sub
Loftesness, Ray	narrator	1972, 76 & 77 guest
Loftesness, Ray	publicity	1983
Loftesness, Ray	vocal duet	1966 & 75 guest
Loftesness, Scott	trombone	1994
Loomis Hansen, Marilyn	flute	1964-66; 85 guest
Lorensen, Leonard	sax	1949
Lotz, Mark	cornet	1973-74
Lotz, Mark	librarian	1974?
Lyman, Susie	cornet	1987, 89
Lynch, Shirley	inst. soloist, euphonium	1941 guest
Lyons, Gordon		1930-31
Madrigal Quartet	vocal group	1930 guest

Name	Instrument	Years
Maher, Nikki	clarinet	1990-94
Mahlsted, Steven?	cornet	1960
Malmin, Olaf	vocal soloist	1975-76 & 80-81 guest
Marimba Trio	inst. group	1942 guest
Marker, Robert W.	percussion	1949
Marvel, James	horn	1981 & 82 sub
Masek, Brian	sound	1990 sub
Masek, Patricia	flute	1968-94
Masten, Monte	sound	1980 sub
Mathers, Norman	vocal soloist	1929 guest
Matthews, Jon	trombone	1972 sub
Matthews, W. T. (Ted)	trombone	1948-49
Matthius, Marciene	vocal soloist	1942-43, **44,** 47-48, **57-64,** 65, 67, 79
Mattice, John	clarinet	1962-67
May, Melissa	oboe	1982
McAllister, Jeff	euphonium	1976 sub; 77
McAllister, Michael	sound	1989 sub; 91
McCabe, Donald	co-conductor	1969
McCabe, Donald	euphonium	1950 sub
McCabe, Donald	horn	1950-69
McCabe, Donald	trombone	1942, 46
McCabe, Terry	cornet	1966-69
McClain, Floyd	clarinet	1975 sub; 76 alto sax, sub
McClain, Kenneth	cornet	1964-67
McClung, Charles F.	conductor	1923-27
McClung, G. C.	conductor	1928-29
McConahie, Deb	trombone	1991 sub; 92-94
McDonald, Mary	horn	1979
McDowell, Robert, Jr.	trombone	1988, 89 sub; 90-93
McDowell, Robert, Sr.	horn	1961-69; 73-76; 77, 78 & 84 sub
McFarland, Jason	horn	1992-94
McGaughey, Ronald	trombone	1963-65; 66 sub
McGuire, Janice	twirler	1954-55 guest
McHardy, Bryson	horn	1970
McKechnie, Marilyn & Mac	dance & bagpipe	1951 guest
McKenzie, Arthur V.	horn	1948
McKenzie	horn	1927-28
McLaren Roach, Linda	bass clarinet	1975-91; 93-94
McLaren Roach, Linda	clarinet	1973-74
McLaren Roach, Linda	librarian	1974
McLaughlin (Hartrich), Loretta	vocal soloist	1941-43
McLinn, Karen	clarinet	1981
McWayne, James	sax, alto	1975-76; 77 part time; 78-80 (bari sax in 79)
McWayne, James	showmobile asst.	1975-76
Medeck, George B.	clarinet	1927-28?; 29, 32-39; 42-43; 47, 48?; 49, 50 & 51?
Meester, Beth	horn	1977 sub
Mehlum, Nancy	twirler	1960-66, 70-72 guest during all years.
Merrill, Tom	clarinet	1986
Metzger, Marson	cornet	1932?, 33-34
Meyer, Kevin	percussion	1994
Meyer, Roy	clarinet	1920-36
Meyer, William D.	clarinet	1920-41; ill in 42; 43-45; 46?
Meyers, Mark	euphonium	1970
Meyers, Nancy	clarinet	1970
Michael, Mary	sax, alto	1979
Miller, David	electric bass	1981
Miller, David	string bass	1984
Miller, Leon	cornet	1948-57; 62; 63-69 sub; 73; 74-79 & 84-86 sub
Miller, Philip	trombone	1963-65
Millie, G. O.		1930-31
Millikan, Amy	sax, tenor	1993-94
Minnehaha Mandskor	vocal group	1930-31, 33, 45 guest
Mitchell, David	trombone	1968; 70 sub; 86 part time
Mitchell, Larry	conductor, guest	1963 guest
Mitchell, Lee	trombone	1920-41
Mitchell, Linda	flute	1968-69
Moberly, Russell	cornet	1931

Name	Instrument	Years
Moe, Debra	clarinet	1972
Moe, Kathy	oboe	1973-76
Moen, Dale	euphonium	1934
Monk, B. G.	horn	1945
Moore, Frances (Miss)	inst. soloist, cello	1922 guest
Moore, Jim Lee	inst. soloist, cornet	1959 guest
Moore, Myron	horn	1942 sub?; 43
Morgan, Glenn (Bud)	horn	1949
Morgan, Glenn (Bud)	sax, baritone	1953 sub
Morris, Robert	vocal soloist	1931 guest
Morris, S. O.		1929
Mosher, Hope	vocal soloist	1965 guest
Mueller, Charles	clarinet	1955-60; 64 sub
Mueller, Marc David	cornet	1985
Mueller, Marvin	cornet	1956
Muldbakken, Rolf	tuba	1978-79 sub
Muller, Oscar	flute	1931-35
Municipi-Pals	vocal group	1962 guest
Munson, Eric	tuba	1987 part time
Muriel's Dramusic Studio	dance	1954 guest
Muxfelt, Janet Whitfield	vocal soloist	1944 guest
Myrabo?, Arnold	bass clarinet	1936?
Naber, Teri	horn	1994
Nason, Mrs. Earl V.	piano soloist	1947-48, 52, 55 guest
Nason, Robert	cornet	1952-57
Natvig, Ann	clarinet	1987-88
Natz, Martha Joan	dance	1941 guest
Nauen, Joyce	vocal soloist	1977 & 78 guest
Negstad, Nancy	clarinet	1981 sub; 82
Nelson, Cindy	clarinet	1971 sub; 72
Nelson, Donald M.	tuba	1969-70
Nelson, Fletcher	euphonium	1936-41
Nelson, Gary	percussion	1966-67; 68 sub
Nelson, Harold	cornet	1942-43
Nelson, Jeffrey (Rock)	trombone	1968-69, 73-74, 77-78, 86-91, all years as sub
Nelson, Lois	horn	1985 sub; 86-94
Neprud, Lori	sax	1988; 89-90 sub
Nevin, Joel	sound	1986 sub; 88-90
Newcomb, Don	sax	1970-72
Newton, John "Jack" M.	cornet	1920-45
Niblick, Robert	percussion	1940-44;46-49; 50? 51-52; 57,59 sub,60;80-81 sub
Nield, David	vocal soloist	1980 guest
Noble, Denise	horn	1986 sub; 87-89
Noble, Denise	librarian	1989
Nock, Clifford	percussion	1988-89
Nogami, Karen	oboe	1983-84
Norlin, Dennis	clarinet	1959-61
Norse Glee Club	vocal group	1932-34 guest
Novak, Todd	sax	1987 sub; 88
Nurses' Chorus, Sioux Valley Hospital	vocal group	1943 guest
Nygard, Jeremy	cornet	1994
O'Brien, Patrick	dance	1956, 57 & 61 guest
Oakland, Viki	inst. soloist, marimba	1946 guest
Ode, James	cornet	1954-57; 1960-63; 65, 71 guest soloist; 75 sub
Odland, Mark	clarinet	1941-43
Ohrland, Curt	trombone	1985
Olawsky, Doug	flute	1969 sub; 70-73
Olawsky, Doug	librarian	1972
Olawsky, Ralph	percussion	1977
Oldenkamp Peterson, Garneth	bass clarinet	1972-73
Oldham, Max	percussion	1969 sub; 70
Oleson, Delorez	twirler	1947 guest
Olkiewicz, Chris	sax, alto	1985-87
Olsen, Colin	bass clarinet	1970; 71 sub
Olsen, Greg	percussion	1979 sub
Olsen, Neal	oboe	1949-52; 54-58
Olsen, Ralph, Jr.	clarinet	1964-67; 68 sub, 71 sub

Name	Instrument	Years
Olson, Dennis	alto clarinet	1959-64
Olson, Don	oboe	1967; 68 sub
Olson, Heidi	euphonium	1994
Olson, Linda	flute	1965 sub; 66-67
Olson, Michael	euphonium	1969-73
Olson, Natalie	clarinet	1970-74
Olson, Pat	twirler	1952 guest
Olson, Rolf	cornet	1981 sub; 82, 85-87 & 89 sub; 90
Olson, Steven	bassoon	1964 sub? 65-66; 67 sub; 68
Oltman, Steve	clarinet	1957-60
Omanson, Darrell	cornet	1991
147th Field Artillery firing squad	drill team	1938 guest
Opland, Allen	cornet	1945
Opland, Allen	vocal soloist	1945 guest
Ordal, Jane	flute	1968
Original Rhythm Band	inst. group	1932-33 guest
Ortman, Robert	euphonium	1963 sub; 64-66; 69 sub; 70, 74-75
Ost, Marian	horn	1993 part time; 94
Oster, Carine	clarinet	1969
Osterberg, Ertis	vocal soloist	1980 guest
Overseth, Julie	vocal soloist	1972 guest
Oviatt, Denny	MC	1981 guest
Owen Hanson, Jolayne	sax, alto	1967 sub; 68-69
Ozolins, Elina	percussion	1978; 79 sub
Pace, Kenneth	clarinet	1949
Pachoud, Julia	MC	1993-94 sub
Pallansch, Lyda	vocal soloist	1921 guest
Palmer, O. W. ("Pic")	flute	1920-63
Palmer Faragher, Ann	flute	1966-67; 71-73; 74-75
Parker, Herbert	showmobile driver	1973-82; 83?; 84
Parker, James	cornet	1984; 85 sub
Patterson, Robert	percussion	1971 sub; 77 part time; 78-79; 82 sub
Paul, Ed	MC	1934-37; 39-64
Paul, Ed	vocal soloist	1934-37; 39-64
Paul, Leonard	clarinet	1935-42
Paulsen, Rick	percussion	1973-74
Paulson, Gary	clarinet	1963 sub
Paulson, Jeanette	oboe	1978 sub; 79-81
Paulson, Jeanette	publicity	1977-81
Paulson, Laurel	bassoon	1974-79
Paulson, Michelle	horn	1986-87 sub
Peck		1923
Peckham, Francis	cornet	1945 sub
Pederson, Gary	tuba	1991-94
Peik, Richard	clarinet	1961-67
Pekas, Janine	dance	1960 guest
Pekas, Quido	sax, baritone	1948, 56
Penn, Patricia	flute	1981-84 sub
Perkins, James	cornet	1979 sub; 80-84; 85 sub; 86-89
Perkins, John	cornet	1990 sub
Perrenoud, Mary	clarinet	1966-68
Person, Janet	sax, alto	1972
Person, Sandra McAllister	sax, baritone	1974-77
Petersen, A. Richard	MC	1964, 66, &72 guest appearances
Petersen, A. Richard	vocal soloist	1966 guest
Peterson, Katherine	bassoon	1982-94
Peterson, Keith	bassoon	1964
Peterson, Keith	clarinet	1966
Peterson, Keith	sax	1965; 67-68 sub
Peterson, Lynn	percussion	1973; 74 sub
Peterson, Lynn	showmobile asst.	1973
Peterson, Raymond	vocal soloist	1980 & 81 guest
Peterson, Shirlene	vocal soloist	1976 guest
Petterson, Linda	percussion	1981
Pfeiffer, Steven	showmobile asst.	1978-79
Pfeiffer, Steven	trombone	1978-81
Phillips, Glen	juggler	1952 guest

Name	Instrument	Years
Phillips, Harvey	inst. soloist, tuba	1988 guest
Piechowski, James	tuba	1968 sub
Pierre Kilties	drill team	1930 guest
Pinard, Jean	percussion	1974-76
Plienis, Shari	oboe	1968 sub; 69
Pole, Andrew	trombone	1992; 93 sub
Polynesian Dance Troupe	dance	1980 guest
Polzin, Brenda	twirler	1977 guest
Polzin, Geraldine	whistler	1942-43, 75? guest
Polzin, Linda	twirler	1977, 79-80 guest
Preheim, Jane	horn	1986
Prescott, Gerald	conductor, guest	1948 guest
Price, David	oboe?	1975 sub
Price, Lawrence	horn	1986-88; 89 sub
Prieb (Olawsky), Suzanne	clarinet	1970; 71 sub; 72-73
Prindle, Roma	library asst.	1983
Prindle, Roma	vocal soloist	1981 guest; 82-85; 86 guest
Pruner, Ray G.	percussion	1945-63
Pythian Drill Team.	drill team	1954 guest
Quail, Jane	flute	1986 sub; 87-92; 93-94 sub
Quanbeck, Lori	bassoon	1979 sub; 80-82; 83 sub; 84-94
Quinn, Janet	whistler	1942 & 47 guest
Raker, R. D.	sound	1966
Rasmussen, Lynda	clarinet	1992-93
Rath, Richard	clarinet	1970 part; 71,73
Rath Richard	oboe	1972 sub
Rauk, Mary	clarinet	1973-74
Rayl, Don	sax	1937 sub; 39
Reagan, Charles	horn	1935
Reagan, Paul	oboe	1935
Reed, John Ross	vocal soloist	1922 guest
Reed, Linda	twirler	1952, 54 guest
Reeg, Paul	trombone	1966, 70, 79, 81, 85, 87 sub; 71-78 & 83 full time
Reeve, Everett J.	percussion	1927; 28-31?; 32-39
Reich, Matt	percussion	1983 sub
Reierson, Kristi	clarinet	1979-81
Reistroffer, Ruth Stene (Mrs. L. J.?)	vocal soloist	1947, 56 guest
Rembold, Jack	cornet	1963-66; 67 sub; 71-74
ReQua, Gertrude (Mrs. E. M.)	vocal soloist	1932 guest
Reyner, Kari	clarinet	1985
Reynolds, Jack	cornet	1970, 71 sub; 71-73; 74 & 77 sub
Rhoda, J. F.	librarian	1921
Richards, John J.	conductor, guest	1948 guest
Richardson, James	trombone	1949-51
Richardson, Ron	horn	1949; 50?; 51-52; 54-56; 59
Rieb, Marlene	twirler	1950 guest
Riemann, James	clarinet	1953-56
Riemann, James	sax	1957
Rimerman, Marvin	cornet	1952-54
Rimerman, Marvin	inst. soloist	1950 guest
Rinder, Steve	MC	1974 guest
Rittman, Walter F.	horn	1920-22; 23-25?; 26-48
Robertson, Lissa	horn	1984
Robertson, Paul	trombone	1957
Rock, Arthur R.	percussion	1931-33
Roesler, Janet	horn	1991 sub
Rogers, Burton S.	trombone	1920?; 21-25; 26-27?; 28-29; 30-31?; 32-42
Rogotzke, Susan	clarinet	1985
Rogotzke, Susan	library asst.	1985
Romans, John	clarinet	1955-56 sub; 62
Romans, John	sax	1958-59
Root, Darlene	flute	1985, 86 sub
Root, Darlene	library asst.	1985; 86 sub
Rosheim, John	clarinet	1945
Rostad, Craig	tuba	1987 sub; 88-90; 91 sub; 92; 93 sub
Roth, Connie	horn	1973-76; 80 sub; 81
Roth, Connie (not same as above)	vocal soloist	1945 guest

Name	Instrument	Years
Roth, John	sax, tenor	1973-76; 80 sub; 81
Rozum, Sally	twirler	1950 guest
Runyan, Dan	clarinet	1965 sub; 66-70
Runyan, George	tuba	1964-67
Runyan, Maud	vocal soloist	1941-43 guest
Runyan, Paul	tuba	1971-75; 76 &79 sub
Runyan, Robert	tuba	1971-72
Ruud, Stuart	trombone	1964 sub?
Ryan, Patricia	vocal soloist	1939 guest
Salem Men's Chorus	vocal group	1986 guest
Sampson, Norman	clarinet	1941-42
Sanborn, Keith	clarinet	1969
Savage, Vicki	cornet	1986; 87 sub
Schaefer, Gary	clarinet	1966-71
Schettler Hoogendoorn, Donna	clarinet	1978-79; 81-84
Schive, Reggie	clarinet	1989 sub
Schlunsen, Ann	twirler	1955 guest
Schmidt, Kathy	trombone	1974-75
Schmuck, Toby	tuba	1981-83
Schoppert, Robert	euphonium	1967 sub; 68-69
Schrank, Darlene	twirler	1953 guest
Schuller, Gustav	bassoon	1959-72
Schuller, Gustav	clarinet	1958, 73
Schuller, Jurgen	oboe	1960-67
Schultz, Dean	vocal soloist	1975 guest
Schultz, Verne	clarinet	1932-35
Schultz, Verne	sax	1927; 28-31?
Schwans, Jason	library asst.	1993-94
Schwans, Jason	sax, baritone	1991-94
Schweim Johnson, Janelle	sax, alto	1982 sub; 83-84; 85 sub; 86
Schyde, Harry Hadley	vocal soloist	1936 guest
Scott, Jill	twirler	1958 guest
Sears, Arthur N.	clarinet	1920-34
Seidel, Joe	clarinet	1969 sub
Sellen, Martha	twirler	1953-54 guest
Seto, Michael	tuba	1974, sub; 75-76
Shelsta, Kay	cornet	1973 sub
Shelsta, Scott	inst. soloist, trombone	86-87 & 94 guest
Shelsta, Scott	trombone	1969-70; 73
Shepard, Susan	twirler	1962-63 guest
Sheppard, Ed	horn	1961
Sherburne, Earl	euphonium	1967
Shrine Chanters	vocal group	1949-52 guest
Siders, Audrey	twirler	1954-57, 59 guest
Simon, Lorie	clarinet	1978
Singing Plainsmen, Canova	vocal group	1962-64 guest
Sioux Emperians Barbershop Chorus	vocal group	1986 guest
Sioux Falls Junior Grenadiers	drill team	1961 guest
Sisson, Pat	vocal soloist	1980 guest
Sittig, Amber	clarinet	1994
Siverson, Glennis	oboe	1987 sub
Siverson, Jay	trombone	1993-94 sub
Siverson, Sayra	cornet	1994 sub
Skattum, Paul	percussion	1964-66
Skatula, Rick	euphonium	1978
Smith, Brian	cornet	1991-93
Smith, C. W.	clarinet	1943-46; 47-48?; 49-51
Smith, Dale	cornet	1938?
Smith, Gregory	tuba	1973
Smith, Michael	percussion	1988-94
Smith, Sandra	twirler	1963 guest
Smith, Tad	tuba	1980
Snowden, Donna Jeanine	twirler	1950 guest
Solberg, John	percussion	1963
Solem, Robert	horn	1957
Sommers, Steven	cornet	1980 sub; 81-83; 84, 86 sub
Sona, Gary	vocal soloist	1965-66 guest

Name	Instrument	Years
Sonnichsen, Joel	cornet	1993 sub
Sonnichsen, Kari	flute	1994 sub
Sonnichsen, Kristen	oboe	1992-94
Sonnichsen, Pam	cornet	1989; 90-91 sub; 93-94 sub
Soper, Cara	oboe	1994 sub
Sorenson, Todd M.	showmobile driver	1973-77
Sorvaag, Joe	sound	1983
Soukup, Judy	clarinet	1980, 86
Spieker, Steven	horn	1991-94
Spieler, Robert	clarinet	1942 & 43 sub?
Spring, Dr. Robert	inst. soloist, clarinet	1992 guest
Stahl (Sarfarazi), Faith	sax, baritone	1980
Stanley, Ira	trombone	1935
Stansbery, Jennifer	clarinet	1985-86
Starks, Mary	cornet	1984 sub
Stauffer Flisrand, Ann	clarinet	1966 sub fall; 67; 68 sub
Steever, Tom	MC	1979, 86 guest
Steever, Tom	vocal soloist	1979 guest
Steiner, Harlan	clarinet	1942 sub?
Steinke, Robin	cornet	1978 sub; 79-80
Stephens, Laurie	clarinet	1982 sub; 83-84
Stephenson, Robert	trombone	1956
Stevenson, Rich	percussion	1964 & 65 sub
Stick or Slick?	clarinet	1924
Stivers, Don	horn	1939-41; 42 sub?
Stocking, Glen	euphonium/trombone	1966 sub
Stoeckmann, Jim	trombone	1961, 62 sub
Stombaugh, Steve	cornet	1986; 87 sub; 88-94
Stombaugh, Steve	librarian	1988
Streemke, Robert	trombone	1984-85; 86 sub
Stringham, Pat	bass clarinet	1968
Stroman, Scott	trombone	1969-71
Sugartone Girls' Quartet, Garretson	vocal group	1958 guest
Sundberg, Ronda	twirler	1962-63 guest
Sunde, Melvin	trombone	1943-55; 57-61
Swanson, Betty	oboe	1980 sub; 81
Swanson (Kuhn), Elizabeth	vocal soloist	1956 regular; 1955, 57-59 guest
Swanson, Hale	sax	1958-60
Swenson Matthius, Marciene	See Matthius, Marciene	
Tanglefoot Dance Studio	dance group	1956-70 guest
Tanouye, Gary	sax, tenor	1977-78; 79 sub
Tapantoe Dance Studio	dance	1938, 40 guest
Taylor, Alan	conductor	1987-91; 94 guest
Taylor, Georgia	cornet	1989 sub
Taylor, Georgia	euphonium	1989 sub
Taylor, James	tuba	1974 sub
Temanson, Mary	sax, alto	1972
Teuber, Fred	horn	1959
Texel, Eddie	tuba	1958-59 sub; 60-62
Tharp McDowell, Kristi	clarinet	1989-94
Thomas, Ted C.	cornet	1930-33; 41-43
Thompson, Bruce	cornet	1950s sub?
Thompson, Joe	bassoon	1935-41
Thompson, Lawrence	euphonium	1934
Thompson, Orville	flute	1936-41
Thompson, ?	trombone	1922
Thostensen, Marvin	clarinet	1943-44
Tiede, Russell	horn	1963; 64 part time; 65
Tiede, Russell	tuba	1957-58
Tietjen, William "Bill" H.	cornet	1943-52
Titus, John	clarinet	1984; 85 sub; 86-87; 88 & 94 sub
Titus, John	librarian	1987
Titus, John	publicity	1986
Tobin, Ruth	vocal soloist	1975-78 guest
Tolpo, Nellyebelle Reardon	vocal soloist	1943 guest
Tork, Erwin	trombone	1989 sub
Tornberg, Connie	horn	1972-73

Name	Instrument	Years
Townswick, Jane	flute	1968-69
Tremere, Douglas	clarinet	1952-53
Tri Valley Chorus, Viborg	vocal group	1956-59, 61 guest
Trumm, Janice	clarinet	1974, 76
Trunnell, Glen	sax	1964 sub; 67-68 sub
Tschetter, Joseph	conductor, guest	1950 guest
Tumblettes	gymnastics	1957 guest
Tunge, Edie	dance	1980 guest
Tyler, Frederick H.	flute	1948-50
Tyler, Ralph	clarinet	1964-65
Tyler, Ralph	flute	1952-63
Valley Male Quartet, Rock Valley, IA	vocal group	1954 guest
Van Bockern Krueger, Donna	flute	1969-70; 74-75; 76 sub; 77-79
Van Egmund		1952
Van Ellis, Mrs. R. L.	vocal soloist	1929 guest
Van Holland, Joan	vocal soloist	1993 regular soloist
Van Steenwyck, Joyce	vocal soloist	1945 guest
Vaska, Kevin	clarinet	1975-79
Vaska, Kevin	showmobile asst.	1975 , 77 sub
Veenker, Ron	oboe	1952-53
Veenker, Ron	percussion	1954-57
Vegge Nelson, Martha	sax, alto & tenor	1973-80;81 sub; 82-84; 86 sub;87-88; 89 sub; 90-92
Veldhuizen, Nancy	clarinet	1971 sub
VFW Drum and Bugle Corps	drill team	1938 guest
VFW Twirling Majorettes	twirler	1942 guest
Vocal trio, Canton	vocal group	1942, 44 guest
Vocal trio, Sioux Falls	vocal group	1942 guest
Vorhes, Anna	harp	1977
Voss, John	vocal soloist	1980 guest
Vugteveen, Linda	twirler	1962-63 guest
Wagner, William G.	horn	1920-57
Wagner, Carl (sp?)		1921
Wakeman, Al		1930-31
Waldow, Dean	sound	1984
Walker, Darwin	conductor, guest	1984, SDSU campus, Brookings, guest
Walter, Terry	clarinet	1976, 78
Walter, Terry	librarian	1980-83, 85
Walter, Terry	library asst.	1975-76; 1978-79
Walter, Terry	sax, alto	1974, 77, 79-85; 87 part time; 88; 91 sub; 94 sub
Waltner, Wallace	library asst.	1989
Waltner, Wallace	tuba	1988-91
Waltner Pfeiffer, Gina	horn	1980-81
Wangberg, Ludwig	horn	1942, 46-47
Waring, James	percussion	1968 sub
Warner, Luanne	percussion	1977 sub; 78
Warner, Vada	inst. soloist, electric organ	1938 guest
Warren, Mary	sax, tenor	1969-71
Warren, Maureen	horn	1968 sub; 69-70
Warren, William	sax	1956; 57 sub
Warttman, George		1930-31
Weber, Jill	sax	1993 sub
Weber, Paul A.	horn	1949
Weber, Vinson	euphonium	1971-72
Webster, Kaye	vocal soloist	1986 guest
Wegner or Wagner?, Carl	vocal soloist?	1922 guest
Wegner, David	cornet	1955-64; 65-66 sub
Wegner, Nathan	cornet	1985-89
Wegner, Tom	clarinet	1959-61
Wegner, Paul, Jr.	bassoon	1955-56
Wegner, Paul, Jr.	clarinet	1954, 57-58
Wegner, Paul, Sr.	vocal soloist	1964 guest; 65-79; 80-82 guest
Wegner, Paul, Sr.	MC	1965-79; 81 guest
Weich, August C.	cornet/horn	1920; 1921-29?; 30-31
Weikel, Paul	euphonium	1980 sub; 81
Weikel, Paul	trombone	1982-83
Weikel, Sandra	horn	1980 sub; 81-83
Weiland, Anne	clarinet	1994

Name	Instrument	Years
Wells, Teresa	clarinet	1979-82
Welter, Kathy	percussion	1986 sub
Wessman, Mark	clarinet	1969
West, Joyce	twirler	1950 guest
Westerlund, Donald	vocal soloist	1954 guest
Westra, Mitzi	vocal soloist	1987 guest
Whalen, Ron	cornet	1951
White, Gene	inst. soloist,trombone	1978 guest
White, Gene	MC	1971
White, Gene	trombone	1971-72 sub
Whitely, Kris	cornet	1992-93
Whittaker, Ella June	vocal soloist	1946, 47 guest
WHS Majorettes	twirler	1953-54, 57-63 guest
WHS twirling duet	twirler	1966 guest
Widness, Brad	showmobile asst.	1979-80
Widness, Brad	trombone	1979-83
Wiehl (Grevlos), Lisa	vocal soloist	1987 guest; 88-92; 94
Wilbert, Vernon	euphonium	1942
Williams, Barbara	twirler	1950-52 guest
Williams, Floyd	clarinet	1928-29
Williamson, I. M.	clarinet	1953 sub; 54-55
Williamson, Mark	horn	1958
Wilson, David	cornet	1952-53
Winden, Arthur Ellsworth	horn	1955-60
Winkel, Muriel	vocal soloist	1956 guest
Winter, Loni	percussion	1980
Winter, Susan	clarinet	1968
Wissink, Phyllis	library asst.	1986-87
Wold, Jeff	clarinet	1961-66
Wold, Steve	clarinet	1958-61
Wombacker Blanchard, Connie	bassoon	1970, 73
Wood, Susan	bassoon	1987 sub
Woodard, Robert	sound	1980 sub
Woolworth, Rich	trombone	1982
Worthington Jr. Col. Male Quartet	vocal group	1958 guest
Wortman, Verne	clarinet	1964 sub
Woster, Jim	MC	1987 guest
Wright, Keith	percussion	1971
Wright, Lon	bass clarinet	1968-70
Wright, Lon	clarinet	1967
Wright, Lon	tenor sax	1967 sub
Wright, Mark	clarinet?	1982 sub
Wulf, Sheila	oboe	1991-94
YMCA Quartet	vocal group	1930 guest
Yoshida, Ken	percussion	1985 sub; 86; 87 sub
Youngquist, Michelle	horn	1982-83; 86-87
Zacharias, Brenda	clarinet	1985-86; 88
Zellers, Everett	clarinet	1928-39?; 1940-42; 46
Zenner, Bobbie	instr. soloist, cornet	1944 guest
Zweifel, Sheila	sax, alto	1994 sub

• • •

Personnel By Year, 1920-94

No complete rosters of the Sioux Falls Municipal Band from 1920-34 have been located. Documentation of those members listed came from Band minutes, programs in which certain players were listed as featured members or in news stories.

In some cases the authors made a presumption of membership. For example, if it were documented that a member played from 1920-26 and 1929-35 it was assumed that he also played in 1927 and 1928. Although there is a possibility that he may have dropped out during those years, there is a greater chance that he continued. A question mark after a name or year indicates that it is likely that the member played that year but that there is a certain element of uncertainty. With some of the early players, it was not possible to document their first names or instruments.

A players name is listed if he/she played one or more concerts. If only a few concerts were played that person is listed as a "sub." If approximately a half season is played, the player is listed as "part time." The band normally began its new rehearsal season in autumn, preparing for the following summer. Often new players joined the Band at that time. The concerts played during the remainder of that calendar year were few — usually on Veterans Day and/or a concert at the Penitentiary. Some of the players listed as "sub" played the autumn season preceding their first full season. These autumn or winter concerts were normally played from Recording Trust Funds (not City funds), and it sometimes is difficult to trace those records. Although attempts were made to locate those records, one may sometimes miss a player who played only one or two concerts near the end of a calendar year.

The following list includes Band members and individuals and group performers who appeared as guests.

Sioux Falls Municipal Band Personnel 1920 (1st season)
Lloyd M. Coppens, Conductor

First name	Last name	Instrument	Year
Raymond G.	Hoyt	bass clarinet	20
Henry T.	Hanson	clarinet	20
Roy	Meyer	clarinet	20
William D.	Meyer	clarinet	20
Arthur N.	Sears	clarinet	20
Lloyd M.	Coppens	conductor	20
Henry	Busse	conductor, guest	20 guest
John "Jack" M.	Newton	cornet	20
August C. "Gus"	Weich	cornet/horn	20
Oril W.	Palmer	flute	20
Walter F.	Rittman	horn	20
William G.	Wagner	horn	20

Guy G.	Anderson	saxophone	20
Fred	Beecher	trombone	20
Oscar G.	Dahl	trombone	20
Jake	Helfert	trombone	20
Andrew K.	Indseth	trombone	20
Lee	Mitchell	trombone	20
Austin K.	Bailey	tuba	20
Walter L.	Kleinheinz	tuba	20
Ole	Holm	vocal soloist	20 guest
Sid	Drew		20
Charles	Hobson		20
Harry	Hobson		20

Sioux Falls Municipal Band Personnel 1921 (2nd season)
Lloyd M. Coppens, Conductor

Raymond G.	Hoyt	bass clarinet	21
Henry T.	Hanson	clarinet	21
Roy	Meyer	clarinet	21
William D.	Meyer	clarinet	21
Arthur N.	Sears	clarinet	21
Lloyd M.	Coppens	conductor	21
John "Jack" M.	Newton	cornet	21
Oril W.	Palmer	flute	21
Walter F.	Rittman	horn	21
William G.	Wagner	horn	21
Johanna	Downs	inst. soloist, piano	21 guest
J. F.	Rhoda	librarian	21
Guy G.	Anderson	sax	21
Oscar G.	Dahl	trombone	21
E. O.	Dietrich	trombone	21
Jake	Helfert	trombone	21
Lee	Mitchell	trombone	21
Burton S.	Rogers	trombone	21
Austin K.	Bailey	tuba	21
Walter L.	Kleinheinz	tuba	21
Community Chorus		vocal group	21 guest
James	Ballard	vocal soloist	21 guest
Royal S.	Barnes	vocal soloist	21 guest
Gerhard H.	Dahl	vocal soloist	21 guest
Roland "Rolla"	Dickenson	vocal soloist	21 guest
Ole	Holm	vocal soloist	21 guest
Lyda	Pallansch	vocal soloist	21 guest
W. J.	Gilbertson		21
Carl	Wagner?		21

Sioux Falls Municipal Band Personnel 1922 (3rd season)
Charles F. Emmel, Conductor

Raymond G.	Hoyt	bass clarinet	22
Henry T.	Hanson	clarinet	22
Roy	Meyer	clarinet	22
William D.	Meyer	clarinet	22
Arthur N.	Sears	clarinet	22
Charles F.	Emmel	conductor	22
John L.	Johnson	cornet	22
John "Jack" M.	Newton	cornet	22
Oril W.	Palmer	flute	22
Walter F.	Rittman	horn	22
William G.	Wagner	horn	22
Frances (Miss)	Moore	inst. soloist, cello	22 guest
Johanna	Downs	inst. soloist, piano	22 guest
Isa	Duncan	inst. soloist, violin	22 guest
Guy G.	Anderson	sax	22?
Oscar G.	Dahl	trombone	22
E. O.	Dietrich	trombone	22
Jake	Helfert	trombone	22
Andrew K.	Indseth	trombone	22
	Landech	trombone	22 guest?
Lee	Mitchell	trombone	22?

Burton S.	Rogers	trombone	22
	Thompson	trombone	22
Austin K.	Bailey	tuba	22
Walter L.	Kleinheinz	tuba	22
D. M.	Hanson	vocal soloist	22 guest
John Ross	Reed	vocal soloist	22 guest
Carl	Wegner sp?	vocal soloist?	22 guest
Jack	Dunn		22

Sioux Falls Municipal Band Personnel 1923 (4th season)
Charles F. McClung, Conductor

Raymond G.	Hoyt	bass clarinet	23
Henry T.	Hanson	clarinet	23
Roy	Meyer	clarinet	23
William D.	Meyer	clarinet	23
Arthur N.	Sears	clarinet	23
Charles F.	McClung	conductor	23
Elmer T. "Eddie"	Edwards	cornet	23
John L.	Johnson	cornet	23
John "Jack" M.	Newton	cornet	23
Arthur	Berdahl	euphonium	23
Oril W.	Palmer	flute	23
Walter F.	Rittman	horn	23?
William G.	Wagner	horn	23
Guy G.	Anderson	sax	23
E. O.	Dietrich	trombone	23?
Jake	Helfert	trombone	23
Andrew K.	Indseth	trombone	23
Lee	Mitchell	trombone	23
Burton S.	Rogers	trombone	23
Austin K.	Bailey	tuba	23
Walter L.	Kleinheinz	tuba	23
Alice	Barr	vocal soloist	23 guest
	Peck		23

Sioux Falls Municipal Band Personnel 1924 (5th season)
Charles F. McClung, Conductor

Raymond G.	Hoyt	bass clarinet	24
Henry T.	Hanson	clarinet	24
Roy	Meyer	clarinet	24
William D.	Meyer	clarinet	24
Arthur N.	Sears	clarinet	24
	Stick or Slick?	clarinet	24
Charles F.	McClung	conductor	24
Elmer T. "Eddie"	Edwards	cornet	24?
John L.	Johnson	cornet	24
John "Jack" M.	Newton	cornet	24
Oril W.	Palmer	flute	24
Walter F.	Rittman	horn	24?
William G.	Wagner	horn	24
Guy G.	Anderson	sax	24
E. O.	Dietrich	trombone	24?
Jake	Helfert	trombone	24
Andrew K.	Indseth	trombone	24
Lee	Mitchell	trombone	24
Burton S.	Rogers	trombone	24
Austin K.	Bailey	tuba	24
Walter L.	Kleinheinz	tuba	24

Sioux Falls Municipal Band Personnel 1925 (6th season)
Charles F. McClung, Conductor

Raymond G.	Hoyt	bass clarinet	25
Henry T.	Hanson	clarinet	25
Roy	Meyer	clarinet	25
William D.	Meyer	clarinet	25
Arthur N.	Sears	clarinet	25
Elmer T. "Eddie"	Edwards	cornet	25?

John L.	Johnson	cornet	25
John "Jack" M.	Newton	cornet	25?
Charles F.	McClung	conductor	25
Oril W.	Palmer	flute	25
Walter F.	Rittman	horn	25?
William G.	Wagner	horn	25
Guy G.	Anderson	sax	25
Jake	Helfert	trombone	25
E. O.	Dietrich	trombone	25?
Andrew K.	Indseth	trombone	25
Lee	Mitchell	trombone	25
Burton S.	Rogers	trombone	25
Austin K.	Bailey	tuba	25
Orral O.	Jackson	tuba	25
Walter L.	Kleinheinz	tuba	25

Sioux Falls Municipal Band Personnel 1926 (7th season)
Charles F. McClung, Conductor

John L.	Johnson	asst. conductor	26
Raymond G.	Hoyt	bass clarinet	26
Henry T.	Hanson	clarinet	26
Roy	Meyer	clarinet	26
William D.	Meyer	clarinet	26
Arthur N.	Sears	clarinet	26
Charles F.	McClung	conductor	26
Elmer T. "Eddie"	Edwards	cornet	26
John L.	Johnson	cornet	26
John "Jack" M.	Newton	cornet	26
Oril W.	Palmer	flute	26
Walter F.	Rittman	horn	26
William G.	Wagner	horn	26
Roger	Brown	publicity?	26
Guy G.	Anderson	sax	26
E. O.	Dietrich	trombone	26?
Jake	Helfert	trombone	26?
Andrew K.	Indseth	trombone	26
Lee	Mitchell	trombone	26
Burton S.	Rogers	trombone	26?
Austin K.	Bailey	tuba	26
Orral O.	Jackson	tuba	26
Walter L.	Kleinheinz	tuba	26

Sioux Falls Municipal Band Personnel 1927 (8th season)
Charles F. McClung, Conductor

Raymond G.	Hoyt	bass clarinet	27
Henry T.	Hanson	clarinet	27
George	Medeck	clarinet	27
Roy	Meyer	clarinet	27
William D.	Meyer	clarinet	27
Arthur N.	Sears	clarinet	27
Charles F.	McClung	conductor	27
Elmer T. "Eddie"	Edwards	cornet	27
John "Jack" M.	Newton	cornet	27
Merlin	Hanson	euphonium	27
Oril W.	Palmer	flute	27
	McKenzie	horn	27
Walter F.	Rittman	horn	27
William G.	Wagner	horn	27
Everett J.	Reeve	percussion	27
Roger	Brown	publicity?	27
Guy G.	Anderson	sax	27?
Verne	Schultz	sax	27
E. O.	Dietrich	trombone	27?
Jake	Helfert	trombone	27
Andrew K.	Indseth	trombone	27
Lee	Mitchell	trombone	27
Burton S.	Rogers	trombone	27?
Austin K.	Bailey	tuba	27

Orral O.	Jackson	tuba	27
Walter L.	Kleinheinz	tuba	27

Sioux Falls Municipal Band Personnel 1928 (9th season)
Gerard C. McClung, Conductor

Raymond G.	Hoyt	bass clarinet	28
Henry T.	Hanson	clarinet	28
George	Medeck	clarinet	28?
Roy	Meyer	clarinet	28
William D.	Meyer	clarinet	28
Arthur N.	Sears	clarinet	28
Floyd	Williams	clarinet	28
G. C.	McClung	conductor	28
Elmer T. "Eddie"	Edwards	cornet	28
John "Jack" M.	Newton	cornet	28
Oril W.	Palmer	flute	28
	McKenzie	horn	28
Walter F.	Rittman	horn	28
William G.	Wagner	horn	28
Roger	Brown	publicity?	28
Guy G.	Anderson	sax	28
James or Rex?	Cloud	trombone	28
E. O.	Dietrich	trombone	28?
Jake	Helfert	trombone	28
Andrew K.	Indseth	trombone	28?
Lee	Mitchell	trombone	28
Burton S.	Rogers	trombone	28
Austin K.	Bailey	tuba	28
Orral O.	Jackson	tuba	28
Walter L.	Kleinheinz	tuba	28
Eugene "Gene"	Cashman	vocal soloist	28 guest

Sioux Falls Municipal Band Personnel 1929 (10th season)
Gerard C. McClung, Conductor

Raymond G.	Hoyt	bass clarinet	29
Allan	Bliss	clarinet	29
John D.	Buus	clarinet	29?
Henry T.	Hanson	clarinet	29
George B.	Medeck	clarinet	29
Roy	Meyer	clarinet	29
William D.	Meyer	clarinet	29
Arthur N.	Sears	clarinet	29
Floyd	Williams	clarinet	29
G. C.	McClung	conductor	29
Elmer T. "Eddie"	Edwards	cornet	29
John "Jack" M.	Newton	cornet	29
M. T. (G?)	Hanson	euphonium	29
Walter F.	Rittman	horn	29
William G.	Wagner	horn	29
Guy G.	Anderson	sax	29
James or Rex?	Cloud	trombone	29
E. O.	Dietrich	trombone	29
Jake	Helfert	trombone	29
Andrew K.	Indseth	trombone	29
Lee	Mitchell	trombone	29
Burton S.	Rogers	trombone	29
Austin K.	Bailey	tuba	29
Orral O.	Jackson	tuba	29
Walter L.	Kleinheinz	tuba	29
Eugene "Gene"	Cashman	vocal soloist	29 guest
Norman	Mathers	vocal soloist	29 guest
Mrs. Roy K.	Van Ellis	vocal soloist	29 guest
A. H.	Hanson		29
S. O.	Morris		29

Sioux Falls Municipal Band Personnel 1930 (11th season)
Otto H. Andersen, Conductor

Raymond G.	Hoyt	bass clarinet	30
Allan	Bliss	clarinet	30
John D.	Buus	clarinet	30?
Henry T.	Hanson	clarinet	30
Roy	Meyer	clarinet	30
William D.	Meyer	clarinet	30
Arthur N.	Sears	clarinet	30
Otto H.	Andersen	conductor	30
Elmer T. "Eddie"	Edwards	cornet	30
John "Jack" M.	Newton	cornet	30
Pierre Kilties		drill team	30 guest
Mike G.	Hanson	euphonium	30
Walter F.	Rittman	horn	30
William G.	Wagner	horn	30
Vernon Herman	Alger	inst. soloist, violin	30 guest
Glen G.	Houdek	percussion	30?
Guy G.	Anderson	sax	30
James or Rex?	Cloud	trombone	30
Jake	Helfert	trombone	30
Andrew K.	Indseth	trombone	30
Lee	Mitchell	trombone	30
Burton S.	Rogers	trombone	30?
Austin K.	Bailey	tuba	30
Orral O.	Jackson	tuba	30
Walter L.	Kleinheinz	tuba	30
Madrigal Quartet		vocal group	30 guest
Minnehaha Mandskor		vocal group	30 guest
YMCA Quartet		vocal group	30 guest

Sioux Falls Municipal Band Personnel 1931 (12th season)
Otto H. Andersen, Conductor

Raymond G.	Hoyt	bass clarinet	31
Allan	Bliss	clarinet	31?
John D.	Buus	clarinet	31?
Henry T.	Hanson	clarinet	31
Roy	Meyer	clarinet	31
William D.	Meyer	clarinet	31
Arthur N.	Sears	clarinet	31
Otto H.	Andersen	conductor	31
Jimmy	Barnett	cornet	31
	Crowley	cornet	31
Elmer T. "Eddie"	Edwards	cornet	31
Russell	Moberly	cornet	31
John "Jack" M.	Newton	cornet	31
Ted C.	Thomas	cornet	31
August C. "Gus"	Weich	cornet/horn	31
Mike G.	Hanson	euphonium	31
Oscar	Muller	flute	31
Oril W.	Palmer	flute	31
C. E.	Bild	horn	31
Walter F.	Rittman	horn	31
William G.	Wagner	horn	31
Vernon Herman	Alger	inst. soloist, violin	31 guest
Ardeen	Foss	oboe	31
Glen G.	Houdek	percussion	31
Arthur R.	Rock	percussion	31
Guy G.	Anderson	sax	31
Jake	Helfert	trombone	31
Andrew K.	Indseth	trombone	31
Lee	Mitchell	trombone	31
Burton S.	Rogers	trombone	31?
Austin K.	Bailey	tuba	31
Orral O.	Jackson	tuba	31
Walter L.	Kleinheinz	tuba	31
Minnehaha Mandskor		vocal group	31 guest
Robert	Morris	vocal soloist	31 guest

Gordon	Lyons		31
G. O.	Millie		31
Al	Wakeman		31
George	Warttman		31

Sioux Falls Municipal Band Personnel 1932 (13th season)
Otto H. Andersen, Conductor

Raymond G.	Hoyt	bass clarinet	32
Allan	Bliss	clarinet	32
Henry T.	Hanson	clarinet	32
George B.	Medeck	clarinet	32
Roy	Meyer	clarinet	32
William D.	Meyer	clarinet	32
Verne	Schultz	clarinet	32
Arthur N.	Sears	clarinet	32
Otto H.	Andersen	conductor	32
Elmer T. "Eddie"	Edwards	cornet	32
Marson	Metzger	cornet	32?
John "Jack" M.	Newton	cornet	32
Ted C.	Thomas	cornet	32
Mike G.	Hanson	euphonium	32
Oscar	Muller	flute	32
Oril W.	Palmer	flute	32
C. E.	Bild	horn	32
L. A.	Lewedag	horn	32
Walter F.	Rittman	horn	32
William G.	Wagner	horn	32
Original Rhythm Band		inst. group	32 guest
Vernon Herman	Alger	inst. soloist, violin	32 guest
Ardeen	Foss	oboe	32
Glen G.	Houdek	percussion	32
Everett J.	Reeve	percussion	32
Arthur R.	Rock	percussion	32
Guy G.	Anderson	sax	32
Jake	Helfert	trombone	32
Andrew K.	Indseth	trombone	32
Lee	Mitchell	trombone	32
Burton S.	Rogers	trombone	32
Austin K.	Bailey	tuba	32
Walter L.	Kleinheinz	tuba	32
Norse Glee Club		vocal group	32 guest
Roland "Rolla"	Dickenson	vocal soloist	32 guest
Florence	Gunderson-Soutar	vocal soloist	32 guest
Gertrude (Mrs. E. M.)	ReQua	vocal soloist	32 guest
Florence (Mrs. F. J.)	Soutar	vocal soloist	32 guest

Sioux Falls Municipal Band Personnel 1933 (14th season)
Otto H. Andersen, Conductor

Raymond G.	Hoyt	bass clarinet	33
Allan	Bliss	clarinet	33
Henry T.	Hanson	clarinet	33
George B.	Medeck	clarinet	33
Roy	Meyer	clarinet	33
William D.	Meyer	clarinet	33
Verne	Schultz	clarinet	33
Arthur N.	Sears	clarinet	33
Otto H.	Andersen	conductor	33
Jimmy	Barnett	cornet	33
Elmer T. "Eddie"	Edwards	cornet	33
Russ	Henegar	cornet	33
Marson	Metzger	cornet	33
John "Jack" M.	Newton	cornet	33
Ted C.	Thomas	cornet	33
Mike G.	Hanson	euphonium	33
Oscar	Muller	flute	33
Oril W.	Palmer	flute	33
Walter F.	Rittman	horn	33
William G.	Wagner	horn	33

Vernon Herman	Alger	inst. soloist, violin	33 guest
Mrs. O. H.	Andersen	inst. soloist, violin	33 guest
Original Rhythm Band		inst. group	33 guest
Ardeen	Foss	oboe	33
Vernon Herman	Alger	percussion	33
Glen G.	Houdek	percussion	33
Everett J.	Reeve	percussion	33
Arthur R.	Rock	percussion	33
Guy G.	Anderson	sax	33
Rudy H.	Dornaus	string bass	33
Jake	Helfert	trombone	33
Andrew K.	Indseth	trombone	33
Lee	Mitchell	trombone	33
Burton S.	Rogers	trombone	33
Austin K.	Bailey	tuba	33
Walter L.	Kleinheinz	tuba	33
Minnehaha Mandskor		vocal group	33 guest
Norse Glee Club		vocal group	33 guest

Sioux Falls Municipal Band Personnel 1934 (15th season)
Otto H. Andersen, Conductor

Raymond G.	Hoyt	bass clarinet	34
Allan	Bliss	clarinet	34?
Ardeen	Foss	clarinet	34
Henry T.	Hanson	clarinet	34
George B.	Medeck	clarinet	34
Roy	Meyer	clarinet	34
William D.	Meyer	clarinet	34
Verne	Schultz	clarinet	34
Arthur N.	Sears	clarinet	34
Otto H.	Andersen	conductor	34
Jimmy	Barnett	cornet	34
Elmer T. "Eddie"	Edwards	cornet	34
Russ	Henegar	cornet	34
Marson	Metzger	cornet	34
John "Jack" M.	Newton	cornet	34
Mike G.	Hanson	euphonium	34?
Dale	Moen	euphonium	34
Lawrence	Thompson	euphonium	34
Oscar	Muller	flute	34
Oril W.	Palmer	flute	34
Walter F.	Rittman	horn	34
William G.	Wagner	horn	34
Harold (Prof.)	Edwards	inst. soloist, violin	34 guest
Ed	Paul	MC	34
Vernon Herman	Alger	percussion	34
Glen G.	Houdek	percussion	34
Everett J.	Reeve	percussion	34
Guy G.	Anderson	sax	34
Rudy H.	Dornaus	string bass	34
Jake	Helfert	trombone	34
Lee	Mitchell	trombone	34
Burton S.	Rogers	trombone	34
Austin K.	Bailey	tuba	34
Orral O.	Jackson	tuba	34
Norse Glee Club		vocal group	34 guest
Ed	Paul	vocal soloist	34

Sioux Falls Municipal Band Personnel 1935 (16th season)
Russ D. Henegar, Conductor

Joe	Thompson	bassoon	35
Ray	Benard	clarinet	35
Allan	Bliss	clarinet	35
Leo	Gossman	clarinet	35
Henry T.	Hanson	clarinet	35
C. R. "Bob"	Larson	clarinet	35
George B.	Medeck	clarinet	35
Roy	Meyer	clarinet	35

William D.	Meyer	clarinet	35
Leonard	Paul	clarinet	35
Verne	Schultz	clarinet	35
Russ	Henegar	conductor	35
Milt	Askew	cornet	35
Jimmy	Barnett	cornet	35
Elmer T. "Eddie"	Edwards	cornet	35
Royal	Ellis	cornet	35
Kenneth	Lane	cornet	35
John "Jack" M.	Newton	cornet	35
Mike G.	Hanson	euphonium	35
Oscar	Muller	flute	35
Oril W.	Palmer	flute	35
L. A.	Lewedag	horn	35
Charles	Reagan	horn	35
Walter F.	Rittman	horn	35
William G.	Wagner	horn	35
Elaine	Larson	inst. soloist, trombone	35 guest
Ed	Paul	MC	35
Ardeen	Foss	oboe	35
Paul	Reagan	oboe	35
Vernon Herman	Alger	percussion	35
Curtis	Beecher	percussion	35 sub
Glen G.	Houdek	percussion	35
Everett J.	Reeve	percussion	35
Guy G.	Anderson	sax	35
Raymond G.	Hoyt	sax	35
Joe	Foss	sax, baritone	35
Rudy H.	Dornaus	string bass	35
Jake	Helfert	trombone	35
Lee	Mitchell	trombone	35
Burton S.	Rogers	trombone	35
Ira	Stanley	trombone	35
Austin K.	Bailey	tuba	35
Orral O.	Jackson	tuba	35
Harmonettes		vocal group	35 guest
Ed	Paul	vocal soloist	35

Sioux Falls Municipal Band Personnel 1936 (17th season)
Russ D. Henegar, Conductor

Arnold	Myrabo?	bass clarinet	36?
Joe	Thompson	bassoon	36
Ray	Benard	clarinet	36
Leo	Gossman	clarinet	36
Henry T.	Hanson	clarinet	36
C. R. "Bob"	Larson	clarinet	36
George B.	Medeck	clarinet	36
Roy	Meyer	clarinet	36
William D.	Meyer	clarinet	36
Leonard	Paul	clarinet	36
Russ	Henegar	conductor	36
Elmer T. "Eddie"	Edwards	cornet	36
Royal	Ellis	cornet	36
Robert	Kindred	cornet	36
Kenneth	Lane	cornet	36
John "Jack" M.	Newton	cornet	36
Justin	Berger	dance	36 guest
Florence Bright School of Dance		dance	36 guest
Pat and Barbara	Holdridge	dance	36 guest
Mike G.	Hanson	euphonium	36
Fletcher	Nelson	euphonium	36
Oril W.	Palmer	flute	36
Orville	Thompson	flute	36
Palmer	Kremer	horn	36
L. A.	Lewedag	horn	36
Walter F.	Rittman	horn	36
William G.	Wagner	horn	36
Ed	Paul	MC	36
Ardeen	Foss	oboe	36

Vernon Herman	Alger	percussion	36
Glen G.	Houdek	percussion	36
Everett J.	Reeve	percussion	36
Raymond G.	Hoyt	sax, alto	36
Joe	Foss	sax, baritone	36
Guy G.	Anderson	sax, tenor	36
Milt	Askew	sax ?	36 sub
Rudy H.	Dornaus	string bass	36
Cliff	Foss	trombone	36
Jake	Helfert	trombone	36
·Lee	Mitchell	trombone	36
Burton S.	Rogers	trombone	36
Austin K.	Bailey	tuba	36
Orral O.	Jackson	tuba	36
Ed	Paul	vocal soloist	36
Harry Hadley	Schyde	vocal soloist	36 guest

Sioux Falls Municipal Band Personnel 1937 (18th season)
Russ D. Henegar, Conductor

Joe	Thompson	bassoon	37
Ray	Benard	clarinet	37
Marlin	Brown	clarinet	37
Leo	Gossman	clarinet	37
Henry T.	Hanson	clarinet	37
Ronald	Lane	clarinet	37
C. R. "Bob"	Larson	clarinet	37
George B.	Medeck	clarinet	37
William D.	Meyer	clarinet	37
Leonard	Paul	clarinet	37
Russ	Henegar	conductor	37
Elmer T. "Eddie"	Edwards	cornet	37
Royal	Ellis	cornet	37
Robert	Kindred	cornet	37
Kenneth	Lane	cornet	37
John "Jack" M.	Newton	cornet	37
Mike G.	Hanson	euphonium	37
Fletcher	Nelson	euphonium	37
Oril W.	Palmer	flute	37
Orville	Thompson	flute	37
Palmer	Kremer	horn	37
L. A.	Lewedag	horn	37
Walter F.	Rittman	horn	37
William G.	Wagner	horn	37
Ed	Paul	MC	37
Ardeen	Foss	oboe	37
Donald	Foss	oboe	37
Vernon Herman	Alger	percussion	37
Glen G.	Houdek	percussion	37
Everett J.	Reeve	percussion	37
Raymond G.	Hoyt	sax, alto	37
Don	Rayl	sax, alto	37
Joe	Foss	sax, baritone	37
Guy G.	Anderson	sax, tenor	37
Edgar	Foss	sax, tenor	37? sub?
Rudy H.	Dornaus	string bass	37
Cliff	Foss	trombone	37
Jake	Helfert	trombone	37
Lee	Mitchell	trombone	37
Burton S.	Rogers	trombone	37
Austin K.	Bailey	tuba	37
Orral O.	Jackson	tuba	37
El Riad Chanters		vocal group	37 guest
Sidney	Jacobs	vocal soloist	37 guest
Ed	Paul	vocal soloist	37

Sioux Falls Municipal Band Personnel 1938 (19th season)
Russ D. Henegar, Conductor

Joe	Thompson	bassoon	38

Marlin	Brown	clarinet	38
Leo	Gossman	clarinet	38
Henry T.	Hanson	clarinet	38
Ronald	Lane	clarinet	38
C. R. "Bob"	Larson	clarinet	38
George B.	Medeck	clarinet	38
William D.	Meyer	clarinet	38
Leonard	Paul	clarinet	38
Russ	Henegar	conductor	38
Elmer T. "Eddie"	Edwards	cornet	38
Royal	Ellis	cornet	38
Robert	Kindred	cornet	38
Kenneth	Lane	cornet	38
John "Jack" M.	Newton	cornet	38
Mike G.	Hanson	euphonium	38
Fletcher	Nelson	euphonium	38
Oril W.	Palmer	flute	38
Orville	Thompson	flute	38
Palmer	Kremer	horn	38
L. A.	Lewedag	horn	38
Walter F.	Rittman	horn	38
William G.	Wagner	horn	38
VFW Drum and Bugle Corps		inst. group	38 guest
Donald	Lias	inst. soloist, cornet	38 guest
Vada	Warner	inst. soloist, electric organ	38 guest
Burton S.	Rogers?	MC	38
Ardeen	Foss	oboe	38
Donald	Foss	oboe	38
Vernon Herman	Alger	percussion	38
Glen G.	Houdek	percussion	38
Everett J.	Reeve	percussion	38
Raymond G.	Hoyt	sax, alto	38
Joe	Foss	sax, baritone	38
Guy G.	Anderson	sax, tenor	38
Edgar	Foss	sax, tenor	38? sub?
Rodney O.	Bray	sound	38
Rudy H.	Dornaus	string bass	38
Cliff	Foss	trombone	38
Jake	Helfert	trombone	38
Lee	Mitchell	trombone	38
Burton S.	Rogers	trombone	38
Austin K.	Bailey	tuba	38
Orral O.	Jackson	tuba	38
El Riad Chanters		vocal group	38 guest
Harmonettes		vocal group	38 guest
William	Dickenson	vocal soloist	38 guest
Sidney	Jacobs	vocal soloist	38
Francis	Loewen	vocal soloist	38?guest
Ed	Paul	vocal soloist	38 on leave

Sioux Falls Municipal Band Personnel 1939 (20th season)
Russ D. Henegar, Conductor

Joe	Thompson	bassoon	39
Marlin	Brown	clarinet	39
Leo	Gossman	clarinet	39
Henry T.	Hanson	clarinet	39
Ronald	Lane	clarinet	39
C. R. "Bob"	Larson	clarinet	39
George B.	Medeck	clarinet	39
William D.	Meyer	clarinet	39
Leonard	Paul	clarinet	39
Russ	Henegar	conductor	39
Elmer T. "Eddie"	Edwards	cornet	39
Royal	Ellis	cornet	39
Robert	Kindred	cornet	39
Kenneth	Lane	cornet	39
John "Jack" M.	Newton	cornet	39
Eddie	Lias	dance	39 guest
Charleen	Holdridge	dance/song	39 guest

Mike G.	Hanson	euphonium	39
Fletcher	Nelson	euphonium	39
Oril W.	Palmer	flute	39
Orville	Thompson	flute	39
Palmer	Kremer	horn	39
Walter F.	Rittman	horn	39
Don	Stivers	horn	39
William G.	Wagner	horn	39
Richard	Lanning	inst. soloist, clarinet	39 guest
Donald	Lias	inst. soloist, cornet	39 guest
Vada	Holdridge	inst. soloist, piano	39 guest
Ed	Paul	MC	39
Ardeen	Foss	oboe	39
Donald	Foss	oboe	39
Vernon Herman	Alger	percussion	39
Glen G.	Houdek	percussion	39
Everett J.	Reeve	percussion	39
Raymond G.	Hoyt	sax, alto	39
Don	Rayl	sax, alto	39
Joe	Foss	sax, baritone	39
Guy G.	Anderson	sax, tenor	39
Rodney O.	Bray	sound	39?
Rudy H.	Dornaus	string bass	39
Cliff	Foss	trombone	39
Jake	Helfert	trombone	39
Lee	Mitchell	trombone	39
Burton S.	Rogers	trombone	39
Austin K.	Bailey	tuba	39
Roy W.	Bailey	tuba	39
Orral O.	Jackson	tuba	39
El Riad Chanters		vocal group	39 guest
Frances	Loewen	vocal soloist	39 guest
Ed	Paul	vocal soloist	39
Patricia	Ryan	vocal soloist	39 guest

Sioux Falls Municipal Band Personnel 1940 (21st season)
Russ D. Henegar, Conductor

Joe	Thompson	bassoon	40
Marlin	Brown	clarinet	40
Leo	Gossman	clarinet	40
Henry T.	Hanson	clarinet	40
Ronald	Lane	clarinet	40
C. R. "Bob"	Larson	clarinet	40
William D.	Meyer	clarinet	40
Leonard	Paul	clarinet	40
Everett	Zellers	clarinet	40
Russ	Henegar	conductor	40
Elmer T. "Eddie"	Edwards	cornet	40
Royal	Ellis	cornet	40
Robert	Kindred	cornet	40
Kenneth	Lane	cornet	40
John "Jack" M.	Newton	cornet	40
Eddie	Lias	dance	40 guest
Mike G.	Hanson	euphonium	40
Fletcher	Nelson	euphonium	40
Oril W.	Palmer	flute	40
Orville	Thompson	flute	40
Palmer	Kremer	horn	40
Walter F.	Rittman	horn	40
Don	Stivers	horn	40
William G.	Wagner	horn	40
Myron	Floren	inst. soloist, accordion	40 guest
Donald	Lias	inst. soloist, cornet	40 guest
Tom	Ellwein	inst. soloist, trombone	40 guest
Ed	Paul	MC	40
Ardeen	Foss	oboe	40
Donald	Foss	oboe	40
Vernon Herman	Alger	percussion	40
Glen G.	Houdek	percussion	40

Robert	Niblick	percussion	40
Milt	Askew	sax, alto	40
Raymond G.	Hoyt	sax, alto	40
Roy	Borneman	sax, baritone	40
Guy G.	Anderson	sax, tenor	40
Cliff	Foss	trombone	40
Jake	Helfert	trombone	40
Lee	Mitchell	trombone	40
Burton S.	Rogers	trombone	40
Austin K.	Bailey	tuba	40
Roy W.	Bailey	tuba	40
Orral O.	Jackson	tuba	40
El Riad Chanters		vocal group	40 guest
Harmonettes		vocal group	40 guest
Ed	Paul	vocal soloist	40

Sioux Falls Municipal Band Personnel 1941 (22nd season)
Russ D. Henegar, Conductor

Floren Accordion Quartet		accordion	41 guest
Joe	Thompson	bassoon	41
Marlin	Brown	clarinet	41
Leo	Gossman	clarinet	41
Henry T.	Hanson	clarinet	41
C. R. "Bob"	Larson	clarinet	41
William D.	Meyer	clarinet	41?
Mark	Odland	clarinet	41
Leonard	Paul	clarinet	41
Norman	Sampson	clarinet	41
Everett	Zellers	clarinet	41
Russ	Henegar	conductor	41
Elmer T. "Eddie"	Edwards	cornet	41
Royal	Ellis	cornet	41
Robert	Kindred	cornet	41
John "Jack" M.	Newton	cornet	41
Ted C.	Thomas	cornet	41
Mike G.	Hanson	euphonium	41
Fletcher	Nelson	euphonium	41
Oril W.	Palmer	flute	41
Orville	Thompson	flute	41
Palmer	Kremer	horn	41
Walter F.	Rittman	horn	41
Don	Stivers	horn	41
William G.	Wagner	horn	41
Myron	Floren	inst. soloist, accordion	41 guest
Donald	Lias	inst. soloist, cornet	41 guest
Eddie	Lias	inst. soloist, cornet	41 guest
Shirley	Lynch	inst. soloist, euphonium	41 guest
Ed	Paul	MC	41
Ardeen	Foss	oboe	41
Donald	Foss	oboe	41
Vernon Herman	Alger	percussion	41
Glen G.	Houdek	percussion	41
Robert	Niblick	percussion	41
Milt	Askew	sax, alto	41
Raymond G.	Hoyt	sax, alto	41
Roy	Borneman	sax, baritone	41
Guy G.	Anderson	sax, tenor	41
James	Berdahl	string bass	41
Cliff	Foss	trombone	41
Jake	Helfert	trombone	41
Lee	Mitchell	trombone	41
Burton S.	Rogers	trombone	41
Austin K.	Bailey	tuba	41
Orral O.	Jackson	tuba	41
El Riad Chanters		vocal group	41 guest
Myrtle Stolt	Kaponin	vocal soloist	41 guest
Loretta	McLaughlin (Hartrich)	vocal soloist	41
Ed	Paul	vocal soloist	41
Maud	Runyan	vocal soloist	41 guest

Sioux Falls Municipal Band Personnel 1942 (23rd season)
Russ D. Henegar, Conductor

Kermit	Harrington	bassoon	42
Douglas	Brooks	clarinet	42
Marlin	Brown	clarinet	42
Leo	Gossman	clarinet	42
Henry T.	Hanson	clarinet	42
C. R. "Bob"	Larson	clarinet	42
George B.	Medeck	clarinet	42
William D.	Meyer	clarinet	42 ?
Mark	Odland	clarinet	42
Leonard	Paul	clarinet	42
Norman	Sampson	clarinet	42
Robert	Spieler	clarinet	42
Harlan	Steiner	clarinet	42
Everett	Zellers	clarinet	42
Russ	Henegar	conductor	42
Elmer T. "Eddie"	Edwards	cornet	42
Howard	Hillman	cornet	42
Robert	Kindred	cornet	42
Harold	Nelson	cornet	42
John "Jack" M.	Newton	cornet	42
Ted C.	Thomas	cornet	42
Alcorn Dance Studio		dance	42 guest
Mike G.	Hanson	euphonium	42
Vernon	Wilbert	euphonium	42
Tom	Hanson	flute	42
Oril W.	Palmer	flute	42
Myron	Moore	horn	42
Walter F.	Rittman	horn	42
Don	Stivers	horn	42
William G.	Wagner	horn	42
Ludwig	Wangberg	horn	42
Bagpipe Band, Winnipeg, Canada		inst. group	42 guest
DAV Junior Drum and Bugle Corps		inst. group	42 guest
Marimba Trio		inst. group	42 guest
Myron	Floren	inst. soloist, accordion	42 guest
Donald	Lias	inst. soloist, cornet	42 guest
Eddie	Lias	inst. soloist, cornet	42 guest
Vada	Holdridge	inst. soloist, piano	42 guest
Ed	Paul	MC	42
Vernon Herman	Alger	percussion	42
Glen G.	Houdek	percussion	42
Robert	Niblick	percussion	42
Milt	Askew	sax, alto	42
Raymond G.	Hoyt	sax, alto	42
Roy	Borneman	sax, baritone	42
Guy G.	Anderson	sax, tenor	42
Cliff	Foss	trombone	42
Jake	Helfert	trombone	42
Donald	McCabe	trombone	42
Burton S.	Rogers	trombone	42
VFW Twirling Majorettes		twirler	42 guest
Austin K.	Bailey	tuba	42
Harry	Ellis	tuba	42
Orral O.	Jackson	tuba	42
Canton Vocal Group		vocal group	42 guest
El Riad Chanters		vocal group	42 guest
Elks Quartet		vocal group	42 guest
Vocal Trio		vocal group	42 guest
Loren	Loe	vocal soloist	42 guest
Loretta	McLaughlin (Hartrich)	vocal soloist	42
Ed	Paul	vocal soloist	42
Maud	Runyan	vocal soloist	42 guest
Myrtle Stolt	Kaponin	vocal soloist	42 guest
Marciene	Swenson Matthius	vocal soloist	42 guest
Geraldine	Polzin	whistler	42 guest

Sioux Falls Municipal Band Personnel 1943 (24th season)
Russ D. Henegar, Conductor

Floren Accordion Quartet		accordion	43 guest
Kermit	Harrington	bassoon	43
Marlin	Brown	clarinet	43
Ernest	Dvoracek	clarinet	43
Ed	Gedstad	clarinet	43
Leo	Gossman	clarinet	43
Henry T.	Hanson	clarinet	43
C. R. "Bob"	Larson	clarinet	43
George B.	Medeck ?	clarinet	43?
William D.	Meyer	clarinet	43 ?
Mark	Odland	clarinet	43
C. W.	Smith	clarinet	43
Robert	Spieler	clarinet	43
Marvin	Thostensen	clarinet (E flat)	43
Russ	Henegar	conductor	43
Elmer T. "Eddie"	Edwards	cornet	43
Willard	Fejfar	cornet	43
John	Howard	cornet	43
Harold	Nelson	cornet	43
John "Jack" M.	Newton	cornet	43
Ted C.	Thomas	cornet	43
William "Bill" H.	Tietjen	cornet	43
Mike G.	Hanson	euphonium	43
Wayne	Krumrei	euphonium	43
Oril W.	Palmer	flute	43
Donald	Halvorson	horn	43
Paul	Hammond ?	horn/cornet	43?
Albert R.	Hillman	horn	43
Palmer	Kremer	horn	43
Myron	Moore	horn	43
Walter F.	Rittman	horn	43
William G.	Wagner	horn	43
Lud	Wangberg (on furlough)	horn	43 sub
Myron	Floren	inst. soloist, accordion	43 guest
Donald	Lias	inst. soloist, cornet	43 guest
Vada	Holdridge	inst. soloist, piano	43 guest
Ed	Paul	MC	43
		oboe not available	43
Vernon Herman	Alger	percussion	43
Marvin	Cooper	percussion	43
Glen G.	Houdek	percussion	43
Robert	Niblick	percussion	43
Milt	Askew	sax, alto	43
Raymond G.	Hoyt	sax, alto	43
Everton	Little	sax, alto	43 sub
Roy	Borneman	sax, baritone	43
Guy G.	Anderson	sax, tenor	43
Cliff	Foss	trombone	43
Jake	Helfert	trombone	43
Harold	Hoover, Sr.	trombone	43
Melvin	Sunde	trombone	43
Austin K.	Bailey	tuba	43
Harry	Ellis	tuba	43
Orral O.	Jackson	tuba	43
El Riad Chanters		vocal group	43 guest
Nurses Chorus		vocal group	43 guest
Donna	Brown (Robinson)	vocal soloist	43 guest
Anne	Bryant Fisher	vocal soloist	43 guest
Arlene	Julson	vocal soloist	43 guest
Marion	Larson	vocal soloist	43 guest
Loretta	McLaughlin (Hartrich)	vocal soloist	43
Ed	Paul	vocal soloist	43
Maud	Runyan	vocal soloist	43 guest
Marciene	Swenson Matthius	vocal soloist	43 guest
Nellyebelle Reardon	Tolpo	vocal soloist	43 guest
Geraldine	Polzin	whistler	43 guest

Sioux Falls Municipal Band Personnel 1944 (25th season)
Russ D. Henegar, Conductor

Kermit	Harrington	bassoon	44
Richard	Colwell	clarinet	44
Ernest	Dvoracek	clarinet	44
Ed	Gedstad	clarinet	44
Leo	Gossman	clarinet	44
Henry T.	Hanson	clarinet	44
William D.	Meyer	clarinet	44 ?
C. W.	Smith	clarinet	44
Marvin	Thostensen	clarinet	44
Russ	Henegar	conductor	44
Elmer T. "Eddie"	Edwards	cornet	44
Willard	Fejfar	cornet	44
Donald	Lias	cornet	44
John "Jack" M.	Newton	cornet	44
William "Bill" H.	Tietjen	cornet	44
Alcorn Dance Studio		dance	44 guest
Claude	Hamilton, Jr.	dance	44 guest
Robert	Aga	euphonium	44
Wayne	Krumrei	euphonium	44
Oril W.	Palmer	flute	44
Donald	Halvorson	horn	44
Paul	Hammond ?	horn/cornet	44?
Albert R.	Hillman	horn	44
Walter F.	Rittman	horn	44
William G.	Wagner	horn	44
Eddie	Lias	inst. soloist, cornet	44 guest
Ed	Paul	MC	44
Milt	Askew	oboe	44
Vernon Herman	Alger	percussion	44
Glen G.	Houdek	percussion	44
Robert	Niblick	percussion	44
Raymond G.	Hoyt	sax, alto	44
Everton	Little	sax, alto	44
Roy	Borneman	sax, baritone	44
Guy G.	Anderson	sax, tenor	44
Cliff	Foss	trombone	44
Jake	Helfert	trombone	44
Harold	Hoover, Sr.	trombone	44
Melvin	Sunde	trombone	44
Austin K.	Bailey	tuba	44
Harry	Ellis	tuba	44
Orral O.	Jackson	tuba	44
El Riad Chanters		vocal group	44 guest
Vocal Trio		vocal group	44 guest
Anne	Bryant Fisher	vocal soloist	44 guest
Nancy	Gardner	vocal soloist	44 guest
Janet Whitfield	Muxfelt	vocal soloist	44 guest
Ed	Paul	vocal soloist	44
Marciene	Swenson Matthius	vocal soloist	44

Sioux Falls Municipal Band Personnel 1945 (26th season)
Russ D. Henegar, Conductor

Henry T.	Hanson	alto clarinet	45
Raymond G.	Hoyt	bass clarinet	45
Richard J.	Guderyahn	cello	45
Robert	Ahlness	clarinet	45
Charles	Baker	clarinet	45
Richard	Colwell	clarinet	45
Ernest	Dvoracek	clarinet (E flat)	45
Ed	Gedstad	clarinet	45
Leo	Gossman	clarinet	45
William D.	Meyer	clarinet	45 ?
John	Rosheim	clarinet	45
C. W.	Smith	clarinet	45
Russ	Henegar	conductor	45

Elmer T. "Eddie"	Edwards	cornet	45
Donald	Lias	cornet	45
John "Jack" M.	Newton	cornet	45
Allen	Opland	cornet	45
Francis	Peckham	cornet	45
William "Bill" H.	Tietjen	cornet	45
Alcorn Dance Studio		dance	45 guest
Fred	Kamolz	euphonium	45
Wayne	Krumrei	euphonium	45
Oril W.	Palmer	flute	45
Albert R.	Hillman	horn	45
B. G.	Monk	horn	45
Walter F.	Rittman	horn	45
William G.	Wagner	horn	45
Dean	Clarke	inst. soloist, saxophone	45 guest
Richard J.	Guderyahn	inst. soloist, violin	45 guest
Ed	Paul	MC	45
Vernon Herman	Alger	percussion	45
Marvin	Cooper	percussion	45
Glen G.	Houdek	percussion	45
Ray G.	Pruner	percussion	45
Milt	Askew	sax, alto	45
Everton	Little	sax, alto	45
Roy	Borneman	sax, baritone	45
Guy G.	Anderson	sax, tenor	45
Cliff	Foss	trombone	45
Jake	Helfert	trombone	45
Harold	Hoover, Sr.	trombone	45
Melvin	Sunde	trombone	45
Austin K.	Bailey	tuba	45
Orral O.	Jackson	tuba	45
El Riad Chanters		vocal group	45 guest
Minnehaha Mandskor		vocal group	45 guest
Helen	Brumbaugh (Hanson)	vocal soloist	45 guest
Anne	Bryant Fisher	vocal soloist	45
Allen	Opland	vocal soloist	45 guest
Ed	Paul	vocal soloist	45
Connie	Roth	vocal soloist	45 guest

Sioux Falls Municipal Band Personnel 1946 (27th season)
Russ D. Henegar, Conductor

Henry T.	Hanson	alto clarinet	46
Raymond G.	Hoyt	bass clarinet	46
Marlin	Brown	clarinet	46
Richard	Colwell	clarinet	46
Ernest	Dvoracek ?	clarinet	46?
Ed	Gedstad	clarinet	46
Leo	Gossman	clarinet	46
C. R. "Bob"	Larson	clarinet	46
William D.	Meyer	clarinet	46 ?
C. W.	Smith	clarinet	46
Everett	Zellers	clarinet	46
Russ	Henegar	conductor	46
Elmer T. "Eddie"	Edwards	cornet	46
Kenneth	Lane	cornet	46
Donald	Lias	cornet	46
		cornet	46
		cornet	46
		cornet	46
Alcorn Dance Studio		dance	46 guest
Wayne	Krumrei	euphonium	46
		euphonium	46
Oril W.	Palmer	flute	46
		flute	46
Albert R.	Hillman	horn	46
Palmer	Kremer	horn	46
Walter F.	Rittman	horn	46
William G.	Wagner	horn	46
Ludwig	Wangberg	horn	46

Eddie	Lias	inst. soloist, cornet	46 guest
Richard	Colwell	librarian	46
Ed	Paul	MC	46
Ardeen	Foss	oboe	46
Vernon Herman	Alger	percussion	46
Glen G.	Houdek	percussion	46
Robert	Niblick	percussion	46
Ray G.	Pruner	percussion	46
Milt	Askew	sax, alto ?	46
Everton	Little	sax, alto	46
Guy G.	Anderson	sax, tenor	46
Jake	Helfert	trombone	46
Harold	Hoover, Sr.	trombone	46
Donald	McCabe	trombone	46
Austin K.	Bailey	tuba	46
Harry	Ellis	tuba	46
Orral O.	Jackson	tuba	46
Anne	Bryant Fisher	vocal soloist	46
Joan	Forrette	vocal soloist	46 guest
Ed	Paul	vocal soloist	46
Ella June	Whittaker	vocal soloist	46 guest

Sioux Falls Municipal Band Personnel 1947 (28th season)
Russ D. Henegar, Conductor

Henry T.	Hanson	alto clarinet	47
Raymond G.	Hoyt ?	bass clarinet	47?
Robert J.	Barnett	clarinet	47
Richard	Colwell ?	clarinet	47?
Ernest	Dvoracek ?	clarinet	47?
Ed	Gedstad	clarinet	47
Leo	Gossman	clarinet	47
C. R. "Bob"	Larson	clarinet	47
		clarinet	47
		clarinet	47
Russ	Henegar	conductor	47
Elmer T. "Eddie"	Edwards	cornet	47
Kenneth	Lane	cornet	47
Donald	Lias	cornet	47
		cornet	47
		cornet	47
		cornet	47
	Alcorn Dance Studio	dance	47 guest
Wayne	Krumrei	euphonium	47
William	Ireland	euphonium	47?
Oril W.	Palmer	flute	47
Albert R.	Hillman	horn	47
Walter F.	Rittman	horn	47
William G.	Wagner	horn	47
Ludwig	Wangberg	horn	47
Mrs. Earl V.	Nason	inst. soloist, piano	47 guest
Ed	Paul	MC	47
Ardeen	Foss	oboe	47
Vernon Herman	Alger	percussion	47
Glen G.	Houdek	percussion	47
Robert	Niblick	percussion	47
Ray G.	Pruner	percussion	47
Milt	Askew	sax, alto	47
Everton	Little	sax, alto	47
Guy G.	Anderson	sax, tenor	47
Harold	Hoover, Sr. ?	trombone	47?
Donald	McCabe ?	trombone	47?
Melvin	Sunde	trombone	47
Austin K.	Bailey	tuba	47
Harry	Ellis	tuba	47
Orral O.	Jackson	tuba	47
American Legion Chorus		vocal group	47 guest
Anne	Bryant Fisher	vocal soloist	47
Ed	Paul	vocal soloist	47
Mrs. L. J.	Reistroffer	vocal soloist	47 guest

Marciene	Swenson Matthius	vocal soloist	47 guest
Ella June	Whittaker	vocal soloist	47 guest
Janet	Quinn	whistler	47 guest

Sioux Falls Municipal Band Personnel 1948 (29th season)
Russ D. Henegar, Conductor

Henry T.	Hanson	alto clarinet	48
Raymond G.	Hoyt	bass clarinet	48
Robert J.	Barnett	clarinet	48
Richard	Colwell ?	clarinet	48?
Ernest	Dvoracek ?	clarinet	48?
Ed	Gedstad ?	clarinet	48?
Leo	Gossman	clarinet	48
C. R. "Bob"	Larson	clarinet	48
	?	clarinet	48
	?	clarinet	48
Russ	Henegar	conductor	48
Lt. Col. Harold	Bachman	conductor, guest	48 guest
Glenn C.	Bainum	conductor, guest	48 guest
Col. Howard C.	Bronson	conductor, guest	48 guest
Carl	Christensen	conductor, guest	48 guest
J. De Forest	Cline	conductor, guest	48 guest
Henry	Fillmore	conductor, guest	48 guest
Dr. Edwin Franko	Goldman	conductor, guest	48 guest
Dr. A. A.	Harding	conductor, guest	48 guest
Capt. R. B.	Hayward	conductor, guest	48 guest
John J.	Heney	conductor, guest	48 guest
Col. Earl D.	Irons	conductor, guest	48 guest
Karl L.	King	conductor, guest	48 guest
Leo	Kucinski	conductor, guest	48 guest
Gerald R.	Prescott	conductor, guest	48 guest
John J.	Richards	conductor, guest	48 guest
Paul	Yoder	conductor, guest	48 guest
Kenneth	Ewing	cornet	48
Robert	Griffith	cornet	48
Donald	Lias	cornet	48
Leon	Miller	cornet	48
		cornet	48
William	Hobson	euphonium	48
Wayne	Krumrei	euphonium	48
Oril W.	Palmer	flute	48
F. H.	Tyler	flute	48
Albert R.	Hillman	horn	48
Arthur V.	McKenzie	horn	48
Walter F.	Rittman	horn	48
William G.	Wagner	horn	48
Myron	Floren	inst. soloist, accordion	48 guest
Mrs. Earl V. Nason	Nason	inst. soloist, piano	48 guest
Ed	Paul	MC	48
Ardeen	Foss	oboe	48
Vernon Herman	Alger	percussion	48
Glen G.	Houdek	percussion	48
Robert	Niblick	percussion	48
Ray G.	Pruner	percussion	48
Milt	Askew	sax, alto	48
Everton	Little	sax, alto	48
Quido	Pekas	sax, baritone	48
Guy G.	Anderson	sax, tenor	48
Harold	Hoover, Sr.	trombone	48
W. T. (Ted)	Matthews	trombone	48
Donald	McCabe ?	trombone	48?
Melvin	Sunde	trombone	48
Austin K.	Bailey	tuba	48
Harry	Ellis	tuba	48
Everitt	Friedhoff	tuba	48
Orral O.	Jackson	tuba	48
American Legion Chorus		vocal group	48 guest
El Riad Chanters		vocal group	48 guest
Donna	Brown (Robinson)	vocal soloist	48 guest

Anne	Bryant Fisher	vocal soloist	48
Ed	Paul	vocal soloist	48
Marciene	Swenson Matthius	vocal soloist	48 guest

Sioux Falls Municipal Band Personnel 1949 (30th season)
Russ D. Henegar, Conductor

Henry T.	Hanson	alto clarinet	49
Raymond G.	Hoyt	bass clarinet	49
Richard	Colwell	bassoon	49
Robert J.	Barnett	clarinet	49
Ed	Gedstad	clarinet	49
Leo	Gossman	clarinet	49
C. R. "Bob"	Larson	clarinet	49
Leland	Lillehaug	clarinet	49
George B.	Medeck	clarinet	49
Kenneth	Pace	clarinet	49
C. W.	Smith	clarinet	49
Russ	Henegar	conductor	49
Kenneth	Ewing	cornet	49
Robert	Griffith	cornet	49
Desmond H.	Kittelson	cornet	49
Donald	Lias	cornet	49
Leon	Miller	cornet	49
William "Bill" H.	Tietjen	cornet	49
Stanley	Brooks	euphonium	49
Wayne	Krumrei	euphonium	49
Oril W.	Palmer	flute	49
F. H.	Tyler	flute	49
Glenn "Bud"	Morgan	horn	49
Ron	Richardson	horn	49
William G.	Wagner	horn	49
Paul A.	Weber	horn	49
Richard	Colwell	librarian	49
Ed	Paul	MC	49
Ardeen	Foss	oboe	49
Neal	Olsen	oboe	49
Vernon Herman	Alger	percussion	49
Robert W.	Marker	percussion	49
Robert	Niblick	percussion	49
Ray G.	Pruner	percussion	49
Everton	Little	sax, alto	49
Milt	Askew	sax, alto	49
Leonard	Lorensen	sax, baritone	49
Guy G.	Anderson	sax, tenor	49
George	Hering	sound	49
John	Brauch, Jr.	trombone	49
Harold	Hoover, Sr.	trombone	49
Donald	McCabe ?	trombone	49?
James	Richardson	trombone	49
Melvin	Sunde	trombone	49
Austin K.	Bailey	tuba	49
Harry	Ellis	tuba	49
Everitt	Friedhoff	tuba	49
Orral O.	Jackson	tuba	49
American Legion Chorus		vocal group	49 guest
American Legion Quartet		vocal group	49 guest
Shrine Chanters		vocal group	49 guest
Helen	Brumbaugh (Hanson)	vocal soloist	49 guest
Anne	Bryant Fisher	vocal soloist	49
Mrs. James	Donahue	vocal soloist	49 guest
Ed	Paul	vocal soloist	49

Sioux Falls Municipal Band Personnel 1950 (31st season)
Russ D. Henegar, Conductor

Henry T.	Hanson	alto clarinet	50
Vernon Hermann	Alger	asst. conductor	50
Raymond G.	Hoyt	bass clarinet	50
Robert J.	Barnett ?	clarinet	50?

Richard	Colwell ?	clarinet	50?
Ernest	Dvoracek ?	clarinet	50?
Ed	Gedstad	clarinet	50
Leo	Gossman	clarinet	50
C. R. "Bob"	Larson	clarinet	50
Leland	Lillehaug ?	clarinet	50?
C. W.	Smith	clarinet	50
Russ	Henegar	conductor	50
Paul	Christensen	conductor, guest	50 guest
Joseph	Tschetter	conductor, guest	50 guest
Robert	Griffith	cornet	50
Desmond H.	Kittelson	cornet	50
Donald	Lias	cornet	50
Leon	Miller	cornet	50
	?	cornet	50
	?	cornet	50
Ament brother & sister		dance and song	50 guest
Donald	McCabe	euphonium	50
Wayne	Krumrei	euphonium	50
Oril W.	Palmer	flute	50
F. H.	Tyler	flute	50
Donald	McCabe	horn	50
William G.	Wagner	horn	50
	?	horn	50
	?	horn	50
Marvin	Rimerman	inst. soloist, cornet	50 guest
Ed	Paul	MC	50
Ardeen	Foss	oboe	50
Vernon Herman	Alger	percussion	50
Glen G.	Houdek	percussion	50
Ray G.	Pruner	percussion	50
Milt	Askew	sax, alto	50?
Everton	Little	sax, alto	50?
Guy G.	Anderson	sax, tenor	50
	?	sax, bari	50
George	Hering	sound	50
John	Brauch, Jr.	trombone	50
Harold	Hoover, Sr.	trombone	50
James	Richardson	trombone	50
Melvin	Sunde	trombone	50
Austin K.	Bailey	tuba	50
Harry	Ellis	tuba	50
Orral O.	Jackson	tuba	50
Betty	Allen	twirler	50 guest
American Legion Chorus		vocal group	50 guest
El Riad Chanters		vocal group	50 guest
Kaiser-Frazer Quartet		vocal group	50 guest
Anne	Bryant Fisher	vocal soloist	50
Donna	Carlson	vocal soloist	50 guest
Ed	Paul	vocal soloist	50

Sioux Falls Municipal Band Personnel 1951 (32nd season)
Russ D. Henegar, Conductor

Henry T.	Hanson	alto clarinet	51
Raymond G.	Hoyt	bass clarinet	51
Charles	Knutson	bassoon	51
Robert J.	Barnett	clarinet	51
Richard	Colwell ?	clarinet	51?
Ernest	Dvoracek ?	clarinet	51?
Ed	Gedstad	clarinet	51
Leo	Gossman	clarinet	51
C. R. "Bob"	Larson	clarinet	51
C. W.	Smith	clarinet	51
	?	clarinet	51
Russ	Henegar	conductor	51
Robert	Griffith	cornet	51
Desmond H.	Kittelson	cornet	51
Leon	Miller	cornet	51
William "Bill" H.	Tietjen	cornet	51

Ron	Whalen	cornet	51
?		cornet	51
Marilyn	McKechnie & father	dance & bagpipe	51 guest
Harvey	Eichmeier	euphonium	51
Wayne	Krumrei	euphonium	51
Oril W.	Palmer	flute	51
?		flute	51
Wayne	Burk	horn	51
Donald	McCabe	horn	51
Ron	Richardson	horn	51
William G.	Wagner	horn	51
Ed	Paul	MC	51
Ardeen	Foss	oboe	51
?		oboe	51
Vernon Herman	Alger	percussion	51
Glen G.	Houdek	percussion	51
Robert	Niblick	percussion	51
Ray G.	Pruner	percussion	51
Milt	Askew ?	sax, alto	51?
Everton	Little ?	sax, alto	51?
Guy G.	Anderson	sax, tenor	51
?		sax, baritone	51
George	Hering	sound	51
E. O.	Dietrich	trombone	51
Harold	Hoover, Sr.	trombone	51
James	Richardson	trombone	51
Melvin	Sunde	trombone	51
Austin K.	Bailey	tuba	51
Harry	Ellis	tuba	51
Orral O.	Jackson	tuba	51
Harvey	Eichmeier	tuba?	51
Leslie	Arneson	vocal soloist	51 guest
El Riad Chanters		vocal group	51 guest
Anne	Bryant Fisher	vocal soloist	51
Donna	Carlson	vocal soloist	51 guest
Ed	Paul	vocal soloist	51

Sioux Falls Municipal Band Personnel 1952 (33rd season)
Russ D. Henegar, Conductor

Henry T.	Hanson	alto clarinet	52
Vernon Hermann	Alger	asst. conductor	52
Raymond G.	Hoyt	bass clarinet	52
Charles	Knutson	bassoon	52
Earl	Colgan, Jr.	clarinet	52
Richard	Colwell	clarinet	52
Ernest	Dvoracek	clarinet	52
Ardeen	Foss	clarinet	52
Warren	Gedstad	clarinet	52
Leo	Gossman	clarinet	52
Dean	Koolbeck	clarinet	52
Douglas	Tremere	clarinet	52
Russ	Henegar	conductor	52
Robert	Griffith	cornet	52
Leon	Miller	cornet	52
Robert	Nason	cornet	52
Marvin	Rimerman	cornet	52
William "Bill" H.	Tietjen	cornet	52
David	Wilson	cornet	52
Harvey	Eichmeier	euphonium	52
Wayne	Krumrei	euphonium	52
Oril W.	Palmer	flute	52
	Van Edmund	flute ?	52
Wayne	Burk	horn	52
Donald	McCabe	horn	52
Ron	Richardson	horn	52
William G.	Wagner	horn	52
Mrs. Earl V. Nason	Nason	inst. soloist, piano	52 guest
Ed	Paul	MC	52
Neal	Olsen	oboe	52

Ron	Veenker	oboe	52
Vernon Herman	Alger	percussion	52
Curtis	Beecher	percussion	52
Robert	Niblick	percussion	52
Ray G.	Pruner	percussion	52
Milt	Askew	sax, alto	52
Everton	Little	sax, alto	52
Guy G.	Anderson	sax, baritone?	52
Lyle	Lien	sax, tenor	52
George	Hering	sound	52
E. O.	Dietrich	trombone	52
	Eberle	trombone	52
Harold	Hoover, Sr.	trombone	52
Melvin	Sunde	trombone	52
Austin K.	Bailey	tuba	52
Harry	Ellis	tuba	52
Orral O.	Jackson	tuba	52
Betty	Allen	twirler	52 guest
Leslie	Arneson	vocal soloist	52 guest
El Riad Chanters		vocal group	52 guest
Anne	Bryant Fisher	vocal soloist	52
Donna	Carlson	vocal soloist	52 guest
Ed	Paul	vocal soloist	52

Sioux Falls Municipal Band Personnel 1953 (34th season)
Russ D. Henegar, Conductor

Henry T.	Hanson	alto clarinet	53
Raymond G.	Hoyt	bass clarinet	53
Charles	Knutson	bassoon	53
Tommy	Knutson	bassoon	53
Robert J.	Barnett	clarinet	53
Earl	Colgan, Jr.	clarinet	53
Ernest	Dvoracek	clarinet	53
Ardeen	Foss	clarinet	53
Warren	Gedstad	clarinet	53
Leo	Gossman	clarinet	53
Oscar	Loe	clarinet	53 sub
James	Riemann	clarinet	53
I. M.	Williamson	clarinet	53
Douglas	Tremere	clarinet/b sax	53
Russ	Henegar	conductor	53
O. A.	Joneson	cornet	53
Leon	Miller	cornet	53
Robert	Nason	cornet	53
Marvin	Rimerman	cornet	53
David	Wilson	cornet	53
Harvey	Eichmeier	euphonium	53
Wayne	Krumrei	euphonium	53
Oril W.	Palmer	flute	53
Ralph	Tyler	flute	53
Wayne	Burk	horn	53
Donald	McCabe	horn	53
William G.	Wagner	horn	53
Ed	Paul	MC	53
Larry	Hartshorn	oboe	53
Ron	Veenker	oboe	53
Vernon Herman	Alger	percussion	53
Buddy	Beck	percussion	53
Glen G.	Houdek	percussion	53
Ray G.	Pruner	percussion	53
Milt	Askew	sax, alto	53
Everton	Little	sax, alto	53
Glenn "Bud"	Morgan	sax, baritone	53
Guy G.	Anderson	sax, tenor	53
George	Hering	sound	53
Lloyd	Kreitzer	string bass	53
E. O.	Dietrich	trombone	53
Harold	Hoover, Sr.	trombone	53
Melvin	Sunde	trombone	53

Harry	Ellis	tuba	53
Orral O.	Jackson	tuba	53
Jeanice	Anderson	twirler	53 guest
Betty	Allen	twirler	53 guest
Sandra Kay	Hart	twirler	53 guest
WHS Majorettes		twirler	53 guest
El Riad Chanters		vocal group	53 guest
Anne	Bryant Fisher	vocal soloist	53
James	Cabbell	vocal soloist	53 guest
Ed	Paul	vocal soloist	53

Sioux Falls Municipal Band Personnel 1954 (35th season)
Russ D. Henegar, Conductor

Henry T.	Hanson	alto clarinet	54
Raymond G.	Hoyt	bass clarinet	54
Charles	Knutson	bassoon	54
Tommy	Knutson	bassoon	54
Earl	Colgan, Jr.	clarinet	54
Ernest	Dvoracek	clarinet	54
Ardeen	Foss	clarinet	54
Warren	Gedstad	clarinet	54
Gary	Harms	clarinet	54
Oscar	Loe	clarinet	54
James	Riemann	clarinet	54
Paul	Wegner, Jr.	clarinet	54
I. M.	Williamson	clarinet	54
Russ	Henegar	conductor	54
A. F.	Aughenbaugh	conductor, guest	54 guest
Carl	Christensen	conductor, guest	54 guest
Robert	Griffith	cornet	54
Leon	Miller	cornet	54
Robert	Nason	cornet	54
James	Ode	cornet	54
Marvin	Rimerman	cornet	54
Harvey	Eichmeier	euphonium	54
Wayne	Krumrei	euphonium	54
Oril W.	Palmer	flute	54
Ralph	Tyler	flute	54
Paul	Anderson	horn	54
Wayne	Burk	horn	54
Donald	McCabe	horn	54
Ron	Richardson	horn	54
William G.	Wagner	horn	54
Ed	Paul	MC	54
Larry	Hartshorn	oboe	54
Neal	Olsen	oboe	54
J. H.	Elgethun	percussion	54
Glen G.	Houdek	percussion	54
Ray G.	Pruner	percussion	54
Ron	Veenker	percussion	54
Milt	Askew	sax	54
William	Kramer	sax	54
Everton	Little	sax, alto	54
Guy G.	Anderson	sax, tenor	54
George	Hering	sound	54
Lloyd	Kreitzer	string bass	54
Joseph	Birkenheurer	trombone	54
James	Boise	trombone	54
E. O.	Dietrich	trombone	54
Harold	Hoover, Sr.	trombone	54
Melvin	Sunde	trombone	54
Harry	Ellis	tuba	54
Orral O.	Jackson	tuba	54
Augustana Vikingette Duo		twirler	54 guest
WHS Majorettes		twirler	54 guest
Four Blue Notes (Pipestone, Minnesota)		vocal group	54 guest
Valley Male Quartet (Rock Valley, Iowa)		vocal group	54 guest
Margaret Barnard	Cavitt	vocal soloist	54 guest
Anne	Bryant Fisher	vocal soloist	54

James	Cabbell	vocal soloist	54 guest
Ed	Paul	vocal soloist	54
Donald	Westerlund	vocal soloist	54 guest

Sioux Falls Municipal Band Personnel 1955 (36th season)
Russ D. Henegar, Conductor

Henry T.	Hanson	alto clarinet	55
Gary	Harms	bass clarinet	55
Tommy	Knutson	bassoon	55
Paul	Wegner, Jr.	bassoon	55
Earl	Colgan, Jr.	clarinet	55
Richard	Colwell	clarinet	55
Ernest	Dvoracek	clarinet	55
Ardeen	Foss	clarinet	55
Warren	Gedstad	clarinet	55
Charles	Mueller	clarinet	55
James	Riemann	clarinet	55
John	Romans	clarinet	55 sub
I. M.	Williamson	clarinet	55
Russ	Henegar	conductor	55
William	Byrne	cornet	55
Robert	Griffith	cornet	55
Leon	Miller	cornet	55
Robert	Nason	cornet	55
James	Ode	cornet	55
David	Wegner	cornet	55
Harvey	Eichmeier	euphonium	55
Wayne	Krumrei	euphonium	55
Oril W.	Palmer	flute	55
Ralph	Tyler	flute	55
Paul	Anderson	horn	55
Wayne	Burk	horn	55
Donald	McCabe	horn	55
Ron	Richardson	horn	55
William G.	Wagner	horn	55
A. Ellsworth	Winden	horn	55
Ed	Paul	MC	55
Richard	Foss	oboe	55
Neal	Olsen	oboe	55
J. H.	Elgethun	percussion	55
Glen G.	Houdek	percussion	55
Ray G.	Pruner	percussion	55
Ron	Veenker	percussion	55
Milt	Askew	sax	55
Robert	Graham	sax	55
William	Kramer	sax	55
Everton	Little	sax	55
George	Hering	sound	55
Lloyd	Kreitzer	string bass	55
Joseph	Birkenheuer	trombone	55
E. O.	Dietrich	trombone	55
Harold	Hoover, Sr.	trombone	55
Melvin	Sunde	trombone	55
Harry	Ellis	tuba	55
Orral O.	Jackson	tuba	55
Anne	Bryant Fisher	vocal soloist	55
James	Cabbell	vocal soloist	55 guest
Ed	Paul	vocal soloist	55
Elizabeth	Swanson (Kuhn)	vocal soloist	55 guest

Sioux Falls Municipal Band Personnel 1956 (37th season)
Russ D. Henegar, Conductor

Henry T.	Hanson	alto clarinet	56
Gary	Harms	bass clarinet	56
Tommy	Knutson	bassoon	56
Paul	Wegner, Jr.	bassoon	56
David	Bane	clarinet	56
Earl	Colgan, Jr.	clarinet	56

Richard	Colwell	clarinet	56
Ernest	Dvoracek	clarinet	56
Ardeen	Foss	clarinet	56
Warren	Gedstad	clarinet	56
Leland	Lillehaug	clarinet	56 sub
Charles	Mueller	clarinet	56
James	Riemann	clarinet	56
John	Romans	clarinet	56
Russ	Henegar	conductor	56
William	Byrne	cornet	56
Robert	Griffith	cornet	56
Leon	Miller	cornet	56
Marvin	Mueller	cornet	56
Robert	Nason	cornet	56
James	Ode	cornet	56
David	Wegner	cornet	56
Tanglefoot Dance Studio		dance group	56 guest
Harvey	Eichmeier	euphonium	56
Wayne	Krumrei	euphonium	56
Oril W.	Palmer	flute	56
Ralph	Tyler	flute	56
Paul	Anderson	horn	56
Wayne	Burk	horn	56
Donald	McCabe	horn	56
Ron	Richardson	horn	56 sub?
William G.	Wagner	horn	56
A. Ellsworth	Winden	horn	56
Ed	Paul	MC	56
Richard	Foss	oboe	56
Neal	Olsen	oboe	56
J. H.	Elgethun	percussion	56
Glen G.	Houdek	percussion	56
Ray G.	Pruner	percussion	56
Ron	Veenker	percussion	56
Milt	Askew	sax	56
Robert	Graham	sax	56
Everton	Little	sax	56
Quido	Pekas	sax	56
William	Warren	sax	56
George	Hering	sound	56
S. J.	Herting	string bass	56 sub?
Lloyd	Kreitzer	string bass	56
Joseph	Birkenheuer	trombone	56
Roland	Chambers	trombone	56
E. O.	Dietrich	trombone	56
Harold	Hoover, Sr.	trombone	56
Robert	Stephenson	trombone	56
Harry	Ellis	tuba	56
Orral O.	Jackson	tuba	56
Tri Valley Chorus (Viborg, South Dakota)		vocal group	56 guest
Anne	Bryant Fisher	vocal soloist	56
Mike	Haley	vocal soloist	56 guest
Ed	Paul	vocal soloist	56
Ruth Stene	Reistroffer	vocal soloist	56 guest
Elizabeth	Swanson (Kuhn)	vocal soloist	56
Muriel	Winkel	vocal soloist	56 guest

Sioux Falls Municipal Band Personnel 1957 (38th season)
Russ D. Henegar, Conductor

Henry T.	Hanson	alto clarinet	57
Gary	Harms	bass clarinet	57
Tommy	Knutson	bassoon	57
Leland	Lillehaug	bassoon	57
David	Bane	clarinet	57
Curt	Brandland	clarinet	57
Earl	Colgan, Jr.	clarinet	57
Ernest	Dvoracek	clarinet	57
Ardeen	Foss	clarinet	57
Warren	Gedstad	clarinet	57

Charles	Mueller	clarinet	57
Steve	Oltman	clarinet	57
Paul	Wegner, Jr.	clarinet	57
Russ	Henegar	conductor	57
William	Byrne	cornet	57
Robert	Griffith	cornet	57
Denis	Kelly	cornet	57 sub
Loren	Little	cornet	57 sub
Leon	Miller	cornet	57
Robert	Nason	cornet	57
James	Ode	cornet	57
David	Wegner	cornet	57
Tanglefoot Dance Studio		dance group	57 guest
Harvey	Eichmeier	euphonium	57
Wayne	Krumrei	euphonium	57
Robert	Foss	flute	57 sub
Oril W.	Palmer	flute	57
Ralph	Tyler	flute	57
James	Adams	horn	57
Paul	Anderson	horn	57 sub
David	Lias	horn	57
Donald	McCabe	horn	57
Robert	Solem	horn	57
William G.	Wagner	horn	57
A. Ellsworth	Winden	horn	57 sub
Ed	Paul	MC	57
Chad	Boese	oboe	57
Richard	Foss	oboe	57
J. H.	Elgethun	percussion	57
Greg	Hall	percussion	57 sub
Glen G.	Houdek	percussion	57
Paul	Hoy	percussion	57 sub
Robert	Niblick	percussion	57 sub
Ray G.	Pruner	percussion	57
Ron	Veenker	percussion	57
Milt	Askew	sax	57
Everton	Little	sax	57
Neal	Olsen	sax	57
James	Riemann	sax	57
William	Warren	sax	57 sub
Kenneth	Busse	sax, baritone	57 sub
George	Hering	sound	57
S. J.	Herting	string bass	57 sub
Lloyd	Kreitzer	string bass	57
Joseph	Birkenheuer	trombone	57
Pat	Boffman	trombone	57 sub
Roland	Chambers	trombone	57
Harold	Hoover, Sr.	trombone	57
Paul	Robertson	trombone	57
Melvin	Sunde	trombone	57
Harry	Ellis	tuba	57
Orral O.	Jackson	tuba	57
Russell	Tiede	tuba	57
WHS Majorettes		twirler	57 guest
American Legion Chorus		vocal group	57 guest
Tri Valley Chorus (Viborg, South Dakota)		vocal group	57 guest
Marty	Braithwaite	vocal soloist	57 guest
Lyndall	Brogdon	vocal soloist	57 guest
Anne	Bryant Fisher	vocal soloist	57 guest
Ed	Paul	vocal soloist	57
Elizabeth	Swanson (Kuhn)	vocal soloist	57 guest
Marciene	Swenson Matthius	vocal soloist	57

Sioux Falls Municipal Band Personnel 1958 (39th season)
Russ D. Henegar, Conductor

Henry T.	Hanson	alto clarinet	58
Gary	Harms	bass clarinet	58
Tommy	Knutson	bassoon	58
Leland	Lillehaug	bassoon	58

David	Bane	clarinet	58
Earl	Colgan, Jr.	clarinet	58
Ardeen	Foss	clarinet	58
Warren	Gedstad	clarinet	58
Charles	Mueller	clarinet	58
Steve	Oltman	clarinet	58
Gustav	Schuller	clarinet	58
Paul	Wegner, Jr.	clarinet	58 part time
Steve	Wold	clarinet	58
Russ	Henegar	conductor	58
Robert	Griffith	cornet	58
Morris	Haanstad	cornet	58
Jackson	Herr	cornet	58
Denis	Kelly	cornet	58
Donald	Lias	cornet	58 sub
Loren	Little	cornet	58
David	Wegner	cornet	58
Tanglefoot Dance Studio		dance group	58 guest
Harvey	Eichmeier	euphonium	58
Wayne	Krumrei	euphonium	58
Oril W.	Palmer	flute	58
Ralph	Tyler	flute	58
James	Adams	horn	58
Samuel	Albert	horn	58
Allan	Boysen	horn	58
David	Lias	horn	58
Donald	McCabe	horn	58
Mark	Williamson	horn	58
A. Ellsworth	Winden	horn	58
Ed	Paul	MC	58
Chad	Boese	oboe	58
Neal	Olsen	oboe	58
J. H.	Elgethun	percussion	58
Greg	Hall	percussion	58
Glen G.	Houdek	percussion	58
Paul	Hoy	percussion	58
Ray G.	Pruner	percussion	58
Kenneth	Busse	sax	58
Everton	Little	sax	58
John	Romans	sax	58
Hale	Swanson	sax	58
George	Hering	sound	58
S. J.	Herting	string bass	58
Arlo	Feiock	trombone	58
Harold	Hoover, Sr.	trombone	58
Larry	Larson	trombone	58
Melvin	Sunde	trombone	58
Harry	Ellis	tuba	58
Eddie	Texel	tuba	58 sub
Russell	Tiede	tuba	58
WHS Majorettes		twirler	58 guest
Sugartone Girls 4 (Garretson, South Dakota)		vocal group	58 guest
Worthington Jr. College, Male 4		vocal group	58 guest
Marty	Braithwaite	vocal soloist	58 guest
Ed	Paul	vocal soloist	58
Elizabeth	Swanson (Kuhn)	vocal soloist	58 guest
Marciene	Swenson Matthius	vocal soloist	58

Sioux Falls Municipal Band Personnel 1959 (40th season)
Russ D. Henegar, Conductor

Dennis	Olson	alto clarinet	59
Gary	Harms	bass clarinet	59
Don	Horsted	bassoon	59
Gustav	Schuller	bassoon	59
David	Bane	clarinet	59
Earl	Colgan, Jr.	clarinet	59
Richard	Colwell	clarinet	59 sub
Ardeen	Foss	clarinet	59
Warren	Gedstad	clarinet	59 part time

Leland	Lillehaug	clarinet	59
Oscar	Loe	clarinet	59 sub
Charles	Mueller	clarinet	59
Dennis	Norlin	clarinet (E flat)	59
Steve	Oltman	clarinet	59
Tom	Wegner	clarinet	59
Steve	Wold	clarinet	59
Russ	Henegar	conductor	59
Vernon?	Ellenbecker	cornet	59 sub
Robert	Griffith	cornet	59
Morris	Haanstad	cornet	59
Jackson	Herr	cornet	59
Donald	Lias	cornet	59 sub?
Danny	Kealey	cornet	59
Loren	Little	cornet	59
David	Wegner	cornet	59
Tanglefoot Dance Studio		dance group	59 guest
Harvey	Eichmeier	euphonium	59
Wayne	Krumrei	euphonium	59
Oril W.	Palmer	flute	59
Ralph	Tyler	flute	59
James	Adams	horn	59
Samuel	Albert	horn	59
Donald	McCabe	horn	59
Ron	Richardson	horn	59 sub
Fred	Teuber	horn	59
A. Ellsworth	Winden	horn	59
Ed	Paul	MC	59
Chad	Boese	oboe	59
J. H.	Elgethun	percussion	59
Greg	Hall	percussion	59 sub
Glen G.	Houdek	percussion	59
Paul	Hoy	percussion	59
Robert	Niblick	percussion	59 sub
Ray G.	Pruner	percussion	59
Milt	Askew	sax	59 sub
Kenneth	Busse	sax	59
Everton	Little	sax	59
John	Romans	sax	59
Hale	Swanson	sax	59
David L.	Johnson	sax, alto	59
George	Hering	sound	59
S. J.	Herting	string bass	59
Harold	Hoover, Jr.	trombone	59
Harold	Hoover, Sr.	trombone	59
Larry	Larson	trombone	59
Melvin	Sunde	trombone	59
Harry	Ellis	tuba	59
Everitt	Friedhoff	tuba	59
Eddie	Texel	tuba	59 sub
Brandon High School Twirlers		twirler	59 guest
WHS Majorettes		twirler	59 guest
Tri Valley Chorus (Viborg, South Dakota)		vocal group	59 guest
Marty	Braithwaite	vocal soloist	59 guest
Marilyn	Fialkowski	vocal soloist	59 guest
Ed	Paul	vocal soloist	59
Elizabeth	Swanson (Kuhn)	vocal soloist	59 guest
Marciene	Swenson Matthius	vocal soloist	59

Sioux Falls Municipal Band Personnel 1960 (41st season)
Russ D. Henegar, Conductor

Dennis	Olson	alto clarinet	60
Ardeen	Foss	asst. conductor	60
Gary	Harms	bass clarinet	60
Don	Horsted	bassoon	60
Gustav	Schuller	bassoon	60
Earl	Colgan, Jr.	clarinet	60
Robert	Drawbaugh	clarinet	60
Ardeen	Foss	clarinet	60

Oscar	Loe	clarinet	60
Charles	Mueller	clarinet	60
Dennis	Norlin	clarinet	60
Steve	Oltman	clarinet	60
Tom	Wegner	clarinet	60
Steve	Wold	clarinet	60
Russ	Henegar	conductor	60
Robert	Griffith	cornet	60
Ronn	Holyer	cornet	60
Danny	Kealey	cornet	60
Loren	Little	cornet	60
Steve?	Mahlsted?	cornet	60 sub?
James	Ode	cornet	60
David	Wegner	cornet	60
Tanglefoot Dance Studio		dance group	60 guest
Harvey	Eichmeier	euphonium	60
Wayne	Krumrei	euphonium	60
Oril W.	Palmer	flute	60
Ralph	Tyler	flute	60
James	Adams	horn	60
Samuel	Albert	horn	60
Paul	Anderson	horn	60
Donald	McCabe	horn	60
A. Ellsworth	Winden	horn	60
Ed	Paul	MC	60
Chad	Boese	oboe	60
Jurgen	Schuller	oboe	60
Jon	Hansen	percussion	60
Glen G.	Houdek	percussion	60
Paul	Hoy	percussion	60
Robert	Niblick	percussion	60 sub
Ray G.	Pruner	percussion	60
Milt	Askew	sax	60 sub
David L.	Johnson	sax, alto	60
Everton	Little	sax, alto	60
Kenneth	Busse	sax, baritone	60
Hale	Swanson	sax, tenor	60
George	Hering	sound	60
Paul	Fialkowski	string bass	60
Richard	Flisrand	trombone	60
Harold	Hoover, Jr.	trombone	60
Harold	Hoover, Sr.	trombone	60
Melvin	Sunde	trombone	60
Harry	Ellis	tuba	60
Everitt	Friedhoff	tuba	60
Eddie	Texel	tuba	60 sub
Nancy	Mehlum	twirler	60 guest
WHS Majorettes		twirler	60 guest
Ed	Paul	vocal soloist	60
Marciene	Swenson Matthius	vocal soloist	60

Sioux Falls Municipal Band Personnel 1961 (42nd season)
Russ D. Henegar, Conductor

Dennis	Olson	alto clarinet	61
Ardeen	Foss	asst. conductor	61
Harold	Gray	bass clarinet	61
Gary	Harms	bass clarinet	61 sub?
Leland	Lillehaug	bassoon	61 part time
Gustav	Schuller	bassoon	61
Robert J.	Barnett	clarinet	61 sub?
Earl	Colgan, Jr.	clarinet	61
Ardeen	Foss	clarinet	61
Oscar	Loe	clarinet	61
Dennis	Norlin	clarinet	61
Richard	Peik	clarinet	61
Tom	Wegner	clarinet	61
Jeff	Wold	clarinet	61
Steve	Wold	clarinet	61
Russ	Henegar	conductor	61

Richard	Berdahl	cornet	61
Robert	Griffith	cornet	61
Ronn	Holyer	cornet	61
Danny	Kealey	cornet	61
Loren	Little	cornet	61
James	Ode	cornet	61
David	Wegner	cornet	61
Tanglefoot Dance Studio		dance group	61 guest
James	Berdahl	euphonium	61
Wayne	Krumrei	euphonium	61
Oril W.	Palmer	flute	61
Ralph	Tyler	flute	61
James	Adams	horn	61
Samuel	Albert	horn	61
Paul	Anderson	horn	61
Donald	McCabe	horn	61
Robert	McDowell	horn	61
Ed	Sheppard	horn	61 sub?
Ed	Paul	MC	61
Chad	Boese	oboe	61
Jurgen	Schuller	oboe	61
Greg	Hall	percussion	61 sub?
Jon	Hansen	percussion	61
Glen G.	Houdek	percussion	61
Paul	Hoy	percussion	61
Ray G.	Pruner	percussion	61
David L.	Johnson	sax, alto	61
Everton	Little	sax, alto	61
Kenneth	Busse	sax, baritone	61
Tom	Little	sax, tenor	61
George	Hering	sound	61
Robert	Collins	string bass	61
Paul	Fialkowski	string bass	61
Harold	Hoover, Jr.	trombone	61
Harold	Hoover, Sr.	trombone	61
Keith	Knoff	trombone	61
Jim	Stoeckmann	trombone	61 sub
Melvin	Sunde	trombone	61
Harvey	Eichmeier	tuba	61
J. H.	Elgethun	tuba	61
Harry	Ellis	tuba	61 was ill
Everitt	Friedhoff	tuba	61
Eddie	Texel	tuba	61 sub?
Nancy	Mehlum	twirler	61 guest
WHS Majorettes		twirler	61 guest
Tri Valley Chorus (Viborg)		vocal group	61 guest
Ed	Paul	vocal soloist	61
Marciene	Swenson Matthius	vocal soloist	61

Sioux Falls Municipal Band Personnel 1962 (43rd season)
Russ D. Henegar, Conductor

Dennis	Olson	alto clarinet	62
Harold	Gray	bass clarinet	62
Leland	Lillehaug	bassoon	62
Gustav	Schuller	bassoon	62
Earl	Colgan, Jr.	clarinet	62
Ardeen	Foss	clarinet	62
Robert L.	Hanson	clarinet	62
Oscar	Loe	clarinet	62
John	Mattice	clarinet	62
Richard	Peik	clarinet	62
John	Romans	clarinet	62
Jeff	Wold	clarinet	62
Russ	Henegar	conductor	62
James	Axelson	cornet	62
Richard	Berdahl	cornet	62 sub
Robert	Griffith	cornet	62
Ronn	Holyer	cornet	62
Danny	Kealey	cornet	62 sub

Loren	Little	cornet	62
Leon	Miller	cornet	62 sub
James	Ode	cornet	62
David	Wegner	cornet	62
Tanglefoot Dance Studio		dance group	62 guest
James	Berdahl	euphonium	62
Wayne	Krumrei	euphonium	62
Oril W.	Palmer	flute	62
Ralph	Tyler	flute	62
Samuel	Albert	horn	62
Paul	Anderson	horn	62
J. H.	Elgethun	horn	62
Gene	Gross	horn	62 sub
Donald	McCabe	horn	62
Robert	McDowell	horn	62
Ed	Paul	MC	62
Chad	Boese	oboe	62
Jurgen	Schuller	oboe	62
Curtis	Beecher	percussion	62
Joe	Bruun	percussion	62
Paul	Hoy	percussion	62
Ray G.	Pruner	percussion	62
Milt	Askew	sax	62 sub
David L.	Johnson	sax, alto	62
Everton	Little	sax, alto	62
Kenneth	Busse	sax, baritone	62
Tom	Little	sax, tenor	62
George	Hering	sound	62
Paul	Fialkowski	string bass	62
Richard	Flisrand	trombone	62
Harold	Hoover, Jr.	trombone	62
Harold	Hoover, Sr.	trombone	62
Keith	Knoff	trombone	62
Jim	Stoeckmann	trombone	62 sub
Harvey	Eichmeier	tuba	62
Harry	Ellis	tuba	62
Eddie	Texel	tuba	62
Nancy	Mehlum	twirler	62 guest
WHS Majorettes		twirler	62 guest
Munici-Pals (from Band)		vocal group	62 guest
Singing Plainsmen (Canova, South Dakota)		vocal group	62 guest
Ed	Paul	vocal soloist	62
Marciene	Swenson Matthius	vocal soloist	62

Sioux Falls Municipal Band Personnel 1963 (44th season)
Russ D. Henegar, Conductor

Dennis	Olson	alto clarinet	63
Harold	Gray	bass clarinet	63
Leland	Lillehaug	bassoon	63
Gustav	Schuller	bassoon	63
Earl	Colgan, Jr.	clarinet	63
Ardeen	Foss	clarinet	63
Robert L.	Hanson	clarinet	63
Gary	Hoiseth	clarinet	63 sub?
Gerald	Kemner	clarinet	63
Oscar	Loe	clarinet	63
John	Mattice	clarinet	63
Gary	Paulson	clarinet	63 sub?
Richard	Peik	clarinet	63
Jeff	Wold	clarinet	63
Russ	Henegar	conductor	63
Paul	Davoux	cornet	63
Ronn	Holyer	cornet	63
Danny	Kealey	cornet	63 sub
Loren	Little	cornet	63
Leon	Miller	cornet	63 sub
James	Ode	cornet	63
Jack	Rembold	cornet	63
David	Wegner	cornet	63

Tanglefoot Dance Studio		dance group	63 guest
Robert	Frick	euphonium	63
Wayne	Krumrei	euphonium	63
Robert	Ortman	euphonium	63
Oril W.	Palmer	flute	63
Ralph	Tyler	flute	63
Paul	Anderson	horn	63
J. H.	Elgethun	horn	63
Scott	Faragher	horn	63
Donald	McCabe	horn	63
Robert	McDowell	horn	63
Russell	Tiede	horn	63
Ed	Paul	MC	63
Chad	Boese	oboe	63
Jurgen	Schuller	oboe	63
Joe	Bruun	percussion	63
Greg	Hall	percussion	63
Paul	Hoy	percussion	63
Ray G.	Pruner	percussion	63
John	Solberg	percussion	63
Milt	Askew	sax	63
John Tom	Dempster	sax, alto ?	63
David L.	Johnson	sax, alto	63
Everton	Little	sax, alto	63
Kenneth	Busse	sax, baritone	63
Tom	Little	sax, tenor	63
George	Hering	sound	63
Paul	Bankson	trombone	63
James	Berdahl	trombone	63
Harold	Hoover, Jr.	trombone	63
Harold	Hoover, Sr.	trombone	63
Keith	Knoff	trombone	63
Ronald	McGaughey	trombone	63
Philip	Miller	trombone	63
Harvey	Eichmeier	tuba	63
Stan	Eitreim	tuba	63
Harry	Ellis	tuba	63
Janine	Johnson	twirler	63 guest
Nancy	Mehlum	twirler	63 guest
Ed	Paul	vocal soloist	63
Marciene	Swenson Matthius	vocal soloist	63
Kristine	Farkas	vocal soloist/dance	63 guest

Sioux Falls Municipal Band Personnel 1964 (45th season)
Dr. Leland A. Lillehaug, Conductor

Dennis	Olson	alto clarinet	64
Harold	Gray	bass clarinet	64
Keith	Peterson	bassoon	64
Gustav	Schuller	bassoon	64
Milt	Askew	clarinet	64 sub
Robert J.	Barnett	clarinet	64 part time
Earl	Colgan, Jr.	clarinet	64 sub
Robert L.	Hanson	clarinet	64
Rex	Hays	clarinet	64 sub
Stan	Hays	clarinet	64 sub
Gary	Hoiseth	clarinet	64
Oscar	Loe	clarinet	64
John	Mattice	clarinet	64
Charles	Mueller	clarinet	64 sub
Ralph	Olsen, Jr.	clarinet	64 part time
Richard	Peik	clarinet	64
Ralph	Tyler	clarinet	64
Jeff	Wold	clarinet	64
Leland	Lillehaug	conductor	64
Russ	Henegar	conductor, guest	64 guest
Paul	Davoux	cornet	64
George	Gulson	cornet	64 sub
Robert	Holyer	cornet	64 sub
Ronn	Holyer	cornet	64

Danny	Kealey	cornet	64 sub
Loren	Little	cornet	64
Kenneth	McClain	cornet	64
Leon	Miller	cornet	64 sub
Jack	Rembold	cornet	64
David	Wegner	cornet	64
Jodie's Dance Studio		dance group	64 guest
Tanglefoot Dance Studio		dance group	64 guest
Richard	Flisrand	euphonium	64 sub
Robert	Frick	euphonium	64
Wayne	Krumrei	euphonium	64
Robert	Ortman	euphonium	64
Kathy	Hays Emmel	flute	64
Marilyn	Loomis Hansen	flute	64
Scott	Faragher	horn	64
John	Fenner	horn	64 sub
Donald	McCabe	horn	64
Robert	McDowell	horn	64
Russell	Tiede	horn	64 part time
Doug	Dean	inst. soloist, cornet	64 guest
Kathy	Hays Emmel	librarian	64
Ed	Paul	MC	64
A. Richard	Petersen	MC	64 guest
Jurgen	Schuller	oboe	64
Alfred	Boysen	percussion	64 sub
Robert	Doescher	percussion	64
Stan	Eitreim	percussion	64
Paul	Hoy	percussion	64
Paul	Skattum	percussion	64
Rich	Stevenson	percussion	64 sub
Glen	Trunnell	sax	64 sub
James	Burge	sax, alto	64 sub
John Tom	Dempster	sax, alto	64
Kenneth	Busse	sax, baritone	64
Everton	Little	sax, tenor	64
Verne	Wortman	sax/clarinet	64 sub
George	Hering	sound	64
Paul	Bankson	trombone	64
Robert	Hansen	trombone	64 sub
Harold	Hoover, Jr.	trombone	64
Keith	Knoff	trombone	64
Ronald	McGaughey	trombone	64
Philip	Miller	trombone	64
Stuart	Ruud ?	trombone	64 sub?
Harvey	Eichmeier	tuba	64
Harry	Ellis	tuba	64
George	Runyan	tuba	64 part time
Janine	Johnson	twirler	64 guest
Nancy	Mehlum	twirler	64 guest
American Legion Aux. 6		vocal group	64 guest
Singing Plainsmen (Canova, South Dakota)		vocal group	64 guest
Ed	Paul	vocal soloist	64
Marciene	Swenson Matthius	vocal soloist	64
Paul	Wegner, Sr.	vocal soloist	64 guest

Sioux Falls Municipal Band Personnel 1965 (46th season)
Dr. Leland A. Lillehaug, Conductor

Harold	Gray	bass clarinet	65
Steven	Olson	bassoon	65
Gustav	Schuller	bassoon	65
Milt	Askew	clarinet	65 sub
John Tom	Dempster	clarinet	65
Robert L.	Hanson	clarinet	65
Rex	Hays	clarinet	65 sub
Stan	Hays	clarinet	65 sub
Gary	Hoiseth	clarinet	65
Oscar	Loe	clarinet	65
John	Mattice	clarinet	65
Ralph	Olsen, Jr.	clarinet	65

Richard	Peik	clarinet	65
Dan	Runyan	clarinet	65 sub
Ralph	Tyler	clarinet	65
Jeff	Wold	clarinet	65
Leland	Lillehaug	conductor	65
Russ	Henegar	conductor, guest	65 guest
Del	Bickel	cornet	65
Paul	Davoux	cornet	65 part time
Clifford	Dyvig	cornet	65 sub
George	Gulson	cornet	65
Robert	Holyer	cornet	65
Danny	Kealey	cornet	65 sub
Harold	Krueger	cornet	65 sub
Loren	Little	cornet	65
Kenneth	McClain	cornet	65
Leon	Miller	cornet	65 sub
Jack	Rembold	cornet	65
David	Wegner	cornet	65 sub
Tanglefoot Dance Studio		dance group	65 guest
Robert	Hansen	euphonium	65
Robert	Ortman	euphonium	65
Kathy	Hays Emmel	flute	65
Marilyn	Loomis Hansen	flute	65
Linda	Olson	flute	65 sub
Scott	Faragher	horn	65
Stephen	Heetland	horn	65
Donald	McCabe	horn	65
Robert	McDowell	horn	65
Russell	Tiede	horn	65 sub
Kathy	Hays Emmel	librarian	65
Dave	Dedrick	MC	65 guest
Paul	Wegner, Sr.	MC	65
Ray	Loftesness	MC?	65 guest
Jurgen	Schuller	oboe	65
Alfred	Boysen	percussion	65
Robert	Doescher	percussion	65
Stan	Eitreim	percussion	65
Paul	Hoy	percussion	65
Paul	Skattum	percussion	65
Rich	Stevenson	percussion	65 sub
Tom	Little	sax	65 sub
Robert J.	Barnett	sax, alto	65
James	Burge	sax, alto	65 sub
Keith	Peterson	sax, alto	65
Kenneth	Busse	sax, baritone	65
Everton	Little	sax, tenor	65
Joel	Gaalswyck	sound	65
George	Hering	sound	65 sub
Paul	Bankson	trombone	65
Tom	Ellwein	trombone	65 sub
Dick	Heinemeyer	trombone	65 sub
Harold	Hoover, Jr.	trombone	65 part time
Keith	Knoff	trombone	65
Ronald	McGaughey	trombone	65
Philip	Miller	trombone	65 sub
Harvey	Eichmeier	tuba	65
Harry	Ellis	tuba	65
George	Runyan	tuba	65
James	Ode	inst. soloist, cornet	65 guest
Nancy	Mehlum	twirler	65 guest
Kathleen	Arend	vocal soloist	65 guest
Roger	Blunk	vocal soloist	65 guest
Kristine	Farkas	vocal soloist	65 guest
Eugenia Orlich	Hartig	vocal soloist	65
Mary Ann	Hohman	vocal soloist	65 guest
Hope	Mosher	vocal soloist	65 guest
Gary	Sona	vocal soloist	65 guest
Marciene	Swenson Matthius	vocal soloist	65 guest
Paul	Wegner, Sr.	vocal soloist	65
Anton "Tony"	Javurek	whistler	65 guest

Sioux Falls Municipal Band Personnel 1966 (47th season)
Dr. Leland A. Lillehaug, Conductor

Harold	Gray	bass clarinet	66
Steven	Olson	bassoon	66
Gustav	Schuller	bassoon	66
Milt	Askew	clarinet	66 sub
Robert L.	Hanson	clarinet	66
Sam	Hasegawa	clarinet	66
Gary	Hoiseth	clarinet	66
Oscar	Loe	clarinet	66 part time
John	Mattice	clarinet	66
Ralph	Olsen, Jr.	clarinet	66
Richard	Peik	clarinet	66
Mary	Perrenoud	clarinet	66
Keith	Peterson	clarinet	66
Dan	Runyan	clarinet	66
Gary	Schaefer	clarinet	66
Ann	Stauffer Flisrand	clarinet	66 sub fall
Jeff	Wold	clarinet	66 sub
Leland	Lillehaug	conductor	66
Del	Bickel	cornet	66
Paul	Davoux	cornet	66 sub
Doug	Dean	cornet	66
George	Gulson	cornet	66
Harold	Krueger	cornet	66
Terry	McCabe	cornet	66
Kenneth	McClain	cornet	66
Leon	Miller	cornet	66 sub
Jack	Rembold	cornet	66
David	Wegner	cornet	66 sub
Dance Quartet		dance group	66 guest
Dody Thill Dancers		dance group	66 guest
Tanglefoot Dance Studio		dance group	66 guest
Richard	Flisrand	euphonium	66 part time
Robert	Hansen	euphonium	66 sub
Dennis	Hegg	euphonium	66 sub
Robert	Ortman	euphonium	66
Mary	Ellefson	flute	66 sub
Marilyn	Loomis Hansen	flute	66 sub
Linda	Olson	flute	66
Ann	Palmer Faragher	flute	66
Scott	Faragher	horn	66
Stephen	Heetland	horn	66
Barbara J.	Johnson Hegg	horn	66
Donald	McCabe	horn	66
Robert	McDowell	horn	66
Barbara J.	Johnson Hegg	librarian	66
Ray	Loftesness	MC	66 guest
A. Richard	Petersen	MC	66 guest
Paul	Wegner, Sr.	MC	66
Jurgen	Schuller	oboe	66
Robert	Doescher	percussion	66
Stan	Eitreim	percussion	66
Paul	Hoy	percussion	66
Gary	Nelson	percussion	66
Paul	Skattum	percussion	66
Robert J.	Barnett	sax, alto	66
David L.	Johnson	sax, alto	66
Kenneth	Busse	sax, baritone	66
Everton	Little	sax, tenor	66
Robert D.	Raker	sound	66
Paul	Bankson	trombone	66
Tom	Ellwein	trombone	66
Keith	Knoff	trombone	66
James	Limburg	trombone	66 sub
Ronald	McGaughey	trombone	66 part time
Paul	Reeg	trombone	66
Glen (Dr.)	Stocking	trombone	66 sub
Harvey	Eichmeier	tuba	66

Harry	Ellis	tuba	66
George	Runyan	tuba	66
Janine	Johnson	twirler	66 guest
Nancy	Mehlum	twirler	66 guest
WHS twirling duet		twirler	66 guest
Ray	Loftesness	vocal duet	66 guest
Eugenia Orlich	Hartig	vocal soloist	66
A. Richard	Petersen	vocal soloist	66 guest
Gary	Sona	vocal soloist	66 guest
Paul	Wegner, Sr.	vocal soloist	66

Sioux Falls Municipal Band Personnel 1967 (48th season)
Dr. Leland A. Lillehaug, Conductor

Harold	Gray	bass clarinet	67
Steven	Olson	bassoon	67 sub
Gustav	Schuller	bassoon	67
Robert L.	Hanson	clarinet	67 sub
Sam	Hasegawa	clarinet	67 sub
Gary	Hoiseth	clarinet	67
Oscar	Loe	clarinet	67 part time
John	Mattice	clarinet	67
Ralph	Olsen, Jr.	clarinet	67
Richard	Peik	clarinet	67
Mary	Perrenoud	clarinet	67
Keith	Peterson	clarinet	67
Dan	Runyan	clarinet	67
Gary	Schaefer	clarinet	67
Ann	Stauffer Flisrand	clarinet	67
Susan	Winter	clarinet	67 sub
Lon	Wright	clarinet	67
Leland	Lillehaug	conductor	67
John D.	Buus	conductor, guest	67 guest
Leo	Kucinski	conductor, guest	67 guest
Del	Bickel	cornet	67
Paul	Davoux	cornet	67 part time
Ray	DeVilbiss	cornet	67 sub
Doug	Dean	cornet	67
George	Gulson	cornet	67
Paul	Hanson	cornet	67 sub
Danny	Kealey	cornet	67 sub
Harold	Krueger	cornet	67
Loren	Little	cornet	67 sub
Terry	McCabe	cornet	67
Kenneth	McClain	cornet	67
Leon	Miller	cornet	67 sub
Jack	Rembold	cornet	67 sub
Tanglefoot Dance Studio		dance group	67 guest
Richard	Flisrand	euphonium	67 sub
Dennis	Hegg	euphonium	67
Earl	Sherburne	euphonium	67 part time
Robert	Schoppert	euphonium	67 sub
Kathy	Hays Emmel	flute	67
Linda	Olson	flute	67
Ann	Palmer Faragher	flute	67
Scott	Faragher	horn	67
Greg	Helland	horn	67
Barbara J.	Johnson Hegg	horn	67
Linda	Johnson	horn	67 sub
Donald	McCabe	horn	67
Robert	McDowell	horn	67
Steve	Seim	horn	67 sub
Barbara J.	Johnson Hegg	librarian	67
Paul	Wegner, Sr.	MC	67
Ray	Loftesness	MC	67 guest
Don	Olson	oboe	67
Jurgen	Schuller	oboe	67
Jon	Berg	percussion	67 sub
Robert	Doescher	percussion	67
Stan	Eitreim	percussion	67

Paul	Hoy	percussion	67
Jon	Jonsson	percussion	67 sub
Gary	Nelson	percussion	67
David	Johnson	sax	67 sub
Keith	Peterson	sax	67 sub
Glen	Trunnell	sax	67 sub
Jolayne	Owen	sax	67 sub
Robert J.	Barnett	sax, alto	67 part time
James	Burge	sax, alto	67 sub
Everton	Little	sax, alto	67
Kenneth	Busse	sax, baritone	67
Lon	Wright	sax, tenor	67 sub (see clar.)
Harry	Ellis	sound	67
Joel	Gaalswyk	sound	67 sub
Robert	Raker	sound	67 sub
Hans	Arlton	trombone	67
Paul	Bankson	trombone	67
Tom	Ellwein	trombone	67
Keith	Knoff	trombone	67 sub
Paul	Reeg	trombone	67
Harvey	Eichmeier	tuba	67
Wayne	Krumrei	tuba	67
George	Runyan	tuba	67
Janine	Johnson	twirler	67 guest
Eugenia Orlich	Hartig	vocal soloist	67
Marciene	Swenson Matthius	vocal soloist	67 guest
Paul	Wegner, Sr.	vocal soloist	67

Sioux Falls Municipal Band Personnel 1968 (49th season)
Dr. Leland A. Lillehaug, Conductor

Pat	Stringham	bass clarinet	68
Lon	Wright	bass clarinet	68
Steven	Olson	bassoon	68
Gustav	Schuller	bassoon	68
Mindy	Braithwaite	bassoon	68 sub
Pat	Anderson	clarinet	68 sub fall
Earl	Colgan, Jr.	clarinet	68 part time
Richard	Flisrand	clarinet	68
Sam	Hasegawa	clarinet	68 sub
Rex	Hays	clarinet	68 sub
Gary	Hoiseth	clarinet	68
James	Johnston	clarinet	68 sub
Ralph	Olsen, Jr.	clarinet	68 part time
Mary	Perrenoud	clarinet	68
Keith	Peterson	clarinet	68 sub
Dan	Runyan	clarinet	68
Gary	Schaefer	clarinet	68
Ann	Stauffer Flisrand	clarinet	68
Susan	Winter	clarinet	68
Leland	Lillehaug	conductor	68
Del	Bickel	cornet	68
Doug	Dean	cornet	68
Merridee	Ekstrom	cornet	68
George	Gulson	cornet	68
Paul	Hanson	cornet	68
Danny	Kealey	cornet	68 sub
Harold	Krueger	cornet	68 part time
Loren	Little	cornet	68 part time
Terry	McCabe	cornet	68
Leon	Miller	cornet	68 sub
Tanglefoot Dance Studio		dance group	68 guest
Mark	Aspaas	euphonium	68
Michael	Olson	euphonium	68 sub
Robert	Schoppert	euphonium	68
Mary	Ellefson	flute	68 sub
Patricia	Masek	flute	68
Linda	Mitchell	flute	68 sub
Jane	Ordal	flute	68
Jane	Townswick	flute	68

Donald	Harris	horn	68 sub Nov.
Greg	Helland	horn	68
Linda	Johnson	horn	68
Barbara J.	Johnson Hegg	horn	68
Donald	McCabe	horn	68
Robert	McDowell	horn	68
Maureen	Warren	horn	68 part time
Doug	Dean	librarian	68
Ray	Loftesness	MC	68 guest
Paul	Wegner, Sr.	MC	68
Ove	Hanson	oboe	68 sub
Oscar	Loe	oboe	68
Don	Olson	oboe	68
Jon	Berg	percussion	68 part time
Robert	Doescher	percussion	68
Connie	Helland	percussion	68 sub
Randy	Hink	percussion	68
Paul	Hoy	percussion	68
Jon	Jonsson	percussion	68
Gary	Nelson	percussion	68 sub
James	Waring	percussion	68 sub
Milt	Askew	sax	68 sub
Glen	Trunnell	sax	68 sub
Robert J.	Barnett	sax, alto	68
Jolayne	Owen Hanson	sax, alto	68
Kenneth	Busse	sax, baritone	68
Everton	Little	sax, tenor	68
Harry	Ellis	sound	68
Hans	Arlton	trombone	68
Paul	Bankson	trombone	68
Tom	Ellwein	trombone	68
David	Mitchell	trombone	68 sub
Jeffrey "Rock"	Nelson	trombone	68 sub
Paul	Reeg	trombone	68
Scott	Stroman	trombone	68 sub
Harvey	Eichmeier	tuba	68
Dennis	Hegg	tuba	68
Wayne	Krumrei	tuba	68
James	Piechowski	tuba	68 sub
Eugenia Orlich	Hartig	vocal soloist	68
Betty (Mrs. August)	Hoeger	vocal soloist	68 guest
Paul	Wegner, Sr.	vocal soloist	68

Sioux Falls Municipal Band Personnel 1969 (50th season)
Dr. Harold Krueger and Donald McCabe, acting conductors

Lon	Wright	bass clarinet	69
Mindy	Braithwaite	bassoon	69
Gustav	Schuller	bassoon	69
Richard	Flisrand	clarinet	69 part time
Kathy	Gerry	clarinet	69 sub
Harold	Gray	clarinet	69
Sheila	Haraldson	clarinet	69
Gary	Hoiseth	clarinet	69
James	Johnston	clarinet	69
Anne	Juul	clarinet	69 sub
Carine	Oster	clarinet	69
Dan	Runyan	clarinet	69
Keith	Sanborn	clarinet	69
Gary	Schaefer	clarinet	69
Joe	Seidel	clarinet	69 sub
Ann	Stauffer Flisrand	clarinet	69 sub
Mark	Wessman	clarinet	69
Harold	Krueger	co-conductor	69
Donald	McCabe	co-conductor	69
Leland	Lillehaug	conductor (on leave)	69
Del	Bickel	cornet	69
Duane	Cook	cornet	69
Doug	Dean	cornet	69
Merridee	Ekstrom	cornet	69

George	Gulson	cornet	69
Paul	Hanson	cornet	69 part time
David	Krueger	cornet	69
Harold	Krueger	cornet	69 part time
Terry	McCabe	cornet	69
Leon	Miller	cornet	69 sub
Tanglefoot Dance Studio		dance group	69 guest
Bruce	Bahnson	euphonium	69 part time
Michael	Olson	euphonium	69
Robert	Ortman	euphonium	69 sub
Robert	Schoppert	euphonium	69 sub
Mary	Ellefson	flute	69
Patricia	Masek	flute	69
Linda	Mitchell	flute	69 part time
Douglas	Olawsky	flute	69 sub
Jane	Townswick	flute	69 sub
Donna	Van Bockern Krueger	flute	69
Donald	Harris	horn	69
Greg	Helland	horn	69
Linda	Johnson	horn	69
Donald	McCabe	horn	69 part time
Robert	McDowell	horn	69 sub
Maureen	Warren	horn	69 part time
Barbara J.	Johnson Hegg ?	librarian	69?
Paul	Wegner, Sr.	MC	69
Ove	Hanson	oboe	69
Shari	Plienis	oboe	69
Robert	Doescher	percussion	69
Stan	Eitreim	percussion	69 sub
Connie	Helland	percussion	69
Randy	Hink	percussion	69
Paul	Hoy	percussion	69
Max	Oldham	percussion	69 sub
Milt	Askew	sax	69 sub
Oscar	Loe	sax	69 sub
Robert J.	Barnett	sax, alto	69 part time
Jolayne	Owen Hanson	sax, alto	69 part time
Kenneth	Busse	sax, baritone	69
Everton	Little	sax, tenor	69 part time
Mary	Warren	sax, tenor	69
Harry	Ellis	sound	69
Paul	Bankson	trombone	69
Tom	Ellwein	trombone	69
James	Limburg	trombone	69 part time
Jeffrey "Rock"	Nelson	trombone	69 sub
Scott	Shelsta	trombone	69
Scott	Stroman	trombone	69 sub
Harvey	Eichmeier	tuba	69
Wayne	Krumrei	tuba	69
Donald M.	Nelson	tuba	69
Marty	Braithwaite	vocal soloist	69 guest
Eugenia Orlich	Hartig	vocal soloist	69
Paul	Wegner, Sr.	vocal soloist	69

Sioux Falls Municipal Band Personnel 1970 (51st season)
Dr. Leland A. Lillehaug, Conductor

Colin	Olsen	bass clarinet	70
Lon	Wright	bass clarinet	70 part time
Mindy	Braithwaite	bassoon	70
Gustav	Schuller	bassoon	70 part time
Connie	Wombacker Blanchard	bassoon	70
Curtis	Braa	clarinet	70
Sheila	Haraldson	clarinet	70
Gary	Hoiseth	clarinet	70 sub
James	Johnston	clarinet	70
Anne	Juul	clarinet	70
Oscar	Loe	clarinet	70 part time
Nancy	Meyers	clarinet	70 sub
Natalie	Olson	clarinet	70

Suzanne	Prieb Olawsky	clarinet	70
Richard	Rath	clarinet	70 sub
Dan	Runyan	clarinet	70 part time
Gary	Schaefer	clarinet	70
Leland	Lillehaug	conductor	70
Del	Bickel	cornet	70
Doug	Dean	cornet	70 sub
Merridee	Ekstrom	cornet	70
David	Gudmastad	cornet	70
George	Gulson	cornet	70
David	Krueger	cornet	70
Harold	Krueger	cornet	70
Loren	Little	cornet	70
Jack	Reynolds	cornet	70 sub
Tanglefoot Dance Studio		dance group	70 guest
Mark	Meyers	euphonium	70 part time
Michael	Olson	euphonium	70
Robert	Ortman	euphonium	70
Robert	Schoppert	euphonium	70 sub
David	Lillehaug	flute	70
Patricia	Masek	flute	70
Doug	Olawsky	flute	70
Donna	Van Bockern Krueger	flute	70
Donald	Harris	horn	70 sub
Greg	Helland	horn	70
Deb	Johnson Helland	horn	70
Donald	McCabe	horn	70 on leave
Bryson	McHardy	horn	70
Maureen	Warren	horn	70
Paul	Wegner, Sr.	MC	70
Ove	Hanson	oboe	70
Jeff	Kull	oboe	70
Ron	Anderson	percussion	70 sub
Greg	Daniels	percussion	70
Robert	Doescher	percussion	70
Stan	Eitreim	percussion	70
Paul	Hoy	percussion	70
Max	Oldham	percussion	70 part time
Jeff	Wold	sax	70 sub
Kristi	Elgethun	sax, alto	70
Don	Newcomb	sax, alto	70
Ralph	Olsen	sax, alto	70 sub
Kenneth	Busse	sax, baritone	70
Everton	Little	sax, tenor	70 sub
Mary	Warren	sax, tenor	70
Harry	Ellis	sound	70
Lon	Alness	trombone	70
Paul	Bankson	trombone	70
Tom	Ellwein	trombone	70
David	Mitchell	trombone	70 sub
Paul	Reeg	trombone	70 sub
Scott	Shelsta	trombone	70
Scott	Stroman	trombone	70
Bruce	Bahnson	tuba	70
Jeff	Bowar	tuba	70
Wayne	Krumrei	tuba	70
Donald M.	Nelson	tuba	70 part time
Nancy	Mehlum	twirler	70 guest
American Legion Chorus		vocal group	70 guest
Joyce	Becker	vocal soloist	70 guest
Marty	Braithwaite	vocal soloist	70 guest
Eugenia Orlich	Hartig	vocal soloist	70
Suzanne	Prieb	vocal soloist	70 guest
Paul	Wegner, Sr.	vocal soloist	70

Sioux Falls Municipal Band Personnel 1971 (52nd season)
Dr. Leland A. Lillehaug, Conductor

Colin	Olsen	bass clarinet	71 sub
Mindy	Braithwaite	bassoon	71

Gustav	Schuller	bassoon	71
Curtis	Braa	clarinet	71 part time
Laura	Frakes	clarinet	71 part time
Gary	Hoiseth	clarinet	71
Anne	Juul	clarinet	71
Jean	Kopperud	clarinet	71
Peg	Larson Cummings	clarinet	71
Oscar	Loe	clarinet	71
Natalie	Olson	clarinet	71
Richard	Rath	clarinet	71
Gary	Schaefer	clarinet	71
Nancy	Veldhuizen	clarinet	71 sub
Leland	Lillehaug	conductor	71
David	Gudmastad	cornet	71
Merridee	Ekstrom	cornet	71
George	Gulson	cornet	71
James	Kirkeby	cornet	71
David	Krueger	cornet	71
Harold	Krueger	cornet	71
Loren	Little	cornet	71 sub
Jack	Rembold	cornet	71 sub
Jack	Reynolds	cornet	71
Michael	Olson	euphonium	71
Vinson	Weber	euphonium	71
David	Lillehaug	flute	71
Patricia	Masek	flute	71
Doug	Olawsky	flute	71 part time
Ann	Palmer Faragher	flute	71
Randy	Bingner	horn	71
Scott	Faragher	horn	71
Donald	Harris	horn	71
Greg	Helland	horn	71
Deb	Johnson Helland	horn	71
Tyrone	Greive	inst. soloist, violin	71 guest
James	Ode	inst. soloist, cornet	71 guest
Barbara J.	Johnson Hegg	librarian	71?
Paul	Wegner, Sr.	MC	71
Gene	White	MC	71 guest
Ove	Hanson	oboe	71
Jeff	Kull	oboe	71
Ron	Anderson	percussion	71 sub
Greg	Daniels	percussion	71
Stan	Eitreim	percussion	71
Paul	Hoy	percussion	71
Keith	Wright	percussion	71
Ron	Anderson	percussion	71 sub
Ralph	Olsen, Jr.	sax	71 sub
Mary	Warren	sax	71
Kristi	Elgethun	sax, alto	71 part time
Don	Newcomb	sax, alto?	71
Everton	Little	sax, baritone?	71 part time
James	Albright	sax, tenor?	71
Harry	Ellis	sound	71
Lon	Alness	trombone	71
Paul	Bankson	trombone	71
Tom	Ellwein	trombone	71
James	Limburg	trombone	71 sub
Paul	Reeg	trombone	71
Scott	Shelsta	trombone	71 sub
Scott	Stroman	trombone	71
Gene	White	trombone	71 sub
Alan	Berdahl	tuba	71
Jeff	Bowar	tuba	71
Paul	Runyan	tuba	71
Robert	Runyan	tuba	71
Nancy	Mehlum	twirler	71 guest
Eugenia Orlich	Hartig	vocal soloist	71
Pat	Hoffman	vocal soloist	71 guest
Paul	Wegner, Sr.	vocal soloist	71
Mary	Harum (Hart)	vocal soloist	71 guest

Marty	Braithwaite	vocal soloist	71 guest

Sioux Falls Municipal Band Personnel 1972 (53rd season)
Dr. Leland A. Lillehaug, Conductor

Oscar	Loe	asst. conductor	72
Garneth	Oldenkamp Peterson	bass clarinet	72
Mindy	Braithwaite	bassoon	72
Gustav	Schuller	bassoon	72
Laura	Frakes	clarinet	72
Thomas Daniel	Hartig	clarinet	72
Anne	Juul	clarinet	72
Peg	Larson Cummings	clarinet	72
Steven	Lillehaug	clarinet	72
Oscar	Loe	clarinet	72
Debra	Moe	clarinet	72
Cindy	Nelson	clarinet	72
Natalie	Olson	clarinet	72
Suzanne	Prieb Olawsky	clarinet	72
Leland	Lillehaug	conductor	72
Carol	Ackerman	cornet	72
Craig	Alberty	cornet	72 sub
Merridee	Ekstrom	cornet	72
George	Gulson	cornet	72
James	Kirkeby	cornet	72
David	Krueger	cornet	72
Harold	Krueger	cornet	72 sub
Jack	Rembold	cornet	72
Jack	Reynolds	cornet	72
Stuart	Evensen	euphonium	72 sub
Michael	Olson	euphonium	72
Vinson	Weber	euphonium	72
David	Lillehaug	flute	72
Patricia	Masek	flute	72
Doug	Olawsky	flute	72
Ann	Palmer Faragher	flute	72 sub
Randy	Bingner	horn	72
Tom	Braithwaite	horn	72 part time
Scott	Faragher	horn	72
Connie	Tornberg	horn	72
Gene	White	inst. soloist, trombone	72 guest
Doug	Olawsky	librarian	72
A. Richard	Petersen	MC	72 guest
Paul	Wegner, Sr.	MC	72
Ray	Loftesness	narrator	72 guest
Ove	Hanson	oboe	72 part time
Jeff	Kull	oboe	72
Richard	Rath	oboe	72 part time
Greg	Daniels	percussion	72
Stan	Eitreim	percussion	72
Jean	Hoiseth	percussion	72 part time
Paul	Hoy	percussion	72
James	Albright	sax, alto	72
Janet	Person	sax, alto	72
Mary	Temanson	sax, alto & tenor	72
Don	Newcomb	sax, baritone	72
Everton	Little	sax, tenor	72 sub
Harry	Ellis	sound	72
Lon	Alness	trombone	72
Paul	Bankson	trombone	72
Tom	Ellwein	trombone	72
David	Evenson	trombone	72
Jon	Matthews	trombone	72 sub
Paul	Reeg	trombone	72
Alan	Berdahl	tuba	72
Mark	Johnson	tuba	72 sub
Paul	Runyan	tuba	72
Robert	Runyan	tuba	72
Nancy	Mehlum	twirler	72 guest
Eugenia Orlich	Hartig	vocal soloist	72

Pat	Hoffman	vocal soloist	72 guest
Julie	Overseth	vocal soloist	72 guest
Paul	Wegner, Sr.	vocal soloist	72

Sioux Falls Municipal Band Personnel 1973 (54th season)
Dr. Leland A. Lillehaug, Conductor

Oscar	Loe	asst. conductor	73
Garneth	Oldenkamp Peterson	bass clarinet	73
Mindy	Braithwaite	bassoon	73
Connie	Wombacker Blanchard	bassoon	73
Thomas Daniel	Hartig	clarinet	73
Yvonne	Johnson	clarinet	73
Anne	Juul	clarinet	73
Steven	Lillehaug	clarinet	73
Oscar	Loe	clarinet	73
Linda	McLaren	clarinet	73
Natalie	Olson	clarinet	73
Suzanne	Prieb Olawsky	clarinet	73
Richard	Rath	clarinet	73
Mary	Rauk	clarinet	73
Gustav	Schuller	clarinet	73
Leland	Lillehaug	conductor	73
Merridee	Ekstrom	cornet	73
George	Gulson	cornet	73
David	Krueger	cornet	73
Harold	Krueger	cornet	73
Mark	Lotz	cornet	73
Leon	Miller	cornet	73 sub
Jack	Rembold	cornet	73
Jack	Reynolds	cornet	73
Kay	Shelsta	cornet	73 sub
Anna	Hamre	euphonium	73
Mary	Larson	euphonium	73 sub
Michael	Olson	euphonium	73
David	Lillehaug	flute	73
Patricia	Masek	flute	73
Doug	Olawsky	flute	73
Ann	Palmer Faragher	flute	73
Susan	Anderson	horn	73
Tom	Braithwaite	horn	73
Scott	Faragher	horn	73
Tom	Keleher	horn	73
Robert	McDowell	horn	73 sub
Connie	Roth	horn	73
Connie	Tornberg	horn	73
Ray	Loftesness	MC	73 guest
Paul	Wegner, Sr.	MC	73
Jeff	Kull	oboe	73
Kathy	Moe	oboe	73
Jean	Hoiseth	percussion	73
Paul	Hoy	percussion	73
Rick	Paulsen	percussion	73
Lynn	Peterson	percussion	73
James	Albright	sax, alto	73
Martha	Vegge Nelson	sax, alto	73
Patsy	Larson	sax, baritone	73
John	Roth	sax, tenor	73
Jon Richard	Erickson	showmobile asst.	73
Lynn	Peterson	showmobile asst.	73
Herbert	Parker	showmobile driver	73
Todd M.	Sorenson	showmobile driver	73
Harry	Ellis	sound	73
Paul	Bankson	trombone	73
David	Evenson	trombone	73
Jeffrey "Rock"	Nelson	trombone	73 sub
Paul	Reeg	trombone	73
Scott	Shelsta	trombone	73
Alan	Berdahl	tuba	73
Paul	Runyan	tuba	73

Gregory	Smith	tuba	73
Deb	Jacobs	twirler	73 guest
Marty	Braithwaite	vocal soloist	73 guest
Eugenia Orlich	Hartig	vocal soloist	73
Paul	Wegner, Sr.	vocal soloist	73
Anton "Tony"	Javurek	whistler	73 guest

Sioux Falls Municipal Band Personnel 1974 (55th season)
Dr. Leland A. Lillehaug, Conductor

Oscar	Loe	asst. conductor	74
Mindy	Braithwaite	bassoon	74
Laurel	Paulson	bassoon	74
Barb	Gilchrist	clarinet	74 part time
Thomas Daniel	Hartig	clarinet	74
Anne	Juul	clarinet	74
Arlene	Kleinsasser	clarinet	74
Jackie	Larsen	clarinet	74 part time
Steven	Lillehaug	clarinet	74
Oscar	Loe	clarinet	74
Linda	McLaren	clarinet	74
Natalie	Olson	clarinet	74
Mary	Rauk	clarinet	74
Janice	Trumm	clarinet	74
Leland	Lillehaug	conductor	74
Tom	Bierer	cornet	74
Ray	DeVilbiss	cornet	74 sub
Merridee	Ekstrom	cornet	74
George	Gulson	cornet	74
Danny	Kealey	cornet	74 sub
David	Krueger	cornet	74
Harold	Krueger	cornet	74
Leon	Miller	cornet	74 sub
Mark	Lotz	cornet	74
Jack	Rembold	cornet	74 part time
Jack	Reynolds	cornet	74 sub
Loren	Fodness	euphonium	74
Robert	Ortman	euphonium	74
David	Lillehaug	flute	74 sub
Patricia	Masek	flute	74
Ann	Palmer Faragher	flute	74
Donna	Van Bockern Krueger	flute	74
Susan	Anderson	horn	74
Tom	Braithwaite	horn	74 part time
Michael	Engh	horn	74
Scott	Faragher	horn	74
Tom	Keleher	horn	74 part time
Robert	McDowell	horn	74
Connie	Roth	horn	74
Mark	Lotz	librarian	74?
Linda	McLaren	librarian	74
Steve	Rinder	MC	74 guest
Paul	Wegner, Sr.	MC	74
Jeff	Kull	oboe	74
Kathy	Moe	oboe	74
Greg	Daniels	percussion	74 sub
Rob	Ferrell	percussion	74 part time
Jean	Hoiseth	percussion	74 sub
Paul	Hoy	percussion	74
Rick	Paulsen	percussion	74
Lynn	Peterson	percussion	74 sub
Jean	Pinard	percussion	74
Patsy	Larson Holzwarth	sax	74 sub
Everton	Little	sax	74 sub
James	Albright	sax, alto	74 sub
Terry	Walter	sax, alto	74
Martha	Vegge Nelson	sax, alto	74
Sandra	Person McAllister	sax, baritone	74
John	Roth	sax, tenor	74
Loren	Fodness	showmobile asst.	74

Herbert	Parker	showmobile driver	74
Tom	Block	sound	74
Paul	Bankson	trombone	74
David	Evenson	trombone	74 sub
Paula	Jorgensen	trombone	74
Jeffrey "Rock"	Nelson	trombone	74 sub
Paul	Reeg	trombone	74
Kathy	Schmidt	trombone	74
Alan	Berdahl	tuba	74
Stan	Eitreim	tuba	74
Mark	Johnson	tuba	74 sub
David	Joyce	tuba	74
Paul	Runyan	tuba	74 sub
Mike	Seto	tuba	74 sub
Greg	Smith	tuba	74 sub
James	Taylor	tuba	74 part time
Diana	Borgum	vocal soloist	74 guest
Eugenia Orlich	Hartig	vocal soloist	74
Shirleen	Peterson	vocal soloist	74 guest
Paul	Wegner, Sr.	vocal soloist	74

Sioux Falls Municipal Band Personnel 1975 (56th season)
Dr. Leland A. Lillehaug, Conductor

Oscar	Loe	asst. conductor	75
Linda	McLaren Faragher	bass clarinet	75
Mindy	Braithwaite	bassoon	75
Laurel	Paulson	bassoon	75
David	Amundson	clarinet	75
Kathy	Bangasser	clarinet	75
Barb	Boschee	clarinet	75 sub
Kenneth	Carpenter	clarinet	75 sub
Barb	Gilchrist	clarinet	75
Barbara	Hanson Johnson	clarinet	75
Thomas Daniel	Hartig	clarinet	75
Rosalie	Jorgensen	clarinet	75
Steven	Lillehaug	clarinet	75
Oscar	Loe	clarinet	75
Floyd	McClain	clarinet	75 sub
Kevin	Vaska	clarinet	75
Leland	Lillehaug	conductor	75
Terry	Anderson	cornet	75
Jeff	Bowen	cornet	75
Janet	Bruns Hallstrom	cornet	75
Ray	DeVilbiss	cornet	75 sub
Merridee	Ekstrom	cornet	75
George	Gulson	cornet	75
David	Krueger	cornet	75
Harold	Krueger	cornet	75
Leon	Miller	cornet	75 sub
James	Ode	cornet	75 sub
Jack	Reynolds	cornet	75 sub
Loren	Fodness	euphonium	75
Robert	Ortman	euphonium	75
Robyn	Lenker Runyan	flute	75 sub fall
David	Lillehaug	flute	75 sub
Patricia	Masek	flute	75
Ann	Palmer Faragher	flute	75
Donna	Van Bockern Krueger	flute	75
Susan	Anderson	horn	75
Tom	Braithwaite	horn	75
Michael	Engh	horn	75
Scott	Faragher	horn	75
Robert	McDowell	horn	75
Connie	Roth	horn	75
Pam	Hansen Barnard	librarian	75
Merridee	Ekstrom	library asst.	75
Steven	Lillehaug	library asst.	75
Terry	Walter	library asst.	75
Ray	Loftesness	MC	75 guest

Paul	Wegner, Sr.	MC	75
Jeff	Kull	oboe	75
Kathy	Moe	oboe	75
David	Price	oboe?	75 sub
Paul	Hoy	percussion	75
Julie	Kahl	percussion	75
Tom	Keleher	percussion	75
Jean	Pinard	percussion	75
Everton	Little	sax, alto	75 sub
James	McWayne	sax, alto	75
Martha	Vegge Nelson	sax, alto	75
Sandra	Person McAllister	sax, baritone	75
John	Roth	sax, tenor	75
Jeff	Bowen	showmobile asst.	75
Loren	Fodness	showmobile asst.	75
James	McWayne	showmobile asst.	75
Kevin	Vaska	showmobile asst.	75
Herb	Parker	showmobile driver	75
Todd M.	Sorensen	showmobile driver	75
Tom	Block	sound	75
Norma	Brick	staff (publicity)	75
Paul	Bankson	trombone	75
Tom	Ellwein	trombone	75 sub
Paula	Jorgensen	trombone	75
Paul	Reeg	trombone	75
Kathy	Schmidt	trombone	75
Stan	Eitreim	tuba	75
David	Joyce	tuba	75
Paul	Runyan	tuba	75
Michael	Seto	tuba	75
Ray	Loftesness	vocal duet	75 guest
American Legion Chorus		vocal group	75 guest
Diana	Borgum	vocal soloist	75 guest
Betsy	Doyle	vocal soloist	75 guest
Eugenia Orlich	Hartig	vocal soloist	75
Olaf	Malmin	vocal soloist	75 guest
Dean	Schultz	vocal soloist	75 guest
Ruth	Tobin	vocal soloist	75 guest
Paul	Wegner, Sr.	vocal soloist	75
Anton "Tony"	Javurek	whistler	75?guest

Sioux Falls Municipal Band Personnel 1976 (57th season)
Dr. Leland A. Lillehaug, Conductor

Oscar	Loe	asst. conductor	76
Linda	McLaren Faragher	bass clarinet	76
Mindy	Braithwaite	bassoon	76
Laurel	Paulson	bassoon	76
David	Amundson	clarinet	76
Mary	Avery	clarinet	76
Kathy	Bangasser	clarinet	76
Lori	Blauwet	clarinet	76
Barbara	Boschee	clarinet	76
Kenneth	Carpenter	clarinet	76 sub
Barb	Gilchrist	clarinet	76
Barbara	Hanson Johnson	clarinet	76
Charlotte	Hedeen	clarinet	76
Steven	Lillehaug	clarinet	76
Oscar	Loe	clarinet	76
Janice	Trumm	clarinet	76
Kevin	Vaska	clarinet	76
Terry	Walter	clarinet	76
Leland	Lillehaug	conductor	76
Terry	Anderson	cornet	76
Jeff	Bowen	cornet	76
Janet	Bruns Hallstrom	cornet	76
Merridee	Ekstrom	cornet	76
George	Gulson	cornet	76
David	Krueger	cornet	76
Harold	Krueger	cornet	76

Clayton	Lehmann	cornet	76
Leon	Miller	cornet	76 sub
Dennis	Hegg	euphonium	76
Jeff	McAllister	euphonium	76
Pam	Hansen Barnard	flute	76
Robyn	Lenker Runyan	flute	76 sub 3-22
David	Lillehaug	flute	76
Patricia	Masek	flute	76
Donna	Van Bockern Krueger	flute	76 sub
Susan	Anderson	horn	76
Tom	Braithwaite	horn	76
Michael	Engh	horn	76 part time
Scott	Faragher	horn	76
Robert	McDowell	horn	76
Connie	Roth	horn	76
Pam	Hansen Barnard	librarian	76
Merridee	Ekstrom	library asst.	76
David	Lillehaug	library asst.	76
Steven	Lillehaug	library asst.	76
Terry	Walter	library asst.	76
Paul	Wegner, Sr.	MC	76
Ray	Loftesness	narrator	76 guest
Jeff	Kull	oboe	76
Kathy	Moe	oboe	76
Greg	Daniels	percussion	76 sub
Paul	Hoy	percussion	76
Julie	Kahl	percussion	76
Tom	Keleher	percussion	76
Jean	Pinard	percussion	76
Floyd	McClain	sax	76 sub
James	McWayne	sax, alto	76
Martha	Vegge Nelson	sax, alto	76
Sandra	Person McAllister	sax, baritone	76
John	Roth	sax, tenor	76
Jeff	Bowen	showmobile asst.	76
James	McWayne	showmobile asst.	76
Herb	Parker	showmobile driver	76
Todd M.	Sorensen	showmobile driver	76
Tom	Block	sound	76
Paul	Bankson	trombone	76
Laurel	Cluts	trombone	76
Paula	Jorgensen	trombone	76
Paul	Reeg	trombone	76
Greg	Duerksen	tuba	76
Stan	Eitreim	tuba	76
David	Joyce	tuba	76
Paul	Runyan	tuba	76 sub
Michael	Seto	tuba	76
American Legion Chorus		vocal group	76 guest
Bicentential Choir		vocal group	76 guest
Diana	Borgum	vocal soloist	76 guest
Eugenia Orlich	Hartig	vocal soloist	76
Olaf	Malmin	vocal soloist	76 guest
Shirlene	Peterson	vocal soloist	76 guest
Ruth	Tobin	vocal soloist	76 guest
Paul	Wegner, Sr.	vocal soloist	76

Sioux Falls Municipal Band Personnel 1977 (58th season)
Dr. Leland A. Lillehaug, Conductor

Oscar	Loe	asst. conductor	77
Linda	McLaren Faragher	bass clarinet	77
Rahn	Anderson	bassoon	77
Laurel	Paulson	bassoon	77
Connie	Wombacker Blanchard	bassoon	77 sub
David	Amundson	clarinet	77
Mary	Avery	clarinet	77
Kathy	Bangasser	clarinet	77
Gayle	Becker	clarinet	77
Lori	Blauwet	clarinet	77

Barbara	Boschee	clarinet	77
Barbara	Hanson Johnson	clarinet	77
Charlotte	Hedeen	clarinet	77
Steven	Lillehaug	clarinet	77
Oscar	Loe	clarinet	77
Kevin	Vaska	clarinet	77
Leland	Lillehaug	conductor	77
Terry	Anderson	cornet	77 sub
Tom	Bierer	cornet	77
Jeff	Bowen	cornet	77 sub
Kellie	Brinkman	cornet	77
Janet	Bruns Hallstrom	cornet	77
Merridee	Ekstrom	cornet	77
George	Gulson	cornet	77
David	Krueger	cornet	77
Harold	Krueger	cornet	77
Clayton	Lehmann	cornet	77 sub
Leon	Miller	cornet	77 sub
Jack	Reynolds	cornet	77 sub
Carl	Hallstrom	euphonium	77
Mary	Larson	euphonium	77 sub
Dennis	Hegg	euphonium	77 sub
Jeff	McAllister	euphonium	77 part time
Pam	Hansen Barnard	flute	77 sub
Mary	Jensen Ryrholm	flute	77
David	Lillehaug	flute	77 sub
Patricia	Masek	flute	77
Donna	Van Bockern Krueger	flute	77
Anna	Vorhes	harp	77 guest
Susan	Anderson	horn	77
Vonnie	Endahl	horn	77
Michael	Engh	horn	77
Scott	Faragher	horn	77
Robert	McDowell	horn	77 sub
Beth	Meester	horn	77 sub
Mary	Jensen Ryrholm	librarian	77
Mary	Avery	library asst.	77
Kathy	Bangasser	library asst.	77
Merridee	Ekstrom	library asst.	77
Paul	Wegner, Sr.	MC	77
Ray	Loftesness	narrator	77 guest
Mary	Auen	oboe	77
Jeff	Kull	oboe	77
Jeanette	Paulson	oboe	77 sub
Paul	Hoy	percussion	77
Julie	Kahl	percussion	77
Tom	Keleher	percussion	77 part time
Ralph	Olawsky	percussion	77
Robert	Patterson	percussion	77 part time
Luanne	Warner	percussion	77 sub
Jeanette	Paulson	publicity	77
Everton	Little	sax, alto	77 sub
Martha	Vegge Nelson	sax, alto	77
Terry	Walter	sax, alto	77
Sandra	Person McAllister	sax, baritone	77 part time
James	McWayne	sax, baritone	77 part time
Gary	Tanouye	sax, tenor	77
Michael	Engh	showmobile asst.	77
Steven	Lillehaug	showmobile asst.	77
Kevin	Vaska	showmobile asst.	77 sub
Herbert	Parker	showmobile driver	77
Todd M.	Sorenson	showmobile driver	77
Tom	Block	sound	77
Paul	Bankson	trombone	77
Laurel	Cluts	trombone	77
Tom	Ellwein	trombone	77 sub
Paula	Jorgensen	trombone	77
Jeffrey	Nelson	trombone	77 sub
Paul	Reeg	trombone	77
Alan	Berdahl	tuba	77

Stan	Eitreim	tuba	77
David	Joyce	tuba	77
Doug	Lee	tuba	77 sub
Mike	Seto	tuba	77 sub
Brenda	Polzin	twirler	77 guest
Linda	Polzin	twirler	77 guest
Diana	Borgum	vocal soloist	77 guest
Eugenia Orlich	Hartig	vocal soloist	77
Joyce	Nauen	vocal soloist	77 guest
Ruth	Tobin	vocal soloist	77 guest
Paul	Wegner, Sr.	vocal soloist	77

Sioux Falls Municipal Band Personnel 1978 (59th season)
Dr. Leland A. Lillehaug, Conductor

Oscar	Loe	asst. conductor	78
Linda	McLaren Faragher	bass clarinet	78
Mindy	Braithwaite	bassoon	78 part time
Carol	Buckwalter Pederson	bassoon	78 part time
Laurel	Paulson	bassoon	78
Susan	Ackerman	clarinet	78
Mary	Avery	clarinet	78
Kathy	Bangasser	clarinet	78
Barbara	Boschee	clarinet	78
Cathy	Clausen	clarinet	78 sub
Barb	Gilchrist	clarinet	78 sub
Marlene	Graber	clarinet	78
Barbara	Hanson Johnson	clarinet	78
Charlotte	Hedeen	clarinet	78
Steven	Lillehaug	clarinet	78 sub
Oscar	Loe	clarinet	78
Donna	Schettler Hoogendoorn	clarinet	78
Lorie	Simon	clarinet	78
Kevin	Vaska	clarinet	78
Terry	Walter	clarinet	78
Leland	Lillehaug	conductor	78
Tom	Bierer	cornet	78
Kellie	Brinkman	cornet	78
Janet	Bruns Hallstrom	cornet	78
Merridee	Ekstrom	cornet	78
David Walter	Erickson	cornet	78
George	Gulson	cornet	78
David	Krueger	cornet	78
Harold	Krueger	cornet	78
Doug	Lehrer	cornet	78 sub
Leon	Miller	cornet	78 sub
Robin	Steinke	cornet	78 sub
Carl	Hallstrom	euphonium	78
Rick	Skatula	euphonium	78
Pam	Hansen Barnard	flute	78 sub
Mary	Jensen Ryrholm	flute	78
Patricia	Masek	flute	78
Donna	Van Bockern Krueger	flute	78
Susan	Anderson	horn	78
Vonnie	Endahl	horn	78
Michael	Engh	horn	78 sub
Scott	Faragher	horn	78
Kathy	Johnson	horn	78
Robert	McDowell	horn	78 sub
Gene	White	inst. soloist, trombone	78 guest
Mary	Jensen Ryrholm	librarian	78
Jeanette	Paulson	library asst.	78
Terry	Walter	library asst.	78
Laurie	Lillehaug	staff	78
Paul	Wegner, Sr.	MC	78
Diana	Borgum	narrator	78 guest
Cindy	Jurisson	oboe	78
Jeff	Kull	oboe	78 sub
Jeanette	Paulson	oboe	78
Mark	Bonfoey	percussion	78 sub

Paul	Hoy	percussion	78
Julie	Kahl	percussion	78
Elina	Ozolins	percussion	78 sub
Robert	Patterson	percussion	78
Luanne	Warner	percussion	78
Jeanette	Paulson	publicity	78
James	McWayne	sax, alto	78
Martha	Vegge Nelson	sax, alto	78
Ramona	Gustafson	sax, baritone	78
Everton	Little	sax, baritone	78 sub
Gary	Tanouye	sax, tenor	78
Tom	Bierer	showmobile asst.	78 sub
Carl	Hallstrom	showmobile asst.	78
Steven	Pfeiffer	showmobile asst.	78
Curtis	Anderson	showmobile driver	78
Herbert	Parker	showmobile driver	78
Tom	Bierer	sound	78 sub
Tom	Block	sound	78 sub
Steven	Lillehaug	sound	78
Kerchal	Armstrong	trombone	78 sub
Paul	Bankson	trombone	78
Laurel	Cluts	trombone	78
Jeffrey	Nelson	trombone	78 sub
Steven	Pfeiffer	trombone	78
Paul	Reeg	trombone	78
Alan	Berdahl	tuba	78
Stan	Eitreim	tuba	78
David	Joyce	tuba	78
Rolf	Muldbakken	tuba	78 sub
Eugenia Orlich	Hartig	vocal soloist	78
Cammy	Iseminger	vocal soloist	78 guest
Joyce	Nauen	vocal soloist	78 guest
Ruth	Tobin	vocal soloist	78 guest
Paul	Wegner, Sr.	vocal soloist	78

Sioux Falls Municipal Band Personnel 1979 (60th season)
Dr. Leland A. Lillehaug, Conductor

Linda	McLaren Faragher	bass clarinet	79
Lori	Quanbeck	bassoon	79 sub fall
Carol	Buckwalter Pederson	bassoon	79
Connie	Wombacker Blanchard	bassoon	79 sub
Laurel	Paulson	bassoon	79
Deb	Aning	clarinet	79
Mary	Avery	clarinet	79
Kathy	Bangasser	clarinet	79
Gayle	Becker	clarinet	79 part time
Lori	Blauwet	clarinet	79 sub
Kathy	Clausen	clarinet	79
Barb	Gilchrist	clarinet	79
Marlene	Graber	clarinet	79
Cathy	Green	clarinet	79 part time
Barbara	Hanson Johnson	clarinet	79
Kristi	Reierson	clarinet	79
Donna	Schettler Hoogendoorn	clarinet	79
Kevin	Vaska	clarinet	79
Teresa	Wells	clarinet	79
Leland	Lillehaug	conductor	79
Phil	Bajema	cornet	79 sub
Tom	Bierer	cornet	79 sub
Kellie	Brinkman	cornet	79
Janet	Bruns Hallstrom	cornet	79
Merridee	Ekstrom	cornet	79
George	Gulson	cornet	79 sub
David	Krueger	cornet	79
Harold	Krueger	cornet	79
Doug	Lehrer	cornet	79
Leon	Miller	cornet	79 sub
James	Perkins	cornet	79 sub
Robin	Steinke	cornet	79

Carl	Hallstrom	euphonium	79
Dennis	Hegg	euphonium	79 sub
Lois	Hendrix	euphonium	79
Martha	Barnett	flute	79 sub fall
Renee	Fillingsness	flute	79 sub
Mary	Jensen Ryrholm	flute	79
Patricia	Masek	flute	79
Donna	Van Bockern Krueger	flute	79
Susan	Anderson	horn	79
Vonnie	Endahl	horn	79 sub
Scott	Faragher	horn	79
Joan	Haugen	horn	79 sub
Kathy	Johnson	horn	79
Barbara J.	Johnson Hegg	horn	79 sub fall
Mary	McDonald	horn	79
Robert	McDowell	horn	79 sub
Mary	Jensen Ryrholm	librarian	79
Mary	Avery	library asst.	79
Jeanette	Paulson	library asst.	79
Terry	Walter	library asst.	79
Paul	Wegner, Sr.	MC	79
Jeff	Kull	oboe	79
Jeanette	Paulson	oboe	79
Daniel	Bailey	percussion	79
Dan	Hatfield	percussion	79 sub fall
David Charles	Hall	percussion	79
Paul	Hoy	percussion	79
Greg	Olsen	percussion	79 sub
Elina	Ozolins	percussion	79 sub
Robert	Patterson	percussion	79
Steven	Lillehaug	sax	79 sub
Everton	Little	sax	79 sub
Gary	Tanouye	sax	79 sub
Mary	Michael	sax, alto	79
Terry	Walter	sax, alto	79
James	McWayne	sax, baritone	79
Martha	Vegge Nelson	sax, tenor	79
David	Joyce	showmobile asst.	79
Steven	Pfeiffer	showmobile asst.	79
Brad	Widness	showmobile asst.	79
Gary	Hood	showmobile driver	79
Herbert	Parker	showmobile driver	79
Tom	Block	sound	79 sub
Evan	Jones	sound	79
Kerchal	Armstrong	trombone	79
Paul	Bankson	trombone	79
Faye	Fossum	trombone	79
Steven	Pfeiffer	trombone	79
Paul	Reeg	trombone	79 sub
Brad	Widness	trombone	79
Stan	Eitreim	tuba	79
David	Joyce	tuba	79
Rolf	Muldbakken	tuba	79 part time
Paul	Runyan	tuba	79 sub
Linda	Polzin	twirler	79 guest
Ann	Bryant Fisher	vocal soloist	79 guest
Eugenia Orlich	Hartig	vocal soloist	79
Dee	Hemphill	vocal soloist	79 guest
Linda	Lang	vocal soloist	79 guest
Tom	Steever	vocal soloist	79 guest
Marciene	Swenson Matthius	vocal soloist	79 guest
Paul	Wegner, Sr.	vocal soloist	79

Sioux Falls Municipal Band Personnel 1980 (61st season)
Dr. Leland A. Lillehaug, Conductor

Pat	Masek	assistant cond.	80
Linda	McLaren	bass clarinet	80
Carol	Buckwalter Pederson	bassoon	80
Robin	Doescher	bassoon	80 sub fall

Lori	Quanbeck	bassoon	80
Laurel	Paulson	bassoon	80 sub
Deb	Aning	clarinet	80
Mary	Avery	clarinet	80
Kathy	Bangasser	clarinet	80
Barb	Gilchrist	clarinet	80
Marlene	Graber	clarinet	80
Cathy	Green	clarinet	80
Barbara	Hanson Johnson	clarinet	80
Charlotte	Hedeen	clarinet	80
Jackie	Larsen	clarinet	80 sub fall
Kristi	Reierson	clarinet	80
Judy	Soukup	clarinet	80
Teresa	Wells	clarinet	80
Leland	Lillehaug	conductor	80
Butler	Eitel	conductor, guest	80 guest
Phil	Bajema	cornet	80 sub fall
Tom	Bierer	cornet	80
Kellie	Brinkman	cornet	80 sub
Janet	Bruns Hallstrom	cornet	80
Merridee	Ekstrom	cornet	80
George	Gulson	cornet	80
Gary	Holman	cornet	80 sub fall
Doug	Lehrer	cornet	80
Mark	Levsen	cornet	80 sub fall
Leon	Miller	cornet	80 sub
James	Perkins	cornet	80
Steve	Sommers	cornet	80 sub fall
Robin	Steinke	cornet	80
Polynesian Dance Troupe		dance	80 guest
Edie	Tunge	dance	80 guest
Mark	Aspaas	euphonium	80 sub
Mike	Dailey	euphonium	80 sub fall
Dennis	Hegg	euphonium	80
Lois	Hendrix	euphonium	80
Paul	Weikel	euphonium	80 sub fall
Martha	Barnett Lyons	flute	80
Mary	Jensen Ryrholm	flute	80
Patricia	Masek	flute	80
Pat	Penn	flute	80 sub
Scott	Faragher	horn	80
Curt	Hammond	horn	80
Joan	Haugen	horn	80
Barbara J.	Johnson Hegg	horn	80
Connie	Roth	horn	80 sub fall
Gina	Waltner Pfeiffer	horn	80
Sandra	Weikel	horn	80 sub fall
Butler	Eitel	inst. soloist, euphonium	80 guest
Warren	Hatfield	inst. soloist, alto saxophone	80 guest
Terry	Walter	librarian	80
Mary	Avery	library asst.	80
Laurel	Cluts	library asst.	80
Merridee	Ekstrom	library asst.	80
Mary	Jensen	library asst.	80
Laurie	Lillehaug	library asst.	80
Jeanette	Paulson	library asst.	80
Robin	Steinke	library asst.	80
Ray	Loftesness	MC	80
Claudia	Hasegawa	oboe	80
Jeanette	Paulson	oboe	80
Betty	Swanson	oboe	80 sub fall
Daniel	Bailey	percussion	80
Dan	Hatfield	percussion	80
Paul	Hoy	percussion	80
Eric	LeVan	percussion	80 sub fall
Robert	Niblick	percussion	80 sub
Loni	Winter	percussion	80
Jeanette	Paulson	publicity	80
Everton	Little	sax	80 sub
Kathy	Kuyper	sax, alto	80 sub fall

James	McWayne	sax, alto	80
Terry	Walter	sax, alto	80
Faith	Stahl	sax, baritone	80
John	Roth	sax, tenor	80 sub fall
Martha	Vegge Nelson	sax, tenor	80
Dan	Bailey	showmobile asst.	80
David	Joyce	showmobile asst.	80
Brad	Widness	showmobile asst.	80
Gary	Hood	showmobile driver	80
Herbert	Parker	showmobile driver	80
Tom	Block	sound	80 sub
Evan	Jones	sound	80
Monte	Masten	sound	80 sub
Robert	Woodard	sound	80 sub
Paul	Bankson	trombone	80
Laurel	Cluts	trombone	80
Faye	Fossum	trombone	80
Steven	Pfeiffer	trombone	80
Paul	Reeg	trombone	80 sub
Brad	Widness	trombone	80
Stan	Eitreim	tuba	80
David	Joyce	tuba	80
Tad	Smith	tuba	80
Linda	Gednalske	twirler	80 guest
Linda	Polzin	twirler	80 guest
Janet	Austin	vocal soloist	80 guest
Monty	Barnard	vocal soloist	80 guest
Anne	Bryant Fisher	vocal soloist	80 guest
Carla	Connors	vocal soloist	80 guest
Joyce	Harris	vocal soloist	80 guest
Eugenia	Orlich Hartig	vocal soloist	80 guest
Olaf	Malmin	vocal soloist	80 guest
David	Nield	vocal soloist	80 guest
Ertis	Osterberg	vocal soloist	80 guest
Ray	Peterson	vocal soloist	80 guest
Pat	Sisson	vocal soloist	80 guest
John	Voss	vocal soloist	80 guest
Paul	Wegner	vocal soloist	80 guest

Sioux Falls Municipal Band Personnel 1981 (62nd season)
Dr. Leland A. Lillehaug, Conductor

Patricia	Masek	asst. conductor	81
Jill	Gibson	bass clarinet	81 sub
Linda	McLaren	bass clarinet	81
Carol	Buckwalter Pederson	bassoon	81 sub
Lori	Quanbeck	bassoon	81
Carole	Ahlers	clarinet	81 sub
Deb	Aning	clarinet	81
Mary	Avery	clarinet	81
Barb	Gilchrist	clarinet	81
Marlene	Graber	clarinet	81 sub
Cathy	Green	clarinet	81
Charlotte	Hedeen	clarinet	81
Mark	Isackson	clarinet	81 sub
Delight	Jensen Elsinger	clarinet	81
Jackie	Larsen	clarinet	81
Oscar	Loe	clarinet	81 sub
Karen	McLinn	clarinet	81
Nancy	Negstad	clarinet	81 sub
Kristi	Reierson	clarinet	81
Donna	Schettler Hoogendoorn	clarinet	81
Teresa	Wells	clarinet	81
Leland	Lillehaug	conductor	81
Phil	Bajema	cornet	81
Kellie	Brinkman	cornet	81 sub
Janet	Bruns Hallstrom	cornet	81
George	Gulson	cornet	81 sub
Gary	Holman	cornet	81
Doug	Lehrer	cornet	81

Mark	Levsen	cornet	81
Rolf	Olson	cornet	81 sub
James	Perkins	cornet	81
Steven	Sommers	cornet	81
David	Miller	electric bass	81 sub
Michael Patrick	Dailey	euphonium	81
Paul	Weikel	euphonium	81
Martha	Barnett Lyons	flute	81
Mary	Jensen Ryrholm	flute	81
Patricia	Masek	flute	81
Patricia	Penn	flute	81 sub
Scott	Faragher	horn	81
Curt	Hammond	horn	81
James	Marvel	horn	81
Connie	Roth	horn	81
Gina	Waltner Pfeiffer	horn	81 sub
Sandra	Weikel	horn	81
Terry	Walter	librarian	81
Mary	Avery	library asst.	81
Martha	Barnett Lyons	library asst.	81
Laurel	Cluts	library asst.	81
Kathy	Kuyper	library asst.	81
Jeanette	Paulson	library asst.	81
Pat	Penn	library asst.	81
Lori	Quanbeck	library asst.	81
Ray	Loftesness	MC	81
Olaf	Malmin	MC	81 guest
Denny	Oviatt	MC	81 guest
Paul	Wegner, Sr.	MC	81 guest
Diana	Borgum	narrator	81 guest
Jeanette	Paulson	oboe	81
Betty	Swanson	oboe	81
Dan	Hatfield	percussion	81
Cathy	Huether	percussion	81 sub
Paul	Hoy	percussion	81
Eric	LeVan	percussion	81
Robert	Niblick	percussion	81 sub
Robert	Patterson	percussion	81 sub
Linda	Petterson	percussion	81
Jeanette	Paulson	publicity	81
Mark	Isackson	sax, alto	81 sub
Kathy	Kuyper	sax, alto	81
Martha	Vegge Nelson	sax, alto	81 sub
Terry	Walter	sax, alto	81
Eddie	Johnson	sax, baritone	81
Gail	Bachand	sax, tenor	81 sub
John	Roth	sax, tenor	81
David	Joyce	showmobile asst.	81
Eddie	Johnson	showmobile asst.	81
Gary	Hood	showmobile driver	81
Herbert	Parker	showmobile driver	81
Mark	Fleming	sound	81
Paul	Bankson	trombone	81
Laurel	Cluts	trombone	81
Faye	Fossum	trombone	81
William	Glenski	trombone	81 sub
Steven	Pfeiffer	trombone	81
Paul	Reeg	trombone	81 sub
Brad	Widness	trombone	81
Stan	Eitreim	tuba	81
David	Joyce	tuba	81
Toby	Schmuck	tuba	81
Brenda	Polzin	twirler	81? guest
Robert	Barnett	vocal soloist	81 guest
Diana	Borgum	vocal soloist	81 guest
Ricki	Bryant (Anderberg)	vocal soloist	81 guest
Olaf	Malmin	vocal soloist	81 guest
Ray	Peterson	vocal soloist	81 guest
Roma	Prindle	vocal soloist	81 guest
Paul	Wegner, Sr.	vocal soloist	81 guest

Sioux Falls Municipal Band Personnel 1982 (63rd season)
Dr. Leland A. Lillehaug, Conductor

Patricia	Masek	asst. conductor	82
Jill	Gibson	bass clarinet	82
Linda	McLaren	bass clarinet	82 sub Nov.
Carol	Buckwalter Pederson	bassoon	82
Katherine	Peterson	bassoon	82 sub Nov.
Lori	Quanbeck	bassoon	82
Carole	Ahlers	clarinet	82
Deb	Aning	clarinet	82
Mary	Avery	clarinet	82
Kathy	Bangasser	clarinet	82 sub Nov.
Kathy	Boullion	clarinet	82 sub Nov.
Judy	Engh	clarinet	82 sub Nov.
Charlotte	Hedeen	clarinet	82
Mark	Isackson	clarinet	82
Delight	Jensen Elsinger	clarinet	82
Jackie	Larsen	clarinet	82
Oscar	Loe	clarinet	82 sub Nov.
Steven	Lillehaug	clarinet	82
Nancy	Negstad	clarinet	82
Donna	Schettler Hoogendoorn	clarinet	82
Laurie	Stephens	clarinet	82 sub Nov.
Teresa	Wells	clarinet	82
Mark	Wright	clarinet?	82 sub Nov.
Leland	Lillehaug	conductor	82
Kellie	Brinkman	cornet	82 sub
Janet	Bruns Hallstrom	cornet	82
George	Gulson	cornet	82 sub
Gary	Holman	cornet	82
Doug	Lehrer	cornet	82
Mark	Levsen	cornet	82
Rolf	Olson	cornet	82
James	Perkins	cornet	82
Steven	Sommers	cornet	82
Vince	Aughenbaugh	euphonium	82
Butler	Eitel	euphonium	82 sub
David	Joyce	euphonium	82
Martha	Barnett Lyons	flute	82
Pam	Hansen Barnard	flute	82
Mary	Jensen Ryrholm	flute	82 sub
Patricia	Masek	flute	82
Patricia	Penn	flute	82 sub
Nancy	Brown	horn	82 sub Nov.
Jeanette	Duerksen	horn	82
Scott	Faragher	horn	82
Curt	Hammond	horn	82
James	Marvel	horn	82 sub
Sandra	Weikel	horn	82
Michelle	Youngquist	horn	82
Terry	Walter	librarian	82
Mary	Avery	library asst.	82
Carol	Buckwalter	library asst.	82
Ray	Loftesness	MC	82
Claudia	Hasegawa	oboe	82 sub
Melissa	May	oboe	82
Dan	Hatfield	percussion	82
Paul	Hoy	percussion	82
Cathy	Huether	percussion	82
Eric	LeVan	percussion	82
Robert	Patterson	percussion	82 sub
Laurie	Lillehaug	publicity	82
Janelle	Schweim	sax	82 sub Nov.
Eddie	Johnson	sax, alto	82
Terry	Walter	sax, alto	82
Gail	Bachand	sax, baritone	82
Martha	Vegge Nelson	sax, tenor	82
Bill	Glenski	showmobile asst.	82
Eddie	Johnson	showmobile asst.	82

David	Joyce	showmobile asst.	82 sub
Gary	Hood	showmobile driver	82
Herbert	Parker	showmobile driver	82
Mark	Anderson	sound	82
Tom	Block	sound	82 sub
Mark	Fleming	sound	82 sub
Paul	Bankson	trombone	82
Brian	Brosz	trombone	82 sub Nov.
Laurel	Cluts	trombone	82 sub Nov.
Faye	Fossum	trombone	82
Bill	Glenski	trombone	82
Paul	Weikel	trombone	82
Brad	Widness	trombone	82
Rich	Woolworth	trombone	82
Stan	Eitreim	tuba	82
David	King	tuba	82
Toby	Schmuck	tuba	82
Monty	Barnard	vocal soloist	82
Roma	Prindle	vocal soloist	82
Anton "Tony"	Javurek	whistler	82 guest

Sioux Falls Municipal Band Personnel 1983 (64th season)
Dr. Leland A. Lillehaug, Conductor

Oscar	Loe	asst. conductor	83
Linda	McLaren	bass clarinet	83
Carol	Buckwalter Pederson	bassoon	83
Katherine	Peterson	bassoon	83
Lori	Quanbeck	bassoon	83 sub
Carole	Ahlers	clarinet	83
Mary	Avery	clarinet	83
Kathy	Bangasser	clarinet	83
Kathy	Boullion	clarinet	83
Judy	Engh	clarinet	83
Charlotte	Hedeen	clarinet	83
Mark	Isackson	clarinet	83
Delight	Jensen Elsinger	clarinet	83
Jackie	Larsen	clarinet	83
Oscar	Loe	clarinet	83
Donna	Schettler Hoogendoorn	clarinet	83
Laurie	Stephens	clarinet	83
John	Titus	clarinet	83 sub Nov.
Leland	Lillehaug	conductor	83
John D.	Buus	conductor, guest	83 guest
Butler	Eitel	conductor, guest	83 guest
Janet	Bruns Hallstrom	cornet	83
George	Gulson	cornet	83 sub
Gary	Holman	cornet	83
Gary	Horsley	cornet	83
Doug	Lehrer	cornet	83
Mark	Levsen	cornet	83 sub
James	Parker	cornet	83 sub Nov.
James	Perkins	cornet	83
Steven	Sommers	cornet	83
Vince	Aughenbaugh	euphonium	83 part time
Rolyn	Beaird	euphonium	83 sub
Fred	Ellwein	euphonium	83 sub
David	Joyce	euphonium	83 part time
Martha	Barnett Lyons	flute	83 sub
Pam	Hansen Barnard	flute	83
Mary	Jensen Ryrholm	flute	83
Patricia	Masek	flute	83
Patricia	Penn	flute	83 sub
Scott	Faragher	horn	83
Curt	Hammond	horn	83
Lissa	Robertson	horn	83 sub Nov.
Sandra	Weikel	horn	83
Michelle	Youngquist	horn	83
Terry	Walter	librarian	83
Curt	Hammond	library asst.	83

Roma	Prindle	library asst.	83
Dave	Dedrick	MC	83 guest
Ray	Loftesness	MC	83
Claudia	Hasegawa	oboe	83
Tami	Huse-Kerr	oboe	83 sub Nov.
Karen	Nogami	oboe	83
Bob	Goheen	percussion	83 sub
Dan	Hatfield	percussion	83
Paul	Hoy	percussion	83
Cathy	Huether	percussion	83
Eric	LeVan	percussion	83
Matt	Reich	percussion	83 sub
Ray	Loftesness	publicity	83
Eddie	Johnson	sax	83 sub
Janelle	Schweim Johnson	sax, alto	83
Terry	Walter	sax, alto	83
Gail	Bachand	sax, baritone	83
Martha	Vegge Nelson	sax, tenor	83
Gary	Horsley	showmobile asst.	83
Toby	Schmuck	showmobile asst.	83
Gary	Hood	showmobile driver	83
Tom	Block	sound	83 sub
Mark	Fleming	sound	83 sub
Joe	Sorvaag	sound	83
Laurel	Cluts	trombone	83
Dan	Engh	trombone	83
Faye	Fossum	trombone	83
Susan	Howard	trombone	83 sub Nov.
Paul	Reeg	trombone	83 sub
Robert	Streemke	trombone	83 sub Nov.
Paul	Weikel	trombone	83
Brad	Widness	trombone	83
Stan	Eitreim	tuba	83
David	King	tuba	83
Toby	Schmuck	tuba	83
Monty	Barnard	vocal soloist	83
Roma	Prindle	vocal soloist	83

Sioux Falls Municipal Band Personnel 1984 (65th season)
Dr. Leland A. Lillehaug, Conductor

Oscar	Loe	asst. conductor	84
Linda	McLaren	bass clarinet	84
Katherine	Peterson	bassoon	84
Lori	Quanbeck	bassoon	84
Mary	Avery	clarinet	84
Kathy	Bangasser	clarinet	84
Kathy	Boullion	clarinet	84
Tami	Dice	clarinet	84 sub Nov.
Judy	Engh	clarinet	84
Charlotte	Hedeen	clarinet	84
Delight	Jensen Elsinger	clarinet	84
Eddie	Johnson	clarinet	84
Kara	Jorve	clarinet	84 sub Nov.
Jackie	Larsen	clarinet	84
Oscar	Loe	clarinet	84
Kari	Reyner	clarinet	84 sub Nov.
Susan	Rogotzke	clarinet	84 sub Nov.
Donna	Schettler Hoogendoorn	clarinet	84
Laurie	Stephens	clarinet	84
John	Titus	clarinet	84
Brenda	Zacharias	clarinet	84 sub Nov.
Leland	Lillehaug	conductor	84
Charles	Erwin, Charles (Lt. Col.)	conductor, guest	84 guest
Janet	Bruns Hallstrom	cornet	84
George	Gulson	cornet	84 sub
Gary	Holman	cornet	84
Eric	Knutson	cornet	84
Doug	Lehrer	cornet	84
Leon	Miller	cornet	84 sub

James	Parker	cornet	84
James	Perkins	cornet	84
Steven	Sommers	cornet	84
Mary	Starks	cornet	84 sub
Vince	Aughenbaugh	euphonium	84
Rolyn	Beaird	euphonium	84
Carl	Hallstrom	euphonium	84 sub Nov.
Martha	Barnett Lyons	flute	84 sub
Pam	Hansen Barnard	flute	84
Mary	Jensen Ryrholm	flute	84
Patricia	Masek	flute	84
Patricia	Penn	flute	84 sub
Wes	Byers	horn	84 sub Nov.
Scott	Faragher	horn	84 sub
Curt	Hammond	horn	84
Tami	Heiden	horn	84 sub
Wayne	Heinemann	horn	84 sub
Robert	McDowell	horn	84 sub
Lissa	Robertson	horn	84
Terry	Walter	librarian	84
Curt	Hammond	library asst.	84
Mary	Jensen Ryrholm	library asst.	84
Ray	Loftesness	MC	84
Tami	Huse-Kerr	oboe	84
Karen	Nogami	oboe	84
James	Carlson	percussion	84 sub Nov.
Dan	Hatfield	percussion	84
Paul	Hoy	percussion	84
Cathy	Huether	percussion	84
Robert	Joyce	percussion	84 sub
Sara	Levsen	percussion	84
Chris	Olkiewicz	sax, alto	84 sub Nov.
Janelle	Schweim Johnson	sax, alto	84
Terry	Walter	sax, alto	84
Gail	Bachand	sax, baritone	84
Kevin	Groskurth	sax, baritone	84 sub Nov.
Martha	Vegge Nelson	sax, tenor	84
Beth	Ahlers	sax, tenor	84 sub Nov.
Eddie	Johnson	showmobile asst.	84
James	Parker	showmobile asst.	84
Gary	Hood	showmobile driver	84
Herbert	Parker	showmobile driver	84
Tom	Block	sound	84 sub
Dean	Waldow	sound	84
Curt	Hammond	staff	84
David	Miller	string bass	84
Laurel	Cluts	trombone	84
Dan	Engh	trombone	84
Faye	Fossum	trombone	84
Bill	Glenski	trombone	84 sub
Dawn	Hanson	trombone	84 sub Nov.
Susan	Howard	trombone	84
Curt	Ohrland	trombone	84 sub Nov.
Robert	Streemke	trombone	84
Stan	Eitreim	tuba	84
David	King	tuba	84
Monty	Barnard	vocal soloist	84
Roma	Prindle	vocal soloist	84

Sioux Falls Municipal Band Personnel 1985 (66th season)
Dr. Leland A. Lillehaug, Conductor

Oscar	Loe	asst. conductor	85
Linda	McLaren	bass clarinet	85
Katherine	Peterson	bassoon	85
Lori	Quanbeck	bassoon	85
Brenda	Bahnson	clarinet	85 sub fall
Kathy	Boullion	clarinet	85
Mary	Fritz	clarinet	85 sub fall
Dennis	Graber	clarinet	85

Charlotte	Hedeen	clarinet	85
Eddie	Johnson	clarinet	85
Kara	Jorve	clarinet	85
Jackie	Larsen	clarinet	85
Oscar	Loe	clarinet	85
Kari	Reyner	clarinet	85
Susan	Rogotzke	clarinet	85
Jennifer	Stansbery	clarinet	85
John	Titus	clarinet	85 sub
Brenda	Zacharias	clarinet	85
Leland	Lillehaug	conductor	85
Merle	Evans	conductor, guest	85 guest
Janet	Bruns Hallstrom	cornet	85
Merridee	Ekstrom	cornet	85 sub Mpls.
William	Freitag	cornet	85
George	Gulson	cornet	85 sub
Gary	Holman	cornet	85
Eric	Knutson	cornet	85
Doug	Lehrer	cornet	85
Leon	Miller	cornet	85 sub
Marc David	Mueller	cornet	85
James	Parker	cornet	85 sub
James	Perkins	cornet	85 sub fall
Nathan	Wegner	cornet	85
Rolyn	Beaird	euphonium	85
Carl	Hallstrom	euphonium	85
Martha	Barnett Lyons	flute	85 sub
Pam	Hansen Barnard	flute	85
Kathy	Hays Emmel	flute	85 guest
Mary	Jensen Ryrholm	flute	85
Marilyn	Loomis Hansen	flute	85 guest
Patricia	Masek	flute	85
Darlene	Root	flute	85 sub
Nancy	Brown	horn	85 sub
Scott	Faragher	horn	85
Curt	Hammond	horn	85 sub
Dennis	Kaufman	horn	85
Lois	Nelson	horn	85 sub fall
Rolf	Olson	horn	85
Terry	Walter	librarian	85
William	Freitag	library asst.	85
Curt	Hammond	library asst.	85
Mary	Jensen	library asst.	85
Susan	Rogotzke	library asst.	85
Darlene	Root	library asst.	85
Ray	Loftesness	MC	85
Ann	Cameron	percussion	85
James Paul	Carlson	percussion	85
Paul	Hoy	percussion	85
Cathy	Huether Moklebust	percussion	85 part time
Robert	Joyce	percussion	85 sub
Eric	LeVan	percussion	85 part time
Ken	Yoshida	percussion	85 sub fall
Mark	Huisman	publicity	85 part time
Mark	Isackson	sax, alto	85 sub fall
Chris	Olkiewicz	sax, alto	85
Janelle	Schweim Johnson	sax, alto	85 sub
Terry	Walter	sax, alto	85
Kevin	Groskurth	sax, baritone	85
Beth	Ahlers	sax, tenor	85
Dawn	Hanson	showmobile asst.	85
Eric	Knutson	showmobile asst.	85
Gary	Hood	showmobile driver	85
Tom	Block	sound	85 sub
Paul Nathan	Hanson	sound	85 part time
Phil	Jankowski	sound	85 sub
Laurel	Cluts	trombone	85
Faye	Fossum	trombone	85
Dawn	Hanson	trombone	85
David	Mitchell	trombone	85 sub fall

Curt	Ohrland	trombone	85
Paul	Reeg	trombone	85 sub
Robert	Streemke	trombone	85
Stan	Eitreim	tuba	85
David	King	tuba	85
Wayne	Krumrei	tuba	85
Monty	Barnard	vocal soloist	85
Roma	Prindle	vocal soloist	85

Sioux Falls Municipal Band Personnel 1986 (67th season)
Dr. Leland A. Lillehaug, Conductor

Oscar	Loe	asst. conductor	86
Linda	McLaren	bass clarinet	86
Katherine	Peterson	bassoon	86
Lori	Quanbeck	bassoon	86
Brenda	Bahnson	clarinet	86
Ann	Barrett	clarinet	86 sub fall
Mary	Fritz	clarinet	86
Dennis	Graber	clarinet	86
Charlotte	Hedeen	clarinet	86
Eddie	Johnson	clarinet	86
Yvonne	Lange	clarinet	86
Jackie	Larsen	clarinet	86 sub fall
Oscar	Loe	clarinet	86
Tom	Merrill	clarinet	86
Judy	Soukup	clarinet	86
Jennifer	Stansbery	clarinet	86
John	Titus	clarinet	86
Brenda	Zacharias	clarinet	86
Leland	Lillehaug	conductor	86
James	Christensen	conductor, guest	86 guest
Conte	Bennett	cornet	86 sub
Ray	DeVilbiss	cornet	86 sub
Janet	Bruns Hallstrom	cornet	86
George	Gulson	cornet	86 sub
Gary	Holman	cornet	86
Eric	Knutson	cornet	86
Doug	Lehrer	cornet	86 sub
Leon	Miller	cornet	86 sub
Rolf	Olson	cornet	86 sub
James	Perkins	cornet	86
Vicki	Savage	cornet	86
Steve	Sommers	cornet	86 sub
Steve	Stombaugh	cornet	86
Nathan	Wegner	cornet	86
Rolyn	Beaird	euphonium	86
Carl	Hallstrom	euphonium	86
Martha	Barnett Lyons	flute	86 sub
Pam	Hansen Barnard	flute	86
Mary	Jensen Ryrholm	flute	86
Patricia	Masek	flute	86
Jane	Quail	flute	86 sub fall
Darlene	Root	flute	86 sub
Mary	Devaney	horn	86
Beth	Duerksen	horn	86
Lois	Nelson	horn	86
Denise	Noble	horn	86 sub fall
Michelle	Paulson	horn	86 sub
Jane	Preheim	horn	86
Lawrence	Price	horn	86
Michelle	Youngquist	horn	86
Scott	Shelsta	inst. soloist, trombone	86 guest
Dawn	Hanson	librarian	86
William	Freitag	library asst.	86
Terry	Walter	library asst.	86
Phyllis	Wissink	library asst.	86
Ray	Loftesness	MC	86
Tom	Steever	MC	86 guest
Ann	Cameron	percussion	86

Dan	Hatfield	percussion	86 sub
Paul	Hoy	percussion	86
Eric	LeVan	percussion	86 sub
Kathy	Welter	percussion	86
Ken	Yoshida	percussion	86
John	Titus	publicity	86
Diana	Christiansen	sax, alto	86
Janelle	Schweim Johnson	sax, alto	86
Chris	Olkiewicz	sax, baritone	86
Beth	Ahlers	sax, tenor	86
Martha	Nelson	sax, tenor	86 sub fall
David	Jans	showmobile asst.	86
Nathan	Wegner	showmobile asst.	86
Eric	Knutson	showmobile asst.	86
Gary	Hood	showmobile driver	86
Tom	Block	sound	86 sub
Phil	Jankowski	sound	86
Joel	Nevin	sound	86 sub
Eric	Christensen	trombone	86 sub fall
Laurel	Cluts	trombone	86
Faye	Fossum	trombone	86
Dawn	Hanson	trombone	86
David	Jans	trombone	86
David	Mitchell	trombone	86 part time
Jeffrey "Rock"	Nelson	trombone	86 sub
Robert	Streemke	trombone	86 sub
Stan	Eitreim	tuba	86
Mark	Johnson	tuba	86 sub
David	King	tuba	86
Wayne	Krumrei	tuba	86
David A.	Larson	tuba	86
Salem Mens Chorus		vocal group	86 guest
Sioux Emperians Barbership Chorus		vocal group	86 guest
Monty	Barnard	vocal soloist	86
Eileen	Bauermeister	vocal soloist	86
Roma	Prindle	vocal soloist	86 guest
Kaye	Webster	vocal soloist	86 guest

Sioux Falls Municipal Band Personnel 1987 (68th season)
Dr. Alan W. Taylor, Conductor

Oscar	Loe	asst. conductor	87 through April
Linda	McLaren	bass clarinet	87
Katherine	Peterson	bassoon	87
Lori	Quanbeck	bassoon	87
Susan	Wood	bassoon	87 sub April
Brenda	Bahnson	clarinet	87
Kathy	Bangasser	clarinet	87
Ann	Barrett	clarinet	87
Mary	Fritz	clarinet	87
Dennis	Graber	clarinet	87
Charlotte	Hedeen	clarinet	87 sub
Linsey	Langford Duffy	clarinet	87
Jackie	Larsen	clarinet	87
Oscar	Loe	clarinet	87
Ann	Natvig	clarinet	87
John	Titus	clarinet	87
Brenda	Zacharias	clarinet	87
Leland	Lillehaug	conductor	87 through April
Alan	Taylor	conductor	87 began in May
Janet	Bruns Hallstrom	cornet	87
Gary	Holman	cornet	87
Eric	Knutson	cornet	87
Doug	Lehrer	cornet	87
Susie	Lyman	cornet	87
Rolf	Olson	cornet	87 sub
James	Perkins	cornet	87
Vicki	Savage	cornet	87 sub April
Steve	Stombaugh	cornet	87 sub
Nathan	Wegner	cornet	87

Craig	Alberty	euphonium	87 sub
Lyn	Alberty	euphonium	87 sub fall
Rolyn	Beaird	euphonium	87
Carl	Hallstrom	euphonium	87
Pam	Hansen Barnard	flute	87
Patricia	Masek	flute	87
Jane	Quail	flute	87
Beth	Duerksen	horn	87 part time
Lois	Nelson	horn	87
Denise	Noble	horn	87
Michelle	Paulson	horn	87 sub fall
Lawrence	Price	horn	87
Michelle	Youngquist	horn	87
Scott	Shelsta	inst. soloist, trombone	87 guest
John	Titus	librarian	87
Phyllis	Wissink	library asst.	87
Ray	Loftesness	MC	87
Jim	Woster	MC	87 guest
Timothy	Clinch	oboe	87 sub April
Glennis	Siverson	oboe	87 sub
Stan	Eitreim	percussion	87
Scott	Fenton	percussion	87
Paul	Hoy	percussion	87
Ken	Yoshida	percussion	87 sub
Todd	Novak	sax	87 sub
Diana	Christiansen	sax, alto	87 sub April
Brian	Knutson	sax, alto	87 sub
Kerry	Kramer	sax, alto	87 sub fall
Chris	Olkiewicz	sax, alto	87
Terry	Walter	sax, alto	87 part time
Cherie	Carlson	sax, baritone	87
Stephanie	Frank	sax, baritone	87 sub fall
Martha	Vegge Nelson	sax, tenor	87
Larry	Bedient	showmobile driver	87
Phil	Jankowski	sound	87
Eric	Christensen	trombone	87
Brian	Dewald	trombone	87
Faye	Fossum	trombone	87
David	Jans	trombone	87
Jeffrey "Rock"	Nelson	trombone	87 sub
Paul	Reeg	trombone	87 sub
Stan	Eitreim	tuba	87
Wayne	Krumrei	tuba	87
David A.	Larson	tuba	87
Eric	Munson	tuba	87 part time
Craig	Rostad	tuba	87 sub
Monty	Barnard	vocal soloist	87
Faye	Hurley	vocal soloist	87 guest
Mitzi	Westra	vocal soloist	87 guest
Lisa	Wiehl	vocal soloist	87 guest

Sioux Falls Municipal Band Personnel 1988 (69th season)
Dr. Alan W. Taylor, Conductor

Linda	McLaren Roach	bass clarinet	88
Katherine	Peterson	bassoon	88
Lori	Quanbeck	bassoon	88
Brenda	Bahnson	clarinet	88
Kathy	Bangasser	clarinet	88
Ann	Barrett	clarinet	88
Mary	Fritz	clarinet	88
Dennis	Graber	clarinet	88
Dan	Irvin	clarinet	88
Linsey	Langford Duffy	clarinet	88
Jackie	Larsen	clarinet	88
Oscar	Loe	clarinet	88
Ann	Natvig	clarinet	88
John	Titus	clarinet	88 part time
Brenda	Zacharias	clarinet	88
Alan	Taylor	conductor	88

Craig	Alberty	cornet	88
Conte	Bennett	cornet	88 part time
Janet	Bruns Hallstrom	cornet	88
Gary	Holman	cornet	88
Eric	Knutson	cornet	88 part time
Doug	Lehrer	cornet	88
James	Perkins	cornet	88
Steve	Stombaugh	cornet	88
Nathan	Wegner	cornet	88
Lyn	Alberty	euphonium	88
Rolyn	Beaird	euphonium	88
Pam	Hansen Barnard	flute	88
Patricia	Masek	flute	88
Jane	Quail	flute	88
Laurie	Jetvig	horn	88 sub
Lois	Nelson	horn	88
Denise	Noble	horn	88
Lawrence	Price	horn	88
Harvey	Phillips	inst. soloist, tuba	88 guest
Steve	Stombaugh	librarian	88
Ray	Loftesness	MC	88
Joe	Lafleur	oboe	88
Stan	Eitreim	percussion	88
Scott	Fenton	percussion	88
Paul	Hoy	percussion	88
Eric	LeVan	percussion	88 sub
Clifford	Nock	percussion	88
Michael	Smith	percussion	88
Cherie	Carlson	sax	88
Kerry	Kramer	sax	88 sub
Todd	Novak	sax, alto	88
Terry	Walter	sax, alto	88
Lori	Neprud	sax, baritone	88
Martha	Vegge Nelson	sax, tenor	88
Larry	Bedient	showmobile driver	88
Tom	Block	sound	88 sub
Joel	Nevin	sound	88
Stan	Eitreim	stage manager	88
Rod	Aasheim	trombone	88 sub
Eric	Christensen	trombone	88 sub
Faye	Fossum	trombone	88
Carl	Hallstrom	trombone	88
David	Jans	trombone	88
Robert	McDowell, Jr.	trombone	88
Jeffrey "Rock"	Nelson	trombone	88 sub
David A.	Larson	tuba	88
Craig	Rostad	tuba	88
Wallace	Waltner	tuba	88
Monty	Barnard	vocal soloist	88
Lisa	Wiehl	vocal soloist	88

Sioux Falls Municipal Band Personnel 1989 (70th season)
Dr. Alan W. Taylor, Conductor

Linda	McLaren Roach	bass clarinet	89
Katherine	Peterson	bassoon	89
Lori	Quanbeck	bassoon	89
Kathy	Bangasser	clarinet	89
Ann	Barrett	clarinet	89
Dennis	Graber	clarinet	89
Barbara	Hanson Johnson	clarinet	89 sub
Cindy	Helwick	clarinet	89
Dan	Irvin	clarinet	89
Mark	Isackson	clarinet	89 sub fall
Linsey	Langford Duffy	clarinet	89
Jackie	Larsen	clarinet	89
Reggie	Schive	clarinet	89 sub
Kristi	Tharp McDowell	clarinet	89
Alan	Taylor	conductor	89
Craig	Alberty	cornet	89

Janet	Bruns Hallstrom	cornet	89
Doug	Lehrer	cornet	89
Susie	Lyman	cornet	89
Rolf	Olson	cornet	89 sub
James	Perkins	cornet	89
Pam	Sonnichsen	cornet	89
Steve	Stombaugh	cornet	89
Georgia	Taylor	cornet	89 part time
Nathan	Wegner	cornet	89
Lyn	Alberty	euphonium	89
Rolyn	Beaird	euphonium	89
Michael	Cwach	euphonium	89
Georgia	Taylor	euphonium	89 sub
Pam	Hansen Barnard	flute	89
Tiffin	Hartwig	flute	89 sub
Mary	Jensen Ryrholm	flute	89 sub
Patricia	Masek	flute	89
Jane	Quail	flute	89
Brett	Austad	horn	89
Sara	Cyrus	horn	89 sub
Scott	Faragher	horn	89 part time
Lois	Nelson	horn	89
Denise	Noble	horn	89
Lawrence	Price	horn	89 sub
Joan	Haaland Paddock	inst. soloist, cornet	89 guest
Denise	Noble	librarian	89
Dan	Irvin	library asst.	89
Wallace	Waltner	library asst.	89
Ray	Loftesness	MC	89
Joe	Lafleur	oboe	89
Stan	Eitreim	percussion	89
Scott	Fenton	percussion	89
Paul	Hoy	percussion	89
Eric	LeVan	percussion	89 sub
Clifford	Nock	percussion	89
Michael	Smith	percussion	89
Lori	Neprud	sax	89
Martha	Vegge Nelson	sax	89
Bruce	Ammann	sax, alto	89 sub
Brenda	Bahnson	sax, alto	89
Cherie	Carlson	sax, baritone	89
Kerry	Kramer	sax, tenor	89 sub
Larry	Bedient	showmobile driver	89
Tom	Block	sound	89 sub
Michael	McAllister	sound	89 part time
Joel	Nevin	sound	89 part time
Stan	Eitreim	stage manager	89
Eric	Christensen	trombone	89
Faye	Fossum	trombone	89
Carl	Hallstrom	trombone	89
David	Jans	trombone	89
Robert	McDowell, Jr.	trombone	89
Jeffrey "Rock"	Nelson	trombone	89 sub
Erwin	Tork	trombone	89 sub fall
David A.	Larson	tuba	89
Craig	Rostad	tuba	89
Wallace	Waltner	tuba	89
Monty	Barnard	vocal soloist	89
Lisa	Wiehl	vocal soloist	89

Sioux Falls Municipal Band Personnel 1990 (71st season)
Dr. Alan W. Taylor, Conductor

Linda	McLaren Roach	bass clarinet	90
Katherine	Peterson	bassoon	90
Lori	Quanbeck	bassoon	90
Kathy	Bangasser	clarinet	90
Lori	Foland	clarinet	90
Mary	Fritz	clarinet	90
Dennis	Graber	clarinet	90

Cindy	Helwick	clarinet	90
Dan	Irvin	clarinet	90
Mark	Isackson	clarinet	90 sub
Delight	Jensen Elsinger	clarinet	90
Linsey	Langford Duffy	clarinet	90
Jackie	Larsen	clarinet	90
Nikki	Maher	clarinet	90
Kristi	Tharp McDowell	clarinet	90
Alan	Taylor	conductor	90
Craig	Alberty	cornet	90
Barb	Bjorklund	cornet	90
Janet	Bruns Hallstrom	cornet	90
Charlene	Dick	cornet	90
Jeremy	Hegg	cornet	90
Doug	Lehrer	cornet	90
Rolf	Olson	cornet	90
John	Perkins	cornet	90 sub
Pam	Sonnichsen	cornet	90 sub
Steve	Stombaugh	cornet	90
Lyn	Alberty	euphonium	90
Rolyn	Beaird	euphonium	90
Heather	Flanery	flute	90 sub
Pam	Hansen Barnard	flute	90
Tiffin	Hartwig	flute	90 sub
Mary	Jensen Ryrholm	flute	90 sub
Patricia	Masek	flute	90
Jane	Quail	flute	90
Brett	Austad	horn	90
Sara	Cyrus	horn	90 sub
Rachel	Dick	horn	90
Scott	Faragher	horn	90 sub
Dennis	Kaufman	horn	90
Lois	Nelson	horn	90
Delight	Jensen Elsinger	librarian	90
Charlene	Dick	library asst.	90
Jackie	Larsen	library asst.	90
Ray	Loftesness	MC	90
Nicole	Barlow	percussion	90 sub
Ann	Cameron	percussion	90 sub
Stan	Eitreim	percussion	90
Scott	Fenton	percussion	90 sub
Paul	Hoy	percussion	90
Eric	LeVan	percussion	90 sub
Michael	Smith	percussion	90
Bruce	Ammann	sax, alto	90
Brenda	Bahnson	sax, alto	90
Laura	Busdicker Britton	sax, baritone	90
Lori	Neprud	sax, baritone	90 sub
Martha	Vegge Nelson	sax, tenor	90
Larry	Bedient	showmobile driver	90
Tom	Block	sound	90 sub
David	Heisel	sound	90 sub
Brian	Masek	sound	90 sub
Joel	Nevin	sound	90 sub
David A.	Larson	stage asst.	90
Stan	Eitreim	stage manager	90
Eric	Christensen	trombone	90
Faye	Fossum	trombone	90
Carl	Hallstrom	trombone	90
David	Jans	trombone	90
Robert	McDowell, Jr.	trombone	90
Jeffrey "Rock"	Nelson	trombone	90 sub
Alan	Berdahl	tuba	90 sub
David A.	Larson	tuba	90
Craig	Rostad	tuba	90
Wallace	Waltner	tuba	90
Monty	Barnard	vocal soloist	90
Lisa	Wiehl	vocal soloist	90

Sioux Falls Municipal Band Personnel 1991 (72nd season)
Dr. Alan W. Taylor, Conductor

Linda	McLaren Roach	bass clarinet	91
Katherine	Peterson	bassoon	91
Lori	Quanbeck	bassoon	91
Kathy	Bangasser	clarinet	91
Lori	Foland	clarinet	91
Mary	Fritz	clarinet	91
Dennis	Graber	clarinet	91
Dan	Irwin	clarinet	91
Delight	Jensen Elsinger	clarinet	91
Linsey	Langford Duffy	clarinet	91
Jackie	Larsen	clarinet	91
Michelle	Lippert	clarinet	91
Nikki	Maher	clarinet	91
Kristi	Tharp McDowell	clarinet	91
Alan	Taylor	conductor	91
Craig	Alberty	cornet	91
Janet	Bruns Hallstrom	cornet	91
Greg	Handel	cornet	91
Stephen	Hartwig	cornet	91 sub
Jeremy	Hegg	cornet	91
Eric	Knutson	cornet	91 sub
Doug	Lehrer	cornet	91
Darrell	Omanson	cornet	91
Brian	Smith	cornet	91
Pam	Sonnichsen	cornet	91 sub
Steve	Stombaugh	cornet	91
Lyn	Alberty	euphonium	91
Rolyn	Beaird	euphonium	91
Heather	Flanery	flute	91 sub
Pam	Hansen Barnard	flute	91
Tiffin	Hartwig	flute	91 sub
Patricia	Masek	flute	91
Jane	Quail	flute	91
Brett	Austad	horn	91
Tiffy	Berg	horn	91 sub
Scott	Faragher	horn	91 sub
Lois	Nelson	horn	91
Janet	Roesler	horn	91 sub
Steven	Spieker	horn	91
Delight	Jensen Elsinger	librarian	91
Jason	Schwans	library asst.	91
Ray	Loftesness	MC	91 guest
Alan	Taylor	MC	91
Sheila	Wulf	oboe	91
Stan	Eitreim	percussion	91
Paul	Hoy	percussion	91
Eric	LeVan	percussion	91 sub
Michael	Smith	percussion	91
Kerry	Kramer	sax	91 sub
Bruce	Ammann	sax, alto	91
Brenda	Bahnson	sax, alto	91
Terry	Walter	sax, alto	91 sub
Laura	Busdicker Britton	sax, baritone	91 sub
Jason	Schwans	sax, baritone	91
Martha	Vegge Nelson	sax, tenor	91
Larry	Bedient	showmobile driver	91
Tom	Block	sound	91 sub
David	Heisel	sound	91 part time
Michael	McAllister	sound	91 part time
David A.	Larson	stage asst.	91
Stan	Eitreim	stage manager	91
Faye	Fossum	trombone	91
Carl	Hallstrom	trombone	91
Gregory	Hill	trombone	91
David	Jans	trombone	91
Deb	McConahie	trombone	91
Robert	McDowell, Jr.	trombone	91

Jeffrey "Rock"	Nelson	trombone	91 sub
Alan	Berdahl	tuba	91 sub
David A.	Larson	tuba	91
Gary	Pederson	tuba	91
Craig	Rostad	tuba	91 sub
Wallace	Waltner	tuba	91
Monty	Barnard	vocal soloist	91
Lisa	Wiehl	vocal soloist	91

Sioux Falls Municipal Band Personnel 1992 (73rd season)
Dr. Bruce T. Ammann, Conductor

Dawn	Dalseide	bass clarinet	92
Britt	Larson	bass clarinet	92
Katherine	Peterson	bassoon	92
Lori	Quanbeck	bassoon	92
Kathy	Bangasser	clarinet	92
Nancy	Barnes	clarinet	92
Mary	Fritz	clarinet	92
Beverly	Gibson	clarinet	92 sub fall
Deann	Golz	clarinet	92
Dennis	Graber	clarinet	92
Barbara	Hanson Johnson	clarinet	92
Dan	Irwin	clarinet	92
Delight	Jensen Elsinger	clarinet	92
Jackie	Larsen	clarinet	92
Nikki	Maher	clarinet	92
Lynda	Rasmussen	clarinet	92
Kristi	Tharp McDowell	clarinet	92
Bruce	Ammann	conductor	92
Craig	Alberty	cornet	92
Janet	Bruns Hallstrom	cornet	92
Greg	Handel	cornet	92
Jeremy	Hegg	cornet	92
Eric	Knutson	cornet	92 sub fall
Doug	Lehrer	cornet	92
Sayra	Siverson	cornet	92 sub
Brian	Smith	cornet	92
Pam	Sonnichsen	cornet	92 sub
Steve	Stombaugh	cornet	92
Kris	Whitely	cornet	92
Lyn	Alberty	euphonium	92
Rolyn	Beaird	euphonium	92
Michael	Cwach	euphonium	92 sub
Pam	Hansen Barnard	flute	92
Patricia	Masek	flute	92
Jane	Quail	flute	92
Carrie	Baird	horn	92
Tiffany	Berg	horn	92 sub
Rachel	Dick	horn	92 sub
Barbara J.	Johnson Hegg	horn	92
Jason	McFarland	horn	92
Lois	Nelson	horn	92
Steven	Spieker	horn	92
Robert, Dr.	Spring	inst. soloist, clarinet	92 guest
Delight	Jensen Elsinger	librarian	92
Jason	Schwans	library asst.	92
Robb	Hart	MC	92
Thomas	Hiniker	oboe	92 sub
Kristen	Sonnichsen	oboe	92
Sheila	Wulf	oboe	92
Mike	Hart	percussion	92
Derek	Hengeveld	percussion	92
Paul	Hoy	percussion	92
Robert	Kramer	percussion	92
Michael	Smith	percussion	92
Mark	Isackson	sax	92 sub
Brenda	Bahnson	sax, alto	92
Laura	Busdicker Britton	sax, alto	92
Terry	Walter	sax, alto	92 sub

Jason	Schwans	sax, baritone	92
Martha	Vegge Nelson	sax, tenor	92
Larry	Bedient	showmobile driver	92
Tom	Block	sound	92 sub
David	Heisel	sound	92 sub
Jason	Hegg	sound	92
Stan	Eitreim	stage manager	92
Faye	Fossum	trombone	92
Mark	Gross	trombone	92
Carl	Hallstrom	trombone	92
Deb	McConahie	trombone	92
Robert	McDowell, Jr.	trombone	92
Jay	Siverson	trombone	92 sub
Michael	Andersen	tuba	92 sub
Al	Berdahl	tuba	92 sub
Stan	Eitreim	tuba	92
Gary	Pederson	tuba	92
Craig	Rostad	tuba	92
Monty	Barnard	vocal soloist	92
Lisa	Wiehl	vocal soloist	92

Sioux Falls Municipal Band Personnel 1993 (74th season)
Dr. Bruce T. Ammann, Conductor

Dawn	Dalseide	bass clarinet	93
Linda	McLaren Roach	bass clarinet	93
Katherine	Peterson	bassoon	93
Lori	Quanbeck	bassoon	93
Kathy	Bangasser	clarinet	93
Lisa	Christensen	clarinet	93 sub
Mary	Fritz	clarinet	93
Beverly	Gibson	clarinet	93
Deann	Golz	clarinet	93
Dennis	Graber	clarinet	93
Barbara	Hanson Johnson	clarinet	93
Dan	Irvin	clarinet	93
Delight	Jensen Elsinger	clarinet	93
Carrie	Koupal	clarinet	93 sub
Jackie	Larsen	clarinet	93
Angela	Larson	clarinet	93 sub
Nikki	Maher	clarinet	93
Lynda	Rasmussen	clarinet	93
Kristi	Tharp McDowell	clarinet	93
Bruce	Ammann	conductor	93
Peter	Afdahl	cornet	93 sub
Craig	Alberty	cornet	93
Roger	Britton	cornet	93 sub
Jim	Gunderson	cornet	93 sub
Janet	Bruns Hallstrom	cornet	93
Greg	Handel	cornet	93
Jeremy	Hegg	cornet	93
Eric	Knutson	cornet	93
Brian	Smith	cornet	93
Joel	Sonnichsen	cornet	93 sub
Pam	Sonnichsen	cornet	93 sub
Steve	Stombaugh	cornet	93
Kris	Whitely	cornet	93
Lyn	Alberty	euphonium	93
Rolyn	Beaird	euphonium	93 sub
Carl	Hallstrom	euphonium	93
Pam	Hansen Barnard	flute	93
Mary	Jensen Ryrholm	flute	93
Patricia	Masek	flute	93
Jane	Quail	flute	93 sub
Carrie	Baird	horn	93
Tiffany	Berg	horn	93 sub
Jim	Gunderson	horn	93 sub
Barbara J.	Johnson Hegg	horn	93 sub
Jason	McFarland	horn	93
Lois	Nelson	horn	93

Marian	Ost	horn	93 part time
Steven	Spieker	horn	93
Paul	Hankins	inst. soloist, trumpet	93 guest
Delight	Jensen Elsinger	librarian	93
Jason	Schwans	library asst.	93
Robb	Hart	MC	93
Dennis	Hegg	MC	93 guest
Julia	Pachoud	MC	93 sub
Kristen	Sonnichsen	oboe	93
Sheila	Wulf	oboe	93
Mike	Hart	percussion	93
Derek	Hengeveld	percussion	93
Paul	Hoy	percussion	93
Robert	Kramer	percussion	93
Michael	Smith	percussion	93
Jill	Weber	sax, alto/tenor	93 sub
Brenda	Bahnson	sax, alto	93
Laura	Busdicker Britton	sax, alto	93
Jason	Schwans	sax, baritone	93
Amy	Millikan	sax, tenor	93
Larry	Bedient	showmobile driver	93
Stan	Eitreim	stage manager	93
Tony	Dresbach	trombone	93
Faye	Fossum	trombone	93
Bill	Gibson	trombone	93
Mark	Gross	trombone	93
Deb	McConahie	trombone	93
Robert	McDowell, Jr.	trombone	93
Andrew	Pole	trombone	93 sub
Jay	Siverson	trombone	93 sub
Michael	Andersen	tuba	93
Al	Berdahl	tuba	93 sub
Stan	Eitreim	tuba	93
Gary	Pederson	tuba	93 part time
Craig	Rostad	tuba	93 sub
Monty	Barnard	vocal soloist	93
Joan	Van Holland	vocal soloist	93

Sioux Falls Municipal Band Personnel 1994 (75th season)
Dr. Bruce T. Ammann, Conductor

Linda	McLaren Roach	bass clarinet	94
Katherine	Peterson	bassoon	94
Lori	Quanbeck	bassoon	94
Kathy	Bangasser	clarinet	94
Charlotte	Hedeen Miller	clarinet	94 sub
Linsey	Langford Duffy	clarinet	94 sub
Mary	Fritz	clarinet	94
Beverly	Gibson	clarinet	94 sub
Deann	Golz	clarinet	94
Dennis	Graber	clarinet	94
Barb	Hanson Johnson	clarinet	94 sub
Delight	Jensen Elsinger	clarinet	94
Patti	Kroth	clarinet	94 sub
Angela	Larson	clarinet	94
Nikki	Maher	clarinet	94
Amber	Sittig	clarinet	94
Kristi	Tharp McDowell	clarinet	94
John	Titus	clarinet	94 sub
Anne	Weiland	clarinet	94
Bruce	Ammann	conductor	94
Leland	Lillehaug	conductor	94 through April
Leland	Lillehaug	conductor, guest	94 guest
Alan	Taylor	conductor, guest	94 guest
Craig	Alberty	cornet	94
Roger	Britton	cornet	94 sub
Jeral	Gross	cornet	94
James	Gunderson	cornet	94 sub
Janet	Bruns Hallstrom	cornet	94
Greg	Handel	cornet	94

Jeremy	Hegg	cornet	94
Eric	Knutson	cornet	94
Jeremy	Nygard	cornet	94
Sayra	Siverson	cornet	94 sub
Pam	Sonnichsen	cornet	94 sub
Steve	Stombaugh	cornet	94
Lyn	Alberty	euphonium	94
Michael	Cwach	euphonium	94
Heidi	Olson	euphonium	94
Pam	Hansen Barnard	flute	94
Mary	Jensen Ryrholm	flute	94
Patricia	Masek	flute	94
Jane	Quail	flute	94 sub
Kari	Sonnichsen	flute	94 sub
Shad	Fagerland	horn	94
Amy	Herman	horn	94 sub
Jason	McFarland	horn	94
Teri	Naber	horn	94
Lois	Nelson	horn	94
Marian	Ost	horn	94
Steven	Spieker	horn	94
Paul	Hankins	inst. soloist, cornet	94 guest
Scott	Shelsta	inst. soloist, trombone	94 guest
Delight	Jensen Elsinger	librarian	94
Deann	Golz	library asst.	94
Jason	Schwans	library asst.	94
Robb	Hart	MC	94
Julia	Pachoud	MC	94 sub
Kristen	Sonnichsen	oboe	94
Cara	Soper	oboe	94 sub
Sheila	Wulf	oboe	94
Kelly	Bradbury	percussion	94
Michael	Hart	percussion	94 sub
Derek	Hengeveld	percussion	94
Paul	Hoy	percussion	94
Robert	Kramer	percussion	94 on leave
Kevin	Meyer	percussion	94
Michael	Smith	percussion	94
Brenda	Bahnson	sax, alto	94
Laura	Busdicker Britton	sax, alto	94
Terry	Walter	sax, alto & tenor	94 sub
Sheila	Zweifel	sax, alto	94 sub
Jason	Schwans	sax, baritone	94
Amy	Millikan	sax, tenor	94
Larry	Bedient	showmobile driver	84
Jason	Hegg	sound	94
Stan	Eitreim	stage manager	94
Tony	Dresbach	trombone	94
Cindi	Ellison	trombone	94
Faye	Fossum	trombone	94 sub
Mark	Gross	trombone	94
Carl	Hallstrom	trombone	94
Scott	Loftesness	trombone	94
Jay	Siverson	trombone	94 sub
Michael	Andersen	tuba	94
Alan	Berdahl	tuba	94
Stan	Eitreim	tuba	94
Gary	Pederson	tuba	94 sub
Monty	Barnard	vocal soloist	94
Eugenia	Orlich Hartig	vocal soloist	94 guest
Lisa	Wiehl Grevlos	vocal soloist	94
Bruce	Thompson	cornet	years unknown

Bibliography

Interviews/Correspondence

Craig Alberty, interview January 27, 1994.
Dr. Bruce Ammann, interview December 29, 1993.
Gladys Bairey, interview January 26, 1994.
Paul Bankson, interview October 4, 1993.
Dr. Monty Barnard, interview January 8, 1994.
Dr. G. L. Barnett, interview January 21, 1994.
Margaret (Mrs. Charles) Barnett, interview January 28, 1994.
The Rev. Steve Barnett, interview January 28, 1994.
Joyce Becker, telephone interview February 26, 1994.
June Beecher, interview January 11, 1994.
Robert Beecher, telephone interview February 25, 1994.
Lawrence Benard, telephone interview March 1994.
James E. Berdahl, letter January 13, 1994.
Gen. Justin Berger, telephone interview October 14, 1993.
Betty Best, telephone interview 1994.
Paul Bierley, telephone interview July 4, 1994.
Elizabeth "Betsy" Doyle Bjorneberg, letter May 1994.
Marguerite Meyer Block, interview February 14, 1994.
Marty Braithwaite, interview October 26, 1993.
Rodney O. Bray, letter March 4, 1994; interview August 18, 1994.
Florence Meyer Brown, interview February 14, 1994.
Marlin Brown, letters 1993; interview January 21, 1994.
James Burge, letter July 14, 1994.
Bill Byrne, telephone interview September 28, 1994.
Margaret Cashman, interview January 9, 1994.
Dr. Richard Colwell, telephone interview August 9, 1994; letter August 26, 1994.
Joe Cooper, interview January 3, 1994.
Doris Henegar Dean, interview September 23, 1993.
Douglas Dean, letter 1994.
Helen De Velde, interview January 26, 1994.
Libbie (Mrs. Ernest) Dvoracek, interview February 1994.
Stan Eitreim, interview October 28, 1993; letter January 7, 1994.
Merridee Ekstrom, letter January 7, 1994.
Edna Ellwein, interview October 12, 1993.
Kathy Hays Emmel, telephone interview March 12, 1994; letter June 8, 1994.
Barbara Everist, telephone interview, 1994.
Scott Faragher, interview January 5, 1994.
Ann Bryant Fisher, letter December 9, 1993; interview February 13, 1994.
Myron Floren, telephone interview March 13, 1994.

Donald Foss, interview February 19, 1994.
Edgar J. Foss, telephone interviews March 19, 1994, and September 28, 1994.
Joe Foss, telephone interview March 21, 1994.
Marcella (Mrs. Clifford) Foss, telephone interview 1994.
Richard Foss, telephone interview March 19, 1994.
Sandra Hart Golding, telephone interview September 11, 1994, and fax September 20, 1994.
Lisa Wiehl Grevlos, interview February 22, 1994.
Bonnie Medeck Griffith, interview October 14, 1993.
Robert Griffith, interview October 14, 1993.
George Gulson, interview November 2, 1993.
Greg C. Hall, letter February 7, 1994.
Carl Hallstrom, interview January 3, 1994.
Janet Bruns Hallstrom, interview January 3, 1994.
Howard Hammitt, letter December 1, 1993.
Curt Hammond, interview January 6, 1994.
Greg Handel, interview January 18, 1994.
Jon Edward Hansen family, letter March 1994.
Helen Brumbaugh Hanson, telephone interview October 1, 1994.
Mary Harum Hart, telephone interview July 19, 1994.
Eugenia Orlich Hartig, interview January 20, 1994.
Loretta McLaughlin Hartrich, interview January 12, 1994; letters 1993 and 1994.
Robert Harum, telephone interview July 11, 1994.
Robert Heege, interview February 17, 1994.
Sylvia Henkin, interview January 14, 1994.
William Hobson, telephone interview December 10, 1994.
Verlyn Hofer, telephone interview January 13, 1994.
Gary Holman, telephone interview January 9, 1994; letter January 1994.
Paul Hoy, interviews 1981 and November 18, 1993.
Maureen Hult, interview January 10, 1994.
Jane (Mrs. Howard) McClung Ice, telephone interview January 2, 1995.
Jennifer Iveland, interview 1993.
Orral O. Jackson, Jr., letter October 6, 1994.
Delmar Junek, telephone interview January 2, 1995.
Coral Kelly, interview February 18, 1994.
Robert Kindred, telephone interview April 2, 1994; letters May 26 and 31, 1994.
Dr. Otis Kittelson, telephone interview 1994.
Rick Knobe, interview November 2, 1993.
Robert Kolbe, interview February 10, 1994.
Jean Kopperud, letter 1993.
Eloise (Mrs. Palmer) Kremer, letter March 24, 1994.
David Krueger, interview January 6, 1994.
Dr. Harold Krueger, interview February 3, 1994.
Wayne Krumrei, interview October 11, 1993.
Leo Kucinski, telephone interview March 14, 1994.
Elizabeth Swanson Kuhn, letter August 16, 1994.
Robert Kunkel, interview 1993.
Ronald H. Lane, letters February 2, 1994 and March 30, 1994.
Doris (Mrs. C. R.) Larson, interview November 4, 1993.
Merle Larson, telephone interview January 24, 1994.
Doug Lehrer, interview January 22, 1994.
Donald Lias, interview January 25, 1994.
David Lillehaug, telephone interview January 23, 1994.
Dr. Steven Lillehaug, telephone interview January 23, 1994.
Dr. Loren Little, letter August 19, 1993; telephone interview January 13, 1994.
Oscar Loe, interviews September 29, 1993 and various other dates; letter January 10, 1994.
Scott Loftesness, interview January 18, 1994.
Tom Long, interview September 9, 1993.
Clifford H. Manderscheid, Jr., telephone interview February 24, 1994.
Leonard Martinek, interview February 10, 1994.
Patricia Masek, interview January 5, 1994.
Marciene Swenson Matthius, interview February 8, 1994.
Hallie McBride, interview January 24, 1994.
Donald McCabe, letter June 20, 1994.
Lila McCammons, interview January 26, 1994.
Earl McCart, interview September 30, 1994.
Virginia (Mrs. James) McClung Maguire, telephone interview, January 2, 1995.
Robert McDowell, Sr., interview October 15, 1993.
George F. Menke, telephone interview January 10, 1994.
Marson Metzger, telephone interview September 29, 1994.
Leon "Curly" Miller, interview October 6, 1993.

Vera Moss, interview January 18, 1994.
Ken Munce, telephone interview September 29, 1994.
Robert Nason, letter February 6, 1994.
Fletcher Nelson, interview September 24, 1993.
John "Jack" M. Newton, telephone interview 1931.
Pat O'Brien, interview April 26, 1994.
Dr. James Ode, telephone interview March 1994.
Ralph Olsen, Jr., interview August 25, 1993.
Al and Nona Ordal, telephone interviews various dates; letter January 1994.
Marge Overby, telephone interview January 1994.
Ed Paul, interviews September 29, 1993, and various other dates.
Jeanette Paulson, letter February 1, 1994.
Francis Peckham, telephone interview September 1993.
Jean Hoiseth Peterson, letter April 30, 1994.
Lynn Peterson, letter April 30, 1994.
Roma Prindle, telephone interview June 6, 1994; letter June 12, 1994.
Thomas E. Pruner, interview, September 10, 1994.
Linda McLaren Roach, interview January 8, 1994.
Glenna Rundell, telephone interview 1994.
Norman Sampson, letter March 1994.
Michael Sauers, interview January 24, 1994.
Anna Schartz, interview January 24, 1994.
John Schilt, telephone interview January 26, 1994.
Mike E. Schirmer, interview September 20, 1993.
Esther Schroeder, interview January 24, 1994.
Lowen Schuett, interview January 12, 1994.
Scott Shelsta, letter 1993; interviews August 7, 1994, and various other dates.
Julie Simko, interview January 8, 1994.
Helen (Mrs. Wilmer) Simmons, interview January 26, 1994.
Betty Slocum, telephone interview 1994.
Johnny Soyer, interview February 15, 1994.
Matt Staab, interview January 28, 1994.
Stephen Stombaugh, letter August 1994.
Tillie (Mrs. Mel) Sunde, interviews January 11, 1994, and January 24, 1994.
Dr. Priscilla Swanson, telephone interview August 1994.
Richard Swanson, interview August 1994.
Manfred Szameit, interviews September 9, 1994, and October 20, 1994.
Dr. Alan Taylor, interview January 17, 1994.
Ralph Tyler, interview November 15, 1993.
Terry Walter, interview December 27, 1993.
Lud Wangberg, letter May 1994.
David Wegner, letters 1993 and 1994.
Paul F. Wegner, Jr., letters 1993 and 1994.
Vivian Wegner, interview 1994.
Gene White, telephone interview January 13, 1994.
Mayor Jack White, interview December 28, 1993.
Harold Wingler, interview October 11, 1993.
Bob Winkels interview, November 3, 1994.
Milo Winter, letter February 15, 1994; interview May 29, 1994.
Everett Zellers, letter December 1993; telephone interview September 27, 1994.

Books

Bachman, Harold B. *The Biggest Boom in Dixie, The Story of Band Music at the University of Florida.* Published by the author, 1968.
Bailey, Dana R. *History of Minnehaha County, South Dakota.* Sioux Falls, South Dakota: Brown and Saenger, printers, 1899.
Berger, Kenneth. *Band Encyclopedia.* Published in the U.S.A., distributed by Band Associates, Inc., Kent, Ohio, 1960.
Bierley, Paul. *John Philip Sousa, American Phenomenon.* Englewood Cliffs, New Jersey: Prentice-Hall, 1973.
Bragstad, R. E. *Sioux Falls in Retrospect.* Privately published, 1967.
Cox, George E. *First Congregational Church — A Congregation of the United Church of Christ, Centennial 1872-1972 / Sioux Falls, SD,* Sioux Falls: First Congregational Church, 1971.
Cowlishaw, Mary Lou. *This Band's Been Here Quite a Spell ... 1859-1981.* Naperville, Illinois: The Naperville Municipal Band, Inc., 1981.
Floren, Myron and Randee. *Accordion Man.* Brattleboro, Vermont: The Stephen Greene Press, 1981.
Foss, Joe, with Donna Wild Foss. *A Proud American: The Autobiography of Joe Foss,* New York: Pocket Star Books, 1992.

Goldman, Richard Franko. *The Concert Band.* New York: Rinehart & Company, Inc., 1946.
Graham, Alberta Powell. *Great Bands of America.* New York: Thomas Nelson & Sons, 1951.
Grimes, Paul L. *The Pride of Arizona, A History of the University of Arizona Band 1885-1985,* privately published, 1985.
Horton, Arthur G., research director and editor. *An Economic and Social Survey of Sioux Falls, South Dakota 1938-39.* Sioux Falls Chamber of Commerce and City of Sioux Falls, official sponsors.
Huseboe, Arthur. *An Illustrated History of the Arts in South Dakota.* Sioux Falls, South Dakota: The Center for Western Studies, 1989.
Jennewein, J. Leonard and Boorman, Jane, eds., *Dakota Panorama,* Dakota Territory Centennial Commission, 1961.
Johnson, Patricia. "Bibliography of Minnehaha County, South Dakota," *Dakota Book News,* Volume 1, October 1966.
Kolbe, Robert, coordinator. *Minnehaha County Historical and Biographical Sketches.* Minnehaha County Historical Society. copyright.
Kremer, L. M. "Barney." *Theatre in Spite of Itself — A Century of Action on Sioux Falls Stages Cues Its Schools' Evolvement in the Fine Arts.* Sioux Falls, South Dakota: Sioux Falls Independent School District, 1976. Quotes used by permission of Mildred Kremer.
Lennox Municipal Band Diamond Jubilee – 1883-1958, published 1958.
Lippincott's Pronouncing Gazetteer of the World. J. B. Lippincott, 1895.
Olson, Gary D. and Erik L. *Sioux Falls, South Dakota, A Pictorial History.* Norfolk, Virginia: The Donning Company/Publishers, 1985.
Parker, Donald Dean, compiler. *History of Our County and State.* Brookings: South Dakota State College, 1960.
Rehrig, William H., ed. Paul E. Bierley. *The Heritage Encyclopedia of Band Music* (two volumes). Westerville, Ohio: Integrity Press, 1991.
Richardson, Jeanne Schulte. *Here Lies Sioux Falls.* Freeman, South Dakota: Pine Hill Press, 1992.
Schwartz, H. W. *Bands of America.* New York: Doubleday and Company, 1957.
Sioux Falls Park and Recreation Board and Department. *Guide to Sioux Falls Park and Recreation Facilities.* Privately printed, 1984.
Smith, Charles A. *Minnehaha County History.* Mitchell, South Dakota: Educator Supply Company, 1949.
Van Der Wert, Lesta, Turchen and James D. McLaird. *From County and Community – A Bibliography of South Dakota Local Histories.* 1979.

City Directories

Sioux Falls city directories, various years.

Official Minutes

Sioux Falls City Commission minutes, various years.
Sioux Falls Municipal Band Board minutes, 1919-94.
Sioux Falls Park Board minutes, various years.

Newspapers/Periodicals

Argus Leader (also known through the years as *The Daily Argus-Leader* and *The Argus-Leader.* For ease of reading, *Argus Leader* has been used in all references).
Musician News Reporter, American Federation of Musicians, Sioux Falls, South Dakota: Sioux Falls Musicians Union, Local 114, September 1927, Vol. IX, No. 9.
Sioux Falls Press
Sioux Falls Tribune.

Miscellaneous Sources

Augustana College *Edda,* 1920.
Census: 1920, Minnehaha County, South Dakota.
El Riad Shrine Band Constitution and By Laws, 1958.
Leland Lillehaug notebooks.
Letters from Arthur Smith to Davis-Schmegler Company.

Letters between Russ Henegar and Lynn Sams, from the Lynn Sams Collection, American Bandmasters Association Library, University of Maryland.

Letter from Col. J. D. Kindred addressed to Sioux Falls City Hall and program from dedication from February 22, 1987, of Bronson Hall band room for 74th Army Band at Ft. Benjamin Harrison, Indiana.

1989 letter from William Byrne supplied by Jacquelyn Gunnarson.

Local 114, American Federation of Musicians, records, courtesy Joseph F. Pekas, secretary/treasurer of Local 773, Mitchell, South Dakota.

Mary Harum Hart's approved biography.

Paul Hoy's scrapbooks.

Program from Sioux Falls Municipal Band annual party, September 27, 1937.

Programs from Sioux Falls Municipal Band concerts, 1935-present.

Program from U.S. Navy Band concert, October 19, 1938.

Russ Henegar funeral bulletin.

Russ Henegar's scrapbook, courtesy of Doris Henegar Dean.

Sioux Falls Municipal Band computerized list of music.

Sioux Falls Municipal Band personnel records.

Sioux Falls Municipal Band scrapbooks.

South Dakota Masons master list, Masonic Temple, Sioux Falls, South Dakota.

Washington Senior High School *Warrior,* 1920-21, 1923, 1925, 1926, 1928, 1931, 1936.

William Meyer correspondence, including letters from Emil Medicus, flute virtuoso, May 8, 1926; from James L. Hansen Sales Company; and from the Selmer Corporation, March 4, 1929, April 2, 1929, and November 21, 1929. His contract with the Sioux Falls Symphony Orchestra.

About the Authors

Dr. Leland A. Lillehaug

Dr. Leland A. Lillehaug of Sioux Falls, South Dakota, served as conductor of the Sioux Falls Municipal Band for twenty-three years, from 1964 through 1986. During those years he conducted more than 900 concerts. He also founded the Sioux Falls Park and Recreation Youth Band in 1971, conducting it through 1977.

Lillehaug is professor emeritus of Augustana College in Sioux Falls, having been a member of the college's music faculty from 1956 through 1991. In addition to serving as director of bands, he was department chairman for several years. While at Augustana, he led the band on several national, three-week tours and produced eleven albums.

Lillehaug was born on a farm near Lane, South Dakota. He received his bachelor's degree, *magna cum laude*, with a major in music from Augustana College. Additional education includes master's and Ph.D. degrees from the Eastman School of Music. He received a diploma from the Academy of Music in Vienna, Austria, where he was a Fulbright Scholar and studied clarinet and bassoon with members of the Vienna Philharmonic.

He has performed professionally on bassoon, clarinet, saxophone and flute. He was a member of the United States Army from 1948 through 1951 and served in the 71st Army Band in the Panama Canal Zone. Professional playing included major ice shows, Canadian National Ballet, Ringling Brothers and Barnum and Bailey Circus bands and various community symphonies. He is the leader of the area backup

481

band for Myron Floren.

Additional conducting experience includes the Waverly, Iowa, High School Band (1953-56), numerous festivals, nineteen productions of Broadway musicals in Sioux Falls and guest conducting the U.S. Marine Band and The U.S. Army Band of Washington, D.C.

Research experience includes a project for the U.S. Office of Education in contemporary music, computerization of music libraries, and sacred music for voices and instruments. Several of the latter have been published by Concordia Publishing House. His work has been recognized by the *School Musician* as one of "Ten Outstanding Music Educators for 1986-87," the Bush Foundation and the Danforth Foundation.

Lillehaug is a member of the American Bandmasters Association and is immediate national past president of the Association of Concert Bands. He is a member of the South Dakota Bandmasters Hall of Fame.

Lillehaug and his wife Ardis are the parents of three grown children: David of Minneapolis, Dr. Steven of Iowa City and Laurie L. Anderson of Sioux Falls. They have two granddaughters, Amy Anderson and Kara Lillehaug.

Laurie L. Anderson

Laurie L. Anderson is a reporter with the *Argus Leader* newspaper in Sioux Falls, South Dakota. She attended Augustana College in Sioux Falls, graduating *magna cum laude* with majors in English and journalism.

She was born in Rochester, New York, in 1959 but grew up in Sioux Falls. Interest in journalism began in high school, where she served as editor of the Sioux Falls Washington High School *Orange and Black*. She continued her journalism endeavors in college, editing the Augustana *Mirror* and working part time at the *Argus Leader*.

Following college graduation, she was a full-time copy editor at the *Argus Leader* for a year. She then married and moved away for ten years, living in Virginia, New York and Minneapolis. She and her husband returned to Sioux Falls in 1992.

Anderson never played in the Municipal Band, but she studied piano and violin for many years, earning a spot in the South Dakota All-State Orchestra all four years of high school. Her interest in researching the history of the Sioux Falls Municipal Band began in 1981, when she did a short history of the Band for a college journalism class.

She and her husband, Jeffrey G. Anderson, have one daughter, Amy.

Index

In addition to the index entries, please see the following listings in the appendix:

Note: Individuals on the Municipal Band pictures are not indexed but are named below the picture. Titles of musical compositions and composer names (except John Philip Sousa and Karl L. King) are not indexed unless they have special significance.